W9-CUB-193

BUSINESS ETHICS
IN BIBLICAL PERSPECTIVE

A Comprehensive Introduction

MICHAEL E. CAFFERKY

IVP Academic

An imprint of InterVarsity Press
Downers Grove, Illinois

InterVarsity Press
P.O. Box 1400, Downers Grove, IL 60515-1426
ivpress.com
email@ivpress.com

InterVarsity Press® is the book-publishing division of InterVarsity Christian Fellowship/USA®, a movement of students and faculty active on campus at hundreds of universities, colleges and schools of nursing in the United States of America, and a member movement of the International Fellowship of Evangelical Students. For information about local and regional activities, visit intervarsity.org.

All Scripture quotations, unless otherwise indicated, are taken from the New American Standard Bible®, copyright 1960, 1962, 1963, 1968, 1971, 1972, 1973, 1975, 1977, 1995 by The Lockman Foundation. Used by permission.

Cover design: Cindy Kiple
Interior design: Beth McGill
Images: Raw Paw Graphics/Getty Images

ISBN 978-0-8308-2474-8 (print)
ISBN 978-0-8308-9866-4 (digital)

Printed in the United States of America ∞

Library of Congress Cataloging-in-Publication Data
Cafferky, Michael E.
 Business ethics in biblical perspective : a comprehensive introduction / Michael E. Cafferky.
   pages cm
 Includes bibliographical references and index.
 ISBN 978-0-8308-2474-8 (casebound : alk. paper)
 1. Business ethics—Biblical teaching. 2. Business—Biblical teaching. 3. Management—Religious aspects—Christianity.
4. Ethics in the Bible. I. Title.
 BS680.B8C34 2015
 241'.644—dc23
                          2015018753

P	26	25	24	23	22	21	20	19	18	17	16	15	14	13	12	11	10	9	8	7	6	5	4	3	2	1
Y	37	36	35	34	33	32	31	30	29	28	27	26	25	24	23	22	21	20	19	18	17	16	15			

For my family.

I am so proud of you.

Contents

Part IV Widening the Perspective

Part V Appendixes and Case Studies

Preface

For a day in Your courts is better than a
    thousand outside.
I would rather stand at the threshold of
    the house of my God
Than dwell in the tents of wickedness.
For the LORD God is a sun and shield;
The LORD gives grace and glory;
No good thing does He withhold from
    those who walk uprightly.
    (Ps 84:10-11)

As an undergraduate student, I found that the course in Christian ethics was the most difficult and least interesting of all required subjects that I completed. In retrospect, if I had been given a choice, I probably would not have enrolled in the course. At the time I lacked the vision to see how practical such a course can be.

Some of the theories were confusing. I had no idea how to reconcile the contradictions or resolve the paradoxes that seemed to plague the discussions of complicated ethical issues. The cases discussed (abortion, euthanasia, lying to protect your family from an evil home invader) seemed to be remote from the world I expected to enter after graduation. No one that I knew ever had an abortion. As far as I knew, it just was not done in our small community. Growing up in Clarkston, Washington, a small town in Asotin County, I had never

heard of anyone who had to defend his or her home against an invader.

Now, many years later, having had the benefit of twenty-five years of experience in leadership in the marketplace in both non-profit and for-profit organizations, and a dozen years teaching management, strategy, organization theory and business ethics, I find the subject to be one of the most interesting of all that I encounter. Given the scriptural perspective, it has become for me the most compelling. More than any other course in the business school curriculum, it is business ethics that offers the potential to challenge us to the core of who we are.

In my other courses in management theory and practice I find more and more that these essentially involve teaching ethics through a different lens. Above all else, for good or for ill, managers are the ethical leaders in their organizations and society as a whole.

An outgrowth of my continued study following the publication of *Management: A Faith-Based Perspective*, this text, *Business Ethics in Biblical Perspective*, attempts to let scriptural thinking represent itself in the conversations about business ethics. It is designed for faith-based colleges and universities that want to offer a business ethics course from a biblical perspective and in doing so engage in a guided conversation about right and wrong in the marketplace.[1]

The book is built on the premise that, while the Bible is the absolute objective authority on ethical matters, it is the members of the faith community who must interpret the Bible through dialogue together under changing historical, social and technological conditions.

Traditionally religious leaders and scholars have taken the lead in this conversation. Other community leaders participate from the point of view of government organizations, nonprofit agencies and for-profit firms. Accordingly, this book is intended to contribute to the faith community conversation on business ethics. Its contribution lies primarily in two areas:

1. An exposition of a dozen biblical story themes that guide thinking and action in the world of business. These themes form the structure of the faith community's conversation from a biblical perspective.

2. An application of the biblical ethics process which involves the community as much as it does the individual.

Most business ethics and social responsibility textbooks approach their subjects from the perspective of Western philosophy, law, economics or management. These books either ignore or gloss over religious values and teachings. Most books on ethics appear hesitant to mention specific religions or the Bible. Yet, religion is considered one of the most important cultural influences in Western society. Even if people do not have in-depth knowledge of what the Bible says, religion remains important for social behaviors.

From the perspective of the Christian college and university, leaders and students desire to experience transformed lives. Studying religion and attending religious services play an important part in this. But who says that the only settings in which personal transformation can occur are located in the college chapel, church or the religion classroom? Isn't it possible that the study of business and business ethics can also contribute to this? If faith comes by hearing the word of Christ,[2] isn't it possible that the study of business can present opportunities to hear the Word and thereby experience faith for the marketplace? Should the problem of biblical illiteracy be given to religion faculty, pastors and priests to correct? Framed in more blunt terms, on what basis should the Christian business classroom abdicate its role (some would say responsibility) in teaching the biblical foundations for business? This book offers an understanding of such a deep foundation.

FEATURES OF THIS BOOK

After all is said about theological foundations for business, ultimately it is what we do in the marketplace that matters, not just what we think about or how we feel. Thus, this book is not merely a book about theology or theory. It is a book that considers moral action guided by scriptural assumptions and scriptural thinking. The section "Down to the Nitty-Gritty" in the various chapters encourages students to engage in community dialogue as part of ethical actions. The collection of interwoven Scripture themes that form the intellectual engine of the book distinguishes it from other substitutes. The opening scenarios of chapters and the end-of-book cases combine with the end-of-chapter exercises and discussion vignettes to total more than eighty different business situations that can be evaluated individually and in small groups using the Bible story themes as guides.

Because of its focus on biblical themes,

something that most other books and articles do not employ, this book makes liberal use of passages from both the Old Testament and the New Testament. Accordingly, this book does not consider the Old Testament irrelevant. The contrast that some Christians prefer to make between the two Testaments of the Bible is not made in this book. For example, the Old Testament is not merely about law and the New Testament is not merely about grace. The Old Testament says as much about God's grace as does the New Testament. The New Testament speaks more about the law of God than some people realize. We see that the authors of the New Testament books quote extensively from Old Testament writings. Jesus was familiar with the Old Testament. He quoted from it, regarded his own work in terms of its message and considered it God's Word. The New Testament way of thinking builds substantially on Old Testament ideas. Thus, the Old Testament is necessary when trying to understand the message about Jesus given in the New Testament. Accordingly, in this endeavor we see a wonderful unity in diversity among Scripture writers.

Most other books merely introduce the various contemporary approaches to business ethics. Little space is devoted to evaluating the pros and cons of these approaches. Little if any space is devoted to critical thinking about these approaches especially as they may or may not align with scriptural thinking. Accordingly, this book will use the biblical themes as a lens through which to evaluate contemporary ethical approaches.

Other books on business ethics devote little if any space to the issues of the ethics of buying and consuming products, the community setting for the ethics process, the fundamental tensions in the ethics process and in the environment of business, and the economic implications of the Ten Commandments. Accordingly, this book will advance the conversation about ethics in the market by addressing these issues.

This book presents scores of ethical situations to consider in light of the biblical themes and contemporary ethical models. It is designed to introduce you, the reader, to the main elements of biblical story thinking so that you can participate in the community dialogue about these and other situations. Some of the work is done for you to show how the biblical story thinking is applied to some situations. Other situations presented do not provide the solution for you. The process of deciding what is right or wrong in the marketplace we call the ethics process. Ultimately, this is a community process as much as it is a cognitive process of individual reflection that leads to decisions and actions.

The style guide for this project is the *Chicago Manual of Style*. This will be of interest to some readers who have particular expectations for spelling of words related to religious belief. For example, words that refer directly to God and Jesus are always capitalized, but pronouns that refer to God or Jesus (he, him) are not. This is consistent with the convention used by most English translations of the Bible. The words *Bible* and *Scripture* are always capitalized, but the words *biblical* and *scriptural* are not. When passages of the Bible are quoted, the New American Standard Version is used except where otherwise noted.

Part I The Fundamentals (chaps. 1–4) provides an introduction to the big issues at stake. This section presents the heart of the intellectual and faith-based engine of the book. The benefits of an ethical approach to business are presented. Four levels of application are introduced: individual, organizational, industry/ profession and the larger economic system. The nature of the ethical, social and legal environment of business is explored in terms of fundamental tensions present there. Spread over two chapters, the biblical themes are introduced as the biblically ideal patterns of marketplace thinking and action.

Part II Contemporary Approaches (chaps. 5–13) evaluates common approaches to ethical decision making by evaluating each in terms of the pros and cons and then through the lens of biblical story themes. Some secular approaches have deep Judeo-Christian roots (e.g., justice and rights); others are *prima facie* at odds with scriptural thinking (e.g., egoism, relativism). The desire in this section is to be fair to Scripture and to contemporary thinking. This requires integrity to acknowledge where Scripture aligns with some elements of the contemporary thinking that is otherwise clearly at odds with the Bible. The following contemporary ethical approaches are evaluated in the light of scriptural themes:

- egoism
- relativism
- common sense
- social contract
- utilitarianism
- universalism
- agency
- justice and rights
- virtues and character

Part III Contemporary Issues (chaps. 14–18) focuses on the application of ethics to the traditional business disciplines at the individual, organizational and industry/professional levels. Accordingly, this section presents several contemporary ethical issues that can be found in various settings of the marketplace:

- consumer ethics seen from the perspectives of the individual, the organization, the industry and the economic system
- management
- accounting and finance
- marketing
- global business

As with the previous section the big issues are considered in the light of the biblical story themes.

Part IV Widening the Perspective (chaps. 19–21) concludes the book by exploring through the lens of biblical story themes the application of ethical decision making and accountability in the larger context of the environment of business, including the physical environment and political-economic systems. In this section the book addresses the topic of corporate responsibility. The morality of the larger economic system also is evaluated. The final chapter challenges readers to work intentionally toward developing a stronger, biblical-theme-based moral imagination for use in responding to pressure-packed situations.

Part V Appendixes and Case Studies contains additional material that readers may find useful. This part presents several appendixes and seventeen case studies designed for discussion, interesting debate topics that represent some of the directions that community conversations about business ethics take, an outline of the ten principles for a flourishing marketplace (the Ten Commandments), the underlying purpose of business as seen through the lens of biblical story themes, a short Bible reference section that contains support for each of the biblical story themes employed in the book and biblical story theme summary tables that can be used for study and review, and a Q & A Bible study on the topic of prosperity.

COLLATERAL RESOURCES

I wrote several practical teaching resources as collateral materials for instructors to use in preparation and delivery in Christian colleges and universities. These include the following:

- instructor's manual containing suggestions for in-class activities and assignments designed to add interest to class periods, supplemental information on various topics covered here and a sample course syllabus

- chapter outlines that can be used in traditional lecture formats that contain additional Scripture passages and more in-class discussion questions

- test item files containing multiple-choice questions and essay questions useful for assessments

- PowerPoint slide sets (one per chapter)

Acknowledgments

This book would not have been possible had I not been given an opportunity to interact with undergraduate students in the course "Ethical, Social and Legal Environment of Business" in the topics course "Capitalism and Its Critics" and in the MBA course "Integrating Faith and Business." The questions that students posed to me spurred my interest to search the Scriptures. Additionally, the doctoral degree courses in business ethics under the leadership of Dr. Sharon Johnson and Dr. Mike Weise at Anderson University Falls School of Business encouraged me to pursue biblical answers to my questions. Dr. Weise gave me valuable guidance early in the process of writing this book.

For years I had been studying several of the biblical themes explored in this book. But the "ah-ha!" moment occurred in 2012 in Bloemfontein, South Africa, while I waited my turn to speak at a conference on biblical foundations of academic disciplines. It was then that it became clear to me which biblical story themes apply to business.

I appreciate the support from the book development and editorial teams at InterVarsity Press and the peer reviewers who provided many helpful suggestions for how to make this book a better product and the peer reviewers in the Christian Business Faculty Association who have made suggestions for improving the papers I submitted for publication or conference presentation.

Tackling a project like this is not easy given the teaching requirements at a small, private university with religious heritage. This requires patience. Moreover, the pain of the opportunity costs incurred from making the commitment to this project I felt on a regular basis. Accordingly, I appreciated when colleagues at Southern Adventist University, both inside and outside the School of Business and Management, encouraged me as I progressed along.

As in previous publishing projects, my wife, Marlene, generously supported this project so that I could stay focused on the work. As a result, she had to endure the sacrifices common to writers' spouses. I appreciated her enthusiasm as each milestone was completed. Thank you!

Outline of the Book

General Introduction

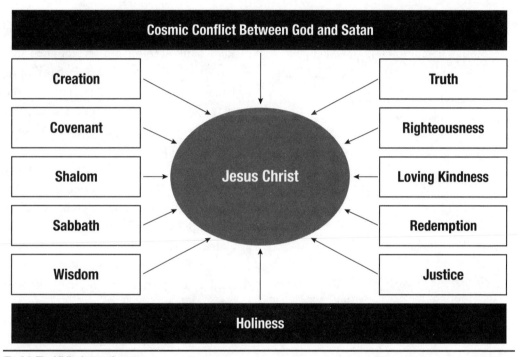

Fig. I.1. The biblical story themes.

SCRIPTURE PASSAGE

How blessed is the man who does not
  walk in the counsel of the wicked,
Nor stand in the path of sinners,
Nor sit in the seat of scoffers!
But his delight is in the law of the Lord,
And in His law he meditates day and
  night.
He will be like a tree firmly planted by
  streams of water,
Which yields its fruit in its season,
And its leaf does not wither;
And in whatever he does, he prospers.
  (Ps 1:1-3)[1]

CHAPTER OVERVIEW

In this chapter we introduce the concept of biblical story themes that are guides to ethical thinking and action in the marketplace. In particular, we will

- contrast the contemporary view on the ethics process with a biblical perspective

- consider the biblical idea of the heart and how this is related to making decisions regarding right and wrong

- introduce the biblical model of the ethics process as seen from the point of view of the person

- consider the biblical model of the ethics process from the point of view of the community

- begin practicing the intrapersonal process and the interpersonal process

- introduce the value of biblical themes and how they were selected

MAIN TOPICS

KEY TERMS

biblical ethics process, community perspective, faith, heart, interpersonal, intrapersonal, personal perspective, story themes

OPENING SCENARIOS

In this book we will consider scores of scenarios from the world of business. These will provide us with many opportunities to think and talk about business from a biblical perspective. Some situations in business are relatively simple. We know what is right and wrong. Other situations are more complicated. Let's start with two short scenarios that illustrate this point.

Scenario A. A group of persons skilled in the creation and use of technology install secret video cameras at automatic teller machines (ATMs) and gasoline fuel pumps for the purpose of recording account information and PINs that customers use to access funds in their bank accounts.[2] They combine this with the technology to create fake bank cards which are then used to take money from the bank accounts of unsuspecting bank customers. Is what these sophisticated operators are doing wrong?

Scenario B. You move into a new apartment. The first night you are there you open your laptop computer and, wonder of wonders, your computer detects an unsecured WiFi available nearby. The WiFi is called JasonC. The signal strength is medium in your living room. But if you sit in a chair facing the wall between the stove and the refrigerator, the WiFi signal strength goes up. The next morning on your way out to work you meet one of the other tenants in the apartment building. He introduces himself to you as Jason C. You immediately think about the name of the unsecured WiFi you found last night. You decide not to say anything about the WiFi signal to Jason right now. Is it wrong to use Jason's unsecured WiFi signal to access the Internet without permission?

What to do in Scenario A is what we might call straightforward. Most people will say that it is clearly and utterly wrong to use someone else's bank account information. Furthermore, it is wrong to create fake bank cards and use these to steal from other people's bank accounts.

What to do in Scenario B is not quite as simple to determine compared with Scenario A. It is a little more complicated, though you might have an initial feeling about what is right or wrong. First is the issue of what is being stolen, if anything. Has Jason lost anything of value as a result of your use of his WiFi connection? Has the Internet provider lost anything of value (lost revenue)? Then there is the issue of who has the responsibility to protect access to the Internet. If Jason or the Internet service provider does not secure his Internet connection, does this give you permission to jump on his router and surf the web without permission? Is this an issue of invasion of privacy or theft, or both or neither? If you jump on his WiFi connection but do not hack into Jason's system, are you invading his privacy? Does it matter whether you live with Jason sharing a room in his apartment or live next door to Jason in a different apartment? Would it matter if you are merely logging on to check email once in a while versus using Jason's connection to run an e-business out of your apartment? What is the central issue? Is this an ethics issue, or is it merely a question of neighborhood courtesy?

While you contemplate the questions relating to Scenario B, consider this: *Deciding what to do in these two scenarios depends on your perspective.* Thus, it is with the issue of perspective that we start this book.

CONTEMPORARY BUSINESS ETHICS PROCESS AND CONTENT

With some exceptions the contemporary business ethics process is often seen through intrapersonal, rational or cognitive dimensions.[3] The process begins when a person encounters a situation in which an ethical choice must be made or when ethical issues are present that require a social response. The person first tries to understand the moral standards that can be used to think through the issues. Moral standards are viewed as personal and person-specific. To resolve the fact that there are personal differences in the moral standards, the person will employ the following process steps:

- *Recognize the moral impact.* Consequentialism or perceptions of social expectations form the basis for the analysis at this and later stages of the process. At this point the person considers the benefits and harms, the rights and the wrongs that result from a particular action. The expected reactions of others may be considered.

- *State the moral problem* in such a way that it persuades others to see the ethical issues in the same way. This step is often implied, but how and when the attempt to persuade is seldom discussed.

- *Determine the economic outcomes* balancing the net good outcomes with the net bad outcomes in order to achieve the optimum result. Here the utilitarian posture, which we will explore later, is hard to miss.

- *Consider the legal requirements.* Laws are formal and specific expressions of social expectations. In addition, society expects its citizens to obey the law. At this step the legal requirements are rationally analyzed.

- *Evaluate the ethical duties.* At this point the person will consider some of the content that has traditionally formed the smorgasbord of duties from which to choose as the situation seems to indicate. Included in this list may be religious beliefs which are placed alongside virtues, utilitarianism, the duty to use reason and avoid contradictions, justice and rights.

As with the other steps in the process, this is dominated by rational, cognitive activity accomplished by the person.

A few observations can be made about this. First, popular contemporary approaches, for most business ethics thinkers, are dominated by the rational, cognitive activity of the person. The social context is not wholly ignored; however, it tends to be de-emphasized in favor of the individual, cognitive activity. At times, this cognitive activity engages others through dialogue or debate and in so doing becomes somewhat political. It is cognitive in that the analysis and decision making occurs primarily in the mind of each person. It becomes political when, as each person follows the analytical steps, he or she realizes that differences of opinion exist. Each attempts to persuade the others of the validity of his or her point of view. This persuasion is seen as primarily a meeting of rational minds but each, at least potentially, that comes from a different starting point. From such dialogue a way through the differences is then negotiated. It is with this typical contemporary individual, cognitive approach that this book is in contrast.

Second, not all contemporary approaches are this cut and dried as portrayed here in the steps of the process. Some contemporary approaches emphasize virtues. Others, such as egoism, emphasize what the person desires to achieve placing this above other concerns. Others, such as relativism and the social contract, emphasize social expectations. Even when the various approaches are considered, the rational, cognitive dimensions tend to dominate.

THE PERSPECTIVE OF THIS BOOK

The goal of the book is to help you understand a biblical perspective so that you can make an informed decision as to what degree this perspective is plausible, defensible and practical in the contemporary market. A related goal is to provide a setting in which you can think carefully about your preferred ethical approach and in the process make a commitment of the heart to an approach which you believe to be best.

Another goal is to provide a framework that you can begin practicing now. This is not just a book about theory. It helps you take the first steps of practice in a social setting.

Some of the ethical issues that companies and their managers face are relatively straightforward. What is right or wrong may seem obvious. With few exceptions the ethical approaches described in the book will all lead to the same conclusion: Do not lie, cheat or steal! However, as you will see, some of the ethical dilemmas that businesses face are more complicated. It is with these more complicated problems and dilemmas where the ethical perspective you believe is best will be tested.

Some ethical decision-making approaches are easier than others. Some focus on a limited set of issues because the definition of what constitutes justice or rights is simple. As we will see, for example, egoism tends to focus on the interests of the person. Utilitarianism attempts to counteract the shortcomings of egoism by placing all relevant stakeholders in the same status with respect to morals.

We use the term *process* to refer to the intrapersonal (within the person) and interpersonal (between persons) activities which lead to a decision for action or the action itself. A process can be thought of as a sequence of action steps that a person takes to accomplish a task. When faced with an ethical choice, the task is to decide and act on the question, What is the right thing to do in this situation? You will be given, through reasoning and discussions with others, a chance to test these approaches on more complicated ethical questions. You should know that a biblical perspective is not necessarily simple. It may be one of the more comprehensive approaches to ethics. It is capable of being applied to a wide variety of situations. Because of this, in some situations the biblical theme approach may require more work than so-called secular, contemporary approaches.

Accordingly this is a book that will guide you in developing critical thinking about the various ethical approaches and how to apply them. Given the theme of this book, some readers may take exception to this suggestion. If you are a Christian and your idea of faith leads you to say something like, "If God said it, I believe it; that's good enough for me," then a suggestion of developing critical thinking to evaluate the biblical approach to ethics may be offensive. The premise of the book should not be forgotten here: A biblical perspective is offered as the comprehensive, authoritative standard of ethics yet one that has the potential to be applied to a wide variety of marketplace situations.

That being said, the natural response of any reader is to think about the plausibility of such a claim. In the process, you will not avoid thinking about the plausibility of your own preferred approach to deciding right and wrong in business. You may find that some of the ideas you have previously held are not biblical. What will you do when you encounter this?

An additional premise is that both Christians and non-Christians take ethical actions and make decisions that can be considered ethical. Christians do not have a monopoly on all things right and wrong. There are some points of alignment between the biblical perspective and some so-called secular approaches to ethics used by non-Christians. Accordingly, this book does not advocate that all non-Christian ways of thinking and acting in the market are wrong.

Another premise of this book is that faith does not do away with the need for the Christian to think. Instead, faith informs reason; it is the foundation for reason. Faith should not destroy cognitive function. Said another way, biblical faith does not do away with the need to ask questions and think carefully especially about issues of faith. On the contrary, biblical faith may spark the Christian to ask more questions that need consideration.

The recommendation to contrast a biblical perspective with contemporary secular approaches was addressed in the Bible itself. The Bible writers were aware that the primary readers (or hearers) of the Bible story were living, buying, selling, working and playing among people who did not accept biblical ideals. Collectively, they present the Bible story itself as an authoritative and plausible alternative to competing worldviews of the days when the various books were written or the narratives recorded took place.

More than 230 times the Bible makes explicit reference to "other gods." The God presented in the Bible story is implicitly compared with the philosophies that embrace the idea of many divine beings. The Scripture passage at the beginning of this chapter is just one illustration among others throughout the Bible (in both Old and New Testaments) where the ways of God are compared with the various ways of people who do not follow God. But nowhere in the Bible are we told to not think about what God says.

Indeed, the entire biblical record is designed for just the opposite! It is as though the Bible writers as a group are saying to us, *Here is the story about God and his ways. Now consider this long and carefully with your whole being before you reject it in favor of something else! Furthermore, don't just* think *about it. Open your whole heart and being to the possibility of embracing the God who is the Author of this way.*

This is not just about using pure reason alone. Talk about it to other people. So, on the one hand, it is about a enjoying a relationship, but relationships involve the whole person in action with others, not just the powers of logic hidden in one person's mind. On the other hand, relationships do not short-circuit rational thinking. Using your whole being with all of its capabilities and faculties, body, mind, spirit, emotions, social awareness, perceptions and economic awareness, learn to accept the gift of faithfulness in a relationship with God and with others in the marketplace even when it is not always crystal clear what should be done.

BIBLICAL PERSPECTIVE ON FAITH

The biblical perspective on business ethics sheds light on the meaning of faith itself. Just as the apostle James wrote to the early Christian church, faith that is not evident in action is not only useless; it is dead![4] This suggests that belief that is not brought in to action is not truly faith. Biblical faith is not mere belief or mental assent to the proposition that God exists or belief in the truthfulness of what the Bible says when it talks about God or belief in Jesus as your personal Savior. This is a part but not the whole. Biblical faith is more!

Biblical faith is not a feeling of certainty that you have correct beliefs. Thus, biblical faith is not a mere sense of psychological certainty which you use to remove all questions, even the difficult ones. Rather, biblical faith involves living a life that is committed to a relationship with God and his way of living even when we do not feel especially close to him and especially when we still have questions. You may encounter a few ambiguous ethical and social situations for which the one "correct answer" is not plain to see. But this does not remove our responsibility to do our best, with the help of the community around us, to make decisions that are faithful.

Like the biblical story themes explored in this book, faith is action-oriented, not just psychological or emotional affection. It involves committed faithfulness of your whole being in a social context. In addition, true faith is not just an individualistic way of personal thinking; it is commitment lived in community where the great biblical story themes are shown in action. Accordingly, faith is not merely what you say; it is what you do with others that shows in action what you say. This level of commitment is not something that humans can produce of their own will. What an amazing gift of God faithfulness is.

Faith: faithfulness in action

All Christians are called to be witnesses of God. However, there are times and places in the business world where it may be inappropriate to openly talk about religious faith. In such situations every Christian can still speak on behalf of the character of God, drawing attention to the amazing principles of a flourishing life. When you promote these principles, advocate on behalf of them in your organization and integrate them into your own habits, you are telling about Jesus Christ just as surely as when you mention his name.

When you promote these principles, advocate on behalf of them in your organization and integrate them into your own habits, you are telling about Jesus Christ just as surely as when you mention his name.

To start the task of critical thinking about the biblical story perspective, let us consider the biblical portrayal of an important process. As you read, reflect and talk with others about the issues raised in this book you may find yourself coming back to this again and again. In fact, it is the biblical portrayal of the process which is one of the central contributions of this book to the field of business ethics.

ETHICS AND THE HEART

That the scriptural approach to business ethics involves more than the use of pure reason alone is addressed in the Bible. The biblical process of making decisions regarding ethics, social justice and social responsibility is rooted in the concept of the heart and its care by a person and by a community of like-minded faithful people.

The heart is the seat of decision making, judgment and moral commitments. It is in the heart that a person deals with personal and perceptual biases, battles the tendency toward self-deception, considers how to relate to other people, evaluates the behavior of others in the community and considers what is right and wrong and provides the courage to act on what the person believes to be right.

The heart, representing the whole person, is the center of the ethical process seen from the perspective of one person in community. The ancient Hebrew idea of the heart means the "inner person" signifying, in part, that all of life's experiences in their totality are embraced by, controlled by and enjoyed in the heart. It is as if a real, whole person and this person's awareness of the entire community resides in the heart directing, evaluating, deciding, acting and responding to the person's actions as well as the actions of others. Ethical action by one person springs from a heart that is transformed

under the power of God and in dialogue with a faith community of persons who are open to being transformed as a community.

Notice how the following Scripture emphasizes the whole person in a social context:

> Hear, O Israel! The LORD is our God, the LORD is one! You shall love the LORD your God with all your heart and with all your soul and with all your might. These words, which I am commanding you today, shall be on your heart. You shall teach them diligently to your sons and shall talk of them when you sit in your house and when you walk by the way and when you lie down and when you rise up. (Deut 6:4-7; see also Ex 18:20; Deut 5:33)[5]

This idea that the whole person engages in a response to God and to the community was also expressed by Jesus Christ:

> And He said to him, "'You shall love the LORD your God with all your heart, and with all your soul, and with all your mind.'" (Mt 22:37; see Mk 12:30-33; Lk 10:27)

Certainly an intrapersonal, cognitive or introspective dimension is important. Humans have an amazing capacity to discern, judge, evaluate, reason, critique, compare and contrast. But the biblical metaphor of the heart communicates that the whole person is involved with ethical decisions and action. The heart is the spring of action.

Further, the heart is located in the person, but it takes into consideration the hearts of other persons in the community. With the whole heart each person is responsible for taking a leadership posture with respect to right and wrong. The whole person is involved in interpreting the statements of God's will. The whole person bears the responsibility for action.

The biblical perspective is that the faithful follower of God will keep the heart. Keeping the heart means allowing God to write on the heart the principles of his character designed for us to imitate for our own well-being:

> Watch over your heart with all diligence,
> For from it flow the springs of life. (Prov
>   4:23; see also Prov 4:4; 28:26; Deut 4:9)

> How blessed is the man who does not
>   walk in the counsel of the wicked,
> Nor stand in the path of sinners,
> Nor sit in the seat of scoffers!
> But his delight is in the law of the LORD,
> And in His law he meditates day and
>   night. (Ps 1:1-2)

> The law of the LORD is perfect, restoring
>   the soul;
> The testimony of the LORD is sure, making
>   wise the simple.
> The precepts of the LORD are right,
>   rejoicing the heart;
> The commandment of the LORD is pure,
>   enlightening the eyes. (Ps 19:7-8)

> The law of his God is in his heart;
> His steps do not slip. (Ps 37:31)

> Your word I have treasured in my heart,
> That I may not sin against You. (Ps 119:11)

> I shall run the way of Your commandments,
> For You will enlarge my heart. (Ps 119:32)

> Your testimonies also are my delight;
> They are my counselors. (Ps 119:24; see
>   also Prov 2:1-12)

These concepts from the Old Testament are consistent with what is found in the New Testament. Jesus taught that it is out of the heart actions in social context come (Mt 12:35; 15:19; Mk 7:21). It is the heart on which God will write his Law to transform us (Heb 10:16).

The Bible story portrays the wise person as one who is diligent in keeping his or her heart because it cannot always be trusted if left merely to human devising. In contrast, in the Bible fools are foolish because they trust their own hearts as they are, they do not care for the heart using the principles of God's commandments and they do not get counsel from Scripture or from other trusted community leaders who are on the pathway to following God's principles for well-being.

The biblical metaphor of the heart refers to the location of several elements of human experience:

- fundamental beliefs
- cognitive reasoning
- judgments and evaluations
- decisions
- virtues
- will
- memory of personal experiences with other people
- perceptions of others in the community
- personal biases
- awareness of interpersonal relationships
- commitments to God and to others
- intuitions
- conscience
- human spirit
- emotions[6]

THE PERSONAL PERSPECTIVE

In biblical perspective, while it is the person's responsibility to watch over the heart diligently, ultimately the faithful heart and all it contains for good comes from and is developed by God. It is worth repeating: Not only is the initial acceptance of God, in Jesus Christ, part of the gift of faith. The transformation of the heart toward the actions of faithfulness also is a gift! Accordingly, the person who desires to keep his or her heart commits this choice of allowing God to work on the heart to transform it. This is the ongoing work of faith (faithfulness). It is God who puts his law in the heart;[7] it is God who enlarges the moral capacity of the heart such that, to use scriptural imagery, the person walks and even runs along the way outlined by God.

Keeping the heart is also achieved through a process of continual reflection on God's Word while living life in community. The foundation for this lies in three areas. First, the explicit biblical directions for action should be followed when the issues are clear. These explicit directions must be allowed into the heart. Second, biblical narratives provide us with examples of lessons that can be drawn for our actions. These stories illustrate the principles in action and the social impact of certain themes. Third, biblical story themes embody both the explicit biblical guidance and the lessons from narratives. These themes carry the essential messages of the narratives and the explicit teachings. It is these biblical story themes that are in focus in this book.

When difficult situations are encountered, listening to others in the community who are also following God becomes an important part of keeping the heart.[8] These wise persons promote a flourishing life in the community by providing counsel that has passed through their reflection of the themes from God's Word. This brings them joy and provides you with wisdom. "A wise man will hear and increase in learning, and a man of understanding will acquire wise counsel" (Prov 1:5).[9] "Deceit is in the heart of those who devise evil, but counselors of peace have joy" (Prov 12:20).

Action begins in the heart. Thus, ultimately it is out of the heart, bathed in God's Word and tested through dialogue with trusted wise persons, that ethical actions flow.[10] But action involves other dimensions of the person, too. This biblical ethics process can be illustrated by figure I.2, which portrays the ethics process as seen from the point of view of a person. As we will see, a biblical perspective on ethics includes the personal (individual) perspective. But it also goes beyond this to embrace a process undertaken in the entire community.

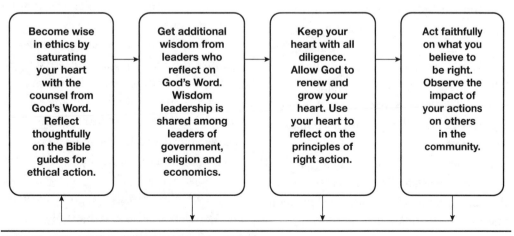

Fig. I.2. The biblical ethics process from a personal perspective.

THE COMMUNITY
(SOCIAL GROUP) PERSPECTIVE

While personal responsibility is part of the context of the biblical narratives, pure individualism is not.[11] Ethical decisions and actions are individual, but this does not mean that the personal perspective is the only viewpoint of Scripture. In spite of this, some Christians approach the ethics process as if it is primarily an individual matter.

While the heart is the metaphor which focuses on the personal perspective, it is the metaphor of walking or "the way" or journey which conveys the community perspective of the ethics process.[12] Walking involves more

---

ETHICS

- thinking and doing
- "the heart" and "the walk"

---

than thinking. It requires action in a community. It means going out among other people, communing with them, engaging them in conversations about life and life activities. It also means taking actions in their presence (after thoughtful consideration) which show who you are and what you stand for. When combined with the personal perspective, as a process ethics becomes both thinking and doing in a community. In this way the action side of ethics is not rash, thoughtless action. Rather, it is action based on thoughtful awareness of how other persons in community see the matter.

The following ideas show that the process of discerning right from wrong in the marketplace cannot be purely an individual matter in complicated situations. First, all ethics involves behavior in a social context. If in a social

context, at merely a glance we are compelled to ask, how can the ethics process be purely a personal matter? In truth, it cannot.

Second, the person contemplating a certain action has a biased point of view representing a particular interest based in personal needs and personal experiences. Other persons (we can call them stakeholders) may have different points of view representing different interests and life experiences. Whenever two sets of stakeholders have competing interests, we get an ethical problem. Finding a way through this problem requires a conversation among the stakeholders who have different interests. An example of competing interests can be found in some buyer-seller relationships, employer-employee relationships and company-society relationships.

Third, the rightness or wrongness of certain marketplace actions is not immediately apparent. Some marketplace actions have both desirable and undesirable consequences. Some decisions may require the decision maker to choose between the better of two good things or the lesser of two bad things. The most complicated ethical dilemmas may require both types of choices. Assuming that more than the decision maker is affected by the action, other people may have an opinion about the decision.

Fourth, shaping public policy (laws and regulations) based on ethical principles to minimize the risks of unethical behavior requires a conversation among lawmakers and interest groups who represent the various points of view on the ethical issues at stake. Shaping international regulations, laws and policies will require a much more complicated, lengthy discussion.

Finally, history reveals that group conversations do take place about ethical matters. Although Christians point to the same biblical

---

INTERPERSONAL AND INTRAPERSONAL

- **Interpersonal:** a process that occurs in the context of one or more relationships between persons through conversations
- **Intrapersonal:** a process that occurs inside a person's thinking or self; cognitive, rational, emotional

---

record as the foundation for their belief and practice, we can see that down through history Christian thinkers who wish to be faithful to that biblical record have had different points of view or points of emphasis when compared with thinkers who lived at different times and places. One might even see the roughly two thousand years of Christian dialogue on ethical matters as being a very slow conversation about difficult ethical matters.

Wisdom for ethics is not limited to what a person in isolation from the community is able to learn. It is a person-in-community process and a collective community process of getting and using wisdom.[13] Through conversations about social behaviors faith community members develop a shared belief regarding the

origin of ethical principles (i.e., God). This is the community's way of voicing a belief in existence of absolute, objective standards of conduct. Further, it is the community's way of positioning this absolute standard outside the persons and the community as a whole while being managed in the community through the participation of persons. In terms of the thesis of this book, it is the collection of biblical story themes which form the content of community dialogue on ethical matters. These themes are the architecture of the narratives which are formed when community members act (see fig. I.3).

Community members accept the Ten Commandments as the fundamental ethical principles that must be followed. But some actions, at least on the surface, need a thorough explo-

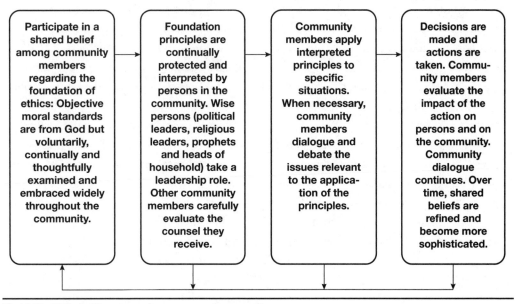

| Participate in a shared belief among community members regarding the foundation of ethics: Objective moral standards are from God but voluntarily, continually and thoughtfully examined and embraced widely throughout the community. | Foundation principles are continually protected and interpreted by persons in the community. Wise persons (political leaders, religious leaders, prophets and heads of household) take a leadership role. Other community members carefully evaluate the counsel they receive. | Community members apply interpreted principles to specific situations. When necessary, community members dialogue and debate the issues relevant to the application of the principles. | Decisions are made and actions are taken. Community members evaluate the impact of the action on persons and on the community. Community dialogue continues. Over time, shared beliefs are refined and become more sophisticated. |

Fig. I.3. The biblical ethics process from a community perspective.

ration of how biblical principles should be applied. This requires members of the community to have conversations founded on the same starting point: the principles that foster a life-giving relationship with God and with each other. This is a community process of testing ideas, reflection, debate, decision making, observing results and further reflection. Thus, ethics is as much a community, interpersonal relational process as it is a cognitive, intrapersonal cognitive process.

> You shall teach them diligently to your sons and shall talk of them when you sit in your house and when you walk by the way and when you lie down and when you rise up. (Deut 6:7)

We see examples of the interpersonal process at work in Scripture. Abraham and Lot have a conversation about what to do regarding the conflict that had arisen over scarce resources for their animals. This was an important economic issue. Through this conversation Abraham takes a leadership position by recommending that a geographic division be made between the two families.[14]

The experience of the exodus, in part, removes Israel from a situation in which their community conversations about ethics were not allowed to a place where it is allowed and encouraged.[15] The people took full advantage of this newfound freedom to talk.[16] In these stories we learn that all persons affected by a situation can become parties to the conversation that takes place regarding what is right and wrong.

The verse from Deuteronomy 6:7 highlighted above refers to the interpersonal dimension. Ethical principles are to be a matter of social

conversation not only within the family but also in society as people went about their business walking "by the way." Moses instituted an organizational restructuring so that leaders among the people who were considered wise in the ways of God would share in the process of giving advice and mediating between disputing parties. "You shall select out of all the people able men who fear God, men of truth, those who hate dishonest gain; and you shall place these over them as leaders of thousands, of hundreds, of fifties and of tens" (Ex 18:21).

Moses warned the people against discontinuing communal dialogue. "You shall not do at all what we are doing here today, every man doing whatever is right in his own eyes" (Deut 12:8). Later, under the judges, Israel learned the hard lesson what happens when people stop taking counsel.[17] Still later Solomon warned, "The way of a fool is right in his own eyes, but a wise man is he who listens to counsel" (Prov 12:15).

Other Bible writers emphasize the importance of counselors. Solomon mentions the importance of seeking counsel from wise people.[18] The king is responsible for advocating on behalf of the poor and anyone who cannot speak for himself or herself.[19] When the civil rulers do not participate in this community conversation about the poor, prophets rise up to rebuke them. The prophet Isaiah foretells the time when God would restore the flourishing life to his people. The presence of counselors was an important step in the process: "Then I will restore your judges as at the first, and your counselors as at the beginning; after that you will be called the city of righteousness, a faithful city" (Is 1:26). Isaiah identified the coming Messiah as a counselor who would come among the people.[20] In contrast to the wise counselors available to help the person who wishes to be faithful to God, the Bible describes the presence of wicked counselors who advise foolish courses of action.[21] Isaiah comments that when the people are taken into captivity, God would remove from them the counselors.[22] Removing the very thing that is needed in complicated ethical decisions is indeed a drastic punishment!

From a practical point of view, simple ethical questions are answered directly by the law of God: Don't kill. Don't steal. Don't tell lies. Don't cheat.[23] The more complicated ethical dilemmas need more thorough exploration of how biblical principles should be applied. A more thorough exploration means that it is more likely that community persons are brought into the conversation.[24] In turn, this means that someone will need to take the lead or share the lead in the conversations. It is in community where decisions are made about the difficult problems, not that every difficult problem needs to be shouted from the town square. Instead, a small group of persons can gather in private around the one tasked with making a difficult decision. The story that emerges from such conversations, and the resulting actions, become evidence of how important is community (even the small-group variety). Furthermore, this story that emerges becomes an important social foundation for the obligations that are shared.

Walking in the community having conversations involves testing ideas, reflection, debate, decision making, observing results and further reflection.[25] It involves putting relationships on the line when injustices occur. It is the relationships themselves that are at stake when ethical issues arise. To nurture and protect the relationship, someone must lead in the conversation. The prophets and Jesus Christ all discerned the validity of what others in the community were putting forward as guidance based on their understanding of God's law. They were not silent; instead, they participated in the community dialogue regarding right and wrong actions.[26] Thus, there is no mechanical process by which we carry with us an outline or list which we apply in a decision-tree fashion for the complex issues.

Such dialogue forms an ongoing broader conversation in and around the community regarding shared concerns.[27] It involves judges at the city gates,[28] the king on the throne,[29] prophets speaking out and parents teaching their children.[30] The process is suited for all social settings in an environment that is continually changing in terms of technology, politics, science, commerce, religion, philosophy, art, music, literature, and every other human endeavor or expression. The process is a form of communion, not only with each other but also ultimately with God. Our walk is not only a journey among humans; it is also a walk that takes place in the presence of God as a person holds on to another person as they walk together.[31]

Ultimately ethics is not just what we think. It is about what we do in a social setting. Accordingly, when we face a complex ethical dilemma and in sorting it out we engage others in the conversation, this becomes the first thing to do in the process. It can be the action step which provides us the wisdom, political support and perhaps courage needed for the other actions which follow. In some cases, this simple action of starting a conversation with others may be the most important action one can take in the ethics process. It is the action step which makes possible the telling of stories which, in turn, communicate character and make possible the transformation of character in others.

To summarize what we have observed thus far, the biblical perspective on deciding what is right and wrong in the marketplace is both an intrapersonal process of our heart and an interpersonal process during our walk in a social context. To the extent to which persons engage in conversations about right and wrong, the communal process occurs at the same time as the personal process. The communal process involves community leaders. In Bible times these were judges, counselors, prophets, teachers, civil leaders, priests and heads of households.

> Initiating a conversation with others about a complex ethical issue is the first *action* step in ethics.

In the personal process simple ethical questions can be answered directly by the basic principles in the Bible. Community leaders participate in conversation with different points of view and when the issues are complicated. To simulate this first action step, the section "Down to the Nitty-Gritty" is offered for the purpose of practicing the process.

DOWN TO THE NITTY-GRITTY

This section of the book will reappear in all but the last chapter. It is modeled after the two interrelated aspects of the ethics process described above. This is where you are given a chance to practice. To spark intrapersonal reflection and the interpersonal community conversation, a few questions will be asked in this feature relating to the practical dimensions of the chapter topic. Here is the first example (see table I.1).

THE CURRENT CRISIS

There is a crisis of business ethics among contemporary businesses and their managers. In spite of calls for reform at all levels including changing what is taught in business schools, it does not appear that the trend will change any time soon. In any given week, we hear stories about people who do unethical things in business. These appear in the local and national news media. Just read the *Wall Street*

Table I.1. The ethics process: intrapersonal and interpersonal.

Keeping Your Heart: An Intrapersonal Process	Walking in the Community: An Interpersonal Process
• What commitment have you made in your heart to be faithful to God? • How do you feel about the two-part process (intrapersonal and interpersonal) when deciding what is right and wrong? • Think about Scenario A at the beginning of the chapter. What makes the actions of the ATM thieves wrong? • Think about Scenario B at the beginning of the chapter: Is it wrong to use Jason's unsecured WiFi signal to access the Internet without his permission? If so, why?	• Has your circle of friends made the same commitment in their hearts to be faithful to God? If not, on what basis do you continue to associate with them? Can you be friends with someone who does not share your level of commitment to God? • When was the last time you and other people got involved in a conversation about something that was right or wrong? What was the topic? Who took a leadership role in the conversation? What, if anything, was the outcome of the conversation? • Think about Scenario A at the beginning of the chapter. In what way, if at all, would it benefit you to talk with someone else about what is right or wrong in this case? • Think about Scenario B at the beginning of the chapter. With whom might you talk about this to more clearly know what is the right thing to do? Get in a group now and discuss this scenario. What is the outcome of that conversation?

Journal or any business weekly magazine and you will see examples.

It has become such a problem that calls for renewed focus on business ethics and business reforms have come from many sectors of society including leaders in business. The calls have become more intense, and for good reason. People in business, customers, media, government, indeed most groups of people in society have experienced an erosion of trust in business primarily because of the scandals, the gross wrongdoing and the blatant disregard for standards of right and wrong. Employees see these things from the inside of their organizations and are disheartened and discouraged.

Business school graduates enter a marketplace in which sensitivities toward ethical scandals have never been higher. Yet, this same marketplace is riddled with persons and organizations that will stretch the ethical boundaries to the edges of what society is willing to tolerate. Young business professionals entering the workforce may be encouraged to take a relativist or egoist approach all in the name of supporting laudable organizational or personal goals.

Just as there is a crisis in business ethics, so too there is a crisis among Christians regarding what is right and wrong. Some Christians, seemingly without thinking, have embraced secular approaches to business ethics. In some cases, they have embraced approaches to ethics that are opposed to the biblical foundation of Christian faith and practice.

Carefully evaluating the commonly accepted secular ways of thinking will give readers a chance to recognize in themselves some of the same patterns of thinking. In this process, the flaws of secular approaches can be evaluated and readers can come to clarify what they believe and why.

This brings us to the engine of this book: The biblical story themes. These are called story themes in this book because they are integral not only to specific stories and teachings of the Bible but also to the overall big story of the Bible, the story about God and what a relationship with God is all about.

THE VALUE OF BIBLICAL STORY THEMES

Scripture story themes are valuable for several reasons. Scriptural themes offer the reader an unusual way to saturate the heart with scriptural thinking. The more we connect Scripture with business thinking and practice (it is assumed), the more we will think and act biblically when we are in the marketplace, the more the Holy Spirit can bring to our memory what we have learned,[32] the more alive our conscience will be to do the right thing, the stronger our defense against doing the wrong thing,[33] the stronger our moral imagination will become, the more capable we will be to counteract our inherent perceptual and judgment biases that lead us unwittingly into unethical practices and the better able we will be to encourage others.[34]

Story themes interrelate, interweave and sometimes overlap each other. At other times they interpret each other. In these ways, they become a complex canvas on which the Bible paints the essential message of God for our times.

Biblical themes promote the movement of learning from schooling into the arena of character education where hearts, minds and whole lives can be transformed.[35] The distinction between schooling and education is an important one. Schooling is the setting in which you learn information such as principles of accounting, economic theory or estimating the investment risks of particular opportunities. Education is the process of having the whole life transformed from the inside out by the renewing, creative power of God. Education is the process whereby the image of God is restored in us for service on this earth and for service in the life to come.[36]

> Education is the process whereby the image of God is restored in us for service on this earth and for service in the life to come.

Biblical themes are valuable for unlocking some difficult, and often misunderstood, passages of Scripture. Without the rich, deep perspective that these themes offer, a superficial reading of Scripture results in the development of bad theology and bad policies.

Scriptural themes are so pervasive throughout the Bible that they help us avoid cherry picking verses here and there to suit our private goals. In short, these themes help us maintain the authority of Scripture.

It has been said that you become like the person whom you admire most. As we spend time admiring the beautiful elements of God's character (expressed in story themes), we become changed. By continually focusing on these themes, especially as revealed in the life of Jesus Christ, we become changed, transformed into his image.[37] Scripture themes continually keep before the mind the character of God in Christ as seen in both the Old Testament and the New Testament.[38] By continually beholding the character of God, the community comes to know God and as a result becomes changed.[39]

Evangelical Christians sometimes refer to this as Christ "living in their hearts." For some this becomes a powerful mystical experience as they sense the close presence of God in their life. They see how their behavior has changed,

and they are energized by the realization that the power of God is at work.[40] This becomes the basis of witnessing.

Others who do not experience the intense mystical presence of God can still come to relate to the idea of an indwelling Christ. These come to understand that the primary characteristics of Christ, and those of God the Father, are starting to take root in their own habits of action. For both types of persons, it is the biblical themes that they start to relate to. Biblical themes reveal the character of God.[41] The interplay of one theme against another shows the aesthetic beauty of God's plan for a flourishing life. Take even one theme away and you are left with a diminished conception of God. Accordingly, the elements of God's character (comprising of the themes) become the basis of our witness in action and witness in words.

Regardless of your religious experience (or lack thereof), you will likely see alignment between some of the biblical story themes and the themes that all humans are interested in. Conversations in the community regarding ethical matters tend to cluster around certain themes present in the community (e.g., justice, rights, loyalty, faithfulness), some of which are the same as the biblical themes.

If just one or two biblical themes are used in the ethics process, the danger is that the more complicated ethical issues will be short-changed. Discussants will oversimplify or miss certain questions. If the full range of biblical themes is employed in discussion of the complicated ethical issues, more of Scripture is available to guide ethical behavior. One thing should become apparent after reading the whole book: Biblical themes form a cluster of perspectives that are very broad in their application. They may be the broadest set of principles compared with any other single system of ethics.

Compressing the twelve themes into just two or three would result in loss of understanding. In our desire for efficiency, we would quickly sacrifice richness and ethical effectiveness. The biblical themes that represent God's character and the believer's conduct are rich in texture. They are interrelated and interdependent but not identical. Because of this, they are difficult to separate.

In addition to these reasons why the themes are important we see an additional rationale. The prospect of becoming familiar with biblical story and its major themes offers the opportunity to saturate the heart with Scripture in a way that reading a few verses here and there cannot do alone. This is considered in several Bible passages:

> These words, which I am commanding you today, shall be on your heart. You shall teach them diligently to your sons and shall talk of them when you sit in your house and when you walk by the way and when you lie down and when you rise up. (Deut 6:6-7)

> You shall therefore impress these words of mine on your heart and on your soul; and you shall bind them as a sign on your hand, and they shall be as frontals on your forehead. (Deut 11:18)

> How blessed is the man who does not walk in the counsel of the wicked,
>
> Nor stand in the path of sinners,
>
> Nor sit in the seat of scoffers!
>
> But his delight is in the law of the LORD,
>
> And in His law he meditates day and night. (Ps 1:1-2)

Saturating the heart with Scripture is particularly relevant to work in the world of business as shown in these passages from one of the most famous portions of Scripture, Psalm 119:

- *Business is where our feet walk every day*: "Your word is a lamp to my feet, and a light to my path" (Ps 119:105).

- *Business requires wisdom from counselors*: "Your testimonies also are my delight; they are my counselors" (Ps 119:24).

- *The business environment offers temptations for false dealing*: "Remove the false way from me, and graciously grant me Your law" (Ps 119:29).

- *Business offers temptations for selfish gain*: "Incline my heart to Your testimonies, and not to dishonest gain" (Ps 119:36).

- *Business results in cash flow*: "The law of Your mouth is better to me than thousands of gold and silver pieces" (Ps 119:72).

THE MORE WE CONNECT SCRIPTURE WITH BUSINESS . . .

- the more we will think biblically when we are in the marketplace.
- the more the Holy Spirit can bring to our memory what we have learned.
- the more alive our conscience will be to do the right thing.
- the stronger our defense will be against doing the wrong thing.
- the stronger our moral imagination will become.
- the more capable we will be to counteract perceptual and judgment biases.
- the more capable we will be to encourage others.

- *Business is a competitive environment that requires wisdom*: "Your commandments make me wiser than my enemies, for they are ever mine" (Ps 119:98).

- *Business requires understanding*: "From Your precepts I get understanding; therefore I hate every false way" (Ps 119:104).

- *Business is an agent of shalom (peace)*: "Those who love Your law have great peace, and nothing causes them to stumble" (Ps 119:165).

Biblical themes reveal that the Bible respects the material and economic dimension of life experience. These themes are integral to life in the marketplaces of the world. Indeed, these themes are relevant to all social relationships. Themes explored in this text are applicable to both buyers and sellers.

The themes are grounded in the writings of Moses but are carried forward from there to more than three-quarters of the books of the Bible. These themes are employed from Genesis through Revelation. They are identified by two important kings in the Psalms and the Proverbs. They are present in the apocalyptic literature as well as in historical narratives and poetry in the Bible. Following the lead of the prophet Moses, the later prophets use these themes as the bases for their messages. Still later, the identity and work of Jesus are based on these themes.

More than five hundred times these themes appear in the Bible in groups. Here are just a few notable examples:

Righteousness and justice are the foundation of Your throne; loving kindness and truth go before You. (Ps 89:14)

But by His doing you are in Christ Jesus, who became to us wisdom from God, and righteousness and sanctification, and redemption. (1 Cor 1:30)

Stand firm therefore, having girded your loins with truth, and having put on the breastplate of righteousness, and having shod your feet with the preparation of the gospel of peace. (Eph 6:14-15)

And they sang the song of Moses, the bond-servant of God, and the song of the Lamb, saying,

"Great and marvelous are Your works,

O Lord God, the Almighty;

Righteous and true are Your ways,

King of the nations!" (Rev 15:3)

We should be cautious about claiming that we know everything about God once we become familiar with these themes. Scripture tells us that the full information about God is not perfectly knowable.[42] This awareness should lead us to humility. What we know of God through Scripture is true, but our knowledge may not be complete.

HOW THE THEMES WERE SELECTED

Scholars have catalogued scores of Scripture themes. But which themes are relevant to business ethics?

Three criteria seemed important when identifying the relevant Bible themes. First, themes identified are those that the Bible itself associates with our conduct. It is our conduct in all spheres of life (including the marketplace) that is considered. Thus, these themes apply equally to family relationships, leisure pursuits and our work in the faith community.

Second, themes associated with the character of God were selected since some of the biggest questions in the Bible relate to his character: Who is God, and what is he like? Is God's way of relating and living the best way to promote a flourishing life in community when compared with other ways? It is the character of God that is in focus in Scripture and that we are encouraged to imitate.[43] When God's image is restored in human beings, it is his character that becomes the key moral dimension.

Third, the themes are associated directly with Jesus Christ and his work. Jesus, the central figure in the biblical story and the author and finisher of our faith, is the clearest expression of what the character of God is like in human experience.[44] If we are to emulate God, we will find the guidance we need in the life and teachings of Jesus. The biblical support for these themes can be found in appendix B and in the notes for chapters three and four.

The intersection of these three criteria can be illustrated by the following diagram (see fig. I.4).[45]

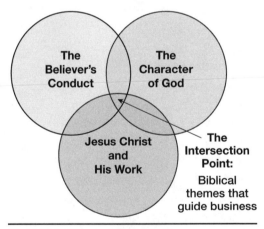

Fig. I.4. Biblical theme selection criteria.

When these selection criteria were applied, the following themes emerge:

- cosmic conflict
- creation
- covenant relationships
- holiness
- shalom

- sabbath
- justice
- righteousness
- truth
- wisdom
- loving kindness
- redemption

In chapter three we will consider the question of why so many themes. For now consider that the biblical story themes are appropriate to consider for specific business ethical dilemmas, so-called dirty tricks, legal issues, social responsibility issues and related case studies. These themes provide the framework to consider practical ethical challenges that organizations face in a global environment. In biblical thinking, business is not separate from the rest of life. Life is an integrated whole experience involving all social relationships, religious faith, economic endeavors, international relations and physical and mental health.

INTRODUCTION REVIEW QUESTIONS

1. What is the particular perspective that this book takes?

2. In Scripture, what is the relationship between ethics and the metaphor of the heart?

3. What does the metaphor of "walking by the way" signify in Scripture?

4. Describe the biblical ethics process from the personal perspective.

5. What is the biblical ethics process seen from the community perspective?

6. What is the current crisis in business ethics for people entering the marketplace?

7. What is the value of biblical story themes for studying business ethics?

8. How were the biblical story themes selected for this book?

DISCUSSION QUESTIONS

1. The book asserts that it is not only acceptable but also required to use our minds to think carefully about God's way of deciding right and wrong. Do you agree or disagree with this?

2. If the principles of right and wrong action are given by God and because of this these principles are objective and authoritative, why does the community need to participate in the ethics process?

3. When might community dialogue be most necessary in the ethics process?

4. Consider the criteria to select the biblical themes explored in this book. Are these three criteria valid?

5. What elements of biblical teaching, if any, seem to be missing from the ethics process described here?

6. After all that is said about the involvement of the community in the ethics process, to what degree is ethics primarily a personal process?

PART ONE

THE FUNDAMENTALS

Ethics is about moral action in a social context, not just moral thinking or correct doctrine considered in private. Accordingly, there is nothing more practical than business ethics when you think that the biggest question that is asked in business ethics is *What should I do in this situation?* At times the answer to the question is clear and easy to give. The tension is that at other times the answer to the question is somewhat more difficult and, at least in the world of business, often more complex.

The biblical perspective presented here provides a plausible structure to consider contemporary ethical ideas and challenges. Followers of God believe that the principles of ethics applying to business come from God. But when these principles are examined rationally, they are plausible explanations for how best to conduct oneself in the marketplace. The biblical themes presented here portray the means by which a person, in community, can be successful in this endeavor.

In chapter one we consider the question, Why is ethics in business important? We in-troduce the basic terms and concepts. Chapter two presents the underlying nature of the ethical, social and legal environment of business in terms of fundamental tensions that must be managed when taking action. As we will see, these fundamental tensions are universal and unending. Chapters three and four present the intellectual engine of the book: twelve interrelated, interwoven and interdependent biblical themes that are used as lenses to think through contemporary business ethics issues (cosmic conflict, creation, holiness, covenant, shalom, sabbath, justice, righteousness, truth, wisdom, loving kindness and redemption). As we will see, many of these themes are action-oriented. Designed for all areas of life's experience, they take us past mere thinking and guide us into the real world of behaviors in a social context. It is vital that the reader understand the essential elements of each theme as these will be used later in the book to evaluate contemporary ethical theories and contemporary ethical problems in business.

1

Why Ethics in Business Is Important

SCRIPTURE PASSAGE

So you shall keep His statutes and His commandments which I am giving you today, that it may go well with you and with your children after you, and that you may live long on the land which the LORD your God is giving you for all time. (Deut 4:40)[1]

CHAPTER OVERVIEW

In this chapter we consider whether or not it is beneficial for an organization, whether for-profit or nonprofit, to allow ethics to be influential in the life and work of the organization. In particular, we will

- introduce the benefits and costs of ethical and unethical actions in business

- examine what contributes to ethical problems occurring in business

- explore the definitions and distinctions of key concepts: morals, ethics, law

- introduce four levels of application of moral principles in organizations: individual, organizational, industrial and economic system

MAIN TOPICS

Is Honesty Always the Best Policy?
Why More Interest in Business Ethics Now?
Benefits of Ethical Business Activities

Costs of Unethical Business Activities
Why Study Business Ethics?
Why Ethical Problems Occur in Business
Basic Concepts
Four Levels of Application
Down to the Nitty-Gritty

KEY TERMS

amoral, communal, dirty tricks, ethics, generally accepted moral principles (GAMP), gray areas, immoral, law, morality, proscribed, prescribed, unethical

OPENING SCENARIO

Exercise and changing your diet to low-fat foods is one way to shed some weight. But some high-fat treats such as doughnuts are difficult to give up completely when you are on a diet. That is when Robert Ligon hit on a powerful target marketing concept: sell low-fat doughnuts to people trying to lose weight. This is just what he did.[2]

The typical doughnut is a sweet-tasting delivery system for a whopping 530 calories lathered in up to 18 grams of fat. As much as 25 percent of the traditional doughnut is fat. That's one reason why it tastes so good. Ligon's low-fat carob-covered version boasted 135 calories and 3 grams of fat. Delivering just one fourth of the calories and 17 percent of the fat, four of Ligon's doughnuts were the equivalent of one traditional doughnut. And Ligon's doughnuts tasted great!

Ligon sold not only low-fat doughnuts but also low-fat cinnamon rolls and low-fat cookies through weight-loss retail centers. Ligon's customers liked his product. A few customers were at first disappointed and then outright concerned when they gained weight instead of losing it. Then someone complained to the US Food and Drug Administration (FDA) that Ligon's doughnuts tasted too good to be of the low-fat variety. One customer noticed that when Ligon's doughnut was placed on a piece of paper it left a grease ring.

In 1997 the FDA began a formal investigation. This is when Ligon's three-year entrepreneurial bakery venture began to crumble. Through their investigation FDA food scientists determined that Ligon's doughnuts carried the same amount of fat and calories as do typical doughnuts. The FDA threshold for claiming that a product is low fat is 3 grams. The investigation revealed that Robert Ligon had been purchasing doughnuts from Cloverhill Bakery in Chicago, contracting with a packaging company to repackage Cloverhill's doughnuts and then selling the repackaged doughnuts under Ligon's brand.

As a result of their investigation the government raided Robert Ligon's doughnut packaging facilities in Kentucky and Illinois; they seized 1,560 dozen doughnuts as well as cinnamon rolls and packaging labels. Ligon was indicted for mail fraud for shipping falsely labeled goods. He pled guilty to one count but probably sold thousands of mislabeled doughnuts, cinnamon rolls and cookies. For his part Ligon claimed that he did not break the law and that he had never heard even one complaint about his doughnuts. He com-

mented that he had been singled out. In January 2004, Ligon began serving a fifteen-month sentence in federal prison.

Ligon was not the first to introduce the low-fat doughnut to the market. Entenmann's bakery tried selling a doughnut with 25 percent less fat, but the product was not successful. Entenmann's attempt was entirely legal and ethical. Not so with Vernon Patterson, the CEO of Genesis II Foods, Inc. who for a time also sold low-fat doughnuts. Patterson served a one-year prison term for mail fraud, misbranding food and unlawful monetary transactions. His crime: selling three varieties of regular doughnuts falsely labeled as low-fat.

Fortunately, the majority of people who start new ventures do not base their strategic commitments on faulty ethical principles. Whether or not they are Christians, many of the business activities are based on solid ethical foundation. If for no other reason, their organizations' survival depends on ethical practices.

IS HONESTY ALWAYS THE BEST POLICY?

Is honesty always the best policy in business? We can say with Benjamin Franklin, yes. But honesty does not automatically mean that you will earn a profit.[3] Looking only from a purely economic point of view over only the short run, being honest can make you money such as when a customer returns because he or she trusts you. Honesty is at the foundation of trust, which is necessary for success in both the short run and the long run. However, when a firm is under pressure to achieve a strong quarterly profit report or when the managers of the firm have an information advantage over a supplier or over a customer, the expected short-run financial benefit of being dishonest can exceed the expected costs. This is especially true if the managers believe there is a good chance they won't get caught.[4]

At other times being honest does not appear to have any direct and immediate measurable financial impact, either positive or negative.[5] Still, at other times honesty can increase your operating expenses, which means that short-term profit would go down if you cannot find other ways to cut costs or pass along the increase in cost to customers.

> Honesty is the best policy.
> But is it always good for profits?

Unethical actions can promote making a short-run profit if customers have no other substitute available and absolutely must have what you sell, if you can avoid detection or if you use physical intimidation of extortion.[6] Likewise, in the short run being dishonest can increase expenses incurred from defending a lawsuit in court. Or, it can mean lost revenue when a customer goes away. At other times being dishonest may have no immediate measurable financial impact one way or the other.

We can see from this brief review that the financial results of ethical and unethical behavior are mixed.

WHY MORE INTEREST IN BUSINESS ETHICS NOW?

If the results of ethical and unethical business action are mixed in terms of short-term profit regardless of your policy on honesty, why are so many people interested in business ethics these days? The answer is what we call ethics scandals, which, in reality, have been a part of business for centuries. In late fifteenth-century

Italy the wealthy Medici bank went insolvent in part because of the personal lifestyles of Medici family members. In eighteenth-century Louisiana, John Law exaggerated his own net worth and the value of a monopoly trade venture. When the proverbial bubble burst, he was expelled from the territory. Closer to our time, in the early 1960s Tino De Angelis defrauded clients and his bank by selling large quantities of water and passing it off as vegetable oil. He would fill his tanks with water and then pour in vegetable oil to cover the water (oil rises to the top). He used the tanks of "oil" as collateral to secure loans and do business deals . . . until he was caught.

Since the beginning of the twenty-first century, unethical behavior of some high-profile firms has severely damaged public trust in particular companies, in whole industries and in business in general. You may have heard about companies like WorldCom (telecommunications company), Enron (energy firm), Arthur Anderson (accounting firm) and Adelphia Communications (cable television company), all of which suffered catastrophic results of ethical-legal scandals.

Thousands of lesser-known companies have been caught in scandals, too. For example, in the mid-1990s Bre-X, a Canadian precious metals mining firm, announced that it had found enormous gold deposits on jungle land that it had purchased in Indonesia. The stock price shot up from pennies to more than CA$280 (Canadian dollars), and in short order Bre-X achieved a market capitalization of CA$6 billion during the investing frenzy. The Indonesian gold turned out to be truly fool's gold. It was not gold; and those who invested in the company became fools. It was not long before Bre-X's claim was found to be fraudulent, and the company collapsed taking billions of investors' money down a deep, dark money pit. In recent decades public outrage for business unethical behavior has peaked sparking calls for business ethics training in companies and in business schools.

Another reason is that people are beginning to realize that short-run profit is not the only time horizon that must considered.[7] Over the long haul it is more difficult to maintain a policy of dishonesty and avoid detection. There are notable exceptions to this, such as the experience of Bernie Madoff, the investment advisor and stockbroker who for many years used a Ponzi scheme to scam investors. True, in some cases the public never finds out about a business's dishonesty. For example, in 1920 an Irish immigrant to Canada signed on as a door-to-door salesman for the J. R. Watkins liniment oil (and other products).[8] He obtained products on account with Watkins and sold the products to local farmers. Apparently he skipped town to avoid paying the Watkins company. His customers may not have found out about his unethical dealing with the company. Watkins did. But why would customers care about it since they got the products they had purchased?

A third reason is that we now realize that business involves more than the purely financial impact. Isolating the financial dimension of ethical or unethical action from all the other dimensions of relationships is artificial and does not reflect social reality. What is considered good business includes how people are treated, how trust is built and maintained and how relationships are managed. Ethical actions play an important role in these other dimensions of business, too.

A fourth reason in alignment with the mission of this text is that people from more than one religion are more interested in living life in the marketplace consistent with their faith. Monotheistic religions such as Christianity, Islam and Judaism all encourage believers to act ethically in business.[9]

BENEFITS OF ETHICAL BUSINESS ACTIVITIES

Can we make a compelling business case for following ethical principles? Some say yes. When considering all the dimensions of business, including financial and nonfinancial, more than one business expert has advocated the importance of acting ethically in business.[10] Research studies have shown that paying attention to ethical issues in business can bring positive benefits to organizations. Ethical organizations have an easier time recruiting good employees. Companies that hold a high ethical standard find that employees want to stay longer working there. Employees are more likely to be productive in ethical work environments. Not surprising to proponents of business ethics, studies also say that attention to ethical issues can improve relationships with customers through improving customer loyalty and the power of the brand, and it can sway customer decision making.

Researchers measured companies with integrity (having attributes such as creativity, emphasis on ethics and allowing employee input) against gains in operating earnings, return on investment and increase in stock prices. Of the 207 major companies studied over an eleven-year period, it was found that the top twenty companies were those that emphasized integrity. They averaged 571 percent higher earnings, 417 percent higher return on investment and increased stock prices of 363 percent when compared with the ones that did not have a strong focus on integrity.[11]

17.8   -0.80   (-4.34)

Sept 25 3:51 p.m. ET

Open: 18.1   **Vol: 22,639**

High: 18.4   **Avg Vol: 15,500**

Fig. 1.1. A daily summary of a stock's performance.

From a biblical perspective, as we will see in the coming chapters, being ethical in business means that you are participating in the community in ways that support a flourishing life. Moral standards for business conduct are not merely arbitrary statements about the will of a capricious divine Being who is self-absorbed. Moral standards portrayed in the Bible, when applied widely across the community, contribute to the best way of experiencing an abundant life in all its dimensions.[12]

COSTS OF UNETHICAL BUSINESS ACTIVITIES

The costs of unethical actions in business can be high.[13] Few things are more time-consuming for a manager than when an employee acts in an un-

ethical manner that results in harm to someone. A customer gets angry and goes away. A supplier retaliates. A fellow employee complains asking for a resolution to a grievance. Productivity declines for all involved. An organization takes you to court. Defending lawsuits brought by aggrieved stakeholders can cost hundreds of thousands of dollars, not to mention the public embarrassment and humiliation. An ethics scandal erupts in the media and triggers civil lawsuits and increased scrutiny by regulators, law enforcement and the public. The organization's reputation can be permanently hurt. The crisis management public relations firm that your company hires to manage public impressions will cost tens of thousands or even hundreds of thousands of dollars. Researchers found that the cost of unethical behavior results in significant negative abnormal financial returns to shareholders. Illustrations of these high costs are provided in table 1.1.

Depending on the intensity of the scandal, it could take years to recover a damaged reputation. The Salomon Brothers Treasury bond bidding scandal shows how unethical (and illegal) actions can cost a firm hundreds of mil-

Table 1.1. Examples of the costs of unethical actions.

Scandal	Cost Estimate
Exxon Valdez oil spill in Alaska[a]	$3.5 billion
Stock options back-dating scandal[b]	$500 million
Manipulation of London Interbank (LIBOR) interest rates[c]	$88 billion
Food Network Paula Deen scandal[d]	$10 million
Penn State Jerry Sandusky sex-abuse scandal[e]	$48 million
Annual aggregate cost of crime to society in the USA[f]	$1.1 trillion

[a]http://money.cnn.com/galleries/2010/fortune/1005/gallery.expensive_oil_spills.fortune/2.html.

[b]E. Dash, "Report Estimates the Costs of a Stock Options Scandal," *New York Times* (September 6, 2006), www.nytimes.com/2006/09/06/business/06options.html?_r=0.

[c]M. Gongloff, "Libor Scandal's Potential Costs Exploding to $88 Billion or More," *Huffington Post* (August 27, 2012), www.huffingtonpost.com/2012/08/27/libor-scandal-bank-cost-estimates_n_1833150.html.

[d]The scandal involved television star Paula Deen making inappropriate racial comments. http://finance.yahoo .com/blogs/daily-ticker/scandal-cost-paula-deen-over-10-million-says-163142039.html.

[e]http://sportsillustrated.cnn.com/college-football/news/20130802/penn-state-scandal-cost.ap.

[f]D. A. Anderson, "The Aggregate Burden of Crime," *Journal of Law and Economics* 42, no. 2 (1999): 611-42.

lions of dollars. In Salomon Brothers' case, the firm was required to pay almost $200 million, and the firm's stock price fell by $300 million. Investors were concerned that the firm might lose customers who distrusted the company.[14]

> Adversity pursues sinners,
> But the righteous will be rewarded
> with prosperity. (Prov 13:21)

In some cases it is impossible for a firm to recover, and the persons involved in unethical or illegal actions must close their business, move away and start again under a different business name. Reputation is, after all, essentially an ethical issue: it is the community's attempt to maintain a current awareness of the firm's behavior. Such damage to reputation may not be directly measured, but the deterioration of relationships, declining employee productivity, creativity and loyalty, ineffective information flow through the organization, absenteeism and difficulty recruiting and retaining the most competent employees are all costs of being uninterested in the application of ethical reasoning at work. In some highly publicized cases, the impact from damaged reputation may be permanent and the company goes out of business. When companies go bankrupt because of ethical lapses and the resulting scandal, the cost of the impact is shared in the wider community: employees lose their jobs, creditors lose money, and strategic alliance partners lose. Everyone pays. Unraveling the consequences of unethical behavioral can be frustrating taking time away from pursuing other worthy goals.

Managers who ignore the ethical dimension to their actions are at an increased risk of incurring personal and corporate legal liability. They could lose their job and find it difficult to get a similar job elsewhere.

Research regarding the effect of employee discrimination, environment pollution, bribery or insider trading shows that the costs of penalties and litigation affect more than the bottom line of profitability, and this is increasingly important as profits are squeezed from increased competition. Such costs also have begun to influence boards of directors to monitor more closely the work of high-level managers. Acting legally and ethically can save billions of dollars each year in lawsuits, settlements and theft. This has an impact on the income statement, balance sheet and statement of cash flows.[15]

> Damage to a firm's reputation may mean the persons involved in unethical or illegal actions must close the business, move away and start again under a different business name.

As the wealth of corporations goes, we might infer, collectively so goes the wealth of their respective industries. And as both corporate-level wealth and industry-level wealth declines, society's resources are destroyed. Put in other words, if the economic profit of a firm is negatively affected by unethical behavior such that the total profit earned is less than the firm's cost of capital, it destroys society's wealth.[16] This community dimension is what places the issue of ethical and unethical behavior squarely in the ethical, social and legal environment of business, and is a major reason why it must be addressed in a book like this.

As unethical behaviors are manifested by upper-level management, workers throughout the organization note them, and unethical behavior becomes an organizational cultural norm. When this happens sometimes we say, "Unethical behavior flows downhill." Ultimately, this culture results in detrimental behaviors such as underdelivering on promises, turf guarding, goal lowering, budget twisting, fact hiding, detail skipping, credit hogging and scapegoating.

Table 1.2 provides a summary of the reasons commonly given by those who advocate being ethical in business.

WHY STUDY BUSINESS ETHICS?

There are several reasons why anyone going into business should think carefully about business ethics and even more reasons why the Christian in business should think about it. We review some of these here.

It is personal. Ultimately the question of whether or not to be ethical in business is personal. Why would *you* want to be ethical in your business activities or not? Do you want a clear conscience and peace of mind? Do you just want

Table 1.2. Why be ethical in business?

Benefits of Being Ethical	Costs of Being Unethical
Effective employee recruitment	Decreased productivity
Higher employee retention and loyalty	Cost of defending lawsuits
Better employee morale	Damaged reputation (brand)
Higher employee motivation and productivity	Absenteeism and low productivity
Better relationships with customers	Difficulty recruiting good employees
Strengthens the reputation (brand)	Cost to wider community: creditors
Influences customer decision making	Personal risks: loss of job, damage to career
Higher operating margins and ROI	Damage to industry profits
Higher stock price	Damage to organizational culture

To be fair in this discussion we should consider the opposite point of view. Those who argue that ethics and business do not mix suggest the following reasons. Some ethical issues can be solved only by spending more money. They say that it is inappropriate to discuss ethical issues at work. Others say that it is impossible to please everyone all the time. If you bring up ethical issues there will be such a diversity of opinion that a discussion of the matter would only divide people and create disharmony among workers. A final argument that you may hear in the market is that if people or companies do wrong, the market will punish them. Consumers will go away, laws will be passed, lawsuits will force changes: all these will produce the desired effects without taking the time to be philosophical.

to stay out of trouble? Do you want to live an authentic life in which your behavior is consistent with your beliefs? Do you want to preserve self-respect? Are you hoping that being ethical will build a positive reputation? Do you just want to do the right thing? Do you want to be a more effective manager? Do you want to comply with the law? Hoping to build positive relationships with others? Do you want to make more money?

> It is personal.
> Why do *you* want to be ethical in business?

Morality is unavoidable. Humans are wired for moral thinking and action! Try to go one full day without making even one moral judgment about someone or a situation. Even if you stay by yourself in a room and do nothing, it is impossible to avoid thinking morally. One reason for this is that we continually face new situations where moral judgment is applicable.[17] Nowhere is this illustrated better than in business situations. New technology, new business methods, new relationships continually emerge in business.

Intense moral issues arise in the marketplace. The more intense the issue, the less likely it can be avoided. Being prepared to discern moral issues and their intensity heightens your awareness as to what people are likely to be talking about. People do not like being lied to, cheated, stolen from, taken advantage of or harmed in other ways. The higher the moral intensity, the higher the visibility of an action, the less likely a person can avoid dealing with the issues.

T. M. Jones proposed that moral intensity is comprised of six factors. Collectively these factors have an effect on ethical decision making.[18] His model is shown below.

1. *Consensus of wrong* (social consensus). How much agreement is there that this action is wrong? The more there is agreement, the greater the intensity.

2. *Probability of harm* (probability of effect). How likely is it that this action will cause harm? The higher the probability that the action will cause harm, the greater the intensity.

3. *Immediacy of consequences* (temporal immediacy). Will harm be felt immediately? The more immediate the consequences, the greater the intensity.

4. *Proximity to victims* (proximity). How close, geographically or relationally, are the potential victims? The closer the proximity, the greater the intensity.

5. *Concentration of effect.* How concentrated is the effect of the action on the victims, that is, will it be quickly and easily observed? The more visible the effects of an action the greater the intensity.

6. *Greatness (severity) of harm* (magnitude of consequences). How many people will be harmed? The more people harmed the greater the intensity.

A question that naturally comes to mind when seeing the Jones moral intensity model is to what degree moral intensity influences the decision that a person makes. For example, if most people believe that a particular action is wrong, are you less likely to take this action? Likewise, if the consequences of an action are quickly and easily observed, are you less likely to take the action if you believe it is wrong? Is it the intensity of an action that makes it wrong or right? Should intensity be used to decide whether an action is permissible?

Education needed. Some unethical business behaviors are clear, yet some people do not know the legal and financial implications of these behaviors in business. Some people do not realize that if detected and convicted, they could pay fines and go to jail for a long time:[19]

- Vernon Matthews owned a company called First Capital Group in Virginia Beach, Virginia. Between 2010 and 2013 Matthews targeted members of the US military with investment schemes. He lured service personnel to his office by offering a free night in a hotel. He told them that the US government paid him for investment advice. This was a lie. He told them that their investment funds would be put in attractive mutual funds and certificates of deposit. In reality, he used their money for personal expenses or his business. He told his clients that there was low risk or no risk but that they would earn between 4 percent and 300 percent on their investment. Matthews was investigated and charged with fraud after he had received hundreds of thousands of dollars from his victims. He pled guilty and received a hefty fine and a forty-eight-month federal prison sentence.

- Russell Wassendorf scammed more than thirteen thousand investors out of millions of dollars over a twenty-year period. He is serving a fifty-year prison sentence.

- In 2007 Jeff McGrue started a foreclosure relief business in Los Angeles. He paid a finder's fee to real estate agents and others who were aware of homeowners who were facing loss of their home because their mortgage bank had given them notice of foreclosure. McGrue contacted the owners and promised to send the mortgage bank "bonded promissory notes" drawn from a US Treasury Department account. This note would pay off their mortgage. The hitch: Homeowners must pay a small fee of $1,500 or $2,500 and sign over the title of their home to McGrue's company. But they could buy back their home from McGrue for $25,000 after the bank was paid off. McGrue was caught after swindling 250 home owners out of more than $1 million. He was sentenced to twenty-five years in federal prison.

Ethical employers are hiring ethical employees. Aware of how important ethical workers are for customer trust, supplier trust and being on the right side of the law, more companies are considering ethics during their new employee recruitment and selection processes.

Ambiguity and debate. Some behaviors are clearly illegal and can land people in jail. There are many other actions where it is not clear whether they are illegal and still more actions where it is not clear whether they are unethical.

Business ethics is a popular topic, but if a person does not know how to think through ethically ambiguous situations or complicated dilemmas, and if viable alternatives are not known, he or she could be skating on thin ice and not really know how or why. Well-meaning persons have differences of opinion on whether certain actions are right or wrong. For example, the following situations illustrate the presence of ambiguous ethical dilemmas.[20]

- In August 2013 it was reported that the US Senate is investigating the use of "slotting fees" that retail food stores charge food manufacturers to gain access to retail shelf space. Grocery store executives say that slotting fees are necessary to offset costs and risks of putting new products on the shelf—products that might not sell as well as expected. Some smaller food manufacturers say that high slotting fees (which can be paid by the larger corporations) are unaffordable and unfair. They also claim that because larger food companies can pay the fees, they are able to squeeze smaller firms out of the market. Is it wrong for food retailers to charge slotting fees that are unaffordable to smaller firms?

- Solyndra, LLC, a solar-panel manufacturing firm, received a $535 million loan guarantee in March 2009 under a US Department of Energy program. One year later, in March 2010, auditors raised concerns about the financial viability of Solyndra. On January 1, 2011, the firm owed the US government $527 million. In August 2011, Solyndra operations shut down, and most workers were laid off. The next month Solyndra filed for bankruptcy protection. Was the US government relationship with Solyndra good thing for society?

Complicated issues. Some issues are more complicated than they first appear. If you write off a complicated issue as being obvious, you will come across to others who are more experienced or more knowledgeable as being uninformed and naive. Studying ethics, especially with respect to the more complicated issues, provides you with an awareness of how complex some issues truly are. This provides an important framework to build wisdom during your career. More than this, studying the ethical issues in the complicated dilemmas can teach you a lot about management and leadership.

Conversations in the public square. Entering into the marketplace to work in business takes you into the public square where, collectively, people talk about everything including ethical, social and legal issues of the situations they or other people are in. Studying business ethics thoughtfully will improve the clarity of your thinking and prepare you to engage in these conversations.

If there are benefits from promoting ethical behavior and if there are significant negative effects from unethical behavior, then why do ethical problems continue to occur in business? To this question we turn next.

WHY ETHICAL PROBLEMS OCCUR IN BUSINESS

It is tempting for the Christian to oversimplify the problem of unethical behavior by blaming the problem on sin, that is, disobedience to God's will. The implication is that if everyone converted to the Christian religion, business ethics problems might suddenly vanish. While sin might be at the root of the moral problems in business from a religious point of view, there are several other factors of the human experience that increase the likelihood that unethical behaviors will occur. Table 1.3 lists some of the reasons by ethical problems occur in business and some of the influences that prevent ethical problems.[21]

BASIC CONCEPTS

Before we go much farther, it is time to define a few ideas. In this section we define and distinguish between three interrelated ideas: morality, ethics and law.

Morality. Morality is the standard of right and wrong behaviors. Immorality is any behavior that does not align with the standard of right and wrong. A moral system is a standard of action or living in general, often encompassing a worldview on which those standards are based.[22] It is the set of fundamental principles that guide behavior.

Morality is a fundamental element in all human communities designed to foster the general welfare of the group. Moral rules form an important part of the structure of society. We can say that the existence of a social group requires a set of basic standards. Moral standards take priority over or override personal preferences and other social expectations. The continued existence of social groups depends on group members following the rules. In Western cultures most social groups consider that the moral standards apply equally to all members of the group. They are part of what are considered personal and social responsibility.

> **Morality** = standards of right and wrong behavior

At the foundation of moral standards are basic principles which are the fundamental rules which form the basis of standards. These are used to evaluate moral standards. Moral standards can vary from society to society or from one cultural group to another. But the basic principles do not change.[23]

Over the centuries various forms of moral standards have been put forward in societies.[24]

Table 1.3. Why ethical problems occur and what prevents ethical problems in business.

Why Ethical Problems Occur	What Prevents Ethical Problems
Narrowly focused and unrestrained self-interest of decision makers; unrestrained ambition and greed	The rule of law in society backed up by an impartial justice system
Ambiguous situations combined with leaders who reframe the interpretation to encourage particular behaviors	Ownership of private property
Code of silence and inaction coupled with penalties for dissent	Restrained and broadly focused self-interest
Competitive pressures mixed with aggressive profit-oriented goals; time pressures	Organizational systems designed for interdependence with the external environment
Organizational structure that undermines accountability	Ethical review processes and impartial grievance procedures
Lack of moral awareness	Individuals committed to maintaining solid personal standards
Organizational culture that allows for moral ambiguity	Selection and orientation of new employees
Cultural diversity	Consistent application of progressive disciplinary procedures
Instability of personal standards of right and wrong	Clearly enunciated statements of values backed up by supportive top-level leader behaviors
Double standards mixed with personal economic pressures (living beyond your means)	Managerial oversight
Biases in perception and judgment	Self-awareness
A sense of personal entitlement: "I deserve this!"	Humility
Trying to implement a great business idea with a bad business plan	Realistic business assumptions
Use of alcohol and drugs	Experience in observing the results of unethical behavior by other people
Personal traits: low conscientiousness, neuroticism, narcissism, use of power to achieve personal goals rather than organizational goals, emotional immaturity	Emotional, social and spiritual maturity
Moral disengagement: placing the responsibility on someone in higher authority; justifying the action as serving a moral purpose; reinterpreting the consequences; blaming the victim	

Contemporary Western organizational cultures have a moral system that is the foundation of the free market economy. Don't steal, don't lie; don't cheat; follow through on your commitments. Interestingly, these simple standards sound very much like what is given in the Bible.

Christians have a moral system that has been established on the Bible:

- the two Great Commands: Love God supremely; love each other unselfishly[25]

- the Ten Commandments[26]

- the many principles and guidelines found in the Bible that are particular applications of the Ten Commandments[27]

Amoral. An act that is amoral is defined as something that is neither moral nor immoral; actions that lie outside the sphere of morality. Some people say that this is true for the business environment. But this is a myth. Ultimately, business actions cannot be separated from moral standards of right and wrong (see fig. 1.2).

Ethics. Ethics is the study of the basic principles for determining conduct. We might say

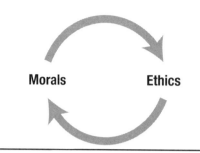

Fig. 1.2. The relationship between morals and ethics.

that ethics is the process of thinking about action and then, on the basis of that thinking, taking action. Ethics is the process of thinking about morality or the application of moral principles to specific situations.[28] Ethics involves the discussions and debates that people have when resolving differences of opinion regarding why some behaviors are wrong and others are right.[29] Any time you have a conversation with someone (or with yourself) about what is the right thing to do, you are engaged in the ethics process.

> **Ethics** = the process of thinking and talking about moral standards

In high school the principal announces a new student policy, and you grumble about this to your friends in the hallway after getting the news. You are "doing" ethics in the hallway during your conversation as you judge the rightness or wrongness of the new policy. Whenever you question why a particular social rule exists and why you have to obey it, you are doing ethics. Ethics involves our attempts to make sense of or justify a particular moral standard. It is the process of trying to be more precise in our thinking about right and wrong behaviors. It is the thought processes involved in understanding and examining moral standards that we hold or that other people agree with. Ethics also has been called moral phi-

losophy. Ethics is personal or social group reflection on moral issues in an attempt to better understand why behaviors are right or wrong.

Law. The nineteenth-century American physician and poet Oliver Wendell Holmes said that law is the "witness and external deposit of our moral life."[30] Law is the collection of formal codes that describe our public, but morally founded, duties that are either proscribed (prohibited, forbidden) or prescribed (required). Law is a contractual obligation that citizens make to each other "in exchange for which every individual has resigned a part of his natural liberty."[31] It is "a principled means of governing individual conduct."[32]

If laws are not obeyed, the citizen is subject to social sanctions and legal consequences.[33] The law should always be taken into consideration for business actions for two reasons: it represents the minimum requirements established by society—failure to obey the law brings undesirable consequences of fines, imprisonment or other imposed limitations; and the law is an indicator of the moral foundation under the law that should be taken into consideration when encountering a situation not explicitly addressed by the law.

> **Law is the collection of formal codes that describe our public, but morally founded, duties that are either proscribed (prohibited, forbidden) or prescribed (required).**

If it were not for Generally Accepted Moral Principles (GAMP), there could be no law. Legal requirements, while reflecting a common minimum level of morality by citizens, do not always define what is moral in the broader sense. The law is limited in its ability to address every

Figure 1.3. The relationship of morals, ethics and law.

possible action in every potential social situation.[34] The law usually addresses very specific behaviors. Some laws are usually made in reaction to specific situations that have occurred. In this way these laws lag the public awareness that certain actions are wrong or right.

> "The law is the witness and external deposit of our moral life. Its history is the history of the moral development of the race. The practice of it, in spite of popular jests, tends to make good citizens and good men."[35]

Many, but not all, laws are written in the form of a negative formulation saying what you must not do. But morality goes beyond the law by having something to say regarding what you should do. Furthermore, a particular behavior may be legally permitted (that is, the law does not explicitly forbid it), but it still might lack in a broader moral foundation (see fig. 1.3).[36]

Most actions in business that are legal also have a solid moral foundation for the law. And most illegal actions have solid moral foundations for the law. However, once in a while you may face a situation in which a particular behavior is illegal but might be the morally right thing to do in a particular circumstance.

Likewise you will likely encounter business situations where it is permissible to act in a certain way but not moral. A person might play a dirty trick on someone but not break the law. Finally, there may be a few areas where it could be debated whether a particular action is legal or illegal and either moral or immoral. These debatable circumstances we call gray areas. They are debatable because all the details may not be known and yet we try to make sense out of them from an ethical point of view (see fig. 1.4).

		LEGALITY	
		ILLEGAL	**LEGAL**
MORALITY	**MORAL**	Running a red light to take someone to the hospital Smuggling medicine into a war-stricken area	Many common actions that are commendable and expected
	IMMORAL	Most actions forbidden by law Dirty tricks such as fraud and extortion	Misleading people when selling a product provided that you do not lie

Gray Areas

Figure 1.4. A matrix of law and morals.

Table 1.4. Definitions and distinctions of three key terms.

	Legal	Moral	Ethical
Definition	Bare minimum set of specific behaviors that are required or forbidden as agreed to by society as written in formal rule of laws and regulations	The fundamental principles that govern social conduct that embrace a wider range of behaviors than the law can cover; based on values implicitly or explicitly embraced by society	How a person or a group of people evaluate right and wrong behavior a specific situation and come to a decision of what to do; the process of justifying an action based on moral standards; evaluating the rightness or wrongness of an action
Enforced by	The justice system; addresses a limited set of specific required and forbidden behaviors	Personal will to follow a strategy of integrity of behavior	Managerial decision-making policies and procedures or by personal will to follow a strategy of integrity of mind and heart; social pressure to conform to Generally Accepted Moral Principles
Examples	Don't commit fraud. Report all your earnings accurately on your tax return. Tell the truth when you advertise. Tell the truth when you report financial statements.	Behaviors that may or may not be specifically mentioned in the local, state or federal law. Be honest; act with integrity toward employees, clients, suppliers, investors and the government.	When faced with a specific (and sometimes ambiguous) situation or question of what to do or not do, how should a person think through the moral issues and come to a decision that guides in how to act with integrity and honesty?

Moral obligations are private, individual rules of conduct.[37] But they are not merely private. These rules are communal in that they are widely accepted across a given society as being valid. They have a communal impact.

> **MORAL OBLIGATIONS**
> - personal, private
> - social, communal

Communal means that it applies to the whole of society or even broader to a whole nation or even internationally. We say that morality is private only in the sense that moral standards for action are processed within a person. They are often commonly shared among many in society, rather than imposed from the outside source such as from the law.[38] While there are some behaviors that are private, the behaviors of individuals in organizational settings are never absolutely or completely private because organizational behaviors have implications for or consequences for others.

Table 1.4 provides a summary of the definitions and distinctions among three interrelated terms: law, moral and ethics.

FOUR LEVELS OF APPLICATION

Considering the range of issues and the broad scope of application of fundamental principles in the ethical, social and legal environment of business leads us to consider four possible levels of application: personal, organizational, industry/profession, and economic system.[39] If we are to strive for consistent integration of our fundamental principles, we will be willing to consider each level. These levels of analysis are shown in figure 1.5.

> **PERSON**
> - beliefs
> - moral values
> - perceptual biases in judgment

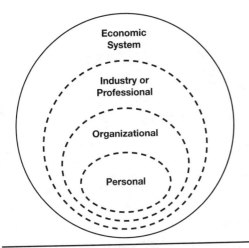

Figure 1.5. Four levels of application of morality, ethics and law.

guide behaviors that affect the organization as a whole (e.g., organizational policies, procedures, work units, departments and many employees). At this level the questions are: How does the person influence organizational decision making regarding pricing, maintaining relationships with customers, suppliers and employees, fulfilling social responsibility, exercising stewardship and care of the environment, and determining the appropriate level of economic return? How can the person work diligently toward effectiveness in pursuing the organizational mission and efficiency in achieving an economic return while also valuing persons? How should the person speak with others in the organization, if at all, regarding right and wrong organizational behavior? Accountability is organizational for actions taken by the organization. When moral problems arise, organizational behaviors should be evaluated and, where necessary, corrected (see fig. 1.6).

Personal. At the personal level we find beliefs, moral values and thoughts guide individual behaviors which affect other persons. Here the ethical, moral and legal questions are: What is required or forbidden by law for the person? How shall a person behave in a moral manner when taking actions in the marketplace? How should the person dialogue with others in the marketplace, if at all, regarding right and wrong behavior? Accountability is personal for actions taken by the person. When moral problems arise, personal behaviors should be evaluated and, where necessary, corrected.

Organizational. At the organizational level we find that beliefs, moral values and thoughts

Industry/professional association. At the level of the industry or professional association we find that beliefs, moral values and thoughts guide behaviors that affect the industry or professional association as a whole (e.g., industry practices) in which the organization or person participates. Here the questions are: How can the person influence the industry or professional association decision making that affect

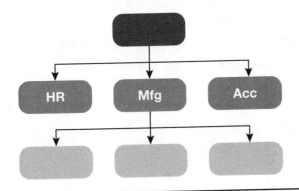

Organizations

- Administrative oversight team
- Use of authority
- Operational coordinating committees
- Policy committees

Figure 1.6. Morals and ethics in organizations.

INDUSTRY OR PROFESSIONAL ASSOCIATION

- officers, leaders
- policy committees
- oversight of activities
- publications
- annual conferences and programs

- liaisons with other industries/professions
- legislation monitoring; lobbying efforts
- licensure standards and control
- ethics standards
- member discipline

---

many persons and organizations? What are the moral values to promote among members? How to manage relationships with other industries or professions? How can the industry or profession exercise social responsibility? How can the person work diligently toward effectiveness in pursuing the industry or professional association mission by fostering the interests of the members? How should the person talk with others in the organization, if at all, regarding right and wrong industry or professional behavior? Accountability is at a broader scale for actions taken by the industry or profession. When moral problems arise, industry or professional behaviors should be evaluated and, where necessary, corrected.

Economic system. At the economic system level beliefs, moral values and thoughts guide behaviors that affect the economic system as a whole. Here the questions are: Is the current economic system moral? What role, if any, exists by the business professional/economist to advocate for or against change in the current economic system? On what moral basis can the person separate the practice of business in the economy from entering the public debate about the morality of the economic system? Should persons use some form of collective action to attempt moral economic reforms? If so, what types of moral reforms should be approached first? If not, why not? Should a person take a stand for or against socialism, or for or against the free market system? If so, in what way and on what basis? How should the person dialogue with others in society, if at all, regarding right and wrong behaviors of the economic system?

ECONOMIC SYSTEM

- planning, coordination and reform
- government-business relationship
- coordination mechanisms for productive enterprises
- factor and product markets
- prices; incentive systems
- national income, product and expenditure
- central bank: money; inflation
- international trade, finance, investment and aid

- consumer economics
- welfare and poverty
- performance monitoring and feedback
- access to natural resources; energy; environment
- political economy; legal institutions, property rights, law, regulation
- organizations: industry councils; government agencies

Accountability is at an even broader scale for actions taken by the economic system as a whole. When moral problems arise economic system behaviors should be evaluated and, where necessary, corrected.

DOWN TO THE NITTY-GRITTY

Think about Robert Ligon's story from the first of the chapter . . . Let's get down to the nitty-gritty (see table 1.5)!

CHAPTER REVIEW QUESTIONS

1. Why is the interest in business ethics growing?

2. What are the benefits and costs of being ethical in business?

3. Why do some people believe ethics are not appropriate in business?

4. What contributes to ethical problems in business?

5. Explain the basic concepts of morality, ethics and law. How can these be distinguished?

6. What are the four levels of application of ethics in business?

DISCUSSION QUESTIONS

1. If everyone professed the Christian faith, would the ethical problems in business go away?

2. Should we praise integrity because it has market value, or should integrity be pursued because it has intrinsic value?

3. Why do *you* want to be ethical in business?

4. If the issues that come up in the ethical, social and legal environment of business can be applied at four levels (individual, organizational, professional/industrial and economic system), on what basis might we say that accountability also is applicable at all four levels?

5. If you worked in a doughnut bakery that inaccurately advertised low-fat doughnuts to customers, what would you say to the owner of the firm? If you were the marketing director for such a bakery, what would you do?

Table 1.5. Applying the ethical process.

Keeping Your Heart: An Intrapersonal Process	Walking in the Community: An Interpersonal Process
• What does your heart tell you about Robert Ligon's goal of helping people who are overweight? • If you worked for Robert Ligon as the marketing director and you realized what was happening before the FDA found out, what would you do? • If you had this great idea for a business to sell low-fat doughnuts, what would your heart say is the right thing to do?	• If you worked for Robert Ligon as the marketing director and you realized what was happening before the FDA found out, with whom might you talk about this? • If you had a great idea to sell low-fat doughnuts to people wanting to lose weight, with whom might you talk about this to create your business plan? Would you discuss the ethics issues with someone? • In what way might a community conversation prevent unethical, illegal activities from coming into your business? In what way might a community conversation not prevent unethical, illegal activities from coming into your business? • Have a conversation with someone now regarding the possible ethical ways to sell low-fat doughnuts to people who are attempting to lose weight. How might an ethical business model be set up?

6. How can it be true, as stated in the previous chapter, that the marketplace is filled with unethical people pushing the boundaries of ethical limits and at the same time, as stated in this chapter, that the marketplace is filled with businesses that act ethically?

ETHICAL VIGNETTES TO DISCUSS

For each of the following vignettes discern what is right and wrong.

1. Richard Schulze, founder and CEO of Best Buy, resigned under pressure from the corporation's board of directors for failing to disclose a personal relationship between Brian Dunn, CEO, and a young subordinate. Such a relationship with a young subordinate is a violation of Best Buy ethics policy. A month before Schulze resigned, Brian Dunn also resigned. Increasingly corporate executive conduct, including behavior off the job, is under greater scrutiny by boards of directors. The use of social media by employees also is under greater scrutiny by mid-level and senior-level managers. Corporations are more sensitive to employees doing things that embarrass the company. Is it right that a company scan social media sites used by its employees and then discipline employees as a result of what appears on these sites?

2. You hire several Cambodian refugees to work in your plant that manufactures chemicals used in industrial coatings. These chemicals are highly toxic. The work is dirty and unpleasant. Mishandling raw materials can lead to serious injury and possibly permanent disability. The Cambodian refugees are willing to work for minimum wage and no health benefits. They seem grateful for their jobs.[40] What is the right thing to do?

2

Fundamental Tensions
in the Environment of Business

SCRIPTURE PASSAGE

Do not merely look out for your own personal interests, but also for the interests of others. (Phil 2:4)

CHAPTER OVERVIEW

In this chapter we grapple with the concept of paradoxical tensions that represent unseen influences on ethical thinking and actions. In particular, we will

- examine the characteristics of fundamental tensions in the business environment
- distinguish the opposing sides of five fundamental tensions in all of business
- explore the scriptural evidence regarding these four fundamental tensions

MAIN TOPICS

The Environment of Business
The Nature of Paradoxical Tensions
Economic Goals Versus Other Goals
Individual Needs Versus the Needs of Others
Short Term Versus Long Term
Duty to Others Versus Consequences
Universal Principles Versus Particular
   Situations

What Adds to Complexity
Down to the Nitty-Gritty
The Bible on Fundamental Tensions

KEY TERMS

casuistry, cognitive tension, deontological ethics, moral reasoning, paradox, right-versus-right dilemma, specious reasoning, teleological ethics

OPENING SCENARIO[1]

Dumping an unwanted employee on another company is not possible . . . unless you worked in the contract catering industry in 2003. Here's how this dirty trick worked.

Contract catering is the business of providing food services on a contract basis. Some contract caterers work for private special events such as weddings, anniversaries and parties. Other, large-scale catering companies serve organizations such as hotels, hospitals, prisons, large companies, schools and colleges on an ongoing basis. Aramark, Marriott and Sodexho Alliance were among the largest catering firms in 2003 serving companies such as Microsoft, Disney, General Electric and IBM. Some catering companies are regional, some national and a few have become global.

Although the details of contract terms differ from company to company, some contract caterers take on all the costs and keep the profit. Others may negotiate profit-sharing arrangements. In some arrangements the food service workers have the option of staying with the host organization if there is a change in contractor. Regardless of the arrangements, catering contracts are often price competitive as the host organizations seek to minimize their costs by outsourcing.

Catering contracts can be won this year and lost next year. It is during the transition from one contractor to another where dirty tricks can be played. In the contract catering industry the dirty tricks had gotten so bad in 2003 that some catering companies began calling for the development of an industry code of practice to bring a halt to the underhanded dealing.

A few weeks before the effective termination date of a catering contract, managers who work for the outgoing company can use scare tactics with food service workers. Maybe the outgoing manager will make statements about what he has heard about how the new company treats food service workers. Or, maybe he will speak disparagingly about how the new company cuts corners in quality. Or, the human resource manager for the outgoing firm might warn workers that their work schedules will be disrupted or claim that the incoming firm is inflexible with employees who have small children.

Employees with the most marketable skills will desire to work for the outgoing company if they get anxious about working for the incoming contractor. This leaves the incoming company with an employee group that in general underperforms, thus making it difficult for the incoming firm to achieve its profit goals. This can have a negative influence on the service quality. As a result, leaders in the host organization have second thoughts about their decision to contract with the new firm. With this scenario in mind, let's consider five fundamental tensions in the ethical, social and legal environment of business.

THE ENVIRONMENT OF BUSINESS

Take a trip in a deep-sea submersible vehicle through the Pacific Ocean and you could travel to the Mariana Trench, the place in the ocean that is closer to the core of the earth than anywhere else. Below the partial ring of the Mariana Islands, the ocean is 36,000 feet deep. What is the environment of the Mariana Trench like?

You can talk about water pressure because that may be what scares you the most. You might remark how dark it is down there. But if you wanted to get the central issues at stake of that environment, you would describe the geophysical plate subduction processes slowly at work changing the shape of the ocean floor. The Pacific Plate is being squashed and pulled under the Philippine Plate. You could also think of this as a very slow but gargantuan waste basket for the ocean. Whatever is on the ocean floor will be inexorably dragged into the underground molten lava pools that are even deeper. At the depth of the Mariana Trench you could also describe a paradox: the huge tension between the molten lava pushing up against the massive water pressure pushing down on the ocean floor. These forces are hidden from view but nevertheless are constantly at work.

If you traveled to the core of the environment of business, what could you observe? You could talk about something personal to you and your goals, such as where the best jobs are or which career will result in the largest life-time earnings, or which career you will find most interesting. Or, you could broaden your scope and look for the processes at work that influence everyone the entire world of business.

You can describe the environment of business in terms of what the average household in the United States spends (more than $6,000 on food, more than $17,000 on housing and utilities, more than $8,000 on transportation). You could mention the average hourly wage or the current unemployment rate. You can discuss the trends in e-commerce by noting that every year almost half a trillion dollars flow through the business-to-consumer (B2C) part of the economy. Some might be surprised when you tell them that nine times that much money flows through business-to-business (B2B) e-commerce transactions. But is this the core of the business environment?

Here an analogy is in order. Think of an ordinary apple. When you look at it, you do not see the core that contains the seeds. Yet, you know from experience that the core is there but hidden from view. As you eat the apple from the outside, you progressively get closer to the core. Think of this chapter as representing the eating of an apple. At your first bite you might get some accounting. At your next bite you might get the taste of marketing or management or how to use a spreadsheet. Keep eating and you are getting closer to the unseen.

Business is a social activity that can be seen. Because of this it is natural to think that business decisions are made based on only observable social behaviors. In business school we learn the activities of business that will help us be successful. We learn how to observe the actions of customers, lawmakers, competitors, and everyone who is relevant to business activity. But where do we learn about the fundamental core of business activities, the center which contains the seeds of everything that we do see? In this book we learn about the core.

To change metaphors, it is like peeling back the layers of an onion. When you look at patterns of behaviors of buyers and sellers, you get nearer to the core of the environment of business. You see that there are patterns of opposing though unseen forces at work. You notice that buyers and sellers are both competing with each other and cooperating with each other. They compete when the buyer wants a product at a lower price and the seller wants to sell the product at a higher price. Yet, they cooperate by meeting in the marketplace of products and services to interact with each other in order to do business. This is one hidden element of the environment of business.

Another hidden element of business is inside every organization: It is the presence of strategic thinking and operational thinking. Managers must keep in mind the big-picture commitments that the organization is making while at the same time stay focused on carrying out day-to-day activities. These and hundreds of other opposing forces are constantly at work

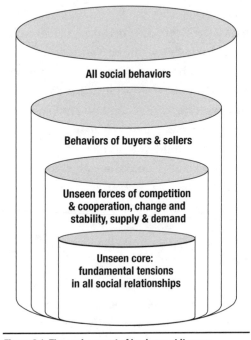

Figure 2.1. The environment of business at its core.

Labels within figure:
All social behaviors
Behaviors of buyers & sellers
Unseen forces of competition & cooperation, change and stability, supply & demand
Unseen core: fundamental tensions in all social relationships

throughout the business environment. Most of them are hidden, yet we experience their effect every day as we go about our work. When you go deeper, you get to the fundamental tensions that affect everyone in all social relationships, including business relationships (see fig. 2.1).

The deep core of all social relationships is important for several reasons, though that is rarely explicitly discussed in other business textbooks and university courses.[2] First, as we will see in this chapter, these fundamental though hidden elements of the business environment have an effect on all behaviors that can be observed. Second, sometimes we may not be aware of how these hidden elements affect us in our work. But this does not mean they are not present and active. The more aware we are of these unseen elements, the wiser we will become in managing the things that we see. Third, name any organization, from a family to a neighborhood watch organization to a for-profit business, a nonprofit organization or a government agency. None of these can escape the influence of these unseen fundamental tensions. The reason is that these fundamental tensions are locked into all social relationships. Fourth, to be successful in business we have to manage these fundamental tensions just as much as we must manage what we can see in our relationships in business. The only problem is that managing the unseen can be far more difficult than managing what we can see. As you gain wisdom for how to manage these fundamental unseen tensions, you are gaining wisdom for how to be successful.

THE NATURE OF PARADOXICAL TENSIONS

This chapter explores five of the fundamental tensions that make up the unseen core of the business apple that we experience all the time. Before we explore these tensions, we will define the concept of paradox. Then we will learn the characteristics of these fundamental paradox tensions.[3]

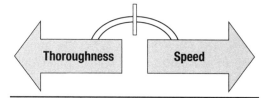

Figure 2.2. A paradox illustrating two opposing forces.

A paradox is a condition where two opposing forces are at work at the same time. A managerial paradox occurs when members of the organization must pursue goals that appear to be in direct conflict with each other. For example, managers are expected to be thorough and fast; however, these dynamics are somewhat opposing.

Four characteristics of fundamental paradoxes in business help us recognize them.[4] First, paradoxes in the world of business are universal in application. Everyone experiences them. This is true for the smallest-scale marketplace exchange between two persons at a garage sale to the largest-scale series of transactions that involve multinational enterprises. At an even larger scale these tensions are present when nations negotiate treaties or try to figure out how to deal with global warming.

Second, these paradoxes involve at least two somewhat opposite (or different) pressures at times counteracting or working against each other. This will be illustrated later in this chapter. Third, these paradoxes are enduring: they do not go away, but they must be managed. The reason for this is the fourth characteristic of social life: Each side of the tension is inseparable from the other. Both sides of the tension are structurally interdependent with each other. Each side has an impact on the other. These characteristics are summarized in table 2.1.

Table 2.1. Characteristics of paradoxes fundamental to business.

Characteristics of the Fundamental Paradoxes
Universal: These paradoxes can be applied in all types and all scales of social situations.
Opposites: These tensions require the action of opposing or different pressures.
Enduring: Paradoxes defy choosing one side over the other.
Interdependence: The opposing sides of paradox are intertwined with and affect each other.

In this chapter we are introducing the five fundamental paradoxes, the unseen tensions that affect all marketplace actions at all levels worldwide:

- economic goals-other goals
- individual-community
- short term-long term
- duty-consequences
- universal principles-particular situations

We will consider each in turn starting with the tension of pursuing economic goals versus pursuing other goals.

ECONOMIC GOALS VERSUS OTHER GOALS

By its very nature business activities of buying and selling involve the pursuit of economic goals (earning money, making a profit, saving money, growing the value of assets). At the same time, the activities of buying and selling involve the pursuit of non-economic social goals (meaning in life, happiness, general well-being, flourishing life, social harmony, satisfaction in personal relationships, meeting the needs of others).

Sometimes economic goals conflict with other goals but we feel compelled to attempt to achieve both. We do not always succeed. Sometimes we value the economic achievements. At other times the other social goals take priority. For some managers achieving a balance in both sides of the tension is an elusive target in every particular situation.

Strangely, economic goals are intertwined with the other goals, many of them social in nature. It is difficult to achieve the other goals without a measure of economic success. And it is difficult to achieve economic goals without achieving other goals. Yet, placing too much emphasis on one side tends to be destructive of the other. Just as interesting is that both types of goals are essentially social in nature. Both usually involve actions with and for other people. Because of this, it is impossible to separate either set of goals from ethics.

You probably know this tension in your own life. For example, you want to complete a university degree. This comes at an opportunity cost of time, money and learning that you might achieve in other settings. The goal of an education competes with the short-term economic goal of earning money. Or, you are a leader in a club. You want the club members to have good experiences. You also want the club to be financially stable. So the competing questions become how much to spend (to be responsible with the money available) and how interesting to make the club experiences, which may require spending more money than you would prefer to spend.

INDIVIDUAL NEEDS VERSUS THE NEEDS OF OTHERS

The individual-community social tension involves what you want to do for yourself versus what you should do for others. You have experienced this, too. It is everywhere in business and can be considered a basic tension in all of life. It is one that is at the root of all other ethical tensions that exist (see fig. 2.3).

THINKING	ACTION
Desire versus duty	Freedom versus responsibility
What I *want* to do versus what I think I *should* do	Private versus collective

Figure 2.3. The individual-community paradox in thinking and action.

You will see this tension in the company lunch room when someone leaves a note like this one on the door of the microwave oven: "If you are going to heat up spaghetti, clean out the microwave when you are done!" Another example at a larger scale is when managers of an automobile assembly plant like General Motors must decide whether or not to initiate a recall of a certain model of car to make a necessary repair. Something as small as an ignition switch, when faulty, can cause fatal accidents. The part might cost less than $1.00 to manufacture, but it will cost tens of millions of dollars in labor costs to change the ignition switches of two million vehicles. Should the managers follow their desire to take care of the profitability of their company or should they follow a duty to watch out for the interests of the two million owners of vehicles who are at risk? At a much larger scale we saw this at work when the group of European nations decided whether or not and how to help Greece during its financial difficulty in 2011–2012. At the same time each nation needs to preserve sovereignty and autonomy, the group of nations also has a responsibility to preserve stability for all. The success and stability of the group is dependent on individual nations watching out for their own interests as well as the interests of the other nations.

A PARADOX

Bear one another's burdens, and thereby fulfill the law of Christ. For if anyone thinks he is something when he is nothing, he deceives himself. . . . For each one will bear his own load. (Gal 6:2-3, 5)

For centuries people who have thought about society, government and how humans get along in marketplaces have considered this to be a fundamental tension. For Jean Jacques Rousseau the tension between the drive toward individual freedom and the need to protect the common good is managed by how we structure our relationship to the government.[5] Closer to our time, business management thinkers such as Henri Fayol have said that this paradox is one of the great difficulties of management.[6] This paradox as the "basic constitutional problem . . . between fragmentary group interests and the aims of the whole."[7] From the perspective of organizations it is the "basic and enduring problem."[8] It is also considered to be a fundamental tension in morality.[9] This tension is shown in figure 2.4.[10]

INDIVIDUAL		COMMUNITY
Freedom, desire		Responsibility, duty
Self-interest	INDIVIDUAL	Other-interest
Freedom of individual	versus	Restrictions of the group
Independence	COMMUNITY	Interdependence
Personal desire		Duty to others
Individual goals		Group's goals

Figure 2.4. Forms of the individual-community paradox.

From this one tension flows some of the most important dynamics in life, including how we get along with each other in a business organization and what form of government we think is best: a constitutional democracy that emphasizes individual interests and freedoms (but does not completely forget group needs) or collectivism that emphasizes the group's interests and responsibilities (but does not completely ignore individual needs) or another type of government. From this one tension comes many, if not most, of the ethical dilemmas we face. Both sides of the tension represent legitimate, positive duties to perform. Additionally, imbedded in this tension is a fundamental element of moral reasoning: At the moment we must decide what to do we not only must consider the effect on ourselves but also not allow self-interest to have any preference over the interests of others. This issue applies to all individuals and all social groups at all levels of society. Notice that each individual unit is part of a larger community context.

SHORT TERM VERSUS LONG TERM

We come now to the fundamental paradox relating to time: the short term versus the long term.[11] This tension refers to the fact that organizational leaders must at the same time make decisions that solve present problems or address the current issues and make decisions that affect themselves and the company in the long run.

The famous writer Ralph Waldo Emerson said, "The present and the future are always rivals."[12] This is true in all of life and especially in our marketplace activities. What is more, the short term and the long run cannot get away from each other.[13] It might seem that we have only the present to think about, but this is an illusion. The present is always connected with the past and the future.

This tension applies to something as simple as deciding what to eat. High-calorie fast food is convenient. After enjoying a late-night fast-food meal you do not wake up the next morning thirty pounds heavier. This will take a few years of late-night high-calorie meals.[14] But if it was not for the ever present, that particular long-run effect would not result.

Consider two examples of situations in which you must make a decision:

- You have ninety minutes of free time in your schedule now. Should you use that time to socialize, to study, to read a good book, to play tennis or to play a video game?

- You are in your first job after graduation. You want to begin putting money away for your retirement and you need cash to enjoy things now.

At first glance your decision may not seem to have any long-run consequences. But a pattern of short-term decisions affects long-run consequences which you may like or dislike depending on results. In any given situation you might want to grant yourself an exception to your rule. But if exception granting becomes the pattern, you should expect to achieve a long-term outcome that is different from your goal.

Now consider an example of a situation in which the short term and long run are inseparable in business.

- Top-level managers must make decisions to adjust the expenses of their company so that the profit earned during this current ninety-day period meets the projections. Achieving this goal will have a direct effect on the estimates that stockholders make of the firm's stock price.

- Managers must be careful where to cut expenses. If expenses are cut too much for the short term to achieve a particular profit goal,

SHORT TERM

SUNDAY	MONDAY	TUESDAY	WEDNESDAY	THURSDAY	FRIDAY	SATURDAY
			1	2	3	4
5	6	7	8	9	10	11
12	13	14	15	16	17	18
19	20	21	22	23	24	25
26	27	28	29	30		

LONG TERM

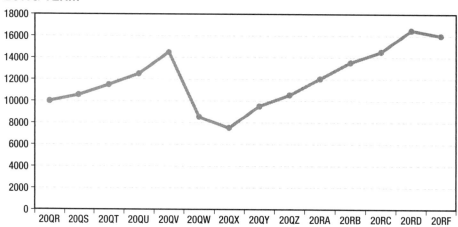

Figure 2.5. An illustration of the short term and the long term.

it could harm the ability of the organization over the long run to achieve its purpose.

On a small scale company performance must be managed operationally today and strategically for the years in the future.[15] At a broad society level, efficient waste handling and disposal today must be weighed against the long-term benefits and costs of recycling and the technologies and capital investments in multiple industries and across many countries.[16] On an even broader international scale, how the community of nations uses energy for the short term will have a long-run impact on the availability of natural resources on the planet as a whole on which we all depend.

Research shows that humans tend to see higher value of the present while discounting the future. Compared with gains and losses that we might experience in the present time, we tend to discount the value of all gains and losses that will come in the future. When we look to the future, we are more likely to focus on what we *should* do. But when considering our options for the present, we tend to do what we *want* to do.[17] Present concerns are far more vivid to us because it is the present that we experience at the moment.

Short-term focus coupled with discounting the future played a role in the global financial crisis of 2008. Real estate developers, government regulators, real estate agents, banks and customers all seemed to discount the future as low-income families tried to buy houses. Lenders offered attractive variable-interest mortgages requiring very small down payments. Policies regarding the earning power of families were relaxed. Many people got into homes they could not have purchased a few years earlier. Lenders then bundled scores of risky loans and resold these to other lenders. When interest rates increased and families could not meet their mortgage payments, the housing bubble burst and the crash affected many other areas of the economy. The culprit: excessive short-term focus by all involved.[18]

Like the previous two paradoxes, this fundamental element applies everywhere in social life. It is never ending. It represents the inseparable interdependence between the past, present and future. In addition, just as the tension between individual and community is often central to the question of what is the ethical thing to do, so is the question of time.

The following observations can be made regarding this time paradox:

- Goods we can obtain now are more highly valued than those we get later. Thus, we tend to value the present higher than the future.[19] When the present is more highly valued than the long-run future, this can make it more difficult to manage this tension.

- Managers are sometimes tempted to focus on today and let tomorrow take care of itself.[20]

- Managers can use the opportunity of the present to infuse the perception among subordinates regarding the long run with meaning.[21]

- In many of our decisions we often want to do something that will satisfy short-term desire when we know we should do differently to achieve a different long-run goal.[22]

- Profit is often of a short-term concern. Ethical considerations often concern both the short term and the long run.[23]

- Decisions today can place unintended constraints on future options. Further, some decisions in the present can be changed while others are unchangeable.[24]

- Decisions made in the short run can bring negative long-run results that are far greater than the short-run benefit we enjoyed.[25]

- When the short run is emphasized to the exclusion of the long run, the risk may increase that individual interests will dominate over community interests.

Several things explain why the short-term focus dominates in the experience of most organizational leaders.[26] Many organizations including for-profit, nonprofit and government are under pressure to do things in the short term.[27] Those who have these expectations may be thinking largely of the short term. Left to themselves today's issues will take so much time that we have little time left to think about strategic concerns. The present is tangible and understandable; the future is vague and abstract. Managers are often evaluated on the short-term performance of their organization. Stockholders monitor the short-term value of stock; executives follow suit in hopes that compensation bonuses will be earned. Like the workers they supervise, managers need feedback that tells them how well they are doing.

We have considered three fundamental tension points present in all of business experiences. We now address two additional fundamental tensions related to the process of deciding what is right and wrong.

DUTY TO OTHERS VERSUS CONSEQUENCES

You are a real estate agent who has just received a visit from an elderly widow who wishes to purchase a condominium. The condominium has been listed by an agent working for another company. You believe that the list price for a condo she is interested in is $5,000 more than what the owner expects to sell it for. But the woman, ignorant of common real estate practices, wants to offer the full list price. Should you tell her to offer less or communicate her uninformed offer to the seller's agent? Should you decide what is right or wrong on the expected outcomes for the seller, the real estate agents and the widow? Should you decide based on duty to a principle of what is the right thing to do?

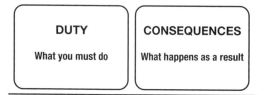

Figure 2.6. The relationship between duty and consequences.

The traditional approaches to deciding what is right and wrong have been put into two broad categories. Some approaches are based mainly on duty or obligations (sometimes called deontological ethics); other approaches take into consideration the consequences or goals of actions (sometimes called teleological ethics). These two broad categories are often contrasted as being, if not opposite, quite different from each other.

In reality these two contrasting approaches can never be completely separated. For example, let us consider again the auto assembly plant that is assessing whether or not to initiate a recall to repair a defective part. On the one hand, managers at the plant have a duty to

obey regulations. They also have duties to product safety for customers. On the other hand, the decision whether or not to recall two million cars must consider the expected consequences of two options: What will happen to drivers if the defective part is not repaired? What consequences will the company experience in terms of the costs of repairing two million vehicles? We will learn in part II of the book that this approach is known as utilitarianism. Likewise, the person who bases decision making on duty to principle cannot consider duty alone without thinking about the consequences of the action. Implicit in the perceived duty to action is an awareness of what happens if the action is or is not taken.

As another example, when a Christian says that he or she has the duty not to steal because this is commanded in the Ten Commandments,[28] this duty is in the larger context of beliefs regarding the nature of human beings created in the image of God and how stealing is an attack on both the image of God (i.e., another human being) and the Creator. Thus, it is not just stealing considered in a vacuum that is the duty but stealing considered in terms of how the outcomes of stealing have an impact on someone.

By analogy, rules in sport become duties but these duties are based on the consideration of consequences of certain actions. The reason the rule was established was because of outcomes that are either desired or not desired. Does the football umpire throw the flag for a foul because the quarterback is hurt or because the defensive player broke the rule by hitting the quarterback on the head? Does the soccer referee show the yellow card because a player tackles a competitor without touching the ball or because one team lost possession to the other or the tackled player got a bruised hip as a result? Does the court judge fine and imprison a felon because the victim was harmed by the felon's action or because the felon acted in a way that is forbidden by law? A company fires an employee for embezzling funds even though the employee pays back the money. Does the firm do this because it has a duty to protect the owner's assets or because the firm suffered financial loss even if for a short term? In these and hundreds of other situations both duty and consequences are considered either implicitly or explicitly.

UNIVERSAL PRINCIPLES VERSUS PARTICULAR SITUATIONS

Like the other tension points explored in this chapter, the fifth and final universal tension in the ethical, social and legal environment of business cannot be avoided.

Acting on what you believe to be right and wrong is rooted in specific situations because business behavior always occurs in a particular social context. But ethics cannot be only about specific situations. Ethics also must take into account certain principles of behavior that apply across many different situations. Any particular ethical dilemma we find ourselves in at the moment is merely one scene in a larger story of which we are also a part. Thus, the principles we use to deal with the current scene must also be the principles that apply in the larger story in other scenes. Such principles require impartial generalizations that transcend particular situations.[29] Thus we have the tension between the particular application of principles and the universal principles.

Attempting to manage this tension alone can be risky. The reason is that the more complicated the ethical problem, the more difficult it will be as one person to think through all the issues that are involved.

By saying that the particular situation is important (and even that it cannot be avoided), we are *not* saying that all ethical principles are situational. Rather, we are saying that all behavior occurs in particular historical, social situations the details of which cannot be ignored when thinking about the broader principles of right and wrong behavior. Examples of the universal-particular tension are provided in table 2.2.

Moral reasoning and casuistry. The process of taking general, universal principles and applying them to a particular, concrete situation in order to discern what is right or wrong is known as moral reasoning or casuistry. It is the ethics process in action. When persons debate the rightness or wrongness of

Table 2.2. Examples of universal-particular tension.

Universal	Particular
Do no harm: A moral principle that is common to all societies.	When repairing someone's car, give the owner a choice before incurring a large expense.
Be fair to your employees.	Give employees what you promised them; however, be careful to minimize the chances that an employee will try to take advantage of the company's policy for reimbursing workers for incurring authorized expenses.
Limit your own freedom so that others have freedom, too.	Stop at the red traffic light.
Interpreting a particular passage in the context of what the rest of the Bible says.	Reading a particular verse from Scripture and applying it to my life.
Remember the sabbath to keep it holy . . .	What specific behaviors are appropriate or not appropriate for sabbath keeping?

a particular action in a particular circumstance and in light of general principles and in the light of previous experiences or cases, they are engaging in casuistry.[30]

Casuistry has both positive and negative connotations. From the positive perspective, casuistry involves engaging in serious reflection and conversations with others to determine the rightness or wrongness of an action by using general principles applied to a specific situation. From this perspective you give yourself no special consideration; you limit your personal biases by including others in the conversation.

In the negative use of the term, casuistry can be used with what is known as specious reasoning, which is an attempt to bias the process of determining what is right and wrong so that a particular ethical outcome is achieved that serves your personal biases.

In the middle of the seventeenth century the philosopher-mathematician Blaise Pascal ridiculed priests of his day who, in his mind, were tolerating lax moral precepts and using a negative form of casuistry to justify their ways. But such a temptation is not limited to priests at a particular time in history. All humans are prone to the personal bias which leads them to self-serving casuistry that supports their personal desires. "When a person uses the particulars of a situation to arrive at a specific ethical judgment that suits his or her own purposes, that person engages in casuistry in the negative sense of the word."[31]

Using casuistry effectively on some ethical issues is relatively easy, such as determining whether or not it is wrong to steal another person's car in order to remove and sell its parts. For other ethical issues that are more complicated, it can be more difficult to determine what is right and wrong. You will more likely need to bring this to other people for counsel.

General principles and concrete situations complement each other. How we see the concrete is influenced by what we believe are the general principles at stake. Likewise, how we understand the general principles is influenced by the concrete situation we face. But this interdependence reveals one of the weaknesses of human moral reasoning: the reasoning process alone may not be absolutely reliable to eliminate personal biases from the process.

WHAT ADDS TO COMPLEXITY

Right-versus-right dilemmas. When applying universal principles to particular situations, an ethical problem can arise when it is not clear what is right because of the complicated nature of the situation. Sometimes we do not know all the information we wish to know. Sometimes we cannot precisely estimate the impact of an action on others. They may not know the full effect on themselves until after the action is taken! Ethical problems can be solved with better information (this does not mean that problems are easy to resolve or that the information is always available).

A more challenging situation occurs when deciding between two or more things that are both right.[32] This is called an ethical dilemma. A right-versus-right dilemma pulls you into two or more different directions at the same time, each of which is a good direction to go, each with its own set of legitimate social obligations on you. For example, you have a duty to sustain the organization you work for. This will require making tough choices which, when executed well, result in profitability. At the same time, you have a duty to take care of the needs of workers, but this can often mean increasing the expenses of the organization which counteracts profitability.

The duty to truth might compete with the duty to loyalty. Or a duty to loyalty to one person or group may conflict with the duty to loyalty to another person or group. For example, because of your position as marketing director you participate in top-level meetings with the CEO when big decisions are made. In one of the meetings you learn that the company is going to lay off personnel and reorganize. This means that another manager with whom you work closely on a regular basis will be laid off. You are suddenly placed in a situation not of your choosing where you have a duty to truth and a duty to loyalty.

Any of the paradoxical tensions represented in this chapter can end up as right-versus-right dilemmas. For example, taking care of the needs of one person is often the right thing to do; taking care of the needs of the organization is also the right thing to do. Promoting economic well-being can be the right thing to do at the same time as achieving other social goals which, depending on the situation, can be in conflict with economic goals.

Right-versus-right dilemmas are often the most serious, hard choices that managers must make. These are the choices that bubble up from lower-level managers because they are more complicated than other ethical issues. Following one duty might mean that you cannot follow the other duty. This would be a tradeoff that a lower-level supervisor will not want to make alone. These dilemmas require making clear organizational priorities and values and personal priorities.

The right-versus-right dilemmas are good evidence for why we need leaders and why leaders must listen to others![33] To be effective, leaders who face these complicated situations should engage the issues with the help of others in the community. Going it alone can be risky!

> Right-versus-right dilemmas are good evidence for why we need leaders and why leaders must listen to others.

Right-versus-right dilemmas are difficult; however, they present opportunities for transformation. And "communal transformation is best initiated through those times when we gather."[34] The community members (other managers in the organization, experienced leaders) gathered in a small group can act as discussants on the issues, testing your theories and your conclusions. In a small group every person will have a chance to speak and be heard. Through the conversation that ensues, group members can affirm each other's contribution. They can provide a setting in which you and they can simulate a decision. They can advocate on behalf of others not involved in the conversation but whose voices need to be heard. They might provide additional information not available to you. They can offer their wisdom based on experience, which may be helpful in managing the tradeoffs embedded in the dilemma. Their perspective may be different. They can offer encouragement and emotional support. They will have their own views challenged. Superiors can lend their political influence in support of the hard decisions, especially those that have unanticipated, unpleasant outcomes. Finally, it is through small-group dialogue that community members experience the belonging that each craves.

The good thing about universal principles is that they apply to many situations. They voice the universally accepted goals for flourishing life. One problem with universal principles is that they are more difficult to use when facing the right-versus-right dilemma alone. In a dilemma it can seem that the universal principles contradict each other. It is the particular details of a right-versus-right dilemma which make application of universal principles so difficult. In addition to the right-versus-right dilemmas, there may also be the need to avoid more than one bad outcome. This is sometimes called making a choice between the lesser of two evils.

Scale. As the scale of an ethical decision increases from the level of the individual to the level of the political-economic system, the complexity of the ethical issues increases (see fig. 2.7).

Scope. As the scope of an ethical decision increases to include more fundamental tensions and stakeholders representing different points of view, the complexity of the ethical issues increases. As scale and scope increase, there seems to be more need for interpersonal conversations about the issues such as in a small group. And with the need for small group conversations comes the need for leadership to be shared in the group (see fig. 2.8).

Complexity of ethical decisions. We can now begin to see several elements that add to the complexity of an ethical decision:

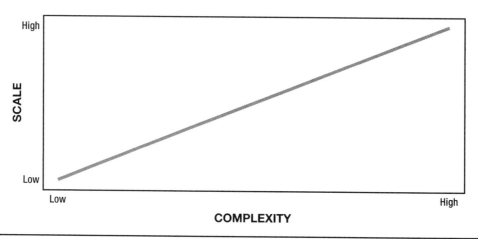

Figure 2.7. An illustration of scale.

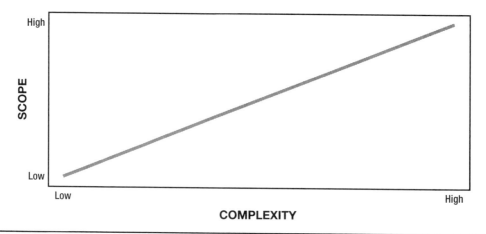

Figure 2.8. An illustration of scope.

- the existence of a greater number of stake-holders

- differences in perspective regarding the meaning or values of the situation among various persons who have an interest in the situation (stakeholders)

- differences between individual needs and community needs

- availability of information relevant to the stakeholders

- clarity of the available information

- complexity of details in the particular situation which makes it different from other situations

- clarity of duties

- clarity of the expected outcomes

- economic outcomes might be mixed: some people are helped while other people are hurt

- needs that arise from short-term goals and from long-term goals

Table 2.3. Levels of complexity to ethical, social and legal issues.

Simple and Easy **Examples:** Embezzling money or resources from your organization, committing fraud.	• Unambiguous right vs. wrong situation. • Straight forward; relatively easy to determine right from wrong. • The answer is immediately evident. • May require seconds, minutes or hours to develop the solution.
Complicated and Difficult **Example:** The story about JasonC and the WiFi connection in the General Introduction.	• One or more ambiguous elements. • Information is lacking or unclear. • Moral impacts are uncertain. • Legal requirements ambiguous. • More than one point of view will see the situation differently. • More than one stakeholder (person, organization) is impacted. • May require days or weeks to develop the solution. • May have time pressure for a quick decision.
More Complicated and Difficult **Examples:** Vignette No. 1, "The New National Park Debate" and vignette No. 3, "Fired for Refusing to Fly" at the end of this chapter.	• One or more ambiguous elements. • Multiple stakeholders impacted. • Right vs. right dilemma, **OR** lesser of two evils dilemma. • Right vs. right dilemma **AND** lesser of two evils dilemma in the same situation. • Requires weeks and months to develop solutions. • May have time pressure for a quick decision.
Even More Complicated and Difficult **Examples** of issues that have an impact on business: The Keystone Pipeline debate in the United States, healthcare reform, welfare reform, revision to the federal minimum wage law, immigration reform, tax reform, balancing the federal budget.	• One or more ambiguous elements. • Multiple stakeholders impacted on a regional or national scale. • Right vs. right dilemma **OR** lesser of more than two evils dilemma. • Right vs. right dilemma **AND** lesser of more than two evils dilemma on a regional or national scale. • Public policy issues that involve multiple stakeholders and several competing interests. • Involve multiple branches of government (state, federal). • Requires months or years to develop solutions. • There may be political pressure to develop a solution as quick as possible.
Most Complicated and Difficult **Examples** of issues that have an impact on business: Global conversations about sustainable development, global warming, eliminating corruption in business and government, Kyoto protocol.	• Ambiguous elements. • Multiple stakeholders in multiple countries impacted. • Cultural differences in the interpretation or meaning of moral principles. • Right vs. right vs. right dilemma **AND** lesser of more than two evils dilemma in an international context or scale. • Public policy issues that involve multiple stakeholders and competing interests among businesses, industries, nations, governments. • Involve multiple branches of government (state, federal, international) and multiple governments. • Requires decades to develop solutions. • There may be political pressure to develop a solution as quickly as possible.

Accordingly, the most complex decisions to make are ones where there is a problem understanding the true nature of the duty, the true outcomes of possible alternatives and the presence of right-versus-right tension, the need to choose between the lesser of two evils, and the meaning of these duties and outcomes for various people. This is the time when talking with other people will help. It is in the ethical dilemma that the ethics process more likely will need to become a small-group conversation. In complex dilemmas that involve international interests, the group conversation needs to expand to include many groups. Such conversations will involve exploring the other paradoxes mentioned in this chapter: the need to take care of individual needs versus the need to care for the community's needs and the short-term outcomes versus the long-term consequences. It is in community dialogue (whether done in a small group or on a global scale) that we gain a clearer understanding of the values that compete with each other. This does not mean that a community conversation will produce a resolution which makes everyone happy. The challenge that can come up here is that talking about sensitive ethical issues is very difficult in a group setting where people of different perspectives are present together.

Considering this relationship between complexity of the issues and the usefulness of engaging others in the conversation, we can draw the following graph to illustrate (see fig. 2.9).

Taking these observations into account we can say, in general, that as the complexity of an ethical decision goes up, the usefulness of any one particular ethical formula goes down. This is illustrated in figure 2.10.

Some of the ethical models explored later in this book have been used to resolve right-versus-right and lesser of two evils dilemmas. But even with the help of these ethical approaches, the answer may not be clear. In truth, in the world of business, the right thing to do can be ambiguous long after the decision is made. We conclude from this that in the world of business simplistic approaches often will not be useful in resolving dilemmas. In addition, as important as it becomes, community dialogue about the complexity of a situation becomes more difficult to achieve because of the sensitive nature of the issues for the people involved. This problem may be the most compelling argument in support of the need for leaders in organizations who have ethical wisdom as much as they have business knowledge. In fact, for the Christian in business, it is in the midst of these complex dilemmas where the work of business and the work of Christian faith cannot be separated.

Leaders who participate in the ethics process with a small group will watch out for the following elements to come up in conversations about ethical dilemmas (see fig. 2.11).

Small-group members can all share in the leadership by asking the following questions:[35]

- What tensions are we not talking about that should be talked about?

- Which biblical themes are we resisting bringing into the conversation?

- Who should be here (or represented by an advocate) who is not currently in the conversation?

- Do we agree which biblical themes are most important in this situation?

- Are we committed together to find a solution after considering all the issues and all the guidance from the biblical themes?

- Is everyone's voice being heard?

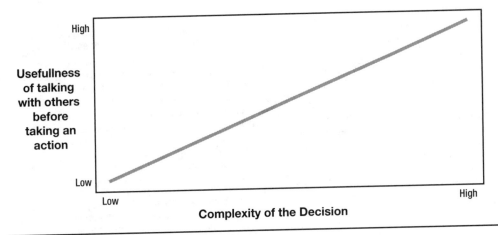

Figure 2.9. A graph illustrating the complexity of decisions.

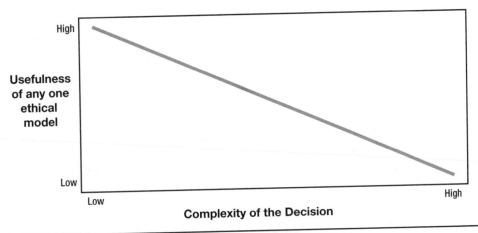

Figure 2.10. The relationship between complexity of decisions and a single ethical model.

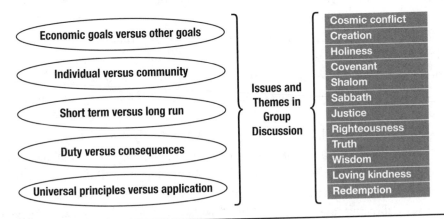

Figure 2.11. Elements to be aware of in ethical dilemmas.

Table 2.4. Applying the ethical process.

Keeping Your Heart: An Intrapersonal Process	Walking in the Community: An Interpersonal Process
• You are the managing chef for a contract caterer serving a large corporation. Your firm has just lost the catering contract to a competing firm. In 90 days you and your team must leave so that the new caterer can move in. What is the right thing to do as you and your team prepare to exit? • What does your heart say is the right thing to do when talking with dietary workers about the change that is coming in 90 days? • What do you believe to be right in this situation that you find yourself resisting?	• You are the managing chef for a contract caterer. With whom might you start a conversation about the problem that is rampant in the industry? • What would give you credibility with others to start such a conversation? • If your boss in the corporate office is resistant to having a conversation about the ethical issues, with whom should you talk, if anyone? • You are about to make the official announcement regarding the change in contract caterers. Who should be present to participate in making statements to employees? • If you have a conversation with someone in the corporate office regarding the problem that the industry is experiencing, which of the fundamental tensions presented in this chapter will come into the conversation? • What right-versus-right dilemmas, if any, can be identified in this story? Have a conversation with someone about this right now. What is the outcome of the conversation? • How might a group conversation help (or not) resolve any right-versus-right dilemmas?

DOWN TO THE NITTY-GRITTY

Think about the contract catering story from the beginning of the chapter. It's time to get down to the nitty-gritty (see table 2.4)!

THE BIBLE ON FUNDAMENTAL TENSIONS

When we look in the Bible we see evidence of each of these tensions.

Economic goals-other goals. Scripture recognizes the legitimacy of pursuing economic goals when this occurs within the broader commitment of serving our own needs and the needs of others. Scripture recognizes that these two sets of goals can be in conflict. An example of this is found in the words of Jesus: "You cannot serve God and wealth" (Mt 6:24). The biblical view of prosperity is the best way to understand how Scripture sees this tension. Prosperity, in the Bible is multidimensional. It encompasses well-being in every part of life, including faithfulness to our commitments to

God and to each other, social harmony, safety, international peace, physical and mental health and economic well-being. Further, prosperity is primarily but not exclusively a community goal. Last, prosperity is multigenerational in perspective. One generation is not prosperous unless the following generation has both the moral foundation for well-being and the economic foundation for the material dimensions of life. For a short Bible study on this topic, see appendix H.

Individual-community. This tension is part of the Scripture's basic guidance to us: "Do not merely look out for your own personal interests, but also for the interests of others" (Phil 2:4). "Scripture affirms the value of the individual, but simultaneously calls each of us to understand that we are part of Christ's body. To allow for simultaneous honoring of *both* individual interests *and* organizational or community interests fosters true integrity."[36] Ancient Israel was about to cross the Jordan River and enter the land of Canaan.[37] Leaders of two tribes, Reuben and Gad, came to Moses and asked permission to stay on the east bank of the river because that was good land for grazing animals. The needs of the larger community would have been served if the two tribes came across the Jordan River and helped establish security for the whole group. The needs of the two tribes would have been served if they remained on the east side of the river. Moses was wise! He told the leaders of Reuben and Gad that if they first came across the river and helped establish security, they could return to the preferred grazing lands on the east side. In this way the needs of both could be satisfied. Another example is found in the writings of Paul the apostle.[38] Paul encouraged believers to get jobs so that they would not be a burden to those who had sources of income. Apparently, some Christians were slacking and benefiting from others who were diligent workers. To watch out for the needs of the community as a whole, each able-bodied person should work his or her fair share.

Short term-long term. Clearly we were created with the ability to anticipate the effect of our decisions and with learning make adjustments so as to see a possible future result. Without a concept of the future, the whole idea of right and wrong would disappear. The giving of the Mosaic law at Sinai is based on the assumption that a future consequence is expected as a result of obedience (or lack thereof).[39] Moral standards would mean nothing without this connection between the present and the future.

Several examples of Scripture illustrate the importance of both the short-term and the long-run. The wise person is one who realizes that future economic stability is uncertain. The economic decisions made today can help the wise person manage uncertainty that comes to-

morrow.[40] In the parable of the builder we learn how important it is to count the cost now before you build so can avoid embarrassment later.[41] Leaders of the early church were admonished to care for the daily needs of members.[42]

Duty-consequences. The inherent tension of both duty and consequences is in Scripture. In Exodus 20 we find the description of covenantal relationship duties; however, the consequences are never far from view. Jesus spoke much about the law of God and encouraged his followers to be true to their duty to love one another.[43] In terms of consequences, unproductive resources are spoken of in disapproving terms in the Bible.[44] The principle of destroying unproductive assets and replacing them with productive assets may be the rationale behind Solomon's wisdom that there is a time to plant and a time to uproot that which is planted, that is, when the asset cannot be salvaged and becomes irreversibly unproductive.[45] Deuteronomy 28 records the clear connection between present actions and future consequences.

Duty emerges from the covenantal nature of relationships. We owe it to others in the community to take certain actions and avoid other actions. Each member of a covenant relationship has responsibility to the others. Duty is social, communal in nature. We are interdependent with each other for flourishing. The primary duty in covenant relationships is the duty of loyalty and faithfulness.

Universal-particular. Moses applies the universal principles of the Ten Commandments to specific situations.[46] Jesus also engages in the reasoning process of applying the general principles of the law of God to a variety of specific situations. He also criticizes Pharisees for their self-serving, biased casuistry.[47]

Complicated dilemmas will seem to arise when there is an apparent conflict between two biblical duties. As we have seen, the biblical perspective is that both an intrapersonal and interpersonal process is involved when making ethical choices. Two examples of dilemmas that involve Scripture themes are also common in secular thinking: justice versus mercy; truth versus loyalty.[48] In this book and some of the cases presented you will be given an opportunity to practice discerning which themes are most directly applicable in a particular situation.

This discussion regarding paradox may unintentionally give the impression that the most important dimension of business ethics is in how you think when facing a tension point. Thinking is important. Ultimately it is what you do in the midst of the tension that matters. Ethics, after all, is about action. But managing these tensions through action is not always simple to achieve.

CHAPTER REVIEW QUESTIONS

1. What is at the core of the environment of business, and why is this important?

2. What is the concept of paradox in the environment of business?

3. Explain the nature of the individual-community tension. Why is this called the fundamental tension in all of life?

4. What is the tension between the short term and the long term, and why is it important?

5. Explain the tension between understanding universal moral principles and applying these principles to a particular situation.

6. How are duty and consequences inseparable in social relationships?

7. What do we learn from the Bible regarding the five tensions explored in this chapter?

DISCUSSION QUESTIONS

1. Can an act be right if it does not simultaneously promote both the interests of the individual and the interests of the larger community?

2. Can an act be wrong if it promotes the interests of either the individual or the larger community but not both?

3. When there is a conflict between the interests of the individual and the interests of the social group, which should acquiesce to the other?

4. Give an example of a situation in which it might be wrong for the individual to acquiesce to the interests of the social group. When would it be wrong for the social group to acquiesce to the interests of the individual?

5. Give an illustration from your experience of the individual-community tension.

6. What is the most complicated ethical decision you have ever had to make? What made this situation complicated? Based on that experience, what could you add to this chapter that reveals other elements which make ethical situations complex?

7. How is the Christian to deal with a complex ethical situation that remains ambiguous even after prayer, reflection on the biblical theme perspective and receiving counsel from other faithful believers who have wisdom?

ETHICAL VIGNETTES TO DISCUSS

For each of the following vignettes discern what is right and wrong.

1. *The new national park debate.* You live in a state where an unusual land formation exists. One of the members of Congress rep-

resenting a nearby state has proposed a bill to the Congress that the land around this unusual geologic formation be officially designated as a national park. Local citizens who live near the spot own businesses that capitalize on the tourists who visit the location every year from out of state. They oppose the national park designation because that would require them to move their businesses several miles away from the site. If a national park is established, some people who live next to the site would be required to sell their homes and move to land outside the park boundaries. Members of Congress desire the national park designation so that the site is preserved for future generations from what they term the "negative effects of commercial interests." They argue that the proposed park would exist for the whole nation and not just for local citizens. They use as evidence the number of vehicles that have been observed traveling to this spot bearing license plates from more than forty different states in the US and six provinces in Canada.

2. Under the leadership of National Park Ranger Ellis Richard, a new organization formed in 2013 calling itself Park Rangers for Our Lands. The goal of the organization is to increase public awareness and to influence the US Congress and the US Bureau of Land Management regarding what they believe to be growing threats to the national parks from private companies that want to drill for oil and natural gas on or near national park lands.[49]

3. *Fired for refusing to fly.* A group of thirteen flight attendants employed by United Airlines walked off the 747 jumbo jet just before takeoff from San Francisco (scheduled to fly to Hong Kong) July 14, 2014, because an employee saw a message written in oil residue on the fuselage tail cone that said, "Bye Bye ☺☺." The tail cone contains an auxiliary engine. The message had apparently been written on the plane by a ground crew member when it was in Korea. The first officer, one of four pilots on the aircraft, had taken a photo of the message and shared what he called a "disturbing image" with the other pilots and then told one of the flight attendants. The first officer requested a visual inspection of the compartment under the tail section. Nothing suspicious was found. When flight attendants saw the message they interpreted it as threatening. They were afraid to fly. One of the face images was a smile. The attendants interpreted the other as having a "devilish" expression. Earlier that same week a bomb warning had been issued to airlines by the Transportation Security Administration. This was just months after the disappearance of Malaysian Airline flight 370. The United Airlines attendants asked that the passengers and crew be put off the aircraft and that everyone and the airplane be searched again before takeoff. When this request was refused and the crew ordered to work by a UA supervisor, the flight attendants walked off the plane refusing to fly. Flight 869 was cancelled. In October 2014 the crew members were fired for insubordination. The employees filed a complaint against United Airlines with the Occupational Safety and Health Administration (OSHA) of the US Department of Labor asking that they be reinstated in their jobs with back pay and compensatory damages. *Was it right that these employees got fired?*

3

Biblical Themes for Business Ethics — Part 1

SCRIPTURE PASSAGE

Let the word of Christ richly dwell within you, with all wisdom. (Col 3:16)

CHAPTER OVERVIEW

In this chapter we introduce the concept of biblical story themes that are guides to ethical thinking and action in the marketplace. In particular, we will explore the essence of four biblical themes that form part of the biblical story framework to guide business ethics: cosmic conflict, creation, holiness and covenant

MAIN TOPICS

Powerful Story Themes
Why So Many Themes?
Cosmic Conflict
Creation
Holiness
Covenant Relationships
Down to the Nitty-Gritty

KEY TERMS

cosmic conflict, covenant relationships, creation, holiness

POWERFUL STORY THEMES

What draws us to stories is not just the twists and turns of plot actions and fascinating story characters that keep us asking, *What will happen next?* At a much deeper level the underlying, intertwined themes of the story touch the core of who we are.[1] Through these themes blockbuster narratives shape our moral sensibilities calling us to discern what is right and wrong in the story. They also confront us to examine what is right and wrong in our own life.

The most popular theme in contemporary stories is the struggle between good and evil. The power of love is a close second. Love is an unstoppable force for good and the most powerful force against evil. Love is the most noble of all quests. It represents the right thing to do and the right way to be in relationships. Other

---

MOST POPULAR STORY THEMES IN LITERATURE

- Good versus evil
- Love
- The great journey
- Coming of age
- Noble sacrifice
- Fall from grace and redemption
- Revenge
- Triumph over adversity

popular themes include the struggle of humans against nature, the internal struggle over right and wrong within a person and the compelling power of revenge (an attempt to make right a wrong). The entertainment and publishing industries earn billions in revenue from the power of these basic, compelling concepts.

This chapter (and the book as a whole) will introduce selected themes of the biblical story that are relevant to the ethical, social and legal environment of business.[2] These are themes that help us listen to the Bible story on its own terms from the perspective of the persons who wrote the story rather than ideas imposed from the outside.[3] Story themes help us become insiders to the story rather than remain as uninformed outsiders. Theme answers the question: Why? Why is the story told? What's the point of the story? Theme is the main concern in the story. It is the main ideas or patterns of thought that are repeated throughout the Bible and dominate the ideas of the Bible. The primary way this comes out in the Bible is when Bible writers focus on the character of God and the character of humans in the narrative, repeating images, phrases and dominant ideas.

In this book the following biblical story themes are introduced:[4]

- cosmic conflict
- creation
- holiness
- covenant relationships
- shalom
- sabbath
- justice
- righteousness
- truth
- wisdom
- loving kindness
- redemption

WHY SO MANY THEMES?

One question that you might have is Why so many themes? Twelve themes seem like a lot to learn! Wouldn't it be easier to just have a few? Twelve is too many to remember when faced by an ethical dilemma! In answer to this question first consider that the Scripture presents these and many other themes that are used across the Bible. If the Bible presents them, on what basis can we say we do not want to use some of them? The themes emerge from Scripture rather than being imposed on the Bible by human devising. We might prefer to have fewer things to remember, but the Bible (apparently) is not concerned about this problem. One possible reason is that it is the community as a whole that is to remember, not just individuals. One person considers some themes more important; another person thinks a different set of themes important. Together with other persons, all of the major perspectives of God's character are brought into the conversation. During this conversation the people involved come to discern which of the themes is most important in the particular situation. There are additional themes that relate to our conduct, God's character and the work of Jesus Christ. These twelve themes are the ones that emerge as the most consistent and dominant when considering the whole Bible.

Second, the Scripture is rich, deep and broad in its application to life. The wonderful unity of Scripture shows how the many Bible writers (mainly prophets, kings and apostles) had similar views on God's character. God's character is multidimensional. One reason humans cannot, of their own power, reproduce these dimensions in their own lives is this very thing: It is complicated! A person might be able to become good at one dimension (such as truth telling or faithfulness to promises), but to be perfect at all dimensions is beyond our capabilities.

Third, Bible writers themselves seem to understand that some ethical decisions are complicated. They address these complex situations with more than one perspective based on God's characteristics.

Fourth, it is the whole person who is in a complex ethical situation, not just the person's power of reason alone. Accordingly, the whole person, more than pure reason alone, is needed to determine what is right and wrong. For this, complicated ethical situations require more than one perspective. The themes offer this variety of perspective.

Fifth, if we try to simplify God and who he is and in so doing simplify our own duties, we will miss important elements of God's point of view in complex human situations. Simplifying God is one way some Christians have attempted (but failed) to control God by forcing him into a box of their own devising.

Sixth, if you had to choose just a few themes that are more important than the others for application across all complicated situations, which ones could be chosen without losing the rich understanding of all of Scripture? Collapsing or compressing some themes into others might be attractive from a practical study point of view, but it will result in diminished understanding. For example, we might be prone to say that covenant embraces several others including sabbath, justice, truth (faithfulness), righteousness and loving kindness. But if we say covenant without exploring the nuanced differences of these other themes that

are part of covenant relationships, we lose the very dimensions of covenant that are important to guide us in actions.

Seventh, collapsing or reducing the number of themes because it seems like too many to learn will result in oversimplifying a complex situation. From this will likely come a bad ethical decision. By way of analogy, if in managerial accounting you simplify by treating all costs as the same, you will end up with incorrect conclusions, bad information and a bad business decision. If in financial investment decisions you treat all investment risks the same, you will make a bad investment decision. While Scripture has much to say about money and business, it does not address all the complicated situations that we face today. The complex ethical dilemmas cannot easily be resolved by a direct quote of a passage of the Bible here and there. What is needed is a deep understanding of Scripture, provided by the themes considered here, that can be applied to the complicated dilemmas.

Eighth, it is the multiple dimensions that give the biblical perspective so much power with respect to complex real-life situations. Furthermore, it is the cluster of themes which sets the biblical perspective apart from secular approaches. Unfortunately, Christians have an inglorious history of repeatedly attempting to oversimplify Scripture and in so doing we have glossed over important scriptural points of view. By analogy, wanting to reduce the number of themes out of concern for the time it might take to study them would be like the people of ancient Israel going to Samson and saying, "We love how you are so strong in defending us against the physical attacks of our enemies, but could you just cut your hair? It's too long!"[5] The very thing that gave him his strength is the thing that you would want taken away. Or, it is like the disciples saying to Jesus, "We appreciate that you are sometimes willing to spend entire nights in prayer or many hours at a time going off by yourself to think, meditate and pray. This time alone seems to energize you, but we think you should get more sleep."[6] Or, it is like an English instructor who says to students, "Your assignment is to write an original creative short story. There is no need to be concerned about plot or characterization. Just simplify your story down to the basics that are most important." And if all we learned in business ethics from a biblical point of view was the following verse from Leviticus, this could be accomplished in one class period wedged into any existing course: "You shall not steal, nor deal falsely, nor lie to one another" (Lev 19:11). Such an oversimplified approach does not reflect the complex nature of many business situations in which right and wrong (in terms of lying, cheating, stealing, and many other actions) are ambiguous.

Ninth, many of these themes are intimately interrelated to each other. Remove one and you remove important linkages between the themes. This is one reason why some people may desire to eliminate some of them. In wisdom we are challenged to consider holiness, covenant, creation, truth, righteousness. In shalom we encounter creation, covenant, sabbath, justice, truth, holiness, righteousness. In the cosmic conflict all other themes are comprehended.

INTRODUCING THE BIBLICAL STORY THEMES

In this chapter we will not take time to apply each theme to the variety of business situations. That will come later. Instead, we will introduce them and consider some of their broad implications in terms of the purpose of business.[7] To begin, we will start with the cosmic conflict between God and his adversary, Satan.

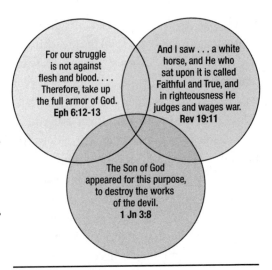

Figure 3.1. The theme of cosmic conflict.

Cosmic conflict. You do not have to look very far to see the conflict between good and evil played out in the environment of business. For example, consider why so many employees hate their bosses. Some bosses cheat and scheme. They verbally abuse subordinates. They try to hurt people. They are vindictive. They disregard the truth. They quickly blame others. They bully, dehumanize and manipulate. They live above the law of the organization. Evil bosses deceive and deny. They are control freaks. Their leadership power is focused on themselves and their wants rather than on the organization and its needs.[8] Move past the employer-employee relationship and you will find a host of other people in the marketplace scheming to take advantage of others, attempting to defraud clients our investors out of money, cheat the government or deceive the public or cook the books to hide unethical or illegal behavior. Look at any major newspaper in any given week and you will see examples of evil doing in the marketplace.

The struggle between good and evil is a theme in the biblical story.[9] The serpent that tempts Eve,[10] the legendary skirmish between the teenage shepherd David and the giant Goliath,[11] the work of Jesus[12] and the preaching of the apostle Paul in Ephesus[13] are just a few examples where this theme can be seen in plot actions. Paul's preaching resulted in certain Gentiles being converted to faith in Jesus Christ. They stopped worshiping and buying idols. The decrease in demand for idols made the local artisans angry. When they found out who had persuaded their customers not to buy idols, the artisans ran Paul out of town. Jesus uses this theme when he tells about the kingdom of God[14] and when he sends his disciples out for ministry.[15] The apostles of Jesus identify this theme when they tell us what Jesus Christ's work means.[16] At times they describe our conduct in terms of this great cosmic struggle.[17]

> And I will put enmity
> Between you and the woman,
> And between your seed and her seed;
> He shall bruise you on the head,
> And you shall bruise him on the heel.
> (Gen 3:15)

In the story, we find on one side of the cosmic conflict God's chief adversary, Satan.[18] The story tells us that he is a murderer. There is no truth in him. A liar and the father of lies, he deceives the world. He steals. He is a master of disguise. He oppresses people to prevent them from having a faith relationship with God. Using the negative politics of discredit, without cause other than his own selfish ambition, he incites questions regarding the validity of God's authority and character: he falsely claims that God does not tell the truth and insinuates that God's commands are too burdensome for humans to keep. He tries to usurp God's authority.[19]

On the other side of this conflict we find the answer: God.[20] Over two hundred seventy times God is referred to as the Lord of Hosts (armies). The central figure is Jesus Christ. He is the Lifegiver and Sustainer of communities. Being fully divine, Jesus Christ demonstrates: God is all powerful. In loyalty to the whole universe he chooses to be bound by the standards of behavior which he provides for created beings.[21] He encourages freedom but not perfect autonomy, which would lead to chaos, lawlessness and anarchy. He desires for all humans a flourishing life of well-being. He encourages. He is patient, merciful and compassionate even to those who reject him. He heals and reconciles. He helps spiritually blind people see. His authority is founded on character traits of wisdom, truth, righteousness, justice, loving kindness and redemption. He judges without bias. He takes responsibility for his actions. He provides no cause to discredit his character.

GOD: "And I will put enmity between you and the woman, and between your seed and her seed; He shall bruise you on the head, and you shall bruise him on the heel."

SATAN

Figure 3.2. The conflict between God and Satan.

In this contest between good and evil we see the characters of God and Satan revealed. In the end of the story God does not allow Satan to have ultimate control; the Creator-Redeemer shows that policies of coercion, intimidation, deception and manipulation fail. Policies of freedom within boundaries, responsibility in community, truthfulness, faithfulness and committed loyalty succeed. Appendix C contains several theme summary tables, each of which shows the contrast between God's program of managing the universe and Satan's program.

> By lovingkindness and truth
> iniquity is atoned for,
> And by the fear of the Lord one
> keeps away from evil. (Prov 16:6)

Implications. What might this cosmic struggle have to do with business? A lot! In light of the cosmic conflict theme, the purpose of business is not just local or even global; business is also cosmic. It is this theme that poses a big question of Scripture: How does God manage when some of his creatures rebel against his plan for a flourishing life? As we will see, the other themes provide an answer to that question. We are called to imitate God. It is his character traits, revealed by how God manages the universe, that are worthy of imitation.[22] It is in business as much as in church where persons demonstrate in their actions God's way or Satan's way. To be equipped to deal with the conflict, believers are encouraged to take on several spiritual weapons and armor. Items that outfit us for battle against evil include truth, righteousness, faithfulness, shalom and redemption. To war against evil we are asked to saturate our minds and hearts with

God's Word.[23] We are called to resist the devil.[24] Thus, we find persons and organizations counteracting these forces by acting decisively to resist evil.[25] Accountants help all of us to develop habits of openness, transparency, truthfulness and trustworthiness. Information systems collect information which is used, in part, to constrain narrow self-interests. As a result these systems protect many people from harming others. Managers foster accountability when they establish policies and procedures and then monitor the behavior of subordinates. Other managers take responsibility to make sure that promises are kept and agreements honored. Ultimately through their actions the market players demonstrate the character of God or the character of Satan. They will foster freedom within boundaries.

With the backdrop of cosmic conflict in place we can now consider the other story themes related to business ethics. We can say with confidence that the other themes find their implicit roots in how God manages the cosmic conflict. The story portrays two contrasting ways of living and interacting. We continue with the theme of creation.

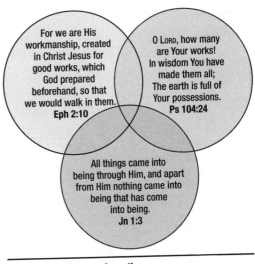

Figure 3.3. The theme of creation.

Creation. According to some surveys, somewhere between one-third and one-half of employees do not like their bosses and quit work because of it.[26] Jaded by their corporate experiences and filled with hope of something better, many bosses do not like their situation either! They want to create a more satisfying, healthier company culture.

What creative entrepreneurs and entrepreneurial-minded managers know is something that God knows all about: creation! When God chose to create, he chose to be faithful. The biblical story begins with creation and ends with re-creation. At creation we learn that God took a chaotic, barren wasteland and transformed it into an orderly, fertile, flourishing space where love (loyalty) can be expressed.[27]

In the creation story we learn that God is the ultimate owner of this earth. We were created in his image to shape our behavior for our relationships after him.[28] This forms the basis for valuing the sanctity of human life.[29] Accordingly, creation is the event whereby humans were chosen to serve and, in service, to become a blessing to others. This follows the model laid down by God himself: It was in creation that God began the process of serving and blessing those he created. One great element of the creation story is that God comes to earth and he comes that he might give abundant life.[30] At creation he founded the blessing-filled principles on which the Ten Commandments would stand.[31] It is in the creation story that we see the most primal

relationship with God, with each other and with the earth expressed. Creation dramatically tells us that we must join in affirming our solidarity with all persons regardless of their religion (or lack thereof). In this we are all equal: We are all God's creatures.

Jesus Christ, the Creator, is the ultimate owner of all raw materials that are used to provide all products and services.[32] He originated the value chain. Everything that humans do involves something that came directly from the hand of Christ. Accordingly, humans will enjoy all that he has made but will also treat his possessions with respect.[33] This is the basis of respect for the property of others. The Creator gave humans the commission to work as he does: as ruler and servant.[34] This is how we can be co-workers with him in realizing the full potential of the earth's fruitfulness.

The social relationships established at creation guide us in the ethical, social and legal environment of business today. God created persons in community, not just individuals living in perfect autonomy from each other. "We are members of one another" (Eph 4:25).[35] We are interdependent. Interdependence means that all persons are mutually dependent on each other. Mutual dependence requires service, freedom and responsibility. A summary of the creation theme is shown in table 3.1.[36]

The major structure of ethical principles and tensions were established in creation. Humans were given a great amount of moral

Table 3.1. Creation theme.

Creation	Chaos
Order; fertile, flourishing land	Chaos; barren wasteland
Dependence and interdependence	Absolute independence
Moral authority of God over all established	Moral authority of God is challenged
Responsible beautifying, sustaining, serving	Irresponsible defacing, withering, abusing
Interdependent freedom within boundaries	Independent freedom without boundaries

freedom. But freedom in God's program has boundaries. Limits to moral relativism are established because all persons are created by God and the basic structure of community relationships is common to all worldwide. Humans have duties to cooperate in sustaining the created order. Humans should expect to see consequences of their actions.[37]

As the story progresses, the theme of creation is transformed into the theme of re-creation and restoration. This theme of restoration, hinted at in the book of Genesis, is taken up by the prophets of the story to be recast later by Jesus and the apostles.[38] God makes humans new putting in them a new Spirit-filled heart, writing on their hearts a transcript of his character.[39] The story concludes when God creates a whole new heaven and a new earth after the final scenes of the cosmic conflict and the problem of sin is taken care of.[40]

Implications. In light of the creation theme, the purpose of business is to provide a setting in which we can be co-workers with God in sustaining and promoting a flourishing life. This means acknowledging the lordship of God over all that business works with: materials, persons and everything in the environment. The earth and all its resources is not merely something to exploit for profit; it is holy, set apart for service to God. The good earth will be cared for as we enjoy its bountiful resources. The great work of those involved in business involves being a co-worker with God in the restoration of the image of God in humans lost in the Garden of Eden.[41] It is at creation where we see the first guidance for ethical decision making that leads to honor and respect for the moral authority of God. Thus, one purpose of business is to act as a community agent of preservation and protection of God's moral authority.[42] Human marketplace players who wish to follow God will take actions that maintain healthy relationships with other humans and with the earth.

Accordingly, the creation theme compels us to ask important questions as we discern right from wrong:

- Will the action I am about to take honor and respect human life? Will it foster a flourishing life in community for the long run, or will it result in harm?

- When we take from the earth, how are we fulfilling our responsibility to care for the earth?

- Will the actions we are about to take contribute to or undermine the process of God restoring his image in people?

With the creation in place we move farther down the pathway of learning what the story says about business ethics as we consider the next theme: holiness.

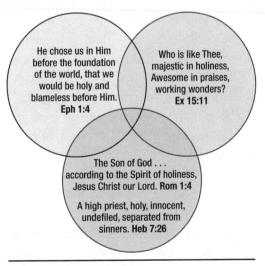

Figure 3.4. The theme of holiness.

Holiness. The idea of holiness encompasses a whole cluster of somewhat mysterious elements indicating the depth and totality of commitment to God.[43] Holiness involves "single-minded devotion to God and absolute ethical purity."[44] It refers to being set apart or consecrated to God,[45] distinctive and different.[46]

Holiness is a central characteristic of God.[47] It is because God is holy and completely separate from moral flaws and sin that his promise keeping can be trusted. God's holiness is the basis of other Bible story themes: his approach in the cosmic conflict, creation, covenant making, fulfillment of shalom, wisdom giving, justice, loving kindness and redemption. Sabbath is designed to remind people of the holiness of God.[48]

It is in the concept of holiness that an important but mysterious tension in the Bible story exists. First, God is so far from sin and evil that he cannot tolerate it. His holiness drives him to act with justice toward evil. Second, and paradoxically, it is his holiness that infuses his love with action of grace toward sinful persons. His loving kindness (loyalty) is an expression of his holiness! Faithfulness and trustworthiness to fulfill his promises also are expressions of his holiness.[49] It was his holiness that motivated him to mercifully give the covenant as a sign that he wanted to dwell with the people in grace.[50] God's desire to be with people is so great that it drove him to send his Son Jesus Christ as the expression of holiness.[51]

In the biblical story people are called holy only as they enter a relationship with God who is holy.[52] People get holiness from God, not from their own behaviors. In this we see another story tension: Humans cannot of their own power attain the level of moral purity that God alone enjoys. It is God's transforming power in the hearts of humans that leads them to walk the journey of a holy life. Accordingly, all God's people are holy, not because they are morally pure in an absolute sense on their own but be-

cause they respond to God's call to follow him, to trust him.[53] In following him God's people are distinctive and set apart for service to him.[54]

Implications. Holiness is not something to experience just at church. God's holiness that we are to mimic in the community is expected to penetrate every area of life.[55] Holiness must be taken into the marketplace. Believers in business have a role to play: not just buying and selling, but buying and selling in a way that demonstrates God's character. In this we see, painted in broad brush strokes, the big picture regarding the purpose of business. This includes activities of commerce:

- fairness in economic relationships[56]
- generosity[57]
- compassion[58]
- integrity[59]
- safety[60]
- ecology[61]
- equality[62]
- personal property[63]
- honesty in trade[64]

In the story, serving God in holiness is not possible when people persist in worshiping idols or following false religion.[65] Thus, all those who respond to God's call to a relationship with him will desire to separate themselves from practices that undermine holiness. At the same time, collectively the people of God are called to represent him to the world. This requires managing an important tension: This call separates his people apart for a distinct service.[66] But it is also a call to live in the world.[67] Faithful obedience to the relationship with God demonstrates the reality of God's awesome creative and redeeming power. This demonstration results in God lifting up his

Table 3.2. Holiness theme.

Holiness	Defilement
Sacred, consecrated fully to God	Common, profane, deconsecrated, ordinary use
Wholly other, separate	Join with evil and unrighteousness
Moral purity	Moral pollution
Break from idolatry and false religion	Acceptance of idolatry and false religion
Cleanness of social justice	Uncleanness of injustice

people to a position of true prosperity that becomes attractive to others.[68]

Caution! There is danger in thinking that holiness is the result of our own behavior.[69] If we believe that total obedience leads to holiness, it is easy for us to think that all we need is a list of rules to follow. And if we master obedience to this list, we will be holy. Holiness is not about making and keeping a list of rules. Rule keeping has no power to influence how God thinks of us. Salvation is not based on our obedience. It is based on God's holy action for us in sending Jesus Christ.[70] He loves us just the way we are! Furthermore, a strategy of obedience designed to gain favor with God is impossible for us to achieve. However, this does not give us license to do whatever we want.[71] If we are holy people set apart for distinctive service to God, our hearts will gradually be transformed and our actions will follow Jesus, who is the clearest expression of holiness.

Another problem with people who strive to be holy is that they think their own behavior is the standard to judge the behavior of all other persons. In a strange way, faithful followers subtly, if unintentionally, place themselves above God in the position of judge of their social world. Still another problem is when faithful followers begin thinking that the only way to attain holiness is to withdraw from engagement with sinful people in the world and live in an isolated community where social behaviors can be more carefully controlled.

As a guide to moral actions in the marketplace, the idea of holiness compels us to ask a few questions:

- Will the action I am about to take communicate God's holiness?

- Will my action be consistent with what I am called by God to reveal about his character?

- Does my action need to be distinctively different from the common actions of the marketplace?

- Will my action merely be a way for me to show how good I am rather than, in humility, foster good for others?

A summary of the holiness theme is given in table 3.2.

Holiness is a wonderful idea: Business is called to be dedicated to serving God in the world. Such dedication is deeper and more absolute than we might first imagine. The staggering implication of this needs further explanation. The depth of dedication comprehended in holiness is described in the concept of covenant. It is in covenant that we find the description of just how we are to be distinctly different. This is the next story theme.

Covenant relationships. One of the deepest desires of the human heart is for love and belonging, health and happiness. We all want an all-around full, satisfying life. We want to belong. This deep desire is encompassed by a story theme recognized by several scholars as being one of the most important in all the

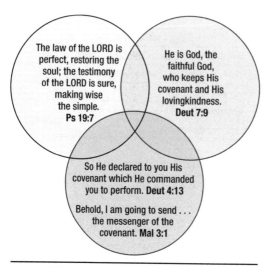

Figure 3.5. The theme of covenant relationships.

Covenant relationships are

- not merely individualistic but also communal in scope

- part of the larger context of community

- formed and maintained in the presence of a higher authority: God, the originator of covenant relationships

- long-term in nature

- preferred over casual, temporary relationships

- vulnerable to being broken if one party is unfaithful

- possible in relationships in which the participants have equal power (symmetrical) or when participants have different degrees of power (asymmetrical)[75]

In the story, God establishes a covenant relationship described as love. Love is best expressed in a covenant, but love is not merely a warm feeling of affection toward someone. Feeling attracted to someone is good, but in the biblical sense when you love someone you make a deep commitment which leads you to behave in particular ways that foster mutual commitment toward each other regardless of how you might feel toward each other at any moment.[76]

Implications. In terms of the purpose of business, the idea of covenant suggests the importance of nourishing faithfulness among community relationships. Indeed, the purpose of business through the lens of the biblical story is that it serves the many relationships embedded in the community. The purpose is not just profit but rather serving the needs of

Bible. It is one that has potential for application for all social relationships, including business.[72]

A covenant is an agreement or a promise to contribute something of value to a long-term relationship that results in a better life for all involved in the relationship. From the story point of view, the ultimate purpose of a covenant relationship is to promote a flourishing life of well-being in the community.[73] Other purposes of covenant are instrumental for achieving this. For example, covenant relationships reveal the character of the participants. A covenant relationship is established so that one party can be a blessing to others.[74] Covenants are for nourishing interdependent relationships with others and with the wider community not only for the present but also for the long term. Covenant provides a means by which at least one participant can act in a redemptive way when the relationship is in need of reconciliation (see table 3.3).

Table 3.3. The purposes of covenant relationships.

The Ultimate Purpose	To create and sustain an abundant, flourishing life in community
Instrumental Purposes	To reveal the character of the covenant participants
	To be a blessing to others in the community
	To nourish long-term interdependent relationships in community
	To provide for reconciliation and renewal of relationships

the relationships. A covenant relationship involves not just general, vague commitments but also specific commitments for particular actions. When both parties act on the commitments, they nourish the relationship. When one or both are not faithful, the relationship breaks down.

A succinct description of ideal covenant relationships is given in the form of the Ten Commandments, the gracious guidelines for a flourishing life.[77] Each of the commandments has implications for business.[78] While each commandment has broad application, there are some fundamental ideas applicable to business. For example, everyone involved in marketplace activities (buyers and sellers), people and organizations would not lie, cheat or steal. They would be faithful to their promises. In the biblical story true obedience to the commandments comes not from the burdened sense of need to fulfill an arbitrary code of right and wrong so that God will love us more or to balance our account with God, but from a faith-based desire to be faithful in all our relationships and thereby foster long-term mutual blessings.[79] The law is not the savior; however, obedience to the law does contribute to community well-being. In the biblical story walking in obedience to the Commandments is a walk of freedom and flourishing life, a walk that restores the soul.[80] Walking apart from the commandments is a walk away from freedom and an abundant life toward chaos, misery and destruction.

Life in the story comes from knowing the other party's faithfulness in the relationship. It comes from what the other participant does to promote well-being, not just what he or she says. Thus, the broadly applicable principles comprehend specific, objective duties of action.[81] These specific demonstrations energize both parties to be faithful to each other.

In the story, the most visible demonstration of the ideal relationship is that of Jesus Christ.[82] Through his ministry of teaching and healing Jesus Christ modeled covenant relationships by showing the deeper and broader meaning of the Ten Commandments.[83]

One of the most famous statements Jesus made about covenant relationships is also the shortest. It is known as the Golden Rule: "Therefore, treat people the same way you want them to treat you, for this is the Law and the Prophets" (Mt 7:12).[84]

Just like his statement regarding the two great commands[85] (love God and love other people as you love yourself), Jesus positions this rule of ethics as the essence of God's law of love.[86] In terms of the story themes, this is not just an isolated wise saying that happened to become popular worldwide. It is a core statement about how people in covenantal relationships can expect to nourish their relationships in a way that results in well-being for all.[87]

The ideal community experience was first seen at creation in the Garden of Eden. Later, it anticipated when God gave his first promise. Still later, it was anticipated when the Law was

Table 3.4. Covenant relationship theme.

Covenant Relationship	Casual Relationship
Long-term concerns	Short-term concerns
Deepening permanent commitment	Shallow, casual commitment
Loyalty	Disloyalty
Respect for the interests of all considered	Self-interest considered
Gives to nourish the relationship	Takes from to deplete the relationship

given. This great anticipation is the concept of shalom (peace). This story theme is taken up in chapter four.

DOWN TO THE NITTY-GRITTY

Think about the Ethical Vignettes to Discuss at the end of this chapter. Think about vignette 2. You work as a real estate agent. A person from out of town calls you representing himself as the executor of the estate of a person from your town who is now deceased. The executor says that he would like to get $150,000 for the property. His job is to disburse the proceeds from the sale of the estate to the beneficiaries of the will. You look at the home and, based on comparable properties in the neighborhood, you believe it is easily worth $200,000. You also realize that this property would be a good match for what your cousin has been looking for. What should you do? It's time to get down to the nitty-gritty (see table 3.5)!

CHAPTER REVIEW QUESTIONS

1. Why are so many themes important when considering the biblical perspective on business ethics?

2. What are the central ideas of the biblical story about the cosmic conflict between God and Satan, good and evil?

3. What does the creation theme tell us about our relationships with God and with each other?

4. What are the basic ideas of holiness, and what might this mean for a faithful believer?

5. What is the nature of a covenant relationship?

DISCUSSION QUESTIONS

1. To what degree or under what circumstances is the concept of the covenant practical for contemporary business?

Table 3.5. Applying the ethical process.

Keeping Your Heart: An Intrapersonal Process	Walking in the Community: An Interpersonal Process
• You are the real estate agent who is contacted by the executor of the estate. What does your heart say is the right thing to do? • Which biblical theme explored in this chapter informs your heart on this situation? (Which theme is the most relevant in this case?) • What other influences in your heart seem to be prominent as you think about this situation? • Fundamental beliefs • Cognitive reasoning • Judgments and evaluations • Decisions • Virtues • Will • Memory of personal experiences with other people • Perceptions of others in the community • Personal biases • Awareness of interpersonal relationships • Commitments to God and to others • Intuitions • Conscience • Human spirit • Emotions	• You are the real estate agent who is contacted by the executor of the estate. Other than the executor who called you, with whom might you have a conversation about this property? • Which of the biblical themes in this chapter would most likely come up either directly or indirectly in the conversation? Why? • If you have a conversation with someone regarding this situation, which of the fundamental tensions presented in the previous chapter might come into the conversation? • What right-versus-right dilemmas, if any, can be identified in this situation? Have a conversation with someone about this now. What is the outcome of the conversation? • How might a conversation with someone else help (or not) resolve any right-versus-right dilemmas? • Have a conversation about this situation with someone now. What different points of view are mentioned? In terms of deciding what is right and wrong, what is the outcome of the conversation?

2. In biblical thinking, business is transacted not only at the local, national and international levels but also before the whole universe. Accordingly, we should look in a wider sphere to find the purpose of business in the context of the cosmic conflict. How would you describe this larger purpose of business?

3. Jesus Christ appeared for the purpose of destroying the works of Satan (1 Jn 3:8). To what degree might this also be the purpose of the believer in business?

4. Consider in turn each of the themes presented in this chapter and discuss the following question in terms of the universal-particular tension point in ethics: Based on the information presented, what is an example of a particular action that might be called for to foster a covenant relationship in the marketplace? Give an example of a behavior that should be avoided in the marketplace.

5. Give an example of a story you have read, heard or seen recently that illustrates one or more of the story themes presented in this chapter. How was this theme portrayed in ways that are the same or different from how the Bible story portrays the theme(s)?

EXERCISES

1. For each biblical story theme presented in this chapter write a summary of how this theme is a guide to ethical behavior in the marketplace. Consider the following questions to help you create this summary: What general ethical principles do you believe God intends for us to use in the marketplace from each theme? How is does each statement describe God's character? How is each principle related to Jesus

Christ and his work for our redemption? What implications does each have for our marketplace conduct?

2. Two Christian entrepreneurs believe differently regarding how to live holy life. One believes that he must hire only Christians to be employees so that together they can create a company which represents God's character to others. The other believes that he should hire only non-Christians so that he can be closer to them and provide them with an opportunity to learn about God's character through his actions. Which approach best fulfills the story message for us to be holy?

ETHICAL VIGNETTES TO DISCUSS

For each of the following vignettes apply the biblical story themes to discern what is right and wrong.

1. You are a staff accountant. Your boss comes to your office one morning bearing an expense report with attached expense receipts. The report describes that these expenses were incurred while entertaining a client at a restaurant and lounge the previous evening. At lunch you hear your boss's wife, who works in a different department, tell another worker what a great time she and her husband had at dinner the previous evening. What should you do?

2. You work as a real estate agent. A person from out of town calls you representing himself as the executor of the estate of a person from your town who is now deceased. The executor says that he would like to get $150,000 for the property. His job is to disburse the proceeds from the sale of the estate to the beneficiaries of the will. You look at the home and, based

on comparable properties in the neighborhood, you believe it is easily worth $200,000. You also realize that this property would be a good match for what your cousin has been looking for. What should you do?

3. Professor Willis was new to academic life. He was surprised to learn during his first semester that textbook publishers send complimentary copies of textbooks to professors to consider when making textbook adoption decisions. A few weeks later he learned that he could turn these books into cash if he sold them to used book buyers who frequented the halls of academia. Some publishers sent books unsolicited. Others sent books only when he asked for a review copy. If he played his cards right, he could get dozens of books from publishers, including books that he did not intend to seriously consider for adoption, and sell them for cash from a book buyer within a few weeks. This put three to four hundred dollars in his pocket each semester. Is his plan to earn extra cash ethically right or wrong?

4

Biblical Themes for Business Ethics—Part 2

SCRIPTURE PASSAGE

Depart from evil, and do good;
Seek peace, and pursue it. (Ps 34:14)[1]

CHAPTER OVERVIEW

In this chapter we introduce additional Bible story themes that provide ethical guidance for business activities. In particular, we will

- explore the essence of eight biblical themes that form the biblical framework to understand business ethics

MAIN TOPICS

Shalom
Sabbath
Justice
Righteousness
Truth
Wisdom
Loving Kindness
Redemption
Down to the Nitty-Gritty

KEY TERMS

justice, loving kindness, redemption, righteousness, sabbath, shalom, truth, wisdom

INTRODUCTION

In the previous chapter we introduced the idea of biblical story themes. We considered four themes relevant to business ethics: cosmic conflict (good versus evil), creation (establishing relationships for a journey), holiness (individually and collectively being deeply consecrated to God) and covenant relationships (living in a relationship of deep commitment to follow Jesus). In this chapter we conclude our introduction of the biblical themes by considering the following themes:

- shalom
- sabbath
- justice
- righteousness
- truth
- wisdom
- loving kindness
- redemption

To segue toward the remaining themes, consider the words of the Preamble[2] to the Constitution of the United States of America:

> We the people of the United States, in order to form a more perfect union, establish justice, insure domestic tranquility, provide for the common defense, promote the general welfare, and secure the blessings of liberty to ourselves and our posterity, do ordain and establish this Constitution for the United States of America.

Table 4.1. Shalom theme.

Shalom	Misery
Abundant life	Stealing, killing, destroying
Justice	Injustice
Whole, complete, strong, healthy, safe	Broken, incomplete, weak, sick, unsafe
Social and political harmony	Social and political disharmony, conflict, strife
Economic prosperity broadly defined	Economic prosperity narrowly defined

Notice the following phrases: "more perfect union," "establish justice," "insure domestic tranquility," "promote the general welfare" and "secure the blessings of liberty." In this chapter we are introducing eight biblical story themes that, by analogy, are elements in the ideal goal of living as seen by the Bible. What the Constitution has in mind for the nation, the Bible writers have in mind for all who desire the same qualities of life. You will notice that in the first theme of shalom, the ideas of welfare and blessings are highlighted just as they are in the Constitution (see table 4.1).

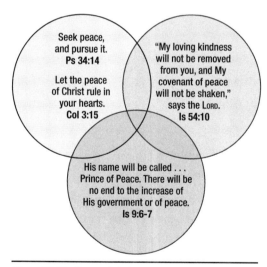

Figure 4.1. The theme of shalom.

Shalom. God's plan for humans at creation was for them to experience complete well-being in all its dimensions. The same experience is desired in covenant relationships in community. This experience came to be called shalom

(peace).[3] Covenant relationships are sometimes called covenants of peace.[4] Accordingly, the law of God is his prescription for how best to walk with God and with each other along the journey toward peace and life.[5] More than one Bible story writer encourages us to pursue the blessings of peace that come from God and to live actively in covenant relationships so that misery and misfortune can be avoided.[6]

The Messiah for whom Israel looked to bring in the promised blessings of shalom is called the Prince of Peace.[7] In the story theme of cosmic conflict it is the God of peace who will crush Satan under the feet of believers.[8] As the fulfillment of God's covenant relationship with us, Jesus took up this same Story theme when he said, "The thief comes only to steal and kill and destroy; I came that they might have life, and have it abundantly" (Jn 10:10).[9] This is consistent with the biblical perspective on the Ten Commandments. Jesus is the best expression of the self-giving law of God. When we have a deep relationship with him, we not only will have the desire to keep the commandments as he did but also will find the power to do so (see fig. 4.2).

People in Bible times believed that obedience to the law of God would foster shalom. "Those who love Your law have great peace, and nothing causes them to stumble" (Ps 119:165).[10] The danger in taking a shalom perspective on obedience to the Ten Commandments is that it is easy to begin thinking that our obedience to the precepts of the commandments is what

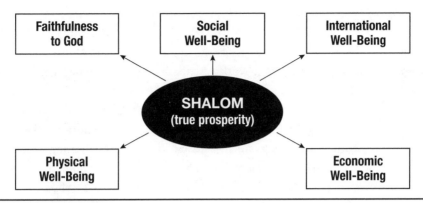

Figure 4.2. The dimensions of shalom.

makes us right with God. The law of God is not the savior; however, from a purely human point of view, when persons in community are obedient to the precepts of the law of God, they will experience many of the blessings of shalom.[11]

Implications. Seen through the lens of this theme, the purpose of business is to provide a structured means in society for people to be a blessing to each other. In this way they extend the experience of shalom to others while experiencing it themselves. Even when one person or one organization cannot create well-being for an entire community all by themselves, they can create a taste of shalom for those with whom they connect. Believers will make business decisions that contribute to well-being in all its dimensions, including economic prosperity. Believers will pray for and pursue true prosperity, not for selfish purposes but for the purpose of sharing it with others.[12]

Seen through the lens of this theme, the big question that guides ethical behavior is Will this action undermine shalom in the community? If the action is expected to undermine shalom, it is unethical. Will the action foster shalom? If it will, then the action is ethical.

In the story, the experience of shalom does not occur by chance or from the arbitrary actions of a capricious God. While the blessings

of shalom ultimately come from God, humans have a role to play in realizing the promised blessings in their relationships. Indeed, in the story, covenant relationships require constant attention. This brings us to the next theme that intersects with several story themes: sabbath.

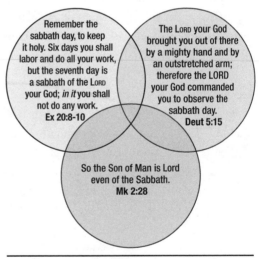

Figure 4.3. The theme of sabbath.

Sabbath. The pinnacle of covenant relationships in the story is the concept of sabbath.[13] Like the other themes we are exploring, sabbath offers guidance for behavior in the ethical, social and legal environment of business.

Sabbath in the story is centered on the community spending a day in community with the Creator-Redeemer.[14] Sabbath is a space in time in which we are free to be fully human as God intended. Accordingly, a major story purpose of sabbath is rest from work starting with the rest of God from his work but embracing rest from our work. The sabbath day is a means for humans to renounce continually human autonomy and acknowledge God's lordship in our life. Sabbath is a brief return to an Eden-like existence where work was free from its burdens. When the shalom experience of Eden was disrupted by sin, the hidden potential of sabbath was revealed: spending time with God and laying aside the burdens of our economic pursuits.

Thus, in sabbath we have a weekly hope of experiencing shalom where all creation receives a benefit.[15] Soon after their departure from Egypt, the children of Israel received the sabbath as a gift. In Egypt, the desires for rest were disrupted by cruel overseers who continually demanded more and more productivity with no rest. Upon leaving Egypt, they received the rest from oppression that they had longed for. For them at that moment, this was shalom! This connection of sabbath with shalom is not lost on Isaiah and Ezekiel, two Old Testament prophets who foretold the renewal of the covenant which would usher in a whole new order for life. This new order for life included sabbath.[16]

Some believe that the sabbath commandment is an arbitrary religious belief that has nothing to do with morality.[17] Such a view superficially sees the commandments as a somewhat random list of unrelated dos and don'ts. The weekly sabbath[18] is inseparable from and interdependent with the story's emphasis on work and the pursuit of shalom. Sabbath refers to commitment to a set of principles designed to foster flourishing life. Thus,

sabbath is a miniature representation of all the principles of a flourishing relationship with God, namely, his law. One might even say that sabbath might lose some its meaning if on the other six days no work was done, or was done in a way that dishonors the covenant relationships in the community. In the story, work loses some of its meaning when what the sabbath stands for is ignored or rejected.

Sabbath is primarily about our living in a relationship with God and resting from our daily work as we are co-laborers with God in sustaining each other, resting in the joy of God's great gifts at creation and redemption. Just as in the story God rested from his work on the seventh day of the creation story, so we rest from our labors on sabbath.[19] Now that sin is present, sabbath involves resting from our works of righteousness as a means to gain favor with God and instead resting in faith that the work of God's grace in Christ on our behalf is sufficient for our salvation. Sabbath became one of the defining characteristics of God's people in the story. Believers act in faith by ceasing from their work on sabbath as a sign of trust in God.[20] Sabbath also involves resting in the hope that one day the peace of Eden will be restored at the consummation of the story.

The idea of sabbath in the story extends to how humans are to manage the productivity of both people and the land which was their primary resource for sustenance and producing the physical and economic dimensions of shalom.[21] The seven-year sabbatical required story participants to demonstrate trust in God's sustaining power. Sabbath also is a limit on unrestrained drive for ever-higher productivity. One-seventh (14.285%) of productive time is put aside for other purposes than economic gain.

Table 4.2. Sabbath theme.

Keeping Sabbath	Breaking Sabbath
Rests from grasping for more	Unrelentingly grasps for more
Fosters diligent work and contentment	Incites discontentment; devalues work
Loyal, trusting	Disloyal, distrusting
Acknowledges God's lordship over all of life	Rejects God's lordship over all of life
Resting in redemption provided by the Creator	Attempting to provide our own redemption

Implications. In terms of sabbath, the purpose of business is to foster both work and contentment. Business managers must encourage diligent work and rest. If we think of sabbath as only a day to go to church each week, after which we watch football, mow the lawn or go shopping, we have lost sight of the deeper meaning of sabbath principles. We take sabbath principles with us wherever we go, even into the marketplace. Without sabbath principles at work in our life continually reminding us of how we are set apart by God for service to others, we can easily use the sabbath day hours to scheme how we might obtain profit by breaking the other principles of covenant relationships.[22]

The next story theme we introduce is that of justice, without which it is impossible to experience true shalom or sabbath.[23]

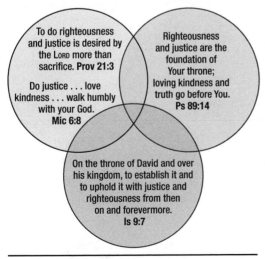

Figure 4.4. The theme of justice.

Justice. We often reduce the idea of justice to a matter of fair play in the market. The Bible's idea of justice is broader, encompassing all aspects of responsibilities to each other and to God.[24] In the story, whenever a person fulfils one's obligations, that person is behaving justly. Justice involves all conduct by someone who is doing right according to the principles of covenant relationships.[25]

Justice is the actions that a person takes to honor the rights of others.[26] Blessings envisioned for one person in the community is of equal value for all. Thus, we pursue covenant relationships together requiring that anyone in authority treat those under their authority with fairness. Likewise, the idea of shalom embraces all persons in the community. Even strangers should be allowed to participate. God does not show favoritism; humans are to follow this model.[27]

In the story, justice is not merely how we think about others. It involves actions we take that open up the channels of shalom blessing to others.[28] In the story, justice is an active distribution system: It must journey throughout the land rather than stay just at the city gate or the throne of the king (the official places of justice). One reason for this may be that those who do evil against orphans and widows will do it far away from the city gate where the judge sits. The most vulnerable in the land must have justice come to them. Thus justice in the Bible narrative is dynamic:

The figure text reads:

To do righteousness and justice is desired by the Lord more than sacrifice. Prov 21:3

Do justice . . . love kindness . . . walk humbly with your God. Mic 6:8

Righteousness and justice are the foundation of Your throne; loving kindness and truth go before You. Ps 89:14

On the throne of David and over his kingdom, to establish it and to uphold it with justice and righteousness from then on and forevermore. Is 9:7

Table 4.3. Justice theme.

Justice	Injustice
Basing actions that affect others on covenant relationship principles of God's law	Basing actions that affect others on personal bias
Heroically intervening to correct injustices	Perpetrating or perpetuating or ignoring injustices
Extending justice throughout the entire community beyond the formal justice system	Limiting justice to what is done in the formal justice system
Honoring the rights of others	Jeopardizing or weakening the rights of others

I [wisdom] walk in the way of
    righteousness,
In the midst of the paths of justice,
To endow those who love me with wealth,
That I may fill their treasuries. (Prov
    8:20-21)[29]

It flows down from those in high authority toward those with low authority and continues out like a life-giving stream to the most vulnerable and needy.[30] It must flow through the marketplace. And justice must nourish everyone present in the community including enemies and visitors from other nations.[31]

The story reveals that we all can become vulnerable to the unjust actions of others even if we are not an orphan or a widow. There may come a day when someone attempts to limit our rights or does something evil toward us. On that day we will want justice. This reveals a practical, utilitarian perspective to story justice in community: If a person acts justly toward others, it will foster a flourishing life in the community; everyone receives a blessing.[32]

Implications. One implication from this theme is that justice is not only the domain of the court system. The purpose of business is to be a channel of justice in the marketplace so that many can receive blessings. In the ethical, social and legal environment of business, faithful followers of God will seek to reveal God's character of love and justice to others in the marketplace. Marketplace

workers will act in just ways to everyone in the community, even to strangers who may be unfamiliar with local customs or standard prices. Business workers will use business technology in ways that foster justice rather than taking advantage of people. Employers will treat workers fairly; companies will treat suppliers fairly; suppliers will treat customers fairly. Goods will be sold at prices that reflect the value of the product. Followers of God will leave vengeance to God; however, they will intervene to correct injustices that are within their sphere of responsibility.

Justice is a concept that is a sibling to our next theme: righteousness. They look so much alike in some parts of the story that they are easy to be confused.

Righteousness. It should be evident by now

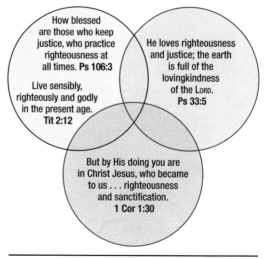

How blessed are those who keep justice, who practice righteousness at all times. Ps 106:3

Live sensibly, righteously and godly in the present age. Tit 2:12

He loves righteousness and justice; the earth is full of the lovingkindness of the LORD. Ps 33:5

But by His doing you are in Christ Jesus, who became to us . . . righteousness and sanctification. 1 Cor 1:30

Figure 4.5. The theme of righteousness.

Table 4.4. Righteousness theme.

Righteousness	Unrighteousness-Wickedness
Firm, straight	Slack, crooked
Strength	Weakness
Endurance, steadfastness	Temporary
Blameless in conduct; aligned with covenant	Conduct out of alignment with covenant
Acting in a way that is faithful to vulnerable	Uncaring toward the vulnerable
Regard for God's character; trusts in God	Disregard for God's character; trusts in self
Acts that honor, preserve and lend stability	Acts that corrupt, violate, destabilize
Interventional—makes right the wrong	Uncaring about righting wrongs

how much these story themes overlap with each other yet are not precisely identical. Each presents a different facet of a unity of thought in the story. Our natural tendency may be to distinguish narrowly between each one, whereas the story writers do not seem to make such precise distinctions all the time. Accordingly, the theme of righteousness is sometimes intertwined with and used as a synonym for other themes such as, justice, loving kindness and redemption.[33]

The story makes clear that ultimately God is the source of doing the right thing. Humans are called on to imitate God's behavior in community. Righteousness in the story conveys a few basic ideas: (a) God's actions which show his faithfulness to his promises (creating, fulfilling promises and making right that which has undermined community relationships); (b) right doing—blameless behavior that is evaluated by the community in terms of the ten covenant principles;[34] (c) actions that promote justice; (d) to be straight and firm or steel-like rather than slack;[35] to be strong and enduring in faithfulness to the principles of the covenant.[36] While humans are called on to behave righteously with one another, the story recognizes that true righteousness is a gift of God.[37] The good news of the gospel is that in his saving acts, God's righteousness is revealed to us.[38] He is faithful to his covenant relationship with us.

Standing opposed to those who do right are the unrighteous or "wicked."[39] These are story characters who disregard God's righteous actions, characters such as Cain (who killed his brother)[40] or Queen Jezebel.[41] They are selfish, greedy and ultimately destructive in covenant relationships. They lack caring for the vulnerable in the community; they may even lead others astray.[42] They fail to act in ways that nourish covenant relationships.

Implications. In terms of righteousness, the biblical purpose of business in society is to lend stability to the larger community by acting in ways that support covenantal relationships. Business will not undermine firmness to principle, but rather will encourage firmness. At times this means that business leaders get involved with issues outside their organization in the larger community they serve. It also means that once leaders of a business set its course and make commitments, they remain faithful to these for the sake of stability.

Like other story themes, the theme of righteousness emphasizes faithfulness in the covenant relationship. A different nuance of faithfulness comes next in the theme of truth.

Truth. One of the biggest problems in the ethical, social and legal environment of business is the challenge of knowing for certain whether or not a person is genuine. Is a person you meet truly what he or she says, or does the person merely say words that are not backed up by action?

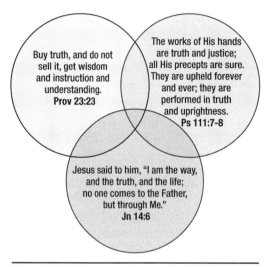

Figure 4.6. The theme of truth.

For example, for years the notorious Bernie Madoff, an expert on Ponzi schemes, carefully managed the impressions that investors had about him. Without such impression management, he would not have successfully committed fraud. Eventually not only was his fraud reprehensible but also his unfaithfulness in managing community impressions.

At a superficial level we can think of the story idea of truth as meaning telling the truth instead of deceiving. But a person's work with respect to truth is not limited merely to pursuit of the abstract idea of truthfulness of information and integrity of speech (as opposed to telling lies).[43] Truth involves this but also has a deeper, more profound meaning in the biblical story.

The story concept of truth means faithfulness of action.[44] Truth means that there is a close correspondence between our actions and what others expect from us. In other words, truth means that we are who we say we are:

faithful in all covenant relationships.[45] Others can rely on a person to act in a consistent manner from one situation to another. When a person or organization behaves in a particular way over time, this leads others around them to develop certain expectations. Then if the person or organization acts contrary to these expectations, apart from what else might be wrong with the unexpected actions, there is an additional problem that is created: inconsistency of behavior. Inconsistency of action fosters distrust.

> Do not let kindness and truth leave you;
> Bind them around your neck,
> Write them on the tablet of your heart. (Prov 3:3)

Implications. In this theme we see that the purpose of business is to be one of the structures in society that encourages faithfulness, trustworthiness and consistency when values are exchanged. In contemporary terms, truth involves living a consistent life over time without hypocrisy.[46] Truth means ensuring that all our actions have lasting reliability. It means that our actions are a reliable messenger about the reality of who we are. For example, in the story when the king, emulating God's character, builds his authority on truth, he builds it on actions of faithfulness to covenant relations and loving kindness.[47] In essence advancing truth means advancing the cause of faithfulness to commitments in and around the community. Anything that undermines this or that presents something that is false in words or actions is detestable.[48] In the story, when young King Josiah embarked on repairing the temple, the

Table 4.5. Truth theme.

Truth	Unfaithfulness
Consistency of behavior from one situation to another	Inconsistency of behavior from one situation to another
Reliable behavior pattern; faithfulness	Unreliable behavior pattern; unfaithfulness
Telling the truth without deception	Deceiving others through our words or actions
Walking in integrity and uprightness	Walking without integrity

persons in charge of paying the workers were implicitly trusted to be faithful with the cash. So consistent was the pattern of their behavior that the community could rely on them to manage the internal cash control.[49]

Truth is one of the big questions of the cosmic conflict in the story: Does God act consistently and reliably? This understanding of truth is a necessary part of covenant relationships that lead to shalom. Reliability, stability and faithfulness in daily actions are a part of complete well-being and true prosperity.

The story idea of truth brings us to another important theme related to the ethical, social and legal environment of business: wisdom. Living a consistent life is the smart thing to do if you are in a covenant relationship that you value. To this story theme we turn next.

Wisdom. Wisdom means being firm and well-grounded first in faithfulness to God and second in the business of living life celebrating all the good that God has given for life.[50]

In the story it is by wisdom that God creates.[51] Wisdom brings blessings.[52] God's action of redemption shows his great wisdom.[53] Ultimately, wisdom comes from God, who continues to be active in the creative process when he creates wisdom offering it as a gift. Wisdom cannot be understood apart from its relationship to covenant relationships.[54] Biblical wisdom is interwoven with faithfulness, justice and other dimensions of moral uprightness.[55] Accordingly, humans on their own are limited in their ability to gather true wisdom for all of life. In this regard, the nature of wisdom is similar to the nature of shalom: it encompasses all dimensions of life envisioned in covenant relationships. By beholding Christ we learn how to reflect his character in our own hearts and actions. With God's power, we learn to live faithfully. This is true wisdom. This is what makes faith so practical!

As applied to practical life, wisdom involves "masterful understanding, skill, expertise."[56] Indeed, one of the fundamental ideas associated with wisdom is the ability to consider something diligently or closely and thereby have insight and understanding regarding it.[57] The wise person is careful in speaking and prudent in doing. The wise person becomes adept at dealing with all things material. But it is also wisdom which leads in the ethics process.

In the story, wisdom is applied to technical and artistic skills,[58] government,[59] diplomacy,[60]

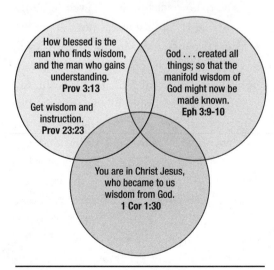

How blessed is the man who finds wisdom, and the man who gains understanding.
Prov 3:13

Get wisdom and instruction.
Prov 23:23

God . . . created all things; so that the manifold wisdom of God might now be made known.
Eph 3:9-10

You are in Christ Jesus, who became to us wisdom from God.
1 Cor 1:30

Figure 4.7. The theme of wisdom.

Table 4.6. Wisdom theme.

Wisdom	Foolishness
Constructive, productive	Destructive, ruinous, unproductive, careless
Uses discretion; communally prudent	Uses indiscretion; communally reckless
Protects self from being misled	Blind to being misled; misleads others
Practical skill mastery used for good, useful	Inept, useless, worthless
Listens to counsel from others	Listens to self; ignores counsel
Being smart in managing covenant relationships based on covenant principles	Morally stupid

war,[61] judging and ruling a nation,[62] cleverness to master how to deal with people and situations[63] and the ability to answer difficult questions.[64] However, these skills are never isolated from the other biblical story themes.

Closely related to wisdom is the story idea of prudence. Having wisdom means being intensely prudent but always mindful of one's relationship with God and the wider community. Prudence means careful discretion when applying knowledge to everyday life; however, prudence is not merely mental activity. It, too, is an action concept.[65] Prudence is the ability to keep oneself from being misled, an important dimension of participating in covenant relationships especially in business.[66]

One risk is that, unguided by truth, justice and righteousness, wisdom will be directed toward selfish means and ends. When this happens it no longer is true wisdom. It is foolishness. The story repeatedly compares the wise person with the foolish person. The foolish person rejects covenantal relationships, attempts to live autonomously from God's principles for living, blames God and is self-centered, proud and destructive.[67] The larger community ridicules fools because, even though they might be intelligent and on the surface appear to be successful in business and activities involving money, in reality they are senseless or stupid from the point of view of the other story themes.[68] "As a partridge that hatches eggs which it has not laid, so is he who

makes a fortune, but unjustly; in the midst of his days it will forsake him, and in the end he will be a fool" (Jer 17:11).

Implications. The purpose of business is not only to be the repository of knowledge about how to efficiently exchange things of value in the market or the most practical ways of doing business. In the biblical way of thinking, business is for the purpose of sharing not only practical wisdom but also wisdom about how life in the community can be improved as business leaders work together with other community leaders to solve community problems. When a business offers training to employees to improve their skills, the training can range beyond just the technical dimensions to include other things represented by the biblical themes.

Exactly how wisdom is achieved in all the varied contexts of business is not a topic that the story explores in depth; however, wisdom is so closely tied to the other themes that we are not left without moral guidance for business.

The theme of wisdom brings us to another core story idea relevant to the ethical, social and legal environment of business: loving kindness.

Loving kindness. What useful value is in a relationship for either party if the main emphasis is on following arbitrary rules imposed by one party on the other? Not much in the long run. Without the story theme of loving kindness, covenant relations would disintegrate. Indeed, loving kindness is one of the most important foundation stones in the building of community.[69]

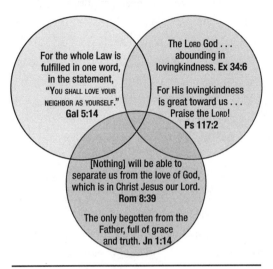

For the whole Law is fulfilled in one word, in the statement, "You shall love your neighbor as yourself." Gal 5:14

The Lord God . . . abounding in lovingkindness. Ex 34:6

For His lovingkindness is great toward us . . . Praise the Lord! Ps 117:2

[Nothing] will be able to separate us from the love of God, which is in Christ Jesus our Lord. Rom 8:39

The only begotten from the Father, full of grace and truth. Jn 1:14

Figure 4.8. The theme of loving kindness.

One surprising thing we learn about the story theme of loving kindness is that, like a finely cut diamond, it has many aspects. We cannot limit the story idea of love to be merely a feeling of affection or emotion toward someone. While there is plenty of evidence in the story that God has affection toward humans,[70] the central idea associated with covenant relationships, shalom, justice, righteousness and the other story themes we are considering is abiding loyalty. When someone in community says, "I love you," in story terms they are saying, "I will remain loyal to you even if you reject me."

Like the theme of truth, loving kindness is an action word wherein a person does not merely talk about loyalty. He or she shows loyalty in action.[71] When story writers like David observed God's action toward his people, he exclaimed that the whole earth was full of God's abiding loyalty.[72] One reason that the whole earth is full of God's love is that actions of justice are allowed to move on its pathway throughout the whole community. If we deeply desire the experience of shalom in covenant relationships, we will pursue abiding loyalty in our relationships.[73]

Covenant commitment and abiding loyalty form the basis of story ideals for relationships between persons and between groups. Covenant commitment is the moral promise; abiding loyalty characterizes the actions in the relationship based on the principles in the Ten Commandments.[74] Thus, when we think of acting on the principles of the Ten Commandments, we are describing what it means to be loyal, faithful and kind to others in the community even if we do not have nice, warm feelings toward them at a given point in time.

Implications. The purpose of business seen through the lens of loving kindness is this: Business is about fostering loyalty in relationships in the community. Loyalty in community relationships (such as the family) has an important economic dimension. Businesses can support interpersonal loyalty by how they structure deals with customers and how they go about attracting customers. Offering deals to customers that tempt them to undermine their relationship with their family undermines

Table 4.7. Loving kindness theme.

Loving Kindness, Loyalty	Capricious Loyalty
Love based primarily on unchanging loyalty	Loyalty based primarily on changeable feelings
Respect for the covenant relationship	Shallow commitment to the relationship
Loyalty that is demonstrated in action	Loyalty in words only
Fostering mutual reciprocity	Promotes selfish gain
Faithfulness in relationships	Unfaithfulness in relationships

loving kindness. Loyalty can be fostered in the employer-employee relationship, too. Companies that are loyal to workers even when the economy tanks foster shalom in the community.

The last story theme considered here is closely related to several other themes, especially loving kindness. It is the theme of redemption that presents something important about the story perspective on business ethics not found in other approaches to ethics.

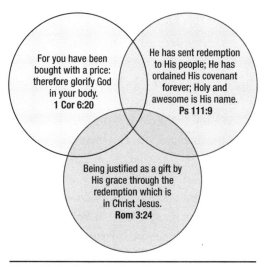

Figure 4.9. The theme of redemption.

Redemption. In the story, ethics is not just a list of rules to follow. Ethics involves an integrated, systemic way of thinking and conduct in community in response to what God has done to redeem us. Whatever God has asked us to do in terms of behavior in community, this is inseparable from the redemption story. Redemption in the story means to act as a kinsman to buy back someone or something, to ransom, liberate or rescue.[75] When God redeems his people, the effects of evil and chaos come to an end. He is the power that transforms them.

By looking at the various story themes we can see that human conduct is viewed as a particular kind of relationship between you and God, be-

tween you and other people and between you and the environment. This relationship is described as being a covenant relationship. Many of the actions envisioned in the story themes are designed to nourish such a relationship.

When we consider the whole biblical story of redemption from both Testaments, we see God's approach to redemption including a few basic elements. (a) The plan for redemption was established on the principles of the character (law) of God designed for happiness in human community. (b) He provided a means for teaching and modeling these principles by example. The Ten Commandments were the first time these were modeled; Jesus Christ was the second time. (c) God provided a means of reconciliation whereby the stakeholders are given a chance to change if they are outside the boundaries of the principles. Such transformation is possible only through faith and the power of God. (d) When communicating the redemption plan in advance, God came close to those with whom he communicated. (e) In the Ten Commandments, as exhibited in the life of Christ, God gave warnings that are based on the principles but rooted in specific observed behaviors. (f) God evaluates impartially. (g) Ultimately, God provides a means for separation for those who choose not to align with his principles. (h) He encourages rather than forces those who align with his principles. (i) He centers the transformation process on a faith relationship between the person and himself through Jesus Christ.

Implications. In terms of the theme of redemption, the purpose of business is to contribute to reclaiming broken relationships. While business organizations should not be expected to repair every relationship, business can do its part by healing economic relationships that involve any of the players in the

Table 4.8. Redemption theme.

Redemption	Bondage
To act as a kinsman to liberate or rescue	To put into bondage, to take, to enslave
Designed to recover lost shalom	Deepens the misery of lost shalom
Not limited to spiritual forgiveness of sins; encompasses the whole earth	Encompasses the whole earth
Humans commissioned to work with God	Humans work with God's adversary
Reconnecting with God	Separation from God

market: employees, customers, suppliers and strategic alliance partners. Business plays a key role in bringing stability to all relationships. It is the redemption theme that suggests that the world of business is one, but not the only, place where the image of God can be restored.

Redemption accomplished by Jesus Christ was not limited to spiritual forgiveness of sins but includes the whole earth (everything that he created).[76] Redemption involves the process (and the result) of finally and completely restoring all dimensions of shalom on a new earth!

Just as humans were commissioned at creation to participate in the ongoing work of God in community, so humans are commissioned at redemption to participate in the ongoing work of God. As agents of redemption, business professionals have the commission to work for the restoration of the image of God in humans. We are called to worship the Creator. We are challenged to make covenant relationships a high priority in the community. Business has tremendous influence for bringing the transforming power of God to communities and to organizations. The person who works in the marketplace playing a role in the manufacture, distribution and marketing promotion of necessary products is working not only with the things that came from the hand of the Creator but also the things that were purchased by the Redeemer.

BIBLICAL PERSPECTIVE AS A PRISM

The major themes of the story that we have considered here are at the intersection of God's character, Jesus Christ's work and God's design for our conduct. We can describe them as a prism.[77] Like a prism that bends incoming light, each theme helps us see a slightly dif-

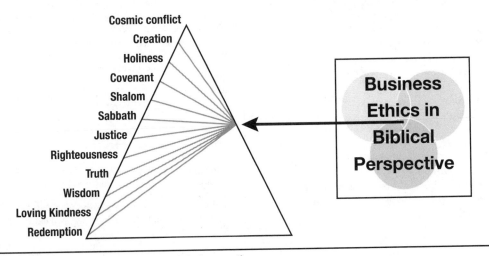

Figure 4.10. The prism of business ethics in biblical perspective.

ferent facet of a unified story ideal for business conduct. Each reveals something slightly different about God. Each connects us with Jesus Christ and his work, since these themes are facets of his character (see fig. 4.10).

These biblical themes give a new perspective on the tension between faith and reason. The themes show a particular type of reasoning in ancient Hebrew life. This is not a bald-faced reason-alone approach to life. Rather, living a life infused with these deep themes is a plausible and reasonable way to approach life's moral challenges. It is the reasoning infused with biblical thinking that becomes the system which organizes thinking and action.

DOWN TO THE NITTY-GRITTY

Think about the Ethical Vignettes to Discuss at the end of this chapter. Think about vignette 1, the story from Cuba. Is it wrong for the sem-

inary to break Cuban law and purchase rice and gasoline on the gray market in Cuba? It's time to get down to the nitty-gritty (see table 4.9)!

CHAPTER REVIEW QUESTIONS

1. What is the concept of shalom, and how is it a guide to decision making?

2. What does the sabbath theme tell us about making business decisions?

3. How does the theme of justice guide business activities?

4. What does the theme of righteousness say about making business decisions?

5. What is the essence of the theme of truth as it applies to business?

6. What does biblical wisdom mean, and how is this a guide in business?

7. What is the core idea of the biblical theme of loving kindness?

Table 4.9. Applying the ethical process.

Keeping Your Heart: An Intrapersonal Process	Walking in the Community: An Interpersonal Process

• You are one of the officials at the seminary in Cuba. What does your heart say is the right thing to do?
 • Which biblical themes explored in this (or the previous) chapter inform your heart on this situation? (Which themes are the most relevant in this case?)
 • What other influences in your heart seem to be prominent as you think about this situation?
    • Fundamental beliefs
    • Cognitive reasoning
    • Judgments and evaluations
    • Decisions
    • Virtues
    • Will
    • Memory of personal experiences with other people
    • Perceptions of others in the community
    • Personal biases
    • Awareness of interpersonal relationships
    • Commitments to God and to others
    • Intuitions
    • Conscience
    • Human spirit
    • Emotions
	• You are one of the officials at the seminary in Cuba. With whom might you have a conversation about this situation? Who else might have a helpful perspective on this type of situation?
	 • Which of the biblical themes in this chapter will most likely come up in the conversation either directly or indirectly? Why?
	 • If you have a conversation with someone regarding this situation, which of the fundamental tensions presented earlier in the book might come into the conversation?
	 • What right-versus-right dilemmas, if any, can be identified in this situation? Have a conversation with someone about this now. What is the outcome of the conversation?
	 • How will you resolve the right-versus-right dilemma(s)?
	 • If the answer to the question (Is it wrong for the seminary to break Cuban law and purchase rice and gasoline on the gray market in Cuba?) is ambiguous even after careful thought and conversation with others, how can you handle this as a Christian?

8. What does the redemption theme say about business activities?

DISCUSSION QUESTIONS

1. Consider in turn each of the themes presented in this chapter and discuss the following question in terms of the universal-particular tension point in ethics. Based on the information presented, what is an example of a particular action that might be called for to foster a covenant relationship in the marketplace? Give an example of a behavior that should be avoided in the marketplace.

2. Give an example of a story you have read, heard or seen recently that illustrates a story theme presented in this chapter. How was this theme portrayed in ways that are the same or different from how the Bible story portrays the theme(s)?

3. Review all the theme summary tables in this chapter (see appendix C). What pattern of recurrence do you see with certain ideas that appear in the tables? Identify which ideas repeat (or are similar) from theme to theme. What might this pattern tell us about the biblical perspective on business ethics?

4. For each theme write a one-sentence summary of one general ethical principle that you believe God intends for us to use in the marketplace. How does each statement describe God's character? How is each principle related to Jesus Christ and his work for our redemption?

5. It has sometimes been said that the essence of God's law is love (Deut 6:5; 10:12; Mt 22:36-40; 1 Jn 5:3). To what degree, if at all, does this limit the law given the other story themes that are found in the Bible?

EXERCISE

For each biblical story theme presented in this chapter write a summary of how this theme is a guide to ethical behavior in the marketplace. Consider the following questions to help you create this summary: What general ethical principles do you believe God intends for us to use in the marketplace from each theme? How does each statement describe God's character? How is each principle related to Jesus Christ and his work for redemption? What implications does each have for our marketplace conduct?

ETHICAL VIGNETTES TO DISCUSS

For each of the vignettes described below, apply one or more of the biblical story themes to discern what is right and wrong.

1. A Christian seminary in Cuba needs to provide food and other resources for the students who are enrolled. For example, the seminary provides a food service and serves rice to students. The seminary also uses a vehicle to complete tasks needed to keep the seminary operating in the community. The problem is that by Cuban law the seminary is allowed to purchase only limited quantities of certain commodities such as rice and gasoline. The seminary needs eight times the amount of rice than is allowed. Interestingly, although it is technically illegal, the gray market in Cuba offers for sale certain commodities such as rice and gasoline. Government officials who receive extra rations of certain commodities sell their surplus to the gray market to make extra money. It can be dangerous to purchase some commodities because it is technically illegal. When managers of the seminary go to the gray market to make purchases, they feel anxious that

they could be arrested by the same government officials who supply the gray market. Is it wrong for the seminary to break Cuban law and purchase rice and gasoline on the gray market in Cuba?

2. A real estate developer is building several condominiums to sell. The list price for a two-bedroom condo is $165,000. The developer knows that, following industry practices after negotiation, the sale price will be more likely $155,000. One day a widow comes to the sales office to enquire about the condos. In the past, her husband did all the real estate negotiations. She is from out of town. Furthermore, she is unfamiliar with the condominium concept. But she likes one of the two-bedroom units. With the cash from her husband's life insurance policy in the bank, she offers the list price for it. Is it wrong for the developer's sales team to accept the widow's offer?

3. One group of Christians say, "We should use this new technology for getting a natural resource out of the earth. Getting the natural resource will result in happier people because the resource is less expensive and more plentiful. Look how the whole economy will be improved! This is shalom." Another group of Christians oppose the first group by saying, "Look at the injury to workers when they use the technology! Look at the people who live near where the technology is used. Their drinking water is unfit for drinking. To use the technology is to undermine shalom." Which group is correct? Why? Is there a dimension of shalom that should be limited? If so, which one?

PART TWO

CONTEMPORARY APPROACHES

Part II explores common secular approaches to ethical decision making by evaluating each through the lens of biblical themes established in part I. Some secular approaches have deep Judeo-Christian roots; others are *prima facie* at odds with Scripture.

The chapters in part II provide introductions and are not intended to be comprehensive reviews of all philosophical questions that have been asked and debated over the years for each approach; however, an attempt has been made to represent each in a fair manner. What we are examining here is the collection of fundamental principles that are often used in the marketplace as the approach to decide what is right and wrong. These so-called secular approaches considered in this book include

- egoism (chap. 5)
- relativism (chap. 6)
- common sense (chap. 7)
- the social contract (chap. 8)
- utilitarianism (chap. 9)
- universalism (chap. 10)
- agency (chap. 11)
- justice and rights (chap. 12)
- virtues and character (chap. 13)

The assumption of this text is that each person develops and uses one or more approaches to ethical decision making. Knowing your own approach, including its strengths and weaknesses, can counteract the tendency (in some people) to uncritically accept an approach.

If you have not studied these approaches before, or if you have had little experience personally dealing with the complex ethical issues that arise in the marketplace, you may not grasp the importance of such a study at first. Thus, one additional reason why this book addresses the commonly used approaches is that it helps readers be aware of the broader conversations taking place, either implicitly or explicitly, in the market and among scholars who have been trying to more clearly understand the right and wrong actions in the marketplace.

The following graphic illustration represents the various approaches in terms of how narrow or how broad the focus of each approach (see fig. PII.1). Laying out the spectrum in this way illustrates how various approaches are seen as progressively more mature than others. Beginning at the bottom center of the spectrum (egoism) and moving outward, we start at the most narrow of all approaches, in which the focus is on the personal and partial perspective. On the outer band we find the approaches that take the broad, impersonal and impartial perspective emphasizing the needs of others with equal weight to our own needs. Another way of saying it is that at the broadest perspective a person has no greater claim to special treatment than anyone else. At this broad perspective the consequences of social actions on others and the duties we have toward others is just as important as the consequences of actions on ourselves and duties we have toward ourselves. Some of the approaches overlap others because they have some elements in common. In other words, some of these approaches are not mutually exclusive of others.

Notice the parameters used to show the relationships among the various models:

- impartiality versus partiality
- immaturity versus maturity (based on Kohlberg's model)
- broad versus narrow (in scope)
- individual versus community (a fundamental tension)

Furthermore, notice the relative positions of the four concentric half circles. On the basis of this illustration, do some ethical models seem to be better than others? On what basis do you think they are better?

Near the end of each chapter, the text will guide you into thinking about some (but not all) of the pros and cons of the approach explored in the chapter. This section of each chapter is not meant to be comprehensive. Rather, it is designed to introduce you to a more advanced discussion that is possible regarding each of the ethical approaches. Another benefit of having some of the pros and cons presented is that these will help the novice reader become aware that the level of complexity for ethical issues may be far greater than first believed. This can contribute to the development of humility and, for some students, the desire to learn more. A final benefit of this section in the chapter is that understanding the pros and cons of various theories will challenge

SPECTRUM OF ETHICAL MODELS

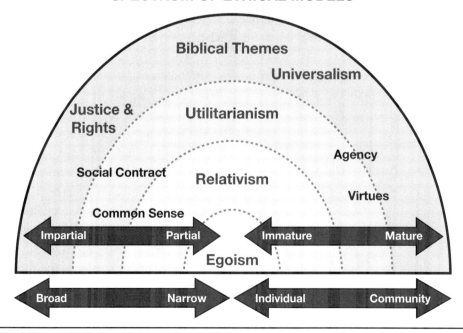

Figure PII.1. Diagram of ethical models.

readers to evaluate their own perspective. Readers will see more clearly how the contemporary models do not align with Scripture.

Additionally, at the end of each chapter the biblical themes are employed to evaluate the theory presented in the chapter. As with the pros and cons, this section is not intended to be a comprehensive review of the biblical perspective on that theory. Rather, this is designed to introduce to the reader the major issues and directions that the biblical perspective is expected to take. The author hopes that this introduction will spark a curiosity among some readers to study the Scripture more thoroughly to evaluate the points that are made or the conclusions that are drawn in this book.

Critiquing the various commonly employed theories will help readers be more astute when in conversations with people who do not share the biblical perspective. Readers will become better skilled in communicating the weaknesses of contemporary theories. They will not tend to oversimplify contemporary theories. And they will recognize the positive contribution that many contemporary theories have made to the ongoing larger human dialog about ethics. Critical thinking about these approaches should improve the sense of self-efficacy for many readers. For example, if you better understand where the relativist is coming from, you can enter a conversation with a relativist more confident that you will be effective in the dialogue.

The goal of part II is to help you advance in the process of developing an integrated understanding of why certain behaviors are right and others are wrong. It will help you develop the ability to have a conversation with someone as to why you believe the way you do.

As important as they are, these approaches can lead to diverse views.[1] Understanding these approaches to ethics is of vital importance. This is not just an intellectual exercise, for it is the questions you ask, how you frame the issues and the overall perspective you take that makes an essential difference in terms of deciding what is right and wrong. Each approach takes a slightly different point of view. Accordingly, the best ethical approach is not merely in taking a little of this and a little of that just to cover the bases.[2] Indeed, if we were to be eclectic in our approach we would find ourselves being self-contradictory.

This portion of each chapter illustrates how some of the various themes are closely interrelated. So, yes, what can be said from the point of view of holiness might in certain instances also be said under truth. This illustrates the power and beauty of Scripture. Some may think that it is acceptable to combine various themes to make fewer elements. The result would be a tradeoff that undermines Scripture.

Ultimately, the content of part II is personal: What approach do *you* believe is the strongest in supporting your worldview? Which approach can you justify to others if asked?

Neuropsychology research has shown that moral development depends on basic physiological elements of the brain being mature and healthy. But this takes time to develop. The prefrontal cortex of the brain, located at the front of the frontal lobes and right under the forehead, acts like the chief executive officer of the rest of the brain's structures.[3] The power of choice in a moral situation (a.k.a. volitional control) depends on having fully functioning, healthy frontal lobes.

The prefrontal cortex of the frontal lobes helps you make predictions regarding the outcomes of anticipated actions. One section of the prefrontal cortex, the orbitofrontal cortex, makes it possible to anticipate whether you will feel positive or negative as a result of taking a certain action. This cortex enables you to discern whether you are likely to be rewarded or punished for an action.

To be fully functional with the ability to consider one's own interests as well as the interests of others in a moral dilemma, the bundles of connector cells between the prefrontal cortex and the rest of the brain need a fatty sheath over them. This sheath is known as myelin and is not fully formed until a person reaches the early to mid-twenties. The myelinization process continues into the thirties and beyond. The physiological maturity of the brain cells is not identical with moral maturity or social maturity; however, without a healthy functioning prefrontal cortex and healthy connector cells bathed in myelin, moral maturity may be difficult to achieve.

One of the dangers of alcohol and drug use is that the frontal lobes become functionally deficient even when the person otherwise seems to be fully functioning mentally. Also, if a person suffers an injury to the frontal lobes such as a closed head injury or brain concussion, this can have an unsavory impact on the ability to predict the outcomes of action, the ability to reason regarding the social rewards and punishments from certain actions and, as a result, the effectiveness of moral reasoning.

Part II also illustrates, to a degree, Lawrence Kohlberg's model of cognitive moral development that describes stages of progressive moral maturity that humans develop from childhood through adulthood.[4] Advancing from one stage to another is a process. Infants and toddlers lack moral development. Egoism is closest to this stage. Very young children react to pleasure and pain, affirmation and punishment and shape their behavior accordingly.

People increase their understanding of morality as they grow and reach Kohlberg's second stage. Family life, experiences in school and with religious organizations begin to shape their understanding of what is right and wrong for behavior, and they continue to shape their behavior in conformity to the moral rules given to them by others in society. Kohlberg believed that this stage persists for many who enter adulthood. Certain behaviors are wrong because these are specified in the formal and informal rules of society.

For Kohlberg, most adults do not progress beyond this stage. Some, however, reach the third (highest) level of moral development by considering the rules imposed by society and developing a personal understanding of why some conduct is right and other conduct is wrong. Such persons develop an ability to provide a justification for why they believe and act the way they do that goes beyond explanations of fear of punishment and beyond simply saying that society says it is right or wrong. In other words, they progress past concern for themselves toward concerns for other people and for society as a whole and integrate their beliefs into their whole view of life.

Kohlberg's model is dominated by an emphasis on the cognitive dimension of the ethics process. Such an emphasis glosses over the other intrapersonal elements and almost completely ignores the community dimension of ethics. In contrast to Kohlberg, this book takes the reader in a different direction by suggesting that the ethics process involves the whole person in a social context and that there is a communal dimension to ethics that is vital especially when the issues become complex.

Even with its deficiencies, a personal question that the Kohlberg model raises is: Where are *you* in your own moral development? Do you tend to take a narrow viewpoint, or do you have a broader viewpoint that you can defend during a conversation with someone?

5

Egoism

Do what you want to do based on what you get out of it.

SCRIPTURE PASSAGE

The generous man will be prosperous,
And he who waters will himself be
    watered. (Prov 11:25)[1]

CHAPTER OVERVIEW

In this chapter we consider a popular approach to making business decisions in the market-place. In particular, we will

- explore the basic ideas of egoism

- distinguish between the narrow and broad definitions of self-interest

- evaluate the pros and cons of ethical egoism as an approach to business ethics

- evaluate ethical egoism through the lens of biblical themes

MAIN TOPICS

Definitions and Distinctions
Egoism: "Look Out for Yourself Only"
Evaluation: Pros and Cons
Down to the Nitty-Gritty
Through the Lens of Biblical Themes

KEY TERMS

altruism, ethical egoism, interdependence, egoist, self-interest

OPENING SCENARIO

In this scenario two roads in southeast Missouri intersect to help illustrate an ethical problem. One road we will name Earthquake Avenue; the other Deficient Bridge Street.[2]

Deficient Bridge Street. Bridges are an integral part of the nation's transportation system. Bridges that connect roads are important for the nation's economy, the national defense and general free mobility of citizens.

In 2012 in the state of Missouri there were 24,334 bridges, as many as 28 percent of which were structurally deficient or obsolete. In Mis-

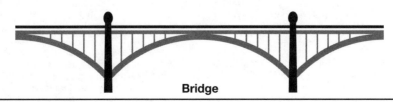

Figure 5.1. Diagram of a bridge.

sissippi County, located in southeast Missouri, more than one hundred bridges exist. Even though this is a rural agricultural area, thousands of people use the bridges of Mississippi County every year.[3]

Earthquake Avenue. Earthquakes occur frequently in the New Madrid Seismic Zone, also located in southeast Missouri.[4] Every eighteen months this region experiences an earthquake strong enough to be felt. From December 16, 1811, to March 16, 1812, a series of strong quakes occurred in this region that affected several states. Some of the quakes may have been as strong as 7.0 or 8.0. Two of the quakes caused massive damage that forever changed the topography in the region. Some experts say that there is a 90 percent chance of a 6.0 or greater earthquake occurring in that same area sometime during the next thirty years.[5]

The intersection. Like other states, Missouri is trying to repair, rehabilitate or rebuild deficient bridges to make them safe for the future.

To do this, government agencies can contract with private construction companies to complete the repair and rebuilding projects.

Now for the ethical dilemma: A bridge construction company contacts Midwest Hardware Manufacturing,[6] a steel supply company, asking it to bid on steel bolts and nuts and other hardware needed to rebuild several bridges in Mississippi County.[7] The salesman for the steel supply company, Sam, likes the opportunity to sell a lot of nuts and bolts. However, bolts manufactured by his company have a 3 percent defect rate, which makes them unsuitable for certain applications like construction projects that will be subjected to severe, sudden stresses, the kind of stresses an earthquake can cause.

If Sam wins the bid for bolts, he will earn a five-figure bonus. Additional bonuses could be earned if the contractor purchases more bolts in future years to repair more bridges. Should Sam tell the bridge construction company that if his bolts fail in an earthquake, the bridge

Table 5.1. Probability of chain of events.

Impact on Sam: Probability Estimate*			
Event	Low Probability	Medium Probability	High Probability
A defective bolt will be used	0.5	0.7	0.9
Defective bolt will be used in critical location	0.2	0.4	0.6
Earthquake occurs near the rebuilt bridge	0.7	0.8	0.9
Earthquake causes damage to rebuilt bridge	0.3	0.5	0.7
Earthquake causes catastrophic bridge failure	0.3	0.5	0.7
Failure occurs on a high-volume traffic bridge	0.2	0.3	0.4
Someone will die from injuries	0.5	0.7	0.9
Bridge failure is attributed to defective bolts	0.5	0.7	0.9
Catastrophe occurs during Sam's tenure	0.5	0.7	0.9
Company will blame the salesman	0.5	0.7	0.9
Company records show salesman to be at fault	0.15	0.2	0.25
Total Probability	0.001%	0.081%	1.562%

*Probability estimates can be changed to see the net result of different assumptions. There are other elements in the scenario that might be factored in but not listed here. The ones listed are hypothetical and used for illustration purposes only. Recall that the failure rate for bolts is estimated at just 3%. This low probability was not factored into the calculations above. The more events that are included in the probability estimate, the lower the total probability that all of them together will bring an unfavorable result for Sam.

could collapse and people could be hurt or even die as a result? If Sam tells the construction company about the defect rate of the bolts, he could very well lose the sale and his sales bonus. One question this chapter addresses is, If Sam is an egoist, what will he do? What is egoism, and how does it direct marketplace conduct? Table 5.1 illustrates the probability of the chain of events that might occur if the bolts from Sam's company are used in bridge rebuilding.

With Sam's ethical choice in your mind, it is time to explore the essence of what it means to be an egoist. To begin we will consider two distinctions. Then we will understand the difference between a psychological egoist and an ethical egoist (the main focus of the chapter). The chapter will conclude with a review of the pros and cons of egoism. Then we will evaluate egoism using the biblical themes introduced in chapters three and four.

truism: wanting to do something for someone else even if doing so brings you nothing in return or if it costs you.

The broad view of self-interest begins with the assertion that humans have several interests that they value and goals that they want to pursue. For example, one goal of most people is to sustain their own life. In order to achieve this they must be participants in the processes related to sustenance. Human interests can span a wide range of endeavors, including religious faith, family, art, hobbies, education, making money, and many other endeavors. Another example is that some people have an interest in science. They engage in activities that contribute to the advancement of science, or they simply

Narrow Self-Interest	Broad Self-Interest
• Selfishness	• The interests you have in life
• Your concern for others is limited to what brings benefits to you	• Potentially a wide range of interests
• Altruism is impossible	• Altruism possible and probable

Figure 5.2. The contrast between narrow and broad self-interest.

DEFINITIONS AND DISTINCTIONS

Egoism is an ethical theory in which the standard of right and wrong conduct is based on self-interest. A person who follows this theory is called an egoist.

The term "self-interest" has two descriptions or views.[8] One is a narrow view; the other is a broad view. The narrow view considers self-interest as essentially selfishness. It is this narrow definition that is of primary concern in this chapter, because egoism is based on the narrow view. In this view, everything that you do is to fulfill personal desires and wants. Your concern for the welfare of others is considered only as such concern helps you get what you want.[9]

The opposite of narrow self-interest is al-

learn more about science. Still other people have an interest in giving to charitable organizations. In this view self-interests are not inherently selfish. This broad view of self-interest includes all the interests that you have as a person.[10] Thus, in the broader view you can express self-interests through altruistic behavior.[11] Because of this, altruism is not the opposite of the broad view but merely one of the many possible expressions of human interest.

A problem with the broad view of self-interest is that while it is appealing, it begs the question regarding the existence of absolute moral standards of right and wrong. It deflects the conversation away from moral standards to something else.

Most people probably agree that narrow self-ishness based on personal feelings is not a valid standard of right and wrong conduct. Furthermore, narrow self-interest based only on what you want, by itself, takes no consideration for what you should do for others. Desire overshadows duty. Individual interests dominate community interests. This approach to decision making will be rejected by most people.[12] We will see several reasons for this near the end of the chapter.

In contrast, the broader definition of self-interest allows for you to consider the needs of others. Most people develop interests in relationship with others in their family and the larger community of which they are a part. In reality humans are not individuals in isolation from others, but rather whole persons with needs and wants in a community of persons.[13]

With these distinctions and definitions in mind we are now ready to explore the theory of egoism.

> Do nothing from selfishness or empty conceit. (Phil 2:3)

EGOISM: "LOOK OUT FOR YOURSELF ONLY"

Egoism is a philosophy of life that holds that you should consider your options and then pursue your own narrow self-interest regardless of how others are affected by your conduct.[14] Framed in the negative, if you do not pursue your own narrow self-interest when you can, it would be wrong.[15]

In egoism we find both duty and consequences intertwined.[16] If you are an egoist, there is but one duty: pursue self-interests regardless of how other persons feel about it. But consequences are not trivial. While you have the duty to watch out for your own interests, you can know whether or not you have achieved this only by seeing the consequences of particular actions on your own welfare. Indeed, egoism is concerned about consequences.[17]

In egoism we also see the presence of short term and long term. If you live consistently according to this philosophy, you will sometimes choose not to attempt to gain pleasure for yourself in the short run if delaying gratification means that a greater benefit for you is achieved in the long run. You may want to do something pleasurable in the short run. But the conduct that brings short-term benefit may have an insidious long-run negative effect on you. In this case, as a true egoist you should and will do what is good for narrow self-interest over the long haul even if it means foregoing some benefit now.

Some people incorrectly believe that egoists are frequently dishonest, lack kindness, are unhelpful or cannot promote other people's interests.[18] Such ways of relating to others would not advance the self-interests of the

---

ETHICAL EGOISM

A theory prescribing that self (and your organization) should be central to all decision making.

You should consider the consequences of action and then pursue self-interest and your organization's interest regardless of how others are affected. What should you do? You should always choose to act in your own narrow self-interest.

egoist. Egoism requires that you do your best to promote your own long-term interests, and at times, this might require you to advance the interests of others also.[19] If you are an egoist, you are concerned primarily about the consequences for yourself. If you see someone in need, you may choose to help such a person as long as in the helping you help yourself. Thus, it is permissible for an egoist to help other people so long as such help is given so that the egoist serves his own interests. It is not the helping of others that makes the action right; from the egoist's point of view, in helping others you have attempted to achieve a gain for yourself. This is what justifies any charitable action toward others.

Egoism also can be seen through the lens of the organization. In this perspective egoism means that you *should* consider your organization's options and then pursue the course of action that is in the interest of the organization regardless of how others are affected by your conduct.

When seen as a process, egoism leads to the steps shown in figure 5.3.

We all have a bias that tends to pull us toward narrow self-interests. Yet, we know that others will respond to us with punishment if we take our self-interests to an extreme. Even so, some people follow egoism whenever they can get away with it.

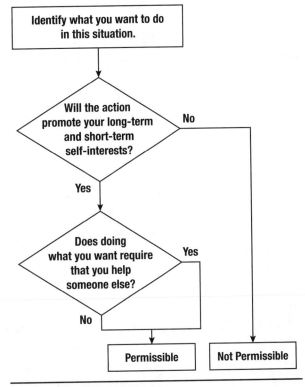

Figure 5.3. The egoism ethical process.

EVALUATION: PROS AND CONS

Appealing to egoism (based on a narrow definition of self-interest) as a standard for right and wrong conduct is an attempt to emphasize the individual. Egoism assumes that each person is autonomous in society.

Ethical egoism is the principle that you should pursue only your narrow (selfish) self-interests. It is wrong to think that egoism teaches that you should never assist others; egoism simply says that you have no moral duty to assist others.[20]

Self-interest can be seen from either a narrow viewpoint of selfishness or from a broader viewpoint of the interests of the self. What seems to make self-interest selfish is when you disregard the interests of others or neglect duties toward others.[21] If you decide to help someone only because such charity will bring you some benefit, you are acting selfishly.

It is time to consider some of the pros and cons of this approach. Pros (arguments in support) will be identified by the symbol (+); cons (arguments against) will be identified by the symbol (-).

(+) Egoism highlights the need to watch out for our own interests; however, many people believe that it goes too far in emphasizing this need.

(+) Egoism is concerned about consequences of action. This represents an important dimension of healthy living: watching out for your own interests, preventing people from taking advantage of you and preventing harm from coming to you. Such a perspective recognizes that other persons in society may not have your best interests in mind when pursuing their selfish self-interests.

(+) Each person is in the best position to understand personal wants because we have an imperfect understanding of what others want.[22] While this may be true, it might also be true that some persons are unable to understand what is best for themselves and may need others in the community to help them see what is best for them.

(+) Looking out for other persons' interests is intrusive. It presumes that one person can adequately understand the needs of another. This is likely a faulty assumption. Altruism degrades the recipient of charity because it communicates to others that the recipient is not competent to care for himself or herself.[23] Doing what is best for others is achieved by fulfilling your own interests in the long run. In answer to this we can say that if a charitable person forces altruism on another to provide care, this would be intrusive and degrading. But assuming that the recipient of charity is allowed a choice, we would be hard pressed to support the claim that altruism is intrusive.

A critique of egoism reveals several flaws and weaknesses.

(-) We are persons physically and mentally separate from each other, even if we are associated in a community. In answer to this, we say that this reveals a basic problem of being or existence. We are separate persons, but we are also persons interdependent *with* each other. Thus, egoism emphasizes the separation from one another but offers little regarding how we are to manage the mutual interdependence with one another. When interdependent beings attempt to interact with others by maintaining their separateness, they destroy the interdependence. Ultimately, it is only within community that we can truly express what it means to be a person; it is only with persons that we can experience community.

> Ultimately, it is only within community that we can truly express what it means to be a person; it is only with persons that we can truly experience community.

(-) Egoism based on a narrow self-interest is self-defeating. Some believe that the purpose of moral standards is that they provide the basic standards for "cooperative social existence and allow us to resolve conflicts by appeal to shared principles of justification."[24] How could egoism, if truly practiced consistently by everyone, help society achieve cooperative social existence? It seems, from a practical point of view, impossible for this to occur. If everyone acted in narrow self-interest, it seems that it would be impossible for anyone other than the very strongest to get their way. Egoism is promoted as the way to achieve happiness across the whole of society; however, if everyone were an egoist, widespread, narrow self-interest would prevail and give rise to conflicts in which egoists would battle with each other for supremacy. Egoists might agree on certain principles so that their existence is more efficient; however, the society would likely be highly unstable because self-interest would trump willingness to live consistently according to agreed-on social standards of conduct. Society would disintegrate into anarchy, chaos and constant danger. Such a social situation, it seems, would make it impossible for egoists to achieve their wants. Conflicts that arise out of a continual contest of wills are more likely to decrease happiness for everyone, rather than increase it. Egoists may respond by saying that even egoists show respect for human life and would not do just anything to get their own way. Egoists realize that they are a person just like other humans and that all persons must avoid actions that harm others so that their own self-interests can be promoted.

(-) Egoism is self-contradictory.[25] If we hold that everyone ought to pursue his own self-interest regardless of how others are affected, then to be consistent we must say that others should follow the same principle toward us. But this is not possible. If one person has a desire to act in such a way that it harms a person, the person toward whom harm is directed has a self-interest duty to attempt to prevent the harm from being done to her; she must not allow the other person to pursue his or her self-interest. Stopping someone from pursuing that person's self-interest is against the very principle of egoism, but not stopping someone from harming you also is against self-interest. It cannot be at the same time both wrong and right to stop a person from doing harm to yourself. Hence egoism is self-contradictory.

(-) Egoism offers nothing by way of explanation for how society is to resolve conflicts of interest that should be expected to arise if everyone truly pursued only his or her self-interest.[26] To resolve conflicts of interest, the participants must turn to a rule that is outside themselves, because their self-interests are in conflict with each other.

(-) Egoism attempts to categorize persons into two groups: yourself and everyone else; however, it offers no rational justification for why one person in a community of persons should be allowed special consideration while all other persons are not allowed the same consideration.[27] Each person, narrowly self-interested, attempts to look on himself or herself as superior to the other members of the community.[28] Such is the ultimate form of "positive illusion."[29] Like other arguments that undermine the validity of egoism, this one turns to the larger community of persons. Such perspective of the larger community indicates that egoism is an arbitrary point of view. In comparison with other persons in the community, what makes the egoist so special? The same issue can be raised when considering one generation and another. "No generation has the right to endanger future people any more than it has the right to endanger present people."[30]

(-) The discussion of egoism raises for consideration the assumption that moral standards require objective, impartial application to all persons impartially. If you make yourself and your wants the standard of right and wrong, for either the long term or the short term, this prevents you from making an objective, impartial application of moral standards across the community.

(-) In terms of the spectrum of moral maturity, egoism fails to move us along the journey toward moral maturity. Its scope is narrow. It exclusively focuses on the individual and sees the community as merely a means to an end of achieving personal happiness.

(-) Egoism says that serving your own

Table 5.2: Applying the ethical process.

Keeping Your Heart: An Intrapersonal Process	Walking in the Community: An Interpersonal Process

• You are Sam. What does your heart say is the right thing to do?
• Which biblical themes explored in this book inform your heart on this situation?
• Which biblical theme, if any, do you feel yourself resisting? Why do you feel resistance?
• How strong are your desires for personal benefit from this situation?
• What other influences in your heart are prominent as you think about this situation?
  • Fundamental beliefs
  • Cognitive reasoning
  • Judgments and evaluations
  • Decisions
  • Virtues
  • Will
  • Memory of personal experiences with other people
  • Perceptions of others in the community
  • Personal biases
  • Awareness of interpersonal relationships
  • Commitments to God and to others
  • Intuitions
  • Conscience
  • Human spirit
  • Emotions
	• You are Sam. With whom might you have a conversation about this situation? Who else might have a helpful perspective?
	• Which of the biblical themes in this chapter will most likely come up in the conversation either directly or indirectly? Why?
	• If you have a conversation with someone regarding this situation, which of the fundamental tensions presented earlier in the book might come into the conversation?
	• What right-versus-right dilemmas, if any, can be identified here? Have a conversation with someone about this now. What is the outcome of the conversation?
	• How will you resolve the right-versus-right dilemma(s)?
	• How might a conversation about this situation with someone else serve as a protection to you? What type of protection are you thinking of?
	• You are in a conversation with an egoist regarding Sam's choice. How could you successfully counteract the egoist's position?

needs is the only reason you should have for taking an action even if such action results in good for someone else. It denies the validity of all other reasons. However, the presence of the community suggests the possibility of at least one other valid reason for conduct, namely, an interest in serving the needs of the community.

(-) Egoism is in open disagreement with the biblical story and its themes. A person cannot be a Christian and an egoist at the same time because these two views are fundamentally incompatible.[31]

DOWN TO THE NITTY-GRITTY

Think about the opening story at the beginning of this chapter. You are Sam. What should you do regarding the sale of steel bolts? It's time to get down to the nitty-gritty (see table 5.2)!

THROUGH THE LENS OF BIBLICAL THEMES

This part of the chapter will use the biblical story themes as a lens through which to evaluate the ethical approach featured in the chapter. Because the themes are interrelated and interdependent, we should expect to see some overlap in the thinking regarding the ethical approach. Some themes will contribute the same thinking as will other themes. The power of these themes comes from their guidance when a community of people talks about complicated ethical dilemmas faced in business practice (see fig. 5.4).

When we put up the twelve biblical story themes in front of egoism, what do we see? At first glance, egoism runs counter to what the Bible teaches. If everyone does what is right in his or her own eyes, life in the covenant community will be chaotic and destructive.[32] Bible narratives describe people who were pursuing self-interest at the expense of morality.[33] The Bible also describes others who pursued self-interest in a narrow, selfish manner.[34] Narrow self-interests that stop a person from acting charitably toward others are contrary to biblical ideals. "In the biblical framework, authentic selfhood is not found in seeking one's own interests but in being other-oriented, yet without negating one's own self."[35] This principle can be seen in the various story themes.

Cosmic conflict. In the conflict between God and his adversary, Satan, it is the egoism of Lucifer that, unchecked but fueled by pride, takes him into open rebellion against God. The serpent's temptation of Eve was an appeal to egoism.[36] Satan's temptation of Christ appealed to his self-interests.[37] Prophets lamented that leaders were hurting the people because they turned to their own interests rather than serving the needs of the people.[38] Paul the apostle reported that there were not more people to share in his concerns for the needs of the church because "they all seek after their own interests, not those of Christ Jesus" (Phil 2:21). Self-interest implies the presence of freedom of choice which can be used for either selfish ends or for altruistic ends.

Creation. Interests of the self are part of the image of God in the creation of humans. Humans were placed in dependent and interdependent relationships in community.[39] Each human is not autonomous with respect to others. Humans were given the task of being co-workers with God and with each other.[40] Some tasks can be done alone, but the results of even these tasks have an impact on the larger community. Other tasks should not be done alone.[41] Both self-love and love of neighbor are appropriate obligations that derive from the equality and solidarity of persons as equals before God. Neither duty is prior to the other. These duties intersect with each other, and they sometimes collide.[42] Egoism is based on an assumption of the autonomy of a person. The biblical perspective is that we are not autonomous individuals but rather persons integral to community. Humans are dependent on God, on each other and on the good earth. Life in community does not require giving up all personal identity, the power to choose or all freedom to act.

Holiness. Consecration to God, set apart for service to him in the marketplace, implies that there is more to be considered than just our own narrow self-interests. Even with a broad view of self-interest (the interests of the self), these interests, too, are consecrated in service to God. This requires the assumption that there is more to ethical decision making than self-interests.

Covenant relationships. In a covenant-relationship community each person is to look out for the interests of others as well as his or her own interests. "Honor your father and your mother, that your days may be prolonged in the land which the Lord your God gives you" (Ex 20:12).[43] Yet Scripture also holds firmly to the idea that self-interest is always seen in the larger context of community. "Not one of us lives for himself" (Rom 14:7). Egoism overemphasizes individualism, and while this promotes a kind of "natural liberty" in the end it undermines faithfulness to the federation of persons in cov-

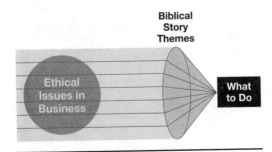

Biblical Story Themes

Ethical Issues in Business → **What to Do**

Figure 5.4. Evaluating an ethical approach.

enant community.[44] Covenant relationships are both individual and communal. As an illustration of ideal covenant relationships, the Ten Commandments reflect how destructive it can be if persons live according to narrow self-interests. The eighth commandment implies a high view of self-interest.[45] The same can be said regarding the third, fourth, fifth, sixth, seventh and ninth commandments.

On the one hand, in covenant relationships there is no room for narrow selfishness. "For this is the message which you have heard from the beginning, that we should love one another" (1 Jn 3:11).[46] We should not be a burden to others.[47] On the other hand, covenant relationships do not work if each party is not watching out for his or her own interests. Scripture portrays God as having self-interest.[48] But God also has ultimate other-interests, interests that are focused on humans and all creation.[49] "He loves righteousness and justice; the earth is full of the lovingkindness of the LORD" (Ps 33:5). The Scriptures support being responsible for yourself and taking care of legitimate personal needs. This is not the same as egoism. If you do not take responsibility for yourself, how will you be responsible for the needs of others?

Scripture recognizes that when a person is charitable toward others, the altruistic person also gains. "The merciful man does himself good, but the cruel man does himself harm" (Prov 11:17).[50] Healthy or proper self-interest is not bad or sinful. It has a valid role in life.[51] We should be aware of the effect of our actions on others and on ourselves. But self-interest should not be the exclusive goal or the single motive for all conduct.

Closely related to self-interest is the term "self-love." As Christians seek to understand the relationship between self and others in the biblical story, four Christian views of self-love have emerged (see table 5.3).[52]

If in the term "self-love" we mean placing the interests of self above the interests of others, then the narrow view of self-love in table 5.3 is clearly opposed to the Scripture record. In contrast, if by the term "self-love" we mean abiding loyalty to one's self, then this is aligned with the Scripture themes of wisdom (prudence) and covenant relationships.

Scripture themes encourage us to see ourselves within a larger context of the community. Beyond this, the biblical context for viewing humans is in the frame of reference of God.[53] Accordingly, story themes encourage a broad view of self-love. When Jesus summarized the point of God's law he said, "YOU SHALL LOVE YOUR NEIGHBOR AS YOURSELF" (Mt 22:39).[54]

Table 5.3. Four Christian views of self-love.

Narrow View	Broad Views		
Self-Love Is Morally Wrong and Sinful	Self-Love Is Morally Neutral	Self-Love Is Integral to Covenant Relationships	Self-Love Is Morally Good, a Religious Obligation
Self-love came after creation, when humans sinned. Self-love = selfishness. It is the basic human problem of sin that can be overcome only by self-sacrificial agape love.	Self-love is a part of how God created humans. Self-love is a necessary and fitting part of human life. Without self-love we are unhealthy. By nature self-love is neither good nor bad.	Self-love is a positive obligation derived from our duties of loving our neighbor. You cannot love your neighbor unless you have positive regard for yourself. Self-love is integral to interdependent relationships.	Self-love is not only an obligation in covenant relations. It also is valid in its own right as a moral-religious obligation to God and to each other. Humans should also love that which God loves.

Shalom. Shalom is not merely an individual experience.[55] The pursuit of community shalom requires each person to move past his or her own narrow self-interests. Pursuit of narrow self-interest is destructive of shalom not only for ourselves but also for the whole community and for succeeding generations.

Sabbath. One of the root principles in sabbath is contentment. Sabbath is a tangible action that structures our contentment. We say by keeping sabbath that life is not all about us. While during the week we work to provide for ourselves and our families, and indirectly to the good of the whole community, on sabbath we lay aside the pursuit of economic elements of our narrow self-interests.

Justice. Justice is the actions that a person takes to honor the rights of others. God does not show favoritism; humans are to follow this model even when we try to place ourselves in a favored position in the community.[56] We are to encourage justice to flow throughout the whole community, affecting high and low, secure and vulnerable, and anyone who is present in the community. Accordingly, justice by nature requires us to think outside our own narrow self-interests toward the interests of others. It implies that we are aware of our own needs.

Righteousness. Those who are opposed to principles of covenant relationships are the persons who make narrow self-interests the main focus of their life. The biblical theme of righteousness (and its opposite, wickedness) shows how destructive selfishness is and how life-giving living for others is.

Truth. Truth means that there is a close correspondence between our actions and what others expect from us. But the larger context of expectations comprehends righteousness, justice and loving kindness. Thus,

narrow self-interest undermines truth in the covenant community.

Wisdom. In the biblical story, narrow self-interest is foolish. From a practical point of view it is stupid. Selfishness is reckless in community. It reveals that the person is blind to the needs of others in the community. It shows a lack of understanding about the nature of covenant relationships.

Loving kindness. Abiding loyalty, faithfulness and kindness to others in the community require the person to move past narrow self-interests. Love "does not seek its own, is not provoked, does not take into account a wrong suffered" (1 Cor 13:5).[57]

Redemption. Humans can and do good things, but humans are also selfish. On our own we are unable to produce shalom in community. We act in untrustworthy ways. We are narrowly self-interested when we should broaden our interests to include others and their concerns. In biblical terms narrowly focused self-interest is an issue of the heart. It is only the grace of God, received by faith in Jesus Christ, whereby you can become transformed by the renewing of your heart.[58] As this renewal process takes place you begin to desire to support the covenant relationships around you. You begin to mature, not walking according to your own selfish interests but according to the interests of also the community.[59] "He died for all, so that they who live might no longer live for themselves, but for Him who died and rose again on their behalf" (2 Cor 5:15). Envisioned here is something different from what psychological egoism espouses.

As a model for human behavior in the marketplace, redemption demonstrates God's character. In the context of the cosmic conflict it is in God's self-interest to redeem. His adversary, Satan, claims that God is unjust, arbitrary and narrowly self-interested. Yet redemption shows that God is other-interested. Scriptural themes suggest that this is the model to follow in the marketplace.

CHAPTER REVIEW QUESTIONS

1. What is the difference between a narrow view of self-interest and the broad view of self-interest?

2. What does it mean to be an egoist?

3. What are the elements of egoism that seem commendable? What are the major criticisms of egoism as a decision-making approach?

4. What can we conclude from the biblical story themes regarding egoism as a decision-making approach in business?

DISCUSSION QUESTIONS

1. In what way, if at all, can self-interest be altruistic?

2. Refer to the introductory scenario regarding Sam the steel bolt salesman. What difference does the total probability make in terms of dealing with the ethical dilemma? Is it natural to take into consideration these and other relevant probabilities? Should Sam take into consideration these probabilities?

3. From the opening scenario, what are Sam's options regarding the issue of disclosing defect-rate information? Using table 5.4, for each option describe how the ethical egoist will view the option in terms of meeting his personal goals. Also, evaluate each option in terms of the biblical story themes.

4. If a person has a healthy regard for self, how could he or she not have some altruistic tendencies also? Likewise, if a person has a healthy regard for the interests of others, how can he or she not experience self-interest also?

5. You are in a conversation with a person about the rightness or wrongness of a certain action. During the conversation you sense that the other person might be an egoist. What approach would you take to challenge egoism?

ETHICAL VIGNETTES TO DISCUSS

For each of the vignettes described below apply the biblical story themes to discern what is right and wrong.

1. Some managers look around them and want to correct what they believe are marketplace injustices.[60] For example, Mia, a manager in a department store, employs workers at minimum wage. One of these low-wage employees cannot afford a new prom dress for her daughter. Mia believes that the low wages she is required to pay are unjust, but she has no authority to raise

Table 5.4. Options in an egoist's decision making.

Option	Personal Goal (Sam's reason for acting in self-interest)	Biblical Theme Perspective on the Option
1. Reveal information about the defect rate.		
2. Hide information about the defect rate.		
3.		
4.		

Table 5.5. Evaluating ethical options.

Option	Mia's and Martin's Personal Goals (reasons for acting in narrow self-interest)	Biblical Theme Perspective on the Option
1. Help employees by giving them company inventory or by padding their wages.		
2.		
3.		

the wages. To counteract the perceived injustice Mia made a few mistakes when she ordered prom dresses: too many were ordered. Some, but not all, were returned. She says, "It got kind of confusing." The employee did not pay for a new dress, but the daughter of the employee looked great in her new dress at the prom. Martin, a manager of a grocery store, adjusts time cards of selected low-wage workers to give them a few more hours of work per pay period. Sometimes he gives them food to take home that he says has been damaged.

- What does the term "subvert" mean?

- Did Mia and Martin truly help their employees in the long run by what they did?

- Will the economic subversion described in this scenario make things better or worse?

- Under what conditions is economic subversion morally justified?

- If Mia and Martin are egoists, what personal goal(s) might they be trying to achieve by their actions? Do biblical themes support their actions? Think of at least two other options that Mia and Martin have when they consider whether or not to help their employees in the way they did. Using table 5.5, for each option describe how the ethical

egoist will view the option in terms of meeting his or her self-interest. Also, evaluate each option in terms of the biblical story themes. To what degree do biblical themes support each option?

- If you disagree with egoism, what would you say to Mia and Martin to persuade them to consider your point of view?

- What is altruism? Under what conditions might altruism be morally wrong?

2. The operations manager of a construction company employs five supervisors ("foremen") to be in charge of construction crews.[61] One of the supervisors is female. She is as qualified as any male supervisor in the company. The problem is that all of her subordinates are male and some of them resent taking orders from a woman. The result is that productivity is lower on this crew compared with other crews. Should the operations manager fire the female supervisor and replace her with a male? Should the operations manager fire the crew members? Should the operations manager have a talk with the crew members and warn them that they will be subject to discipline if their productivity does not get up to par? On what basis do you make your recommendation? If the operations manager is an egoist, how might he act? How would you apply the Golden Rule to this situation?

6

Relativism

When in Rome, do as the Romans do.

SCRIPTURE PASSAGE

So you shall observe to do just as the Lord your God has commanded you; you shall not turn aside to the right or to the left. (Deut 5:32)

CHAPTER OVERVIEW

In this chapter we explore another popular approach to ethical decision making found in the marketplace. In particular, we will

- explore the basic idea of cultural relativism

- distinguish between the descriptive relativism and cultural relativism

- evaluate the pros and cons of relativism as an approach to business ethics

- evaluate relativism through the lens of biblical story themes

MAIN TOPICS

Challenges to Traditional Ideas
Definitions and Distinctions
Four Levels of Relativism
Evaluation: Pros and Cons
Down to the Nitty-Gritty
Through the Lens of Biblical Themes

KEY TERMS

absolutism, cultural relativism, descriptive relativism, ethnocentrism, objective morality, social role, subjective morality

OPENING SCENARIO

In September 2013, a United Nations work group known as Better Factories Cambodia announced that it had plans to publicize the degree to which certain Cambodian garment and shoe manufacturers comply with minimum standards of safety.[1] The Better Factories group inspects factories looking for what it believes are violations of child labor laws and unsafe working conditions. The group plans on collecting and reporting to the public information about fire safety, wages and workers' rights violations. The group hopes that shining the spotlight on certain factories that are out of compliance will encourage all factories to make changes in their employment policies. It is estimated that only about 3 percent of the hundreds of garment and shoe factories in Cambodia are two standard deviations below the mean on compliance issues.

Factory owners and the Cambodian government claim in response that publicity will result in factories being shut down and moved to other countries where oversight is not as aggressive. Walmart released a statement in support of the Better Factories plan saying that public monitoring of safety conditions is important for improving working conditions for factory workers.

Is it right or wrong that Better Factories Cambodia imposes its values regarding worker safety on factories in a particular nation without consent of that government or without the consent of the industry group represented by the factories?

In this chapter we move a little farther away from egoism by broadening our perspective to include the point of view of others in our social group or within the larger cultural group.

CHALLENGES TO TRADITIONAL IDEAS

Traditional characteristics of moral standards include the following: (1) Judgment about what is right and wrong must be universally applicable to all persons. (2) Standards of right and wrong override all other considerations. (3) Knowledge about right and wrong comes with social responsibilities. (4) The primary focus is on behavior.

When we come to relativism, we find some of these traditional characteristics being challenged. Relativism is the belief that judgment about what is right and wrong cannot be universally applicable. The rightness or wrongness of an action is defined by other considerations. Such considerations define what is right and wrong. Relativism is less concerned about behavior and more concerned about culturally shaped opinions and feelings of persons in a given culture.

How this view developed is a result of scientific anthropology. Cultural anthropologists in the nineteenth and early twentieth centuries studied a variety of cultural groups around the world. Some of them noticed the differences between cultural groups regarding what is considered right and wrong conduct.

Anthropologists like Ruth Benedict and others concluded that just as societies have different styles of food and clothing, so also they have different standards of right and wrong.[2] These scientists found a plurality of moral standards around the world. They concluded from this that objective, absolute standards of conduct do not exist. Instead, standards of right and wrong are shaped by culture. Moral conduct is based solely on an individual's self-interest and values and feelings shared in his or her society at a particular time.

Anthropologists raised our awareness of the difference between what we can see in another culture and what we cannot see. We can see art work, food, clothing, religious ceremonies, music, drama, leisure activities and artifacts such as tools. What we cannot see are the elements of culture where the standards of right and wrong reside deeply in the minds and hearts of people in that culture. It is at this deep level where the meaning of what is visible resides.

Scientists also noticed that when people from one culture visit another culture, they tend to judge the rightness or wrongness of what they find. This bias, known as ethnocentrism, is the belief in the inherent superiority of one's own culture. Anthropologists set about to counteract this bias because they believed this bias gets in the way of scientific endeavor. The way to be on guard against this intellectually arrogant point of view is to embrace relativism. "When it comes to ethnocentrism, relativists are absolutists," but not in a *moral* sense.[3] In other words, these scientists believe that ethnocentrism is the wrong approach to doing good science.

In spite of what the anthropologists promoted for the cause of good science and toleration, some now believe that relativism is the best guide for conduct. Relativists are not merely concerned about enthnocentric biases; they promote the belief that moral standards from one cultural perspective are simply statements of opinion, feeling or emotion. Because moral standards are culturally determined, judging another culture is arrogant because there is no way of knowing for sure which moral standard is correct. Criticisms of another culture's standards are based not on truth (whether philosophical or religious) but on individual, societal or cultural preference. Relativists also find support from history which, they say, is filled with examples of individuals who acted in the name of infallible truth. Later, these actions were judged by society to be wrong. Two societies might disagree about what is morally permissible, and both can be right. For example, one society believes that slavery is permissible while another society believes that slavery should be forbidden. In the United Kingdom, before a parliamentary law was passed, it was permissible to sell your wife. After the law was passed, it was no longer permissible to do this. This illustrates how formal changes can take place in society regarding what is right and wrong.

Finally, relativists believe that because objective authority for moral standards has never been scientifically proven, it does not exist.

> The way of a fool is right in his own eyes. (Prov 12:15)

DEFINITIONS AND DISTINCTIONS

The attempt to describe the standards of right and wrong in a given culture (the work of cul-tural anthropologists) is called descriptive relativism. Descriptive relativism is "not a statement *of* morality, but a statement *about* morality [in a given cultural context]."[4] De-scriptive relativism is what anthropologist sci-entists do as they observe various cultures. They observe and describe what they find. In business, descriptive relativism is helpful. By knowing cultural standards of people in dif-ferent cultural groups the business profes-sional can be wise in business dealings.

In contrast, cultural relativism is a nor-mative statement *of* morality. It is the belief that objective, universal moral principles do not exist in an absolute sense. It claims that when any two cultures or people hold different views on what is moral, both can be right. In this view, standards of right and wrong are developed and shaped solely by culture. Thus, when you say that your neighbor cheated someone when he sold his used lawn mower, all you really can say is that the person who sold the lawn mower violated a precept of his own culture.

> ## THE CLAIM OF RELATIVISM
> When any two cultures or people hold different views on what is moral, both can be right.

Relativists believe that we acquire standards of right and wrong not by means of a truth-finding process but by the process of cultural conditioning. For the relativist, we cannot speak of right and wrong in any other terms except that persons who do right are behaving consistently with their culture and those who do wrong are going against the grain of their culture.[5] If we find common standards of conduct across cul-tures, this is merely the result of humans having a shared capacity for moral standards. Those who hold to this view believe that there are no absolute moral standards that cross all cultures, locations, situations and times.

You may hear people refer to relativism in various ways: "Everything is relative." "Moral standards are rules of thumb but can change if you are in a new situation." "People have differences of opinion." "When in Rome, do as the Romans do." What the Romans do is presumed to be moral for Romans. If a visitor to Rome wishes not to engage in Roman conduct because he considers it to be immoral, it is arrogant—if not imperialistic—for the visitor to criticize Roman culture as being morally inferior to his own culture.

The opposite of cultural relativism is absolutism. This is the belief that objective standards of right and wrong exist and as such are independent of culture. Absolutists distinguish between what people believe to be moral standards and absolutes. What people believe to be right is called subjective morality. But what we think is right may be wrong. Absolute standards of right and wrong are based on the belief that an objective standard of right and wrong exists outside the person or cultural group. Well-meaning persons will disagree regarding what should be allowed as the objective standard. Some will turn to humanism or other philosophy as the source. Others turn to religious beliefs.

Relativism depends on our ability to identify the social setting or group which shares certain

Relativism	Absolutism
There are no objective standards; all standards are subjective and culturally determined.	Objective standards exist and are not culturally determined.

Figure 6.1. A comparison of relativism and absolutism.

values of right and wrong.[6] At the level of the person, personal relativism says that it is up to the person to decide what is right or wrong and whatever the person decides is right for him or her.[7] Do not judge the person for what he decides.[8] It would seem on the surface that personal relativism is not different from egoism.

Another level of relativism depends on defining the social role that a person is in. Social role is the collection of expectations that others have regarding a person in the role that the person plays for others. Social role is often determined by the profession or professional group. If chief financial officers are expected to define right and wrong in a particular way regarding financial statements, then whatever these managers decide is right for them. Someone outside the profession should not presume to judge those inside the profession because they are simply doing their jobs.[9] For another example, a manager's role is to carry out the legal and financial responsibilities to the shareholders. Whatever promotes shareholder value takes precedence over other concerns.[10] In the social role a person can easily appeal to the job: "I was only doing my job!"

FOUR LEVELS OF RELATIVISM

- Personal relativism
- Social role relativism
- Company or industry relativism
- Cultural group relativism

Another social group that is appealed to for moral standards is the company or industry in which one works.[11] Each company and industry develops a set of standard or accepted practices. If in the industry it is accepted practice to use the fact that customers lack knowledge about costs and value, managers are expected to follow this even though the customers perceive it to be unfair. For example, managers are expected to follow these practices. A manager in such a situation will be concerned about how others in the social group would act.[12] It becomes easy to define right and wrong if it is part of a person's job or appears to be necessary to get the job done efficiently.

On a larger scale it is the cultural group or larger culture in the country whose citizens share certain values that are written into civil laws and regulations. Relativism holds that outside a particular culture there are no objective standards which are valid for judging the culture. For example, relativism says that if you want to do business in a particular country that treats certain ethnic or social groups in ways that are different from how your culture treats these groups, your job is to understand the morality of the country so that you can be smart. But do not presume to judge how business is conducted in the other culture.[13]

Perceptions of ethical issues do vary to some degree by country and industry.[14] Managers in the United States in practice are more likely to be concerned about employees' use of company information and personnel issues compared with European managers. Wholesaling and retailing companies show greater concern for employee conduct. Agriculture and manufacturing businesses tend to have greater concerns regarding the role of government and relations with foreign governments. As one might expect, insider trading is

an important issue in finance companies. However, the fact that there are differences in approaches and differences in concerns does not mean that there should be fundamental country differences regarding right and wrong. When seen as a process, relativism uses the steps shown in figure 6.2.

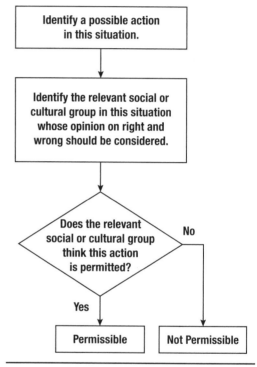

Figure 6.2. The relativism ethical process.

From this flow chart and from thinking about the foundation ideas of relativism, it should become clear to the reader that relativism is not the same as being charitable or tolerable toward other people who disagree with us. To be tolerant toward someone does not mean that we accept their approach to ethical decision making.

EVALUATION: PROS AND CONS

A question in cultural relativism is not whether or not different moral standards exist. They do. Another question is whether there is any commonality that overrides the differences—any universal truths, any common principles—that unifies us all. Many experts and many people who have traveled extensively believe there are common principles.

Ethics scholar LaRue Hosmer believes that there is at least one moral principle that exists across all groups, cultures and times—the irreducible minimum common denominator that binds all humans everywhere: members of the group have responsibility for the well-being of other group members. Because of the nature of being human, cooperation is necessary for survival. Thus, even in this humanistic perspective, some basic standards of behavior are required to ensure such cooperation.[15]

This chapter introduces the idea of relativism as a moral standard of right and wrong. It is time to consider some of the pros and cons of this approach. Pros (arguments in support or strengths) will be identified below by the symbol (+) while cons (arguments against or statements of weakness) will be identified by the symbol (-).

(+) Ethnocentrism bias is not good. Scientists who observed differences in moral standards have raised our awareness to the problem of ethnocentrism.

(+) Relativism raises our awareness of the importance of toleration.[16] However, toleration is not mutually exclusive of discerning the behavior of others. Toleration requires community conversation so that shared understanding emerges even if shared values are not always agreed on. Furthermore, relativism offers no basis from which to criticize intolerance.

(+) Relativism respects diversity. Relativism highlights an important dimension of human life: diversity. The world is a community of value diversity. However, if we allow toleration to the extreme, this will tend to excuse any action regardless of how harmful it might be.

(+) Relativism emphasizes commonness. The diversity of the human community does not overshadow our commonness. It is our awareness of how we are the same as humans, how we share the same space, the same resources for a flourishing life that ultimately defeats relativism as a serious contender for our worldview. Humans live in community; we communicate with each other. These elements show that humans have a common basis for exploring common principles of right and wrong conduct.[17]

If we meet someone who does not agree with us regarding standards of right and wrong, we should be cautious not to label the whole culture. Every society has persons who choose to behave inconsistently with the shared values of the culture.

A critique of cultural relativism as a way to decide right and wrong reveals several flaws and weaknesses.

(-) Relativism argues from a position of weakness. Moral relativism can be used to justify almost any action in a social setting. Because of this, appealing to relativism makes an argument weaker rather than stronger.

(-) Relativism is silent regarding injustice. Relativism focuses primarily on the interests of the person in relation to norms of the social reference group. But it is silent when discerning whether or not justice or injustice has occurred. All one can say is whether or not the person acted consistently with the norms of the social reference group.

(-) Social role relativism assumes that we know what the role requires and that this role depends on a valid standard of conduct outside the role.[18] Such a position is not a relativist position because a standard of right and wrong must exist. If a manager states that his role requires him to take a certain action but that he would not do such an action if it were not for the role he is in, then the manager is saying that the social role is not a valid standard of conduct at least with respect to the particular action. Either moral relativism based on a social role is correct and we act on it, or we believe it is not correct. But if it is not correct, then the basis for this approach itself is not valid; that is, the social role itself may be flawed. But if the role is flawed, then its basis as a moral standard also is flawed.

(-) Relativism cannot resolve social role conflicts.[19] Each person plays more than one role at a time. Which role should be the moral guide when there is a conflict in roles? Relativism offers nothing to resolve social role conflicts of interest. The person is more than a mechanical collection of social roles. Social role, as the basis for a standard of conduct, requires us to think of the human person as a collection of fragmented pieces rather than as a whole person in community.

(-) Under relativism socially accepted practices are immune from careful evaluation.[20] Cultural relativism requires that when any action is classified as an accepted practice, it is immediately immune from being evaluated or judged. This tends to produce a status quo existence. If new social norms can never be established (because new norms would go against established norms), the whole idea of social leadership becomes impossible.

(-) Relativism fosters an uncritical acceptance of a perception of what other people think. Appealing to cultural relativism is the easy way out of complicated situations. It shortens and simplifies the ethical process by attempting to bring an end to the discussion.

(-) When two different cultures interact for trade, some middle ground of standard must be established for business to be accomplished. There needs to be a moral standard line drawn somewhere; otherwise it will be somewhere between difficult and impossible to transact business on a routine basis. Moral relativism offers nothing in answer to the question, *Where should the moral line be drawn?*

(-) Relativism allows for cultural interpretation only. Relativism implies that personal views of right and wrong cannot be rationally defended but rather only culturally interpreted. However, it is common that during disputes, rational arguments are employed in an attempt to convince someone of what is right or wrong. Humans do attempt to resolve moral differences through cross-cultural dialogue.

(-) Relativism confuses tolerance and plurality. Relativists confuse an interest in tolerance for diversity with moral absolutes. Understanding norms in their cultural contexts can deepen social bonds and promote tolerance. This is not the same as using ethical relativism to make moral decisions. Pluralism exists. There are different points of view; however, in relativism all you have is alternatives to choose from or various opinions. Pluralism means that various points of view contend to be the best during the conversations that take place. From community conversations, at least in the business and political arenas, come a shared consensus for the practical way to live together. This is pragmatic, but it does not, by itself, define what is right or wrong. It is only that there are commonly shared values (even if these are few in number), so that we can get a pragmatic solution. The point is that basic values must exist in order to find consensus. This, it would seem, demonstrates the need for fundamental values common to all who want to live together. Relativism is not the same as toleration. Toleration of others is important, regardless of where they come from or their cultural group. By exercising toleration we promote human freedom to choose. But, this does not require us to agree with their choices. Permitting someone to have a difference of opinion does not mean that you agree with or accept their opinion. In relativism, there is no more reason to be tolerant than to be intolerant. Under relativism neither is morally right or wrong. Furthermore, relativism offers no basis for criticizing intolerance.

(-) Relativism is in open contradiction with the biblical perspective as well as most other ethical models.

(-) Relativism is subject to logical fallacies. Cultural relativism depends on several logical fallacies:

- The mere fact that two groups disagree regarding a certain action does not prove that there is no objective truth in the matter.[21] Relativism does not logically follow from observations of diversity. The fact that

people do not agree on what is the moral standard does not mean that such a standard is objectively absent.

- Because an absolute truth is difficult to find does not prove that it does not exist.

- Simply because most people think a statement is true does not make that statement true. Simply because most people think something is right does not make it right.

- Is relativism true, or only relatively true? If it is absolutely, universally true, then not all truth about ethics is relative.

- True moral relativists attempt to make an absolute, universal claim that everyone should follow the moral standards of his or her culture. But if this is absolute, then moral relativism as a universal standard

Table 6.1. Applying the ethical process.

Keeping Your Heart: An Intrapersonal Process	Walking in the Community: An Interpersonal Process

• You are a general manager in charge of one of the Cambodian factories. What does your heart say is the right thing to do?
• Which biblical themes explored in this book inform your heart on this situation?
• Which biblical theme, if any, do you feel yourself resisting? Why do you feel resistance?
• Do you want to see two sets of moral standards apply in this situation?
• What other influences in your heart are prominent as you think about this situation?
  • Fundamental beliefs
  • Cognitive reasoning
  • Judgments and evaluations
  • Decisions
  • Virtues
  • Will
  • Memory of personal experiences with other people
  • Perceptions of others in the community
  • Personal biases
  • Awareness of interpersonal relationships
  • Commitments to God and to others
  • Intuitions
  • Conscience
  • Human spirit
  • Emotions
	• You are a general manager in charge of one of the Cambodian factories. With whom might you have a conversation about this situation? Who else might have a helpful perspective?
	• Which of the biblical themes in this chapter will most likely come up in the conversation either directly or indirectly? Why? Which one(s) will be the most influential in the conversation?
	• If you have a conversation with someone regarding this situation, which of the fundamental tensions presented earlier in the book might come into the conversation?
	• What right-versus-right dilemmas, if any, can be identified here? Have a conversation with someone about this now. What is the outcome of the conversation?
	• What benefit and what cost might be incurred by having a conversation with others about the issues?
	• You are in a conversation with a relativist regarding this situation. How could you successfully counteract the relativist's position?

must be false. Also, such a claim ignores the possibility that standards of right and wrong in a particular culture may be contradictory or inconsistent.

DOWN TO THE NITTY-GRITTY

Think about the opening story at the beginning of this chapter. You are a general manager in charge of one of the Cambodian factories. Is it right or wrong that the United Nations group Better Factories Cambodia impose its values regarding worker safety on factories in a particular nation without consent of that government or without the consent of the industry group represented by the factories? It's time to get down to the nitty-gritty (see table 6.1)!

THROUGH THE LENS OF BIBLICAL THEMES

This part of the chapter will use the biblical story themes as a lens through which to evaluate the ethical approach featured in the chapter. Because the themes are interrelated and interdependent, we should expect to see some overlap in the thinking regarding the ethical approach. Some themes will contribute the same thinking as will other themes. The power of these themes comes from their guidance when a community of people talks about complicated ethical dilemmas faced in business practice.

The biblical story recognized that the faith community would have constant interaction with peoples who did not share their standards. The standards of conduct in the faith community were believed to come from God himself through Moses. The story recognizes that people are sometimes born into a culture that is against the principles of covenant relationships. This can offer no excuse for following culturally shaped practices.

Cosmic conflict. The Scripture story begins with the assumption that it is God who established absolute ethical standards. God's way of managing the economy of the universe is to foster freedom within the boundaries of these standards. He fosters relationships with all persons regardless of social status. In contrast, relativism confronts God in three ways. First, it assumes that humans create their own valid standards. Second, because of the differences among social groups, there cannot be any absolute standards. Third, relativism gives preference for persons of a particular social status. It is the person's social group which becomes the arbiter of ethical standards. This, in effect, gives preference to that social group. Because of this, relativism is another form of egoism at the social group level.

Creation. Regardless of what people from other cultures do or how they believe, the creation story teaches us that we all share a common bond: We are all children of God made in his image.[22] All humans have been given royally delegated responsibilities. Humans are not the originators of objective standards of right and wrong. But we do attempt to change the standards.

Holiness. Deep consecration to God is completely contradictory to the principles of cultural relativism. A deeply consecrated person will be tolerant of others and their views; however, the deep commitment that comes with consecration to God is the starting point for being faithful to the guiding principles found in covenant relationships.

Covenant. Covenant relationship principles should be commonly shared; however, it is not the commonness of sharing that makes the principles valid. Validity of standards stems from the absolute source, God. The biblical story recognizes that faithful people will interact with peoples who have different standards of conduct. The biblical story refers to these as strangers and aliens. What does the Bible require of you when dealing with strangers? Whatever the Law says for the covenant community it applies also to how members of the faith community are to relate to strangers. The community of faith and the community of strangers are equal in God's sight: both are aliens in the land.[23] Followers of God should allow strangers to worship with them.[24] They should teach the principles of the covenant relations to aliens.[25] Participating in certain practices known to be part of the culture, such as eating food that had been offered to idols, was forbidden.[26] The welfare system included strangers.[27] God's people were to be careful to keep the principles of the covenant to avoid becoming slaves of strangers.[28] It was permissible to charge interest to strangers when loaning them money.[29] Aliens were to be treated the same as anyone else; they were not allowed to blaspheme the name of God.[30]

Shalom. In the Bible story shalom is hardly possible if each person does what is right only in his or her own eyes.[31] Awareness of how others in one's social group view moral standards is important; however, the social group is not the standard but rather the principles of covenant relationships given in the Ten Commandments.[32] The social group has the responsibility of protecting, preserving and interpreting the principles of covenant. Faithful followers of God should be on guard against other peoples who would destroy shalom. Strangers must not pursue religious practices in the land that would tempt faithful followers of God. It is not good if strangers are allowed to plunder the good things that come from shalom.[33]

Justice. Justice in the biblical story was to be extended to anyone present in the community.

Followers of God were expected to treat strangers fairly, allowing them to enjoy the fruits of shalom without regard to their standards of right and wrong.[34] Likewise, by implication, strangers in the land were not allowed to impose their beliefs of right and wrong on God's people. The justice system that provided for the protection of criminals also protected strangers.[35] Justice is blind to cultural context or individual characteristics.

Wisdom. Followers of the covenant should be cautious (wise) about entering into economic arrangements with strangers unless they agree with your values.[36] Not everyone is trustworthy. Covenant followers were to live so that their reputation was positive among strangers.[37] Solomon counseled that the way of the fool is right in his own eyes.[38] There is always the risk that what we think is right is what will take us to destruction.[39] Making judgments about strangers requires active discernment. Community members must maintain awareness of who is among them in the community. This implies the need to gather information from each other regarding the reputation of all in the community. With this shared information, the community can protect itself. These principles for discernment, caution and choice of whom to associate with implies the shared awareness that some peoples they encounter will not share the covenant relation principles. This raises a tension point of judging and discerning. The biblical story provides two perspectives regarding judging others. On the one hand, we should not attempt to take the place of God, who alone has the prerogative to judge between what is right and wrong. God has absolute authority over standards of right and wrong, and this authority is not shared with humans. On the other hand, we must discern the behavior of others so as not to be taken in by false belief or act in unjust ways toward others.[40]

Loving kindness. God's love is not limited to his faithful followers; this was a model for the people to follow even though strangers and aliens did not have the same rules of conduct. The people were to remember that they were once aliens in Egypt.[41] God's people were to allow strangers to glean in the fields with the poor.[42] The Scripture story warns about following the standards of right and wrong found in other cultures.[43] God's people were expected to go into other lands, but they were expected to remain faithful to the principles of the covenant at all times and places.[44] This counsel was not heeded.[45] They were not to intermarry with strangers who worshiped other gods, but they did anyway.[46] Above all, God's people were to guard against participating in the worship of Baal, the god of prosperity and wealth.[47]

Redemption. The redemption theme assumes the commonness of all humans in all cultures and all places. In the biblical story, all cultures are subject to the principles at stake in the character of God; all are in need of redemption. This undermines the basis of cultural relativism because no person, no work group, no industry group or no cultural group is able to establish moral superiority over any other.

CHAPTER REVIEW QUESTIONS

1. How does relativism challenge the traditional ideas about right and wrong?

2. What is the difference between descriptive relativism and cultural relativism as an approach to decision making?

3. How is relativism applied to four social levels?

4. What are the pros and cons of cultural relativism?

5. To what conclusion regarding relativism do the biblical story themes lead?

DISCUSSION QUESTIONS

1. What, if any, moral principles might be shared worldwide?

2. Visit the website of Transparency International (www.transparency.org) and view the most recent Corruption Perceptions Index rankings by country. Countries listed at the top of the table have the least amount of corruption; countries at the bottom of the list have the most. The Corruption Perception Index is based on data gathered through surveys of people doing business in various countries. Measures include bribery, kickbacks, embezzlement of public funds and estimates of the strength and effectiveness of a country's efforts to stop corruption.

3. Is it possible to be a moral relativist and still believe that God has established moral absolutes that everyone should follow?

4. When you compare personal relativism and egoism what, if any, differences do you find?

5. You are in a conversation with someone who advocates cultural relativism. How would you challenge this perspective in a way that shows respect to the person?

ETHICAL VIGNETTES TO DISCUSS

For each of the vignettes described below apply the biblical story themes to discern what is right and wrong.

1. Your firm needs more land to build more apartment buildings and homes adjacent to the first phase of one of your major land investments now up and running.[48] A

private developer who has heard about your plan secretly secures a five-year option from the owners on the adjacent land. He then offers to sell the land to you at a substantial mark-up over its original value. The owners claim their hands are tied and the option agreement is legally binding. What, if anything, is wrong with what the private developer did on the land option? What is dirty about his dirty trick? What might your company have done to minimize your vulnerability to such an action by a private developer? What level of relativism might be in play here (individual, social role, company/industry, cultural group)? How would a moral relativist private developer think about secretly buying land next to your property?

2. News Flash: Savar (near Dhaka), Bangladesh, Wednesday, April 24, 2013 . . . Bangladesh Factory Building Collapses Killing More Than 1,000; Government, Western Retail Brands React . . . [49] The multistory Rana Plaza garment factory building housing five different garment manufacturing companies collapsed within hours after workers notified supervisors that large cracks had appeared in walls. The garment industry accounts for more than 80 percent of Bangladesh exports. Each company in the building manufactures textile products which are exported to Western countries. Europe is the major importer of Bangladesh apparel products. But retailers in the United States such as Walmart and Kmart are popular outlets for Bangladesh clothing products. The building collapse has been called the worst industrial accident in the country's history. European and North American brands do not own the factory, but some claim that they have a moral responsibility by being complicit in the lax approach to workers' protection. Others say that the factory building was illegally constructed. What, if anything, might a cultural relativist say about the standards of right and wrong that may have led to the building collapse?

7

Common Sense

Just use common sense!

SCRIPTURE PASSAGE

Do not be wise in your own eyes;
Fear the Lord and turn away from evil.
(Prov 3:7)

CHAPTER OVERVIEW

In this chapter we will explore common sense as an ethical guide for actions in the marketplace. We will wrestle with the various ways that people define common sense when applied to ethical decision making. In particular, we will

- explore various ways the term "common sense" is used

- review the pros and cons of common sense as an ethical decision-making approach

- evaluate common sense through the lens of biblical themes

MAIN TOPICS

Gut Instinct
Intuition
Practical Judgment
Generally Accepted Moral Principles (GAMP)
Evaluation: Pros and Cons
Down to the Nitty-Gritty
Through the Lens of Biblical Themes

KEY TERMS

common sense, generally accepted moral principles, gut instinct, intuition, practical intelligence

OPENING SCENARIO

One of the responsibilities of a professional architect is to contribute to the development of new customers for the firm. This involves schmoozing clients by taking them out to eat for dinner in hopes that the relationship developed during the meal will result in the client signing the contract.

Schmoozing clients is an acceptable marketing practice. This activity may occur prior to or after signing a service contract with a new client. Schmoozing clients involves the company paying for meals and drinks. The problem: alcoholic drinks are available during the meal. The Christian architect who believes that drinking alcohol is conduct unfaithful to his relationship with God faces a dilemma. He may not want to order alcoholic drinks. But clients may not see anything wrong with drinking. They may be looking forward to the architectural firm picking up the tab for their food and drinks. Paying for drinks and food is the responsibility of a gracious host.

A Christian might prefer not to pay personally for alcoholic drinks that others consume. If the architecture firm is hosting the event, it would be socially rude and marketing suicide for the architect to ask the prospective clients to pay for their own alcoholic drinks.

If the Christian in this scenario used common sense, what would be his decision regarding paying for alcoholic drinks?

Have a conversation with someone about a dilemma like this and notice how quickly other persons refer to common sense when describing what should be done. Right and wrong can seem so clear to some persons that common sense appears to be the obvious approach to justify an action. In spite of the various ethical theories and formulas that are available to people, some boil it all down to a simple dictum: "Just use common sense!"[1]

To say that something is common sense is to state that the proposed action or thought is so obvious, at first glance so self-evident, that it hardly deserves further investigation or analysis.[2] But is this always valid?

This chapter will review various uses of the term "common sense" when applied to the process of deciding what is right and wrong. Each of the following will be explored as a moral guideline: gut instinct, intuition, consensus, practical judgment, social reasoning and generally accepted moral principles. As you will see, some of these are closely related.

GUT INSTINCT

When we experience certain emotions, feelings in reaction to a situation, we sometimes feel it in our stomach (gut). What we feel, some say, is closer to our instinct to take a particular action. We observe the behavior of someone and make a judgment about what that behavior means. We experience an emotional response in our gut, which in turn influences our action.

One problem with this is that two people can experience the same situation and yet have two distinctly different, and sometimes opposing, gut instincts for action because they interpret the facts of the same situation differently. Making this worse is when only partial information is available. When there are gaps in the information available, we must make assumptions about what we do not know. But people may make two sets of assumptions that are in disagreement.

Gut instincts may be subject to biases resulting from temperament, self-interest or competitive pressures. Note also the comments by Laura Nash regarding the weaknesses of gut instinct when it comes to complicated moral issues: "In many ethics issues such a response is about as adequate as an aspirin in a car accident. Gut instinct alone hardly copes with the moral complexities of PACs [political action committees], random drug testing, wage gaps, or environmental responsibility."[3]

The larger the organization, the greater the diversity of perspective will be present. Nash explains that gut instinct does not provide the organizational leader with the voice that is needed for the complexity of issues that large organizations face. What one person believes is smart marketing another person believes is morally reprehensible. The larger the organization, the more likely the need to achieve profit will put increasing pressure on managers to compromise integrity. What a person will not do with his or her family acting alone (such as falsifying an accident report), that person might be willing to do at work if a reasonable justification can be found and if he or she participates with a group whose members have no problem with falsifying details on a report. Nash cites the example of "church going executives at a major food processor [that] not only failed to investigate clear indications that their 'apple juice' concentrate was 100 percent chemical but later shipped cases of the chemical cocktail off to Puerto Rico in an effort to evade the FDA and sell the product anyway."[4]

If we have faced a particular situation before and experienced the outcomes of decisions, and have had a chance to reflect on the action in terms of standards of right and wrong, our gut instinct may indeed be reliable assuming two things: (1) that we know enough information on which to make a moral judgment; and (2) that previously we applied the standards of right and wrong appropriately. But if the current situation is different from what we have experienced before, if it is more complicated than we expect, if key information is lacking, if our assumptions regarding what we cannot observe are invalid and if we have something personally at stake in the situation, our gut instinct may just as likely be incorrect as correct.

Scripture[5] and contemporary research both attest to "the innate tendency for individuals to engage in self-deception."[6] Thus, some gut instincts may be morally sound; others might be unsound. When seen as a process, the gut instinct view of common sense is a series of steps (see fig. 7.1).

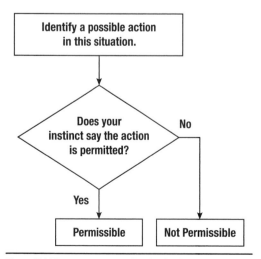

Figure 7.1. The common sense (gut instinct) ethical process.

INTUITION

Perhaps related to gut instinct is the idea of intuition. Some believe that at the most fundamental level the ethics process is first of all an emotional process.[7] It is our emotions that form the first ethical reasoning that we develop from childhood that lead to developing intuitions.

Emotions arise because of the innate abilities of our perceptions to tell us when someone is caring (or uncaring and even harmful), fair (or cheating us), loyal (or a betrayer), respectful of hierarchical relationships (or subversive), dominant and perhaps abusive (or submissive) respecting the sanctity of humans (or degrading humans). The emotional responses we experience as a result of our social interactions then teach us what is right and wrong.[8] But this moral learning cannot be solely the result of the individual experiencing and learning from the emotions. Learning the meaning of these emotions requires guidance from the larger community.

Accordingly, this view claims that the basic moral principles are self-evident to all persons who become mature adults. Conduct that is right or wrong is conduct that is socially approved.[9] Intuitively we all sense that pleasure is good while pain is bad. We know that when someone has treated us badly, our power of empathy helps us intuit that other people would feel the same if we treated them badly.

Like emotions on which our moral intuitions are based, intuition is fast. It is the ability to connect deep understanding of patterns and structures with emotional reactions to our judgments. Intuition is sometimes seen as a shortcut to making judgments about a complex situation. But using such a shortcut is not always advisable because speculation often leads to severe errors in judgment.[10]

Intuition is not free of values. Values must be a part of all our judgments. Instead, intuition is a "composite of cultural lessons that carry with them political judgments representing specific values and ideologies."[11] The danger in relying on intuition when making decisions in an organization is that intuition is dominated by the ideologies of the organization that holds power over its employees.

What a person automatically feels about an action will vary from person to person.[12] Complicated cases are more likely than simple cases to reveal competing considerations. In addition, the more complex the situation, the more difficult it may be to identify the elements on which the decision of right and wrong turn. The more unusual the case, the more difficulty will be encountered in determining what is right and wrong. We may have a strong opinion but at the same time be unfamiliar with the crucial elements which, with more thorough study, may reveal that our opinion is flawed. For example, some workers employed by Amazon.com regional distribution centers in the United Kingdom complained that the company forces them to work too hard. During the busiest shopping season (November and December), employees who fulfill customer orders must walk many miles through the large warehouse each day. What does intuition tell you regarding whether their claim is valid or invalid? Some might argue that Amazon.com fully informs job applicants of the intensity of the work. Others might argue that the company's push for higher efficiency requires them to mistreat employees, who must work harder than is reasonable.

PRACTICAL JUDGMENT

By common sense some people mean sound practical judgment useful in everyday life when making decisions that we expect will result in desired outcomes or practical consequences.[13] "The common sense person is practical, making his or her choices in terms of means and ends, choosing the most effective and efficient means to reach desired goals."[14]

During informal conversation you will hear people say something like, "It is common sense to do such and such in that situation," or "It makes sense to not do that because of what will happen." When we use the term in this way, we refer to practical intelligence or experiential knowledge regarding what works or what does not work in a given situation.[15]

Practical common sense in business is based on knowledge of marketplace behaviors of customers, workers, competitors, managers, owners, and other stakeholders. Practical common sense is also based on knowledge of how mechanical or electrical devices, natural laws (such as gravity) or materials operate under certain conditions or on the requirements of work processes. For example, we might say, "If you raise prices, you will sell fewer units of the product." Or, "If you put that bucket of paint at the edge of the table, it is common sense to think that someone might knock it over and spill paint on the floor."

Practical judgment common sense may have some, though limited, ethical use in situations where there is an emergency with no time for systematic analysis. A common sense approach can provide an initial indication, based on experience, whether a proposed action is similar to actions taken in the past where positive outcomes were experienced. Or it might indicate that negative outcomes are probable.

Common sense from this point of view contains some weaknesses. It may merely express a subjective perception of the environment. But perceptions change, and with them so does common sense.[16] Every time we use common sense and then experience an outcome, we risk modifying common sense in favor of the positive business outcomes without taking into consideration the effect of the decision on important stakeholders. Gradually common sense may include behaviors that previously we would have identified as immoral but are now merely common sense. Thus, this problem may be revealed on a day when business outcomes are held in such high priority that just about any means to accomplish the outcome might be used, even though such means are not moral while they now appear as common sense.

The greatest weakness of this use of the term is that it glosses over the moral issues at stake in a situation. It essentially leads to the "ends justify the means" utilitarianism. While the business outcomes of a particular decision cannot be ignored and should be considered, business outcomes alone cannot be the ultimate standard of right and wrong.

Perhaps the benefit of common sense is that it is integral to, but not the only step in, a larger process of ethical decision making. There is a lot of practical business wisdom in the larger community that has been reliable through the years to be factors in business success. There also may be a lot of practical business wisdom that is nonsense!

> A wise man will hear and increase in learning,
> And a man of understanding will acquire wise counsel. (Prov 1:5)

GENERALLY ACCEPTED MORAL PRINCIPLES (GAMP)

Another use of the term common sense is centered on what we might call generally accepted moral principles. For example, we might subscribe to the idea that most people in most places on earth would agree that conduct should be guided by what is fair and what is respectful to others because they are human beings.[17] One problem with such an approach is that to put ethical principles into two broad, relatively undefined ideas oversimplifies business situations.

We might boil down the minimum basic principles required in the marketplace to just three.[18] First, when someone is in need, it is commonly believed that one ought to give assistance if the cost is minimal. We call this the principle of mutual aid. The second principle is to do no harm to others. Third, it is commonly believed that each person should respect the autonomy of other persons.

Bernard Gert and others go beyond these three basic principles. They believe that there is a set of moral principles that is commonly accepted to be valid across most of society. Gert's belief is that all humans share a "universal human nature."[19] "Common morality is the moral system that people use, usually not consciously, in deciding how to act when confronting moral problems and in making their moral judgments."[20] For example, some people think that it is common sense to believe that we should "balance our own interests against the interests of others."[21] "The commonsense assumption in this is that other people's interests count, for their own sakes, from a moral point of view" just as much as their own interests.[22]

According to Gert, such a moral system is based on the desire to avoid doing harm—

Table 7.1. Common morality.

1. Do not kill.	**Basic**
2. Do not cause pain.	
3. Do not disable.	
4. Do not deprive of freedom.	
5. Do not deprive of pleasure.	
6. Do not deceive.	**Derivative**
7. Keep your promises.	
8. Do not cheat.	
9. Obey the law.	
10. Do your duty. Here "duty" is used in its "everyday sense to refer to what is required by one's role in society, primarily one's job, not as philosophers customarily use it, which is to say, simply as a synonym for 'What one morally ought to do.'" "These rules are not absolute; they all have justified exceptions, and most moral problems involve determining which exceptions are justified." (Gert, "Common Morality and Computing," p. 60)	

death, pain, disability, loss of freedom and loss of pleasure. From these five harms we get ten moral rules that capture the core of common morality. Using these common principles, "all rational people will agree on the answers to most moral questions, [but] they need not agree on the answers to all of them."[23] Gert's list of moral rules is shown in table 7.1.

Thomas Beauchamp has a slightly different way of describing common morality which he refers to as universally admired traits of character or virtues:

> The common morality contains . . . 10 examples of moral character traits (virtues) recognized in the common morality: (1) nonmalevolence; (2) honesty; (3) integrity; (4) conscientiousness; (5) trustworthiness; (6) fidelity; (7) gratitude; (8) truthfulness; (9) lovingness; and (10) kindness.[24]

Using another approach to identifying generally accepted moral principles by surveying what various organizations[25] and researchers have found, Mark Schwartz identified six elements of a common moral framework:[26]

- Trustworthiness (including notions of honesty, integrity, transparency, reliability, and loyalty);

- Respect (including notions of respect for human rights);

- Responsibility (including notions of accountability, excellence, and self-restraint);

- Fairness (including notions of process, impartiality, and equity);

- Caring (including the notion of avoiding unnecessary harm); and

- Citizenship (including notions of obeying laws and protecting the environment).[27]

Surveys, by themselves, do not provide sufficient justification for the universal authority of such lists. It is only the observations that there are commonly shared principles that make this list worthy of consideration. Some scholars say that it is the commonly shared humanness in community life (a universal experience worldwide) that makes such lists normative.

When comparing the three sets of lists, it can be seen how closely they align with the Ten Commandments, as is shown in table 7.2.

Table 7.2. Commonly accepted moral principles compared with the Ten Commandments.

Ten Commandments	Gert	Beauchamp	Schwartz
Have no other gods	—	—	—
Worship no idols	—	—	—
Do not make false promises invoking God's name	Keep your promises	Trustworthiness	Trustworthiness
Keep the sabbath holy	—	—	—
Honor your parents	Do your duty	—	Respect
Do not commit murder	Do not kill; do not cause pain; do not disable	Non-malevolence; lovingness; kindness	Respect; caring
Do not commit adultery	—	Fidelity	—
Do not steal	Do not cheat; do not deprive of freedom; do not deprive of pleasure	Conscientiousness	Respect
Be a trustworthy witness	Do not deceive	Honesty; integrity; truthfulness	Fairness
Do not covet	—	Gratitude	—
	Obey the law		Responsibility; citizenship

Other thinkers have suggested fundamental principles assumed to be present in efficient markets. Each of these, one could argue, is similar to the principles found in the Ten Commandments: honor agreements, tell the truth, respect the autonomy of others and avoid doing harm to others.[28] Hosmer sees being truthful and honoring contracts as the minimum necessary ethical basis of the market.[29] Hare sees "honesty, truthfulness and fair dealing" as the minimum standards.[30]

The lists of generally accepted moral principles have been called hypernorms. These are moral principles that are believed to be the deepest moral values that result when you combine principles of conduct from a variety of perspectives.[31]

EVALUATION: PROS AND CONS

In an informal conversation, to say that something is common sense is to state that the morality of an action is so obvious and at first glance so self-evident that it hardly deserves further analysis. Two people can experience the same situation and yet have two distinctly dif-

ferent, and sometimes opposing, gut instincts for action because they interpret the facts of the same situation differently. When there are gaps in the information available, we must make assumptions before we can discern whether or not what we sense regarding right and wrong behavior is commonly shared or merely a personal idea. Intuition is not free of values. Intuition regarding what is morally good or bad in complex situations is less trustworthy than intuition that arises in simple cases. As complexity increases, confusion about right and wrong also increases. Appealing to social reasoning appears to be an appeal to the power or politics of a given situation: Whoever has the power in a given situation will have the influence over what is considered common sense.

Making a list of principles is an attempt to define common sense by identifying particular moral standards of right and wrong conduct that are common across social groups. But, by itself, does this make a list of values a valid standard for conduct?

This chapter introduces the idea of common sense as a moral standard of right and wrong. It is time to consider some of the pros and cons of this approach. Pros (arguments in support) will be identified by the symbol (+) while cons (arguments against) will be identified by the symbol (-).

(+) If we say that common sense is the collection of generally accepted moral principles, many countries have similar standards. Thus, this is a system that can have practical utility in many places on earth in many cultures. But the question must be asked: On what basis should practical utility be the deciding factor on whether or not common sense is appropriate?

(+) Look at any professional code of ethics (many are available on the Internet), and you will see common sense imbedded in many provisions. Codes of ethics typically have in view the good of the community of those served by the profession rather than merely individual professionals.

(+) Having said all this about common sense, we are not ready to throw out common sense altogether. As a completely reliable moral standard, we conclude that it is not satisfying; however, what common sense highlights is that moral principles must be applied to a particular time and place and social setting. Common sense takes into account the rational actions that are possible and foresees the consequences of such actions. It also comprehends the general principles that the person believes to be valid. Common sense may form an important link between what we believe to be right and wrong (moral standards) and our attempts to apply the moral standard in real life. It may provide a needed logic map for judgment.[32]

Common sense also reveals some weaknesses.

(-) To appeal to common sense as justification for conduct may be nothing more than saying, "I believe other people will agree with my moral standard in this situation." But even if this is true, on what basis can we say that agreement among persons is the only valid criterion for discerning right from wrong? And if it is not true that other people agree with an action, does disagreement make the action wrong?

(-) To argue in favor of consensus (majority opinion) is to imply that standards of right and wrong are ultimately subjective.[33] According to this view, whatever people feel is right for them and if most people feel that a particular behavior is right, this will make it right. But if the standards of right and wrong are only subjective, how can they be standards? They would not apply to everyone but only to those who share the opinion on those standards.

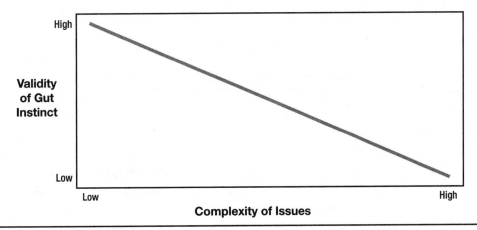

Figure 7.2. Complexity of issues and validity of gut instinct.

(-) Common sense as a moral decision-making model on its own does not answer the complex questions of morality in business. It requires the existence of a standard of right and wrong that is commonly accepted. For example, common sense does not answer for us the question of how far we may be permitted to hurt some stakeholders while bringing benefit to others. Consensus can be achieved regarding what is moral as long as it is built on general, vague propositions. Careful reflection on the details of specific cases tends to unravel the consensus. As the complexity of a situation increases, the validity of gut instinct as a reliable standard of right and wrong decreases (see fig. 7.2).

(-) Some have argued that common sense ethics is at best utilitarianism and at worst egoism or relativism whereby the outcomes of a proposed action are evaluated in terms of the perceived net positive and negative outcomes.[34]

(-) Things that are self-evident in theory are not quite as self-evident when we apply the theory to a specific situation. Furthermore, our intuitions can sometime be conflicting and as a result be an unreliable guide all the time. Thus, the test of a moral theory is not its "initial plausibility, but whether a careful examination uncovers implications that clash with our intuition."[35] Truths considered to be self-evident, learned by sensing what society expects, are vague and disputed because persons interpret truths differently. Thus, the appeal to common sense (the intuitive sense of what is held in common) is an appeal to a socially conditioned way of thinking. The reliability of socially conditioned self-evident truths must be questioned.

DOWN TO THE NITTY-GRITTY

Think about the opening story at the beginning of this chapter. You are the architect. What is the right thing to do? It's time to get down to the nitty-gritty (see table 7.3)!

THROUGH THE LENS OF BIBLICAL THEMES

This part of the chapter will use the biblical story themes as a lens through which to evaluate the ethical approach featured in the chapter. Because the themes are interrelated and interdependent, we should expect to see some overlap in the thinking regarding the ethical approach. Some themes will contribute the same thinking as will other themes. The power of these themes comes from their guidance when a community of people talks about complicated ethical dilemmas faced in business practice.

If we evaluate the common sense approach to ethical decision making through the lens of biblical themes, what will we find?

Cosmic conflict. Two interesting forms of common sense are revealed in the biblical story themes. First, God's plan is for all creatures to accept his principles for a flourishing life. He desires for this to become common among all who desire flourishing well-being. As the dimensions of his character are integrated into the hearts of people, they are transformed into his image. When spread across social groups, transformation occurs more widely. Second, when God's principles for flourishing life are properly understood in their interrelationships with each other, it is common sense that this is how human beings interact together for well-being.

Creation. The creation theme of Scripture is openly opposed to common sense when creation asserts the lordship of Jesus Christ over all. Humans are not given the prerogative of their Creator to determine moral standards of conduct. If Adam and Eve had used common

Table 7.3. Applying the ethical process.

Keeping Your Heart: An Intrapersonal Process	Walking in the Community: An Interpersonal Process

• You are the architect. What does your heart say is the right thing to do?
• Which biblical themes explored in this book inform your heart on this situation?
• Which biblical theme, if any, do you feel yourself resisting? Why do you feel resistance?
• What is the common sense thing to do? How are you defining "common sense"?
• What other influences in your heart are prominent as you think about this situation?
   • Fundamental beliefs
   • Cognitive reasoning
   • Judgments and evaluations
   • Decisions
   • Virtues
   • Will
   • Memory of personal experiences with other people
   • Perceptions of others in the community
   • Personal biases
   • Awareness of interpersonal relationships
   • Commitments to God and to others
   • Intuitions
   • Conscience
   • Human spirit
   • Emotions
	• You are the architect presented at the first of the chapter. With whom might you have a conversation about this situation? Who else might have a helpful perspective?
	• Which of the biblical themes in this chapter will most likely come up in the conversation either directly or indirectly? Why? Which one(s) will be the most influential in the conversation?
	• If you have a conversation with someone regarding this situation, which of the fundamental tensions presented earlier in the book might come into the conversation?
	• What right-versus-right dilemmas, if any, can be identified here? Have a conversation with someone about this now. What is the outcome of the conversation?
	• What benefit and what cost might be incurred by having a conversation with others about the issues?
	• If five people participated in the conversation about this situation, how many different views on "common sense" might be expressed? Why?

sense, the majority opinion would have overruled God. The biblical story portrays human happiness as achieved when we are in service to God and to each other, not based on popular ideas of what is right and wrong but based on the whole system of principles for living established by the Creator.

Holiness. Being fully consecrated to God while living in this world will require of us to be uncommon, especially when the prevailing opinions of right and wrong are not based on principles of covenant relationships. Merely following popular opinion will lead us away from deep consecration.

Covenant relationships. The generally accepted moral principles put forward by contemporary thinkers, while going a long way to support the principles of right and wrong offered in the Bible story, ignore religious faith in a Supreme Being. Similar to the Ten Commandments, contemporary generally accepted principles include both positive (prescriptive) and negative (proscriptive) principles. But they also lack the depth and breadth of the relationship described in the Ten Commandments that is applicable in a wide variety of different situations. The lists put forward by scholars appear on the surface to be a simple collection of unrelated rules. These lists fail to recognize the comprehensive, integrated moral system of which they were a part thousands of years ago.

If you look at any of the Ten Commandments, each one has an element of common sense when you think of the goal of community-wide prosperity and how the behavior described in the commandment contributes to such a goal. For examples, it makes common sense that people in a community

- honor promises because this promotes economic commitments and psychological well-being (third commandment)

- work diligently to contribute their fair share to the community but also be content with what they earn so that they do not infringe on property rights of other persons (fourth commandment; tenth commandment)

- honor each other, as this prevents retaliatory behaviors which are destructive in society (fifth commandment)

- do not kill or injure each other because so doing creates instability for the whole community (sixth commandment)

- honor their marriage commitments because doing otherwise is disruptive to family and community well-being (seventh commandment)

- do not steal from each other, as this undermines general well-being, but instead help each other (eighth commandment)

- are trustworthy when disputes are resolved by independent third parties such as the formal system of laws and courts (ninth commandment)

In this regard the biblical standards of morality contain common sense when you consider the common good of the whole community rather than merely what is good for a single person.

While the Bible recognizes a community process of giving and sharing wisdom (see below on wisdom), the capacity for discernment comes primarily from God as he teaches our hearts. This process requires spending time with the principles of covenant relations so that the principles of the Ten Commandments are written in our heart.[36]

Shalom. The experience of shalom is dependent on following not what is popular but rather the principles of covenant relationships referred to above.

Sabbath. At its root sabbath is about renouncing human autonomy. It is God who is the ultimate objective standard of right and wrong conduct.

Justice. While in a perfect world people would follow the covenant relationship principles, reality is otherwise. God's indicative statements of what he has done for us are always followed by imperative statements of what we are called to do for him, including extending justice throughout the land. This implies that when injustice is common sense, followers of God will depend not on popular ideas of what is justice but instead will depend on biblical ideals of justice and will intervene where possible to correct injustices. People who claim to be followers of God are not immune to having incorrect moral beliefs. For example, American Christians justified slavery during the sixteenth to nineteenth centuries.[37] Further, Christians can and do disagree among themselves regarding moral principles. Thus, the appeal to common sense even among those who claim to be followers of God can be an appeal to an erroneous authority.

Righteousness. As with justice, the biblical standard of right doing lies outside the human person objectively and authoritatively in the character of the Creator-Redeemer. Right doing is not defined by popular opinion.

Truth. The principles on which the standards of right and wrong are based do not change even though the situations we are in do change. If popular opinions about what is acceptable or unacceptable change, the person who aligns with truth will remain steadfast in the midst of pressure to conform to popular opinion.

Wisdom. Wisdom in the Bible story comes from God, and his wisdom is mediated through those in the community who are acknowledged to be experienced followers of God and who have shown by their lives that they support covenant relationships. This is the biblical idea of common sense. It is not foolproof in that those who are seen as trustworthy guides to the community may, in fact, be untrustworthy. In spite of this risk, it is wise to listen to counsel from others in the community as long as these persons are faithful exhibitors of biblical standards. This discernment requires each rational person in the community to judge to what degree counselors are aligned with God's principles for living. The Bible admonishes us to choose our counselors carefully.[38] "A wise man will hear and increase in learning, and a man of understanding will acquire wise counsel" (Prov 1:5). And if others in the community ask for our counsel, we should be careful to guide them in terms of biblical right doing.[39] When we listen to counsel from those who do not follow the Creator's principles of conduct, we are in danger of becoming foolish.[40] In addition, we can deceive ourselves into thinking that we know what is right and wrong on our own, and such self-deception is dangerous: "There is a way which seems right to a man, but its end is the way of death" (Prov 16:25).[41] King Solomon describes such persons as lacking a center of moral judgment.[42] They may follow others in the community who agree with them, but from the point of view of biblical covenant relationships they are senseless.

Redemption. Popular opinion regarding what is right and wrong may lead some in the organization into problems. Mistakes can be made. The faithful manager will encourage others to move toward fundamental principles. If mistakes are made, someone needs to take a leadership position to correct the mistake.

CHAPTER REVIEW QUESTIONS

1. Describe common sense from the point of view of gut instinct.

2. What is intuition as an approach to deciding what is right and wrong?

3. How does practical judgment form the basis of common sense?

4. What are generally accepted moral principles, and how can these be considered common sense?

5. What are the pros and cons of common sense as an approach to business ethics?

6. What perspective do the biblical story themes provide us regarding common sense?

DISCUSSION QUESTIONS

1. What additional arguments would you give either in support of or in challenge to common sense as a method for deciding what is right and wrong in the business environment?

2. Consider the opening scenario of the chapter. Using one or more approaches to common sense, what should the professional architect do in a setting where providing alcohol for clients is expected? Which definition of common sense are you using? On what basis should common sense be sufficient justification for your decision in the scenario?

3. What is the difference between intuition and the biblical metaphor of the heart?

4. Compare the formal code of ethics from three different professions. What are the commonalities in these codes of ethics? What do the commonalities suggest regarding a common sense moral standard?

5. How much agreement must exist in a population regarding a particular moral standard

before we can say with certainty that it is in fact a common sense moral standard? If the proportion of the population that agree regarding a particular moral standard of conduct is not the valid basis for the standard, of what value is the knowledge regarding the extent to which a population agrees?

6. You are in a conversation with someone regarding the rightness or wrongness of a particular action. The person says, "Just use common sense." How would you respond to this person?

ETHICAL VIGNETTES TO DISCUSS

For each of the vignettes described below, apply the biblical story themes to discern what is right and wrong.

1. *The best person for the job.*[43] You have an open position in your company and have gone through the recruiting and selection process. The group of finalists is composed of good candidates, though none is a standout. You could decide to open the search process again, but this would take valuable time. Instead, you decide to make a job offer to the person who is the best of the group. You call the winning candidate and make the job offer. Together you agree on the start date, which is late next week. The next day you get a phone call from a trusted friend who tells you that she has just met the perfect candidate for the job you had open and that you really need to meet this person. You explain that you have already made the job offer. Your friend insists that you must meet this person. Reluctantly, you agree to at least talk with the person. Lo and behold, this person indeed is the standout candidate for the job. This person's training, experience, personality and values all surpass your expectations. You have the budget to hire only one person. What is the best business decision? What is the best moral decision? Can you think of a creative approach whereby you honor your commitment to the person to whom you offered the job and do what is best for the organization?

2. *Upgrade the rental car!* You are the customer service agent for Shazaam Rental Car Company. It is late at night. Most of the flights have arrived carrying rental car customers. All of the small cars—the most popular vehicles you rent at that particular airport—have been rented. All you have left in the lot are full-sized sedans, SUVs and minivans. You know this, but the customer in front of you does not know it. The customer has reserved one of the small, lowest-priced cars—having agreed to a price quoted by the online marketing company that your company is affiliated with. The customer will be using the car for a full week. You try twice to get the customer to upgrade to a full-sized sedan for a very low (around two dollars) per-day upgrade fee even though you know that you will have to rent a full-sized sedan at the agreed-on lower price anyway. When the customer rents the full-sized sedan, that car will not be available for a full week to other customers who might be willing to pay a higher price for a larger car. The customer declines the upgrade offer that you make and is pleasantly surprised to learn that he will be driving a full-sized sedan when you hand him the rental agreement. Is it ethical for you to attempt to capture a small increase in revenue when you know that the customer will get the upgraded car anyway? If the customer suspects that there are no very small cars left on the lot at that time of day, is it ethical for the customer to accept the larger vehicle without paying the upgrade fee?

8

Social Contract

Do what society expects.

*To be truly free you must give up
some freedom.*

SCRIPTURE PASSAGE

For you were called to freedom, brethren;
only do not turn your freedom into an opportunity for the flesh, but through love
serve one another. (Gal 5:13)

CHAPTER OVERVIEW

In this chapter we will wrestle with the idea
called the social contract as an approach to deciding right from wrong in the marketplace. In
particular, we will

- explore the idea of the social contract as it
  applies to the environment of business
- evaluate the pros and cons of the social contract as an approach to ethical decision
  making in the marketplace
- evaluate the social contract idea through the
  lens of biblical themes

MAIN TOPICS

Definition of Terms

Historical Roots of the Social Contract

Application to the Business Environment

Evaluation: Pros and Cons

Down to the Nitty-Gritty

Through the Lens of Biblical Themes

KEY TERMS

community, Thomas Hobbes, John Locke, psychological contract, Jean Jacques Rousseau,
social contract, social norms

OPENING SCENARIO

Everything seems to be going well right after
you purchase the multifunction laser printer
for home use.[1] You are glad that the machine
is a laser printer, a digital copier and a
scanner. After successfully printing a document, copying a magazine article to give to
a friend and successfully scanning a few old
photographs of your great-grandparents,
you conclude that the machine works
properly. It warms up quickly. The printing
speed is reasonable for home use. It has a
small footprint on the desk top next to your
computer. The slide-out tray at the front
makes it easy to add paper. The toner cartridge is easy to change.

Speaking of the toner cartridge, this is the first thing that gives you some concern two months later when you see a warning notice appear on the digital display: "Toner is low. Replace cartridge soon." After talking with your spouse, you estimate the number of pages you have printed since installing the printer. The total seems to be fewer than fifty pages. You begin to wonder how much toner has been used. You print a page and inspect it. The print is as sharp and clear as on the first use of the machine. There are no indications that the toner is low.

You decide to wait a while before responding to the warning notice with a trip to the office supply store. You decide to make that shopping trip when the pages clearly have less toner applied.

Days go by. A few weeks go by. A new warning message appears on the display: "Toner is empty. Replace cartridge now." Yet, you detect no difference in the quality of printed pages compared with when the machine was new. You decide to wait a little longer before driving downtown or ordering a cartridge online.

A whole year later . . . the display on the printer conveniently provides the same warning message as before, but you have not changed the cartridge: "Toner is empty. Replace cartridge." Now you begin to wonder about the warning message. Is there an error? You also wonder whether the printer manufacturer intentionally programmed the machine so that unsuspecting customers end up purchasing toner cartridges before they need to. Then you begin to think that there might be other possible reasons for the warning message.

This situation gives us an opportunity to consider the set of unwritten, often unspoken expectations that customers have of businesses that make printers, toner cartridges and other products that enhance our lives.

Business is an activity of society that enables members of society to provide for general welfare or in other ways attempt to increase happiness. Members of society exchange goods and services because it is difficult for a person alone to provide for all personal and family needs. This makes business inseparable from other social goals and activities. It follows that ethical choices that we make in business cannot be separated from this larger social environment.[2]

This chapter is concerned with a fundamental, implicit agreement that members of a community make with each other. Without this agreement, it would be difficult if not impossible to have a real community. Without such an agreement, laws would cease to have the impact they are intended to have. This agreement is called a social contract.[3]

DEFINITION OF TERMS

According to Donaldson and Dunfee, two proponents of the social contract theory of business ethics, a community is a "self-defined, self-circumscribed group of people who interact in the context of shared tasks, values or goals and who are capable of establishing norms of ethical behavior for themselves."[4] What this means is that when persons form a community they define the ground rules or expectations of each other as they try to meet commonly shared needs. The self-defining elements of a group of people include not only those particular to one group but also those that are common to all human social groups. We might even say that by definition a community is a group of people who voluntarily commit to certain obligations to each other, without which there can be no community.

The heart of the social contract is voluntary consent to follow social norms coupled with an expectation that other people will follow the same norms. Social norms are rules of conduct that are present even when formal laws are not. We feel guilty when we break one of the social norms; yet, we still break some rules sometimes if we think we can go undetected or if the social group we are in at the time breaks some rules. We do not like it when other people do not follow the social norms that we expect of them.

company. The supervisor also says that the subordinate is expected to perform other job-related duties that the supervisor asks of him or her. In the mind of both persons an agreement is made that establishes the relationship. Even though not every detail is discussed, not every situation is evaluated, voluntary assent to the relationship is a key element.

THE HEART OF THE SOCIAL CONTRACT

Voluntary consent to follow formal and informal social norms by limiting personal freedom; an implicit expectation that others will do the same

---

Applied to the individual level. At the individual level the social contract is essentially a psychological contract infused with ideology held by the person. "In short, the psychological contract is the set of perceived, but unwritten, obligations" to someone. "In a sense, an individual's psychological contract represents a customized working map of the macro-social contract by which that individual evaluates and seeks to maintain the morality of his or her institutional context."[5] At this level the contract is a set of beliefs in the mind of the person that have developed because of promises made or statements made by those in authority in the organization.

Psychological contracts exist in any organized social group, including the company you work for, the nonprofit organization you volunteer for, the town softball league you participate in, the political party you support and the church you belong to. During the orientation of a new employee, a supervisor and the subordinate have a conversation regarding the scope of authority of the employee. They discuss the range of tasks for which the employee is responsible. They talk about the core values of the

Psychological contracts involve the development of beliefs about each other. For example, a belief exists that the new employee will not act carelessly to damage equipment and materials owned by the company. The supervisor will not act carelessly to damage the resources that the employee is expected to use. The employee expects that the supervisor will provide adequate job- or task-related information to the employee. The supervisor expects that the employee will provide adequate job- or task-related information. Both parties have mutual expectations of each other and rely on their understanding of these mutually expected norms when making choices of behaviors in the future. But both parties also realize that not everything in the relationship can be made explicit at the beginning. Some things cannot be known about the mutual expectations until specific situations arise.

Applied to a social group. When a group of people, such as a work team or department, or people in a neighborhood, share the same common beliefs regarding promises made by an organization and the norms of behavior expected of each other, the psychological contract exists.[6] Members of the group tend to reinforce the expectations of each other to follow the group's norms. They are interdependent with each other and because of this rely on each other to fulfill their various obligations.

Applied to society as a whole. When we broaden the idea of voluntary agreement to follow certain social norms, we arrive at the idea of social contract, an implicit agreement among members of society, a set of fundamental social expectations that we have of each other. Perhaps the easiest way to understand this level is to see that the laws in society would be worthless if there was not an implicit understanding among citizens that the laws are meant to be obeyed. It is this understanding that we share with each other which is part of the social contract.

Historically, a few widely spread social expectations have existed in all societies. For example, one expectation is that if you expect others to provide aid to you, you should help others. This is the idea of reciprocity. Closely related to this is the idea of indebtedness. Until a favor is returned, the recipient of a favor feels indebted to the giver of the favor. The more distant the relationship, the more the parties expect a speedier repayment of the debt. The closer the relationship, the less likely it is for persons to keep an accounting of who has given more (or less) to the relationship. Social contracts influence how we interpret promises we make to each other. Second, societies expect that persons among them will not harm each other. This can be called the "do no harm" rule.

> Love does no wrong to a neighbor; therefore love is the fulfillment of the law. (Rom 13:10)

HISTORICAL ROOTS OF THE SOCIAL CONTRACT

It has not been many years since business scholars have been discussing the idea of the social contract as a guideline for business ethics, but the idea of a social contract has ancient roots. Since ancient times the idea of the social contract has been central to discussions about how citizens should structure their government. And it is these ideas that form the basis of the social contract at work in the ethical, social and legal environment of business. In addition, it is these ideas that form an important linkage in the relationship between business and government.

We explore briefly the ideas of the social contract that apply to society as a whole and then as applied to the ethical, social and legal environment of business. Why consider society as a whole? First, it is in this larger society context that business operates. Second, the discussion of the relationship between business and government later in this book depends on a knowledge of this social contract idea.

Plato.[7] For Plato in ancient Greece, the fundamental problem for which the solution is the social contract is above all else that people want freedom to commit injustices on other people. But their greatest fear is that someone will treat them unjustly without an opportunity to punish the wrong-doer. The solution to this tension is that citizens voluntarily submit to the city's system of laws, which is the basis of justice.

Greatest Human Desire	Greatest Human Fear
Freedom to treat others unjustly.	Other people will treat me unjustly.

Figure 8.1. Fundamental issues addressed by the social contract.

Hobbes.[8] For Thomas Hobbes, the social contract involves an agreement among citizens for how to govern themselves so that they can live at peace with one another. By nature humans are narrowly self-interested. Yet, in order to live at peace they must have a minimum level of agreement for cooperation so that society is preserved. Without some form of government, anarchy would reign and people would destroy each other. Such anarchy reveals that some mechanism is needed because no person would be capable of defending his or her life unless he or she joined in some kind of federation with others for their common defense. Persons in conflict would be unable to completely trust their enemy. Thus, what is needed is some way to provide assurance that persons can be trusted and that promises are kept. That assurance mechanism is the government which the citizens implicitly agree to obey.

Political authority and obligation are based on the individual self-interests of members of society who are understood to be equal to one another; all share a basic drive to preserve life and avoid death. No single person is invested with the authority to rule over the rest; however, the sovereign must be obeyed when that sovereign's interests are the same of his or her subjects. Thus (in Hobbes's day) the king must be allowed to have absolute authority in order for society to survive. And citizens enter into an implicit voluntary contract to obey the king in exchange for the king acting on their behalf to protect and preserve their life. Thus, all citizens voluntarily submit to enforcement mechanisms that a society puts in place to stop people from acting opportunistically at the expense of others. At the same time citizens agree to allow each other the same degree of liberty as they want for themselves. This requires of citizens to allow a person or a small group of persons the power to establish laws and enforce them. But this requires giving up some liberty.

Locke.[9] The idea of voluntary commitment on the part of citizens also appears in the writings of John Locke, an English physician and philosopher. Locke believed that the natural condition of humankind is a state of perfect and complete liberty to conduct one's life as one best sees fit, free from the interference of others. All humans share equally in the status of being human because all were created equal with certain inalienable, natural rights such as the right to life, the right to own property and the right to freedom. The state's function is to protect these natural rights. However, persons are not free to do anything they please, or even anything that they think is in their self-interest. All citizens must voluntarily limit their freedom by obeying the law.

Table 8.1. Freedom: humanism and biblical perspective compared.

The work of Plato, Hobbes, Locke, Rousseau and others have highlighted the importance of freedom in civil society. But what do we mean by the term "freedom"? The humanistic description of freedom is quite different from that of the Bible.	
Humanism	**Biblical Perspective**
Humans have ultimate autonomy.	Under the guidance of the Holy Spirit, we have liberty (2 Cor 3:17).
Humans are free to choose moral standards.	Freedom was created by and mediated through a relationship with Jesus Christ (Lk 4:18; Jn 8:32-36; Gal 5:1).
Independence from God: humans are autonomous individuals.	Freedom is to be used to serve others (Gal 5:13).
Freedom must come by voluntarily constraining our behavior to a rule of law or generally accepted moral principles.	Freedom occurs within the boundaries established by the truth about God and serving him (1 Cor 9; 1 Pet 2:16).

Rousseau.[10] Jean Jacques Rousseau (1712–1778) also developed ideas regarding this voluntary commitment to each other. The government and society are united in a general will based on common interests and equal rights. In *The Social Contract* Rousseau described an interesting paradox: the state has a pact with society to give citizens true freedom in exchange for citizens to obey a self-imposed rule of law. "Man is born free; and everywhere he is in chains."[11] The will of the individual and the will of the state are not separate and self-sufficient but rather are interdependent and complementary.

Common interests sometimes conflict with personal interests. Rousseau reasoned that when citizens form a government, they agree to submit to the laws that are established. In return the citizens get to participate in establishing the principles and laws on which the government operates. This is a community process of conversations among the citizens. Individual citizens are encouraged to express their individual will as society as whole comes to understand the collective will of the people. The state, thus formed, becomes the expression of the sovereign and general will of the people. When the state exercises its power against a citizen who does not comply with the rules, it is the citizens as a whole who are exercising their power against the ones who refuse to live up to the terms of the social contract.

Later political philosophers such as Rawls and Habermas have built on the basic ideas of the social contract theory applied to government.[12] Whereas the earlier discussions of social contract sought to justify how government can legitimately establish and enforce laws, more recent discussions tend to emphasize the obligations of government to foster social justice.[13]

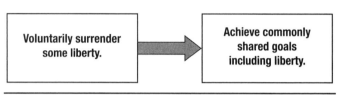

Figure 8.2. The relationship between liberties and the social contract.

Applied at the level of society as a whole the social contract is an implicit agreement among citizens related to how true liberty can be achieved and the basis on which government can be established and maintained. Each person in society has liberties, but these liberties are constrained by the obligations to serve the common good. The common good is defined through the community process of conversations among citizens.

The contract we make with each other is that all must voluntarily surrender some of their liberty in exchange for protection and to

---

THE SOCIAL CONTRACT IN SOCIETY

- Every citizen has certain natural rights or liberties.
- Citizens desire to pursue self-interests but also to be protected from other persons who pursue self-interests.
- Citizens need a third party to act on behalf of everyone to assure protection.
- Citizens form an organized community (government) by consenting to give up some individual freedom in exchange for protection and the achievement of common general welfare.

achieve other commonly shared goals and resources. This summary prepares us to consider the concept as it has been applied to business.

APPLICATION TO THE BUSINESS ENVIRONMENT

An implicit agreement among citizens that supports the rule of law and the foundation for government is one thing. But does this apply to the ethical, social and legal environment of business? Some people say yes.[14] Social contracts "often comprehend standards of right behaviour" and "constitute a significant source of ethical norms in business."[15] In turn, these standards of conduct create a duty of compliance.

Members of society associate together for the purpose of mutual protection, to promote freedom and to foster the ability of families to pursue family-related goals such as raising children, caring for each other and engaging in friendship with others. Members of society expect that the activities of the marketplace will assist citizens in accomplishing these goals.

Existing among members of society is an implicit belief that businesses have the right to engage in trade in exchange for certain benefits that society expects. Society gives businesses the legal permission to own and use assets, to hire citizens as employees and to gain access to and refine natural resources into products and services that enhance the welfare of society.

Society expects that consumers will gain from the activities of business increased efficiencies (better prices), improved access to goods and improved stability of distribution of goods.[16] Businesses are expected to live up to basic moral codes relevant to honesty and loyalty to commitments and fostering marketplace justice.

Businesses also are expected to operate within generally accepted moral principles of justice.[17] This requires that managers avoid fraud and deception. Managers are expected to see that the organization avoids harming persons.

A business must be free to pursue its goals without interference; however, it is not free to do anything its managers desire. When a business is given permission to operate in society, it surrenders some liberties to serve the common good. Accordingly, business should not rule over consumers by being so dominant that customers lose their freedom to exchange in the marketplace. No organization should be given so much power that the equality of persons served by the business is undermined.

> No one should have so much economic power that equality is undermined.

True freedom in the marketplace means obeying a self-imposed constraint that respects the interests of others. The nature of the constraints is contained in an implicit agreement between society and business organizations. This agreement can be explicit or implicit, but it is always based on mutual trust. It contains a quid pro quo provision: Society gives permission for the business to exist, and in return the business watches out for the interests of society (see fig. 8.3).

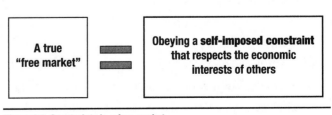

Figure 8.3. Constraints in a free market.

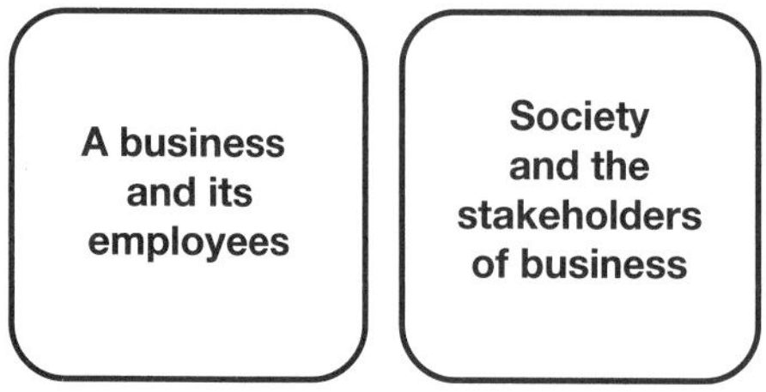

Figure 8.4. Parties to the social contract in business.

Society develops laws and regulations that govern the operation of businesses. The law is the mechanism that is used to socially enforce limits on freedom. Society assumes that businesses voluntarily submit themselves to the rule of law; however, the expectations in the social contract go deeper than what is provided for in the law. The law contains some, but not all, of society's expectations. Where the law does not cover some specific actions, society expects business to choose to conform to fundamental generally accepted moral principles. These broader moral principles are moral constraints to which society expects business voluntarily to submit. These broader moral principles are essentially community- or group-focused rather than individualistic.

The social contract in business is always conditional. "If an organization fails to adhere to these terms and an alternative entity (e.g. state controlled production) is perceived as preferable, then society might force a change."[18] Put in other words, ultimately a firm's repu-

tation (brand) is held in trust by and belongs to the community. When the business lives up to the expectations of society, the community loans a good reputation (brand) to the business. A good reputation allows the firm to share in the community's common interests. But when the conditions of the loan are breached, the reputation suffers.

How the social contract is used as a decision-making method is becoming clearer. How do you decide what is right or wrong in a given situation? An action that is right is an action that, paradoxically, constrains freedom so that it also promotes freedom. The right action is one that avoids one party ruling over the other. An action that is wrong is one where one party interferes with the other, undermines marketplace equality or undermines marketplace freedom. When seen as a process, the social contract leads to the steps shown in figure 8.5.

EVALUATION: PROS AND CONS

Some key assumptions are at the root of the social contract idea. First, the social contract assumes that a society in which individual citizens are free to pursue their own interests is good. Persons in society are dependent on an implicit agreement among themselves to voluntarily submit to certain social expectations. A good society is one in which individual citizens are free to pursue their own

---

THE SOCIAL CONTRACT APPLIED TO BUSINESS

- Pursue the interests of the firm.
- Contribute to the positive general welfare of citizens.
- Minimize negative externalities.
- Offer benefits to employees: income, diffusing legal liability.

- Act justly by avoiding harm, deception and fraud.
- Voluntarily submit to the rule of law and law enforcement.
- Voluntarily limit freedom in order to foster a free market.

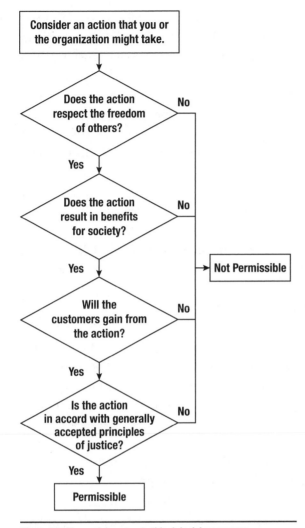

Figure 8.5. The social contract ethical decision process.

This chapter introduces the idea of the social contract as a moral standard of right and wrong. It is time to consider some of the pros and cons of this approach. Pros (arguments in support or strengths) will be identified by the symbol (+) while cons (arguments against or statements of weakness) will be identified by the symbol (-).

(+) Social contract attempts an elegant articulation of the basis of moral authority that is applicable to many situations.[19] Such authority is based on voluntary consent. It is possible to articulate a set of universal agreements that set the ground rules for ethical behavior and that the moral authority of these agreements "derives from the assumption that humans, acting rationally, would consent to the terms of some particular societal agreement."[20]

(+) Interdependence is embedded in and honored by the social contract. Only when one person is willing to limit personal freedom can the freedoms of others be ensured. Only when business constrains its behavior can the marketplace be truly free.

(+) The social contract is a collection of implicit agreements among members of society which contain norms of behavior "derived from shared goals, beliefs and attitudes of groups or communities or people."[21]

(+) The social contract is different from the formal agreements used in society. This is why it is called social as contrasted with legal contracts. Because it is a different form of expectation does not mean that the concept is invalid.

The idea of the social contract as a standard of conduct in business has been criticized by some. Here is a summary of the weaknesses of the social contract.

(-) The social contract is not really a contract. It is not an explicit contract in that it is

interests. The social contract assumes that everyone shares the belief that liberty is the goal. The social contract also assumes that all should be equal. It includes an element of duty to others while not undermining freedom.

Further, in order for the social contract to be practical, the whole fabric of a free society depends on consistent application of the contract. If one business organization is allowed to have an exception, this undermines true freedom for all the rest of the organizations in the marketplace.

not in writing anywhere. Members of society and owners businesses do not sign a document saying that they agree to certain things in exchange for considerations. It is not an implied contract in the same way that implied contracts operate in society. For example, if the time of an agreement between two parties expires and the two parties continue to do business with each other, there is an implied agreement to renew the contract. There is no "meeting of the minds" per se. Society and the business owners do not speak with each other regarding mutual expectations. Most people who start a business simply comply with the provisions of the law for business license, filing articles of incorporation, establishing a relationship with state and federal taxation authorities and meeting other requirements. Business owners are not aware of other expectations to serve society's interests other than what is required in the law.

(-) If a business is already large and powerful with respect to customers, suppliers or society in general, there is no incentive for it to consent to limit its freedom other than the economic incentive to act in its own narrow self-interest.[22] The social contract is based on the principle of consent.[23] If consent is given, a moral obligation is established in the relationship. However, there is no evidence that consent is given between the parties. Contract terminology is used to describe obligations when, in fact, no agreement has been established between the parties other than an expectations that both parties agree to obey public law. Further, consent is required but the social contract theory offers nothing substantial for why a person or business should consent when it might be in their best self-interest not to consent.[24] If the only goods in view in the social contract are those goods that

can be obtained in this life, the social contract is a flawed concept because it is not always in the best interest of a marketplace actor to curb self-interest and to be moral.[25]

(-) As a valid ethical theory the social contract does not define what is right and wrong by itself but instead leaves the definition of right and wrong ambiguous. If ethics is based on the social contract which is based on someone's perception of what others in society expect, is this a valid standard? Perception of what others believe makes it little different from common sense or cultural relativism. For the reason that common sense is weak, the social contract also is weak.

DOWN TO THE NITTY-GRITTY

Think about the opening story at the beginning of this chapter. You are the product manager for the computer printer company. What is the socially expected right thing to do? It's time to get down to the nitty-gritty (see table 8.2)!

THROUGH THE LENS OF BIBLICAL THEMES

This part of the chapter will use the biblical story themes as a lens through which to evaluate the ethical approach featured in the chapter. Because the themes are interrelated and interdependent, we should expect to see some overlap in the thinking regarding the ethical approach. Some themes will contribute the same thinking as will other themes. The power of these themes comes from their guidance when a community of people talks about complicated ethical dilemmas faced in business practice.

Some elements of the social contract are consistent with biblical themes. After reviewing the biblical themes, we can say that these themes envision an implicit agreement

Table 8.2. Applying the ethical process.

Keeping Your Heart: An Intrapersonal Process	Walking in the Community: An Interpersonal Process
• You are the product manager for the computer printer company. What does your heart say is the right thing to do regarding the presence of warning messages to consumers? • Which biblical themes explored in this book inform your heart on this situation? • Which biblical theme, if any, do you feel yourself resisting? Why do you feel resistance? • What implicit social contract does your company have with society? Does this contract include displaying warning messages? • Is the social contract sufficient on its own to guide you to decide what is right and wrong? If not, what additional perspective is needed?	• You are the product manager for the computer printer company. With whom might you have a conversation about the issue of warning messages? Who else might have a helpful perspective? • Which of the biblical themes in this chapter will most likely come up in the conversation either directly or indirectly? Why? Which one(s) will be the most influential in the conversation? • If you have a conversation with someone regarding this situation, which of the fundamental tensions presented earlier in the book might come up? • What right-versus-right dilemmas, if any, can be identified? Have a conversation with someone about this now. What is the outcome of the conversation?

among members of society that each will act in such a way so that the benefits envisioned for one are experienced by all. But the question becomes whether or not the so-called secular social contract by itself goes far enough to define what is right and wrong.

Cosmic conflict. Voluntary consent is at the heart of the issues in the cosmic conflict. Without voluntary consent, God would not be worthy of our worship and loyalty. God's ideal for his creatures is to foster freedom of choice, but in order for freedom to be truly enjoyed it must have limits. Thus, true freedom is achieved by constraining behaviors so that the freedom of others is preserved. Consent in the biblical view is not merely an arbitrary rational decision but rather consent made in the context of the larger shared goals of the faith community.

Creation. Interdependence is at the root of human relationships at creation. Humans are helpers for each other and co-workers with God in serving. The community at creation was placed in an environment designed to foster a flourishing life. To achieve this, humans were given freedom, but within constraints. Humans also had responsibilities to God, to each other and to the earth.

Holiness. Deep consecration to God does not require that we separate ourselves from or become insensitive to how other people in our social group or society in general believe regarding right and wrong. Being aware of what others expect of us is important so that we can be thoughtful in our consecration to God. The idea of commitment to following a set of important, fundamental principles is important in our relationship to God and with others. Followers of God should be known for their stable commitments. However, commitments are not made superficially or thoughtlessly. They are made after having considered the potential costs that might be incurred especially when other persons are not as committed.

Covenant relationships. Covenant relationships are both individual and communal in nature. The covenant relationship is built on an implicit agreement by members of the community that the principles of the covenant will guide their lives. In order for individuals to flourish, they must be in a community where they contribute to flourishing of others. In order for the community to flourish, the community must allow for individuals to choose actions that are designed to promote community well-being and allow for individual well-being, too. In order for covenant relationships to be maintained, each individual in the relationship must give up a certain degree of individual freedom. It is the principles of covenant relationships that comprise the covenant social contract from the biblical story point of view. Observing covenant principles in all our relationships is the pathway to true way to freedom.[26]

> Interpreting the principles of the covenant relationship brings us to an important but challenging problem: the subjectivity with which we read Scripture. Accordingly, the biblical approach to counteract subjectivity is to have a community of faith participate together in conversation about the Word of God and what it means for our life today.

Shalom. Shalom envisions the covenant relationships that demonstrate the flourishing life of well-being. The implicit understanding in covenant social contract is that in order to experience the blessings of shalom, each person must contribute by being a blessing to others.

Sabbath. Meaningful work contributes to well-being of the worker and those whom he or she serves. By keeping sabbath, each worker continually acknowledges that Jesus Christ is Lord of life. Sabbath means contributing to the rest that others may experience. It means renouncing human autonomy.

Justice. Biblical justice involves continually honoring the rights of others. It means actively taking actions that promote fairness at all levels and all corners of society. This requires an implicit agreement that our relationships

with each other are impartial, that is, we do not place our self in any advantageous position with respect to any other person. Justice is fostered in both the formal justice system and the informal relationships in community.

Righteousness. Faithfulness to promises and acting in ways that are right for the other person are at the foundation of the biblical social contract. A person who brings righteousness to the marketplace acts with honor and preserves and lends stability to covenant relationships. Such a person invests in community by placing the interests of others above narrow self-interests.

Truth. Biblical ideals for relationships hold that there needs to be a close correspondence between actions and expectations of others in the community. Community members depend on this consistency and reliability. Accordingly, faithfulness is a key element at the basic level of relationships. It is part of the social contract.

Wisdom. The wise person in the Bible story is the person who listens to the community, who watches out for the community but also protects himself or herself from being misled. Getting counsel from others who are committed to being faithful to covenant principles assumes that these others have your best good in mind. Furthermore, this requires an implicit trust at the root of the social contract. Wisdom is not merely skill mastery for personal good isolated from faithfulness, loyalty and respect to relationships. Wisdom means taking actions that serve the good of others.

Loving kindness. Love in the biblical story is always other-focused. It never seeks its own in isolation from social relationships. Love means being loyal to certain principles even when someone else makes us angry. The implicit agreement in love is that we will continue to show respect to each other even when we have differences of opinion. The covenantal social contract involves an implicit expectation that each person will love even his or her enemy by declining to take vengeance. Each will follow the Golden Rule. A person's enemy is also part of the community and part of God's children. Loving others involves fostering mutuality and demonstrating loyalty in action.

Redemption. In spite of the implicit covenantal agreement to foster relationships that promote well-being and flourishing life, the reality is that the implicit contract is broken. When this happens, the covenant principles have one additional provision contained in this theme of redemption: Take a leadership position to recover lost shalom. One Christian philosopher argues that without a belief in the afterlife with expectations of happiness, the social contract has limited value to offer happiness. "Only if there is a next life in which virtue is attainable and issues forth in happiness, may one be properly motivated to be moral."[27] This view seems to gloss over or ignore the principles contained in the biblical story themes. Story themes encourage not only looking to the future to the ultimate redemption but also looking to the present to see how we can contribute to redeeming relationships now by fostering well-being through covenant relationships.

CHAPTER REVIEW QUESTIONS

1. What is the definition of the term "community"?

2. What is a psychological contract?

3. What contribution did Plato, Hobbes, Locke and Rousseau provide for our understanding of the social contract?

4. Describe the social contract in terms of the business relationships.

5. What are the pros and cons of the social contract as an approach to decision making?

6. What perspective do the biblical story themes provide when considering the idea of social contract?

DISCUSSION QUESTIONS

1. What additional arguments might someone put forward in support of or in challenge to the social contract as an approach to decision making?

2. Do you think that social contracts exist in society? If so, what is the content of this contract?

3. What is the difference between social contract and covenant? Between the social contract and cultural relativism?

4. If civil law and enforcement mechanisms are required to deter persons from acting opportunistically toward other citizens, what barriers are possible for multinational enterprises?

ETHICAL VIGNETTE TO DISCUSS

For the vignette described below, apply the biblical story themes to discern what is right and wrong.

1. Your firm, an outsource partner under contract with a large corporation, provided a specialized set of tasks that helped them manage the supply chain more efficiently. The mantra around your company has been, "Never Forget: Our Customers Can Always Do What We Do!" In one staff meeting you heard the top boss remark that if your firm did not do its job, your customers would find a way to do the work themselves. "Just remember that every day

we do our job well, we teach them how to do the same work without us," he said. Some employees' employment status was recently changed from hourly employee to exempt professional employee, meaning that exempt employees are not paid overtime pay. Lately managers have been asking these professional employees to put in longer hours to get the work done. Obviously, no one is talking about raises, and this stands to reason given that your firm is an outsource partner and must perform the tasks for less money than it would cost the corporation who contracts for your services. Plus, your firm must interact with the employees of the corporation as if your team were insiders but be more polite with them than they are with you. Lately, your boss has been making statements about the need to "make changes" if the team cannot get its work done with less. He sent around an article about rising un-

employment. The previous month he sent around an article on the state of the economy. During staff meeting he hinted of the possibility of layoffs, but when staff members asked about the specifics, he denied that a specific layoff had been planned. Then one day you notice on his desk a copy of *The Black Book of Outsourcing*, an annual survey report that evaluates the satisfaction that corporations have with their outsource partner contractors.[28] You notice a piece of paper sticking out of the report marking one page. On the top of the book mark is written "Staff meeting agenda." You have heard other employees talk about looking for work elsewhere. One said openly in the lunch room the other day, "I'm not going to wait around for this company to axe me. I'm out of here the first chance I get." You are getting concerned. What is the psychological contract that is at stake here?

9

Utilitarianism

Do what is best for the most people.

Do the most good.

SCRIPTURE PASSAGE

Our people must also learn to engage in good deeds to meet pressing needs, so that they will not be unfruitful. (Tit 3:14)

CHAPTER OVERVIEW

In this chapter we will introduce one of the most popular approaches to making decisions in the environment of business. In particular, we will

- explore the distinction between utility and utilitarianism

- explain the concept of utilitarianism as a moral decision-making method

- critique utilitarianism in terms of its benefits and objections

- evaluate utilitarianism through the lens of biblical story themes

MAIN TOPICS

Historical Roots of Utilitarianism
Definitions and Distinctions
The Utilitarian Analysis Process
Evaluation: Pros and Cons
Down to the Nitty-Gritty
Through the Lens of Biblical Themes

KEY TERMS

act utilitarianism, aggregate welfare, ends, means, mutual advantage, rule utilitarianism, utility, utilitarianism

OPENING SCENARIO

Your company manufactures wood chipper machines that lawn and garden maintenance companies, municipalities and hardware retailers purchase.[1] One of the key components of the chipper is the engine. Your company also rebuilds and resells used lawn and garden tractors and other items. One of the ways you keep the unit costs low is by purchasing gasoline engines from a liquidator, a firm that cuts deals with manufacturers to buy their unsold inventory (last year's models, close-out models, etc.) which the liquidator sells to companies like yours.

The salesman for the liquidator calls you on the telephone. "I found the lot of engines that you need for your next run of wood chippers. We just took shipment of these little numbers into our warehouse yesterday afternoon. But here's the deal: I know we agreed on a price of $250 per unit, but come to find out this price was below cost for the manufacturer. I think this is one reason why this manufacturer is filing for bankruptcy. We are suing the supplier. I know you need your engines, but I got to charge you a little more than the original quote."

"What?" you ask. "We had a price agreement! I don't care if that engine manufacturer is financially collapsing. Anyway, this is the nature of liquidation. You make deals with companies that want to unload inventory, and we along with hundreds of other customers take these products and find a way to add value. I'm not paying the higher price!" Your company has made promises to several retailers and other organizations that sell to thousands of lawn and garden maintenance contractors.

"I'd like to ship these to you, but I just cannot do that unless we get a revised price," is his reply.

"Send the engines. We'll pay," you say, discouraged because this will make the unit costs go up by at least fifty dollars each.

"Okay, but we will need a certified check, or we can send the units C.O.D. [cash on delivery]," he says.

"What?" you shout. "We are always good for payment; you know that!"

"Nothing I can do about it this time. My boss is saying certified check or C.O.D. or no engines," he says.

Reluctantly you agree but fume about it in the lunch room.

One way to look at this situation is to determine what outcomes result for all involved. This gets to the heart of what is known as utilitarianism.

HISTORICAL ROOTS OF UTILITARIANISM

Utilitarian ideas are fundamental to economic theory.[2] As a philosophy or model of ethical decision making utilitarianism is popular among some people who do not fully understand it. The problem often is, however, that some persons want what they believe is the benefit of utilitarianism without doing the work of a true utilitarian. "With noted exceptions, most free market economists have been utilitarians; they have made Utilitarianism an intrinsic part of their explanation of how the economy works and should work."[3]

Utilitarianism is based on an ancient Greek concept regarding happiness (*eudaimonia*). For the Greeks, happiness included enjoyment, pleasure, human fulfillment and the capability of realizing satisfactions to or achievements of basic interests.[4] For example, being loved and respected and achieving knowledge and understanding are basic human interests which, when fulfilled, bring happiness.

Utilitarianism emerged in Great Britain among social reformers who realized that to be effective in reform they had to engage in dialogue with leaders of key stakeholder groups that would be affected by their reform efforts. One of the most vocal supporters of the idea was Jeremy Bentham (1748–1832), a social and legal reformer who "laid down the principle that one should act so as to produce the greatest good for the greatest number of persons in the long run."[5] In his plan for prisons, workhouses and other institutions, Bentham devised compensation programs, building designs, worker schedules and even new accounting systems. He advocated a government which provided guaranteed employment, minimum wages and social benefits.

Bentham had a large influence on a group of economists, including James Mill and his

---

JOHN STUART MILL'S RELIGIOUS BELIEFS

• Utilitarianism started at creation: God wants us to be happy!
• Utilitarianism is the essence of the Golden Rule.

---

son John Stuart Mill. John Stuart Mill refined and popularized utilitarian concepts. He became the most persuasive proponent of the ideas of his time.

John Stuart Mill based his ideas of utilitarianism on the Bible story of creation. As Mill interpreted the Bible he believed that at creation God showed that he wants humans to be happy. "If it be a true belief that God desires, above all things, the happiness of his creatures, and that this was his purpose in their creation, utilities is not only not a godless doctrine gone, but more profoundly religious than any other."[6] Humans should follow this and seek to foster the greatest happiness possible and to prevent as much pain as possible. This is the standard of morality.

Mill also saw in the teachings of Jesus Christ the essence of utilitarianism: "In the golden rule of Jesus of Nazareth, we read the complete spirit of the ethics of utility. To do as one would be done by, and to love one's neighbor as oneself, constitute the ideal perfection of utilitarian morality."[7]

Mill recognized that humans have the power and will to sacrifice their personal good for the good of others; however, the sacrificial act is not the good, but rather the consequence of the self-sacrifice is. Self-sacrifice that does not result in more happiness for others is wasted.

For most Christians a key question is to what degree a person subordinates utility considerations to other principles of right and wrong as described in God's law. On this issue Mill held to a hierarchy of principles. He be-

lieved that some principles (such as justice) take precedence over other considerations. These principles provide a social utility that sometimes are vastly more important. For example, in Mill's mind saving a life is more important than telling the truth. In some cases, it is not only allowable but also a duty to steal or tell a lie in order to save someone's life.[8]

Every tree that does not bear good fruit is cut down and thrown into the fire. (Mt 3:10)

DEFINITIONS

Utility is not identical with utilitarianism. Utility is an economic idea: it is a measure of satisfaction we gain from certain marketplace choices we make.[9] Utility also means being useful. We calculate or estimate (even if it is not numerical) the expected satisfaction of an action. After taking the action, we evaluate to what degree the expected satisfaction was the same as the actual satisfaction. We balance our wishes when we cannot get everything we want, but we try our best to get what we want. Utility may or may not consider outcomes to other people or organizations. When utility is concerned only for the consequences that affect the decision maker, it is essentially egoism in practice.

Utility requires us to compare the present short term with the future long run. We remember the outcomes from past choices and apply memory to today. Personal utility is what people do when considering what they want to achieve for themselves. We come up with a cost-benefit evaluation and weigh the result of an action as it affects our self. Utility can be applied to yourself or to an organization. The point is that the guiding principle is in finding the way to optimize the good for oneself or for one's organization.[10]

By itself, utility does not recognize other universal moral standards as being valid for guiding behavior unless these standards have been found to produce optimal behavior. Concerned about the impact of an action on the decision maker, utility may end up sacrificing justice for expedience. Isolated from other dimensions of life and value, with personal utility there are no moral differences between goods and harms. Taken to its logical extreme, personal utility would on occasion require the taking of innocent lives to save the lives of others. Accordingly, if maximizing utility is life's guiding principle, it essentially reduces to egoism.

In contrast, utilitarianism is concerned about the impact of an action on all affected stakeholders, not just the decision maker. This difference between the effect on just the decision maker and the effect on all stakeholders who are affected by the decision is important.

Utilitarianism is "an ethical theory that holds that an action is right if it produces, or if it tends to produce, the greatest amount of good for the greatest number of people affected by the action. Otherwise the action is wrong."[11] Utilitarianism, when properly applied, impartially applies the analysis of outcomes.

For the utilitarian, justice is defined by the consequences of an action. Thus, utilitarianism is based on the effect of consequences on people and organizations. It is collective consequences that make an action moral or immoral. This

requires making an assumption that current actions will have future consequences. This requires us to assume that humans can correctly anticipate the consequences.[12]

Utilitarianism requires an impersonal approach. No person or organization, even the decision maker, gets a preferential treatment. A particular person's or organization's good counts for no more than that experienced by others. Furthermore, all outcomes, whether good or bad, must be considered. In the environment of business, outcomes may be mixed: for some people the outcomes are good, and for other people the outcome is bad. Utilitarianism says that for an action to be morally right, the total good outcomes must outweigh all the bad outcomes for everyone who is affected.

For example, Solyndra, LLC, a solar-panel manufacturing firm, received a $535-million loan guarantee in March 2009 under a United States Department of Energy program. One year later, in March 2010, auditors raised concerns about the financial viability of Solyndra. On January 1, 2011, the firm owed the US government $527 million. In August 2011, Solyndra operations shut down and most workers were laid off. The next month Solyndra filed for bankruptcy protection. Was it right that the US government helped Solyndra? The utilitarian will first identify the key stakeholders. In this case the major stakeholders are the executive branch of the federal government, Solyndra as a company, the managers and workers at Solyndra and their families, the taxpayers, Solyndra's suppliers and competitors both domestic and global.

Next the utilitarian will be as fair as possible in estimating the consequences of the government loan. Some stakeholders (Solyndra and its managers and workers) will be helped. Others might be harmed (taxpayers). Still other stakeholders will have no particular positive or negative consequences. For the utilitarian it is the cumulative net impact of the action on all stakeholders that matters, not just the local impact on a particular stakeholder.

Next, the utilitarian will think of an alternative action and conduct the same analysis using the same stakeholder groups. There may be other alternatives to consider. Finally, the net consequences of each of the various alternatives will be compared. The one to choose is the one that will result in the most good and least harm collectively. If the utilitarian believes that more good is accomplished in the long run by the government offering the loan, this is the morally just thing to do. However, if the utilitarian believes that another alternative, such as not offering a loan, is better over the long run, then this is the right thing to do.

Notice that the utilitarian anticipates and calculates the outcomes of a particular action and its best alternatives.

Actions that are taken by others can change the level of well-being of themselves and of others either by improving it or making it worse. Humans may or may not be correct in evaluating their current state of well-being. Even if a human is incorrect in judging the current state of well-being, there is an objective truth regarding that person's well-being. Some qualities of well-being are higher in value than other qualities. For example, it is generally considered better if a person is employed than unemployed.

DISTINCTIONS

A few additional distinctions can be made when studying utilitarianism. First is the distinction between duties and consequences. Duties are obligations we have based on principles that are not dependent on outcomes or consequences. Consequences are the expected outcomes of an action. Utilitarians emphasize consequences of actions. Interestingly, utilitarians say that it is our duty to consider the consequences of our actions on all relevant stakeholders! But the actual decision-making approach is based not on duties but rather on expected outcomes.

> For the utilitarian, justice is defined by the expected consequences of an action.

Second, we need to distinguish between ends (goals) and means (actions taken to achieve the goals). Utilitarians emphasize the goals, thus seeking to maximize the net aggregate good. The means used to achieve a goal become important only if the means breach some obvious goal which has a known outcome which must be either avoided or achieved. Otherwise it does not matter what means are used to achieve the goal.

Sometimes you might hear the phrase "the ends justify the means." This is used to describe a person who decided to achieve a worthy goal but used an action that otherwise would be considered unethical. The person then tried to give a rationale for the action based on the goal.

Third, we must distinguish between mutual advantage and aggregate welfare. This is an important distinction! Utilitarians emphasize the effect of actions on the aggregate welfare of all those affected by the action. Aggregate welfare may be offset by some stakeholders obtaining an advantage over other stakeholders. Utilitarianism is built not on mutual advantage for stakeholders but rather aggregate welfare of stakeholders. The mutual

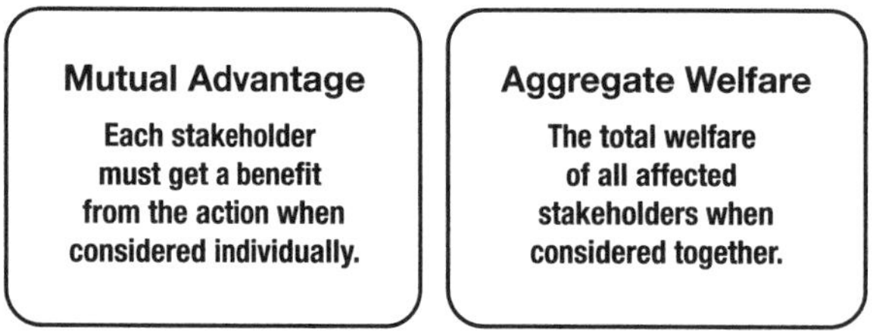

Figure 9.1. The distinction between mutual advantage and aggregate welfare.

advantage viewpoint holds the following: "in order for something to be justified as a common good, each person involved must be shown to derive some benefit from it. On an aggregate-welfare view, what matters is the overall total welfare, regardless of whether the position of every individual is improved."[13]

Fourth, utilitarianism emphasizes thinking about the rightness or wrongness of an action before taking it. When attempting to evaluate the goodness or badness of an action based on its consequences, we must evaluate the *expected* consequences rather than the *actual* consequences. In other words, goodness or badness is anticipated. Of course, retrospectively we can evaluate the outcomes of an action and from this learn for the future.

Fifth is the distinction between act utilitarianism and rule utilitarianism. Should an action be considered (in comparison with reasonable alternatives) by itself, or should an action be considered as part of a class or category of actions? Act utilitarianism is the belief that each action should be evaluated using the test of utilitarianism. Rule utilitarianism is the belief that "we ought to act in accordance with a rule such that if everyone were to abide by it, the sum total of welfare would be maximised."[14] In other words, we should test the overall consequences of the relevant class of actions to

which a particular action belongs rather than test a particular action. For example, if we wanted to test whether it is wrong for a thief to break into a particular person's house and steal something, the rule utilitarian would test the general consequences of stealing things that people have in their homes. In contrast, the act utilitarian would use the utilitarian test for the particular situation and the particular house in question.

Rule utilitarianism makes it easier for us to be impartial and apply the utilitarian test universally to all persons in similar situations as well as in the particular situation. This minimizes the chances that we will want to impose a personal bias using the utilitarian test. We may not be able to precisely anticipate the specific outcome for the particular person, but we are more likely to be able to anticipate the general consequences which are reasonable to expect.

THE UTILITARIAN ANALYSIS PROCESS

Following utilitarianism is, from one perspective, straightforward.[15] When considering an action, the utilitarian will place the action in the context of choosing from among reasonable alternatives available. The consequences of each must be assessed. This is done so that we can be assured that the choice we make is compared with the outcomes of other

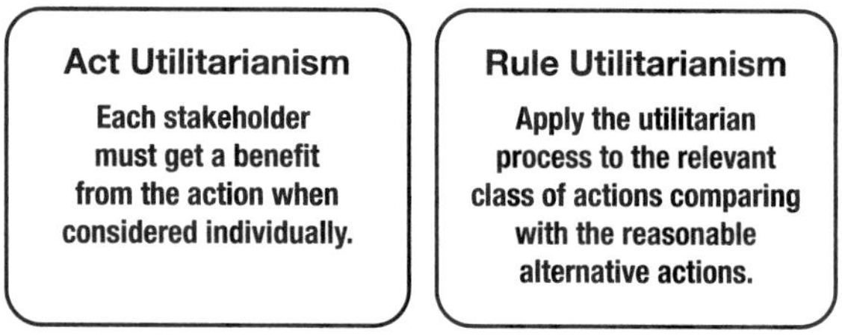

Figure 9.2. A comparison of act utilitarianism and rule utilitarianism.

choices available to us. Indeed, it would be impossible for the utilitarian to evaluate the moral goodness or badness of an action unless the goodness or badness of alternative actions also is considered.

Of course it is a little more involved than this, because determining or estimating the benefits and costs can be difficult prior to experiencing the consequences of an action.

Utilitarianism must consider the impact of an action on all affected stakeholders. Accordingly, we must identify who are the stakeholders. Who will be affected by the action?

Next the utilitarian will estimate the good and bad consequences for each stakeholder or stakeholder group for each relevant alternative. Good outcomes will be impartially weighed against bad outcomes. To do this, the utilitarian must use the information that is available before the choice is made. But the job is not done yet! We must also consider the impact of the outcomes on stakeholders who are indirectly affected by the action.

Using an impartial approach to weigh the good and the bad outcomes so as not to bias the results in our own favor or in the favor of any particular stakeholder, next we estimate the net or total outcome for each stakeholder. We use the same stakeholders or stakeholder groups for evaluating the outcomes of the action and each of the alternatives. The utilitarian process can be summarized in this way:

- Identify the possible courses of action that appear feasible.

- Identify the stakeholders who are affected.

- Fairly estimate the foreseeable benefits and harms that would result from each action.

- Choose the course of action that provides the greatest benefits after the costs have been estimated.

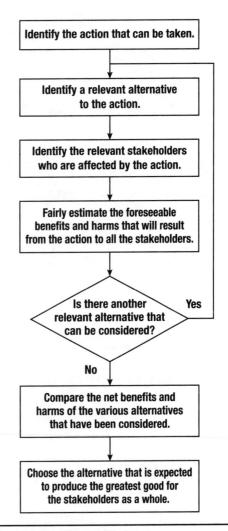

Figure 9.3. The utilitarian ethical process.

The utilitarian ethics process is illustrated in figure 9.3.

If the action we are considering produces more good than bad compared with what is produced by the outcomes of other actions, the action is morally right. Comparing different actions, the action with the most positive outcome for the most people is the right one. This procedure is illustrated in table 9.1, Utilitarian Worksheet 1, and table 9.2, Utilitarian Worksheet 2. Only two worksheets are shown here. If additional alternatives are considered, a worksheet might be prepared for each. The

Table 9.1. Utilitarian worksheet 1: action A.

Action A			
State a summary of the action being evaluated.			
Identify a key stakeholder who is affected by the action.	Good Consequences	Bad Consequences	Net Outcome
Identify a key stakeholder who is affected by the action.	Good Consequences	Bad Consequences	Net Outcome
Identify a key stakeholder who is affected by the action.	Good Consequences	Bad Consequences	Net Outcome
What is the net outcome of your analysis, and what is your recommendation in terms of this action?			

Table 9.2. Utilitarian worksheet 2: action B.

Action B (the alternative to A)			
State a summary of the alternative action being evaluated.			
Identify a key stakeholder who is affected by the action.	Good Consequences	Bad Consequences	Net Outcome
Identify a key stakeholder who is affected by the action.	Good Consequences	Bad Consequences	Net Outcome
Identify a key stakeholder who is affected by the action.	Good Consequences	Bad Consequences	Net Outcome
What is the net outcome of your analysis, and what is your recommendation in terms of this action?			

results of each worksheet are then compared to determine which action is morally right.

EVALUATION: PROS AND CONS

Utilitarianism is an ethical theory that is closely associated with business activities. Considering the costs and benefits of an action is standard procedure for many managerial decisions. As an ethical decision-making approach utilitarianism may be one of the most popular.

The thesis of utilitarianism is that when faced with a decision you should decide in favor of the action that will produce or tend to produce the greatest amount of good for the most people who are affected. Utilitarianism is not the same as egoism, because it considers the effect of an action not only on the actor but also on all affected.

One problem with utilitarianism is that you cannot always be sure of a favorable outcome

your action. Sometimes an unfavorable consequence can result from what you expected would be a right action.

Utilitarianism offers much that is attractive in the world of business. Lawmakers at the local, state and national level may use utilitarian principles when creating or amending laws.

(+) It takes into consideration that many people or organizations can be affected by a business decision. This is one of the ethical theories that respect the interests of all key stakeholders in a given situation. Moral principles are equally applicable to all persons. In this, utilitarianism broadens the scope of those considered and moves away from egoism. "Utilitarianism, far from being a self-serving approach to moral issues, demands careful, objective and impartial evaluation of consequences."[16]

(+) It recognizes that in reality some marketplace actions bring benefits to some people and harm to others.

(+) It weighs the costs and benefits of an action to the organization and thereby considers the goals of the organization. This promotes being a responsible steward of organizational resources.

(+) This method takes into consideration the consequences of our actions. Consequences are important to our understanding of responsibility.[17] Humans have the ability to anticipate the effect of our actions on others and foresee what can happen that is helpful or hurtful. If we do not consider the consequences of our actions, we gloss over an important dimension of social life.

(+) Utilitarianism assumes that the persons deciding the rightness or wrongness of an action will take responsibility to watch out for the interests of stakeholders other than themselves.

Utilitarianism, if used alone, also shows some weaknesses.[18] Some objections to utilitarianism include the following:

(-) Utilitarians hold that the end justifies the means; however, this is clearly wrong. An "act is not automatically good simply because it has a good goal. The means to achieve it must be judged good by some objective standard of good."[19] "Something is not good because the intentions underlying it are good; it is good only if the actions are also good."[20] Utilitarianism has no need for absolute moral standards of right and wrong apart from consequences. It offers nothing substantial for how to define what is good or bad. What is good for one person may be bad for another. Thus, right and wrong are defined in terms of culturally determined or individually determined standards of good and bad.

(-) Utilitarianism usually leads to majority rule; however, "certain principles of right and justice should be respected even if they do not always benefit the majority."[21]

(-) How can a person possibly foresee all of the consequences of any particular action and as a result calculate all the consequences? History teaches us that some consequences are unintentional. Humans might not anticipate the most important consequences. Proponents of utilitarianism argue that we can foresee a large number of expected consequences because we have the benefit of having learned from experience. If we take an action and later learn that one or more consequences were unexpected, we can change for the future taking into consideration the new information. We are not required to calculate all the consequences before we act. Using rule utilitarianism we have our collective memory of the likely impact of similar actions.

(-) If we must consider the effect of a decision on all the people that might be affected by an action, such a task is practically beyond the time and resources that most people have available for making business decisions in a fast-paced environment. When used correctly utilitarianism is intellectually demanding. Evidence must be gathered and interpreted without personal bias (which is difficult in itself). There may be differences of opinion regarding the interpretation or meaning of certain facts or expected outcomes from an action. In addition, if we are unable to bring about the amount of positive welfare (or prevent an unfavorable amount of harm), we would fail in using this approach in practice. If it is difficult always to successfully use this method in practice, it is an unrealistic approach. Utilitarians may grant that it is difficult work to gather information and make decisions under time pressure, but just because it is difficult does not mean we should abandon the method.

(-) Utilitarianism apparently pays no attention to how welfare is distributed. Achieving the net positive welfare for the most will sometimes require that some people get a great amount of welfare and some people get a little amount, or worse yet, get a bad result from an action.[22] If those who get more welfare from an action already are in an advantageous position with respect to welfare (in comparison to people who are generally disadvantaged), it does not seem right that they get more welfare at the expense of others. Further, such an action would do nothing to alleviate chronic maldistributions of resources.

(-) Utilitarians' emphasis on aggregate welfare rather than mutual advantage "opens them to the charge that they could allow the imposition of unreasonable sacrifices on the few in order to promote the welfare of the many."[23] "The utilitarian injunction to maximize aggregate welfare requires that the welfare of the few be sacrificed for the sake of the welfare of the many."[24] Utilitarian arguments are based on the assumption that what a person does for himself or herself (choose to give up some good in one part of life in exchange for good in another part of life) a community can also do in the same way. But the aggregate of persons is not a super "aggregate person" who can seek to maximize its own welfare without regard to the welfare of individual persons. Aggregates of persons are made up of separate, individual persons.

DOWN TO THE NITTY-GRITTY

Think about the opening story at the beginning of this chapter. You are a sales person wanting to sell small gasoline engines to the wood chipper assembly company. What is the right thing to do? It's time to get down to the nitty-gritty (see table 9.3)!

THROUGH THE LENS OF BIBLICAL THEMES

This part of the chapter will use the biblical story themes as a lens through which to evaluate the ethical approach featured in the chapter. Because the themes are interrelated and interdependent, we should expect to see some overlap in the thinking regarding the ethical approach. Some themes will contribute the same thinking as will other themes. The power of these themes comes from their guidance when a community of people talks about complicated ethical dilemmas faced in business practice.

Cosmic conflict. God's idea of utility is different from that of humans. God found it

Table 9.3. Applying the ethical process.

Keeping Your Heart: An Intrapersonal Process	Walking in the Community: An Interpersonal Process
• You are a sales person wanting to sell small gasoline engines. What does your heart say is the right thing to do regarding the issue of the agreement and pricing? • Which biblical themes explored in this book inform your heart on this situation? • Which biblical theme, if any, do you feel yourself resisting? Why do you feel resistance? • What stakeholders should you consider in this situation? What effect will this situation have on each depending on what you do? • Is utilitarianism sufficient on its own to guide you to decide what is right and wrong? If not, what additional perspective is needed?	• You are a sales person wanting to sell small gasoline engines. With whom might you have a conversation about the issue of the agreement and pricing? Who else might have a helpful perspective? • Which of the biblical themes in this chapter will most likely come up in the conversation either directly or indirectly? Why? Which one(s) will be the most influential in the conversation? • If you have a conversation with someone regarding this situation, which of the fundamental tensions presented earlier in the book might come up? • What right-versus-right dilemmas, if any, can be identified? Have a conversation with someone about this now. What is the outcome of the conversation?

useful to allow Satan and sin to coexist with righteousness in the universe for a time in order to show the true nature of his character. In his infinite wisdom, God has the unique ability that humans do not have: to foresee the end from the beginning. His ability to anticipate the ends of an action is perfect. Humans do not share this level of absolute perfection. The cosmic conflict shows that God has in mind beings other than himself in the universe. He does indeed desire the greatest happiness for his creatures; however, his definition of happiness is different from ours.

Creation. It was at creation that we see God's wisdom in action. He first prepared the environment in which covenantal relationships can flourish, and then he placed humans in a social context in that environment. Creation narrative shows that God desired the greatest good for all, not just the most. After sin, the great object was the restoration of broken relationships. Thus, utility, however God conceives of it, must be considered in this larger context of God's plan for restoration.

Holiness. The Bible is clear: We should look for ways to be useful to others. It is by being useful that we best serve God as his hands and feet to sustain and foster flourishing life. Usefulness is one way in which our consecration to God can be exhibited. Usefulness must be set apart for service to God, not merely for our own self-interests (though we should not forget our own needs either) but also for the good of others. Usefulness for the good of others is defined not in merely economic terms or cost-benefit terms but in terms of covenant relationships.

Covenant relationships. Covenant envisions outcomes in all dimensions of life, not just economic. Humans have been created with the ability to anticipate our effect on others.

Consequences are important because they have an impact on other human beings ability to experience freedom and flourishing life. Consequences change the nature of a relationship. Relationships cannot merely be built on the immediacy of the process but also must include consideration of short-term and long-term outcomes. Some consequences may be difficult or impossible to restore. Outcomes may affect stakeholders who are beyond the immediate relationship. Duty without consequences leads to uncaring. Consequences without duty lead to egoism. Some actions are wrong simply because of the effect of the consequences on the community. Some duties are required because of the risk of consequences. The Bible condemns utility if it is achieved immorally (e.g., stealing).

Shalom. Shalom was not just the ideal for the most people. Every person is to keep in mind shalom and to act in such a way that all persons benefit from it. In contrast to utilitarianism, which emphasizes aggregate welfare, shalom promotes aggregate welfare and mutual advantage. Poverty is not God's plan for humans. The whole community has a responsibility to contribute to the alleviation of poverty. Shalom means safety from harm. Thus, decision makers in the community will ensure that community decisions do not bring harm.

Sabbath. Sabbath involves resting from grasping for more. Persons could be harmed because of the utilitarian actions of others who desire for more. Thus, followers of God will rest from this. Sabbath, a miniature representation of the entire covenant relationship with God to be imitated, encourages decision making such that flourishing life in all its dimensions is promoted. Sabbath is a structural way to place limits on the constant push for more economic wealth. It encourages the pursuit of the other dimensions of shalom.

Justice. Justice in the Bible is not defined by generating the most good for the most people. Justice requires that good be shared even with the most disadvantaged and vulnerable. Even the minority who might be harmed by a utilitarian action must be preserved from harm. Accordingly, utilitarianism is an incomplete definition of justice.

Righteousness. Righteousness is not limited to the net positive outcomes when considering the negative consequences. Any utility that is calculated for self or for others is accomplished in the larger context of considering the impact on the covenant relationships with all and with God. Righteousness means taking actions that honor, preserve and lend stability to covenant relationships. This is the definition of common good regardless of the economic utility outcomes. It is not enough to calculate the aggregate welfare if we anticipate that some are harmed in the process. Decision makers will work so as to do no harm to any affected stakeholder.

Truth. On the one hand, truth (faithfulness) is meaningless unless consequences are considered. On the other hand, if only the consequences for the most people are considered, we are not being truthful for those who might be harmed in the process.

Wisdom. "Many scriptural texts run counter to utilitarian reasoning."[25] God has a concern for each individual person.[26] Jesus interacts with social outcasts.[27] Jesus treats children with care.[28] Jesus praises the action of the shepherd who seeks the one lost sheep.[29] Balancing these passages, we find other Scriptures that appear to support utility and usefulness.[30] Wisdom is a community resource, but individuals are not completely discounted for the good of the com-

munity. The Scripture assumes that humans will attempt to be as productive as possible. But this is not the same as utilitarianism. For example, humans are encouraged to be diligent in their work. In the Bible both economic gain and economic loss are seen as gifts from God.[31] As a result, unless circumstances outside the control of the diligent worker come up, the diligent should lack nothing and will be able to help others.[32] Diligence that makes for progress reflects the character of God to others. Yet some humans are more productive than others. Diligence is positively commanded while sloth is forbidden.[33]

Usefulness is prized in Scripture.[34] Pruning fruit-bearing plants results in higher production.[35] The implication is that higher production is better than lower production. Careful breeding of sheep will result in a healthier flock.[36] Grain farmers were aware of the factors that increase yield.[37] However, unproductive resources are spoken of in disapproving tones in the Bible.[38] It is unwise to use technology that is inefficient or useless. When a resource became unproductive, it was expected that the owner of the resource would get rid of it. Some activities are impractical and because of this are valued less than other, more practical activities.[39] This principle was used by Jesus to illustrate an important spiritual truth.[40] The principle of destroying unproductive resources may be the rationale behind Solomon's wisdom that there is a time to plant and a time to uproot that which is planted (i.e., when it becomes unproductive).[41] Christians are encouraged to make the most of every opportunity for the sake of the kingdom.[42] Implied in this are two fundamental concepts of efficiency and diligence. At the same time the Bible condemns utility if it is achieved immorally; stealing, which in some instances is the most efficient way to obtain goods, is condemned. For example, Ahab's stealing Naboth's vineyard was wrong.[43]

Loving kindness. Through the lens of biblical themes we see that acquiring resources, deciding how to use resources and distributing resources are actions designed to foster loving kindness in covenant relationships. Utilitarianism is silent on most of these actions. Utilitarianism seems to be less concerned about the loyalty to commitments we make in relationships. Thus, when an action is taken that may cause harm, loving kindness will direct decision makers to create mutual advantage rather than purely aggregate welfare.

Redemption. Redemption calls on us to rescue those who are harmed by marketplace decisions. While pursuing utility is important, also important is the recovery of lost shalom that results from decisions we make.

CHAPTER REVIEW QUESTIONS

1. What are the root ideas of utilitarianism as espoused by the English thinkers of the eighteenth and nineteenth centuries?

2. What distinction can be made between the concept of utility and utilitarianism?

3. What distinction is made between duty and consequences?

4. What is the difference between act utilitarianism and rule utilitarianism?

5. Describe the process that a utilitarian uses to make a decision regarding what is right and wrong.

6. What are the pros and cons of utilitarianism as an approach to making decisions?

7. How do the biblical story themes inform us regarding utilitarianism?

DISCUSSION QUESTIONS

1. Evaluate the pros and cons of utilitarianism. What would you add to the evaluation discussion?

2. What is the difference between egoism and utilitarianism?

3. What is the difference between utilitarianism and the biblical idea of wisdom?

4. Utilitarianism tends to contrast "being moral" with selfishness and egoism.[44] Is this a fair contrast?

5. Utilitarianism requires a person to take an impartial perspective of a situation, giving no special priority to self compared with other people. Doesn't the need to preserve life require a person to place himself or herself in a position of higher priority than is given to others?

ETHICAL VIGNETTES TO DISCUSS

For each of the vignettes described below, apply the biblical story themes to discern what is right and wrong.

1. Christians differ in their interpretation of Scripture on the economic concept of utility maximization, a concept related to the topic of this chapter. Jonathan Leightner argues that economic utility maximization is completely contrary to the scriptural principle of self-sacrificing love. He says, "If the maximizing of utility is my primary goal, then I will not love as Christ loved."[45] The two great commands say nothing about maximizing utility: love God, love others. Jesus commands us to feed the hungry, give water to the thirsty and shelter the stranger. "All these acts reduce the amount of income and time we have to spend on ourselves and, consequentially,

reduce our utility in the Neoclassical sense."[46] In contrast, John Rose argues that utility maximization is not moral philosophy. It is "simply a descriptive concept, and in no way is it intended to condone or encourage self-centeredness in personal behavior."[47] Economics does not say whether utility maximization is good or bad. Instead, it assumes that people tend to act in ways that maximize their utility. Jesus recognized utility maximization "as normal, instinctive human behavior and used the concept as a backdrop to emphasize how God intended for believers to behave toward others."[48] We should love others as we love our self. If love of self is the standard for loving others, Jesus must implicitly accept the idea that each person should seek his or her self-interest. Furthermore, he did not tell us to not be self-interested. Which of these points of view do you take? What is your rationale?

2. You are a partner in a start-up software development firm. The other partner is the software developer; you oversee the business side of the company, including marketing, contracting and accounting. One day you announce to your partner that you have received a request for software development services from a Christian nonprofit organization. They need their website updated. Their stated goal is to generate more interest from members of the community to attend their church. You describe all the things your firm does and make an offer. The person representing the Christian nonprofit organization verbally accepts your offer on the spot. When you report this to your partner, he asks, "What church is this?" When you tell him, he says, "My conscience does not allow me to do any work for a church that believes differently from how I believe. We cannot do work for this client."[49]

10

Universalism

*You cannot say yes and no
at the same time and mean it!*

SCRIPTURE PASSAGE

Do not be conformed to this world, but be transformed by the renewing of your mind, so that you may prove what the will of God is, that which is good and acceptable and perfect. (Rom 12:2)

CHAPTER OVERVIEW

In this chapter we will wrestle with one of the most insightful approaches to ethical decision making: universalism. In particular we will

- explore the connection that Immanuel Kant makes between religious beliefs and moral reasoning

- explain how Kant's categorical imperative works as a guide to ethical decision making

- evaluate the benefits and objections to the categorical imperative

- evaluate the categorical imperative through the lens of biblical story themes

MAIN TOPICS

Immanuel Kant's Religious Beliefs
Immanuel Kant's Teaching on Ethics
The Three Rational Tests of Morality
Evaluation: Pros and Cons
Down to the Nitty-Gritty
Through the Lens of Biblical Themes

KEY TERMS

autonomy test, categorical imperative, humanity test, king-subject rule, logical contradiction, supreme limiting condition, universalism, universal test

OPENING SCENARIO

Three and a half months before the scheduled December wedding, the parents of the groom asked a family member, who lived in the town where the wedding ceremony was to occur, to research the costs and menu options for catering the wedding rehearsal dinner. The groom was interested in serving Thai food to the wedding party and related persons the night before the wedding. The family's agent did just this. In September she contacted the only two Thai restaurants in the town and discussed with each the total price for food for forty guests and menu options, and the logistics of food delivery from restaurant to the site for the rehearsal dinner.

After discussing this, the decision makers narrowed the choice to one of the two restaurants. The groom was familiar with this restaurant and stated that this was his first choice. On a per-guest basis the total price was reasonable.

In November, the family's agent placed a specific order with the selected restaurant. The total price was agreed on, as were the details regarding delivery of food. It was later learned that the other Thai restaurant went out of business in November.

On Friday, the day before the rehearsal dinner, the family's agent called the restaurant to confirm the details of the order, including the number of guests who would be served which, the agent informed the restaurant owner, had been reduced from forty people to thirty-five people, and the logistics such as what time the food would be picked up and when and where the serving pans would be returned to the restaurant. It was during this phone call that the restaurant owner informed the family's agent that the total cost of the dinner would be two hundred dollars more than the original price quote even though the guest list had been reduced by five persons. The family's agent made a quick call to the groom's family reporting what had just happened. The groom's father said, "We have too many details that we are taking care of right now to make alternative plans. Plus, on what basis do we think we will get a better price if we contact another restaurant at this late date? If we switched suppliers, we will most likely pay an even greater premium at this last minute. The restaurant may have to race out and purchase extra food at the last minute just for this event. In the great scheme of things, this is a minor matter. Go ahead with the order."

KANT'S RELIGIOUS BELIEFS

For Immanuel Kant, the founder of universalism, all humans everywhere have the same needs, the same drives to coexist and cooperate in peace. All humans have the ability to use their God-given power of reason. This power provides the most fundamental principle and the irreducible minimum basis of all moral standards in all cultures and all times and circumstances. To grasp the power of Kant's ideas we will explore his religious beliefs and his beliefs regarding ethics.

Kant believed that the earth and all living things were created by God.[1] He reasoned that if humans continually expect to achieve happiness as a result of their actions, this requires us to believe that God exists who gives happiness to humans. He also reasoned that human power of reason must ask the question why the natural world exists. This reveals the God-given power to consider the question of purpose. The very fact that humans can ask such a question is an indicator that humans also have the ability to imagine the existence of God who created everything for a purpose. Kant also believed that humans were created with a special gift that animals do not have, namely, the powers of logical reasoning. Thus, humans have a fundamental duty to honor and respect all humans because all have this gift.

In spite of the ability of humans to use the gift of reason to make sense out of our reality, ultimately God's existence is a matter of faith. In his *Critique of Pure Reason*, Kant states that human beings cannot know with our senses that God exists. All human knowledge is a function of the limits to which our senses can experience reality. Humans were created with limits to our powers of logical reasoning. This allows room for religious faith. Table 10.1 provides a summary of Kant's beliefs regarding morality.

Table 10.1. Immanuel Kant's beliefs regarding morality.

God is the Creator of this world.	God's existence cannot be known by our senses or by reason alone. Faith is required to accept this. The limit to human reasoning is God's design which allows for faith.
God created human beings with the power of rational thought. This sets us apart from all other living creatures and is the basis of all choices we make.	Humans have a fundamental duty to use reason when deciding right from wrong. The purpose of rational thought is to align our intentions and commitments with our duty to relate to other humans in ways that support them.
God is the supreme head of the "kingdom of ends (purposes)." He has given all humans duties related to how we relate to each other in this kingdom.	By nature humans are members of this kingdom. Humans have the duty to treat all other rational beings with respect (as "ends in themselves" and never as "a means to an end"). When we treat another person as having a purpose in himself or herself and as having the same power of reasoning as we do, we share in the other person's purpose. This duty goes against the natural human tendency to selfishness.
To fulfill God's purpose for their lives, humans must obey the duties that God has given them.	Obedience to duty is not a mechanical formula to achieve happiness ("obey and God will reward you"). Instead, fulfilling our divinely ordained duties is to be pursued for its own sake because this is the right thing to do when living a life consistent with God's plan.
But knowing what our duties are cannot be known directly from God or from human experience.	Discerning our duties must be a process of using God-created rational thought.
Humans ought to obey these duties, but "ought" implies that we "can" do so. The problem is that humans, of their own will, cannot consistently obey these duties.	It is God who, by grace alone, works in us to change the natural tendency to live for our own happiness. Only by divine assistance can we be transformed to consistently live a life according to our God-given duties. This occurs by transforming our powers of reason. Because it is impossible for a person to know for certain whether or not God is transforming our minds, we must accept this by faith and use our reason to determine right from wrong.

KANT'S TEACHING ON ETHICS

Consistent with his Lutheran roots, Kant believed that moral goodness is not the number of good deeds one performs. Rather, moral goodness is the constant readiness to do what is called for by universal duty even if such actions are difficult or unpleasant or require us to lay aside our personal desires. How do we know which duties are universal? Only those duties that stand up to pure reason are universal.

For Kant, human beings all share the same fundamental characteristic of rational thought. Morality requires rational thought prior to action. This brings us to the most important assumption for Kant's ethics: Moral rules must apply impartially to all humans regardless of circumstance, location, ethnicity, personal desires or any other consideration.

Moral rules are the ones that are truly universal. If a rule does not apply universally, it is not a moral rule. According to Kant, knowledge of moral laws is imbedded in the conscience of every human being.[2] It includes such fundamental duties as "do unto others as you would have others do unto you; be a man or woman of your word; do not lie or steal or murder or break covenants."[3]

Using his system of moral reasoning Kant illustrates that it is always our moral duty to tell the truth, respect ownership of private property, charge fair prices to everyone, develop one's talents to serve society, help the needy, support lawful government, honor marriage commitments, make a truthful promise and then fulfill the promise. Likewise, it is always wrong to tell a lie, make a false promise, take someone's life including our own, overcharge an inexperienced customer, neglect one's talents, steal someone's property, attempt to overthrow lawful government, have sex outside marriage and refuse to help those in need.

How did he conclude these things? Kant believed that a supreme principle of morality exists, one that is so fundamental that it is universal applying everywhere for all people and for all time.[4] Such a fundamental principle must be common to all persons, the type of thinking that most rational humans use in everyday life. This is the supreme rational duty (see table 10.2).

on that maxim that can at the same time make itself into a universal law."[7] In other words, moral rules must be universally applicable without exception.

THE THREE RATIONAL TESTS OF MORALITY

Kant proposed three tests to discern whether any particular action is a universal, and because of this, a moral duty. We will consider each of three tests in turn.

Table 10.2. Characteristics of the supreme rational duty.

Universal	Applying everywhere and to everyone
Comprehensive	Applicable to all moral decisions
Basic	Not derived from any other principle
Supreme	Not needing any other principle to balance it
Common	Commonly used effectively by rational humans in everyday life
Categorical	Valid for all people under all circumstances; not applicable based on personal, biased, private interests or personal desires

Kant found what he believed to be that supreme principle based on the reasoning ability of humans as created by God. He called this the categorical imperative, that is, an imperative which determines all other duties. Simply put, this categorical imperative is to use rational thought alone to discern right from wrong.[5]

The starting point, then, is that whatever is a moral duty for one human being must be a universal moral duty for all human beings. By definition a rule is not a moral duty unless it applies equally to all persons. Thus, the categorical imperative rules out policies that are logically inconsistent or impossible to act on. "For example, a company which announced as its hiring policy, 'We are an equal opportunity employer: no women, blacks or Native Americans need apply,'" would be inconsistent with itself.[6] Kant gives the universal formula of the categorical imperative: "Act

1. Universal test: No exceptions or contradictions are allowed. In Kant's words: "Act as though the maxim of your action were to become by your will a universal law of nature."[8] Two possible interpretations exist for the idea of contradiction: logical contradiction and practical contradiction.[9]

Logical contradictions. Making an exception for yourself creates a logical contradiction, and the action is wrong. This is called the universal test because the point is that the basic moral principles must apply equally and impartially to all persons at all times and all circumstances. Said another way, only duties that can qualify as completely universal are moral duties.[10] Moral duties must apply to all persons. Simply from the point of view of rational thought, it is impossible for a person to follow logically opposing moral rules of action at the same time. If we generalize an action for everyone and then say that we want an exception for ourself

---

A LOGICAL CONTRADICTION

Proposition A: A universal moral duty is that no person may steal a possession belonging to another.

    1. To be a moral duty it must be universal in application: All humans must obey this rule.

    2. I am a human person.

    3. Therefore, this rule applies to me and I must obey it.

Proposition B: This universal moral rule does not apply to me right *now*: I deserve an exception to it. Thus, it is permissible for me to steal a possession belonging to another person right now.

Proposition A and **Proposition B** are in logical contradiction to each other. Both cannot be true at the same time.

---

to do the opposite, this is a logical impossibility. You cannot say yes and no at the same time and have both be true (see above).

We are compelled to say with Immanuel Kant emphatically and categorically, "You can't have it both ways!" Either Proposition A is true and the duty applies to all persons, including yourself, or it does not apply to everyone and Proposition B is true.[11] But if it does not apply to everyone, it cannot be a true moral duty because moral duties must apply to everyone. From a pure logic point of view Proposition A excludes the possibility of Proposition B because it is impossible for a rational human being to refrain from stealing and at the same time to steal. To say that both are true at the same time

is to create a logical contradiction.[12] It is this logical contradiction which shows that your action of stealing, an exception to a universal duty, is immoral. This is further illustrated using an analogy from soccer (see fig. 10.1).

Practical contradictions. When considering what will happen if everyone did a certain action, we might also consider the underlying practical purpose of the action. If the underlying practical purpose is thwarted when the action is taken by everyone, the action becomes self-contradictory and because of this, is immoral. If the action no longer is able to achieve its intended purpose when everyone does it, in a practical sense, it is wrong. In the case of making false promises, the purpose of

A. Tripping foul rule in soccer applies universally all the time		**B. Tripping foul rule in soccer does not apply universally all the time**
"No player on either team may trip any player on the opposing team." This rule applies to everyone all the time during the game!		The tripping foul rule does not always apply during the game. It is permissible for me to trip a player on the opposing team if he is trying to score a goal!

A and B cannot both be true at the same time and be logically consistent.

Figure 10.1. The impossibility of logical contradiction on moral matters.

PRACTICAL CONTRADICTION

A practical incompatibility of two propositions (ideas). When taken together these two propositions result in two outcomes that are opposite of or inconsistent with each other. If one idea becomes universally true in practice, the other becomes, practically speaking, inconceivable or impossible. If one idea is reality and everyone did it, in the logical sense people could not follow the one idea and its opposite because, in a practical sense, attempting to follow one rule and its opposite would be self-defeating.

Example: Kant gives examples of how this first test works in practice. His best example seems to be based on the issues of promise making and promise breaking. Consider a person who finds himself in need of money. So this person, knowing full well that he will be unable to repay a loan, asks a friend for money anyway, promising to pay it back. Asking for a loan is compatible with the duty to foster personal welfare and happiness; however, asking for a loan knowing that you cannot repay it cannot possibly be a universal law of nature because it becomes self-contradictory. Applying this action universally permits anyone in need to make a promise he does not intend to fulfill. But if this happens, no one would believe such promises but would laugh at such requests. The whole idea of a promise to repay would become meaningless and self-contradictory because the practice of offering to repay a loan would eventually not be accepted in society because too many people violated the principle of promise making. Thus, we are imagining a world in which someone makes a certain type of promise but the same world in which there could not be such a thing because this type of promise would not be accepted by anyone. Because of this, it would be immoral to make a false promise.

making false promises is thwarted when everyone realizes that promises of this type are false and people are no longer willing to accept such promises. In the case of stealing property for the purpose of obtaining a good at no cost, if everyone did this, they would be unable to keep property (others would steal it!) and, practically speaking, their purpose could not be achieved. In the case of someone who decides not to help another in need, if everyone took this approach, no one would ever receive assistance even at the time when he or she needs it the most for himself or herself. Accordingly, Kant's point in this first test is that to try to live in the middle of a logical contradiction or a practical contradiction regarding a universal moral duty is impossible!

This first test of right and wrong can be illustrated by the flow chart in figure 10.2.

2. Humanity test. Again, in Kant's words: "Act in such a way that you treat humanity, whether in your own person or in any other person, always at the same time as an end, never

In everything, therefore, treat people the same way you want them to treat you, for this is the Law and the Prophets. (Mt 7:12)

TEST NO. 1: The Universal Test

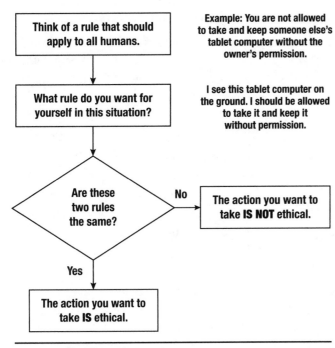

Figure 10.2. The universal test.

merely as a means."[13] This test of morality is essentially the same as the Golden Rule: Do unto others as you would have them do unto you.[14] And it is another way of saying the first rule. Kant called this test the "supreme limiting condition on every person's freedom of action."[15] It may be one of the most famous propositions of ethics of all time, perhaps even the most important rule of life in general.[16]

This duty is based on the assumption that the rational nature of human beings has a purpose in itself and that one human is not merely a means to another human achieving a goal. To be assured of acting morally we will be sure to treat other rational beings with the same type of respect and dignity that we would treat ourselves. Why? All humans have inherent worth and should be given respect because all humans share this same characteristic that distinguishes them from all other living things: Humans are rational agents and have purpose to their decisions.[17] We all share in common the freedom to decide for ourselves what to do. Put a slightly different way, we will act in such a way that preserves the right of all persons, including ourselves, to fully use our power of rational thinking to decide what to do. Kant called this the supreme limiting condition.

This test can be stated in either the positive or negative frame. Framed from a positive perspective, our duty is to do unto others what we would want for ourselves; that is, do what we can

---

SUPREME LIMITING CONDITION

Supreme Limiting Condition: A condition applying equally to all humans whereby we limit our own freedom of action in terms of what we would want done to ourselves.

Example: Consider the possibility of wanting a cash loan and making a false promise to repay the money. If we were to make such a false promise, we would be taking advantage of the person who loans us money, using her as only a means to an end. This would disrespect her as a rational person: if we deceive her, it would disrespect her rational ability to decide whether or not to loan us money (that we will not repay the loan).

TEST NO. 2: The Humanity Test

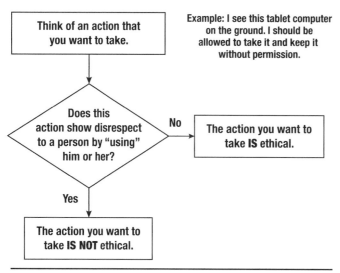

Figure 10.3. The humanity test.

Because we share the same nature as other humans, the humanity test shows that suicide, murder, theft, fraud, promise breaking and many other things are immoral. The humanity test can be further illustrated by figure 10.3.

3. Autonomy test. The third test requires a person to take an action only if such an action is consistent with someone who requires the duty for all others to follow and at the same time who is subject to that duty if it were made to be a rule for him or her by all other people. This autonomy test requires that the human act in an impartial way with regards to duties: True moral principles apply equally and impartially to all humans regardless of the personal interest or bias that a particular person might have.

to foster both in ourselves and in other rational beings their ability to use freedom of rational choice. We should develop our talents, act with charity and provide emotional support and sympathy to those in need. Framed from the negative point of view, we should not do to others what we would not want done to ourselves. All humans have the duty to refrain from deliberately harming the ability of yourself or others to make free choices which would bring happiness.

This means that a person must choose duties to follow from the point of view of both yourself (as if you were the active rule maker and as the passive rule receiver) and from the perspective of other rational beings who also

---

KING-SUBJECT RULE

Act in such a way that if you were both king and subject, you would agree to the action. If only one of the two is likely to agree to the action, the action is wrong.

Example: Consider the temptation to take without permission a printer toner cartridge from your employer and use it in your printer at home. Such an action is moral if and only if both you and your employer are willing to make that a universal law. Because the expenses of the organization would go up if the employer encouraged this among all employees, it is unlikely that such an employer would make it a universal law. You might feel like taking a toner cartridge, but you have a duty not to take it because, using your rational thought, you would have to acknowledge that if you were the employer, you would probably not want all your employees to take toner cartridges without permission.

TEST NO. 3: The King-Subject Rule

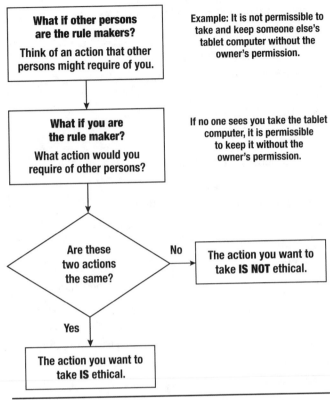

Figure 10.4. The king-subject rule.

both subject to and a source of the laws of the community."[18] In this rational test, each member of the community holds a double relationship to universal, impartial moral standards. First, each makes the standards for all others. Second, each is a receiver of moral standards made by others. Kant assumes that because all members of the community are rational persons, all will legislate the identically same moral standards for all other persons (see fig. 10.4).

Table 10.3 provides a summary of the three tests.

Recall from Kant's religious beliefs that it is impossible for humans, of their own power, to follow the ideal rationally determined moral standards on a consistent basis. But inability to consistently follow ideal standards does not mean that the standards should be changed (lowered). Rather, humans need to be changed through the power of God's grace and thereby become transformed in their ability to use rational thought to derive duty

are rule makers to whom you must be subject. This is also called the king-subject rule.

With this test Kant attempts to "complete his theory by introducing the idea of a moral community of rational agents, each of whom is

Table 10.3. Kant's rational tests for morality.

Categorical Imperative	Humans must use reason alone to determine moral duty.
1. Universal Test	Act as if your action were to become by your will a self-consistent universal law without contradiction when applied impartially to yourself as well as to all others. Test yourself using Kant's basic idea: Is the action you are about to take an exception to the rule that you would make for everyone else? To make an exception for yourself is logically contradictory, and because of this is it is wrong.
2. Humanity Test	Treat all human persons, including yourself, with dignity and respect. Never use a person as merely a means to an end. Test yourself using Kant's approach: If I do this action, does the action respect the dignity and autonomy of other persons? Only if the answer is yes can the action be said to be moral.
3. Autonomy Test	Do only what you would do if you were both the active lawmaker and the passive receiver of laws made by others. Test yourself using Kant's approach: If I do this action, is the action something that both I and another person would want? If another person were to make the rule for this action, would I agree?

TO THE MANAGER

It sometimes pays to use Kant's arguments at work when faced with a superior who asks you to do something immoral.

- Is this how you would want me to act toward our company?
- Is this how we would want our customers (or suppliers) to act toward us? If not, then how is it right for us to do this?
- Won't this undermine the trust that others have in us that we will treat them the same way we would want to be treated?
- Would taking this action make us look rationally stupid to others and because of this harm our reputation?

This is not always effective as when your boss openly uses double standards.

---

and their willingness to follow rational duty regardless of whether they felt like it (see sidebar for an application of the principle).

EVALUATION: PROS AND CONS

This chapter introduces the idea of universalism as a moral standard of right and wrong. It is time to consider some of the pros and cons of this approach. Pros (arguments in support or strengths) will be identified by the symbol (+) while cons (arguments against or statements of weakness) will be identified by the symbol (-).

(+) The universally binding nature of morality is appealing.[19] Moral duties must be impartially applied to all people everywhere including yourself. It is impossible for a rational person to believe that all persons should avoid a particular behavior and at the same to believe that the behavior is permissible for you. In addition, it is wrong to give yourself an exception to the rule so that the decision comes out in your own favor.

(+) Universalism helps us evaluate actions that we have never considered before. With this approach, we have no need of other elaborate schemes of morality. Simply test for logical contradictions when an action is made universal.

(+) Universalism recognizes the unity of all humans and the egalitarian nature of the most fundamental moral principles, that is, that these apply equally to all persons regardless of their personal biases or interests. Thus, it is one of the approaches to decision making that counteracts self-interest.

(+) Universalism is a reasoned approach to control self-interests because it points out the inconsistency of wanting one rule for other persons and a self-interested rule biased in favor of your own interests. Thus, universalism moves us away from and becomes the antidote for the tendency toward egoism.

(+) The power to think helps us evaluate beliefs, assumptions, conclusions, evidence and the logic used to explain and persuade. Universalism has a positive emphasis on reason that is necessary for general living. This is encouraged in Scripture.

Several challenges and objections have been raised regarding universalism.[20]

(-) The categorical imperative places human reason above all other authorities, including the Bible. This is an attempt to make reason (and humans) independent of God. Modern Christians are intellectually uncomfortable with the proposition that reason is placed above Scripture. In effect, this disconnects rationality from religion, an idea that seems contrary to the teaching of Scripture.[21] By assuming that it is reason alone that can be used to determine what is right and wrong, it allows for the rejection of or attacks on Christianity through reason. Reason becomes a substitute for Christianity.

(-) Kant's approach gets stuck in one of the fundamental paradoxes that we considered in chapter two (universal—particular). If we think of a particular duty, it is impossible to universalize this into a general rule because it is based on a specific situation or action. The assumption is that every social situation is unique from all others. Every instance where an action is conceived will be slightly different from every other instance (even for the same action) because the action will take place in a different social circumstance. However, without the specific content, the universal duty cannot be conceived.[22]

(-) Acting out of sympathy and compassion are not moral in Kant's theory. Only acts which fulfill moral duties are morally worthy. Saintly acts and heroic acts which go above and beyond the call of duty have, in his theory, no moral worth, yet surely such actions have moral worth if they further the happiness and well-being of other humans or help prevent the loss of well-being of others.

(-) Duty cannot be separated from consequences. "Kant is totally concerned with consequences, for he believes that a moral agent should be moved by the thought of the good at which his actions aim."[23] While duty is the prime importance in Kant's system, it is impossible to consider duty apart from consequences when attempting to apply the three tests. Kant's system does not recognize the potential good that can come from an action.

(-) Is it truly possible to contradict reason?[24] On the occasion of stealing someone's property, does the thief really contradict reason? Does he or she, at that moment, believe that the rule "do not steal" should be universalized and at the same time believe that he or she should be granted an exception? Or is the thief merely saying that the rule "do not steal" should not be a universal, moral rule?[25]

DOWN TO THE NITTY-GRITTY

Think about the opening story at the beginning of this chapter. You are the owner of the restaurant. What is the right thing to do? It's time to get down to the nitty-gritty (see table 10.4)!

Table 10.4. Applying the ethical process.

Keeping Your Heart: An Intrapersonal Process	Walking in the Community: An Interpersonal Process
• You are the owner of the restaurant. What does your heart say is the right thing to do regarding the agreement and pricing? • Which biblical themes explored in this book inform your heart on this situation? • Which biblical theme, if any, do you feel yourself resisting? Why do you feel resistance? • What stakeholders should you consider in this situation? What impact will this situation have on each depending on what you do? • Is universalism sufficient on its own to guide you to decide what is right and wrong? If not, what additional perspective is needed?	• You are the owner of the restaurant. With whom might you have a conversation about the issue of the agreement and pricing? Who else might have a helpful perspective? • Which of the biblical themes in this chapter will most likely come up in the conversation either directly or indirectly? Why? Which one(s) will be the most influential in the conversation? • If you have a conversation with someone regarding this situation, which of the fundamental tensions presented earlier in the book might come up? • What right-versus-right dilemmas, if any, can be identified? Have a conversation with someone about this now. What is the outcome of the conversation?

THROUGH THE LENS OF BIBLICAL THEMES

This part of the chapter will use the biblical story themes as a lens through which to evaluate the ethical approach featured in the chapter. Because the themes are interrelated and interdependent, we should expect to see some overlap in the thinking regarding the ethical approach. Some themes will contribute the same thinking as will other themes. The power of these themes comes from their guidance when a community of people talks about complicated ethical dilemmas faced in business practice.

When considering the fundamental principles at stake in the biblical story themes, it is possible to see the rationale for these (see, e.g., appendix D). Once the larger picture of covenant relations and the envisioned shalom are considered, biblical story rational thought is logically consistent with itself. Some aspects of Kant's theory are appealing. The Bible story indicates that moral principles are universally applicable. The story theme of covenant clearly supports Kant's humanity test and the king-subject rule test. However, when taken to an extreme, the issue of the role of reason, seemingly stripped of covenantal thinking, may be the most troubling dimension when seen from the viewpoint of biblical themes.

Kant's conception of moral duty is based on the beliefs that to be moral a duty must be

- universally applied to all persons without exception or contradiction
- impartially applied to all persons

After scanning the entire biblical story, it seems that these two assumptions are shared in Scripture. Some will argue that the basis of moral duty in the Bible is different from the basis proposed by Kant, namely, that moral duties are established by God, not humans.

Cosmic conflict. Kant's emphasis on freedom of choice is consistent with story of the cosmic conflict. However, placing reason above the revealed will of God as the standard of right and wrong is essentially to fall into the trap laid by Satan in the Garden of Eden when he tempted Eve and Adam to place themselves in the position of absolute moral authority equal to that of their Creator. God values the freedom to make choices, but within boundaries. Pure reason alone, unguided by moral principles, may lead a person to choose an action which is contrary to God's will. But by the same token, applying moral principles requires the use of rational thought processes.

Creation. Kant bases his theory of ethics on his creation theology, which respects humanity as bearers of the image of God: human persons are rational beings capable of making choices for their behavior that is independent of what other persons decide. Kant believed that God created us with the inherent ability to make free, rational choices for our behavior, and when we apply rational thinking, we are making choices that align with God's will for humans on earth. As an approach to making decisions about what is right and wrong universalism has a certain appeal for the Christian. For Kant, it is the God-given ability to reason that gives humans their true worth. However, the creation narrative tells us that it is not the power of reason alone that provides the worth but rather the origin in God's creation. Universalism emphasizes high regard for the ability of humans to use their minds to think. Kant's point about humanness is well taken: because all humans have the power to think and reason, all humans deserve the same degree of dignity.

Holiness. Consecrating our minds in service to God is an important foundation for committing to follow covenant relationships. It is in submitting our minds to be transformed by the power of the Holy Spirit that we will find understanding of what is right and wrong. We will also find the power to do what we know to be right. When we consecrate ourselves, we do not look for an easy way out by exception for ourselves when it is convenient. We hold to principle. Consecrating ourselves to God means, in part, that we respect the autonomy of others. We do not attempt to sidestep the thinking processes of others. When we are faced with an ethical dilemma, we take the perspective of the other person in the relationship to see it through their eyes.

Covenant relationships. The Christian today may view universalism as insufficient because it has been applied by many without reference to God and the moral duties outlined in the Ten Commandments. Kant based his approach on pure reason. Such an approach can easily be stripped of its creation roots and applied by secular humanists. The humanity test is consistent with the Golden Rule, the scriptural principle of loving your neighbor as you would love yourself.[26] "Therefore, treat people the same way you want them to treat you, for this is the Law and the Prophets" (Mt 7:12). In the Scripture story it is not reason alone that is valued, but reason that is shaped and guided by fundamental covenantal principles embodied by the biblical themes.

Shalom. Shalom is both a guiding principle and the hoped-for community experience of those in covenant relationships. Thus, it is not duty alone that is followed, but duty that is designed for a particular set of outcomes in the community that are described as shalom.

Sabbath. Sabbath thinking illustrates the opposite of how reason alone can lead a person away from covenant relationships. Reason alone would likely lead a person, at least in the short run, to skip sabbath and keep working to grow economic wealth. On the surface there appears to be no reason for putting a limit on economic activities. At a deeper level, however, limiting personal desires for wealth have a positive effect not only on a person but also on the whole community. It is in the sabbath that we see a bit more clearly that reason, in the biblical sense, is not just logic born of mental activity. Instead, reason takes into consideration a wider field of thinking than logic alone.

Justice. Biblical-theme morality is not just based on reason apart from God. At stake are fundamental principles such as rights of other people not to be harmed. A particular action may not seem like the reasonable thing to do, but the biblical story would ask, *What is the fair thing to do, not the logical thing to do?* In other words, the principle of justice trumps logic when we apply rational thought to deciding what is right and wrong.

Righteousness. Acting in a way that is faithful to promises is fundamental to covenant relationships. Actions that keep the interests of others in focus in a way that does not put self in a favored position should guide our reason. In this, Kant's approach aligns with biblical themes. As suggested in the other themes, deciding what is right and wrong depends on comparing actions with the principles outlined in the covenant and in particular, the Ten Commandments.

Truth. In the biblical story, truth calls for consistency and faithfulness as the guiding principles. These are to guide our rational thought processes. Reliability and correspondence between what we say we believe and what we do is just as important as the decision we make, using rational thought when considering the covenant principles.

Wisdom. Clearly the use of reason is valued in the biblical story! However, reason is never viewed in the Bible apart from its place in the human heart along with faith commitment to God and a diligent keeping of the heart by focusing on the principles of covenant relationships. Reason that is separated from covenant principles is foolishness in the Bible. But rational thought bathed in covenant principles reflects divine wisdom. Furthermore, wisdom means that persons will avoid having others harm them just as they will avoid harming others. This is the prudent way to live and is an important contributing element to shalom.

Loving kindness. The categorical imperative requires humans to subordinate their personal desires for happiness when there is a duty to serve others. Love means applying rational thought to a situation where we do not feel affectionate toward someone but still treat even an enemy with respect and consideration that we would give to a friend.

Redemption. As Kant pointed out, humans by themselves are unable to use their God-created reason flawlessly. Humans are hopelessly biased in the self-serving direction. They are inconsistent in their beliefs and actions. "For the good that I want, I do not do, but I practice the very evil that I do not want" (Rom 7:19). Humans are in need of radical transformation that is available only through the grace of God. Only through faith in the rejuvenating power of the Holy Spirit can such a transformation take place. "Do not be conformed to this world, but be transformed by the renewing of your mind, so that you may prove what the will of God is, that which is good and acceptable and perfect" (Rom 12:2). Furthermore, reason alone may not dictate that we act redemptively toward another person who has

wronged us, but the biblical story indicates that we will follow God in becoming a co-worker to heal human relationships.

CHAPTER REVIEW QUESTIONS

1. What were Immanuel Kant's religious beliefs regarding ethics?

2. What does the concept of categorical imperative mean?

3. How does each of Kant's three tests of morality work?

4. What are the pros and cons of universalism as an approach to ethical decision making?

5. How do the Scripture themes guide us regarding universalism?

DISCUSSION QUESTIONS

1. How important is the idea that in order to be valid moral duties must apply universally to all without partiality? What would result in society if persons were allowed to grant themselves an exception to a moral rule any time they wanted?

2. What is the role of reason in Christian experience?

3. Evaluate the objections to Kant's theory. Which objection seems to be the strongest? Which one is the weakest? Why?

4. From the opening scenario: The day before the wedding rehearsal dinner, what options did the groom's family have for catering a dinner that served thirty-five guests? Did the groom's father have the right understanding of the bargaining position that the family was in at that moment on Friday afternoon? Based on the facts that are presented in this case, can we hold the family's agent responsible for this unfavorable

outcome? What, if anything, was wrong with the action of the restaurant owner?

5. Can you think of a situation where Immanuel Kant's three tests do not apply? What issues arise when you apply his three tests in this situation?

6. Read James 2:1-13. Can you identify one or more of Immanuel Kant's tests or morality embedded in this passage?

ETHICAL VIGNETTES TO DISCUSS

For each of the vignettes described below, apply the biblical story themes to discern what is right and wrong. How would universalism answer each one?

1. *Beating the price on Priceline.com.* Priceline, a website that sells hotel rooms, airline tickets and other services at a discount, offers great deals on travel-related products and services. But they have rules. For example, when you place a bid on a hotel room, you must change one of the parameters if you want to submit a second bid. Or you must wait a period of time before bidding again. Parameters are things like the quality of the hotel or the date of your stay; usually parameters exclude changing the price. Some consumers found that if they erase the cookies from their computer after they make a bid on the website, they are treated as if they are a new customer. The customer then can enter the website immediately and change the price a little (without changing the other parameters) to see if his or her bid will be accepted.

2. *Tapping into insurance.* A pedestrian walking across the street in a crosswalk was hit by a motorist who had not scraped the frost from the front window of the car. The driver was given three citations by the police. After the trip to the hospital and doctors' offices, the insurance company of the driver contacted the injured person and offered a cash payment of fifteen hundred dollars for "pain and suffering" over and above paying for all the medical bills. A friend of the injured party suggested that he contact a personal injury attorney because the insurance company offer seemed quite low. The injured person contacted three lawyers, and each one had the same response: The only way the attorney would be able to get more money is by contacting *the injured person's* car insurance company and get them to pay for the pain and suffering. His car insurance may cover him even if his car was parked in his garage at the time of the accident. The lawyer would agree to represent him only if 33 percent of the money obtained in the settlement was then paid to the attorney. The injured person did not think this was the right thing to do because his car was not involved. The injured person negotiated with the insurance company by himself and increased the payment for pain and suffering payment to six thousand dollars. Is it ethical for a personal injury attorney to tap into the car insurance company of the injured person even though his car was not involved in the accident?

11

Agency

Do what you are told by your boss.

SCRIPTURE PASSAGE

It is required of stewards that one be found trustworthy. (1 Cor 4:2)

CHAPTER OVERVIEW

In this chapter we will take a deeper look at one of the most common ways of thinking about right and wrong in the marketplace: agency. In particular, we will

- explore the basic relationship of agency
- consider the moral foundation for the agency relationship
- evaluate the pros and cons of agency as an approach to business ethics
- evaluate agency through the lens of biblical themes

MAIN TOPICS

Historical Background of the Agency
   Concept
Contemporary Concept of Agency: Duties
For Whom Does the Agent Work?
The Moral Foundation for Agency (Three
   Views)
Agency Problem and Agency Cost

Stewardship
Evaluation: Pros and Cons
Down to the Nitty-Gritty
Through the Lens of Biblical Themes

KEY TERMS

agency, agency costs, agency problem, agent, express agency, creative accommodating purist approach, fiduciary, implied agency, law of agency, market stakeholders, nonmarket stakeholders, principal, purist approach, subagent, submissive approach

OPENING SCENARIO

When Extended Stay America emerged out of bankruptcy, its chief executive officer, Jim Donald, realized that the employees were still frozen by fear.[1] Afraid of making a mistake that might make the financial struggles of this national hotel chain worse, employees waited to be told what to do. Mr. Donald needed a way to unfreeze them.

He printed and then began handing out "Get Out of Jail Free" cards reminiscent of the Parker Brothers (Hasbro) Monopoly® game. He hoped that the cards would be a sort of safety net to encourage employees to innovate. If an employee saw an opportunity to help the company but the action was risky, the employee could use the "Get Out of Jail Free" card and avoid managerial criticism.

What Donald may not have counted on is the types of risks that employees might be willing to take. One manager heard that a movie film crew would be in the area. She found their phone number and called them to see what kind of accommodations they needed. The phone call resulted in booking many rooms for many nights with a dollar value of $250,000. Perhaps this was not much of a risk, but it was a good way to cash in her card and at the same time show that she could move quickly to capture unanticipated demand.

Now, consider the risk that another Extended Stay America hotel manager took: She visited the lobby of a nearby competing hotel and without permission took twenty business cards of the competitor's guests that had been dropped into a container destined for the competition's marketing and sales department. Innovative, for sure. Risky, for sure! She could use her "Get Out of Jail Free" card to avoid punishment.

When companies are battered by chaotic markets, hypercompetition and unbearable pressures to reduce expenses and capture customer demand, top-level managers end up giving mixed messages: Take risks, innovate, but be cautious! Don't be unethical in the process. Telling employees to "feel empowered" sometimes is insufficient to get employees moving. Top-level leaders must take action themselves. Jim Donald modeled risk-taking behavior by handing out lime-green safety-net cards. He expected his managers to follow suit.

In this chapter we will address the questions related to doing what the boss says. It is called agency theory, and it is one of the approaches to ethical decision making that is currently popular in the marketplace.

HISTORICAL BACKGROUND OF THE AGENCY CONCEPT

The expectation that employees follow the directions and commands of their employers is very old. We find evidence of this in writings from the ancient Near East. Egyptian viziers were responsible for the Egyptian treasury and other operational matters of state.[2] Ancient Mesopotamian hired shepherd contracts show how detailed these arrangements could be.[3] If a shepherd wanted to build his wealth, he needed to expand his flocks. As the number of sheep exceeded available sons and daughters, the owner hired other shepherds to manage flocks in order to keep growing. These he placed under contract for a year with expectations that the hireling would protect the sheep and increase the number of sheep. The agreement specified payment terms, expected return on investment and provision for risk management.

> You shall not see your countryman's ox or his sheep straying away, and pay no attention to them; you shall certainly bring them back to your countryman. (Deut 22:1; see also vv. 3-4)

A fiduciary relationship is an official relationship in which one person agrees to manage another party's financial resources. Modern fiduciary relationships are secularized versions of ancient religious covenant relationships described in the Bible.[4] Most people see the fourteenth-century English common law, itself based on ancient Roman and Hebrew legal principles, as the foundation for modern fiduciary relationships.[5] English common law required an employee to act loyally and primarily for the employer's benefit. The principle of agency emphasizes faithfulness to the one in the position of economic authority. The feudal lord (employer) had disproportionate amount of power and could fire the vassal (worker) at will. This possibility constantly constrained the employee to think twice about being disloyal.

CONTEMPORARY CONCEPT OF AGENCY: DUTIES

Current law that specifies official fiduciary responsibilities is called the law of agency. In the agency relationship there are two parties that must agree. The principal is the one who asks the agent to act on his or her behalf. In this the principal allows someone else to be responsible for some of his or her financial interests. An agency relationship can be created only to accomplish a lawful purpose; agency contracts that are created for illegal purposes are not valid.[6]

A common form of agency is called express agency, when the authority to act is expressly stated in a written or verbal agreement. In an implied agency, the agent's extent of decision-making authority is determined by the circumstances of the situation. Implied agency can be inferred from commonly accepted industry practices, prior dealings between the parties or the agent's position in the company.

Whether agency is express or implied, principals ask agents to do things they do not have time to do or do not have the capability to do. This creates interdependency that has a two-way moral dimension. The principal is dependent on the agent but has responsibilities to the agent; the principal must trust the agent and uphold his or her end of the agreement. The agent depends on the principal for compensation and must be trustworthy. The agent must voluntarily agree to take the responsibility given by the principal, and the principal must retain the freedom to discharge the agent.

An agent may be a person, a partnership or an organization that has legal capacity to have rights and accept responsibilities to act on behalf of another. An agent may appoint someone else, called a subagent, to perform some or all of the services that the principal expects will be accomplished.

In the principal-agent relationship, both parties have duties. We will consider first the duties of the agent.

Duties of the agent. Having accepted the principal's request to act, the agent faithfully acts on this. In an employer-employee relationship,

Table 11.1. Duties of the agent.

The Agent Must	The Agent Must Not
Use granted authority to take actions which advance the legal and fiduciary interests of the principal	Exceed the scope of his or her authority
	Take an action that the principal would not take
Use diligence, skill and knowledge to the best of his or her ability when serving the principal	Act adversely toward the principal
	Act in a way that damages the principal's endeavors
	Compete with the principal or help a competitor
Notify the principal of facts that the principal would be interested in that affect the principal's endeavors	Use the principal's property for personal purposes or for a third party's personal purpose
	Represent the principal's property as his own
Keep accurate accounting of the principal's finances	Mingle the principal's property with anyone else's property
	Disclose confidential information to a third party
	Personally gain from a third-party transaction taken on behalf of the principal

Table 11.2. Duties of the principal.

The Principal Must
Exercise due care in selecting, training, communicating expectations, supervising and controlling the agent
Accept vicarious liability when the agent performs assigned work
Indemnify (protect against damage) the agent when the agent makes a payment on behalf of the principal
Treat the agent fairly
Fulfil all terms of the agency agreement
Make restitution if the agent enriches the principal at someone else's expense
Fulfil agreements made by the agent on behalf of the principal's financial and legal interests
Compensate the agent according to what was agreed on

an employee is either an agent or a subagent and in taking actions that the employer expects the employee represents the employer. The agent uses skills and knowledge and diligence to the best of his or her ability. The agent must notify the principal regarding facts that the principal would be interested in. And the agent must keep accurate records of the principal's finances. These duties are summarized in table 11.1.

Things the agent must not do. The agent may not exceed the scope of granted authority. The agent also has the duty not to act adversely toward the principal or to deal with a third party that is known to be adverse to the principal. The agent must not act in a way that is likely to damage the principal's endeavors. Similarly, the agent cannot compete with the principal or help a competitor. The agent cannot meet the duty of loyalty to two parties who have conflicting interests. The agent cannot use the principal's property for his or her own purposes or for the purpose of a third party. The agent cannot represent the principal's property as his or her own or mingle the principal's property with anyone else's. The agent cannot communicate confidential information to a third party. Some of these forbidden actions can be taken if authorized by the principal, but the agent must deal fairly and cannot deceive the principal when obtaining permission. The agent has a duty not to personally gain from a third-party trans-

action that was taken on behalf of the principal.

Duties of the principal. The principal has responsibilities to exercise due care in selecting, communicating, training, supervising and controlling the agent. If the agent makes a mistake, the principal is still responsible. The principal is liable when an employee takes an authorized action that results in harm. The principal must reimburse the agent for authorized expenses incurred on behalf of the principal. The principal must treat the agent fairly. This involves informing the agent of risks associated with performing work. If an agent takes an action that results in the principal becoming unjustly enriched at someone else's expense, the party that has been harmed has a right to restitution. When an agent makes an agreement on behalf of the principal, the principal is party to the agreement and is obligated to fulfil the agreement. The principal must pay the agent according to what was agreed on at the time the agent accepted responsibility. In other relationships, the agent may agree to act on behalf of the principal without compensation. Table 11.2 summarizes the duties of the principal.

Examples of agency relationships are everywhere in commerce: A company hires an employee to be a manager or supervisor of other workers. A large manufacturing company hires a person to be a front-line

Table 11.3. Applications of agency.

Principal	Agent
Manufacturing company	Component supplier providing goods
Company A	Company B (provides Company A with services)
Citizens	Elected officials
England	United States agrees to defend England in World War II
Constituents	Nonprofit organization leaders
Nonprofit organization trustees	Nonprofit organization administrator
Husband or wife	Wife or husband

worker on the assembly line (subagent). The salesperson accepts a job selling goods for a retail store. A computer programmer agrees to act as an independent contractor for a company to develop an application (app). A partner in a business acts on behalf of the partnership. An attorney represents a client. A real estate broker negotiates the sale or purchase of a house or other property. A hospital grants a physician privileges to admit and treat patients in the facility. A small business contracts with a temporary employment agency to bring in an accountant. A company signs an agreement with an advertising agency to promote the company's products. Table 11.3 gives additional examples of how the agency relationship can be applied.

Agency is a concept that applies across a wide spectrum of social situations. In its broadest sense, "an agency relationship exists whenever there is an arrangement in which one person's welfare depends on what another person does"[7] or that involves cooperative effort.[8] For example, roommates are agents of each other. One roommate invites several friends over to the apartment for a relaxing party when the other roommate is trying to study. When an officer of a student club asks a club member to take an action on behalf of the club, the club member is an agent for that task.

FOR WHOM DOES THE AGENT WORK?

In a privately owned company the company owner is the principal and anyone this person hires is an agent. But who does an agent work for in a large publically traded corporation where there are thousands of shareholders, few of whom are closely related to the firm or where some of the shareholders are also employees (other agents) of the firm?

Some people think that the agent works directly for the shareholders of a corporation. In this view shareholders are seen as the owners of the corporation because they hold the stock. Their agents are to promote the financial interests of the shareholders.[9] It is the wise management of agents whose decisions have an influence on the stock price. Thus, agents have the responsibility of doing all in their power to increase the value of the stock. This viewpoint tends to support a narrow view of the moral basis of the agency relationship, which we will address later in this chapter.

Others say that the agent works for the corporation and only indirectly for shareholders. Yes, shareholders hold stock and benefit from increasing stock value, but in a corporation all agents work for the success and continuation of the corporation as a whole, and not individual shareholders. No explicit contract exists between the shareholder and the managers.[10] Shareholders choose the directors

CRUCIAL ELEMENTS IN THE DEFINITION OF AGENCY

Three crucial elements define the agency relationship. First, agency results from the consent of one person to another to act on behalf of the other. Second, the agent is given the authority to act on behalf of the other party. Third, the principal exercises control over the agent.

who, as their agents, hire the managers. Most shareholders purchase stock from previous owners of stock, not from the corporation.[11] Shareholders have an arm's-length relationship with the corporation. They expect to be treated as investors and bondholders. Few shareholders have face-to-face meetings with managers. Managers make no specific commitments to individual shareholders.

The relationship between a corporation's agent and the shareholders does not meet the legal requirements of an agency relationship. Individual shareholders are not given consent power when a manager is hired. Many of the financial responsibilities of managers involve activities that are not directly related to shareholders. And these responsibilities do not include looking after the interests of shareholders in all matters. Shareholders do not supervise managers. Yes, shareholders elect directors who establish policies that are used to monitor the work of managers. But individual shareholders do not have the right to come into the corporation and ask the managers to complete particular duties.

Furthermore, managers cannot act directly on behalf of a shareholder to change the legal relationship of the shareholder with a third party such as in pursuing a merger or by changing the corporation's by-laws. Shareholders are not allowed to act on matters that managers do not bring to them. If the board of directors does not like the fact that the managers are not bringing matters of vital interests to the corporation, the board can fire the man-

agers. This argument is summarized above.[12]

The discussion regarding who the agent works for is directly related to the question of the moral foundation for the agency relationship. To this we turn next.

THE MORAL FOUNDATION FOR AGENCY (THREE VIEWS)

A debate exists among business scholars regarding the moral foundation for the agency relationship. Although there are more than three views, for simplicity we can characterize the debate as being between those who hold a narrow view, those who hold a broader view and those who hold a very broad, or stakeholder, view.

Narrow view. One perspective, called here the narrow view, considers the moral foundation for the agency relationship as whatever the principal requires of the agent within the law. In this view, the moral foundation is determined by the wishes of the principal. The agent's role is limited to legal and financial matters, which trump any other concerns. Actions are situationally determined based on the effect the action is likely to have on financial goals.[13] Shareholders are viewed as synthesizing all interests of anyone who has any legal, financial or any other interest in the corporation. Whatever the principal wants done to advance the financial interests, if it is a legal action, the agent will carry out. Other than that specified in the law or the minimum moral standards required for the market to operate relatively efficiently, moral standards are not considered in this viewpoint.

When faced with a moral choice, the agent in the narrow view will ask the following questions:

- Will taking this action fulfill my financial and legal responsibilities to the principal in the short term and the long run?

- Will this action increase the liabilities of the principal?

Broader view. An alternative perspective is that agents have broader moral standards that must be followed in all their work. These standards exceed what is in the law regarding financial obligations. Agents must honor agreements, avoid lying, respect the autonomy of others and avoid doing harm. They must act with higher morals for one of two reasons. They must act as they would in any other situation in society as the principals are expected to act in relationship with any other interested party.[14] This requires a broader set of moral standards that are higher in priority than mere financial goals.[15] Or they must have broader moral standards because the moral basis of agency relationship is defined more broadly than purely financial terms in the law.[16] In this view a distinction exists between financial and nonfinancial obligations to shareholders. Financial accountability must be preserved; however, in the "ordinary business operation" the interests of many stakeholders must be considered (see fig. 11.2).[17]

When faced with a moral choice the agent with a broader view of the moral foundation will ask the following questions:

- What would the principal do in this situation to honor commitments to others?

- What is legal?

- What are my obligations to advance the financial interests of the principal?

- Are there moral requirements that go beyond pursuing just the financial interests of the principal?

The stakeholder view. The broadest view of the question is known as the stakeholder view.[18] In this perspective agents have many duties to all interested parties (stakeholders). Stakeholders can have a direct interest in the transactions of the company. These are market stakeholders or primary stakeholders. For example, customers, employees and suppliers are market stakeholders because they have something directly to gain or lose in transactions with the company.

Other stakeholders have an indirect interest in the activities of the firm. These are known as nonmarket stakeholders. Nonmarket stakeholders are secondary stakeholders. For example, government regulators, the media and the general public have some interest in the firm's activities but based on transactions with the firm.

In this broadest view all stakeholders are treated as having equally important interests.[19] Shareholders are one category among many stakeholders that the agent must be respon-

Narrow View

Serve the interests of your boss.

Figure 11.1. A narrow view of agency.

Broader View

Serve the interests of your boss and do not hurt your customers or your employees.

Figure 11.2. A broader view of agency.

Stakeholder View

Serve the interests of your boss and fulfill your responsibilities to all other stakeholders.

Figure 11.3. The stakeholder view (the widest view).

Table 11.4. Three moral foundations of agency.

	Narrow View	Broader View	Stakeholder View
Responsibility	Agents have but one responsibility: serve the interests of the principal.	Agents have responsibilities to the principal and to others in the business relationship.	Agents have responsibilities to all market and nonmarket stakeholders.
Value and Goal Priority	Financial goals trump all values.	Financial goals coexist with (equal to) all other values.	Other values trump financial goals if financial goals require compromise.
Moral Foundation	The moral foundation is determined in each situation by what is legal and what will favorably advance the financial interests of the principal within the law.	Agents must honor agreements, avoid lying, respect the autonomy of others and avoid doing harm. Agents have financial and nonfinancial obligations to principals and to other stakeholders. By law there is a distinction between the agent's financial and nonfinancial obligations.	Agents must follow a whole range of moral principles to all stakeholders. There is no distinction between financial and nonfinancial obligations. The agent resists putting financial duties above nonfinancial duties.

sible to. Accordingly, this broadest view tends to resist putting financial duties above nonfinancial duties to others.

When faced with an ethical choice, the agent with the broadest view will ask the following questions:

- Who are all the stakeholders, and what are my obligations to all of them?

- How can I balance the interests of all stakeholders when some of their interests conflict?

- In achieving the financial goals, what stakeholder interests might have to be compromised? How can compromise be avoided?

These three views are summarized in table 11.4.

When seen as a process the narrow view of agency has the steps shown in figure 11.4.

AGENCY PROBLEM AND AGENCY COST

When a principal asks an agent to serve, even though the principal has supervisory responsibilities, there is no way to be absolutely certain that the agent will do what the principal wants. To get the agent's help the principal must give up some control.

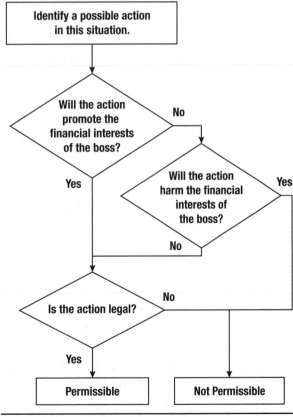

Figure 11.4. The narrow agency ethical process.

A narrow viewpoint of agency leads some to assume that agents usually act in opportunistic ways toward the principal and that they are not capable of refraining from selfish behavior.[20] This gives rise to the agency problem and agency costs.

Agency problem. The agency problem is that agents sometimes do not advance the financial and legal interests of the principal. Instead, they advance their own interests.[21] They will take actions that result in higher pay even though such actions are not in the best interest of the corporation. For example, the top managers may convince the board of directors to merge with another company or to diversify into a new product even though this may not be in the firm's long-term best interest.[22] The agency problem occurs when the interests of the principal and those of the agent conflict or when it is difficult for the principal to verify exactly what the agent is doing.

Agency problems are more likely to arise when stock is widely held by many people and no one shareholder owns more than a small percentage of the total common stock, when the directors of the corporation do not know much about the company or its industry, there is a close personal relationship between directors and top managers, when most of the directors have a direct inside relationship with the company and when the goals of the organization are ambiguous or when some organizational goals are in conflict with other organizational goals.

Agency costs. The principal must be diligent to know that the agent is acting in the principal's best interest and when this is not happening, to make correction to the agent's actions. There is a cost to ensure this. The principal might hire consultants to evaluate the operational activities of the company. An investment banking firm is retained to guide

decision making. The directors of the board require that internal controls on cash and inventory are maintained. The agents are required to produce monthly financial statements and management reports. The principal hires auditors to confirm the validity of financial reports. Members of the board of directors spend their time and expense to discuss financial and operational matters with top managers. Directors establish executive bonuses to incentivize managers to pursue financial and strategic goals.

STEWARDSHIP

In contrast to the agency model, some have proposed an alternative which is based on the recognition that agents are not always self-serving. This model is called the stewardship model.[23] In this approach the steward attempts to widen his or her understanding of whom he or she serves to include the whole organization in the long run. The steward tries to improve financial performance at the same time as trying to satisfy the interests of other stakeholders.

EVALUATION: PROS AND CONS

Appealing to agency as a standard for right and wrong conduct is an attempt to emphasize a person's responsibility to legal authority. By law agents have certain financial and non-financial duties they must fulfill for principals. Depending on how narrowly or how broadly you view agency, the moral foundation is accordingly narrow or broad.

It is time to consider some of the pros and cons of this approach. Pros (arguments in support) will be identified by the symbol (+) while cons (arguments against) will be identified by the symbol (-).

(+) Agency emphasizes the importance of incentives to align the agent's behavior with that of the principal.[24] Much of organizational life is centered around self-interest, and agency takes this into consideration by reminding both principals and agents that they must be mindful of the power of self-interest to divert an agent from loyal fulfillment of duties.

(+) A principal's financial situation plays an important part of the principal's ability to continue a flourishing life, one piece of which is economic. Agency, whether broadly or narrowly defined, emphasizes faithfulness to financial and legal responsibilities. By law agents are required to be good stewards of the principal's financial matters.

(+) Although self-interest is emphasized in agency, paradoxically agency is also concerned about the interest of others, namely, the principal and all those with whom the principal does business.[25] Duty to loyalty and duty to care are legal duties that are other-focused.

(+) A parallel exists between the biblical idea of covenant and the secular idea of fiduciary agency. Agents and principals are to relate to each other in a covenant-like relationship.

(+) Agency is the place where legal duties and fundamental moral principles meet in business ethics.[26] It is in the agency relationship that we find the keys to understanding the fundamental moral codes that are expected in business: honor agreements, avoid lying, respect the autonomy of others and avoid doing harm. These are the indicators where the major points of tension are expected.

A critique of agency as a moral theory reveals several flaws and weaknesses.

(-) The narrow view of agency emphasizes only the financial responsibilities to the person with primary importance, that is, the principal. Other ethical principles are useful only as they facilitate the financial performance.[27] The narrow view of agency uses net present value (NPV) as the yardstick for measuring the moral foundation of the relationship.

(-) The agency model, even the broadest, does not completely answer the question, How does the agent manage the tension when financial interests compete with the duty to others? Additional moral values are needed to guide both agent and principal.

(-) Agency is essentially situation ethics built on love to the principal. The agent who acts only out of concern for the principal's financial well-being will have an advantage in many circumstances; however, if circumstances change, the advantage might be lost unless the agent also changes to preserve the principal as the most important person.

(-) Avoiding harm to others, respecting autonomy and preserving liberty are moral duties that come before and supersede the agency relationship.[28] Without the recognition that there are other, higher, moral principles at stake in all business relationships, agency as a moral principle cannot work because it is dependent on these other moral foundations to work. When an agent is induced to compromise these other more fundamental moral principles, this leads the agent toward self-interest. As a result the agent contradicts the very role of the agent—namely, to serve the interests of another.

(-) The agent cannot ignore other moral obligations in order to fulfill obligation to promote the financial interests of the principal. The same moral logic used to support one moral obligation is the same as that used to say that one has any moral obligations. Accordingly, how can a person be bound by one moral obligation to ignore other moral obligations?[29]

(-) Financial relationship cannot serve as the source of moral obligations.[30] Financial obligations may serve as the vehicle through which the more fundamental principles are transmitted, but they may not serve as the means to avoid responsibility ("I was only following orders!").

DOWN TO THE NITTY-GRITTY

Think about the opening story at the beginning of this chapter. You are the hotel manager. You are thinking about taking business cards from the lobby of a competing hotel nearby. What is the right thing to do? It's time to get down to the nitty-gritty (see table 11.5)!

Agency is a concept that is addressed in Scripture. All of the things we enjoy are God's personal possessions which he as entrusted to us to manage as good stewards.[31] As agents of each other's resources we are ultimately serving as servants of God. Our faithfulness in serving others is rooted in our awareness that God was faithful in keeping his promises. Accordingly, we should care for the assets that we own[32] while we contribute to the sustenance of the assets that belong to other people (even our enemies).[33] Faithful agents are highly prized.[34]

Table 11.5. Applying the ethical process.

Keeping Your Heart: An Intrapersonal Process	Walking in the Community: An Interpersonal Process
• You are the manager of a hotel in the chain. What does your heart say is the right thing to do regarding taking business cards from the lobby of a competing hotel? • Which biblical themes explored in this book inform your heart on this situation? • Which biblical theme, if any, do you feel yourself resisting? Why do you feel resistance? • What might your boss do in this situation? • What other stakeholders deserve considerations before you take action? • Is agency sufficient on its own to guide you to decide what is right and wrong? If not, what additional perspective is needed?	• You are the manager of a hotel in the chain. With whom might you have a conversation about the issue of your idea to take business cards from the lobby of a competitor? Who else might have a helpful perspective? • Which of the biblical themes in this chapter will most likely come up in the conversation either directly or indirectly? Why? Which one(s) will be the most influential in the conversation? • If you have a conversation with someone regarding this situation, which of the fundamental tensions presented earlier in the book might come up? • What right-versus-right dilemmas, if any, can be identified? Have a conversation with someone about this now. What is the outcome of the conversation?

THROUGH THE LENS OF BIBLICAL THEMES

This part of the chapter will use the biblical story themes as a lens through which to evaluate the ethical approach featured in the chapter. Because the themes are interrelated and interdependent, we should expect to see some overlap in the thinking regarding the ethical approach. Some themes will contribute the same thinking as will other themes. The power of these themes comes from their guidance when a community of people talks about complicated ethical dilemmas faced in business practice.

Scripture also recognizes that agents are sometimes unreliable. At times, they will watch out for their own interests at the expense of the interests of the principal.[35]

In response to what he perceived is the dominant model of agency (the narrow view) in Western society, Alexander Hill reviewed three possible responses of the Christian when the principal asks the agent to do something that is against principles.[36] First, the Christian agent can submit to the employer, within the bounds of the law. Hill calls this the submissive approach. This perspective emphasizes the Scripture that emphasizes honoring authority.[37] Acquiescing to the boss's authority minimizes conflict of loyalty. The flaws in this approach are that it overemphasizes the duty of loyalty. While loyalty is an important virtue for the faithful follower of God, it can be dangerous if taken to the extreme. Also, loyalty can change to servility making the agent an unthinking, amoral technician for the principal with little or no obligations to others, much less to God.

Second, when faced by a moral dilemma, the loyal Christian agent can choose to remain pure to biblical principles by refusing to compromise. Hill calls this approach the purist approach. This approach honors the narratives of Scripture that emphasize being true to God.[38] Such a person will tend to be confrontational with the principal, choosing to obey God rather than man. The purist who sees everything in black and white will tend to have a simple solution even to complicated problems. In Hill's model such a person tends to lack creativity in seeking solutions.

Third, the faithful believer who wishes to avoid compromise but also remain loyal will attempt to be creative in accommodating requests for action. Hill calls this the creative accommodating purist approach. Such a person will not be insensitive to the principal's authority but also will attempt to avoid confrontation. Hill sees this person as approaching an ethical dilemma as a neighbor rather than as simply an agent of the principal. Such an agent might give the principal the benefit of the doubt when details of the dilemma are unclear. He or she will accommodate whenever possible. This agent is tolerant in morally ambiguous situations. He or she is not interested in quickly compromising but works diligently to find a creative solution that does not require either compromise or disloyalty. However,

when a creative solution cannot be found, the faithful agent may, on rare occasions, have to make a choice between honoring the principal's request and serving God by ending the agency relationship.

Cosmic conflict. A major principle at stake in the cosmic conflict is that of freedom within boundaries. Persons in relationship must preserve freedom, even freedom that results in one party being unfaithful to the other party. Both parties have the responsibility to watch out for the reputation of each other so that no cause is given to discredit either party. When an agent or principal is unfaithful, this often comes about as a result of one party grasping for more than was agreed on. Unfaithfulness is destructive.

Creation. It is at creation that we see established the larger framework for agency: God is the principal owner of all things he created. The earth and its resources he entrusted to humans as his agents. He has placed humans on earth to work with his assets in order to maintain a flourishing life in community. Only when humans properly care for and share these resources can the true wealth of the whole community be enhanced. We conclude from this that agency relationships are inherently good because they are intended to preserve and foster relationships.

Holiness. When we consecrate ourselves to God, we are signing up to be his agents in the marketplace: representatives in the cosmic conflict, agents of creation, and agents of shalom, sabbath and the other themes (justice, righteousness, truth, wisdom, loving kindness and redemption). It is to these guiding principles that we commit ourselves.

Covenant relationships. A fundamental principle of covenant relationships is that of loyalty or faithfulness. Each party is expected to be loyal to the other. Further, the covenant relationship is for the primary purpose of fostering flourishing life not only of each party but also for the wider community. Covenant principles are broadly applicable and essentially spiritual in nature, yet they comprehend specific duties. The long-term relationship is just as important as what can be gained in the short run. Accordingly, an agency relationship must be based on a broader set of principles than what will contribute only to financial goals of one party.

Shalom. Through the lens of shalom, we must see that agency relationships have a larger purpose, namely, the fostering of flourishing life in community. Both principal and agent will keep this in view. Because the larger community must be kept in focus, an agent's relationship with a principal must be widened to consider the interests of other principals in the community. When the financial interests of the principal who is closest in proximity and directly related to the agent are considered to the exclusion of other principals, the economic dimension of shalom becomes isolated from the full definition of prosperity.

Sabbath. In the sabbath we continually acknowledge God's lordship in all of our life. All relationships are established under and are subject to his authority. Sabbath celebrates God's creative power and redemptive faithfulness. By keeping sabbath we renounce human autonomy and recognize God's continued presence sustaining our lives. Sabbath also encourages diligent work in serving each other.

Justice. Through the lens of justice we see that agency relationships should be structured so that justice can flow through the relationship to all affected parties in the community. When either agent or principal identifies an injustice, they should use their relationship to correct it.

Whenever the principal or the agent engages in injustice or ignores an injustice done by someone else, they undermine the stability of the wider community of which the agency relationship is a part.

Righteousness. Through the lens of righteousness we see that the agency relationship is founded on something deeper and broader than financial interests. This wider perspective on agency means that both agent and principal will engage in acts that honor, preserve and lend stability to covenant relationships. They will see the agency relationship as a means to invest in community. They will place the interests of others above narrow self-interests. Conversely, they will avoid acts that corrupt, violate, destabilize and ultimately destroy covenant relationships or that take from community.

Truth. The agency relationship that is founded on biblical principles is one in which the agent and principal strive for a close correspondence between actions and expectations. Behaviors will form a pattern of reliability. Through this both parties come to trust the other, and those in the wider community will trust that the agency relationship will foster the interests of all.

Wisdom. Agency relationships that are formed and maintained in wisdom are those in which both parties watch out for the interests of all involved, including their own interests. They will attempt to be constructive and productive in their dealings. They will use their practical skills for good and useful purposes. They will not allow themselves to be taken advantage of, nor will they try to take advantage of others.

Loving kindness. The dominant principle at stake in loving kindness for the agency relationship is that both agent and principal will respect the relationship and will foster commitment even when they do not feel affection toward the other.

Redemption. Scripture recognizes that sometimes one party, or both, in a relationship will take an action that undermines the relationship. Through the lens of redemption we see that either party can initiate a redemptive act if the other has acted unfaithfully. The dominant party to the relationship, often the principal, has a dominant leadership role to play in redeeming a broken relationship recognizing that it is not only the immediate parties who need redemption but also the whole community which can benefit from redemption.

CHAPTER REVIEW QUESTIONS

1. Describe the historical roots of the agency concept.

2. What duties do the parties in the agency relationship have?

3. For whom does the agent work?

4. Differentiate between three views of the moral foundation for agency.

5. What is the agency problem? What is agency cost?

6. How does the idea of stewardship differ from agency?

7. What are the pros and cons of agency as an ethical decision-making framework?

8. What is the biblical theme perspective on agency?

9. What three approaches for the Christian agent are described by Hill?

DISCUSSION QUESTIONS

1. Is morality an end in itself regardless of what it contributes to the performance of the business, or is the value of morality de-pendent on what it contributes to the performance of the business?

2. Does the goal of the stockholder trump moral standards or vice versa?

3. Are investors exempted by property ownership from general business ethical standards?

4. Does an agency relationship exist in a nonprofit organization? If so, how?

5. "Some have gone so far as to blame agency theory—and the teaching of agency theory in business schools—for creating the corporate culture that led directly to the scandals."[39] Is it fair to blame ethical scandals on business schools for teaching agency theory?

ETHICAL VIGNETTES TO DISCUSS

For each of the vignettes described below, apply the biblical story themes to discern what is right and wrong.

1. Read 1 Samuel 15:35–16:5. God sent the prophet Samuel[40] on a mission to select a new king of Israel. This assignment occurred before the death of King Saul. Samuel, God's agent, was afraid that if the king learned of the true nature of this mission, the king would kill him. What did God tell Samuel to do? On what basis might this be considered deception? How could one argue that God's guidance was ethical? Is this an example of how to be prudent and shrewd without compromising a principle of covenant relationships?[41] Didn't Samuel have a duty to be loyal to the king whom God had appointed over Israel?

2. Some employees, known as "pickers," at the Amazon.com Swansea, United

Kingdom, distribution facility have complained that Amazon makes them work too hard. These pickers claim that they are to collect items to fulfill a customer's order every 33 seconds from the 800,000 square foot facility. The employee must carry a handset that monitors the time it takes to collect an order. When the allotted time has passed and the order has not been collected, the handset beeps at the picker.

One person who went undercover to document the situation stated that in one 10-and-a-half hour shift, he walked almost 11 miles gathering items to fulfill customer orders. An Amazon spokesperson is reported to have said, "Worker safety is our number one priority." Is it ethical for Amazon managers to require such high-intensity work from pickers in its UK distribution facility?

12

Justice and Rights

*It is more important to be fair
than to be right!*

Be impartial!

SCRIPTURE PASSAGE

How blessed are those who keep justice,
Who practice righteousness at all times!
(Ps 106:3)

The Nature of Rights
Positive Rights and Negative Rights
Evaluation: Pros and Cons
Down to the Nitty-Gritty
Through the Lens of Biblical Themes

CHAPTER OVERVIEW

In this chapter we explore two interrelated approaches to making business decisions: justice and rights. In particular, we will

- explore the basic ideas of justice and rights

- distinguish between the various types of justice

- distinguish between positive rights and negative rights

- evaluate the pros and cons of justice and rights as an approach to business ethics

- evaluate justice and rights through the lens of biblical story themes

MAIN TOPICS

The Nature of Justice
Types of Justice

KEY TERMS

commutative justice, compensatory justice, contractarian method, distributive justice, egalitarian method, entitlement, equity, fairness, impartiality, intuitionist method, justice, libertarian, negative claim rights, positive claim rights, procedural justice, retributive justice

OPENING SCENARIO

Evaluate the degree of fairness for each of the following items from a survey shown in table 12.1.[1]

What is it that makes a particular marketplace situation just and another unjust?[2] Why do some people consider the same situation to be unfair and others consider it fair?

THE NATURE OF JUSTICE

Justice involves several interrelated ideas: equity, impartiality and fairness, with fairness being

Table 12.1. Fairness experiment.

Item	Completely Fair	Acceptable	Unfair	Very Unfair
1. A hardware store has been selling snow shovels for $15 each. The morning after a large snow-storm, the store raises the price to $20 each.				
2. A company is making a small profit. It is located in a community experiencing a recession with substantial unemployment but no inflation. There are many workers anxious to work at the company. The company decides to decrease wages and salaries 7% this year.				
3. A company is making a small profit. It is located in a community experiencing a recession with substantial unemployment and inflation of 12%. There are many workers anxious to work at the company. The company decides to increase salaries only 5% this year.				
4. A landlord owns and rents out a single small house to a tenant who is living on a fixed income. A higher rent would mean the tenant would have to move. Other small rental houses are available. The landlord's costs have increased substantially over the past year, and the landlord raises the rent to cover the cost increases when the tenant's lease is due for renewal.				

the closest to the root idea.[3] Justice is based an important assumption: society is a fair system of social cooperation between free and equal persons. Social cooperation is guided by widely accepted social rules that members of society believe are valid for regulating conduct. Cooperation also assumes that all persons look on cooperative behavior as mutually beneficial for everyone involved. Cooperation also requires that cooperative action will create a positive benefit for each person when seen from the point of view of each person. In order for this to work, each person must have the capacity to discern when actions are just or unjust. They must also have the capacity to know when good results from an action.

Justice involves all persons in society or in an institution (such as in business transactions in the marketplace) making an implicit agreement among themselves regarding access to rights and liberties. This agreement is a basic social contract.

Justice also is concerned with correcting injustices when wrongs have been done in the context of social groups and social institutions such as business, government and nonprofit organizations.

Impartiality requires you to be at a mental distance equal to that of other people so that you can view the situation through their eyes. This requires a degree of empathy with other points of views. To explore this consider that a person, called here the actor, proposes to take an action that has an effect on another person whom we will call the respondent. Justice requires seeing the action through both sets of eyes. As seen through the eyes of others, impartiality requires that whatever action is being proposed, both the actor and the respondent must mutually acknowledge the benefits and burdens of the action. But justice is not merely seen through the eyes of these two persons. There are other persons in the larger community who are potentially affected by the proposed action, too. This conversation about actor and respondent suggests that consequences are important when considering whether or not justice has been done in an action (see fig. 12.1).

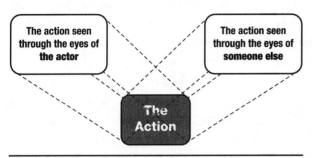

Figure 12.1. Justice as seen from different perspectives.

Perspective matters. One problem with justice is that what we see is influenced by where we stand in relation to the issue. We can see from this that the sense of justice is influenced by the perception of the consequences of the action.

By way of analogy, when we stand on the earth, the moon and sun appear similar in size. But if we were to stand on the moon, the moon and sun seem different in size because you are closer to the moon.[4] Accordingly, when you discern whether or not justice is followed in a social situation, if you take the point of view of one person, actions may appear just. Take the perspective of another person who has opposing goals and you may see that the actions do not appear just. Thus, as we look at justice, we quickly see that it is more complicated than merely saying, "Just be fair!" An example of this is the issue of fairness itself.

Fairness, it can be said, is in the eye of the beholder, meaning that each person has a different perspective or a different priority when determining what is fair.[5] Yet, every society on earth has a sense of fairness. But what shapes the buyer's perception of fairness of the actions

taken by a seller? There are several factors: (a) the reference transaction; (b) the outcomes of the transaction on the seller; and (c) the situation the seller is in.[6]

Reference transactions. If a firm increases its profits by raising its prices (or lowering its wages), most people will think this is unfair, because customers judge fairness with respect to the most recent information about prices based on memory of transactions. If the customer has no experience transacting business with the firm, perceptions of the prevailing prices are used to judge fairness. An employee's current wage is a reference point used to judge the fairness of any changes to the wage. The employee thinks of this as an entitlement. However, if a new person is hired, such a person does not have an entitlement to the former worker's rate of pay. The same principle is at work when a

> Do not withhold good from
> those to whom it is due,
> When it is in your power to do it.
> (Prov 3:27)

new person rents an apartment. A rent increase for the existing renter will be seen as unfair while the same increase in rent to a new renter is acceptable. People usually compare what happens to them with what happens to other people in their company or in their industry rather than with what happens to people in other industries.

Transaction outcomes. The fundamental principle of fairness with respect to outcomes is that one person or company should not gain at the expense of someone else's corresponding loss. Beyond this people tend to be more sensitive to justice issues if it involves an out-of-pocket cost rather than a lost opportunity. They tend to be "more sensitive to losses than to foregone gains."[7] If a firm takes an action that results in a loss to a person, it is more likely to be judged unfair than if it cancels or reduces possible gain that someone else could have had. And a company's action is more likely to be considered unfair if the firm gains by it than if the firm avoids a loss. The change in real income is essentially the same, but what people consider fair and unfair is very different. When a person experiences a loss it is unfair, but when the same person experiences an elimination of a gain, it is acceptable even if the value of each is equal. "Thus, there may be less resistance to the cancellation of a discount or bonus than to an equivalent price increase or wage cut."[8]

The situation. People take into account the situation when forming judgments regarding fairness of actions. For example, people usually think it is fair when a company protects itself against loss by trying to pass along to customers because of increases in the company's wholesale costs or operating costs. When the company's profit falls below its most recent reference level, employees are more likely to accept a reduction in wages. The acceptability of self-protection applies only when it is directly related to the transaction. But it is unacceptable when the company raises prices in one product in order to make up for a loss in revenue from other products or services. People tend to work with a cost-plus rule of fair pricing. When a company sells a product or service, it is expected to earn a profit by passing along marked-up costs. But when a company's costs go down, many people believe it is acceptable for the company to retain the benefits of cost reduction.

Many people believe that it is unfair if a company raises its prices just because there is a temporary increase in demand for its products. People generally consider it even worse when a company exploits a customer for no other reason than a change that has occurred in the customer's situation. Retail customers tend to view a price increase as acceptable if it is done by the manufacturing company instead of the retailer. If the price increase is believed to have been chosen by the retailer, the customers tend to view it as unfair. Retail customers often do not take into consideration the effect on other customers when a company increases its prices. They just want the lower price for themselves. If the store does not increase its price when demand is greater than supply, many customers who would be willing to purchase the product at a higher price will be unable to do so because other customers purchased the product at the lower price. If supply is limited, some customers get the product while other customers do not.

Customers tend to place a lower value on something they do not own and a higher value on the same product once they own it.[9] A person selling a used car tends to view it as more valuable than does the person considering purchasing the car.

The introductory ideas about justice are summarized in table 12.2.

TYPES OF JUSTICE

The idea of justice as fairness in the marketplace leads us to consider the five types of justice. Some of these distinctions were first recognized by the ancient Greek scholar Aristotle.[10] These distinctions are based on the fundamental difference between justice of procedures and justice of outcomes, or justice from what we do versus justice from what happens

Table 12.2. Justice and injustice.

Justice	Injustice
Fairness: like cases are treated the same except where there is a relevant difference	Unfairness: like cases are not treated the same
Impartiality: treatment of others not dependent on personal relationship or characteristics	Partiality: treatment of others dependent on personal relationship or characteristics
Consistency: implementing policies and decisions the same way, for the same circumstances, over time	Inconsistency: implementing policies and decisions in different ways, for the same circumstances, over time
Equality: treating people in ways that reflect a belief in their fundamental moral equality	Inequality: treating people in ways that reflect a belief in their fundamental inequality
Rights: making rights more certain; not interfering with someone's rights	Lack of rights: depriving a person of rights or making rights less certain
Resources: impartiality in distribution of resources and responsibilities or costs	Resources: partial distribution of resources and responsibilities or costs

as a result. We can restate these two broad categories to be similar to the poles of the fundamental tension introduced earlier in the book: duties versus consequences.

In addition to these two broad categories, we recognize five types of justice.

One type of justice involves actions to make corrections for injustices that occurred in past actions. This is called compensatory justice because it involves compensating parties that have suffered an injustice. When someone has broken the law, a different kind of justice is involved where retribution prescribed for in the law is enacted against the law-breaker(s). Thus, it is called retributive justice.

Two other types of justice involve business transactions and the running of social organizations. When people exchange goods and services for money or other things of value, commutative justice requires that the exchange of values is fair for all parties in the transaction.[11] Another type of justice is considered in all types of organizations and formal social groups where decision making is in focus. The fairness of decision-making procedures are in focus here. Thus, this type of justice is called procedural justice. Procedural justice designates fair-decision procedures, practices and agreements. Procedural justice involves fairness in

the organizational or governmental decision-making processes.[12] Six elements are involved. First, organizational procedures designed to allocate resources and influence should be consistent across people and over time. Second, leaders involved in decision making must take steps to suppress their personal biases when allocating resources. Third, decisions must be based on good information so as to be accurate. Fourth, opportunities must exist to modify or reverse a decision when the decision was based on inaccurate information. Fifth, the resource allocation process must be representative of the key stakeholders. Sixth, the allocation process must be compatible with prevailing moral and ethical standards.

Distributive justice involves making decisions about how to allocate economic and political resources and how to ensure that a fair distribution of social responsibilities also is accomplished.[13] This sounds like the right thing to do, but given the nature of human beings, how can this be done?

One method is called the intuition approach to fairness. For example, should distribution of resources be made on the basis of who is most deserving? If so, how will the community determine who is most deserving? Should the decision be made on the basis of who needs the resource the most? Intuitively this sounds right. But this begs the question, How do you determine need in a fair manner? Perhaps intuition tells us that the decision should be made based on who would benefit the most. This requires stakeholders to make a judgment with which others might strongly disagree. A fourth intuitionist perspective is to divide the resource based on a mathematical equality formula.[14] In this approach justice is managed by individuals. The problem is that managing the balance of interests on the basis of intuition means managing conflicting interests of individuals. Also, each of these bases could be used, but there is no clear way forward to apply one approach over another. Thus, intuition seems inadequate.

Another approach to distributive justice is to use the utilitarian definition of fairness. With the utilitarian approach any given person's interests count for no more than for other persons' interests. Fairness is considered from an overall perspective and not from the point of view of any particular person. Thus, as we have seen in a previous chapter, utilitarian fairness might very well require one person to give up something so that the overall good of many other persons can be achieved. Further, if giving up something for the overall good of the many creates an inequality for the one person, utilitarianism is unconcerned about this.

A third approach to distributive justice, called the contractarian[15] or egalitarian method to fairness espoused by John Rawls, is to organize the distribution of resources so that the following principles can be assured.[16] First, use individual liberty as the fundamental principle that defines justice. Each person is to have an equal status and equal right to the total system of basic liberties compatible with a similar system of liberty for all. This principle fosters equality. Second, we must recognize

that some persons are born into situations of inequality. Thus, if any inequality exists, society has a responsibility to manage the distribution of resources so that the least advantaged persons in society can still enjoy equality of liberty and status. This would require that impartial representatives of citizens be chosen to organize the distribution of wealth and opportunity in a fair, impartial manner.

In this approach persistent inequalities of wealth and influence would be allowed so long as basic political rights and civil rights are preserved. Inequalities would not be allowed to be detrimental to the least advantaged citizens. All persons would be given equal opportunities for education and access to occupations which afford them opportunities to participate in society on the same footing as citizens who enjoyed more advantages from birth. In this approach justice is managed by leaders in the community, essentially making it part of the democratic political processes and government bureaucratic processes. Revenue from taxes would be used to distribute to the least advantaged and to manage the distribution process.

For Rawls, justice is not merely about marketplace transactions. It is a social structure problem. Accordingly, government would need to be restructured. Representatives of the least advantaged would be given basic information about the most disadvantaged citizens but not information about race, skin color, or other particular characteristics which could bias the decision making of representatives. Some of the least advantaged might have to be given preferential treatment for entrance into universities and particular jobs so that their economic disadvantage is corrected. At the least the right thing to do is that action which avoids harming some people.

> ## FOUR KINDS OF DISTRIBUTIVE JUSTICE
> - Intuition
> - Utilitarian: the most good for the most stakeholders
> - Contractarian (egalitarian)
> - Entitlement (libertarian)

A fourth approach is the entitlement or libertarian approach espoused by Robert Nozick.[17] In this view liberty is the fundamental value, the first requirement of society. Justice consists of "permitting each person to live as he or she pleases."[18] The libertarian view does not require that persons promote positive rights but instead focuses on noninterference with the rights of others.[19] Any action that interferes with someone's liberty to pursue his or her rights, even if such action is designed to foster the general welfare of society, is unjust. Any law that violates individual liberty to enjoy one's rights, even if such law is designed to foster well-being of many, also is unjust. Rights are part of being human and are not available just because there is a certain law or government in place.

Nozick frames the theory in terms of justice with respect to "holdings." Holdings (property, income, goods, power) must be acquired and transferred in a just manner. If a person obtains a holding in a just manner, he or she is entitled to keep it. When exchange of holdings occurs, such as through buying and selling property, the exchange must be done voluntarily. If someone believes that his or her right has been violated in the marketplace and as a result an injustice occurs, then the person is entitled to restitution as long as the correction is accomplished in a just manner.

The five types of justice are summarized in table 12.3.

The topic of justice has raised the issue of rights which is closely related. To this we turn next.

THE NATURE OF RIGHTS

All persons have rights! Because we are human beings, we have an important claim on our own existence. In other words, each human has the right to life. We have the right to be free from harm caused by others. Correspondingly others have a duty with respect to certain rights. Thus, rights are tied to rules of social conduct. Such rules either allow a person to act in a particular way, to enjoy a particular liberty, or require other persons to act in particular ways with respect to a person's rights. Moreover, certain rights and certain duties or liabilities are often paired with each other.[20] The social rules may be in the form of formal laws or nonlegal informal social expectations.

The basic natural or human rights to life, liberty and the pursuit of happiness are

Table 12.3. Types of justice.

Type of Justice	Description
Commutative	Fairness in marketplace transactions of buying and selling, exchanging things of value
Compensatory	Compensating someone for a past injustice or making right a wrong
Retributive	Punishing someone who has broken a law
Procedural	Fair-decision procedures, practices and agreements in social groups
Distributive	Allocating resources (benefits) and responsibilities (costs) in a fair manner (review the four kinds of distributive justice)

common to all persons regardless of legal status, gender, national origin, race, age and religion. We speak of human rights as being *prima facie*, that is, at first examination it appears to be self-evident. Moral or human rights transcend national boundaries or the type of government that is in power. Moral rights or human rights are rights that can be justified on moral grounds. "Unlike legal rights, human rights are held independently of membership in a state or other social organization."[21]

Humans meet certain criteria based on law such as age (the right to vote). These are civil or legal rights that are protected by law. Civil rights are legal rights that usually apply to citizens but not necessarily all human beings. The right to freedom of religion is both a civil right and a human right.

Some legal rights are related to liberties that all humans expect that they can enjoy. A liberty right means that a person is at liberty to take a particular action. But other people do not have the duty to help them to take the action. A liberty right is a privilege.

Another commonly accepted description of a right is that it is a valid or justifiable claim on other persons in terms of how they should be treated. Some rights require that other persons stop preventing us from exercising our liberties or from taking a particular action on which we have a legitimate claim. These are known as negative claim rights. For example, persons have a right to freedom of speech, freedom of movement, to come and go as they like and freedom of association without interference from others. Unreasonably confining a person to his or her home, kidnapping a person or falsely imprisoning a person are violations of this right. The negative right is that others are forbidden from interfering with the person's right to movement. The right to freedom of speech forbids others from preventing a person from speaking.

The opposite is known as a positive claim right. A positive claim right is a right that requires others (the government or persons) to help you achieve what you have the right to do. Thus, a positive right is a valid claim on goods or services.[22] For example, one of the legal rights in the United States is the right to primary and secondary education. Other people are duty bound to assist in helping persons obtain such an education. The distinction between a negative right and a positive right is illustrated below.

Some rights involve both negative and positive dimensions. For example, an entrepreneur has the right to invest her savings in a business of her choice. She has the negative claim right that other persons will not interfere with her investment endeavors. If you have the legal right to start your own business, others have the duty to permit you to start your own business if you meet the legal requirements. The right to life prevents others from taking the life of a right-bearer. But the right to life requires that government to provide basic protections so as to make the right more easily accessible.

NEGATIVE AND POSITIVE RIGHTS

Negative Right: Requires others not to interfere with you get something you are entitled to receive.

Positive Right: Requires others to help you achieve something you are entitled to receive.

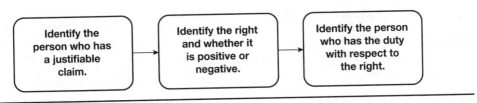

Figure 12.2. An analysis of a claim right.

Power rights are rights that when exercised by the right-holder, one has in order to have an influence on the rights and duties of another right-holder. For example, when a person enters into a business agreement, this binds both parties. Such an agreement may create duties but also liabilities in that one or both of the right-holders is liable to have their rights and responsibilities changed because of entering into the contract.

Yet another type of right is known as immunity rights. These are protections for right-holders so that their other rights and duties are not changed by persons who exercise their power rights over them.

Each person has rights which require other persons to fulfill certain relevant duties, either positive (helping you do what you have the right to do) or negative (not interfering with you as you attempt to do what you have the right to do). The process of analyzing a person's right is illustrated in figure 12.2.

Rights are like the trump card in a card game: they override all other considerations, including the consideration of generating maximum utility. They define the veto power that forbids us from taking particular actions toward other persons.

Rights are not the same as interests or wants. A person can have an interest in pursuing a certain action, such as stealing someone else's property. He may want to steal but not have the right to do it. Property ownership and possession rights mean that if a person has obtained the property in a just manner, he should be allowed to keep that property.

When seen as a process justice and rights lead to the steps shown in figure 12.3.

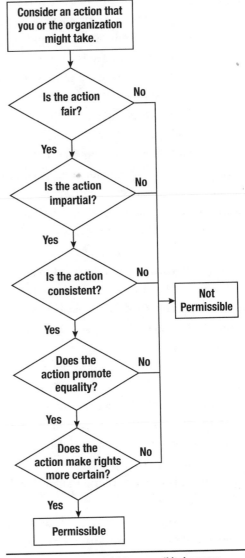

Figure 12.3. Justice and rights as an ethical process.

EVALUATION: PROS AND CONS

This chapter introduces the ideas of justice and rights as the moral standards of right and wrong. It is time to consider some of the pros and cons of this approach. Pros (arguments in support or strengths) will be identified by the symbol (+) while cons (arguments against or statements of weakness) will be identified by the symbol (-).

(+) Justice widens the perspective from egoism and embraces the point of view of all people who are affected by an action. Justice requires that you take a broad view of a particular situation and consider not only your own needs but also the needs of others. Accordingly, justice is considered morally more mature than most other ethical approaches.

(+) The essence of justice is fairness. All persons who have the ability to anticipate the effect of another person's actions on themselves can make an independent judgment regarding the fairness of an action. Persons who lack the ability to understand the effect of another person's action on themselves need an advocate to serve their interests.

(+) Every human can understand the basic idea of justice. We understand when someone has been unjust toward us; we have the ability to empathize with someone else who has been treated unjustly.

(+) Justice is fundamental to cohesive society. Without justice flourishing life of well-being is not possible: "No justice; no peace!"

(+) Justice takes into consideration not only the interests of one person but also the interests of others in society.

(+) The idea of justice is closely aligned with Scripture principles.

Justice and rights as standards of right and wrong also show some weaknesses, which include the following.

(-) Each person's idea of fairness is different from an opposing person's idea. The contemporary view of justice assumes that there is more than one good that can be attained as persons interact in society. This plurality of goods means that what one person considers good may be in direct opposition to what another person considers good. If both are to pursue good freely with equal access to rights, if two persons have opposing views of what is just, and if these persons cannot come to agreement on what is just, achieving justice will require that the conversation extends outward in the community. But at this, the ethics process becomes political. The intervention of a third party of higher authority in the community, such as the court system, may be needed.

(-) Justice assumes the presence of other universally applicable moral standards that must be agreed to by all parties. Without an objective standard of right and wrong that lies outside personal definitions of fairness, justice can degenerate toward relativism or egoism.

(-) Definitions of human rights that are culturally determined reduce the basis of rights to cultural relativism.

(-) Civil rights based on law are inherently limited in terms of their applicability because law is limited in its ability to define right and wrong considering all types of circumstances and situations.

DOWN TO THE NITTY-GRITTY

Think about scenario 4 at the beginning of this chapter. You are a landlord who owns and rents out a single small house to a tenant who is living on a fixed income. A higher rent would mean the tenant would have to move. Other small rental houses are available. Your costs have increased substantially over the past year, and you raise the rent to cover the cost increases when the tenant's lease is due for renewal. Is this the right thing to do? It's time to get down to the nitty-gritty (see table 12.4)!

THROUGH THE LENS OF BIBLICAL THEMES

This part of the chapter will use the biblical story themes as a lens through which to evaluate the ethical approach featured in the chapter. Because the themes are interrelated and interdependent, we should expect to see some overlap in the thinking regarding the ethical approach. Some themes will contribute the same thinking as will other themes. The power of these themes comes from their guidance when a community of people talks about complicated ethical dilemmas faced in business practice.

The ancient Hebrew ideas of justice predate those of the Greek scholars.[23] While the Hebrew writers did not analyze justice systematically in an academic way, their writings show that they understood much of what sophisticated approaches understand today. Their focus is on the practice of justice in the context of a covenant community.

Cosmic conflict. The cosmic conflict centers around the question of God's justice. Satan claims that God unjustly keeps things from his creatures, that God is arbitrary and capricious. Speaking of God in the Scripture story King David said, "Righteousness and justice are the foundation of Your throne; lovingkindness and truth go before You" (Ps 89:14). Justice is an attribute of God.[24] "The works of His hands are truth and justice; all His precepts are sure" (Ps 111:7).[25] "For the biblical writers, the meaning of justice is not discovered through abstract philosophical speculation. It is known primarily through God's revelation in history, and the biblical writings comprise the record of that revelation."[26] God does not show favoritism. Humans are to follow this model.[27] Accordingly all actions that the person or organization takes with respect to either fostering or limiting rights will reflect on or detract from God's character of justice and mercy.

Creation. As the Creator-King with a throne built on justice and righteousness, God established the universe "in a manner that expresses and depends upon" these two principles.[28] Creation is the setting in which justice is to be displayed: his justice and our justice toward each other. When injustice is allowed to occur uncorrected, the foundation of all creation and all relationships is under attack. The biblical context for rights is theological and began at creation. God created humans in his

Table 12.4. Applying the ethical process.

Keeping Your Heart: An Intrapersonal Process	Walking in the Community: An Interpersonal Process
• You are the landlord. What does your heart say is the right thing to do regarding raising the rent? • Which biblical themes explored in this book inform your heart on this situation? • Which biblical theme, if any, do you feel yourself resisting? Why do you feel resistance? • What is the fair thing to do? • What other stakeholders deserve considerations before you take action? • Is justice and rights sufficient on its own to guide you to decide what is right and wrong? If not, what additional perspective is needed?	• You are the landlord. With whom might you have a conversation about the issue of your idea to raise rent? Who else might have a helpful perspective? • Which of the biblical themes in this chapter will most likely come up in the conversation either directly or indirectly? Why? Which one(s) will be the most influential in the conversation? • If you have a conversation with someone regarding this situation, which of the fundamental tensions presented earlier in the book might come up? • What right-versus-right dilemmas, if any, can be identified? Have a conversation with someone about this now. What is the outcome of the conversation?

image.[29] God is the originator of rights. Further, he gives rights to all members of his kingdom.[30] Therefore they are endowed with certain rights. "Humans are created to be representatives of God—a kind of icon of God in the world. They are the means by which God's loving rule is to be made visible on earth. Since God is a God of justice, those who bear God's image must also be agents of justice. They are to learn from God what justice means and to reproduce what they learn in all their activities in the world."[31]

Holiness. The basis of God's justice and his faithfulness to us is his holiness.

If we expect to act in just ways, we must first consecrate ourselves to following the elements of justice as outlined in the principles of covenant relationships.

Covenant relationships. God loves justice. "He loves righteousness and justice; the earth is full of the lovingkindness of the LORD" (Ps 33:5). Justice and righteousness are the two foundation stones for the divine and human kingship.[32] The Law, a clear expression of God's desire for covenant relationships, is identified as being justice.[33] We can also say that justice is a sign of the covenant in action.[34] "The meaning 'law, commandment' occupies an important place in the usage of mishpat. When it denotes that which has been established, the law, mishpat usually appears in the plural. God's mishpatim are the individual commandments as well as the summary of the entire law."[35] "Justice flows from a life of obedience to the law of God, a law that derives its character from a larger vision of shalom, of God's intentions for human life. Law, justice and covenant are thus overlapping or interpenetrating concepts in the Bible."[36] Justice, the basis of law, is a concept central to those who expect to be blessed under the covenant.[37] God expected to see justice enacted throughout the covenant community, including anyone present such as visitors from other nations and the disadvantaged.[38] Workers are to be paid for their work.[39]

Shalom. Justice is inseparable from shalom. Shalom "combines in one concept the meaning of justice and peace. To know shalom requires the achievement of *both* justice *and* peace. They are inseparable ingredients of the same reality."[40] Faithfulness to the covenant relationship with God and with each other, living according to his law, will result in shalom and justice. When injustice exists, shalom needs to be restored, but this can occur only as injustices are corrected and justice is allowed to flow throughout the land.

Sabbath. Sabbath involves both rest and action. Sabbath means resting from our own attempts to achieve God's justice. But it also means taking action to extend God's justice to others in the community. Sabbath is the symbol of this and a structured time set apart for contemplation of how we can extend God's redemption to others.

Justice and righteousness. Justice involves the day-to-day conduct of persons and social institutions when they show in action their righteousness.[41] When people pursue justice through their actions with each other, this is the recipe for living in well-being (shalom).[42] It is the pathway to blessing. "How blessed are those who keep justice, who practice righteousness at all times!" (Ps 106:3). The theme of righteousness is sometimes substituted for the idea of justice. These two words sometimes occur together, having "virtually identical meaning."[43]

Justice also involves decision making by persons who are acting on behalf of the entire community (or portion of the community).[44] It refers to the entire judicial procedure of interpreting laws in particular cases. It also involves the formal social expectations (civil laws) that are established by community leaders. "Woe to those who enact evil statutes and to those who constantly record unjust decisions, so as to deprive the needy of justice and rob the poor of My people of their rights, so that widows may be their spoil and that they may plunder the orphans" (Is 10:1-2).

The biblical idea of justice also is associated with the principle of rights. "Justice also contains the notion of entitlement, privilege, or the claim that an individual has a legal right to something. This phenomenon finds its clearest expression in Deuteronomy 18:3-5."[45]

Justice flows downhill in organizational hierarchy. "If you see oppression of the poor and denial of justice and righteousness in the province, do not be shocked at the sight; for one official watches over another official, and there are higher officials over them" (Eccles 5:8). Thus, one of the most insidious problems in a community is when corrupt leaders are allowed to practice injustice. Other leaders lower in authority follow their example until eventually injustice is rampant. Corrupt leaders show partiality during the mediation of disputes; they take bribes which blind them to the actions required to enact justice.[46]

Prophetic references to the injustices perpetrated by corrupt leaders are the most frequent use of the Hebrew term for justice.[47] One of the things we learn from the writings of the prophets is that justice is a political issue, not just a religious belief issue. This is illustrated by two things. First, justice requires action in a social setting where people disagree regarding whose self-interests should prevail over others' self-interests. Second, when someone speaks out against injustice, those in position of power and authority respond by attempting to stop the dissent.

Truth. The biblical concept of truth is a concept of action.[48] When the king, emulating God's character, builds his throne on truth, he builds it on actions of faithfulness to covenant relations. In essence advancing truth means advancing the cause of faithfulness to commitments in and around the covenant community. Without faithfulness, justice would become a hollow promise and the very idea of justice would be undermined.

Wisdom. There is a practical perspective to justice: "Justice, and only justice, you shall pursue, that you may live and possess the land which the LORD your God is giving you" (Deut 16:20).[49] Wisdom is interwoven with faithfulness, justice and other dimensions of moral uprightness.[50] Sometimes it is not clear which is the just action to take. This requires the wisdom of the community from those who have faced difficult, complex situations. Thus, wisdom is one way that the community shares in the work of justice.

Loving kindness. Behaving justly is one way love your neighbor as yourself. When a judge enacts justice he is expressing loving kindness.[51] Market workers will act in just ways to everyone in the community, even to strangers who may be unfamiliar with local customs or standard prices. Business workers will use business technology in ways that foster justice rather than taking advantage of people. Market workers will promote impartial arbitration and equitable treatment. The business professional will (a) not show favoritism or take bribes; (b) provide fair grievance procedures; and (c) avoid undermining legitimate processes established by those in authority. Organizations will maintain fair processes for mediating disputes among workers or between the organization and its customers or suppliers.

Companies will treat suppliers fairly; suppliers will treat customers fairly. Goods will be sold at prices that reflect the value of the product. Those in business will not withhold products from the market for the purpose of raising prices. Sellers will be transparent in their dealings. Sellers will avoid coercing customers. Customers will avoid taking advantage of sellers. Employers will treat workers fairly. Employers will use progressive discipline processes that are fairly applied across the organization. Employers will not deprive workers of their rights. Instead, they will foster the rights of workers. Employees will avoid taking advantage of employers.

Redemption. Like its relationship with the other story themes considered here, justice is interwoven with redemption. The foundation for God's action of redemption is rooted in justice. God's expectation of humans in the covenant community to keep justice is that God is the Redeemer. "You shall not pervert the justice due an alien or an orphan, nor take a widow's garment in pledge. But you shall remember that you were a slave in Egypt, and that the Lord your God redeemed you from there; therefore I am commanding you to do this thing" (Deut 24:17-18). In a similar way, when leaders act to recover justice in the human sphere, they are participating with God in the work of redemption. The other way to see is this is to see that an action of redemption that a human takes on behalf of another is essentially an act of justice.

CHAPTER REVIEW QUESTIONS

1. What does the idea of justice mean?

2. Differentiate between the various types of justice.

3. What does the concept of rights mean?

4. Distinguish between positive rights and negative rights.

5. What is a power right?

6. What is an immunity right?

7. What are the pros and cons of justice and rights as an ethical decision-making framework?

8. What perspective do the biblical story themes offer for understanding justice and rights?

DISCUSSION QUESTIONS

1. Is it possible to be truly objective when you need to be impartial? If not, is justice ever possible if you do not involve persons from the larger community?

2. Which is better:
   - Act so as to correct an injustice (but risk increasing the desire for vengeance)? or,
   - Do not act; be passive (but risk allowing the injustice to continue)?

3. Is it right that a person acts in a way that places the needs of family above the needs of others? Why? Does this apply equally well to the needs of close friends? Why?

4. Is it right that the self-interest of some uninformed customers be allowed to be the standard for what is fair when other customers may have a different opinion?

5. Consider one of the items in the table 12.1. Compare how a utilitarian would answer the question, What is the right thing to do? with how someone applying justice might answer it.

ETHICAL VIGNETTES TO DISCUSS

For each of the vignettes described below, apply the biblical story themes to discern what is right and wrong.

1. As a manager you hear by the grapevine that some of your workers are dissatisfied with some of the things at work. You hear that some workers want more participation in management decisions. Some workers have expressed the thought that participation in management decisions is an ethical issue, meaning that it is wrong not to allow workers to participate. Others say that it is a matter of feasibility and practicality, meaning that sometimes it makes sense to allow participation because it is more efficient and other times it is not practical to allow worker participation and doing so is less efficient. What do you think?[52]

   - *It is a moral issue.* The decision of whether or not to ask employees to participate in managerial decisions has an impact of worker alienation, that is, when workers are not allowed to participate, they become alienated. Alienation is a preventable condition at work, and if managers do nothing to prevent this, it is unethical. Alienation is one of the observed consequences of managerial practice. "Alienation at work is the most pervasive phenomenon of the post-industrial society and management in both the private and public sectors are engaged in a constant struggle against it for their own survival."[53] Alienation can and should be avoided. It is morally wrong to participate in managerial practices which contribute to alienation.

   - *It is a practical issue, but not a moral issue.* The decision of whether or not to ask employees to participate in managerial decisions is one of feasibility, practicality and efficiency. The ethical guide that we must follow is that of behaviors constrained by law. It is law which is the boundary. Allowing workers to participate in decision making takes time, and this costs the organization. However, in some situations, decision making that involves workers saves time later, and in the long run this is more efficient. We must recognize that some workers do not want to participate in some decisions. They just want to be told what to do and how to do it. Asking them to participate may cause alienation because it is not what they prefer. Such alienation may result in reduced performance, and this is undesirable.

2. On Friday, February 21, 2014, the Arizona state legislature delivered a bill to Governor Jan Brewer for signature. The controversial Arizona bill, SB 1062, was similar to laws also being proposed in other states. The bill, if signed into law by the governor, would make it permissible for a business to refuse service to a customer who is gay. Proponents of the bill say it is designed to protect religious freedom. Opponents say that the bill would foster discrimination. Regardless of either the positive or negative economic impact that the bill might have if signed into state law, should business owners be permitted to deny service to customers based on sexual orientation? What is the ethical basis for your perspective? What elements of justice and rights are at stake here?

13

Virtues and Character

Be who you are!

Be authentic.

SCRIPTURE PASSAGE

For there is no good tree which produces bad fruit, nor, on the other hand, a bad tree which produces good fruit. For each tree is known by its own fruit. For men do not gather figs from thorns, nor do they pick grapes from a briar bush. The good man out of the good treasure of his heart brings forth what is good; and the evil man out of the evil treasure brings forth what is evil; for his mouth speaks from that which fills his heart. (Lk 6:43-45)[1]

CHAPTER OVERVIEW

In this chapter we will introduce an approach to ethical action that is different from the others: Virtues and character. In particular, we will

- explore the basic ideas of virtue and character as ethical standards

- evaluate the pros and cons of virtue and character as an approach to business ethics

- evaluate virtue and character through the lens of biblical themes

MAIN TOPICS

Virtue Ethics

Communal Influences on Virtues

A Curious Double Paradox

Aristotle on Virtues

Character

Evaluation: Pros and Cons

Down to the Nitty-Gritty

Through the Lens of Biblical Themes

KEY TERMS

character, virtue

OPENING SCENARIO

Samantha Harley is chief executive officer of Connect.com, an Internet marketing company that offers an online dating service.[2] Ms. Harley is considering whether or not to contribute cash from her company to the nonprofit community shelter for battered women. Women who manage to escape out of their home when they are assaulted by their significant other often are taken by a friend or by the police to the shelter, where they are interviewed. If they have nowhere else they can go for safety, they are admitted to the shelter until other resources can be found to provide a place of safety. Here they are provided with legal counsel to help them through the process when their significant other goes through the judicial system. They receive counseling, food and encouragement.

If Samantha is a utilitarian, she will consider whether giving to the charity will have an outcome that promotes the greatest degree of happiness for all stakeholders. If she is a universalist following Immanuel Kant's deontological ethics, she will consider what her duty is in terms of helping the nonprofit organization. What these two perspectives ignore is Samantha herself: who she is, her motivations, her intentions and desires. These perspectives also gloss over the particular situation Samantha is in.

If we do not consider Samantha herself, how do we judge what is right and wrong in this situation? Considering only the outcomes of making a corporate charitable contribution or considering only her theoretical duty tends to isolate our discernment of right and wrong from the social, interpersonal and intrapersonal dynamics.

INTRODUCTION

One thing is clear from what we have explored regarding ethics: Ethics involves actions in a social setting. Accordingly, the four basic elements to think about when considering right and wrong are the following:[3]

- the action taken
- the outcome of the action
- the social setting or situation in which the action occurs
- the person who acts

Ethics requires the use of guiding moral principles to analyze and interpret a situation and then decide what is right and wrong.[4]

Ethics also requires the community having a conversation about social actions and the principles that should guide community members. These guiding moral principles have sometimes been identified with virtues. What other ethical theories gloss over, the focus on the person who acts and the social setting, virtue ethics takes into account. It can be argued that virtue ethics attempts to include all four elements in its perspective.

Virtue ethics is concerned with actions because actions come from who the person is and the social context that influences who the person is in the short run and who the person has become in the long run. Virtues are connected with our sense of duty because it is the virtues that make possible being true to duty. Virtue ethics also is concerned with the consequences of the actions in terms of the actor's motives and intentions. Thus, as with other ethical models we have considered earlier in the book, virtue ethics is one way that the fundamental tension of duty and consequences is managed.[5]

In Samantha's case, if she considers ethics as being virtues, she will think about her personal desires, what she wants to get from donating cash. She will think about not only the good that the charity is doing in the community but also the viable alternatives available and how these alternatives compare in terms of providing for needs of battered women or for other needs in the community unrelated to the problem of domestic violence. She will consider other funding sources (such as government allocations of tax revenue) that can provide operating funds for the shelter. She will consider the situation that her company and the shelter are both in at present. She will go deeper and consider the degree to which her desires to spend corporate funds in this way come from a good faith effort to help or from motives tied to desires for personal acclaim. For example, is she favoring this use of funds because she expects that she will become recognized in the community for the donation? She will also consider her current identity and the identity she aspires to have in the future, what she wants to be known for in the community, what will give her the greatest sense of accomplishment when looking at the journey of her whole life.

VIRTUE ETHICS

We have learned that morality is concerned with standards of behavior in a social setting. In seeking a norm, we are really seeking a rule or a principle that will guide our actions. We use such norms to evaluate behaviors of those around us in the environment of business. Accordingly, when we think about ethics in the context of business, it is easy to concentrate on questions like, What should I do? or How should I act?

There is another tradition that de-emphasizes the importance of rules and principles and instead focuses on the character and virtues of the person. Virtue and character ethics argues that the traditional approaches to ethics ask the wrong questions. The key question is not, What ought we to do? but rather, What ought we to be?[6]

Informally we refer to the virtues and character of a person when we say, "He has a heart of gold," "There's not a mean bone in her body,"

"They're rotten to the core," or "We're going to show them what we're made of."

> Watch over your heart with all diligence,
> For from it flow the springs of life. (Prov 4:23)

Virtue ethics is based on the premise that a person acts primarily because of who he or she is in community: being precedes doing.[7] Secular virtue ethics specialists believe that who you are is shaped by the community around you, the actions you take, the feedback you get from these actions and how this changes you over time so that you gradually become transformed into a person guided primarily by virtues or a person guided primarily by vices.

Who you are as a reflection of the cumulative community influences is a primary influence on the actions you take in particular social situations. Repeated over time, the actions you take and the reactions you get from others for these actions gradually shape your character. Accordingly, it has an effect on who you are becoming in the future. This relationship is illustrated in figure 13.1.

Virtue ethics is about the process of improving who you are in a social context. When the soul matures and otherwise improves, the person is happier and the whole community

Figure 13.1. Influences in virtue ethics.

benefits.[8] From the wider perspective, virtue ethics is not merely an individual process. It is a process where the community shares in the development of and the expression of virtues.

COMMUNAL INFLUENCES ON VIRTUES

Recent secular and Christian ethics scholars have emphasized the importance of community in the formation of virtues. Virtues are rooted in community and are never entirely just individual in nature.

A virtue is something that involves the whole person in the social context. It is more than merely a dispositional state. It involves the use of reason.[9] It involves self-awareness. Virtue involves motives and commitments. It involves a fundamental commitment to be a particular type of person. To use a business marketing analogy, it involves establishing a particular position in the marketplace of persons, what you are known for who you are. In a way, then, a virtuous person is a self-interested person but not so in a narrow way. A virtuous person is concerned about living a happy, fulfilled life in community, concerned about his or her continual position in the community with respect to how the person conducts himself or herself.

The social situations we get ourselves into and how we respond to them come about in part because of who we are.[10] Thus, as we mature through life, we reflect on how we get ourselves into the kinds of situations that create ethical dilemmas. From this we learn how to avoid certain situations. If certain situations cannot be avoided, we come to understand better how to address them.

Choosing who we spend time with in the community has a large influence in our own attitudes and conduct. The social group we spend time with will play a role shaping our self-perceptions and our values. The social group will provide positive reinforcement for certain behaviors and attitudes. The group may also have an influence on extinguishing other actions and attitudes.

For example, we might feel attracted to a certain person who has charisma and who makes suggestions regarding where to go and what to do. We might even feel a little uncomfortable at first going to a certain place. If we choose to go along, we learn that not all is as bad as we had anticipated. But once we begin forming a social bond with the person and others who are there, it becomes more difficult to resist the social pressure to engage in other actions that we believe are wrong. In some situations, persons can unwittingly get pulled into dangerous, illegal activities that they did not expect. If they are fortunate enough to not get caught, later they may reflect on the experience and decide that it was not as bad as they had expected. The person may decide that additional social contact with that group of persons is acceptable. In contrast, on reflection of the event, they may decide that it was far worse than they had expected and resolve not to spend time with this group of people in the future.

You may be able to notice the narrative (story) nature of this process of developing virtues. We encounter persons and situations that result in actions and in our own reflection of the meaning of these situations. We experience an internal adjustment either in favor of or in disfavor of what we experienced. This has an influence on our degree of interest in interacting with the social group again.

A CURIOUS DOUBLE PARADOX

In virtue ethics we see a curious double paradox. On the one hand, it is the influence of context and of others in our community that

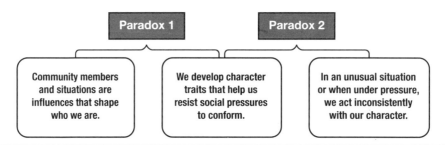

Figure 13.2. The double paradox of community influences.

shapes our character traits. On the other hand, character traits such as honesty and trustworthiness are resistant to social pressure to conform.[11] Yet, when placed in an unusual environment where the person is pressured to behave in a particular way, the person may act inconsistently with character. This paradox is illustrated in figure 13.2.

How a person frames a situation affects what direction will be taken to resolve the ethics questions. For example, a situation can be framed in terms of human rights, and if this is done, then the person will tend to discern whether a positive or negative right is involved and who has the responsibility for respecting that right. Moreover, several influences are at work when a person frames an ethical situation.[12] The social environment a person is in is an influence. Furthermore, the person's ego tends to influence one toward a self-serving bias. A person's interests affect the frame also. Persons normally are more interested in moral issues that affect themselves than they are of issues that affect other people.

ARISTOTLE ON VIRTUES

Virtue and character as the bases of behavior in community goes back a long way in history.[13] Personal virtue or virtue ethics, often associated with the ancient philosopher Aristotle, asked not *What should I do?* but rather, *What type of person should I be?* Aristotle's writings on ethics are still studied today.

For Aristotle (384–322 B.C.), the founder of Greek character/virtue ethics, a trait of character is a virtue only if its expression contributes to the overall well-being of the person in community. Aristotle seems to assume that for any given person, the long-term well-being of the person and of those around that person is what is being considered when a person thinks about a particular action.[14]

Aristotle taught that virtues are habits of being: thinking, emotion and action.[15] Ethics is the process of discerning and developing the highest good possible for humans in society. Living a life characterized by virtues is the surest pathway to happiness and general well-being.[16] Aristotle used the word *eudaimonia*, which means blessedness, well-being, happiness and prosperity in all dimensions of life. This Greek concept is similar to the Hebrew concept of shalom. When we live a life of virtue, we are acting in a way that conforms to what is excellent. This will bring about the desired result of well-being.[17]

To achieve well-being requires humans to use on a continuous basis their higher, rational abilities. Thus, for Aristotle virtue ethics is a duty which is focused on achieving a general result of a good life not just for ourselves but also for the community of which we are a part.

We develop virtues in three ways.[18] Virtues require habits. Habits require practice. Second, habit formation requires freedom to choose rationally particular behaviors. Third, the use of reason to discern and choose behaviors which promote well-being requires participation of others in society. Persons may need the help of others to discern and choose good habits.

Virtues have a certain flexibility and freedom in that there are no specific rules that must be followed in given circumstances. Instead of looking for a rule to follow or assess the outcome of action in a particular situation, the virtuous person strives to become morally sensitive to the situation. Moral sensitivity develops with feedback from others, such as one's parents, with time and with life experience. Thus, the focus of virtues is on character and motives for action in a social context. It is not the duty to act or the result of action per se that is the measure of an ethical person, but rather the motives and character traits and the direction of the entire life of the person that are the foundations for action.[19]

Virtues are not passions like fear or anger, but instead are the character traits that promote a meaningful and worthy human life.[20] An honest person is not someone who wants to steal but decides not to. A person with the virtue of honesty does not want to steal. A person sometimes acts out of character, as when an otherwise loyal friend betrays our trust. Virtues are habits, and a virtuous person is someone who has developed personal habits that promote honor and pride of the kind of life that is considered the best.

The most well-known of the ancient virtues are honesty, courage, temperance and reason.

Other virtues included prudence, magnanimity and contemplation.[21] One of Aristotle's best-known teachings is that the virtues are somewhere near the midpoint between a trait that is in excess and a trait that is deficit. Take, for example, courage, which became one of the cardinal virtues in the Christian church. It is somewhere in between two extremes of foolhardiness (the excess) and cowardice (the deficit). Compassion is between patronizing pity and cold-heartedness. Table 13.1 provides additional examples.

Even after discussing virtues and character, establishing precise definitions is not easy. We have seen that the word *virtue* is sometimes used as a synonym for character. There is wide disagreement as to what virtues are. Accordingly, we are often left with the challenge of describing virtues instead of precisely defining them. Virtues give a person strength to do what a less virtuous person finds difficult. Being virtuous requires taking risks when facing trouble that otherwise would go unrecognized. Having virtue is more like having power to authentically be who you are and less like merely making a choice of what to do in a situation.[22]

CHARACTER

Character[23] has been informally defined as "the inner and distinctive core of a person from which moral discernment, decisions, and actions spring. It is an enduring configuration of the intentions, feelings, dispositions, and perceptions of any particular self."[24] Character, it

Table 13.1. Virtues as midpoints.

Excess	Midpoint	Deficit
Self-indulgence	Temperance	Insensibility
Prodigality	Liberality	Meanness
Vulgarity	Magnificence	Pettiness
Irascibility	Patience/Good temper	Lack of spirit
Buffoonery	Wittiness	Boorishness
Shyness	Modesty	Shamelessness

can be said, involves the typical patterns of who we are in relationship to other people. Character includes the sum of the patterns of thoughts, feelings, passions and values in a social context. It involves the capacity for goal-oriented, purposeful action.[25]

The definition of character defies precision; however, many believe that the content of character heavily overlaps that of virtues. One view is that the virtues that are habitual in a person constitute that person's character.[26]

The assumption common to those who accept virtues and character as valid influences on ethical decision making is that who we are drives how we think and ultimately how we behave.

EVALUATION: PROS AND CONS

This chapter introduces the idea of virtues as a moral theory of right and wrong. It is time to consider some of the pros and cons of this theory. Pros (arguments in support) will be identified by the symbol (+) while cons (arguments against) will be identified by the symbol (-).

(+) Compared with utilitarianism (Jeremy Bentham and John Stuart Mill) and universalism (Immanuel Kant), virtue ethics has a more positive view of the role of emotions in the context of social relationships.[27]

(+) Virtue ethics shifts the focus from merely action to the whole person in community. "If we focus only on actions without attention to character, we lose sight of this dimension of ethics."[28] Virtue conceives of the person as an actor in community. Community helps shape each person's virtues. The person takes action in the community and with patterns or habits of action, the person gradually changes the virtues (or vices) which guide future action. Thus, of less importance is any particular action but rather the whole pattern of actions, what this pattern reveals about the person and what is

present in the community that was an influence in the pattern of actions.[29]

(+) Virtue ethics emphasize the behavior, intentions and motives of people, not just the rational processes of duty (Kant) or the consequences of action (Mill).[30]

(+) Virtue ethics emphasizes authentic consistency between how a person thinks in his or her heart, desires and action.[31] The virtuous person does not experience the conflict that the person who acts simply from duty might experience, that is, feeling compelled to do what he or she does not want to do. In this way virtue ethics supports healthy wholeness and integrity of the whole person in community.

(+) Virtue is not just a rational process of thinking about what is duty or what might happen if the person takes a certain course of action. Virtue emphasizes the doing that is consistent with being. Moreover, virtue is seen in action, not just in words. People who display patterns of action that reveal the virtues are the persons who are looked up to as role models and mentors.[32]

(+) Virtues emphasize the communal exchange of wisdom about how to live an excellent life that contributes in a positive way to society. Virtuous persons contribute to the overall well-being of their community so that others desire to be around them.[33]

A critique of virtues reveals several criticisms.

(-) Virtue ethics that is based on the ancient Greek ideas embraces the influence of community on the person, but it avoids dealing with the political process at work in the community when issues of justice and rights are addressed. Virtues are appropriate when talking about individual persons but inadequate when talking about the struggle for dominant influence in organizations when competing interests are at stake.[34]

(-) Virtues alone are not sufficient. Some virtues, if taken to excess, can bring a person to actions that have unsavory consequences. For example, conformity and obedience has been linked with tragic consequences when taken to an excess.

(-) Virtue ethics are not specific in terms of how to apply any particular virtue in a given context. There is no easy formula to follow to know how much courage to display, the degree of compassion that is appropriate or the amount of generosity to exhibit toward someone in need. Moreover, when two principles are in conflict, there is no method for resolving the conflict.[35]

(-) While the virtues approach emphasizes the formation of habits and character traits, it is also dependent on the social conditioning that occurs on the individual.

(-) If virtues are ultimately dependent on the community's moral vision, is there no transcendent reality, ultimate authority beyond the community? If virtues are ultimately dependent on the community's moral vision, there is no transcendent absolute standard of right and wrong. This line of reasoning has led some to criticize virtue ethics as being little more than cultural relativism.

DOWN TO THE NITTY-GRITTY

Think about scenario at the beginning of this chapter. You are Samantha Harley, considering whether or not to contribute cash from her company to the nonprofit community shelter for battered women. What is the right thing to do? It's time to get down to the nitty-gritty (see table 13.2)!

Table 13.2. Applying the ethical process.

Keeping Your Heart: An Intrapersonal Process	Walking in the Community: An Interpersonal Process

• You are Samantha Harley. What does your heart say is the right thing to do regarding making a contribution?
• Which biblical themes explored in this book inform your heart on this situation?
• Which biblical theme, if any, do you feel yourself resisting? Why do you feel resistance?
• Which virtues might spur you to make the donation? Which virtues might keep you from making the donation?
• Is virtues and character sufficient on its own to guide you to decide what is right and wrong? If not, what additional perspective is needed?
• What other influences in your heart seem to be prominent as you think about this situation?
  • Fundamental beliefs
  • Cognitive reasoning
  • Judgments and evaluations
  • Decisions
  • Will
  • Memory of personal experiences with other people
  • Perceptions of others in the community
  • Personal biases
  • Awareness of interpersonal relationships
  • Commitments to God and to others
  • Intuitions
  • Conscience
  • Human spirit
  • Emotions
	• You are Samantha Harley. With whom might you have a conversation about the issue of making a contribution? Who else might have a helpful perspective?
	• Which of the biblical themes in this chapter will most likely come up in the conversation either directly or indirectly? Why? Which one(s) will be the most influential in the conversation?
	• If you have a conversation with someone regarding this situation, which of the fundamental tensions presented earlier in the book might come up?
	• What right-versus-right dilemmas, if any, can be identified? Have a conversation with someone about this now. What is the outcome of the conversation?

THROUGH THE LENS OF BIBLICAL THEMES

This part of the chapter will use the biblical story themes as a lens through which to evaluate the ethical approach featured in the chapter. Because the themes are interrelated and interdependent, we should expect to see some overlap in the thinking regarding the ethical approach. Some themes will contribute the same thinking as will other themes. The power of these themes comes from their guidance when a community of people talks about complicated ethical dilemmas faced in business practice.

The idea of virtues is true to the biblical teachings about the heart. "The focus on character is akin to the biblical language of the heart with a strong emphasis on actions springing naturally from the inner core of a person."[36] "These words, which I am commanding you today, shall be on your heart. You shall teach them diligently to your sons and shall talk of them when you sit in your house and when you walk by the way and when you lie down and when you rise up" (Deut 6:6-7).[37] The Bible sees virtues as the result of the work of the Holy Spirit working in a person to transform him or her. Virtues are evidence of spiritual growth.[38]

The concept of virtues from the ancient Greeks was brought into the Christian church and became what has been called the seven cardinal virtues. These seven virtues are comprised of two types: natural virtues common to all persons and biblical virtues that are part of the religious experience of Christians. The natural virtues are prudence, justice, fortitude and temperance; the biblical virtues are faith, hope and love (charity).

In contrast to virtues, vices are those character traits that undermine the ability of persons to live a good life. The Christian church has traditionally recognized seven vices:

- pride
- envy
- wrath
- sloth
- avarice
- gluttony
- lust

The virtues as taught by Aristotle have been compared with virtues as taught by Jesus Christ.[39] This is illustrated in table 13.3.

Table 13.3. Comparing Aristotle with Jesus Christ.

	Aristotle	**Jesus Christ**
Context	Polis (city)	Ekklesia (church)
Purpose	Virtues to serve the greater good of the city	Virtues to live and serve the larger purpose of the kingdom of God
The norm for virtues	The elite in society	Jesus Christ
Kind of community to serve	Highly stratified society; lower classes expected to serve the elite	Everyone, including those on the margins of society
Development process	Citizens must intentionally nurture and practice habits that result in virtues; fellow citizens participate in the process by dialogue with each other; this promotes a good life	Followers of God must intentionally nurture and practice virtues; fellow believers participate in the process by giving encouragement and guidance; this is the process of sanctification
What thwarts the development of virtues	Social location: lower classes have more difficult time developing virtues	Sin thwarts the development of virtues
Highly prized virtues	Courage, temperance, honesty, prudence	Faith, hope, love, humility

Cosmic conflict. Many of the biblical story themes are, in essence, virtues that are prized in the kingdom of God. As we have seen, the question of character is central to the conflict between God and Satan. God's character of faithfulness, justice and loving kindness has been questioned by Satan. All of God's actions begin with who he is: being precedes action, and action reveals character. Humans, created in the image of God, are called to reflect his character through our actions in the social environment. It is character that is revealed in the midst of conflict. The marketplace is a setting in which the character of God is constantly under attack by those who live according to the principles opposed to freedom. It is the faithful believer's responsibility to participate in combating these principalities and powers.

Creation. At creation we see the virtues of respect, mutual service and accountability. We are called to foster freedom within limits. Living successfully in a setting where social relationships are interdependent means that dependence is shared by all. No one can live autonomously to the extent that he or she can live above the principles of a flourishing life. In fact, it is the attempt to live autonomously that contributes to the opposite of a flourishing life.

Holiness. Consecration to God is the starting point for developing the types of virtues that help us align ourselves with the principles of a flourishing life.

Covenant relationships. One of the purposes of covenant between persons is to reveal the character of both persons. Covenant relationships are maintained by persons who exercise their covenant-oriented virtues of generosity, reconciliation, loyalty and faithfulness. Maturity of character contributes to a flourishing covenant relationship. Persons who covenant together agree to nourish the relationship by giving and receiving. The biblical virtues require not just the community around us to shape the virtues and our character but also the influence of a community whose members are also striving to follow God.

Shalom. Shalom is a community experience as well as the contributions that persons make to the experience along the way. Fostering life of the community means giving oneself for the needs of others. It means living in such a way that your life, like a life-giving stream, becomes a blessing to those around. It is the good of the entire community that is at stake here.

Sabbath. Sabbath calls for loyalty and trust among members of the community. Six days we are diligent in our labor of service to others. One day per week God has set aside for worship to him. Sabbath promotes the virtue of contentment. It fosters humility in the realization that humans, of their own power, cannot sustain their own life.

Justice. Justice promotes honor to God and honor to each other. Justice is action-oriented. It sometimes requires courage to intervene on behalf of those who are disadvantaged or suffered under injustice. It may, on occasion, require confronting persons in positions of power. It may require conducting a community conversation about what is right and wrong.

Righteousness. Righteousness requires the virtues of firmness, unselfishness and faithfulness.

Truth. As with righteousness and covenant relationships, truth requires the virtues of faithfulness to promises and honesty with oneself and with the larger community. Truth is action-oriented. Thus, the person of truth will move courageously to nourish the land with justice. Truth also calls for consistency in action across time. With truth there is integrity that fosters a close correspondence between actions and expectations. The truthful person is one who is reliable.

Wisdom. Wisdom is one of the prized virtues in the marketplace. Wisdom is not merely knowledge of how to attract customers, how to make appealing products and how to be profitable. The foundation of wisdom is honor to God. Wisdom, and its close relative prudence, involves the expression of humility, practical skill and discretion. But the foundation of wisdom is the whole collection of principles embodied in the covenant relationships. "The wisdom from above is first pure, then peaceable, gentle, reasonable, full of mercy and good fruits, unwavering, without hypocrisy" (Jas 3:17). Here wisdom leads to shalom (peace) and involves the virtues of loving kindness, loyalty and faithfulness.

Loving kindness. Biblical love is based primarily on the virtues of unchanging loyalty (in action) and kindness. Loving kindness fosters mutual reciprocity. Biblical love is not just a feeling of affection toward someone. It means taking an action that is right thing to do, an action that we would want done for us if we were in the other person's shoes.

Redemption. To act redemptively is to take (sometimes) big risks to reclaim that which was lost. Redemption requires taking responsibility to foster long-term covenant relationships that give life to all those who are related. This involves an incarnational approach to communication and self-sacrifice for the good of others.

Based on this review of the biblical story themes, table 13.4 of relevant biblical virtues is offered for consideration.

CHAPTER REVIEW QUESTIONS

1. In what ways is virtue ethics different from other approaches to ethics?

2. How does the social community have an effect on the development of virtues?

3. Describe the double paradox involved with virtues.

4. What did the Greek thinker Aristotle teach regarding virtues?

5. What is character?

6. What are the pros and cons of virtues and character as an approach to ethical action?

7. What perspective do the biblical story themes offer regarding virtues and character?

Table 13.4. Biblical virtues related to biblical themes.

Biblical Theme	Related Virtues
Cosmic Conflict	faithfulness, justice, loving kindness
Creation	respect, mutual service, accountability, sharing dependence
Covenant Relationships	generosity, reconciliation, loyalty, faithfulness
Shalom	oneself for the needs of others
Sabbath	loyalty, trust, diligence, contentment, humility
Justice	courage
Righteousness	firmness, unselfishness, faithfulness
Truth	faithfulness to promises, honesty, integrity, reliability
Wisdom	prudence, humility, discretion, honor, loving kindness, loyalty, faithfulness
Loving Kindness	mutual reciprocity, loyalty, kindness
Redemption	risk taking, responsibility, self-sacrifice

DISCUSSION QUESTIONS

1. To what degree do our social surroundings have an influence on what we think is a person's character? (See Solomon, "Victims of Circumstances?," p. 45.)

2. Can you tell by looking at a person whether or not that person has the virtue of integrity? Is integrity a virtue that is on the inside or something that is visible?

3. Are there certain types of people who have the virtues prized in business? If so, how can we find these persons?

4. If the Christian uses the Bible as the guide for developing virtues, does this adequately address the weaknesses of virtues as an ethical approach?

5. To what degree is the idea of virtues and character in harmony with the biblical story themes?

ETHICAL VIGNETTES TO DISCUSS

For each of the vignettes described below, apply the biblical story themes to discern what is right and wrong.

1. Delmer works as a stock clerk for a local discount store that is part of a nationwide chain, but he is looking for another job. After sending his resume to several companies, he gets a response from another chain store. The only problem is that the manager at the local store wants him to come in for an interview on a day when he is scheduled to work at his current job. Delmer is worried that if he tells the truth about why he will not be at work on the day of the interview, his manager will not grant him the time off. He is also worried that if he tells the other firm that he cannot come for the interview on that particular day, he will not have a chance to interview and as a result will not get the job. Is it ethical for Delmer to lie to his current manager regarding the reason he is not coming to work on the day of the interview?

2. Bill and Mary are a retired couple. Three or four times a week they walk for one hour with a small group of friends at the local shopping mall. While walking through the mall one morning Mary noticed some unusual Italian flowering plants that had been placed around the mall. She stopped and admired these. Later that day she and Bill visited local garden supply stores to search for this plant. None of the stores had any in stock. Because she is an amateur horticulturist, Mary knew that she could grow her own plant from cuttings from someone else's plant. She returned to the mall with scissors and plastic bags. Without getting permission from the mall management, she took one cutting each from three of the many plants. Mary knew that these few cuttings would not harm the plants in any way. She also knew that growing new plants is a way to enhance the environment. Was Mary wrong in taking these cuttings without permission?

PART THREE

CONTEMPORARY ISSUES

This section explores contemporary ethical challenges that businesses and customers face. As we did in part II, we will consider these through the lens of biblical themes. Accordingly, we move to a process that involves applying the general principles embedded in the biblical themes to specific situations. This part applies the principles to the individual and organizational and industry/professional levels.

When we consider applying the general principles to specific situations we must remember that there at least two parties involved with every business transaction: buyers and sellers.

Some business relationships involve more than just two parties. Most business ethics books focus on the actions of sellers in the market but devote little if any space to consider the ethics of the buyer (even professional buyers who work in businesses). Ironically, when it comes to the employee-employer relationship inside organizations, the situation is reversed. Most, if not all, of the attention is paid to the buyer (the employer) while little, if anything, is said about the seller (the employee).

While we cannot forget the ethical actions of sellers, we must also include the actions of those who buy from businesses.[1] Why would we address only half of the relationship?

To be consistent with a biblical perspective, this topic must be included. From a practical point of view all those who serve in commerce also are customers. If the Christian is to make any progress toward integrating faith in business, if the faithful believer is to avoid the criticism of Christians that they are hypocrites, then business ethics for the buyer must be one of the first places we apply biblical principles. From a purely statistical basis there are far more customers in the market than there are businesses. Through the misdeeds of Christians in the marketplace it could be that the power of the church has been weakened, the power of the gospel has sometimes been undermined and the unity of the faith community has chronically been disrupted.

The scope of ethical issues that we face in the marketplace is wide. No customer is without the opportunity to take advantage of others in the market, even if businesses are learning how to prevent this. No business function or role is spared, though it is possible that some functions traditionally have been associated with ethical problems more than others (marketing and finance). Every profession faces certain ethical tensions, dilemmas and temptations. Every industry faces some ethical challenges among the industry firms.

Every organization in every sector of the economy should be considered: for-profit, nonprofit and government.

You may have heard the principles of business ethics simplified down to "Don't lie, cheat or steal."[2] While these may be the most common categories of ethical problems from ancient times, there are variations on these: giving false impressions, hiding information when you should reveal it, giving information when you should not, taking unfair advantage of someone, personal behavior that places at risk the company's reputation or increases the risk of loss and harm, abusing people, violating laws and regulations and permitting or even condoning unethical actions by other people.[3]

Accordingly, in part III we will first apply the biblical themes to selected issues in consumer ethics. Following this we will apply the biblical themes to some of the ethical issues that businesses and business professionals have faced in recent times. We organize contemporary ethical issues into the following categories:

- consumer ethics (chap. 14)

- management (chap. 15)

- accounting and finance (chap. 16)

- marketing (chap. 17)

- global business (chap. 18)

14

Ethical Issues in Consumer Behavior

SCRIPTURE PASSAGE

"Bad, bad," says the buyer,
But when he goes his way, then he boasts.
(Prov 20:14)

CHAPTER OVERVIEW

In this chapter we explore how ethics applies
to buyers and their behavior just as much as it
applies to sellers. In particular, we will

- consider the characteristics of consumerism
  and the consumer society

- understand selected purchasing ethics issues:
  consumer buying and business buying

- evaluate selected purchasing behavior ethics
  issues through the lens of biblical themes

MAIN TOPICS

The Consumer Society
Consumer Purchasing Ethics
Ethical Ideology Types
Neutralization Tactics
Business-to-Business (B2B) Purchasing Ethics
Consumption Behavior at the Industry
    and Economic System Levels
The Influence of Religion
Down to the Nitty-Gritty
Through the Lens of Biblical Themes

KEY TERMS

absolutists, consumers, consumer ethics scale,
consumerism, consumer society, ethical ideology, exceptionists, idealism, neutralization,
purchasing agents, relativism, situationists,
subjectivists

OPENING SCENARIO

You just purchased a used motorcycle from
someone. Your dream has been to use the motorcycle for road trips. This particular model
came complete with motorcycle accessories
such as saddle bags and a beautiful leather tail
bag. You put the title to the motorcycle into
your pocket and enjoy your first ride home.

After you get home, you decide to give your
new machine a thorough cleaning and polishing. Sifting through the bits and pieces of
trash in the saddle bags you come across a
small, hard-shell, velvet-covered box. Inside
the box is a beautiful diamond ring. The diamond ring alone is probably worth a good
portion of the price of the cycle.

Clearly the previous owner was not very
careful when preparing the cycle for sale. You
now own the machine and everything on it.
You would not take the motorcycle saddle bags
back to the owner and say, "Oops! You sold me
saddle bags when I only paid for a motorcycle.
I'm bringing them back to you. Oh, and here is

A BIBLICAL METAPHOR

Thy word is a lamp to my feet,
And a light to my path. (Ps 119:105)

A biblical metaphor for ethical conduct is walking on a journey. This passage from Psalms suggests that the Word of God has practical application for every step of our journey.

---

the half-gallon of gas that was in the tank when I bought the bike." The ring, however, seems to be in a different category from accessories that belong on a motorcycle. Do you seriously think that the previous owner intended to sell you a diamond ring with the motorcycle? When you negotiated the price of the bike, did you take into consideration the value of the diamond ring? Is the probability that the owner was forgetful or negligent a valid reason for you to keep the ring? Should you take it back to the previous owner, or should you consider it rightfully yours to keep?

Most of the emphasis of business ethics is typically placed on the (un)ethical producing and selling behaviors of businesses or the people representing them. But what about unethical buying behaviors? It has only been since the 1980s that research on the ethics of buying behavior of customers has become popular. Because of this, the ethics of buying remains underdeveloped and less well-known than other dimensions of business ethics.

In this book we recognize that the ethics of buying and consuming is just as important as the ethics of producing and selling. We do this for the following reasons. First, from one obvious point of view, if ethics is important in the exchange relationships of the marketplace, there are always at least two parties involved in the exchanges: a seller and a buyer. If we leave half of the exchange relationship out of our consideration of ethics, we are limiting our un-

derstanding of business ethics in its totality.[1]

Second, is it fair to expect companies and managers to behave in ethical ways toward customers and not expect the same of customers in their actions in the marketplace? Ethics, after all, is a two-way marketplace street and applies equally to all parties regardless of their marketplace role.

Third, if the marketplace is to function effectively, ethical behavior of both seller and buyer is necessary. The shared interests of both must be reflected in our thinking and behavior.[2]

Fourth, business has long been considered to be the dominant party in the exchange relationships; however, the power of customers should not be discounted.[3] Depending on the structure of the marketplace, customers have the power to use their buying behavior to influence the kinds of products that are made, the prices that are charged, how products are distributed and the marketing communication approaches that companies employ.

Last, the Christian who is serious about living a life consistent with faith all the time will be concerned about the ethics of purchasing activities just as much as selling activities.

Just as the ethics of producing and selling can be applied at four levels, so too can the ethics of buying and consuming, as table 14.1 shows.

THE CONSUMER SOCIETY

People who observe the historical trends in consumerism in Europe and the Western

Table 14.1. Ethics of buying and consuming.

Buying and Consuming Behaviors Seen at Four Levels			
Individual and Family	**Organizational: Nonprofit, For-Profit, Government**	**Industry/Professional Association**	**Economic System**
Buying materials, equipment, services and other resources such as property for personal and family use. Consumption and disposal of resources in the course of living life. Family systems and values that encourage or discourage certain individual purchasing and consumption practices.	Buying materials, equipment, property, rights of access, services and other resources used in the production of goods and services that are sold to other organizations or to individual consumers and their families. Consumption and disposal of resources in the course of operating the organization. Organizational systems and policies that support organizational purchasing and use behaviors.	Purchasing practices that are common across the industry or profession. Patterns of consumption and disposal of resources across industries or professions. Systems or standards that encourage or discourage certain purchasing and consumption practices.	Broad patterns of resource acquisition and consumption across countries or regions of the world. Infrastructure systems and public policies of countries or regions that encourage or discourage certain purchasing and consumption practices in an international context.

hemisphere over the last few centuries see broad trends occurring.[4] Consumerism is an attempt by consumers to increase their influence with sellers of products and services. It is also the search for self-identity involving a cluster of influences that shape the self-awareness of persons through their market activity of buying and using products and services. The process of personal identity being more and more influenced by buying and consuming (the use of products) behaviors emerged in the eighteenth century in Western Europe. Prior to this personal identity was shaped to a large degree by a person's work, who you were married to and your relationship to a religious organization.

With the Industrial Revolution came the development of technology for more efficient production. Communication systems and transportation systems rapidly developed. Correspondingly, prices for consumer products dropped. Consumers could more easily and increasingly get access to a wide variety of products that had previously been available only to the elite landowners and royalty.

Some of the first characteristics of the consumer society that remain to this day include the following:

- *Novelty and pleasure.* Consumers engage in a continual search for novelty of product variation and pleasure by purchasing and using consumer products.

- *Insatiability.* Possession of novel products fails to satisfy the growing desire.

- *Mental images.* Consumers try to create in their own minds images of the ideal life which are increasingly difficult to live up to even when products are possessed.

- *Growing individuality.* Consumers experience a growing sense of individuality defined by product purchases and use.

- *Debt management.* Consumers are increasingly willing to incur debt that is difficult to manage in order to obtain highly desirable products.

- *Overconsumption.* As spending power increases, consumers tend to purchase more products than are necessary.

- *Work and leisure.* The traditional Protestant work ethic (hard work and strict constraints on spending) gave way to a revised work ethic and growing leisure ethic: Work just enough so that there is time for leisure pursuits. Identity came proportionately less from work and increasingly from leisure time.

At first these trends were observed among the higher socioeconomic groups, but as the middle class emerged, the same trends were seen across an ever wider spectrum of society.

I am a consumer.

I am the center of the known universe.

Figure 14.1. An example of a consumer attitude.

You shall not covet . . . anything that belongs to your neighbor. (Deut 5:21)

During the last decade of the nineteenth century, consumers were concerned about the growing power of big business and wanted protections against monopolistic pricing. In the 1930s consumers became interested in being protected against dangerous and unhealthful products.[5]

The term "consumerism" emerged during the 1960s. During this decade the emphasis by consumers was on protecting themselves from the abuses of corporations, getting adequate information on which to make purchasing decisions and being protected from the results of their naive marketplace decisions. Consumers became interested in unit pricing so that one brand and its package contents could be more easily compared with competing brands. Consumers became more interested in the useful life of durable goods. They wanted the truth about contract arrangements with mortgage lenders. They wanted the truth to be told on product packaging.

Consumers gradually began to place time at the center of their thinking. Any activity that took the place of spending free time came to be seen as a sacrifice of leisure time, the desirable alternative to work. Thus, every activity that was not free time was seen as an opportunity cost.

In the twentieth century, paradoxes of consumerism have developed.[6] Consumers began to feel stronger social pressures to be more like their neighbors through buying and using new products. At the same time, working from an opposite direction as social forces increased to conform to what others were doing, consumers feel the struggle to preserve their individuality and autonomy. In a strange way individuality has become one way in which social belonging has been fostered.

Consumers also are developing more of a conscience as they realize that their purchase actions have an effect on other people such as workers in developing countries who work in factories. Purchasing also has an impact on the environment in terms of the packaging that is thrown into landfills or the use of energy which dumps pollutants into the atmosphere. At the same time consumers seem to be more interested in the pleasure gained from purchasing. These paradoxes are illustrated in figure 14.2.

With this paradox in mind, we are prepared to consider how in the twenty-first century we have seen more facets of consumerism emerge. First, we have seen a refinement of consumer behaviors where purchasing and use of products and services became more symbolic

Individual Expression	**Community Affinity**
Shopping for personal pleasure emphasizing individuality	Shopping to conform or belong to social group

Figure 14.2. Individual-community paradox of consumerism.

of the image that consumers wanted to present to each other. At the same time some products, such as cell phones, diffused worldwide even into developing countries. Innovation in many consumer products has resulted in new products rapidly coming to market every few months in the fashion, food marketing, telecommunications and other consumer product industries. These and other products became the means by which consumers could think about themselves and other people. What you wear and what you use to have conversations over long distances both are symbolic ways to communicate with other people.[7]

Second, insatiable desires for highly visible, novel products has increased. Some consumers developed greater difficulty restraining their purchasing desires. Conspicuous consumption has diffused to even the lower socioeconomic groups.[8] Third, consumerism has expanded beyond traditional consumer products to include consumer interaction with other industries and

endeavors such as health care, higher education, politics and travel. Fourth, some consumers are getting more cynical about marketplace behaviors.[9] Consumers are now more savvy and are less likely to fall prey to scams.[10] Fifth, consumers are taking their expanded global awareness and translating this into desires to have less of a negative impact on the environment. This has come to be called green consumerism.

Sixth, consumers are increasingly aware that they are citizens of a world community. They have a growing sense of the solidarity between themselves and their counterparts in

I am a consumer.
I want to be the same as others.
I want to be different from others.

Figure 14.3. Another example of a consumer attitude.

other parts of the globe. Furthermore, there is a growing awareness that personal consumption has an impact on citizens in developing countries where corporations exert their influence on the politics of these regions. A summary of the various dimensions of consumerism, some a legacy from the past, is provided in table 14.2.

Table 14.2. Facets of consumerism.

Protection against abuses by corporations	Continual search for novel products
Desire for better marketplace information	Insatiable desire for more
Time placed at the center of decision making	Attempt to create images of an ideal life
Strong pressures to conform	A difficult time living up to the image
Struggle to preserve personal identity	Willing to incur excessive debt
Greater difficulty restraining purchase desires	Overconsumption
Expanding expectations into services	Redefinition of work and leisure
Growing solidarity with global community	Desire to have less impact on environment

In addition to these broad patterns of consumer behaviors, we recognize that consumers are prone to exhibit ethically questionable behaviors.

CONSUMER PURCHASING ETHICS

Over the years a variety of ethically questionable consumer behaviors have been observed. To provide examples of these, we start by exploring the Muncy-Vitell Consumer Ethics Scale. Then we will explore some of the factors that seem to influence consumer attitudes toward these behaviors.

The variety of ethically questionable consumer activities caught the attention of James Muncy and Scott Vitell, two researchers who developed what is known as the Muncy-Vitell Consumer Ethics Scale to study the factors that influence consumers' ethical beliefs.[11] They divided the scores of ethically questionable consumer activities into groups of items related to avoiding doing the wrong thing: (a) activities where the consumer can actively benefit by doing something illegal; (b) activities where the consumer can passively benefit from the mistakes of business; and (c) questionable activities that the consumer perceives as not causing any harm. Years later the Consumer Ethics Scale was modified by updating the wording of certain items, adding new ethically questionable items, adding activities related to environmental awareness and adding activities that involve doing good.[12] The items in the scale are scored using a Likert scale of 1 (strongly believe it is wrong) to 5 (strongly believe it is *not* wrong). The items in the Consumer Ethics Scale are seen in table 14.3.

To these items we can add others:[13]

- cell phone fraud that involves illegally cloning or using a cloned cell phone that has the factory-set electronic serial number or

phone number reprogrammed, or purchasing a cell phone from a discount retailer using false identification and then reselling the phone to someone at a higher price

- finding an item that was mismarked at a lower price but not saying anything about it

- switching price tags at the store so that items are marked as cheaper than they should be

- switching clothing set sizes so that the top is one size and the bottom another

- not contacting the company that sends you two of an item when you ordered one

- deshopping, or purchasing an item of clothing to wear to a special event or another product you intend to use once and then returning it to the store for a refund

- purchasing an item of clothing, wearing it and then returning it when you find the same item for sale at a different store at a lower price

- tampering with a product so as to report it as faulty to gain a refund

- purchasing merchandise from a store that sells it at a lower price but returning it to a store that sells it at a higher price

- purchasing an essay online and turning it in as your own for a university assignment

- getting an exam back from a professor and realizing that one of the answers is marked correct when it is not, but not telling the professor about the error

At the end of the chapter we will evaluate consumer behaviors through the lens of biblical themes.

ETHICAL IDEOLOGY TYPES

One factor that seems to influence attitudes toward ethically questionable consumer activ-

Table 14.3. Consumer ethics situations.

Category of Activity	Consumer Activity
Actively benefiting from an illegal action	Returning damaged goods when the damage was your own fault
	Giving misleading price information to a clerk for an unpriced item
	Using a long-distance (telephone) access code that does not belong to you
	Drinking a can of soda in a grocery store but not paying for it
	Reporting a lost item as stolen to an insurance company in order to collect the insurance money
Passively benefiting from an unethical action	Moving into a new residence and finding that the cable television service is still hooked up but not telling the cable television company about it
	Lying about a child's age to get lower price
	Not saying anything when the waiter or waitress miscalculates a bill in your favor
	Getting too much change and not saying anything
	Joining a CD club just to get some free CDs with no intention of buying any
	Observing someone shoplifting but ignoring it
Actively benefiting from an ethically questionable, but legal, action	Using an expired coupon for merchandise
	Returning merchandise to a store by claiming that it was a gift when it was not
	Using a coupon for merchandise you did not buy
	Not telling the truth when negotiating the price of a new automobile
	Stretching the truth on an income tax return
Believing that the action does no harm	Installing software on your computer without buying it
	Copying a CD rather than buying it
	Returning merchandise after buying it and not liking it
	Recording a movie off the television
	Spending more than an hour trying on clothing and not buying anything
Downloading or buying counterfeit goods	Downloading music from the Internet instead of buying it
	Buying counterfeit goods instead of buying the original manufacturers' brands
Environmental awareness activities	Buying products labeled as "environmentally friendly" even if they do not work as well as competing products
	Purchasing something made of recycled materials even though it is more expensive
	Buying only from companies that have a strong record of protecting the environment
	Recycling materials such as cans, bottles and newspapers
Doing good or doing the right thing	Returning to the store and paying for an item that the cashier mistakenly did not charge you for
	Correcting a bill that has been miscalculated in your favor
	Giving a larger than expected tip to a waiter or waitress
	Not purchasing products from companies that you believe do not treat their employees fairly

ities is known as ethical ideology.[14] An ethical ideology is a person's ethical preference when facing an ethical choice. The Ethics Position Questionnaire is one of the tools that has been used to study consumers' ethical ideology.[15] Data on the questionnaire are generated from two categories of ethical measurement scales known as idealism and relativism. Idealism refers to the belief that for every ethical dilemma there is a correct choice that can be made which will result in no harm to stakeholders. Idealism is consistent with the belief

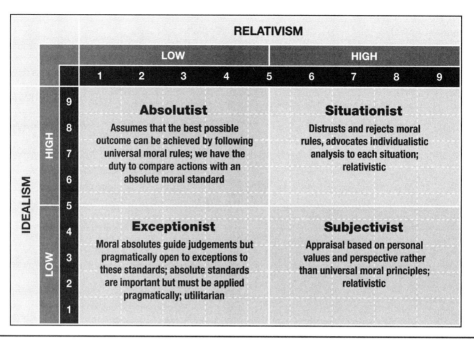

Figure 14.4. Ethical ideology types.

that there are absolute universal moral principles that can be applied across all situations. In contrast, relativism refers to the belief that there are no moral absolute principles that can be applied across all situations. Instead, each situation must be evaluated differently in terms of the social consequences of particular actions. From these two categories come four ideologies that have an effect on ethical attitudes.

- *Absolutists* (persons who score high on idealism and low on relativism) believe that they must follow absolute moral principles. Absolutists tend to have the most rigid moral belief system.

- *Exceptionists* (persons who score low on idealism and low on relativism) believe that there are moral absolutes which should be followed; however, exceptions to moral rules are permissible depending on the situation.

- *Subjectivists* (persons who score low on idealism and high on relativism) believe that

there are no absolute moral rules. They base their decisions on their feelings. Subjectivists have the most flexible moral belief system.

- *Situationists* (persons who score high on idealism and high on relativism) believe that there are no absolute moral rules. They base their decisions on how the best outcomes can be achieved.

These four ethical ideology types are shown in figure 14.4.

The importance of the four ideology types comes into play when considering consumer ethics.[16] Ethical ideology has a mediating influence on ethical beliefs. Persons with an idealistic ethical viewpoint are least likely to do something illegal in order to benefit personally. Compared with relativists, they are also more likely to have a negative view of passively benefiting at someone else's expense through consumer actions. Furthermore, they are more likely to reject the notion of actively benefiting from legal, but ethically questionable, consumer activities. Idealists are more willing to accept a consumer activity if they believe that no harm would result. Many persons, whether they are idealists or relativists, tend to view debatable consumer activities that do no harm as being acceptable. While idealism seems to have a positive effect on ethical consumer behavior beliefs, relativism's negative influence on ethical beliefs is less than what might be expected.

NEUTRALIZATION TACTICS

It is safe to assume in Western cultures that most persons, for the majority of the exchanges that they transact in the marketplace, act ethically. In focus in this chapter are the consumers who misbehave by acting unethically. These consumers find ways to counteract what they believe to be right by neutralizing their moral consciences and thereby justifying behaviors in particular circumstances that help them pursue more selfish goals.[17] Neutralization is the mental and emotional process of justifying a purchase behavior that goes against what the consumer thinks that others might believe is ethically wrong.[18] Consumers seem to use five different neutralization tactics. First, consumers might try to deny personal responsibility by blaming someone else. If people believe that the situation is not of their own doing

or a problem that they did not cause, they can more easily act unethically. Second, if consumers believe that no one will be harmed as a result, they will more likely have a justification for acting in a particular way. Third, if consumers believe that they have been served an injustice, the use of unethical behavior is used as a reason for responding. For them, they are entitled to engage in unethical behavior if the circumstances are right. Fourth, consumers may try to deflect blame by pointing out the faults of others. Fifth, consumers may attempt to appeal to a bigger reason as justification for unethical behavior. These five neutralization tactics are illustrated in table 14.4.

Ethical issues do not stop with the process of purchasing clothing, food, automobiles, computers, cell phones and other things that consumers use. Consuming and disposal of products also has ethical dimensions. How much consumers purchase and consume and how much of their purchases are thrown away are two core ethical issues in the consumer behaviors.

Participation in recycling programs and limiting purchases and consumption to only that which is really needed are two perspectives to consider. Both have an economic effect. Recycling has an impact on sanitary landfills.

Table 14.4. Neutralization tactics.

Neutralization Tactic	Illustration
Deny personal responsibility.	"It's not my fault if the clerk wasn't paying attention when he gave me too much change back." "I didn't make the counterfeit product. I just bought it."
Believe that no one will get harmed.	"So what if I copy this movie. No one gets hurt because of it." "This is a huge company. They won't miss a few items here and there."
Attempt a payback for an injustice.	"The store manager treated me disrespectfully."
Deflect blame.	"Businesses should not be so quick to blame consumers for trying to get a good deal; after all, businesses will try to take advantage of the customer any chance they get." "Tell me the name of one person who has not copied some software for free instead of paying for it!"
Appeal to a higher principle.	"I did it for my family."

Gradually, the interest in recycling has spawned the development and growth of new businesses and industries. Consuming less would have a negative impact on the economy. Demand for products and services would be less. Manufacturing and service firms would have to cut back production. Jobs would be lost. A sustained pattern of consuming less would eventually result in an equilibrium and stabilization of prices.

BUSINESS-TO-BUSINESS (B2B) PURCHASING ETHICS

Buying products and services is not limited to consumers interacting with companies in the retail market.[19] Organizations of all kinds purchase products and services. Many of these are handled in exchanges that require the use of written purchase orders (PO) and sales contracts that describe in detail the specifications of the products and services, delivery terms and payment terms. Contact between buyers and sellers can be frequent as sellers follow up with buyers to see that their expectations have been met and to determine if there are additional opportunities to make sales. Just as consumers face situations in which they consider acting unethically, the same applies in the context of business-to-business purchasing.

Some unethical behaviors in organizational settings are similar to those that exist among consumers. In addition to these, examples of unethical buying behavior in organizations include the following:

- asking a sales rep for a personal favor, gift, hospitality or concessional travel, gratuity, remuneration, benefit, advantage or promise of further advantage in exchange for an order; accepting offers of gifts and gratuities from sales reps

- sharing confidential pricing information with another vendor

- attempting to by-pass competitive bidding processes by offering a bribe or kickback to decision makers

- engaging in a conflict of interest without first obtaining approval from higher level of authority; for example, awarding a contract to a family member who is trying to start a construction business

- using an unauthorized PO

- imposing a time pressure on the sales professional to present an offer

- suggesting that if the supplier does not offer a favorable price, the contract could be canceled

- telling a supplier that a better price can be obtained elsewhere when this is not true

- creating an impression that there are other vendors available when there may not be

- disclosing the bids of other suppliers in an attempt to get a lower price

- purchasing a larger amount than is needed in order to earn a kickback

- keeping important information from the supplier in order to keep the supplier at a disadvantage

A person who does the buying for an organization plays a key boundary-spanning role by coordinating the ordering and receipt of goods and services that the organization needs to serve its customers or constituents (for non-profit organizations). Buyers are the counterparts to the supplier's sales force in that they represent the organization to suppliers. Their actions, ethical or unethical, speak for the organization they represent.

When purchasing managers engage in unethical behaviors they put their own careers at risk. Furthermore, they increase the risk that their organization will be the recipient of retaliation by a supplier who was harmed.

CONSUMPTION BEHAVIOR AT THE INDUSTRY AND ECONOMIC SYSTEM LEVELS

Much of what is explored in this chapter focuses on the ethics of individual and organizational buying behaviors. We should not forget to ask, Do the ethics of buying and consuming matter at the level of the industry (or professional association) and the economic system? It is the thesis of this book that the answer is yes.

Industry level. Resources are used for many things by industries. Raw materials are used to create physical products. Energy is used to extract raw materials, refine them, transport them, transform them into other products, assemble products and package them, just to name a few categories.

Since 1970 "the transition away from heavy industry and towards the commercial and service sectors has contributed to slower energy consumption growth in the industrial sectors of the U.S. economy. At the same time, the industrial sector remains the largest end user of energy."[20] How industries use energy has an ethical dimension as well as an economic dimension.

Another example of a key resource is fresh water: 97 percent of the water available to us is sea water, but fresh water is just 0.5 percent of all the water on the earth.[21] The largest source of fresh water is water from aquifers (under the surface), which are the earth's natural water storage system.

In some regions persistent drought has raised awareness to water use practices of both consumers and industries. Besides the fresh water that is used in domestic daily life, water is also used in agriculture, chemical processing, manufacturing, services, and many other industries. In the future, water may become one of the most sought-after commodities. Keeping in mind the opportunities for salvaging, treating and reusing water, keeping in mind the fact that the population is growing and keeping in mind the global climate changes now taking place, how consumers and industries access and use water will likely be a much bigger issue in the future than it is today. This will bring to the surface the moral issues involved with resource acquisition and disposal both at the industry level and at the economic system level.

Economic system level. Consumption patterns in a country have been used as one measure by economists. As consumption increases for things like natural resources and energy, we take this to indicate a positive trend toward a better quality of life. It also can indicate increases in population. But consumption of certain resources corresponds with negative externalities that society as a whole must deal with. Furthermore, as the use of these things increases, scarcity of finite resources and distribution also become problems. Public policies (laws and regulations) may create incentives for society as a whole to acquire certain resources. Likewise, policies may influence the disposal of consumed resources, which places a greater or lesser burden on society.

One example of consumption is the total energy use by country.[22] As one might expect, total energy use depends on population size and how well developed an economy is in terms of manufacturing and other uses of energy. According to Enerdata Global Energy Statistical Yearbook online, the following were the top-ranked countries in terms of total energy consumption in 2013:

China
United States
India
Russia
Japan
Germany
Brazil
South Korea
Canada
France

Forecast estimates for total energy use provided by the US Energy Information Administration show that countries participating in the Organization for Economic Cooperation and Development (OECD) will increase their energy use by 0.5 percent between 2009 and 2040. For non-OECD countries, energy use is estimated to increase by 2.2 percent.[23] In 2009 as a group OECD countries represented 53.2 percent of total world energy use. This is expected to drop steadily down to 34.7 percent by the year 2040. In contrast, as a group non-OECD countries are expected to increase the proportion of total world energy use from 47.7 percent in 2009 up to 65.3 percent in 2040.

On a per capita basis, energy consumption by country is illustrated in table 14.5.[24]

The per capita energy consumption can also be shown by region, as illustrated in table 14.6.[25]

World per capita consumption of energy has remained relatively stable. In some regions per capita use has increased, and in other regions consumption has decreased.

These statistics suggest a few challenging ethics questions:

- Is it fair that on a per capita basis the persons in North America consume ten to fifteen times as much energy as persons living in Africa?

- What moral obligations, if any, do people living in a region of high energy consumption have toward the energy consumption in other regions?

- For a person living in a high energy consumption region, what responsibility, if any, does each person or the person's family have to consume less energy?

- For a person living in a low energy consumption region, what responsibility, if any, does each person or the person's family have to consume less energy?

- What responsibilities, if any, do high water-use industries have for managing their water consumption?

The consumption patterns of water and energy are part of a broader discussion of sustainable development, which will be addressed in another chapter.

THE INFLUENCE OF RELIGION

Does one's religious faith have an effect on the perception of unethical consumer behavior?[26] The answer seems to be both yes and no. Religious faith is believed to be one of the strongest determinants of personal values. Some research has shown that, in general, it has a positive influence on both attitudes and behavior. Some consumer ethics studies indicate that participating in religion has no effect on ethical attitudes; however, the more often a person attends church worship in a given month, the more likely the person will view questionable consumer activities as unacceptable. Stronger religious beliefs seem to promote stronger ethical norms. In a study in which extrinsic religiosity (where a person uses religion) is distinguished from intrinsic religiosity (where a person lives one's religion), researchers found that extrinsic religiosity is not a factor influencing attitudes

Table 14.5. Energy consumption by country.

	Total Primary Energy Consumption per Capita (Million BTU per Person)				
	2005	2006	2007	2008	2009
Virgin Islands, U.S.	2122.00	2218.25	2011.05	2145.88	2091.74
Qatar	911.41	848.79	781.75	806.63	692.98
Kuwait	508.18	489.08	473.42	471.64	488.14
Singapore	442.22	441.99	468.77	499.39	574.62
Iceland	440.11	478.53	547.63	700.18	692.61
Norway	428.56	392.17	418.86	418.20	408.68
Canada	427.42	420.60	413.05	404.09	389.05
United States	339.34	333.90	336.34	326.52	308.36
Australia	287.82	287.85	292.38	290.94	288.59
Saudi Arabia	276.01	284.37	252.45	284.84	285.26
Sweden	260.02	247.14	249.78	244.28	227.34
Finland	242.49	253.78	255.11	248.77	230.68
Russia	194.63	194.00	200.79	208.07	188.46
Korea, South	191.85	194.08	201.36	204.54	205.72
Austria	190.53	189.69	187.27	186.90	179.48
France	180.44	179.69	175.74	176.23	166.54
Japan	176.76	179.25	178.12	171.18	161.79
Germany	171.08	173.89	168.13	172.15	161.94
United Kingdom	162.27	159.58	152.99	150.36	140.97
Ireland	158.27	162.13	156.68	153.64	135.74
Spain	149.20	147.85	148.97	142.24	131.89
Italy	137.69	136.23	133.60	131.54	121.61
Ukraine	134.74	125.14	135.64	134.59	98.08
Greece	134.54	138.35	140.10	137.18	130.64
Venezuela	115.42	123.18	117.82	136.92	113.32
Argentina	75.42	79.14	81.62	82.47	80.38
Mexico	63.18	64.61	65.92	66.16	62.55
Brazil	50.26	51.52	53.23	52.68	53.73
China	49.47	53.97	57.12	59.98	65.73
India	14.97	15.92	16.74	17.25	18.71
Philippines	13.44	13.07	12.53	12.78	11.67

Table 14.6. Energy consumption by region.

	Total Primary Energy Consumption per Capita (Million BTU per Person)				
	2005	2006	2007	2008	2009
North America	278.3	274.3	275.6	268.2	253.8
Eurasia	149.2	148.0	152.8	156.3	137.1
Europe	143.6	143.9	142.3	142.1	133.7
Middle East	119.3	122.3	119.2	128.6	131.2
Central and South America	52.0	53.8	54.3	55.8	54.1
Asia and Oceania	40.0	42.1	43.7	44.6	46.8
Africa	15.9	15.7	15.8	16.6	16.1
World	70.1	71.0	71.8	72.3	70.7

Table 14.7. Applying the ethical process.

Keeping Your Heart: An Intrapersonal Process	Walking in the Community: An Interpersonal Process

• You are the buyer of the used motorcycle. What does your heart say is the right thing to do regarding what you found?
• Which biblical themes explored in this book inform your heart on this situation?
• Which biblical theme, if any, do you feel yourself resisting? Why do you feel resistance?
• What other influences in your heart seem to be prominent as you think about this situation?
  • Fundamental beliefs
  • Cognitive reasoning
  • Judgments and evaluations
  • Decisions
  • Virtues
  • Will
  • Memory of personal experiences with other people
  • Perceptions of others in the community
  • Personal biases
  • Awareness of interpersonal relationships
  • Commitments to God and to others
  • Intuitions
  • Conscience
  • Human spirit
  • Emotions
	• You are buyer of the used motorcycle. With whom might you have a conversation about the issue of what you found? Who else might have a helpful perspective?
	• Which of the biblical themes in this chapter will most likely come up in the conversation either directly or indirectly? Why? Which one(s) will be the most influential in the conversation?
	• If you have a conversation with someone regarding this situation, which of the fundamental tensions presented earlier in the book might come up?
	• What right-versus-right dilemmas, if any, can be identified? Have a conversation with someone about this now. What is the outcome of the conversation?

toward potentially unethical consumer activities. People who live their religion tend to view questionable consumer activity as wrong. The exception is for activities that consumers perceive to cause no harm or very little harm. In this case, there is no significant difference between consumers who display extrinsic religiosity and those who display intrinsic religiosity.

DOWN TO THE NITTY-GRITTY

Think about scenario at the beginning of this chapter. You are the buyer of the used motorcycle. What is the right thing to do? It's time to get down to the nitty-gritty (see table 14.7)!

THROUGH THE LENS OF BIBLICAL THEMES

This part of the chapter will use the biblical story themes as a lens through which to evaluate the topic featured in the chapter. Because the themes are interrelated and interdependent, we should expect to see some overlap in the thinking regarding the issues. Some themes will contribute the same thinking as will other themes. The power of these themes comes from their guidance when a community of people talks about complicated ethical dilemmas faced in business practice.

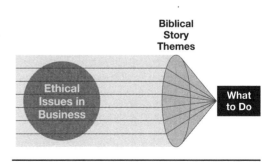

Figure 14.5. Evaluating an ethical approach.

The issue of consumer ethics is important in the Bible. Selling and buying both occur under the watchful eye of the community and of God. If the faithful believer is to live under the rulership of God in ethical matters, then the believer must apply biblical principles to personal conduct in the market. Furthermore, one motive for acting unethically (greed) in the marketplace is not limited to actions of sellers. Buyers, too, wrongly act out of greed.

Cosmic conflict. The person who deceives and defrauds another person is called a "son of the devil" and an "enemy of all righteousness."[27] These are strong words! Under the watchful eye of all the beings in the universe, consumers demonstrate through their actions which principles they align with: principles of God's character or principles of Satan's character. The person (whether seller or buyer) who acts unethically to fulfill greed is not behaving unjustly only toward the other party. Greedy, unethical behavior is a sign that the person is treating with contempt the Creator and Redeemer. "For the wicked boasts of his heart's desire, and the greedy man curses and spurns the LORD" (Ps 10:3).

Creation. It was at creation when God instituted an amazing display of material goods, all at the fingertips of the humans. In the creation account we see that the first sin involved consumer behavior! Moreover, this is the first instance where we see the consumer attempting to deflect blame as justification for unethical behavior.[28]

Holiness. Consumer ethical issues arise because of the problem of fully consecrating ourselves to God. When we are consecrated to God, we will avoid neutralizing tactics that make it seem as if it is permissible to lower our standards or grant ourselves an exception to principles of right and wrong that, down in our hearts, we know should be followed.

Covenant relationships. The covenant implicitly shows awareness of purchasing behaviors, and because of this, includes these human endeavors within its scope of application.[29] The neutralization tactics that researchers have found among consumers when they attempt to justify their unethical actions run counter to the biblical theme of covenant relationships. Covenant relationship emphasizes taking personal responsibility under God and within the context of the larger community. Taking advantage of the other party in an exchange, whether you are the buyer or the seller, goes against covenant: "If you make a sale, moreover, to your friend or buy from your friend's hand, you shall not wrong one another" (Lev 25:14). The same sentiment is stated in the New Testament:[30] covenant relationships in Scripture are multigenerational. Consumption should be limited to what is really needed.[31] Waste should be avoided.[32]

Shalom. It seems clear that buyers have just as much responsibility for contributing to a flourishing life in community as do sellers. When buyers deceive, defraud or take advantage of those who provide products and services, they are destroying the relationships with important stakeholders whose role is to make available the material things on which a flourishing life depends. These buyers make it more difficult for shalom to be extended throughout the community. "Those who love Your law have great peace, and nothing causes them to stumble" (Ps 119:165).

Sabbath. The prophet Amos speaks against those in business who spend the hours of the sabbath plotting how they can take advantage of buyers when the sun goes down.[33] There is no basis for thinking that this problem is limited only to people who sell. Worshiping God on sabbath is nothing but a sham if during the rest of the week both buyers and sellers act in unjust ways to each other.

Justice. We pursue covenant relationships together, which requires that persons in a position of authority treat those under their authority with fairness. The biblical themes go beyond the "buyer beware, seller beware" admonitions. Instead, buyers and sellers are called to be fair and responsible.[34] At the time of the purchase transaction, the consumer is usually in a unique position of authority with respect to the seller: the buyer has discretionary choice what to buy, when to buy, how much to buy. In the story, justice is not merely how we think about others. It involves actions we take that open up the channels of shalom blessing to others, and consumers play a key role as a channel of blessing to sellers. Consumers may perceive that the business they buy from has most of the power. This glosses over the bargaining power of the consumers who use their buying power to influence the companies from which they buy.

Righteousness. The application of righteousness to the issues of consumer behavior follows directly from what has been said above. Doing the right thing in the marketplace is based on the norms of our covenant relationship with God and with each other. When a consumer is in the buying relationship, certain explicit or implicit promises are made to the seller during transactions. When the consumer has an opportunity to take advantage of the seller, the seller is vulnerable. Treating the seller honestly is one way of regarding God's character of righteousness.

Truth. The story concept of truth means faithfulness of action. The majority of consumers in the marketplace act with integrity toward sellers. Sellers rely on a person to act in a consistent manner from one situation to an-

other. When a consumer acts in an inconsistent manner such that the seller is deceived, the buyer breaks truth with the seller. Truth involves living a consistent life over time without hypocrisy. This means that consumers will act toward sellers just as if they were the seller expecting integrity from the buyer.

Wisdom. "'Bad, bad,' says the buyer, but when he goes his way, then he boasts" (Prov 20:14). This is a one-of-a-kind passage of Scripture that reflects the idea of biblical wisdom. It describes a customer who attempts to take advantage of the seller in order to enhance personal economic prosperity. The biblical idea of prosperity has a broad meaning that encompasses spiritual well-being, social harmony, international harmony and economic success. Accordingly, when a person obtains wealth fraudulently, he or she makes the other dimensions of prosperity dwindle even if the economic dimension increases.

Loving kindness. Compared with sellers, buyers are in a unique position to respect covenant relationships in the marketplace. It is up to the customer, through loyalty of action, to provide the value he or she promises in exchange for the value that the seller offers. Loving kindness, in terms of consumer behavior, means loyalty in fostering mutual reciprocity by how consumers act. Accordingly, the customer will exhibit loving kindness on every transaction so that the action in that one transaction represents the best that the relationship can have for the long run. In contrast, a customer who treats the relationship as if it is a one-time event and as if there is no relationship will likely try to take advantage of the seller, not caring whether or not she does business with the seller ever again.

Redemption. Every material that is used in making and selling products, every good that humans enjoy for the sustenance of life was created by God. All have been included in the plan of redemption. In the same way, buyers who embed story themes into their behaviors will be alert to situations to help redeem the seller who makes a mistake in giving change or giving too much product or services not paid for. The buyer will act redemptively by avoiding fraud and deceit. Also, if the buyer makes a mistake with respect to the seller, the buyer will take responsibility to correct the error.

CHAPTER REVIEW QUESTIONS

1. What are the characteristics of the consumer society?

2. Why is it important to consider consumer ethics when studying business ethics?

3. Describe the consumer ethics scale and what it measures.

4. What is the concept of ethical ideology types?

5. What are examples of business-to-business purchasing ethics?

6. What influence does religion have on consumer ethical behavior?

7. What is neutralization, and how does it work?

8. What are two key resources that have moral implications in terms of acquisition, use and disposal at the industry level or economic system level?

9. What guidance do the biblical story themes offer for consumer ethics?

DISCUSSION QUESTIONS

1. What might be new characteristics of consumerism emerging in social groups that you observe? What challenges do these

present to your generation?

2. Is it right to hold businesses to a higher standard of morality than the standard to which we hold customers?

3. If a sales clerk makes a mistake in a transaction with a customer such that the customer receives an unexpected good (e.g., too much money back, too much product or service delivered), does the buyer deserve to get the benefit?

4. Make it personal: What questionable ethical consumer behavior have you engaged in? How did your conscience react at the time?

5. What responsibilities does each family have for conserving water and energy?

ETHICAL VIGNETTES TO DISCUSS

For each of the following vignettes, apply the biblical story themes to discern what is right and wrong.

1. You work as a purchasing agent for a department store. You know that the company has a policy that employees may not accept gifts from customers or from vendors. You also know that some employees have received from salespeople tokens of appreciation such as gift certificates to restaurants, tickets to professional sporting events, and other gifts. One day you get home and your spouse says, "We just received a new Blu-ray player delivered today. Did you order this?" You say, "No." You open the box and inside you see a note from the salesman who works for a clothing distributor that reads, "We value your business. Enjoy this small symbol of our deep appreciation for your business over the years." What will you do?

2. "A purchaser learns that prior to executing a long-term agreement with a supplier, a revised forecast on projected demand will not be as high as specified in the request-for-proposal and negotiations. If the new forecast is correct, the supplier may not be able to recover tooling costs during the term of the agreement. By executing the agreement, the buying firm will be more competitive. Both the buying firm and the supplier belong to the same industry, and both have a keen interest in seeing its survival since it has been slowly losing market-share, to foreign manufacturers."[35] Is it right that the purchaser signs the agreement?

3. For thirteen years Marc Benihoff worked in the Silicone Valley company Oracle. He was mentored by Oracle's top-level executive Larry Ellison. When Benihoff left to start his own company, Ellison invested two million dollars in Benihoff's venture. Benihoff asked Ellison to be a member of the board of directors. All went well until Benihoff learned that Ellison was trying to develop a product that competed directly with Benihoff's product: a web service for sales professionals. Benihoff asked Ellison to resign from the board. Was it wrong for Ellison to use his seat on the board to get information that would be useful for creating a competing product?

15

Ethical Issues in Management

SCRIPTURE PASSAGE

Do not withhold good from those to
 whom it is due,
When it is in your power to do it. (Prov 3:27)

CHAPTER OVERVIEW

In this chapter we explore selected contemporary ethical issues that managers face. In particular, we will explore selected ethical issues in management through the lens of biblical story themes.

MAIN TOPICS

Overview of Ethical Issues in Management
Employment at Will
Rights: Before Hiring and After Hiring
Employment Discrimination and Reverse
 Discrimination
Employee Rights of Privacy
Bullying
Down to the Nitty-Gritty
Through the Lens of Biblical Themes

KEY TERMS

affirmative action, asymmetrical relationship, bullying, discrimination, employment at will

OPENING SCENARIO

Amazing Heirlooms, Inc., is a manufacturing company that makes and sells replicas of popular antique furniture pieces.[1] Over a period of months, several events occur that raise issues with respect to ethical issues in management.

- *February*: The company signed a distribution agreement with a national furniture distributor to carry a new line of furniture.

- *March*: Equipment and materials are purchased, and two new production lines are established. Plans are made to hire thirty new employees to work these production lines.

- *April*: The human resource department recommends to the top executives that credit histories, drug screens and criminal background checks be performed on all new employees prior to employment because some employees will be handling dangerous power equipment. The policy is approved. Thirty new workers are hired and trained.

- *June*: Production slows because a supplier is slow in getting materials to the factory.

- *July*: One of the new employees hired to work on the new production line is let go because of poor performance. His supervisor had been following the company policy on progressive discipline. He is given his final paycheck and is told not to show up for work at the next shift.

- *September*: A new computerized manufacturing process is purchased and installed by upper management for one of the older production lines. The new computerized system uses 30 percent fewer employees.

- *November*: Senior management purchases a new type of glue that contains a chemical that speeds up the drying process. The new chemical releases fumes that are irritating to some employees' skin and eyes.

- *February*: An employee shows up to work impaired. The supervisor believes that he might be under the influence a drug. The employee is sent for drug testing. Members of the senior management team develop and implement a random drug testing program to deter other employees from using drugs.

- *April*: The chief financial officer produces a list of telephone extensions in the company that shows how many long-distance calls were made at each extension and the dollar value of these calls. This list was sent to the appropriate supervisors.

- *August*: Senior-level management establishes a new policy regarding smoking that requires cigarette smokers to smoke in a designated area outside the building. This change seems to be acceptable to employees until someone raises the question of what will happen in the winter.

- *September*: The supervisor for Employee A warns him that he must stop sending damaged materials to the next work station. Employee A explains that fellow employee B has repeatedly damaged some of the materials that employee A has worked on before sending it on to the next work station. Employee B also has damaged employee A's tools. Employee A identifies by name other employees who have seen this happen but have kept silent.

- *October*: Sales are lower than expected for the products being made in the two new

production lines. Senior management decides to cut its losses and shut down one of the new lines at the end of November. This will require laying off fifteen employees.

What are the ethical issues in this company? What rights does the company have with respect to employees? What rights do employees have with respect to management decisions? With the experience of Amazing Heirlooms, Inc., in mind we will consider some of the ethical issues in management that arise.

OVERVIEW OF ETHICAL ISSUES IN MANAGEMENT

Most of the ethical issues traditionally addressed in the work environment emphasize the employer's treatment of the employee. Perhaps this is because the employer is seen as the dominant party in the relationship. Where the employer is the dominant party, we call this an asymmetrical relationship. Here the employer is economically more powerful. The employer can choose to hire or discharge one or more employees if doing so helps the organization achieve its goals. Owners of a for-profit organization and the board of trustees in a nonprofit organization have the delegated authority to pursue the goals of the organization. Organizations hire and fire workers. To be fair, we must not limit ourselves to the point of view of the company. We must also see the issues from the perspective of workers. Figure 15.1 provides a summary of this relationship.

Does the employer have the right to engage in surveillance of employee activities? Surveillance can involve using video cameras and monitoring what websites the employee visits using company computers. Is it right that the employer monitors the employee's use of the Internet at work? Is it right for an employer to

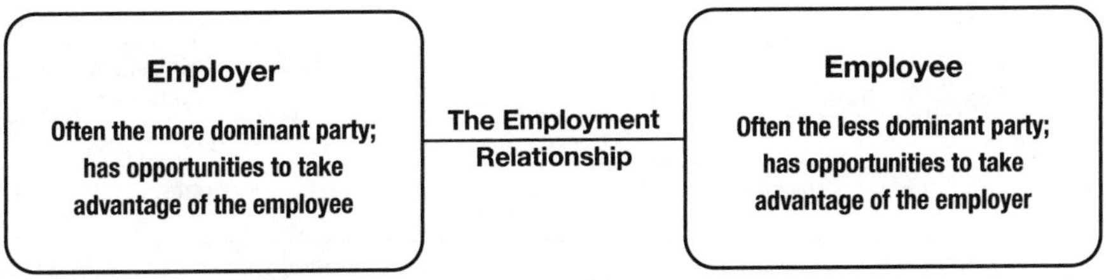

Figure 15.1. Ethical issues involve in the employment relationship.

monitor the use of the organization's telecommunication systems? Is it wrong for the employer to monitor the content of emails that are sent and received by employees? Is it fair that the employer establishes policies that limit employee use of company resources prohibiting use of these for personal benefit? What, if any, are the limits of managerial control that should be placed on workers? Employers and their agents (managers and supervisors) might have many opportunities to exercise managerial control over employees, but such opportunities might also be abused to take advantage of employees by invading their privacy.

These questions can be seen from the opposite point of view, too. Is it right that the employee uses the employer's Internet connection to surf the web for personal purposes while being paid to work? Is it right for the employee to use the company telephone to make personal long-distance telephone calls? Employees have many opportunities to take advantage of the employer.[2]

> The wages of a hired man are not to remain with you all night until morning. (Lev 19:13)

Ethical behavior is not limited to the employer-employee relationship. We must also see that employees have relationships with each other. One employee might undermine the quality of work done by a fellow worker (damaging or destroying the work in progress). Another employee might steal from a fellow worker. At a more subtle level one worker may attempt to say false things about other persons to damage the reputation in order to advance his or her own career. Another person might attempt to take credit for someone else's work.

Collectively, all these questions naturally raise the larger question about rights. What are the rights of the employer with respect to employees? What are the rights of employees with respect to the employer? What are the rights of the strategic business partner or outside organization with whom the company does business? Table 15.1 illustrates the scope of management ethical issues involving management relationships inside the firm.

In this chapter we will select a few of these questions to explore before evaluating them through the lens of biblical themes.

EMPLOYMENT AT WILL

Employment can be seen as an agreement between employer and employee.[3] Both parties must be able to enter into the arrangement voluntarily and without coercion. Both parties must get some benefit from the relationship. In some cases a formal (written) employment agreement is drawn up that both parties sign. Or the agreement can be as

Table 15.1. Scope of management ethical issues.

Employer (or Supervisor) Relationship with Employees	Employee Relationship with the Firm and with Each Other
Employee rights	Employer rights; fellow workers' rights
Discrimination in hiring and promotion	Conflicts of interest; moonlighting without permission
Providing fair compensation	Providing fair value of work for agreed-on compensation; abuse of expense accounts
Deception	Deception; resumé fraud; abuse of expense accounts
Bullying subordinates; unfairness in performance reviews	Bullying fellow workers; shirking legitimate duties
Retaliation; anti-union activities	Retaliation; anti-employer union activities
Employee privacy: monitoring telephone, email and Internet; drug testing, background checks, gathering personal health information; confidentiality; psychological testing	Use of company telecommunication systems; breach of security; confidentiality; employer privacy; copyright infringement; whistleblowing; working while impaired
Oppressive goal setting; rewards and incentives	Goal manipulation, working the system for incentives; cheating on reports goal attainment
Unsafe working conditions	Employee safety practices that increase risk
Employment at will, downsizing, plant closures; self-perpetuating corporate directors; using an employee to get more than is bargained for in the relationship	Using the employer to further personal career interests; terminating employment without notice
Sexual harassment	Sexual harassment

simple as a conversation between the employer and the job applicant. It often involves a written letter describing the job the employee is being hired to do, when the employee will start working and the compensation that will be given to the employee. Or the agreement may be formalized into a multiple-page written document spelling out many terms and conditions.

Figure 15.2. Humorous caution sign about working at will.

When no formal written contract exists other than an implicit agreement made during a conversation, the law in much of the United States provides for what is known as employment at will. Employment at will means that the employer is free to hire and free to fire employees. A company president believes there is good reason to think that future demand for products and services will grow. He decides to hire more employees to perform the work. If the demand is not as he expects, the company is free to lay off workers that it hired. The underlying assumption is that the goals of the company take precedence. These goals include the firm's ability to remain in business and to meet its financial obligations to existing employees and to its suppliers. If there are too many workers, company managers will lay off some workers to reduce expenses. This places the laid-off workers in a difficult position of having to find another job. Employment at will also considers the rights of the employee. The employee is free to take a job and to voluntarily quit that job at any time.

The employee may get other job opportunities.

The employment at will concept assumes that both parties enter the employment relationship voluntarily and that both parties can end the employment relationship at any time for any reason. Further, this concept assumes that the relationship is symmetrical in terms of the degree of influence that each party has. For these reasons employment at will seems fair at first glance.

Look a little deeper into the relationship, however, and you realize that the assumptions of employment at will may not be valid in every situation. It is the company's needs and goals with respect to its marketplace obligations that take precedence over the needs and goals of employees. While companies need workers, firms need qualified workers who will carry out particular tasks under specific working conditions and on a work schedule that supports the firm's ability to fulfill its obligations to marketplace stakeholders such as customers and suppliers. The company managers have the authority to discern which workers are best suited for the company given the goals of the firm and its obligations. They have the flexibility to respond to changing market conditions. Employees do not have this authority. Thus, there is an inherent hierarchy of authority that is established by the top-level managers of the firm with respect to how much discretionary choice they will allow employees to have.

Add to this that a person has no legal right to walk into a company and demand a job. It is not the job applicant who has the right to tell the employer who is the best match for the job. To require a firm to hire a particular employee because this person needs and wants a job is to overstep the rights of the firm with respect to marketplace stakeholders. The worker is not the one with the relationship with the customer and has no authority to decide which workers are either underqualified or overqualified for the work assignment.

RIGHTS: BEFORE HIRING AND AFTER HIRING

Every new employment situation carries unknowns for both the employer and the employee. From the employer's perspective, little is known about the employee's motivation to work or the employee's desire for high performance and high quality in the work that is produced. Little is known about the employee's honesty and faithfulness. Little is known about the employee's goals for the future. Little is known regarding how the employee works with other people. The employee could be using the job as merely a stepping stone to a better job at a company that pays better or merely to get access to healthcare benefits. For example, a female employee may be planning to start a family and want access to quality healthcare paid for by an employer. But she is not required to tell her employer this when hiring on. Another employee may take the job to learn about the business because he has plans to start a similar business as soon as he gains experience. He wants access to inside information regarding how to deal with suppliers and customers and how to manage business operations. But he is not required to disclose this to the employer. From the employer's perspective the employee holds private information that gives the employee an advantage in certain respects.

From the employee's perspective, unless the employer reveals information about its plans for downsizing,[4] the employee will not know when the company plans to downsize because of unfavorable changes in market demand.[5] The job applicant may not have complete information about the working conditions until after accepting a job and working in it for a while. Employees may not know how the personality and temperament of the supervisor affects them until they are on the job for a while. What it is like to work with other employees in the same work unit will not be known until experiencing them. The employee also may not know how difficult the work is or what the company values are in practice. From the employee's point of view the employer holds private information that gives the employer an advantage in certain respects.

Because employment is so often asymmetrical in terms of bargaining power, concerns should be raised regarding what rights the employee has under such circumstances. Couple with this the fact that employers have been constrained by law from obtaining certain information from the employee such as age and religion. For some employees who were let go, employer action has caused unfair results. Table 15.2 provides a summary of some of the rights of the employee during the hiring process.

Certain exceptions apply to the employment at will principle. Federal law prohibits an employer from letting go members of a labor union. The Civil Rights Act forbids employers from

firing a person based on discrimination based on religion, race, sex, age, disability, and other situations. If an employee refuses the request of the employer to act in violation of a law or a regulation, the employer cannot fire the worker.[6]

With these principles in mind it is relatively straightforward to see that deception regarding working conditions, discipline, promotion, pay increase and firing decisions based on non-job-related criteria such as age, gender, race, religion, and other criteria is unethical. This brings up the issue of discrimination, which we consider next.

EMPLOYMENT DISCRIMINATION AND REVERSE DISCRIMINATION

Since the early 1960s discrimination in employment practices has been an important topic. In 1962 a Civil Rights Act was passed by Congress that forbid discrimination based on race, color, religion or national origin. In this section we will consider some of the ethical issues related to this topic.

Definition. By one use of the term, discrimination means to make a distinction or recognize the difference between two things or two ideas. You are at the local farmers' market to purchase apples. You want to get good apples

Table 15.2. Employee rights before hiring and after hiring.

Before Hiring: The employee has the right to	**After Hiring:** The employee has the right to
Know what the working conditions are like	Job-based performance criteria used as the basis for discipline and firing
Know whether the job is temporary	Know when job expectations have changed
Know whether there is a probationary period and how long that is	Know the job-related criteria used to evaluate work performance
Know what the job entails (the job description) and what other duties are expected	Know the disciplinary process and how it is used; know the reason for termination
Know the job-related criteria that are used for determining the hiring, promotion and pay increases and terminations	Promotion and pay increase decisions that are made based on job-related criteria
Know what the pay and benefits are	A fair and impartial performance review of work; equal treatment; fair implementation of pay increases in the organization

and avoid getting bad apples. To achieve this, you discriminate. Under this definition, when we are careful to distinguish between a product or service that is high in quality or one that is comparatively lower in quality, we are discriminating or discerning. In economics, the term "price discrimination" is used to denote the action of a company that sells the same product or service to different buyers at different prices. For example, airline companies and hotels use price discrimination to sell seats on airlines and hotel rooms at different prices to different groups of people. On a flight you could be sitting next to a person who paid a lot more or a lot less than you did to get the same class of seat as you purchased. The person who purchased a ticket at the last minute likely paid more than the person who purchased the ticket thirty days in advance. Selling tickets in advance improves the company's cash flow. Price discrimination tactics include things like peak pricing versus off-peak pricing, early-bird discounts, and other approaches.[7]

The other definition of the term "discrimination" refers to the practice of unjustly treating one category of person differently from other persons based on the grounds of some personal characteristic such as age, race, religion, skin color, and so forth. Accordingly, changing the price or quality in buying-selling transaction based on a personal characteristic of the other party or changing a employment practice because of a personal characteristic is discriminatory.

Types of employment discrimination. In the arena of employment, unjust discrimination can occur when a firm selects one person over another for a job based on a personal characteristic or a superior chooses not to promote one equally-qualified person based on gender. If the company must downsize and

lay people off, selecting persons of a particular group, such as those who are near retirement or women, is another example. Another firm treats an employee differently who has a disability or who has a spouse with a disability. If a firm pays one employee less because the person is younger or is female, even though the job the person does is the same as that performed by an older person or a male, this is a form of discrimination, too. Thus, employment discrimination can occur for hiring, firing, compensation, benefits, promotion, training and any other condition of employment.

Subtleties of employment discrimination. It is sometimes difficult to identify observable employment discrimination. More subtle forms of discrimination include requiring persons of one group to take a pre-employment test that was designed for another group of persons or writing a job description in such a way that only a male could do the work. If advertising for a job opening is kept to publications read primarily by white males, women and members of minority groups might not get the information about the job. If training programs designed to help managers get prepared for senior-level leadership are offered only to persons whose job is flexible enough to allow them time to participate and other persons who are members of a minority group do not have the flexibility in their jobs to participate, discrimination may be occurring.

Why discrimination is wrong. It is illegal to practice discrimination in employment practices. But an ethical reason is at the foundation of the law. The harm done to potential workers, to their families and to society (when carried out in a widespread manner) compared with the benefits that accrue to the firm when employers are allowed to discriminate shows the disutility of discrimination. Harm done is one reason why laws exist that forbid discrimination. Discrimination treats people as a means to an end rather than an end in themselves. People are treated as a member of a certain group that shares a particular non-job characteristic. Because they have this characteristic, they are not given equal treatment compared with other people who do not have this characteristic. If we ask the employee and the employer whether they would want to have employment discrimination, clearly these two might disagree, because the employee would tend not to want it even if the employer did. From a justice point of view, the most disadvantaged people in society would be better off if discrimination was not permitted than if it was permitted. Discrimination does not foster freedom equally across the population, nor does it foster equality of opportunity. The biblical story reasons will be considered below.

Affirmative action. Affirmative action is an effort to make corrections with respect to recruiting women and members of minority groups to become new employees and helping them become qualified for promotion into positions of leadership.

Reverse discrimination. One problem that has developed with the use of affirmative action programs is reverse discrimination. When women or minorities are recruited for employment or are provided opportunities for training that will help prepare them for top-level leadership positions, it can also be unjust to block others who are not women or part of a minority group. Reverse discrimination is when white males are discriminated against because they are not women or members of a minority group.

EMPLOYEE RIGHTS OF PRIVACY

Employees have rights in society regardless of the activities they are engaged in at any particular time, whether at work, at home or at leisure. One of these rights is the right to privacy. But what this right means is not always clear.

The right to privacy is supported by laws that prevent others from entering your home without your permission unless the court has granted a warrant for this purpose. The right to privacy means that the employee must be allowed to make choices regarding how to spend leisure time away from work.

Personal time off. If an employee decides to go to a party at night during the work week, the employer has no right to forbid such action. However, if the late-night party results in loss of sleep such that the employee's performance at work suffers, the employer should discipline the employee. If the employee decides to join a club, organization or church, go the symphony, attend a live theater performance or join a community softball league, the employer has no right to forbid such activities. The employee has a strong argument that he or she should be able to do anything he or she wants during personal time off as long as it does not interfere with his or her performance at work.

But does employee rights mean that the employee can do anything he or she wants during personal time away from work? For example, in most organizations an employee does not have the right to show up for work under the influence of alcohol or another drug.[8] But what about drinking alcohol on personal time? While drinking alcohol on personal time may be a person's right, the effects of drinking such as engaging in lewd social behaviors, assault and battery, drunk driving, trespassing, and other actions will be of concern to the employer because it is disruptive in the community and reflects negatively on the employer's brand.

Furthermore, even though the employee is on his or her own time, one could argue that because the employee has formed a working relationship with an employer, that relationship is representational even during leisure time. Humans do not live in isolation from each other. We are not islands unto ourselves. Instead, we are always interconnected. Your associations with others are affected by your behavior. And it is artificial to try to break the interconnections when you want to behave as you wish on your own time.

Another employee joins the company softball team that competes with other amateur teams in the community. The employee does not have the right to act out in anger by bullying or physically fighting with members of the opposing team if he or she gets angry over events that happen during the game. Even when an employee is on personal time away from work, such as at night or on the weekends, the employee must respect the rights of others in the community. Furthermore, the employee's actions, as a member of the company's softball team, reflect on the employer's reputation. In such a case the employer has the right to discipline the employee.

Drug testing. Does your employer have a right to know whether or not you use drugs or alcohol? The only way that the employer can truly know this is if the employee is subjected to drug testing through urinalysis, a blood test or some other medical laboratory analysis. Because use of drugs such as alcohol and marijuana can affect work performance, some employers want to hire people who are not drug users.

Although medical laboratory tests for the presence of drugs are highly accurate, mistakes sometimes are made, such as when the laboratory test incorrect identifies someone who has a drug in his or her system when no drug is present.

But is drug testing a breach of the right to privacy? If the employee voluntarily agrees to be tested, most people would say that in this voluntary agreement, the employee has given up some right to privacy. The problem gets more complicated when we consider the possibility that the company requires drug testing. In some work tasks, workers who are impaired from drug use are a safety concern not only for themselves (such as using dangerous equipment) but also for fellow workers, customers and anyone the organization deals with. In such a situation, it can be argued, the employer has the right to protect not only the worker but also other persons that the worker's performance can affect.

Other rights of privacy that come up in the discussion about employee rights include the following:

- monitoring the content of emails and telephone calls made to or from company telephones

- monitoring US postal mail that is received by employees

- monitoring employees through the use of closed-circuit video surveillance systems

- monitoring which Internet websites are visited by an employee during work hours

- monitoring the content of social media pages

- requiring pre-employment polygraph tests, psychological tests and ethics tests

- using software to analyze video from pre-employment interviews

- using personal medical information gathered by the health insurance company to determine how much the employee must pay for health insurance premiums

BULLYING

Anytime you have a group of two or more people who are interdependent, you will have occasion for conflict to arise. Workers may disagree over the best methods to get work done. They may disagree over what worker gets which resources to accomplish tasks. Workers will be tempted to protect their control over key resources that they believe might be threatened by someone else's influence. At the top level of leadership there may be conflict over which strategic commitments the organization should make: One leader does not like the tradeoff that results from a commitment that is suggested by another leader. In these types of conflict the focus is on the work, the goals, work processes or on misunderstandings regarding expectations, roles, responsibilities and authority.

Conflict can also become personal and as a result, become dysfunctional. One worker attacks another with hurtful words or shows disrespect to a fellow worker. A worker undermines another worker's relationship with the supervisor. A worker openly questions the motives, character, intelligence or personality of another person. Workers may escalate the conflict by resorting to acts of incivility such as intimidation, ridicule, sarcasm, humiliation or loud vulgar language. When conflict escalates into open aggression toward another person, it becomes a form of bullying.[9] In extreme situations one worker may start a physical fight with another person. Bullying occurs between workers at the same level of authority. But bullying can also occur between supervisors and subordinates.

Bullying is "*repeated* and *persistent negative actions* towards one or more *individual(s)*, which involve *a perceived power imbalance* and *create a hostile work environment*. Bullying is thus a form of interpersonal aggression or hostile, anti-social behavior in the workplace."[10]

Bullying usually involves four characteristics:

a) more than one uncivil or victimizing behaviors, b) that are repeated, c) over a period of time, d) and involve the abuse of differences in power.[11] The following are the common types of behaviors reported by workers who believed that they experienced bullying at work:

- information was withheld that affected your performance
- exposure to an unmanageable workload
- ordered to do work below your level of competence
- given tasks with unreasonable/impossible targets/deadlines
- opinions and views were ignored
- work was excessively monitored
- reminded repeatedly of your errors or mistakes
- humiliated or ridiculed in connection with your work
- gossip and rumours spread about you
- insulting/offensive remarks made about you[12]

What is defined as bullying is far from clear when considering the range of behaviors described above. It might be fair to say that in some cases bullying is in the eye of the beholder. What a manager considers prudent oversight might seem to the subordinate to be excessive monitoring of behavior. A supervisor considers it well within the bounds of legitimate authority to delegate a particular task to a subordinate. The subordinate is offended and considers it bullying because the task is below his competence.

DOWN TO THE NITTY-GRITTY

Think about scenario at the beginning of this chapter. You are a manager in Amazing Heirlooms, Inc. Take the question of laying off

Table 15.3. Applying the ethical process.

Keeping Your Heart: An Intrapersonal Process	Walking in the Community: An Interpersonal Process

• You are a manager in Amazing Heirlooms, Inc. What does your heart say is the right thing to do regarding laying off fifteen persons?
• Which biblical themes explored in this book inform your heart on this situation?
• Which biblical theme, if any, do you feel yourself resisting? Why do you feel resistance?
• What other influences in your heart seem to be prominent as you think about this situation?
  • Fundamental beliefs
  • Cognitive reasoning
  • Judgments and evaluations
  • Decisions
  • Virtues
  • Will
  • Memory of personal experiences with other people
  • Perceptions of others in the community
  • Personal biases
  • Awareness of interpersonal relationships
  • Commitments to God and to others
  • Intuitions
  • Conscience
  • Human spirit
  • Emotions
	• You are a manager in Amazing Heirlooms, Inc. With whom might you have a conversation about the issue of what you found? Who else might have a helpful perspective?
	• Who should take a leadership role in the conversation about the ethics of laying off fifteen people?
	• Which of the biblical themes in this chapter will most likely come up in the conversation either directly or indirectly? Why? Which one(s) will be the most influential in the conversation?
	• If you have a conversation with someone regarding this situation, which of the fundamental tensions presented earlier in the book might come up?
	• What right-versus-right dilemmas, if any, can be identified? Have a conversation with someone about this now. What is the outcome of the conversation?

fifteen employees. What is the right thing to do? It's time to get down to the nitty-gritty (see table 15.3)!

THROUGH THE LENS OF BIBLICAL THEMES

This part of the chapter will use the biblical story themes as a lens through which to evaluate the topic featured in the chapter. Because the themes are interrelated and interde-

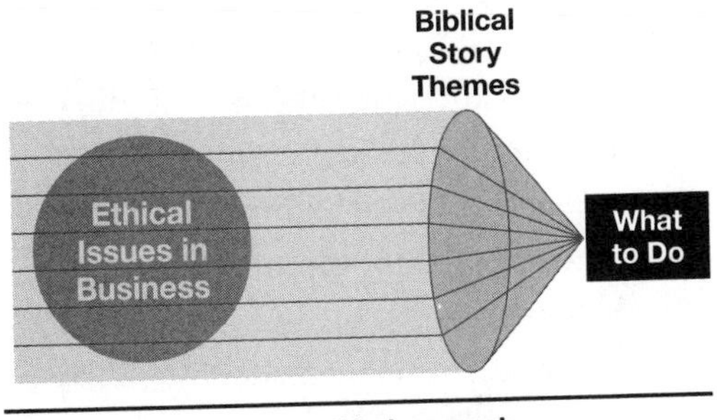

Figure 15.3. Evaluating an ethical approach.

pendent, we should expect to see some overlap in the thinking regarding the issues. Some themes will contribute the same thinking as will other themes. The power of these themes comes from their guidance when a community of people talks about complicated ethical dilemmas faced in business practice.

The application of the biblical story themes provides an interesting perspective to the ethical issues in management.

Cosmic conflict. The central message of the Bible is a story about God's character and great works. God is a God of peace and not chaos.[13] He pursues freedom within boundaries instead of coercion or anarchy. God is sovereign and could have chosen immediately to wipe evil out of existence using brute force. Instead, he sets in motion a great plan of redemption.[14] Employees should not to be terminated arbitrarily. They deserve fairness and impartiality in performance reviews, disciplinary actions and termination procedures, as God's character reveals. For example, reasons given to the employee for termination for cause should not come as a surprise to the employee. Further, reasons for firing, even if for cause, should be strong enough to stand up to scrutiny by an impartial judge. Discrimination against people does not glorify God.[15] It involves hiding and partiality. Like bullying, it is cruel. Followers of Christ will not "lord it over" others, that is, impose their will arbitrarily or abuse their authority over subordinates. Rather, they will serve with compassion and humility.[16]

Creation. At creation we learn that all are created in the image of God. To disrespect some by discrimination, bullying or other ways that avoid honoring their rights is to disrespect all. Leaders who serve God are the type of people who treat others with love, respect and dignity.[17] Workers who take the creation theme with them to work will foster flourishing life rather than leave behind them a wasteland. Discrimination and bullying involve a distortion of relationships. They deface and destroy the image of God in human soul rather than work toward its restoration.

Holiness. Both managers and subordinates are set apart for service to God. This service is most often expressed by serving other people and organizations. Managers, following God's example, should be among subordinates in order to be available to guide, teach, organize, coach, support and encourage. Both managers and subordinates should keep the employer-employee relationship on a professional level and avoid inappropriate relationships and actions. Taking a leadership role, managers and subordinates will both be interested in cleaning up relationships and behaviors in organizations.

Managers will not hesitate to use the progressive discipline process to eradicate unethical behavior from the organization while they show respect and dignity to those involved.

Covenant relationships. When an employer and employee form a relationship, the story theme of covenant looks attractive. Employment at will under covenant thinking will involve a creative tension. On the one hand, both parties will want to test the relationship before making a long-term commitment. On the other hand, building a covenant commitment will involve building in some important dimensions to the relationship recognizing the asymmetry that exists. The employer will look out for the interests of the employee and will even give training to the employee to help him or her succeed. Both parties will respect and nourish the relationship. The Golden Rule, a succinct statement of covenant living, is breached if an employer discriminates against a person for any reason.[18] Prior to employment when the employer discriminates, the message is given that the employer is more interested in taking from than giving to the relationship. The emphasis is on the short-term, narrow self-interest. The Golden Rule also applies to the issue of bullying.

Shalom. The ideal in life is that we live at peace with one another. But reality is usually far from the ideal. Whether because of pride, envy or greed, unwise talking, anger, scarcity of resources, ideology or differences in perspective, conflict is an unavoidable part of life.[19] In the experience of Jesus and the early church leaders, we find a curious mix of conflict avoidance and resolution. But other times these individuals appear to stir up controversy.[20] Sometimes Jesus is outspoken in his judgment of the religious leaders of his day. At other times, his soft-spoken manner turns away their wrath.[21] On the one hand, respecting the rights of another person contributes to shalom. Privacy fosters flourishing life as long as privacy does not mean isolation from community. On the other hand, rights of privacy are important as long as such rights do not interfere with the rights of the community for safety and security.

Sabbath. Sabbath through the lens of story themes involves several things. It involves honoring the place of productive work in society and doing what is possible for unemployed persons to gain meaningful employment. When opportunities to hire workers come, the employer will seek to exercise the right to hire and in so doing help someone experience part of the sabbath principle ("six days you shall labor"; Ex 20:8-11). Sabbath involves managers helping employees celebrate work while experiencing the joy of work for the greater good of the community. By helping each other have joy in work, people are God's servants in bringing one of his gifts.[22] Discrimination and bullying both are forms of breaking the sabbath principles.

Justice. Scripture clearly teaches fairness in dealing with others across a wide spectrum of behaviors, including the employment relationship. Foreshadowed in the sabbath theme, justice involves honoring persons' rights. It means opening the way so that rights can be enjoyed and the persons flourish. The justice-thinking manager will not ignore the injustice of discrimination and bullying and other actions but will become an advocate on behalf of justice. In this way the manager will carry throughout the organization, and by extension into the larger community, the life-giving water of justice.

Righteousness. Much like its first cousin justice, righteousness lends stability to covenant relationships. It invests in the community and builds up rather than destroys. If a worker carrying righteousness theme with him to work notices someone bullying a worker, he will do the right thing and advocate for safety. Doing the right thing means impartially establishing new employee selection criteria that is not narrowly focused on a personal characteristic. Rather, righteousness keeps in view the relevant tasks needed to serve society and will encourage selecting new workers who can best serve regardless of the personal characteristics of the job applicant.

Truth. Truth means faithfulness of action. Faithfulness in action must embrace the needs of the organization as well as those of individual employees. In this Scripture theme we see the individual-community tension as a reflection of God's glory. When the worker and the manager who represents the organization consider forming an employment relationship, truth must be carried into the interview and the selection process. Indeed, like God's throne, the employment relationship is established and maintained on the principle of truth! Truth carried into the workplace will honor employee rights.

Wisdom. Wisdom contains an interesting mix of practical prudence that helps protect a person (and an organization) from being misled or taken advantage of by another party. But covenantal wisdom means others are looked after so as not to be taken advantage of, too. Wisdom is relationship-centered and humble. Wisdom is the ability to consider something diligently or closely and thereby have insight and understanding regarding it in a practical way. Wisdom knows that it is both covenantal and the smart thing to do to honor a person's rights. In terms of the topics of this chapter, wisdom helps both employer and employee make the decision whether or not to commit to a long-term employment relationship. Wisdom helps both to know when it is best to sever the relationship in a way that is respectful for both. Wisdom directs a manager to select the best person for the long-run relationship based on criteria other than personal characteristics.

Loving kindness. The loving kindness of God is demonstrated every time an employer takes a risk in offering a job to someone. The organization and the employee work diligently to be loyalty to each other. Faithfulness and loyalty of the employee require a corresponding posture by the employer. Many employers do not want to consider tenure when laying off workers; however, if employees who have demonstrated loyalty of service need to be laid off, their years of loyalty must not be ignored. Every time an organization must lay off a worker, it is done with as much compassion as possible. Both parties will respect the relationship. This involves mutually honoring each other's rights. It is probably obvious by now that the act of bullying is far outside the biblical ideal. Certainly, showing loving kindness is the opposite of bullying.

Redemption. Believers in business will see in their work opportunities to communicate about the character of God (a) in excellence of the work; (b) in attempts to redeem fallen organizations; (c) in attempts to restore persons to harmony (shalom) with the community of work and the larger community in which they live; (d) where appropriate by being a voice on behalf of the gospel; and (e) being an advocate for restoration of principles founded on the law of God. Employer-employee relationships are ready for redemption. Instead of intensifying the misery by coercing, bullying and discriminating, persons who follow covenantal relationship thinking will work to restore, heal, liberate and rescue. Instead of fostering a culture of intimidation, redemption thinking promotes reconciliation and procedures for fairly and safely airing grievances. Carrying redemption to the marketplace is practical when considering an employment termination. Both parties can act redemptively by giving reasonable notice of the intent to terminate the relationship. This provides the other party with time to begin preparing for the transition.

CHAPTER REVIEW QUESTIONS

1. What is the concept of employment at will? What are the ethical issues at stake?

2. Describe the concept of rights in the employment relationship. What rights do employees have?

3. What is employment discrimination and reverse discrimination?

4. What ethical issues are relevant to employee rights of privacy?

5. What is bullying, and why is it a problem?

6. What do the biblical story themes guide us regarding management ethical issues?

DISCUSSION QUESTIONS

1. This chapter has reviewed just a few of the many ethical issues that can arise in and around organizations. Consider the issue of employee rights after hiring. Using the lens of biblical themes, how would you evaluate this issue?

2. Are the rights of workers only those things that they agree to at the time they hire on as an employee?

3. Is it wrong for a company not to promote a worker into a management position because the person uses a form of English that is commonly found among inner-city youth?

4. Using the Internet, research the meaning of the term "preferential hiring." Is preferential hiring right or wrong?

5. Is it bullying to be ordered by a supervisor to do work below your level of competence?

ETHICAL VIGNETTES TO DISCUSS

For each of the following vignettes, apply the biblical story themes to discern what is right and wrong.

1. One of your high-performing employees comes to your office one day to ask for a raise. You know that she often goes beyond what you expect to help on projects that are outside of her job description. You also know that she has two small children. Your employee states that she is aware that someone doing similar work in a similar organization in a larger town thirty miles away earns 20 percent more pay than she gets. Your organization has a wage and salary scale that applies to every position in the company. You also know that, in general, your company pays less to its employees than the company in the larger town. What is the right thing to do?

2. A university graduate got a job working for a Christian nonprofit organization (NPO) as a policy analyst.[23] Her first major project involved analyzing data and writing a careful analysis that was to be published for the NPO's constituents. When she com-

pleted writing the report, the administrator told her that he would be putting his name as the author. He explained that with his name on the product, it would gain more attention and the organization would sell more copies. This way the impact would be greater. The ministry of the organization could be advanced. Eventually he agreed to include her name on the cover. Was it wrong for the administrator to put his own name on the cover to enhance the impact of the product for the constituents? Was it deceptive that he used his name as one of the authors even though it was the new employee who had done the work?

3. Dudley and Derrin were given a performance goal to achieve by the end of the month.[24] If the goal was achieved, they would get recognition but not a monetary bonus. Dudley did not even get within 10 percent of his goal. But he had an explanation for this that he discussed with his supervisor: There were some elements that were outside of his control. Derrin got very close to his goal. He would have gone past the goal, but he was still waiting for someone else to get part of the project finished by the end of the month. This person was delayed. Derrin reasoned that the project was as good as finished, and he decided to report that the project was complete. Reporting it complete would put him over the line for goal achievement.

16

Ethical Issues in Accounting and Finance

SCRIPTURE PASSAGE

You shall not steal, nor deal falsely, nor lie to one another. (Lev 19:11)

CHAPTER OVERVIEW

In this chapter we will explore issues in accounting and finance. In particular, we will

- explore selected ethical and legal issues in accounting and finance through the lens of biblical story themes

- increase awareness of the criminal penalties for committing white-collar crimes

MAIN TOPICS

The Essence of Fraud

Cheating in Financial Management and Investing

Characteristics of Fraudsters

Catching and Punishing White-Collar Criminals

Down to the Nitty-Gritty

Through the Lens of Biblical Themes

KEY TERMS

back-dating, cheating, collusion, deception, false sales, fictitious revenue, forward-dating, fraud, insider trading, overvalued assets, stock options, tax evasion, white-collar crime

OPENING SCENARIO

If Mathew Martoma had told you in 2008 that he had one of the hottest investment opportunities around, you might have gone away thinking, *If it sounds too good to be true, it probably is.* And you would have been right.

Martoma began working for a hedge fund company called SAC Capital Advisors in 2006, three years after he graduated from Stanford University Graduate School of Business with a master of business administration (MBA) degree.[1] Mathew was placed in charge of a portfolio of investments in the healthcare industry. Quickly he became interested in pharmaceuticals.

In order to keep current on the industry he hired consultants to bring market research data and information related to research and developments in the field of pharmaceuticals. Any investment firm can do the same. It is not illegal to hire consultants to conduct market research using information available to the public.

But Martoma wanted to go farther. In the market research information he gained, Martoma identified two companies, Elan and Wyeth, that were doing promising research on new drugs to treat Alzheimer's disease. From another source he identified the names of two physicians who were involved in cutting-edge research on these new drugs. Martoma wanted to dig deeper and get information that was not available to the public.

Over the course of nearly two years Martoma contacted the two physicians many times to discuss the status of their research. He paid the physicians a secret consultation fee to get the inside information on the status of the research. During one of the early visits he learned that the drug was safe with patients who had been in the testing phase.[2] Based on this confidential information Martoma purchased shares of stock in Elan and Wyeth. He convinced his firm to purchase more stock. By 2008 SAC Capital owned more than $700 million of the stock.

In the summer of 2008 Martoma got bad news from one of the doctors. Alzheimer's patients taking the new drug were getting worse, not better. The doctor had been asked to make a public announcement about this information. On July 19, 2008, a few days before the scheduled announcement, Martoma flew to Detroit and met with the doctor who gave him details. The next day Martoma had a short conversation with his boss at SAC Capital who, after the conversation, directed that SAC Capital traders sell most of the Elan and Wyeth stock. Just as Martoma had worried, after the public announcement on July 29, the value of the stock fell and investors started selling stock.

Mathew Martoma may have thought he had escaped detection. But four and a half years later he was arrested by the FBI for insider trading. The investigation had taken more than three years. After his arrest, the legal process took more than a year, but eventually Martoma was convicted of one count of conspiracy to commit securities fraud and two counts of securities fraud. The maximum penalty for Martoma was five years for the conspiracy charge and twenty years each for the two securities fraud charges.

This case is what the FBI called the most lucrative insider trading scheme it had ever charged until that time. More than $275 million in illegal profits had been earned by SAC Capital, while losses had been avoided by dumping the stock before the rest of the market was aware of the bad news. Martoma had earned more than $9 million in bonuses by cheating the investment system where others lost money. During the case the FBI revealed that Martoma had been expelled from Harvard Law School fifteen years earlier for forging the transcript of his grades, which he may have used to get into the Stanford business school.

If we look closely at the SAC Capital case and the actions of Mathew Martoma in particular, we can see how it parallels many similar cases of unethical and illegal behavior. To understand how Martoma and others try to circumvent the systems designed to protect investors, we will briefly explore the most popular areas of accounting and finance that become targets of unscrupulous activities. The pressure to show that the firm is performing well can become intense and lead some managers to be unethical in their activities.[3] In this chapter we will briefly consider two of the more common unethical and illegal actions that have been observed in accounting and finance: fraud and cheating.

It would be great if newspapers, magazines and electronic media published stories about the ethical practices of businesses. Unfortunately, these do not make the evening news. One reason is that in developed economies the majority of business transactions are carried out in an ethical manner. Standard business practices become routine. They are no longer newsworthy. In contrast to the common ethical practices that are present in most industries on a routine basis, we get sensational news stories about ethical violations. Thus, it is not surprising that the ethical violations become the backbone of case studies and illustrations when studying ethics.

THE ESSENCE OF FRAUD

When a basketball player fakes his opponent, we are amazed and cheer. When the hockey player on a breakaway gets the goalie to move to the left and then shoots to the right, we love the athletic ability. We thrill at the momentary deception that has just occurred. The referees do not care if players fake each other out as long as the other rules are followed.

When faking it happens in finance and accounting, we are not nearly as pleased. When it happens to us in business, we get angry. In sport we call it a fake and encourage our favorite team to do it as often as possible; in business, we call it fraud and maintain laws against it.

> Wealth obtained by fraud dwindles,
> But the one who gathers by labor
> increases it. (Prov 13:11)

Fraud is an attempt to trick or deceive someone to gain an advantage or get money. It involves deception and stealing.[4] Over the thousands of years that humans have engaged in trade, schemers have developed many ways to deceive. When you think about it in financial statement terms, only two ways exist to cook the books: make the revenue or cash look better than it is or make the expenses and liabilities look better then they truly are. Out of these two ways we report here the most common approaches to accounting fraud.[5]

Income statement fraud via fictitious revenue. Many organizations use accrual accounting rather than cash accounting. The revenue that is recorded in the accounting ledger can be manipulated to look better than it truly is. Revenue can be over-reported by placing fictitious numbers in the general ledger. Perpetrators put into the files a few phony invoices to divert the auditors and think they have a recipe to avoid detection.

False sales. Under pressure to perform, someone may ask an accountant to record sales that have not occurred. It may be easy for one manager to bully an employee or to persuade the employee that the deal is done and the contract will be signed tomorrow or by the end of the week, just after the close of the accounting record. After all, the work to close the sale was done during the current period, meaning that the expenses incurred in generating the sale will be booked now, so why not book the revenue booked now, too. Boosting revenue numbers with information representing false sales to existing customers can turn even more evil when a person fabricates false information regarding sales from nonexistent customers with fake addresses.

Balance sheet fraud via overvalued assets. At the end of the fiscal year the current inventory is counted and valued. Fraud schemers can temporarily boost the number of items on the shelves by borrowing inventory from a supplier by asking the supplier to bill them later. Or, after the inventory in one location has been counted, employees might be asked to pack and transport some of it to another location just before inventory is counted there. This has the effect of increasing the current assets on the balance sheet.

Holding the books open for revenue or delaying liabilities. Some fraud schemers may ask accountants to hold the books open a few days into the next fiscal period in order to book the revenue from part of that next period. Waiting until the following fiscal period to book liabilities under-represents true liabilities and makes the owner equity appear better than it is.

Not recording liabilities. It is one thing to delay the recording of liabilities. It is quite another thing to not record them for a very long time, such as for many years or not at all.

Collusion. When two or more persons conspire to commit fraud by circumventing the financial protection systems, it can be more harmful than if a person acting alone attempts fraud. Persons acting in collusion can combine their efforts to override the controls that are in place to prevent fraud. In the United States approximately one-third of fraud cases studied in 2010 involved collusion. Outside the United States collusion is more prevalent (56 percent).[6]

What makes fraud wrong is that deception usually results in financial harm, undermining a person's autonomy and violating a person's property rights.[7] Deception also is a violation of generally accepted moral principles related to cheating, coercion, disloyalty and breaking promises.

CHEATING IN FINANCIAL MANAGEMENT AND INVESTING

Many of the unethical actions in financial management involve cheating. They can involve some form of fraud. They often require the use of false information in accounting records or management records or both. The more complicated unethical and illegal financial schemes require collusion.

Cheating is an attempt to live above the rules of the game. It involves violating a rule that others are expected to follow.[8] The presence of cheating implies that there are other entities (persons or organizations) that are obeying the rules. It also implies that one party is cheating another party. By cheating, the person or organization gains an unfair advantage over the obedient parties. In sport, faking is acceptable, but cheating is not. We might debate whether or not a certain rule in sport gives the offense player an advantage over a defense player, but the official rules of the game apply equally to all players all the time.

Cheating usually involves deception. A broad category of actions, deception "can come in a variety of different forms. One can deceive by making a statement, asking a question, issuing a command, stating an opinion, displaying a picture, making a facial expression or gesture, or engaging in various other forms of verbal and non-verbal behavior."[9] One person can mislead another person without telling a lie. The receiver of a misleading statement bears some responsibility for discerning the truth or falsehood that exists in a statement.

In what follows we briefly explore a few examples of ethical and legal issues in financial management.

Insider trading. The case of Mathew Martoma is a case that involved insider trading and corruption. Insider trading involves trading stock using nonpublic information.[10] Insider trading involves breaking a promise to shareholders not to use information they gain for private benefit. Insider trading involves either fraud, deception or both. In Martoma's case it also involved corruption when he paid the doctors for confidential information.

Mortgage banking ethical lapses. Managing risk usually involves more than one organization that contracts to share the risk. If managers believe that organizations other than their own will bear the major portion of the risk, or if they attempt to structure the contract relationships in such a way that risk is simply passed along to others, they believe that their own exposure to risk is minimized. An example of multiple organizations sharing risk in ways that ended in disaster is that of the subprime mortgage loan financial crisis of 2008. It resulted from the actions of several groups of stakeholders: eager home buyers (some of whom fudged the numbers), eager mortgage loan sales personnel (who either fudged the numbers or falsified the information on loan application forms), eager commercial banks (that did not have the primary job of vetting the ability of home buyers to make loan payments), investment banks (that developed complicated mortgage-backed securities), eager bond rating agencies (that seemed to exaggerate the ratings but did not have the primary data regarding collateral), the incorrect assumption on the part of most people that real estate values would continue to go up and weak government oversight.[11] When enough people bend the rules the impact can be the same as either fraud or cheating or both.

Tax evasion. Bending the rules on mortgage loan applications is one form of cheating. Evading taxes is quite another, bolder approach to cheating the system. The tax laws allow for legal ways that taxpayers can legally avoid paying taxes. Loopholes in the law allow for lawful deductions from taxable income or for tax credits. Either way the tax liability can be lawfully decreased. When persons or for-profit organizations choose not to file a tax return, they are in defiance of the law. Some file a tax return but, in hopes that they will not be audited, do not report all income or overstate expenses that reduce the tax. In essence, both nonpayment of taxes and tax evasion is theft from not only from the government but also from society as a whole because the tax revenue collected by the government is used to pay for things that are designed to benefit society.

Dating stock options.[12] Stock options have become an important element in executive compensation. "A stock option, which is a financial contract between a firm and an employee, gives the employee the *right, but not the obligation* to buy an agreed-upon number of shares of stock from the firm, at an agreed-upon price after a specified period of service during which time, it is expected that the firm performance will eventually lead to an increase in the stock price."[13] Back-dating a stock option means finding a date from the past when the stock price was at its lowest point and using this as the benchmark. The low point in price is the most attractive point to purchase stock and gives the executive the greatest possibility that if the executive purchases at the lowest price the sale of the stock, profit is almost guaranteed. This information is not reported to stockholders. But the scheme is designed to help executives accumulate wealth whether or not the firm's performance improves. The executive would benefit even though he or she has had no effect on company performance. Forward-dating a stock option means that the executive delays the filing of the application for stock options with the Securities and Exchange Commission (SEC) until the stock has decreased to a low point. This gives the executive the same benefit. Whether back-dating or forward-dating, the practice involves manipulating the value of the stock for the benefit of the person who holds the option, a privilege that other stock holders do not have available to them.

Accounting and finance professionals who engage in unethical actions most often are also breaking either a state law, federal law or both. This is an area of criminal behavior known as white-collar crime.

CHARACTERISTICS OF FRAUDSTERS

The characteristics of persons who engage in fraud and cheating have been identified.[14] Fraud is usually committed by an employee who is a middle manager or even an owner or executive of the company. When fraud is committed by an owner or a top-level executive, the losses to victims is usually far greater than losses incurred by others. For example, in the United States, the median loss created by fraud by a manager in 2010 was $150,000. During the same year the median loss caused by an owner or executive was more than double, at $373,000.

In the United States, two-thirds of those committing fraud are men. Outside the United States, the proportion of men who commit fraud is much higher. In addition, fraudulent activity by men usually results in much higher losses to victims. In terms of age, it is middle-age persons who engage in fraud more often than either younger or older persons. Perpetrators of fraud are more likely to have a college or graduate school degree than others. The fraud they commit is more likely to result in heavier losses for victims. Most perpetrators work in accounting, operations, sales, the executive management office, customer service or a purchasing department. More than 80 percent of those who commit fraud (and get caught) have never previously been charged or convicted of a crime. They had never before been punished or terminated from their job.

This may be one reason why some people believe that the primary motive for these types of ethical-legal lapses is greed. A person sees an opportunity to gain personally by fraud and takes the chance in hopes of not getting caught. Other persons may intentionally structure their whole business around a fraud and systematically takes advantage of people through the use of a business model that relies on illegal or unethical activities. There are other reasons, too. For example, when a person has an opportunity to steal and other people trust that person, there is more likely to be a lapse of ethical behavior. Sometimes managers who are trying to further the success of the organization they work for will engage in unethical or illegal activities. They do not think of themselves as doing wrong but rather as doing the thing that is expected of any good manager who wants to succeed.

Most people committing fraud feel under financial pressure. They may be given an aggressive or unreasonable financial performance goal by superiors and then are left with the perception that failure to meet the goal is unacceptable. Under pressure, they might display behavioral traits that indicate being under stress. The common red flags or indicators of stress associated with higher risk of committing fraud include[15]

- living beyond their means (a house and car and other things that are too expensive for them to support given the level of their income)

- experiencing financial difficulties

- having an unusually close relationship with a customer or vendor

- being unwilling to share control with other people

- experiencing marriage and family problems

- being a wheeler-dealer who presents great-sounding ideas for money-making schemes

- seeming to be irritable, suspicious or defensive

- having an addiction problem

- having past employment-related problems

- complaining about inadequacy of compensation

- refusing to take vacations

- experiencing excessive pressure from within the organization

- having prior legal problems

CATCHING AND PUNISHING WHITE-COLLAR CRIMINALS

Business schools have been teaching business law and business ethics courses for years, but white-collar crime is still a problem in the United States. Of course, not every business professional went to business school where he or she had a chance to learn the law and ethics. But even so, awareness of the importance of business ethics has increased in society. Lapses of ethics are quickly picked up and reported in the news media. Leaders of professional associations are emphasizing the professional codes of conduct to their members. In spite of this, a few of the thousands of business professionals, including business school graduates, still go to prison for violations of the law.

A white-collar crime is classed as a nonviolent crime committed by someone who is interacting in the marketplace (or in an organization) to deceive, cheat or steal. A white-collar crime takes unfair advantage of someone such as in a financial transaction or a marketing activity or takes some other illegal action in commerce.[16] The goal of the crime is to achieve a financial gain.

The most common type of white-collar crime is fraud, which is an attempt to deceive someone and in so doing steal from that person in order to achieve a financial gain. There are dozens of different types of fraud perpetrated every year.

Examples of white-collar crimes related to finance, accounting and investments include[17]

- falsification of financial information of public and private corporations

- embezzlement

- insider trading[18]

- kickbacks[19]

- misuse of corporate property for personal gain

- mortgage fraud[20]

- insurance fraud[21]

- Ponzi schemes[22]

- affinity fraud[23]

- pyramid schemes[24]

- prime bank investment fraud[25]

- advance fee fraud[26]

- promissory notes[27]

- foreign currency exchange fraud[28]

- precious metals fraud[29]

- obstruction of justice

Between 2007 and 2012 the US Attorney's office reported white-collar crime statistics, some of which are shown in table 16.1.[30]

A wide range of penalties are imposed on convicted white-collar criminals: fines, home or community confinement, restitution and prison terms. How stiff the penalty is depends on the magnitude of the crime and its effect on victims. Most states have laws forbidding white-collar crimes.

If a person is convicted of a white-collar crime in federal court, the federal judge will follow sentencing guidelines. These guidelines allow the judge some discretion to make adjustments to the sentence based on several factors such as whether this is the first-time offense, the degree of involvement in the crime, how many victims were affected and whether the safety of an organization (especially a

Table 16.1. Selected white-collar crime statistics.

	2007	2008	2009	2010	2011	2012
Conviction rate all white collar crime cases	90.4%	90.2%	.90%	91.1%	91.5%	90%
Most common white collar crime	Fraud	Fraud	Fraud	Fraud	Fraud	Fraud
Securities fraud defendants	259	182	224	250	320	250
Healthcare fraud defendants	786	797	803	872	1,430	833
Corporate fraud defendants	84	74	91	131	107	77
Tax fraud defendants	830	810	865	896	1,000	886
Identity theft defendants (all types)	579	1,060	940	949	1,452	1,002
Mortgage fraud defendants	Data not available	216	492	1,197	947	764

Table 16.2. Maximum federal penalties for selected white-collar crime.

White-Collar Crime	US Law	Maximum Federal Penalty
Fraud and swindles: mail fraud that affects a financial institution	18 U.S. Code § 1341	Fine of not more than $1,000,000 or imprisoned not more than thirty years or both
Wire fraud: defrauding or obtaining money or property by means of false or fraudulent pretenses by wire, radio, television	18 U.S. Code § 1343	Imprisoned for not more than twenty years
Bank fraud: defrauding a financial institution	18 U.S. Code § 1344	Fine of not more than $1,000,000 or imprisoned not more than thirty years or both
Tax evasion	26 U.S. Code § 7201	Fine of not more than $100,000 ($500,000 in the case of a corporation) or imprisoned not more than five years or both, together with the costs of prosecution
Economic espionage	18 U. S. Code § 1831-1839	Fine of not more than $5,000,000 or imprisoned not more than fifteen years or both
Violation of domestic securities law Violation of trust indentures	15 U.S. Code C 2A, Subchapter I § 77X & 77YYY	Fine of not more than $10,000 or imprisoned not more than five years or both
Healthcare fraud: defrauding a healthcare benefit program	18 U.S. Code § 1347	Fined or imprisoned not more than twenty years or both; if the violation results in death, the person will be fined or imprisoned for any term of years or for life or both
Insider trading	15 U.S. Code § 78U–1	Fine of $1,000,000 or three times the amount of the profit gained or loss avoided as a result of the violation
Securities fraud	15 U.S. Code § Chapter 2B § 78FF	Fine of not more than $5,000,000 or imprisoned not more than twenty years or both
Violation of corporate responsibility for financial reports	Sarbanes-Oxley Act, Section 906	Fine of not more than $1,000,000 or imprisoned not more than ten years or both

financial institution) was jeopardized. The typical conviction rates for federal white-collar crimes are between 90 percent and 91 percent.

In a national effort to catch criminals in Ponzi schemes, in 2010 the US attorneys found and charged more than 340 defendants who represented more than $8 billion in Ponzi-scheme losses to investors.[31] Defendants for these and related civil cases spend up to five or more years defending themselves when they could be engaged in more productive work. They spend many more years in prison if convicted.

Maximum federal penalties for a conviction of a white-collar crime can be heavy. Table 16.2 gives some examples of the discretion allowed.[32]

Megan Graham, an undergraduate student at the University of New Hampshire, researched the overall economic impact of white-collar crime in the United States.[33] She concluded that when the ripple effects of white-collar crime are factored in, the negative impact on the whole economy is in the hundreds of billions of dollars annually. Although it is impossible to calculate precisely the total loss to victims because of white-collar crime, it represents a proportion of the gross domestic product (GDP).

DOWN TO THE NITTY-GRITTY

Think about the scenario at the beginning of this chapter. You are a manager in a hedge fund investment firm. In order to keep current on the industry, you hire on a contract basis consultants to bring market research data and information related to research and developments in the field that you specialize in. You are thinking about hiring a contract consultant who works for one of the firms in the industry in order to get firsthand information that investors might

Table 16.3. Applying the ethical process.

Keeping Your Heart: An Intrapersonal Process	Walking in the Community: An Interpersonal Process

• You are a manager in a hedge fund investment firm. What does your heart say is the right thing to do regarding hiring someone who works for a firm in the industry you specialize in?
• Which biblical themes explored in this book inform your heart on this situation?
• Which biblical theme, if any, do you feel yourself resisting? Why do you feel resistance?
• What other influences in your heart seem to be prominent as you think about this situation?
  • Fundamental beliefs
  • Cognitive reasoning
  • Judgments and evaluations
  • Decisions
  • Virtues
  • Will
  • Memory of personal experiences with other people
  • Perceptions of others in the community
  • Personal biases
  • Awareness of interpersonal relationships
  • Commitments to God and to others
  • Intuitions
  • Conscience
  • Human spirit
  • Emotions
	• You are a manager in a hedge fund investment firm. With whom might you have a conversation about the issue of hiring a consultant who works for one of the firms in the industry that you specialize in? Who else might have a helpful perspective?
	• Who should take a leadership role in the conversation about obtaining information to pass along to investors?
	• Which of the biblical themes in this chapter will most likely come up in the conversation either directly or indirectly? Why? Which one(s) will be the most influential in the conversation?
	• If you have a conversation with someone regarding this situation, which of the fundamental tensions presented earlier in the book might come up?
	• What right-versus-right dilemmas, if any, can be identified? Have a conversation with someone about this now. What is the outcome of the conversation?

want. What is the right thing to do? It's time to get down to the nitty-gritty (see table 16.3)!

THROUGH THE LENS OF BIBLICAL THEMES

This part of the chapter will use the biblical story themes as a lens through which to evaluate the topic featured in the chapter. Because the themes are interrelated and interdependent, we should expect to see some overlap in the thinking regarding the issues. Some themes will contribute the same thinking as will other themes. The power of these themes comes from their guidance when a community of people talks about complicated ethical dilemmas faced in business practice.

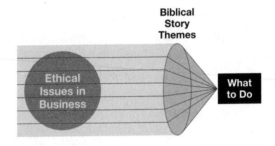

Figure 16.1. Evaluating an ethical approach.

Cosmic conflict. The great conflict between Christ and Satan was leveraged on a deception about God's character. Fraud devalues the meaningfulness of honest work. In comparison, honest work seems meaningless toil. Fraud usually stems from an unrestrained desire to grasp for more power through deceit. It is a subtle form of coercion. It is an attempt to circumvent the authority of the rule of law and ethical principles so that the perpetrator can live above the principles of the law.

Creation. What theft of real goods is to the legitimate owner, fraud is to the marketplace of investors, owners and employees. The fraudster wishes to suspend temporarily the

rules of the market to exhibit independent freedom. Fraud irresponsibly snubs the reality of interdependence for the sake of self-gratification. In usurping authority, the fraudster distorts the divine plan for relationships.

Holiness. The biblical story themes are a high standard to follow. They tell us that to be wholly committed to God we will not combine honest practices with dishonest practices or cheating with rule keeping. Furthermore, God's call to faithful followers is to avoid all appearance of evil and consistently choose not to engage in cheating, fraud, manipulation and other forms of dishonesty.

Covenant relationships. Fraud, cheating, stock price manipulation, securing mortgage loans and other forms of deception have as their basis a short-term outlook. These actions assume that the relationships involved are short-term and shallow and that being disloyal in the relationship is consistent with the nature of the relationship. These actions are narrowly self-interested. They reveal that the perpetrator wants to take from the relationship rather than nourish and give to the relationship.

Shalom. Who can fault someone for wanting to experience shalom? But when someone wants shalom all to themselves and in the process requires others to bear the cost or to have an unfair disadvantage in experiencing the blessings of shalom, or when someone attempts to isolate the economic dimension of shalom from all the other dimensions, this leads to lying, cheating, stealing, manipulation and fraud. All of these actions openly undermine shalom for the entire community.

Sabbath. Sabbath keeping is one of the best deterrents to greed. Sabbath fosters contentment while encouraging hard work. Cheating, stealing, fraud, forms of deception and manipulation of risk are attempts to sidestep the intended blessings of sabbath. Economic deception places human autonomy above our relationship with God. It attempts to provide for our own redemption and temporarily suspends the awareness that human power has limits.

Justice. The accounting, finance and investing ethical issues are contrary to the biblical idea of justice. The cheater and fraudster attempt to place themselves above all others, thus creating a special, personal category for themselves. These actions ignore the injustices they cause and the injustice that is allowed. They jeopardize or weaken the rights of others so that the perpetrators can make rights that do not exist.

Righteousness. The fraudster intentionally looks for the cracks in the protective system designed to preserve trust and the property owner relationships. Everyone in society is vulnerable to being taken advantage of; however, the fraud perpetrator creates vulnerability by exploiting even the most protected persons and organizations. Fraud is uncaring to both the least and the most vulnerable by taking advantage of the tremendous trust that employees and investors place in them. Fraud destabilizes relationships in the marketplace. In order to carry out their deceit, frauds sometimes need accomplices to collude with them.

Truth. Fraud is the failure to act in a way that the person is expected to act after being tested. In the marketplace, fraud is one ultimate form of unfaithfulness. It is the actions of the fraud perpetrator that are the core of deception. Without the actions of the fraudster to avoid detection by auditors, fraudulent financial statements could be quickly be shown to be false. In order to have the financial statements (and other reports) to appear what they are not, the perpetrator

of fraud must commit other actions that are at the root of unfaithfulness.

Wisdom. The biblical story distinguishes between people who are wise in the true sense of being smart about covenant relationships and people who are shrewd and crafty. Crafty people are destructive of covenant relationships. They are self-centered, proud and reckless. Truly wise people know that lying, stealing and cheating undermine community relationships. Wisdom means that a person is faithful to the principles of the Ten Commandments.

Loving kindness. Fraud is considered a white-collar crime. Fraud is usually contrasted with so-called violent crimes such as armed robbery or murder; however, fraud is violent in its own way by destroying trust, killing hope and stirring anger and desires for retaliation. Tweaking the financial records, regardless if it is done by an accountant or a senior manager, is the ultimate form of disloyalty to the financial stakeholders of the organization. The person committing fraud uses the business relationship not for blessing others but in feeding cold-hearted greed.

Redemption. Lying, cheating and manipulation create the need for redemption. These are the things that deepen the misery of lost well-being. People who resort to these activities are enslaved in their own greed or need for control. Redemption involves the community correcting injustices by recovering lost funds (where possible) and by removing these destructive persons from economic relationships for a time.

CHAPTER REVIEW QUESTIONS

1. What is the essence of fraud?

2. Describe some of the ways that people cheat in financial management and investing.

3. What are the characteristics of people who commit fraud?

4. Describe the legal penalties for white collar crime in the United States.

5. What guidance do the biblical story themes provide regarding accounting and financial ethics?

DISCUSSION QUESTIONS

1. When a certified public accountant (CPA) is presented with a situation where the client's interest is in conflict with the public interest, the CPA is presented with an ethical dilemma. In which constituency's best interest should the CPA act?

2. Conduct some research on the Internet: Where is Mathew Martoma today? What was the sentence he was given for the crime of insider trading? Do you think his MBA degree should be taken away if it can be proven that his forged transcript of grades from Harvard played a part in him being accepted as a student into Stanford University Graduate School of Business?

3. Why do you think that the writer of Proverbs says, "Wealth obtained by fraud dwindles"?[34]

ETHICAL VIGNETTES TO DISCUSS

For each of the following vignettes, apply the biblical story themes to discern what is right and wrong.

1. In 2005, Dennis Kozlowski and Mark Swartz, former executives of Tyco corporation, were found guilty and subsequently sentenced for their crimes of twenty-two counts of grand larceny and conspiracy for stealing hundreds of millions of dollars from the corporation. Both men received the same sentence: eight to twenty-five years. They were ordered to pay $134 million back to Tyco. In addition, Koslowski was fined $70 million and Swartz was fined $35 million. During the criminal trial that led to a guilty verdict, prosecutors brought forward evidence that, among other things, showed Koslowski had spent $2 million of Tyco funds to throw a birthday party for his wife on the Italian island of Sardinia. Allegedly he also purchased a $6,000 shower curtain with company funds. Was the sentence too harsh?[35]

2. Bill Harley is a financial analyst for Allstar Alliance, Inc., a company that is on the verge being acquired by General Enterprises, Inc.[36] Negotiations have been going well between the executive teams of both firms. The process has entered the final phase of valuation of the stock for the expected sale. Bill's current task is to work with a team of other staff members to prepare updated financial projections. The financial projections will be given to both sets of executive team members. The night before the big meeting where everyone is expecting that a final sale price is finalized, Bill realizes that there has been a mistake in the estimate of depreciation, which has the effect of overstating the company's projected value. It is not just a small mistake. His chief financial officer has already printed a corresponding support document that provides the buyers with a description of the assumptions on which the financial projections are based. Bill can see the stack of reports sitting on the executive secretary's desk. What should Bill do about the error that he found?

3. A policy of BigFirm, Inc., is that no employee of the firm may receive gifts of any value or of any kind from any outside person or organization with which BigFirm does business.[37] Furthermore, employees are required to inform leaders of BigFirm of any attempt on the part of an outside person or organization to give a gift. James ("Big Jim") Roberts works closely with the production department to procure special materials used in the fabrication of Big-Firm's extra-large, heavy-duty attachments to earth movers. Recently he negotiated the purchase of specialized heavy-duty coil springs from CoilHardeners, Inc. After the purchase agreement was signed and the purchase order submitted to CoilHardeners, CoilHardeners, Inc., sent an envelope via FedEx to Big Jim. The envelope contained several thousand dollars in cash. In the same envelope was a handwritten, unsigned note: "Thanks for ordering the hardened springs from us!" Whether or not Big Jim accepts the cash or sends it back has no effect on the price that BigFirm, Inc., pays for the coil springs. What should Big Jim do with the cash? Is there a gain to any party if the cash is accepted? Is there a victim in this scenario? Is there a loss to any party? Does fraud require a gain, a loss, both or neither? Does the biblical principle of "unjust gain"[38] require that a tangible loss has occurred?

4. When you need a loan for a new car, you can sometimes get financing at the car dealer, at your local bank or at your local credit union. But when you need just a little cash right now, where do you go? You can go to a payday loan company, give them your paycheck and agree to repay the loan within a few weeks or days. No

problem, right? Not so fast. Interest rates that you pay at the neighborhood payday loan store can be 400 percent or higher when figured as an annual percentage rate (APR). Payday loan companies are legal, but is it ethical that these stores charge such high interest rates?

5. Ruben Martinez and Charles Segal have at least one thing in common in spite of the fact that Ruben lives in Staten Island, New York, and Charles lives in Cape Coral, Florida: As of September 2011, neither of them had been paying his mortgage payments for years.[39] In the aftermath of the sub-prime mortgage banking crisis of 2008, these and thousands of other families began defying lenders by refusing to pay their mortgage payments. However, they continued to stay in their homes for free. While some seem to have a cavalier attitude toward it, other homeowners seem genuinely concerned and do not like the situation they are in. The reason: One or both of the adults is out of work. By September 2011, some four million mortgages were delinquent in the United States. The resolution process can take years to be completed. There are several reasons for the delay in getting the foreclosure processes completed in good order. First is the sheer magnitude of the problem. Second, some mortgage companies are suspected of intentionally delaying resolution of claims until conditions are more favorable. They seem uninterested in adding to their rosters of repossessed homes. Third, paperwork process systems in the banks were complicated. Some families, like those of Martinez and Segal, hire lawyers to represent their interests. In some cases, homeowners intentionally attempt to slow down

the system because they believe that the longer it takes to resolve, the more months they might be able to live for free. In some communities, nonpayment of mortgages means a higher financial burden on community members in the condominium neighborhoods where homeowner association fees are paid annually. Bankers estimate that the cost of families living in their homes for free would be shared by future homeowners as interest rates go up. What, if anything, is wrong with what these homeowners were doing by not paying their mortgage payments? Does the fact that mortgage banks played a part in the sub-prime mortgage crisis sufficient reason for consumers to "stick it to the bank" when the banks are in a vulnerable position in terms of managing the foreclosure resolution processes?

17

Ethical Issues in Marketing

SCRIPTURE PASSAGE

Turn away my eyes from looking at vanity,
And revive me in Your ways. (Ps 119:37)

CHAPTER OVERVIEW

In this chapter we will explore selected issues
in marketing. In particular, we will explore selected ethical issues in marketing through the
lens of biblical story themes.

MAIN TOPICS

Marketing as a Social Process
Price
Promotion
Product
Distribution
Down to the Nitty-Gritty
Through the Lens of Biblical Themes

KEY TERMS

bait advertising, cartel, multilevel marketing,
price fixing, price gouging, product dumping,
product recalls, pyramid schemes, sweepstakes

OPENING SCENARIO

Uncertainty: One of the final frontiers to
conquer in business. Where uncertainty exists,
business risks increase; when we can reduce uncertainty, we all do better in business. Accord-

ingly, one of the most difficult problems for
marketing professionals to deal with is the vola-
tility of the market. With market stability comes
better forecasting of demand. Better forecasts
translate into better budgeting of projected
revenue and lower costs. This is true for just
about any product. It is especially true for commodities where economic profits head toward
zero under conditions of perfect competition.

After all is said and done about it, reducing
uncertainty is a community effort. Each
business entity watches other relevant business
entities and customers for signals which help it
predict what will happen in the short run.
Businesses watch each other's prices, products,
promotional efforts and distribution systems.
This effort is not organized within any given
industry. When companies are in proximity to
each other in many geographic markets or
among the same market segments, this market
commonality tends to increase the intensity of
the rivalry among them.

If businesses could organize their collective
efforts, all the firms operating in a given market
could benefit, wouldn't they? Furthermore,
wouldn't the customers benefit, too?

In terms of reducing uncertainty, this might
sound good on paper, but highly organized efforts to improve marketing efficiency have an
unsavory side effect on competitors who do

not participate in the organized efforts. Furthermore, it does not remove uncertainty for the buyers. It has an unpleasant effect on customers. This is what happened when twenty-six rubber component manufacturers serving the automobile industry decided to work together in an organized way to reduce uncertainty in the markets for their products.[1]

Between 1999 and 2007, leaders at Bridgestone and the other rubber companies had meetings to agree which company would get which segment of the market and what prices to charge for the products. This reduced a lot of the uncertainty. But it meant that in order for the agreement to work, all the business from customers would have to be channeled to the participating firms. If a customer, such as an automobile assembly plant that needed rubber parts to reduce vibration and sound in vehicles, asked a participating firm to bid on selling rubber products but that customer was outside of the assigned market segment, the firm was required to give a bid much higher so that the firm assigned to that market could win with a lower bid. In effect the higher bid was a false bid.

It sounds like the customers, in this case automobile manufacturing firms like Toyota and Nissan, were getting a better deal in the form of lower price. But it meant that competition based on price was reduced and the winning bids were higher in price than they otherwise would have been.

If this story sounds like something you might have heard in a business law class, you are on the right track. This organized approach to achieving market stability is called conspiracy and price fixing. After several months investigation, the US Department of Justice charged Bridgestone and other companies. Bridgestone pleaded guilty, thus avoiding a long, messy trial, and agreed to pay a $425-million fine and cooperate with investigators. This was one of the largest fines ever imposed in a price-fixing case. Part of the punishment required that some company executives and board members would forfeit some personal compensation.

This is not the only price-fixing scheme by rubber companies that has been uncovered and prosecuted. The United States is not the only country whose Justice Department charged rubber companies with price-fixing schemes.

MARKETING AS A SOCIAL PROCESS

Marketing is a social process. Much of the marketing process involves attracting customers to exercise trust and loyalty. Marketers desperately want to achieve this; customers are wary. And if for no other reason than this, we should expect that ethical issues will arise with marketing activities. Additionally, the importance of marketing in the business processes underscores that it is especially vulnerable to unethical practices in any of the major elements: price, product, promotion and distribution systems. We will explore some of these in this chapter. At the same time, we should realize that some marketing ethical issues are more complicated than in the accounting or finance processes. Marketing is vital to the success of many businesses.

As we will see, establishing the ethical boundaries is sometimes difficult to do. The reason is that marketing is about managing value-exchange relationships.[2] It includes exchange of goods and services for money, but it is larger than that.[3] The company goes to the market and establishes a presence to offer value in the form of products and services. The buyer goes to the market and offers values in the form of cash in exchange for these products and services.

A product is not all the value it can be until the consumer begins using it for its purpose, begins the enjoyment of owning it or creates a whole new use for it that is beyond what the firm had in mind when it offered the product. Only when the product is used or possessed does it become value to the customer, and by so doing the customer ends up co-producing part of the full value in collaboration with the firm. This can be illustrated by the formula shown in figure 17.1.[4] Some will say that it is only after the product is used up and disposed of or recycled that its full value has been co-created and enjoyed.

Here is why this is important for marketing ethics. If the consumer is a co-producer of value, then

- the consumer has some influence in the marketing process

- the consumer has some control in the marketing proces.

- the consumer is a resource on which the success of the product or service is dependent

- the customer has some responsibility for interpreting the signals about a product's value that are given by the seller

- the customer has some responsibility in the exchange of values and the adding of value during ownership and use

- the customer plays an important role in discerning the nature of a product's value and its meaning

- each customer's contribution to value may be different

- truthfulness or certainty regarding what is value may be difficult to establish objectively and statements about value will be difficult to verify

- faithfulness in representing value must be a collaborative process between seller and buyer

Accordingly, what constitutes ethical actions cannot be separated from what the customer thinks and does in co-producing value during the marketing process. This makes the marketer's job of determining ethical right and wrong more difficult. But it does not mean that marketing professionals should ignore ethical issues in marketing. If anything, the difficulties in pursuing ethical marketing activities should spur us to careful consideration.

Notice the various ways that co-producing involves customer responsibility. We should not forget that the marketer may have more complete information than the customer. Customers with little or no experience with a product are at a disadvantage. Marketers may be able to take unfair advantage of this in how they manage the price, the product, the promotion and the distribution. What follows provides a few examples of when this and other ethical issues are a problem.

PRICE

Product pricing is an area in which ethical issues sometimes arise in the marketplace. We will consider four examples.

Price fixing. Price fixing requires that two

Company creates value when product is made and offered for sale
+ Customer creates value when product is used or owned
_____
= Total value over the full life and use of the product

Figure 17.1. The formula that shows how value is created.

or more companies agree to keep prices at a particular level. Sometimes companies that price fix also agree regarding what geographic areas or which market segments to target. Price fixing usually results in buyers having to pay higher prices than they would pay if free competition was allowed.

> My eyes shall be upon the faithful of the land, that they may dwell with me;
> He who walks in a blameless way is the one who will minister to me. (Ps 101:6)

Price gouging. Mother Nature has a way of bringing out the best and worst in people. A tornado rips through a community and within hours strangers from out of town approach residents whose property sustained damage. The strangers offer to clean up the damage for exorbitant prices. In some cases these smooth operators have not obtained a local business license. Before the law can catch up with them, they leave town. A similar tactic is sometimes used by retailers who hike prices of key resources after a storm such as suppliers of rock salt used in treating icy roads, food, building supplies, lodging and gasoline. When an official state of emergency exists, price-gouging laws protect buyers form opportunistic behavior.

The precise point where the price becomes a gouge is not always clear. In some states price-gouging laws define it to be from 10 percent to 25 percent increase in price compared with the average price one month before a natural disaster. But even the law is not perfect: It does not take into consideration two things: the knowledge that people have re-garding the probability of certain disasters in certain regions and the changes in perception of value that customers place on products and services. After a disaster the customers' perception of value of certain goods and services increases. They are willing to pay more for certain things.

Price scalping. Price scalping involves a person or organization that purchases at the regular price large quantities of products expected to be in high demand; the person or organization believes that the products will sell out quickly. Even though this person has purchased at retail prices, he is hoping that desperate buyers will be willing to pay the higher price when the shortage occurs.

Price-matching policies. In some retail markets competition is largely based on price. Some shoppers are keenly aware of differences in prices when comparing retail options. Some retailers offer a price-matching policy to entice customers to shop at their store. Price-matching policies typically state that if the customer finds the exact same product offered for sale in the market for a lower price, the retailer will match that lower price. In some instances price-matching becomes price-matching plus an additional discount of, say, 10 percent if the customer finds the same product at a better price elsewhere.

One problem that some big-box retailers have gotten into with price matching is that if a customer tries to cash in on the policy, the customer encounters a manager who resists honoring the offer. Another problem that can occur is if the retailer cuts a deal with the manufacturer, for example, of a large home appliance such a washing machine to make the same model as sold at other retailers but with different model numbers than are shown on the competing store's appliances. The machine might have the same size motor, the same control features and the same options for load size, water temperature settings and so forth. But for the model numbers the machine is the same as that sold by another retailer who sells that same brand. When the customer finds the same machine at a competing store for a lower price and then attempts to get the price match plus 10 percent, she is told that it is not the same machine because the model numbers are not the same.

PROMOTION

Customers desire value, and when a company presents its messages to potential customers, it attempts to signal customers that the value they desire can be met by the products and services that the firm offers. While price is an important consideration for customers, especially in competitive markets, promotion also is important. Promotional messages fuel hope in the customer. They heighten desire for value fulfillment. But the minority (20 percent) of people trust advertising most of the time.[5] Thus, the faithfulness with which the company represents the truth about the value it offers is central to the ethical marketing promotion. Accordingly, we review here some of the specific ethical and legal issues that arise.

Truth in advertising. When what customers want is in alignment with the values that the firm offers, customers are willing to make purchases. One practical problem that marketing and advertising professionals face on a daily basis is how to illustrate the truth about a product or service. What is a company to do when it realizes that the value it offers does not exactly match up with the value interests of the customers? The answer is often not very clear, yet the public and the law expect the company to tell the truth in all its messages. In addition,

the majority of companies do not outright tell lies about their products and services, at least not for very long. One reason is that the law prohibits lying, and companies can be fined for lying. The United States Federal Trade Commission (FTC) regulations require that no statement or illustration should be used that creates a false impression of the product. The other reason is that customers would quickly find out, and strong but negative word of mouth would undermine the company's promotional efforts.

Another complicating factor is that value is not limited to what is physically in or on the product. Some of the value is in the meaning of the product for the customer. How does an advertiser represent this intangible element of value in a truthful way especially when there is a variety of customer perspectives and thus a variety of definitions of meaning for any particular product? One customer may purchase a soft drink because of the refreshing taste on a hot day. Other customers will purchase the same drink because it reminds them of good times on the beach in their youth. What is the truth about refreshing taste? Isn't it in the eye of the beholder? What is the truth about that elusive memory of a summer on the beach that the customer wants to recapture?

Another factor is that the consequences of using a product are not always favorable. Should the company disclose to customers the unsavory consequences in their promotional messages? For example, food and drink marketing companies emphasize taste and texture because they know that customers are interested in these. You do not see an advertisement that says, If you eat too much of this over many years, it will increase the chances that you will develop diabetes, heart disease or cancer. You do not see advertisers show the consequences of drinking alcoholic beverages. Showing a drunken person in an advertisement will communicate something that will counteract the signal the company wants to send to customers. Is this unethical?

Product placement. Some marketing promotional efforts are primarily about managing impressions that customers get when they see the product rather than a promotional message about the product. When customers get the impression that a certain product is cool or trendy, their desire for the value imbedded in the product increases. This is one reason why companies try to get new products used as props in movies. Millions of people will see the movie and leave the theater with an impression about the product. Actors in the film are not promoting the product. They do not say something like, "Try this new product. You'll enjoy owning and using it as much as I enjoy using it as a prop in this film." The actor is paid to act the part in a realistic manner. This places the product in real-to-life setting which gives a certain desirable impression attractive to the movie customers.

Whether or not it is ethical to place products as props in movies is one question. But what if a company gives its new products to people who are frequent customers of a popular club? They show the product and talk about it to people at the club. Customers of the club go away talking about it to their friends and family. Is this ethical? Some say that this is deceptive in that the product company compensated their agents to talk about the product in a setting where customers have their guard down. This brings up the issues related to word-of-mouth marketing.

Word-of-mouth marketing. Not many things are more valuable than a firm's positive reputation spread by word of mouth. For some consumer decisions word of mouth is either the primary or secondary source of information on which they make purchase decisions. Word-of-mouth marketing is the only marketing promotion that is of the customers, by the customers and for the customers. When one customer gets advice from another customer, the one giving advice has no stake in the outcome of the conversation. This is an important element in the trust that the customer places in the one giving advice.[6] When a customer talks about your company's products and services, the one listening assumes that the one talking gets nothing in return except a good feeling after helping someone.

When a firm encourages customers to make referrals or inspires them to refer new customers, this is based on a voluntary choice on the part of the customer. Customers understand that a company pays a celebrity to endorse its product. Paying someone to endorse a company or its products when the person is not a celebrity spokesperson is another matter. As mentioned above, some firms have been known to pay people to visit social settings such as bars, clubs and parties and while there to talk about the product. But the unsuspecting friends of these paid talkers have no idea that their helpful friend is being paid.

Some companies have asked their employees to post on the Internet positive things about the company, thus passing these off as comments from happy customers. Essentially this is marketing fraud and is against the law.[7]

Word-of-mouth marketing efforts are sometimes combined with paid advertising in an attempt to leverage the power of word of mouth for greater impact. For example, a television advertisement depicts two persons at a store shopping for dish soap. One says to the other how much cleaner her dishes are since she switched to this brand of soap. Furthermore, the new brand does not irritate her skin as the competing brands do. If the advertisement says that these two persons are customers, this must be a truthful claim.

The Word of Mouth Marketing Association code of ethics stipulates that persons who act on behalf of a company must disclose the material nature of their relationship with the company and if they are being compensated to represent this information truthfully.[8]

The FTC has published guidelines for using endorsements and testimonials in word-of-mouth marketing.[9] Among other things this regulation requires endorsers be truthful in what they say. When a promotional message states that the endorser uses the product, the endorser must really be product users, not just spokespersons.

Advertising to children. Some population groups are especially vulnerable to advertising messages.[10] For example, children are inexperienced in the marketplace. They lack knowledge and wisdom to discern the validity of claims about a product. Their cognitive development is not complete. Very young children have difficulty distinguishing between fantasy and reality. They may not know when an advertiser is exaggerating a claim. They have difficulty distinguishing between news and advertising. Because of this, ethical questions have been raised regarding advertising of products designed for children. For example, is it ethical to advertise foods high in fat and sugar on television programs that children watch or video games they play?

Advertising medicines. Children represent just one population group where advertising ethics is important. Another is the group of people who have a particular disease. People with disease or chronic health conditions are vulnerable because the desire is high to get well

or manage the condition. Pharmaceutical companies have sometimes advertised medicines approved by the Food and Drug Administration (FDA) for one use to patients with a different need. This is called off-label promotion. One of the largest legal cases involved Johnson & Johnson. In 2013, the Department of Justice fined Johnson & Johnson $2.2 billion in civil and criminal penalties for promoting the drug Risperdal.

Telemarketing. Considering the volume of promotional messages that customers are bombarded with on a daily basis, it is no wonder that companies continually seek ways to break through all the clutter to get their message to customers. One approach is telephone marketing.

The downside is that the Federal Communications Commission (FCC) reports that an increasing number of consumers are complaining about unwanted telemarketing efforts by commercial organizations.[11] The law says that if a consumer has established a business relationship with a company, the company has the right to use telephone marketing to solicit consumer actions. What constitutes a business relationship? If a customer makes one purchase, does this constitute a business relationship? If the customer makes a telephone call to a cruise ship company for the purpose of getting information regarding cruises to Alaska, does this constitute a business relationship?

Federal telemarketing rules stipulate that telephone solicitation efforts must not be employed before 8:00 a.m. or after 9:00 p.m. Consumers have the right to register their phone number with the national Do Not Call Registry. Companies that use telemarketing are required to search the registry every thirty-one days and drop from their database any numbers that appear on the registry. They are not allowed to call anyone who is on the registry.

The Do Not Call Registry provides consumers one way to block telemarketers from getting access to their landline telephone number. Some home telephone systems have a feature to block unwanted phone numbers.

Certain organizations are exempt from some provisions of the Telephone Consumer Protection Act of 1991. For example, tax-exempt nonprofit organizations are exempt from following the rules of the Do Not Call Registry. Does this mean that a nonprofit fund raising organization can continue to use telemarketing after target customers ask to have their phone numbers removed from their telemarketing database?

Bait advertising. Sometimes called bait-and-switch advertising, this involves the promotion of a product that the company has no intention to sell. It may not have the product in stock. But the advertising is designed to lure customers to the company in hopes that once there, the customer will purchase something else sometimes at a higher price. This tactic is illegal; however, it is sometimes difficult to detect when it occurs among low-profile organizations among unsuspecting customers.

Fake sweepstakes. You are in your office, and the phone rings. The caller represents a company that sells promotional products (things that you can purchase bearing your company logo and contact information). Promotional products are used in business-to-business marketing. You can give them away at trade shows and conventions. The caller tells you that you have won a 37-inch flat-screen television. The only requirement is that you must place an order with their company for a promotional product. You protest and say to the caller, "If I won the flat-screen TV, just send it to me." The caller explains that you can claim your prize if you place an order with their company. Requiring payment is one of the classic signs of the sweepstake scam. Sweepstake contests are not allowed to charge a fee to participate or to win.

PRODUCT

The product includes several elements, any one of which might raise ethical issues.

Packaging. Many customers do not realize that a product's package is integral to the product. The package protects or preserves the product. It helps the retailer display the product. It provides information to help the customer make an informed decision. It can provide instruction for how to use the product. It carries important promotional signals about the value of the product. The customer may find other uses for the package that are unrelated to the product that came in the material. Plastic and glass containers that were sold containing food can be cleaned and reused to store many other things. Boxes that carry consumer goods can be used for other purposes.

Product packaging also carries some risks. Packaging material can be harmful to young children who are at the age of putting everything in their mouth. Some packaging is not biodegradable.

Ethical issues have surfaced over the years regarding product packaging. For example, in the 1980s software companies were packaging their software floppy disks in very large plastic and cardboard packaging that could not be used for many other things after the software was purchased. Environmentally conscious consumers complained about the unnecessary material that was being thrown into landfills. For another example, a customer sees the images of the product on the outside of the package, but after the product was purchased and the package opened, the product did not match closely with the image portrayed on the outside.

Product labels carry valuable information to customers. For some products customers have complained that labels are inaccurate, incomplete or outright false.[12] Sorting out product labeling requirements or changing packaging to materials that are more environmentally friendly is not always easy to do. The choice of packaging materials comes with tradeoffs and an economic impact. Customers may be upset that a company uses a lower-cost but environmentally unfriendly plastic, but they do not want to pay the higher price for biodegradable materials used in packaging, and they still want their products to be protected and preserved.

Product content. Should some products be removed from the market because of the harm that users experience? Game developer Dong Nguyen thought so when he pulled his wildly popular, enjoyable and yet infuriating game "Flappy Bird" from the market just when it was generating wealth beyond belief.[13] The reason: Nguyen believed that the game was too addictive, an unintended side effect. Should other companies pull their products when consumers use or misuse them to their own harm or if other people believe the products are harmful?

Product safety. Some products are required to meet minimum product safety standards. This means that the product producer must conduct routine quality-control procedures involving inspection and correction when problems are found. When companies are lax in their quality-control processes, it can prove deadly to consumers. Or, when the specific requirements for safety are not sufficient, it can spell trouble for both the company and the customers. For example, Jack in the Box restaurants learned this in 1992. Customers ate hamburgers purchased from Jack in the Box that were tainted with harmful bacteria. Hundreds of customers got ill. A few died. Jack in

the Box seemed to have a solid legal ground on which to stand. At the time the FDA regulations for cooking meat stipulated that meat must be cooked at 140 degrees Fahrenheit (60 degrees Celsius) in order to kill harmful bacteria. After this horrible situation, new regulations were established requiring restaurants to cook meat at 155 degrees (68 degrees Celsius). Later the required temperature was increased to 160 degrees (71.1 degrees Celsius). In spite of the regulation Foodmaker, Inc., the parent company of Jack in the Box, lost hundreds of millions in lost revenue and paid tens of millions to customers who had been harmed.

The experiences of tainted products undermine customer trust. They also raise ethical questions. For example, how much should a company be expected to spend to prevent injury? Makers of food products go to great lengths to remove harmful substances such as metal and glass from the food before it is packaged. Batches of product are identified, recorded, labeled and then tracked through the distribution channels. If a product causes harm, the manufacturer can quickly identify every retail store that purchased the product. This brings up the issue of product recalls.

Product recalls. Taking a computer with you increases efficiency as it allows you to keep working no matter where you are (within reason). But what if your Notebook computer bursts into flame when you are trying to work? Your efficiency suddenly drops to zero. This is what happened to owners of the Dell Notebook computer. In 2006 Dell cooperated with the United States Consumer Product Safety Commission and recalled thirty-three thousand machines worldwide that were using the Sony lithium-ion battery.[14] It cost Dell and Sony hundreds of millions of dollars. The recall process took months to complete. In some cases the recall process can take years, and even then there is no assurance that 100 percent of the customers who are affected complete the recall offer.

Deciding when to initiate a recall is not always easy. Making the decision to recall requires rapid and highly organized action. Managing a recall requires many people to spend a lot of time and money. For companies that sell products worldwide, one recall can cost hundreds of millions of dollars.[15]

DISTRIBUTION

Gaining access to products and services is just as important as pricing, promotion and the product itself. Distribution is hidden in the marketing mix.

Pyramid schemes. Pyramid schemes are fraudulent attempts to scam people out of their money. The organizers will spend money to create the impression of a legitimate business. Promotional materials are professionally produced. Happy investors are enlisted to give testimonials of how much money they earned after joining and how easy it is to succeed with the program. Everyone who signs up is taught how to recruit others to participate under them. When questioned about the details of the company, promoters are vague on the specifics of who, when and where the company is located. Promoters use subtle yet psychologically powerful tactics to recruit people who are interested in starting a business. Promoters sometimes hold seminars giving their pitch and showing how much money can be made for those who invest. Then the promoters require investors to pay a fee to join. It turns out that this is the way the most of the money is made: by getting other people to sign up. In the most blatant cases, no

product is ever produced other than the product samples that are shown during recruitment sessions. When well-meaning joiners try to start selling products, they learn the truth. The first sales orders for products might be processed or not. They might receive the first shipment of products or not, but before long the scheme falls apart as those who joined realize that they are unable to get the products that were promoted. Customers who placed orders are left in the lurch, and the person who joined loses his or her reputation. The pyramid company never intended to produce and sell products. The promoters simply wanted to sell the idea for membership fees and then leave. The promoters quietly move out of their offices and cannot be found.

Pyramid schemes should not be confused with legitimate multilevel marketing, direct marketing or network marketing companies. The two concepts sometimes look alike in the sense that there are multiple levels of persons involved, often family and friends. The structure of a multilevel marketing company looks like the structure of a pyramid scheme company. One big difference is that the multilevel marketing firm sells products, not just memberships. People who work hard selling the products of the multilevel marketing firm

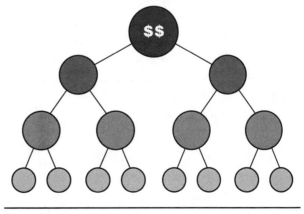

Figure 17.2. A pyramid scheme.

can make money through their own direct sales efforts. Another difference is that a legitimate multilevel marketing firm will not ask for a joining fee. Critics of the multilevel marketing companies claim that the problem that plagues the pyramid scheme is also a problem, though more subtle, than in the fraudulent pyramid company. Critics say that the success of most multilevel marketing firms depends on the constant recruitment of new sales persons to join.

Here are five points for how to determine whether a multilevel marketing company is legitimate or merely a pyramid scheme:[16]

- Find out how the money is made. If it is made by selling real products and services to customers, it is more likely legitimate. If the money is made by selling memberships, it is more likely not legitimate.

- Understand the product. Are the products legitimate? Do the products offer quality and benefits comparable to that of products available through other distribution channels? Are customers getting products they pay for? Are the prices competitive with prices of similar products available elsewhere?

- Understand the up-front financial commitments. How much money is required to participate? The more money required, the more likely it is a pyramid scheme and not a legitimate company. Does the company require the new recruit to purchase a large amount of inventory and thereby incur a great risk? If there is a training fee, is it appropriate for the training that is provided?

- Understand the commitment of effort that is required. How much work is required? Schemes that make it seem very easy to earn money through the sales efforts of other people are often fraudulent. Direct marketing requires a lot of hard work in direct sales. Get-rich-quick schemes are appealing, but they misrepresent the time-tested principle of risk and reward. If you are offered a high reward without risk, be wary! It could be a fraudulent offer.

- Consider the company's history. How long has the company been around? Look for hard evidence of the claims that are made. The best companies are not just the new ones. If the promoters emphasize that the opportunity is for you to get in on the ground floor, be wary. In a pyramid scheme the possibilities of reward decreases the more people get involved. In a legitimate multilevel marketing firm, it should not matter whether or not you get in on the ground floor. You should be able to make sales and earn from your own sales efforts later as well as sooner. Very few legitimate network marketing firms succeed. Thus, the ground-floor opportunity time period is the riskiest time for people who are involved in the firm.

Slotting fees. In the food marketing industry, food manufacturers are often required to pay the retail stores a slotting fee in order to guarantee shelf space for its products. One difficulty is that while large food marketing companies have the cash to spend on slotting fees, small start-up firms find it difficult to pay. For them, slotting fees are large in proportion to their overall marketing budget. Slotting fees help retailers manage the risk that new products pose. If a new product sits on the shelf because customers are not attracted to it, the shelf space could have been used by another product to generate revenue. Thus, every product that just sits on the shelf represents an opportunity cost to the retailer. Food manufacturing companies have been willing to share this risk by paying the slotting fee. But some small food companies claim that large slotting

Table 17.1. Applying the ethical process.

Keeping Your Heart: An Intrapersonal Process	Walking in the Community: An Interpersonal Process
• You are a manager in a raw material firm. What does your heart say is the right thing to do regarding reducing uncertainty by segmenting the market with your two competitors? • Which biblical themes explored in this book inform your heart on this situation? • Which biblical theme, if any, do you feel yourself resisting? Why do you feel resistance? • What other influences in your heart seem to be prominent as you think about this situation? • Fundamental beliefs • Cognitive reasoning • Judgments and evaluations • Decisions • Virtues • Will • Memory of personal experiences with other people • Perceptions of others in the community • Personal biases • Awareness of interpersonal relationships • Commitments to God and to others • Intuitions • Conscience • Human spirit • Emotions	• You are a manager in a raw material firm. With whom might you have a conversation about the issue of segmenting the market? Who else might have a helpful perspective? • Who should take a leadership role in the conversation about obtaining information to pass along to investors? • Which of the biblical themes in this chapter will most likely come up in the conversation either directly or indirectly? Why? Which one(s) will be the most influential in the conversation? • If you have a conversation with someone regarding this situation, which of the fundamental tensions presented earlier in the book might come up? • What right-versus-right dilemmas, if any, can be identified? Have a conversation with someone about this now. What is the outcome of the conversation?

fees undermine fair competition. In effect, they say, large companies are able to keep new companies out of the market because they are willing to pay high slotting fees.

Product dumping. We live in a global market. Competition is not merely between firms but between countries. For years Americans periodically complained about companies from outside the country distributing products at prices lower than it costs to produce them. This marketing ploy is intended to help get products established in markets that are already well developed and served by other firms. Recently India accused Chinese companies of dumping low-cost silk into a country that is also one of the world producers of silk. One response by countries is to protect their domestic industries from foreign incursion. Is it wrong to distribute a product for less than it costs to produce it in order to help get the product established in highly competitive markets? This could be a pricing ethics issue as much as a distribution issue. In a competitive world market for certain commodities, how else is a company to penetrate and build market share?

DOWN TO THE NITTY-GRITTY

Think about scenario at the beginning of this chapter. You are a manager at a company that supplies raw materials to computer chip manufacturers. At an industry trade show, two persons who work for competitors approach you with a proposal that your three companies segment the market and agree on the prices to charge for the materials. What is the right thing to do? It's time to get down to the nitty-gritty (see table 17.1)!

THROUGH THE LENS OF BIBLICAL THEMES

This part of the chapter will use the biblical story themes as a lens through which to evaluate the topic featured in the chapter. Because the themes are interrelated and interdependent, we should expect to see some overlap in the thinking regarding the issues. Some themes will contribute the same thinking as will other themes. The power of these themes comes from their guidance when a community of people talks about complicated ethical dilemmas faced in business practice.

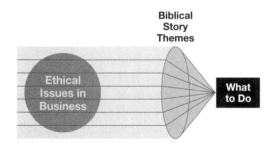

Figure 17.3. Evaluating an ethical approach.

The practical implications of the biblical story themes for ethical conduct in marketing are exciting to see.

Cosmic conflict. Attracting created beings to exercise trust and loyalty to God has been a central issue in the cosmic conflict. Deception, discrediting (by competitors), force and coercion sow seeds of disharmony but faithful marketers will foster freedom to choose. They will imitate the incarnation by coming close to customers to communicate to those who need the value their products offer. They will model God's program by providing substance in the values offered in the market.

Creation. In creation God brought order and clarity out of chaos. Creation-oriented marketers will follow this example by removing the chaos of confusing promotional messages.

They will clarify, not cover up or hide the value they and customers see in the products and services. Products and services that marketers produce and offer will be able to withstand the test of use, reuse and eventually recycling. Products will foster interdependence among members of the community. They will contribute to rather than detract from the restoring of the image of God in humans.

Holiness. Following the principle of holiness begins with being wholly consecrated to following God. Thus, the work of a marketing professional, sales person, retail worker, product developer and market researcher will strive not to be ordinary or to cut corners. Rather, they will offer their daily work and efforts for the glory of God. While the purity of a marketing signal can be ambiguous especially when customer perceptions are a part of the process, faithful marketers will take their responsibility not to mix truth with error in their promotional messages, product packaging and labeling. In some markets and for some products and services this will require transparency between seller and buyer.

Covenant relationships. The principles of the covenant apply as much to marketers as they do to accounting and investing professionals. Lying, cheating and stealing have no place in the journey of faith for marketing. More than this, the faithful marketer will work diligently to foster a covenant relationship with customers. If the marketer has no direct contact with the end-user consumers, he or she will do all that is reasonable to help organizations that distribute the product to end users manage covenant relationships. This will involve honoring warranties and product returns, as well as generous customer service. Product producers and distributors will be loyal to each other. They will consider that the agreements they have between themselves have an effect on the larger community of suppliers and customers.

Shalom. Product designs and styling will beautify and serve flourishing life for not only people but also the whole environment. Marketing efforts will contribute to physical and mental health, social harmony and international peace. They will foster spiritual meaning rather than be cheap substitutes for meaning in life. Products should be of the highest quality that is feasible. And where product quality is less than is available elsewhere, marketers will help customers decide whether the lower quality is truly for them and some of the tradeoffs that may be incurred if the lower-quality product is purchased.

Sabbath. Faithful marketers will desire success. They will work hard; however, they will curb greed by choosing instead to be content with the blessings that accrue from their labor and that come from the efforts of customers who add value to the marketer's effort. Grasping for more market share at the expense of customers or by using deception or fraud breaks the fundamental principle at stake in sabbath.

Justice. How we treat other people when we exchange things of value is a matter of justice. What we say about the product, how we create access to the product, the price we ask for the product, the quality of the product itself, and all other dimensions of marketing involve fairness and being impartial. Following justice might create business opportunities to correct market injustices perpetrated by others who are being unfair or discriminatory.

Righteousness. Faithfulness in our relationships with customers and suppliers is a way of living our faithfulness to God and his way of ethics in the marketplace. Righteousness does not require weakness. In fact, the opposite is in view. As with justice, standing firm on principles of right action may create business opportunities. In a marketplace where buyers and sellers are taking advantage of each other, righteousness contributes to not only the economic dimension of shalom but also the social harmony dimension.

Truth. Faithfulness in representing and delivering value should be the motto of every marketing professional. As product messages and the products themselves are tested by customers, marketers will get the feedback from the market and make improvements where feasible. Advertising messages will be as accurate as possible. The expectations spawned in the hearts and minds of customers must meet with substance. Lower-quality products cannot be represented being high in quality.

Wisdom. The biblically smart thing to do (being fair, being impartial) is often also the economically smart thing in a marketplace where buyers and sellers are doing wrong. Biblical wisdom requires understanding in how covenant relationships work in many directions, relationships not only between sellers and their buyers but also relationships in the larger marketplace such as the relationships between one seller's customers and competitors and relationships with suppliers. Following biblical wisdom, both sellers and buyers will protect their own interests and not get taken advantage of.

Loving kindness. Operating a business with loving kindness means that you will constantly have respect for the covenant relationship that is at stake. Loyalty to the relationship is shown in action as much as it is told in words and images (such as in promotional messages). Loyalty means not only positioning the products, pricing, distribution and promotional messages so that they are consistent with target customers and their needs but also being loyal to the kind of relationship these customers desire. It means entering and leaving every transaction in a way that fosters loyalty for both buyer and seller.

Redemption. Sometimes it is the customer who is the prophetic voice from the marketplace for the seller to make a correction. Redemption suggests that in this situation the seller will have the humility to serve the customer by incorporating the message (when it is true) into the performance improvement systems of the organization. Where the customer's message is not true, the seller will act redemptively and respectfully to help broaden the customer's perspective. This will go far beyond engaging the customer in a debate and will involve giving the customer something to recognize the value that the customer has brought when giving the message, faulty as it might be, to the company. Through this means recovering a relationship with the customer not only fosters economic prosperity but also enhances the customer's enjoyment of life overall.

CHAPTER REVIEW QUESTIONS

1. What are some of the ways that companies can take advantage of customers through pricing policies?

2. What are the ethical issues related to marketing promotion?

3. What are the ethical issues related to product policy decisions?

4. What ethical problems come up in the distribution of products and services?

5. What ethical issues arise in the relationships with competitors?

6. Give examples of how a company's relationship with customers gives rise to ethical issues.

7. What are some ethical issues related to conducting market research?

DISCUSSION QUESTIONS

1. Is it ethical for a salesperson to make statements about a service's outcome when consumers lack the expertise in evaluating that service's end result?

2. Why do laws forbidding price fixing exist? Why are these laws important for an effective free-market economy?

3. Conduct some research on the Internet: What happened to the stock price soon after Bridgestone pleaded guilty to price fixing? Were any executives or managers fired as a result of the case? How much money were executives and board members required to give up as punishment?

4. What is a company to do when it realizes that the value it offers does not exactly match up with the value interests of the customers?

5. What biblical story themes seem to stand out as especially important for marketing and advertising ethical issues?

ETHICAL VIGNETTES TO DISCUSS

For each of the following vignettes, apply the biblical story themes to discern what is right and wrong and in so doing to answer the questions at the end of each vignette.

1. A customer comes to your store stating that he desires to purchase a certain product. When he sees the price, he says, "I can't afford that!" You know that a competitor in your area sells the same product for 10 percent less. Do you refer the customer to

the competitor, try to sell him a different product or just wish the customer well?

2. You live in Seattle and cannot avoid hearing people around you rave about the Seattle Sounders Football (soccer) Club. Seattle soccer fans love their team like no other group of fans in the United States. After hearing about the club from several co-workers, you decide to go to a match. But you arrive late and the stadium is sold out. The ticket windows are closed. You see a few ticket scalpers hanging around ready to help you with your problem. The only trouble is that in solving one problem for you (access to tickets), they have caused another: high prices. Now that you have driven all the way to the stadium, you do not want to go home unsatisfied. You do not want to tell all your friends that you arrived too late and couldn't get in. So you cave in and pay the high price, three times what you would have paid had you arrived early. Is ticket scalping at sporting events unethical?

3. Early in 2014, CVS Caremark, one of the largest chains of retail pharmacies, decided it would stop selling cigarettes and other tobacco products later in the year. Referring to the corporate strategic commitment to get more involved in providing health care, company spokespersons said that selling these products are not consistent with that commitment. In making this commitment the retail chain of drug stores expected to lose billions of dollars annually from lost revenue. However, CVS also has made a commitment to establish in-store medical clinics and offer smoking cessation programs in stores. Clearly, it wanted to move away from being a pill-dispensing store to a healthcare delivery organization. Tobacco is the number one cause of preventable disease and death in the United States. Is the CVS Caremark decision purely a strategic decision, or is it also an ethical issue? In what way, if at all, can it be said that other retail pharmacies are being unethical if they continue to sell tobacco products while at the same time providing customers with health-related products and services? Conduct some Internet research: What happened to the CVS Caremark stock price after the announcement? What has been the trend in the stock price since that major decision?

4. In 2013 Australian consumers were upset that they had to pay almost 70 percent more on average to download from iTunes compared with what customers paid in the United States. Prices for some computer software products were also much higher in Australia compared with prices in the United States. Australian lawmakers were considering making changes to the Australian Copyright Act and the Competition and Consumer Act to stop what they believe to be unjustified price discrimination. Is it wrong for iTunes to charge Australians almost 70 percent more than it charges Americans for downloading the same iTunes product?

18

Ethical Issues in Global Business

SCRIPTURE PASSAGE

And I will bless those who bless you,
And the one who curses you I will curse.
And in you all the families of the earth
will be blessed. (Gen 12:3)

CHAPTER OVERVIEW

In this chapter we will consider global business as the context for ethical issues. In particular we will explore selected ethical issues in global business through the lens of biblical story themes.

MAIN TOPICS

Challenges of Globalization
Corruption
Gift Giving and Bribery
International Ethical Standards and Oversight
Down to the Nitty-Gritty
Through the Lens of Biblical Themes

KEY TERMS

bribery, corruption, foreign corrupt practices act, grease payments, International Court of Justice (ICJ), multinational corporations (MNCs), United Nations (UN), World Trade Organization (WTO)

OPENING SCENARIO

According to a *New York Times* investigative report, a former Walmart executive alleged that the company breached the US Foreign Corrupt Practices Act by paying more than $24 million (US) in bribes to government officials disbursed in more than 440 payments throughout Mexico to secure building permits for its stores. When the news broke about the allegations, Walmart stock price fell by 4.6 percent.[1]

Allegedly the payments stopped only after construction of new Walmart stores was complete in Mexico. Near the center of the allegations is Eduardo Castro-Wright, who was in charge of the Walmart operations in Mexico.

The alleged illegal payments may have been authorized by Walmart general counsel. Written evidence that was uncovered in the scandal by 2006 seemed to support the claim that Walmart's highest-level leaders, including the company lawyers and the chief executive officer, Mike Duke, knew about the payments and the internal investigation but instead of using their authority to stop the activities, attempted to delay and then deflect the investigation away from top-level leaders by placing in charge of the investigation one of the persons who was a primary target in the allegations.

La mordida (Spanish, "the bite" [bribe]) is quite frequently referred to as the customary way of getting things accomplished either in the government sector or the private sector. The question is whether or not *la mordida* is illegal under the Foreign Corrupt Practices Act (FCPA). Whether or not the alleged payments are illegal is debated. It is possible that the payments fall under the provision of the FCPA which allows for some "grease payments" (a.k.a. facilitating payments) under certain conditions which may be made to speed up government processes. Legally, these are not the same as bribes, which are intended to circumvent government regulations. If Walmart concealed the payments by not recording them in the accounting records, this could pose another problem form the point of view of the FCPA.

Officials from Mexico signed documents in 2003 stating that they intended to participate in the UN Convention Against Corruption. Officials from the United States also signed. The Mexican legislature ratified the agreement in July 2004; the US Congress ratified the agreement in October 2006.[2]

If the US Attorney's office determines that no laws have been broken, another question that remains is whether or not the alleged payments are unethical.

Founded by Christian businessman Sam Walton, Walmart is a company that has publicized its high moral standards. It is estimated to be one of the largest employers in Mexico with more than two hundred thousand employees.

CHALLENGES OF GLOBALIZATION

All the ethical issues that we have explored in previous chapters are also issues that managers and their firms face when engaging in global business. While the ethical problems that global businesses face are similar to those that domestic companies face (management, marketing, accounting, finance), there are problems that only global businesses must contend with. For example, even though every nation works hard to preserve its sovereignty separate from other nations, travel, banking and communication systems make it easier to transact business across national borders. This means that national borders, while still important, are less important influences on social activities, including business.

For another example, consider that global business operations result in the creation of new social networks that are not limited by national boundaries. In addition, doing business globally means that new and more complex interdependencies are created. The significance of the individual-community tension we have explored in this book is stretched. Among those doing business globally and their strategic alliance partners, even those who are domestic, there is a growing awareness of the extent and interconnectedness of business relationships worldwide.

The questions that are begged by the development of global business include, What ethical standards should apply, and How do you decide what applies in a given situation? Is there an objective standard by which we can determine how to make right decisions in an international context? How do business leaders manage the pressures of globalization? Figure 18.1 illustrates some of these pressures on stakeholders.

A multinational corporation (MNC) faces conflicting pressures from stakeholders in its home country (expatriates) as well as from those in each of the host countries in which it operates (host-country nationals). The pressures also affect people who come from a third country to work in a country that is different from where

Figure 18.1. Pressures of globalization on stakeholders.

the MNC is based and different from their own home country (third-country nationals). Multiply this by the number of different countries that the firm operates in and you have a recipe for complicated decision making.

For example, a business based in the American system of free enterprise is situated within the context of the American legal, political, generally accepted moral standards, social systems and business systems. Canada, Australia and Great Britain have laws similar to those in the United States, but even with this there is no international context that is exactly the same. If this firm operates in Africa, Southeast Asia, Russia and Western Europe, the challenges increase. Furthermore, the company must obey both sets of laws. There are few organizations and legal standards that govern the operations of business worldwide. Countries and companies must navigate the difficult waters of governance without the help of a worldwide government.[3] To make its way in the international arena, an American business must create multiple approaches to doing business which are quite different from how business is operated in the United States.

Business in the United States is constrained by the rule of law, established customs and conventions, an integrated cluster of shared values that are commonly accepted in the market, organized labor groups, consumer groups, media groups, environmental groups, and many other stakeholders. The establishment and maintenance of infrastructure for trade is slightly different from country to country. This background set of influences, resources and structures is not identical in other countries. Restraints tend to be fewer in developing countries. One of the biggest noticeable differences is the comparative lack of background or support institutions to control and guide the development and operation of business. In some countries this creates an opportunity for abuses.

The expansion of corporations operating in many countries has its proponents and its opponents.[4] Let us look at each point of view.

> The expansion of corporations operating in many countries has its proponents and its opponents.

The benefits of globalization. Proponents of multinational corporations (MNCs) say that their host countries get several benefits:

- MNCs create jobs for local workers.

- Some MNCs pay higher wages than workers could get in their domestic companies.

- MNCs stimulate the local economies. They attract new businesses needed in support for either inbound or outbound logistics.

- MNC joint ventures with local entrepreneurs give local investors access to technology, management expertise, capital and ready markets for their products. Joint ventures lower the risk of doing business.

- The cross-cultural contact that MNCs create enriches the cultural understanding among all people who participate in business activities.

- MNCs attract additional capital investments to projects they start.

- They provide business skills and learning that spill over onto other industries in the host country.

- MNCs increase the industrial output of host countries.

- They help host countries leverage their inherent competitive advantages compared with other nations.

- The intensified competition results in lower prices for consumers everywhere.

- Productivity in all strategic alliance partner businesses is improved.

- The standard of living for many workers in the host country improves.

- MNCs create environments that support the rule of law and human freedom of expression.

- The interconnections between businesses and governments that come as a result of MNCs doing business establish interdependences that cannot easily be broken without risking the loss of the benefits gained. This reduces the probability of armed conflicts arising.

- Minor players (small firms) can more easily get involved in international business as their larger corporate global partners expand.

- New, flexible organizational structures have been created to be in alignment with a global environment.

- A rapid electronic connectivity is occurring between businesses, small groups and businesses and governments. This is creating access to worldwide expertise and contacts, as well as new channels for spreading the influence of business and new distribution channels for products and services.

For all the good that global businesses do, the process of globalization also has its critics.

Criticisms of globalization. Partly because of the pressures MNCs have not always covered themselves in glory. Critics are quick to point out the problems:

- MNCs are not forthright about their practices.

- MNCs place profits above the interests of local people.

- They do not fulfill their part of the social contract expectations to do no harm and respect the rights of others.

- They can avoid paying taxes in their home country.

- Global firms are having an increased influence on the governments of small developing countries. Some corporations' balance sheets are larger than the gross national product (GNP) of the nations in which they do business.

- In some host countries MNCs can engage in practices that harm the environment or destroy local ecosystems—activities they would be forbidden to do in their home country.

- These corporations dominate and protect their core technologies and do not allow companies in their host countries to share.

- Global business has led to consolidations in industries which result in corporations with increased influence in the market and with governments.

- MNCs destabilize national sovereignty by dictating the economic terms. This disturbs local government economic planning.

- MNCs create a national brain drain by hiring the best people, training them to be effective managers and leaders and then creating opportunities for them to transfer to other countries.

- Operating MNC businesses creates an imbalance of national cash outflows over inflows.

- Globalization has resulted in an increase in crime and corruption for the sake of profit and greed.

- Corporations place at risk thousands of workers and their families when they hold out hope for a brighter future and then reorganize by executing massive layoffs.

- Western corporations and their Western managers are either intentionally or unintentionally "westernizing" other national cultures. This undermines cultural diversity.

- In order to stay in the good graces of their host nation, some MNCs ignore human rights violations.

- Global interdependence can be felt any time the stock market of another country changes due to an unfavorable event. This increases vulnerability of large portions of the world during business cycles and political upheaval.

One of the main charges against multinational corporations is that they adopt a double standard, doing in less developed countries what would be regarded as wrong if done in a developed country.[5] Some criticized practices are legal in a host country and are not considered to be unethical by local standards. The home country might consider it both illegal and unethical. Should MNCs be bound by the prevailing morality of the home country and act everywhere as they do in their own country? Or should they follow the practices of the host country? Or are there special ethical standards that apply when business is conducted across national boundaries? If so, what are these standards?

Another charge is that because there is no central world government to oversee global business, MNCs have the luxury of operating independently of the social rules in some countries.[6]

Sometimes the MNCs based in the United States are criticized regardless of what they do. For example, when an American company pays the same wages as local firms, it is criticized for not paying a living wage. But when the company pays a higher wage, it is accused of trying to attract the best workers away from local companies.[7]

A related debate is over the differences in moral standards when we compare one country with another. As a result, different points of view have developed: absolutism and relativism.

Absolutism holds that business ought to be conducted in the same way the world over with no double standards. In other words, "When in Rome, do as you would do at home." Some suggest that the home country's standards are morally correct or superior and should be used as the standard to judge the standards of other countries. It also tends to gloss over the cultural differences between countries. What is considered a sign of respect, honor and a symbol of the desire to establish a long-lasting relationship in one country may be considered a bribe in other country. Some also suggest that the absolutist position limits local influence on decision making regarding business conduct. If the MNC imposes its ethical principles on stakeholders in the host country, locals in the host country will have little influence on decision making. Some see this as ethical imperialism. Counteracting this concern is the awareness that respect for local influence and decision making should not be used as an excuse to do anything that the company wants in order to accomplish business goals. If the host country has a low set of standards regarding human rights, should this be used as license for the MNC to harm innocent people?

In contrast, relativism holds that the only guide for business conduct abroad is what is legally and morally acceptable in the host country where the firm operates. In other words, "When in Rome, do as the Romans do." As we have seen in chapter six, proponents of relativism believe that standards of morality become legitimate only through a socio-cultural process of people in society coming to embrace certain standards and rejecting other standards. In short, "all intercultural comparisons of values are meaningless."[8] A true relativist must reject any objective standard of right and wrong. Critics of relativism suggest that this opens wide the door for all kinds of abuse of people.

A third perspective is that moral standards are absolute but with exceptions. In other words, some practices may be justified where local conditions require that corporations engage in them as a condition of doing business: "We don't agree with the Romans but find it necessary to do things their way in this particular instance. Otherwise, business wouldn't get done!"

These issues are not unique to doing business internationally, but they continue to represent a global problem. Having seen some of the big issues, we will explore two of the specific issues that MNCs have had to deal with for decades: corruption and bribery. These are not the only ethical issues, but they represent some questionable practices that are the most firmly embedded in world cultures, the most damaging to economic development and the most difficult to eradicate.[9]

CORRUPTION

The national governments of the world and the trade organizations conducting global business are becoming more aware of the dangers and costs of corruption in the world economy.

Corruption (a.k.a. graft) is any dishonest or fraudulent use of legitimate power to gain a personal economic benefit or advantage. Corruption often involves bribery (which we will address below). But sometimes it merely involves the person in power using legitimate authority to acquire personal gain.[10]

Corruption is bad for governments. It

> impedes economic growth by diverting public resources from important priorities such as health, education, and infrastructure. It undermines democratic values and public accountability and weakens the rule of law. And it threatens stability and security by facilitating criminal activity within and across borders, such as the illegal trafficking of people, weapons, and drugs. International corruption also un-

dercuts good governance and impedes U.S. efforts to promote freedom and democracy, end poverty, and combat crime and terrorism across the globe.[11]

Business is harmed by corruption, too. Corruption undermines fair competition. It places honest businesses at a disadvantage. It results in distorted market prices. Corruption increases uncertainty in the market. Favors obtained by unlawful payments may lead to business deals that cannot be enforced because enforcement would reveal the illegal nature of the corrupt actions. Once a corrupt relationship is established, there is often choice but to continue the relationship. The problem is not only legal but also economic. Officials who benefit personally from the corrupt relationship are likely to demand increasing amounts of money or goods.

Transparency International, headquartered in Berlin, Germany, annually surveys business leaders' regarding their perceptions of corruption in nations where they do business.[12] The organization then publishes a "corruption perception index" for the world showing which countries are perceived to be the most corrupt and least corrupt. In 1995 TI published the results of their survey. In that year New Zealand was perceived to be the least corrupt while Indonesia was the worst. In 2013 Denmark, New Zealand, Finland and Sweden were seen as the least corrupt countries to do business. The United States ranked nineteenth, behind Japan. Nations that were perceived to be the most corrupt were Sudan, Afghanistan, North Korea and Somalia.

Provisions in the law. The FCPA prohibits anyone acting on behalf of US companies to pay a foreign government official for the purpose of obtaining or retaining business. The law prohibits

the willful use of the mails or any means of instrumentality of interstate commerce corruptly in furtherance of any offer, payment, promise to pay, or authorization of the payment of money or anything of value to any person, while knowing that all or a portion of such money or thing of value will be offered, given or promised, directly or indirectly, to a foreign official to influence the foreign official in his or her official capacity, induce the foreign official to do or omit to do an act in violation of his or her lawful duty, or to secure any improper advantage in order to assist in obtaining or retaining business for or with, or directing business to, any person.[13]

The law applies to US firms doing business in other countries, and it applies to firms from other countries doing business in the United States.

A related provision in the law is that US companies must maintain accounting "books and records that accurately and fairly reflect the transactions of the corporation" and maintain "an adequate system of internal accounting controls."[14]

Making grease payments that facilitate "routine government actions" are permitted. Routine government actions include issuing permits, licenses or other official documents. Here, payment is not an attempt to circumvent the law or create a subjective reciprocity action on the part of the host country official. Accordingly, there is some ambiguity in the FCPA.

Because there is some ambiguity with some elements of the FCPA, it pays to become educated and to have available experienced counselors to interpret the law for you. Guidelines for interpreting the FPCA have been produced by the US Department of Justice and are available free to the public on the Department of Justice website.[15]

Penalties. The law stipulates that each violation of the FPCA can result in a criminal penalty fine to the business or corporation of up to $2 million. Additionally, officers and employees of the business may be fined up to $250,000 and serve a federal prison sentence of up to five years. Federal judges have the discretion to increase the penalty by imposing a fine that is up to twice the value that the criminal obtained by breaking the law. Furthermore, employees or agents of the company are not allowed to have their company pay fines for them. It becomes a personal responsibility.

In addition to the criminal penalties, under the law the Department of Justice and the Securities and Exchange Commission (SEC) are allowed to pursue a civil penalty served against convicted corruption criminals. Both the business and the person can be fined up to $16,000 per violation. This means that every time a manager illegally pays a government official, the civil penalty can be as much as $16,000. Acting corruptly is one thing, but failing to keep accurate accounting records that fairly reflect the corrupt nature of the actions can result in additional fines of up to $150,000 for the responsible person and up to $750,000 for the company. So, it is not only against the law to act in a corrupt manner. It is also against the law to not document the corrupt actions in the accounting and business records of the firm!

This is not the end of the story in terms of penalties. Firms that are convicted of breaking the FPCA may have their export privileges revoked and be barred from being a contractor for the US government.

Protections for whistleblowers. Persons, whether an employee, agent or anyone else, are allowed to notify the SEC if they have information about a possible violation of the FPCA. This can be done anonymously through the SEC's Tips, Complaints and Referrals (TCR) Intake and Resolution System online. Persons can also report a FCPA violation via email to FCPA.Fraud@usdoj.gov. Whistleblowers who alert authorities are protected from retaliation under the law.

GIFT GIVING AND BRIBERY

Few international ethical issues are as controversial as gift giving, bribery and kickbacks. As we will see, it is not always clear whether corruption has taken place. We start our exploration of this with the issue of gift giving.

> Many will seek the favor of a
> generous man,
> And every man is a friend to him
> who gives gifts. (Prov 19:6)

Gift giving.[16] Giving gifts is a symbol of the desire on the part of the gift-giving party to build goodwill with the other party. We can say that a gift is something of value offered without any explicit mutual agreement to receive something in exchange. However, there is often a psychological expectation that develops on the part of the gift giver and the recipient. It has to do with reciprocity. When you give a gift to someone you feel affection toward, don't you hope for some gesture of goodwill in return over time? By doing something that shows a favored relationship, doesn't this show the desire to receive favorable treatment? Giving a gift can create the tendency toward an unspoken desire to see reciprocity from the party receiving the gift. In most societies around the globe, reciprocity is an important rule of life. Without reciprocity, community bonds would be fragile; with reciprocity, communities maintain covenant relationships. Without reciprocity the desire to foster goodwill by giving a gift would be meaningless. Likewise, from the gift receiver's point of view, accepting a gift tends toward a sense of obligation to show reciprocity.

The other side of this discussion is that a true gift, by definition, is given without expectation of anything in return. If there is a mutual understanding that a response (other than a genuine statement of gratitude) is expected, then it is no longer a gift. It would seem that this is the sufficient distinction between a gift and a bribe. However, it is not always possible for the gift giver to tell to what degree the gift has resulted in a sense of obligation to reciprocate. Furthermore, the giving and receiving of a gift can promote self-deception where at a later date, when the interests of the gift giver are being considered, the gift receiver cannot forget the gift. It may very well have a subtle impact on the decision. At this point it becomes difficult to distinguish between a gift and a bribe.

Bribery.[17] Bribery is when someone offers something of value with the understanding that in exchange the person receiving the value will promote the interests of the person or will violate a duty of loyalty owed because of legitimate authority.[18] A bribe involves an agreement to exchange value.

With all the attention that bribery has attained and all the international efforts to combat bribery, it might be surprising to learn that it is still a major problem.[19]

What is wrong with bribery? The answer can be seen from several points of view. One point of view is that a bribe is an attempt to create divided loyalties: loyalty to the principal

and loyalty to the one who is offering the bribe. Divided loyalty, it is believed in this view, requires the one receiving the bribe to breach the fiduciary obligations to the principal. Another point of view is that bribery violates the notion of equality.

A third point of view is focused on the public institution or government agency where the bribe receiver works. Bribery, it is believed, undermines the vitality of the broader social purposes of these institutions because accepting the bribe destroys the impartial point of view that the person must keep when serving everyone. In the context of public institutions, bribery destroys trust because the discretion of the public servants is undermined, discretion required by the very nature of the agency.

A fourth point of view is economic. In the short run, a bribe may seem to be the best alternative; however, in the long run bribes are bad for business. Bribery demoralizes employee confidence that the firm will thrive without the benefit of dishonest activities. Bribery tends to fuel a corporate culture that permits other unethical behaviors such as self-dealing, embezzlement and fraud.[20] This increases the risk that a business will fail, or to avoid failure business managers feel obliged to turn to other unethical or illegal activities to manage the risk created by bribes. Overall, bribery undermines the responsibility that the company has toward investors.

When it comes to bribes, the international business operative may be between a rock and a hard place: refusing a request for a bribe may lead to resentment on the part of the host country; paying a bribe will likely lead to prosecution under the FCPA. This leads to a fifth perspective that is debatable. Some say, perhaps to justify bribery, that the competitive advantage of one company is undermined when it does not pay bribes. Likewise, the competitive advantage of the whole country (that observes anticorruption laws) is reduced when companies from other countries pay bribes. Others disagree, suggesting that the opposite might be true.[21] Refusing to pay a bribe might create a positive competitive advantage. If competitors pay bribes, this drains cash from their operations. In addition, a reputation for being ethical can pay dividends in terms of increased trust by local suppliers, customers and especially government officials.

Instead of paying a bribe, businesses may want to consider

- Making a highly visible donation of cash or goods to a local charity (hospital, clinic, school, NGO service organization) and state that paying a bribe is in violation of the FCPA. Warning! Making charitable contributions can be done improperly. The risk in this is that a public official still may be able to benefit personally from a donation because of his or her relationship with the charity. Goods can be sold on the black market and quickly turned into cash.

- Donating services that can be of value to others besides the host country official.

- Creating jobs that are offered to persons in the host country.

Paying an official out of personal funds is the same as the company breaking the FPCA law. Thus, this is not an alternative to consider. The provisions of the FPCA are sometimes ambiguous; however, to be safe it pays to seek counsel from the Department of Justice or an experienced attorney before choosing an alternative to paying a bribe.

INTERNATIONAL ETHICAL STANDARDS AND OVERSIGHT

Each country has its own laws and regulations that constrain international business activities undertaken by companies based there but that operate in other countries. One example is the United States FCPA. More will be said about this below.

Ethical and legal principles that exist in one nation are common to many other nations. Although there is no central world government, there are international organizations that play a role in oversight of international business. Treaties and conventions between two or more countries have for many years served as the authority for international trade cooperation among the states that participate. The International Court of Justice located in the Netherlands is operated by the United Nations.[22] It provides a means for nations to resolve disputes that involve international trade. In addition, the World Trade Organization (WTO) Dispute Settlement Body helps member nations resolve trading disputes.[23]

The principles on which the Dispute Settlement Body operates are principles of law that are common to all the nations who participate in the WTO. The WTO enforces hundreds of international trade agreements (treaties). The member nations of the United Nations signed a pact called the UN Convention on Contracts for the International Sale of Goods (CISG). The European Union (EU) is one example of dozens of regional organizations that serves the interests of a group of countries. The EU Commission serves the international trade interests of member countries. It has power to enact and enforce trade laws that the member nations abide by.

Organization for Economic Cooperation and Development (OECD).[24] The Organization for Economic Cooperation and Development, with headquarters in Paris, France, was established in 1961 for the purpose of promoting economic stability of Europe.[25] In 1997, more than thirty member states negotiated an agreement for a Convention on Combating Bribery of Foreign Public Officials in International Business Transactions. Nation signatories to the treaty each agreed to enact legislation making bribery of public officials a punishable crime. Furthermore, members agreed to actively prosecute bribery offenses. Perpetrators of bribery crimes are subject to extradition so that they can stand trial in their home country, and member states are expected to cooperate with orders for extradition.

Council of Europe Criminal Law Convention on Corruption.[26] In 1999 the Council of Europe agreed to a treaty designed to fight corruption.[27] More than forty nations signed the treaty, which requires each nation to enact legislation prohibiting corruption and requiring penalties for corruption crimes.

The UN Convention Against Corruption (UNCAC).[28] International sentiment regarding the evils of corruption continued to grow. In 2004 the United Nations published a Convention Against Corruption to reinforce the importance of all UN member nations to support common standards and rules designed to prevent and eliminate corruption. The convention requires member nations to return to their country of origin all assets obtained by corrupt actions. Like laws of some countries, bribery in the UNCAC is not limited to relationship between business and state officials. Bribery in the private sector is also forbidden. As with other international conventions, because there is no international police force and

justice system that covers all international crimes, enforcement remains a challenge.

Thus, most countries that have signed agreements related to corruption have laws against bribery, lying and stealing, but not every country enforces these laws with equal vigor. These and other similar organizations in other regions are not only concerned about the law but also are concerned with the ethical foundation of laws.[29] These international efforts go beyond concerns about corruption to include a variety of issues such as working conditions, human rights and protection of the environment.

Recall that in chapter seven we introduced the idea of common sense defined as generally accepted moral principles (GAMP). We considered some of the fundamental principles across many countries. To these, others could be added which illustrate that for a large portion of the world, there are fundamental principles on which many agree. This is illustrated in the fact that over the years several international codes of conduct for international business have been developed. Examples of these will be introduced here.

CAUX Round Table.[30] If you believe that businesses should do more than just earn a profit, you are in the company of many business executives worldwide. This is illustrated by the CAUX Round Table organization. The CAUX Round Table was founded in 1986 by Frederick Phillips, former president of Phillips Electronics, and Olivier Giscard d'Estaing, former vice-chairman of INSEAD.[31] They formed a network of business leaders to promote ethical business practices worldwide. The purpose of the organization was to establish a comprehensive set of ethical norms which, when followed broadly across many nations, would reduce tensions in trade and foster economic development. They use the concept of moral capitalism, which means to broaden everyone's understanding that purpose of business is not just for the generation of profit by any means, but rather to encourage the development of "humanity's more noble possibilities."[32] Out of the dialogue came principles for businesses, governments, nonprofit organizations and owners of wealth. The principles for responsible business include the following:

- Respect stakeholders beyond the shareholders.

- Contribute to economic, social and environmental development.

- Build trust by going beyond the letter of the law.

- Respect rules and conventions.

- Support responsible globalization.

- Respect the environment.

- Avoid illicit activities.

UN Global Compact. What private business leaders began promoting, government leaders also support. Launched in 2000, the United Nations Global Compact is a voluntary set of social and ethical principles that for-profit companies and nonprofit organizations agree to follow. The compact outlines ten principles. Businesses should:[33]

- support and respect the protection of internationally proclaimed human rights

- make sure that they are not complicit in human rights abuses

- uphold the freedom of association and the effective recognition of the right to collective bargaining

- eliminate all forms of forced and compulsory labor

- abolish of child labor

- eliminate discrimination in respect of employment and occupation

- support a precautionary approach to environmental challenges

- undertake initiatives to promote greater environmental responsibility

- encourage the development and diffusion of environmentally friendly technologies

- work against corruption in all its forms, including extortion and bribery

These are more than mere lists. They represent thousands of hours of discussion and negotiation among business leaders and thinkers as they attempted to develop common guidelines that many voluntarily support.

DOWN TO THE NITTY-GRITTY

Think about scenario at the beginning of this chapter. You are a manager of a company that wants to expand internationally. To accomplish some of your company's goals, you are required to make grease payments to speed up the work of government officials. What is the right thing to do? It's time to get down to the nitty-gritty (see table 18.1)!

THROUGH THE LENS OF BIBLICAL THEMES

This part of the chapter will use the biblical story themes as a lens through which to evaluate the topic featured in the chapter. Because the themes are interrelated and interdependent, we should expect to see some overlap in the thinking regarding the issues. Some themes will contribute the same thinking as will other themes. The power of these themes comes from their guidance when a community of people talks about complicated ethical dilemmas faced in business practice.

Table 18.1. Applying the ethical process.

Keeping Your Heart: An Intrapersonal Process	Walking in the Community: An Interpersonal Process

• You are a manager of a company that wants to expand internationally. What does your heart say is the right thing to do regarding making grease payments?
• Which biblical themes explored in this book inform your heart on this situation?
• Which biblical theme, if any, do you feel yourself resisting? Why do you feel resistance?
• What other influences in your heart seem to be prominent as you think about this situation?
  • Fundamental beliefs
  • Cognitive reasoning
  • Judgments and evaluations
  • Decisions
  • Virtues
  • Will
  • Memory of personal experiences with other people
  • Perceptions of others in the community
  • Personal biases
  • Awareness of interpersonal relationships
  • Commitments to God and to others
  • Intuitions
  • Conscience
  • Human spirit
  • Emotions
	• You are a manager of a company that wants to expand internationally. With whom might you have a conversation about the issue of grease payments? Who else might have a helpful perspective?
	• Who should take a leadership role in the conversation about grease payments?
	• Which of the biblical themes in this chapter will most likely come up in the conversation either directly or indirectly? Why? Which one(s) will be the most influential in the conversation?
	• If you have a conversation with someone regarding this situation, which of the fundamental tensions presented earlier in the book might come up?
	• What right-versus-right dilemmas, if any, can be identified? Have a conversation with someone about this now. What is the outcome of the conversation?

One of the most challenging things for a Christian in global business is how to manage the dilemmas in a way that you can be true to your religious beliefs while being tolerant of others who have different beliefs. Here the biblical story themes provide some guidance.

Cosmic conflict. The scope of the great conflict between God and Satan is global and beyond.[34] Evil on this earth has no boundaries either social or geographic. Scripture does not say, "Resist the devil when he torments your efforts in your own nation." The implication is that Satan is to be resisted regardless of location on earth. Likewise, as the psalmist wrote, God's relationship with this earth is not confined with a small group of people or just one nation. "Let all the earth fear the Lord; let all the inhabitants of the world stand in awe of Him" (Ps 33:8.) Satan's temptation of Jesus included an offer of a bribe: "The devil took Him to a very high mountain, and showed Him all the kingdoms of the world and their glory; and he said to Him, 'All these things will I give You, if You fall down and worship me'" (Mt 4:8-9).[35] This reveals Satan's program. He seeks to circumvent the rules of relationships by appealing to narrow self-interest. This and other temptations are tests of a person's faithfulness when under pressure.[36]

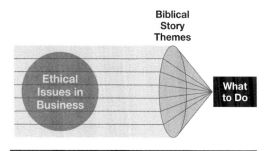

Figure 18.2. Evaluating an ethical process.

Creation. The Scripture story teaches that "we are His workmanship, created in Christ Jesus for good works, which God prepared beforehand so that we should walk in them" (Eph 2:10). One of the purposes of creation is that it offered a venue for the demonstration of God's love. And that venue is worldwide in scope. Accordingly, good works, for which we were created, are to be expressed worldwide. The earth is full of the materials used in business value chains. All of these, regardless of location or national origin, belong to God. Accordingly, our use of the materials in a way that brings glory to God is not limited to what we find in our nation but includes what we acquire and use from all other places on earth.

Holiness. The call to holiness is the call to work in opposition to all which goes against God's way but to work in such a manner that does not compromise the principles envisioned by the other biblical story themes such as justice, truth, wisdom, loving kindness and redemption. One of the problems that some Christians have fallen into is that of working vigorously to eradicate evil (in other people's behavior) but with methods which are against the other biblical themes.

Covenant relationships. To foster covenant relationships on an international scale requires one party to give up the comforts of home and domestic life and to travel and live, perhaps for an extended period of time, in other countries. Covenant living was intended for worldwide enjoyment, not just local enjoyment. One important aspect of developing deep relationships internationally is in showing favor. Showing favor to another is part of developing and repairing broken covenant relationships.[37] Favor from God is highly desirable, but social favor is also highly valued.[38] Accordingly, the Bible record has a place for gift giving. God is the great gift giver who gives life, sustenance, grace and power. It is in a gift where his character of holiness, justice, loving kindness and redemption is shown.[39] Solomon recognizes that a person's "gift makes room for him and brings him before great men" (Prov 18:16). People who give gifts tend have friends.[40] In contrast to the biblical idea of gift giving, bribes divert attention from the community's needs to the individual's needs. The person desiring a bribe thinks primarily about himself or herself and the personal benefit he will receive by accepting the offer. Such self-focus becomes blindness to the needs of the community.[41]

Shalom. It is the whole earth that is to enjoy shalom.[42] It is the whole earth that is comprehended in God's plan of salvation.[43] For the fulfillment of God's plan to be complete, shalom is not complete until it affects everyone on earth. As faithful followers of God go out to many lands and places, they can carry the seeds of shalom to be planted and nurtured in the soil of marketplace activities of buying and selling. One way to nurture these seeds is to collaborate with others of like mind such as in supporting the CAUX principles.

Sabbath. Having the means and developing the capabilities to do business on an international scale can create an international arrogance which works against the biblical story themes. Sabbath is a constant reminder of our need to renounce human autonomy. We may have means and ability, but God is the ultimate author of our success. It is God who is Lord of all of life. Though we can travel around the globe, we do not have the power of God to travel and transact business with other distant planets. In terms of business, this world is the limit. Thus, sabbath should be a constant reminder of our need for humility.

Justice. Most of the Bible verses that mention bribery explicitly are in the context of the justice system.[44] We should not conclude from this that bribery does not apply to business. The principle at stake in bribery applies to all social relationships regardless of setting. Bribery is wrong because it blinds the eyes of the wise person and undermines the cause of justice.[45]

Righteousness. Nowhere is righteousness more important than in doing business internationally. The reason is that dealing with international suppliers and customers continually tests commitment to following God's way of living. It is relatively easy to follow the commands "do not lie; do not steal; do not cheat" when most of the customers and suppliers agree with these. It is more difficult to remain firm when traveling to other places where these commands mean something entirely different or where other principles are used that do not align with biblical principles.

Truth. When you move from your home country where you are known to a place where people do not know you, there is an opportunity and a risk for truth. The risk for truth is that you may be tempted to be unfaithful to who you are and what you stand for. The opportunity for truth is that others need a basis to trust you but have no knowledge of who you are when tested by time and circumstance. Following the theme of truth is more important in global business than in domestic business for this reason alone.

Wisdom. Global business requires a degree of wisdom that might, in some instances, surpass the wisdom required for doing business domestically. Global business tests prudence, discretion and smartness (to follow God's way) in ways that domestic business does not. We have not only to continue to learn God's ways but also see how these ways are perceived through the experience and understanding of people from other cultures.

Loving kindness. Just as covenant may be much more difficult to establish in international business, so to loyalty may be much more difficult to establish and maintain at the international scale of relationships. In most places of the world, reciprocity is a principle that most people understand. Thus, the reciprocity principle inherent in loving kindness can be used as a powerful tool in managing relationships.

Redemption. God was in Christ, sending him to earth to reconcile us to him. We call this the incarnation of God: God became human flesh and dwelt among us, humbling himself even to the covenantal death on the cross.[46] This aspect of redemption is important for carrying on international business. Faithful followers will act incarnationally by going to others and serving them. Acting redemptively and in loving kindness, while being careful not to be taken advantage of, is one of the most powerful forces for the sake of the gospel.

CHAPTER REVIEW QUESTIONS

1. What are the main ethical issues in the debate over the processes of globalization?

2. What is corruption and why is it so dangerous in international business?

3. What is bribery and why is it unethical and illegal?

4. What is the nature of international ethical oversight of ethical principles related to business?

5. What guidance do the biblical story themes provide us in terms of global business ethics?

DISCUSSION QUESTIONS

1. Which of the benefits of globalization is the strongest argument in favor of it? Why? Which of the criticisms is the strongest argument against globalization? Why?

2. Workers in some countries such as Indonesia will use their employment relationship as an opportunity to enhance their personal living conditions: selling company inventory and keeping the money, siphoning fuel oil from company tanks and selling it on the black market, or selling access to the bidding process to potential suppliers. How would you handle the situation if you were a manager working in that type of culture and found your workers doing this?

3. Should MNCs be bound by the prevailing morality of the home country and act everywhere they do in their own country? Or should they follow the practices of the host country? Or are there special ethical standards that apply when business is conducted across national boundaries? If so, what are these standards?

4. If you accept a gift but resist the temptation to treat the gift giver with favoritism in future business dealings, how might it be argued that you are still participating in and even making stronger a corrupt system that undermines freedom of competition?

ETHICAL VIGNETTES TO DISCUSS

For each of the following vignettes, apply the biblical story themes to discern what is right and wrong.

1. You work for an international NGO that, among other things, manages the logistics of obtaining and delivering food to persons who have suffered after catastrophic weather events around the world.[47] After a devastating earthquake in a mountainous region of a developing country, your organization arranges for several truckloads of food and water to be sent to the villages directly affected. Two armed factions have been fighting in this region for a decade. One faction is supported by the government. The other is considered rebels by the government. It is your job to see that the food and water gets through. Your trucks are loaded and have traveled to the region. But you need to get permission to get the trucks to the final destination. A local official says that to make sure the food is delivered safely in a timely manner to the people who need it most, and delivered so that the resources do not fall into the hands of the rebels, you need to pay him. Delivery of a large quantity of food and water is not a routine government action. From one point of view, it seems like the right thing to pay some money so that the suffering people can get food and water. Yet you know that if the money you pay is a large sum, it could be used in the armed struggle even against innocent people. These resources may be just what are needed to save some people from dying. Yet, under the FCPA, paying money might be cause for prosecuting you. What is the right thing to do?

2. Your firm, West African Oil & Gas, Inc., has just secured the rights to explore for and drill to extract crude oil and natural gas off shore from Togo, West Africa.[48] Your company lawyers are well aware of the Foreign Corrupt Practices Act. They require your accountants to document in great detail every meeting with Togo government officials. You make an audio re-

cording of every meeting and then make written transcripts of the meetings. These are placed on file for later reference. During the negotiations with the Togo government Minister for Natural Resources, you learn that your company is required to work in partnership with a local Togo energy firm named Togo Gas & Oil. You are given the name of the president of this firm but no other information. Your lawyers conduct a thorough investigation into this firm but find little information that is substantial. All of the results of this research are carefully documented also. Months later your exploration and drilling teams have identified the best spots off shore to start drilling. The first oil and gas drilling platforms have been built. Your investors, who collectively have placed billions of dollars at risk by investing in your firm, are eager to see what kind of cash is generated from these new off-shore operating units. It is at this point that someone in your firm finds out that the Togo firm is really owned by the Togo Minister for Natural Resources. It is a private firm. Your lawyers counsel you that the revenue generated from the oil and natural gas will likely be used by him and his family rather than for the benefit the citizens of Togo. He is about to become wealthy beyond belief as he shares in the revenue from all the oil and gas that is sold from the off-shore drilling sites. Coincidently it is within a few days of this that you receive a call from the US Attorney's office. The attorney says that his office saw a notice regarding the firm Togo Gas & Oil doing business with your firm. The attorney would like to know the details of the relationship. Your attorneys turn over all the records related to this project to the US Attorney's office. Your attorneys believe that based on the information available to you at the time the deal was struck and after your firm conducted its diligent investigation, your company has not broken any provisions of the Foreign Corrupt Practices Act. But you wonder about something else: Should West African Oil & Gas, Inc., continue its relationship with Togo Gas & Oil now that you believe the Togo firm is privately owned by the very official who negotiated the deal with your firm?

PART FOUR

WIDENING THE PERSPECTIVE

Part IV explores the application of ethical decision making and accountability to the larger level of society and the economic system.

Social responsibility is a popular topic among faith-based universities. The fundamental issues in social responsibility are introduced in chapter nineteen. This chapter will clear up some misunderstandings that some Christians have regarding the proponents of the narrow view.

Another debatable issue for Christians involves the question of how much government involvement is appropriate. Evaluating the morality of economic systems is a debated issue among Christians as they search for ways to live the life of faith in a global context. These issues are introduced in chapter twenty.

Chapter twenty-one introduces the ideas of moral muteness and how to counteract pressure from others to compromise values. We employ the biblical story themes one last time to consider some of these central issues.

19

Corporate Responsibility

SCRIPTURE PASSAGE

Thus says the LORD,
"Preserve justice, and do righteousness,
for My salvation is about to come
And My righteousness to be revealed."
(Is 56:1)

CHAPTER OVERVIEW

In this chapter we wrestle with the issues in the debate over corporate responsibility. In particular we will

- review how corporate responsibility became a popular concern

- explore the complexity of measuring the business reasons for and against engaging in responsible actions

- review the arguments for and against the broad view of corporate social responsibility

- introduce the idea of sustainable development

- explore corporate responsibility issues through the lens of biblical story themes

MAIN TOPICS

How Corporate Responsibility Became Popular

The Business Case for Corporate Responsibility

What Have We Learned?
Arguments in Favor of a Broad View
Arguments Opposed to a Broad View
Sustainable Development
Down to the Nitty-Gritty
Through the Lens of Biblical Themes

KEY TERMS

business case, corporate responsibility, eco-efficiency, market stakeholders, non-market stakeholders, negative externalities, sustainable development, triple bottom line

OPENING SCENARIO

Meet two executives: Andrew C. and Julius R. Each has a different opinion regarding how his businesses should help society.[1]

Andrew has the firm belief that the best way business can help society is for his company to make as much money as possible and then to give away as much money as possible to help with communities. Money from the profits earned by the firm should be donated to help build community resources such as hospitals, schools and museums. Andrew even believes that this is a religious duty before God. Some of his executive friends are not Christians, but they agree with Andrew regarding how their companies should help society: make money and then become philanthropists by giving money to worthy causes.

Julius is of the mind that his company can prosper only if the well-being of his customers' businesses can be fostered. He sets about to identify a few of the key issues that his target customers are struggling with in their businesses. He provides opportunities to learn better techniques. He provides training in new technology. He encourages young people to work for his customers' business or to start a small business of their own in the same industry. As the prosperity of his customers' businesses increases, Julius begins selling them products which will make their work and the lives of their families even better. And he becomes wealthy doing it.

Which approach to corporate responsibility is best?

Andrew C. is none other than Andrew Carnegie (1835–1919), the owner of Carnegie Steel Company in Pennsylvania. Carnegie was known for his ability to make healthy profits making and selling steel and then for giving away to communities millions of dollars of his personal wealth.

Julius R. is Julius Rosenwald (1862–1932), a clothing manufacturer. In 1895, along with a partner, Rosenwald purchased Sears Roebuck & Company, one of the companies that had been distributing clothing made by his factory. It was during his leadership at Sears that Rosenwald began to help family farm businesses to flourish. Along the way his mail-order business mushroomed into a multimillion-dollar business.

Fast forward a hundred years, and we can see that the variety of corporate responsibility initiatives has increased. Some firms give money or other resources toward the alleviation of a social problem that may or may not be related to the firm's products and services. Microsoft Youthspark program links young people with educational and vocational opportunities. The Hershey Company, makers of chocolate, supports Family Health International, which helps to address the problem of malaria by distributing thousands of mosquito bed nets to families.

Other companies make changes to how they do business with suppliers or customers so that the impact of just doing their business has a positive effect on society. Companies like Ben and Jerry's Ice Cream believe that purchasing ingredients through fair trade practices expresses corporate responsibility.[2] Best Buy, a popular retailer of electronics products, expresses corporate responsibility through participating in technology recycling programs. People can bring their old electronics products to Best Buy stores. Kellogg's, maker of popular breakfast cereals, promotes sustainable agriculture by helping to minimize the environmental impacts of agricultural production, assisting the agricultural sector in being more sustainable and promoting and supporting sustainable growing practices.

Another way to express corporate responsibility is to address one or more social issues that are important to the strategic commitments the firm is making in its market.[3] For every pair of shoes that Toms Shoes sells, it gives a pair away to a child who needs shoes. North Face sells outdoor clothing and equipment. By partnering with BlueSign, North Face was able to control the amount of water, chemicals and energy used in production processes. They reduced the use of solvents and water and reduced the amount of carbon dioxide produced. These improvements also saved the firm $5 million per year.

The issues surrounding corporate responsibility are sometimes complicated. An executive might refrain from increasing the price of a product in order to contribute to the social concern of preventing inflation even though a price increase would be in the best interests of the company. In a competitive environment, such a decision might come at a cost. Out of altruism an executive might authorize capital expenses to reduce pollution beyond the amount that is in the best interest of the corporation or that required by law to contribute to the improving of the environment.[4] This decision will almost assuredly increase the cost of doing business. Is this what the executive should do? What are the limits of what a company is expected to do in society? These and other questions continue to be asked in society.

HOW CORPORATE RESPONSIBILITY BECAME POPULAR

If we have a broad definition of corporate responsibility such as one that includes any ethical concerns about business in society, it is safe to say that corporate responsibility has been a concern of some people for hundreds if not thousands of years. It might not be an exaggeration to say that as long as there has been the social activity of trading, there have been social concerns over the impact of business on society.

In the sixteenth century, Martin Luther wrote about his concerns regarding business activities of his day.[5] Among other things, Luther was concerned that international trade was draining local currency in exchange for luxury goods from South Asia and the Far East. Pricing policies of local merchants also concerned Luther. He described several dirty tricks that merchants were pulling on customers. Before Luther and since his day, Christians have had a difficult time accepting the organizations in the marketplace.[6]

The impact on society of the Industrial Revolution has included reactions from humanists and Christians alike. Business has a mixed effect on society. Advancements in technology, some say, have resulted in increased efficiencies and wider distribution of products formerly available only to the wealthy and have increased the wealth of everyone. Technological advances in one industry encouraged applications in other industries. But business, others claim, has also had a negative impact on society in terms of its effect on the environment and its influence on community life.

Concerns over social responsibility might more properly be called concerns over corporate social irresponsibility. Eastern logging companies swoop into the Appalachian Mountains, buy up large forests, clear-cut them for wood and leave the mountains exposed to damaging soil erosion. Alongside the concerns over business irresponsibility we find examples of companies who seem to be ahead of their time in terms of interests in communities and social causes.

It was in the 1950s and thereafter when concerns over the responsibilities of business in society gathered momentum.[7] Public awareness of unintended side effects—negative externalities—became more focused.[8] Paper factories were polluting the air and water. Clearing land for the construction of a new factory has an impact on the local habitat of animals and birds. The smoke from iron ore refineries fell in the form of acid rain, which harmed the trees in New England states.

Rachel Carson's *Silent Spring* helped launch the modern environmental movement.[9] The pollution in the Cuyahoga River near Cleveland, Ohio, was so great in 1969 that chemicals in the river caught fire. The event sparked outrage. Media coverage of situations involving ethical lapses, mistreatment of workers or environmental catastrophes fueled public outrage of what were increasingly being considered irresponsible behaviors.

Using copy machines, fax machines and telephones, college students and activists joined with sympathetic lawmakers to organize and promote the first Earth Day on April 22, 1970, in the United States. The rising tide of public sentiment found a corresponding debate among scholars of several disciplines, including business. This had the effect of firmly establishing a stream of publications which had a corresponding impact on how business courses and other subjects were taught in universities.[10]

Momentum increased in the 1990s as independent organizations formed for the purpose of monitoring, reporting, certifying and accrediting the corporate responsibility actions of corporations who voluntarily chose to participate.[11] For example, the CAUX Round Table and other organizations were established to promote a set of measurable corporate responsibility standards.

Corporate responsibility[12] refers to a broad range of issues relevant to the ethical, social and legal environment of business and the impact of business on this environment. Accordingly, business has responsibilities that span a broad array of relationships with stakeholders. Market stakeholders (suppliers, customers, strategic business partners, investors) are those who have business relationships with the firm. Non-market stakeholders (society in general, media, government) do not transact business with the firm but have an interest in the firm as it has an impact on their experience in society.

Corporate social responsibility (CSR) has been defined in terms of the "means that a corporation should be held accountable for any of its actions that affect people, their communities, and their environment. It implies that harm to people and society should be acknowledged and corrected if at all possible. It may require the company to forgo some profits if its social impacts seriously hurt some of its stakeholders or if its funds can be used to have a positive social impact."[13] Social obligations often come down to deciding what actions to mandate. The challenge is that social choices may involve the balancing of competing values, interests and costs.[14]

One of the obligations of a for-profit organization is to generate a return on investment to the investors. Responsible profit making benefits not only the investors. It also benefits the relationship that the organization has with other key stakeholders. Only by earning a profit can an organization remain in business to serve customers and employees. There is value in profit. But the organization is not obligated to maximize its profit at the expense of other stakeholders.

These descriptions reflect a broad view of corporate responsibilities. A narrower view limits corporate responsibility to earning a profit within the guidelines of the law and generally accepted moral principles. As we will see below, the narrow view sees profit making as an inherently socially responsible action.

> For every beast of the forest is Mine,
> The cattle on a thousand hills.
> I know every bird of the mountains,
> And everything that moves in the
> field is Mine.
> If I were hungry, I would not tell you;
> For the world is Mine, and all it
> contains. (Ps 50:10-12)

THE BUSINESS CASE FOR CORPORATE RESPONSIBILITY

One of the most important issues in the debate over corporate responsibility is the impact on the businesses whose managers take responsible actions.

Elements of corporate responsibility. As we have seen, corporate responsibility means different things to different organizations depending on their situation. Companies in some industries are concerned about the environmental impact of business operations. Others, because of social pressures, are more concerned about human rights of employees. Corporate responsibility is multidimensional; it has potential impact on economic performance of the firm, political influence in society, making contributions to social welfare and affecting the natural environment. Considering these differences and the variety of issues the companies face, we note the broad scope of corporate responsibility actions.[15]

Actions that promote eco-efficiency illustrate the two major viewpoints regarding corporate responsibility and the environment.[16] In one view, economic prosperity for the firm is the focus. In this view, actions that a company takes to minimize its impact on the natural environment are actions which result in a reduction of economic waste. When a company changes its energy use so that it leaves a smaller carbon footprint from company operations, it is lowering its operational expenses. Eco-efficiency is little more than doing the smart thing in order to maximize profit. In the other view, reducing harmful emissions into the environment and recycling waste materials are actions that reduce the harmful by-products of economic prosperity. In this view, the eco-efficient actions are the responsible thing to do for the good of the environment.

SCOPE OF CORPORATE RESPONSIBILITY

- Corporate ethics and principles guide overall company actions
- Accountability and transparency in reporting corporate responsibility to others such as by using a triple bottom line approach for reporting. Triple bottom line reports include reports of financial results (traditional financial statements), reports of social impact and reports of environmental impact.
- Minimizing the impact of company operations on the environment (eco-efficiency)
- Designing products to have reduced impact on the environment during manufacture, use and disposal or recycling
- Contributing to the social and economic development of the communities in which the company does business
- Protecting human rights of workers
- Promoting a healthful, safe work environment
- Encouraging business partners to participate in corporate responsibility initiatives
- Having a responsible corporate influence on stakeholders that are external to the business relationship (society as a whole, government organizations)

Measuring the impact on business. The two perspectives described in the paragraph above illustrate the importance of knowing the financial and social impacts on the business when it engages in corporate responsible actions that benefit others.[17] Support for corporate responsibility has become widespread and commonplace among many businesses; however, it is irresponsible to think about all the good the firm should do for others in society without considering the impact of its actions on itself.

Walmart found a way to save hundreds of thousands of dollars from its stores' operational expenses by removing light bulbs that illuminate the inside of the food vending machines located in its stores. Manufacturing companies such as Ford are finding ways to reduce the amount of water used, which results in savings of hundreds of thousands of dollars. These are two of the many examples that can be found by reviewing company reports of their corporate actions that can be considered responsible.

For some actions it is relatively easy to measure the impact on the operational efficiency of the firm (its expenses). But there are many other possible business impacts that are more difficult to measure objectively. These include the following:[18]

- Improving the performance of the company's stock price. It may be difficult to show causal relationship between specific corporately responsible actions and stock price.
- Increasing revenue.
- Reducing the cost of and improving the access to capital from selling stock or getting loans.

REGARDING MEASURES

You manage what you measure.

Your measures reveal your priorities.

- Stimulating customer demand. For some products customer demand may be stimulated because of corporate socially responsible actions. But for other products it is much more difficult to measure demand that is caused by such actions.
- Strengthening the reputation of the brand.
- Improving the ability to recruit and retain knowledgeable employees.
- Reducing risks.
- Contributing to innovation of new products or new ways of doing business.

From this we learn that measuring the impact on a firm is not as straightforward as we might prefer. Data used to evaluate impacts are not always as objective as we might prefer. Companies use different measures to report the impact of their actions. This makes it difficult to compare the impact on similar companies. When firms report, they may select only certain measures that contribute to a positive perception of the firm and not report other measures that might show the firm in a less positive light.

Measuring impact quantitatively depends on the situation the company is in, the geographic location of its operating units (or of those of its close business partners) and its relationship with particular stakeholder groups, each of which has a different set of interests.

The variety of business measures illustrates that each stakeholder group has something slightly different in focus when it is concerned about corporate responsibility. Each stakeholder group wants to evaluate a slightly different set of information. One stakeholder group might be concerned about how the firm (or its suppliers) treats employees. Another stakeholder group is interested in the impact of that firm's actions on the natural environment. Still another stakeholder group will be concerned about the long-term commitment of a firm to move toward renewable, sustainable sources of energy. Another stakeholder group will be concerned with minimizing expenses, improving the revenue stream or both.

WHAT HAVE WE LEARNED?

What have we learned in terms of the measurable impacts of corporate responsibility? In summarizing the results of many studies and many corporate reports of social responsibility, scholars conclude that corporate responsibility has a positive impact on the firm under some circumstances but not others.[19]

Some positive effects can be measured that seem to be caused by corporate responsible actions. Notably, the dimensions of social responsibility that have had the strongest positive impact on the firm are eco-efficiency initiatives such as changes made in the use of materials, recycling and reductions of harmful emissions to air, land and water. Protection of human rights, improving the working conditions for employees, relationships with strategic business partners and improving the transparency of reporting the impact of the firm also have a strong positive impact on firms. Managing risks is generally improved when firms are more eco-efficient, protect human rights, protect the corporate reputation by responsible actions and develop products that are environmentally friendly.

Some corporate responsibility initiatives have either a neutral or negative impact on the performance of the firms. For example, encouraging strategic business partners (suppliers, buyers) to engage in corporate responsible action has a weak impact on the business's performance. Participating with nonbusiness

stakeholders in corporate responsible activities has no impact on the firm's performance. Some responsible actions by some firms have a negative impact on firm performance.

Primacy of business benefits debated. For many the business benefits from engaging in corporate responsible actions should be first in importance. Managers have stewardship responsibility to watch out for the interests of the organization. The organization cannot serve society effectively if it is hamstrung financially because it spends too much money on actions that benefit others. Thus, when socially beneficial actions are criticized, it is often concern over the financial well-being of the firm that is in focus, and such concerns are launched mostly from outside the firm by stakeholders who have no stewardship responsibilities over the company's assets.

Some criticize firms for not engaging in socially responsible actions or for holding to the primacy of the business benefits for responsible actions. Their concern is that the economic performance of the firm is too dominant in the decision-making processes of company managers. Focusing too strongly on the economic and political interests of the firm, they argue, is what leads firms to take actions that are irresponsible.

Doing well versus doing good. Another point of discussion worth considering here is the question of causation.[20] The practical outcome of this issue is that managers' choice of activities will be influenced by which assumption they hold to be true. Does doing well financially makes it possible for the firm to do good (in society, such as through corporate philanthropy)? Or is it that doing good for society makes it possible for a company to do well financially? This discussion is illustrated by figure 19.1.

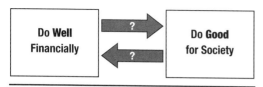

Figure 19.1. Doing well or doing good: Which should be the priority?

Some people suggest that in the long run, as businesses learn how to do good and at the same time find opportunities to do well financially, they will make lasting contributions to society. But without the ability to make a profit, business is shackled in its ability to serve social interests.

Morality versus immorality of profit. In some discussions of corporate responsibility it is assumed that making a profit is incompatible with carrying out social responsibilities.[21] This often unspoken assumption may be at the root of some of the disagreements over corporate responsibility.

These issues in the debate illustrate the variety of perspectives that can be used when deciding the limits of a company's responsibilities. Some support a broad view while others support a narrower view. The broad view is that, in addition to pursuing profit within the law, the firm has responsibility to the broader society in which it operates. Such responsibility, though often ambiguous, is to contribute to the overall well-being of society apart from the profit that might be made by the firm. The narrow view is that responsibility is limited pursuing profit within the constraints of the law and generally accepted moral principles.

ARGUMENTS IN FAVOR OF A BROAD VIEW

Those who support the idea that corporations should be socially responsible in ways that exceed the law represent several points of view.

Social contract.[22] The fundamental social contract between society and businesses is based on the fact that society gives business license (permission) to operate through government administrative procedures. Such permission is a privilege that comes with expectations to live up to the terms of the moral demands of the social contract. It is true that managers have responsibilities to stockholders. However, the stockholder can always sell the stock. Society is stuck with the enterprise. Business has a relationship with society that surpasses minimum legal requirements. The identifying of moral responsibilities may be the most fundamental of all management actions. Similar to the idea of social contract is that of covenant. Humans organize their efforts for the purpose of serving humans—business is a social enterprise. The minimum standard beyond the law, while it may be slowly changing as culture changes, is relatively easy to define.

The Golden Rule.[23] The Golden Rule has practical and biblical dimensions: "Do unto others as you would have them do unto you." If we desire others to treat us in a manner that is right, just and fair, then we should be concerned about how we treat them. The practical fallacy in this is that the world is full of people who might well say, "We'll take our chances on your treatment of us in the future, after we try to get what we want now. And if we get what we want now, we won't have to worry about how you will treat us in the future." Unless you have the biblical foundation integrated into your belief structure as part of your whole outlook on life, reciprocity alone can be an unsatisfying solution.

Law is limited.[24] It would be nice if the law were complete. It is not. Laws are insufficient as a guide because they do not cover all aspects or gray areas of a problem. Regulations are not complete either.

Corporate power must be balanced with responsibility.[25] Businesses have been given (loaned) social power. With power comes the iron law of moral responsibility to act in ways that use the power in a just manner. This is a principle that has come down to us from the Judeo-Christian tradition: To whom much is given, much will be required.[26] Businesses have a role as one of the trustees of society's resources. Businesses operate in a two-way, open system with their environments. Because of this businesses should disclose relevant information to the environment with which they have an interdependent relationship. The analysis of economic costs and benefits of key decisions needs to be balanced with an analysis of the social costs. Businesses need to build into the price of products the social costs of product consumption. Businesses develop areas of competence that should be used for social involvement in places where the social needs can be met by these competencies. When the action a business takes is economically important, the moral duties with that action also become more important.

The long run.[27] Here proponents sometimes follow the principle of enlightened self-interest. Companies must meet their short-term obligations, but at the same time they have a responsibility to sustain a viable future for the environment. Business is in an interdependent relationship with society. Successful businesses need a successful society. If business makes decisions at the expense of society, its success will be only temporary. Ultimately such businesses will become weakened and will be less capable of serving society. Beyond reciprocity is the concern for the quality of our own lives and that of succeeding generations. If we have any thoughts about the kind of society we are structuring for both the near term and the long term, we should think about our responsibilities to others. A basic question is, Do we have an obligation to leave the world a little better than when we found it, or may we take what we want now and let other people, including the next generation, worry about making up for any shortfall?

Prevents the need for government regulation.[28] When businesses take a proactive stance, society will not pressure lawmakers to set the minimum legal standard. It is only when companies act against the interests of society that lawmakers must step in and restrain business.

Reputation of the firm.[29] On the positive side, businesses should view altruistic behaviors as an investment in future goodwill of society. Doing the right thing matters to many people these days. Public awareness is higher than it has been in several years. Incorporating social responsibility concerns into business decision making has good public relations value. Damage to reputation cannot be directly measured, but the deterioration of relationships, declining employee productivity, creativity and loyalty, ineffective information flow through the organization, absenteeism and difficulty recruiting and retaining the most competent employees are all costs of being uninterested in social responsibility at work. Business is a social process. It is becoming increasingly difficult to succeed in the marketplace. This increased difficulty presents the challenge of individuals and groups working in collaboration. When businesses act in socially responsible ways, this builds community cooperation and support. Socially responsible action provides the basis for the community to trust the business. Without trust, commitment cannot follow.

Corrects social problems caused by business.[30] Businesses that act responsibly will correct their mistakes and not leave to another generation or to society negative economic externalities to clean up after them.

ARGUMENTS OPPOSED TO A BROAD VIEW

Opponents of the broad view of corporate responsibility also come from a variety of perspectives. Their view is narrower; it limits the responsibility of business to the pursuit of profit under the law and within generally accepted moral principles. Some base their arguments on two pillars of a free-market economy: property rights and economic theory. Others turn to a discussion of the primary purpose of business.

Primary responsibility.[31] Managers have direct, legal responsibilities to the owners of the corporation. The manager has been hired as an agent of the principal. That responsibility is to conduct business in accordance with the owner's desires, which generally means to build economic performance in lawful ways and to conform to the principles embodied in ethical custom. Correspondingly, management's first responsibility to society is to shareholders by working hard to generate a economic performance. A business that does not show a profit that is at least equal to its cost of capital is socially irresponsible because this is a waste of society's resources. Without positive economic performance a company cannot fulfill any of its other responsibilities. Wealth is a primary consideration, but it is not the only consideration. The rule of law must be followed when determining business conduct. But the rule of law must not be allowed unnecessarily to interfere with the workings of the market.

Property rights. If the market system is expected to grow the wealth of society, owners of property must be protected from illegitimate claims against that which they own. It is the manager's job to protect the property of the owner. Taking actions that support social causes lowers economic efficiency and profits that rightfully belong to owners.

Costs and stakeholders.[32] The more socially responsible your firm becomes, the higher the unit production costs become compared with competitors; this fact gives competitors an unfair advantage. Supporting social causes by spending the firm's capital is a form of discretionary altruism that becomes an illegitimate claim on (theft of) the property that belongs to owners. If such an action results in lowering wages, the manager is stealing from employees. If the action results in higher prices, the manager is stealing from customers.

Authority of business.[33] Business is just one social institution among many. All social institutions have responsibilities toward society. Other social institutions (e.g., government, education, religion) do not always fulfill their responsibilities to society. It is inappropriate for leaders in these other social institutions to point fingers at business in an attempt to saddle business with a disproportionate amount of responsibility when other social institutions are unwilling to exercise their social responsibilities. Society is too complex to put social responsibilities on just one of the social institutions.

The route to social welfare.[34] Business may not be the best entity for discharging the duties of stewardship and philanthropy. Company managers are individuals who can decide how to spend their personal earnings. As such they are acting as a principal and not an agent. But if the manager makes a decision to expend cash for the purpose of social responsibility, this is tantamount to taxation without representation. This is a government function.

Punishment for corporate wrongdoers. The market may be the best place to carry out punishment of irresponsible firms. When a company crosses the line to social irresponsibility, consumers will go away, people will lobby lawmakers, and aggrieved plaintiffs will bring lawsuits to force the firm to make changes. This will be reflected in the organization's balance sheet and income statement. Liabilities will be incurred. Legal expenses and potentially punitive fines will increase expenses. The market is a wonderfully efficient mechanism to weed out the firms that mishandle their social responsibility. Where the market is unable to punish wrongdoers, government regulations can.

Confronting power.[35] Socially focused behaviors of the firm may not be the best way to confront corporate power. External monitoring groups can do no more than to call for voluntary submission to corporate responsibility standards. And a very small proportion of all companies worldwide voluntarily participate. Proponents of corporate responsibility hope that businesses will foster justice; however, without confronting the power of the firms, justice will not be achieved. Furthermore, when pressure comes from society for companies to change social behaviors, some firms look for a different setting in which they do business. They move their company operations to developing countries that have less scrutiny over the social impact of business.

Inappropriate executive dilemma. The executive role is inappropriate to handle the difficult dilemmas posed by social ills. How can we expect company executives to decide which social causes to support and which ones not to support? On what basis should we expect business executives to be competent in righting social ills such as poverty, inflation or pollution? On what basis would the corporate executive make the decision as to which social cause is better than another?

SUSTAINABLE DEVELOPMENT

If you take the idea of corporate responsibility and scale it up and extend it to a full scope of applications, where do you end up? You end up with the concept of sustainable development.

Embedded in the phrase "sustainable development" are two kernels of truth. "Sustainable" refers to providing care for the entire earth such that the present generation and future generations can enjoy the rich, bountiful earth at the same time as conserving resources and sustaining the ecology. "Development" recognizes the need for humans to use earth's resources to meet the economic needs of an ever-expanding population but in a way that supports persons in community while caring for the environment. Accordingly, sustainable development has been defined as "meeting the needs of the present generation without compromising the ability of future generations to meet their own needs."[36]

There are a variety of perspectives on the elements of sustainable development objectives.[37] Justice, ecosystem resilience, economic progress, durability and efficiency are commonly mentioned as values. When considering the various points of view the common denominators seem to be the dual ideas of justice, ecosystem resilience and efficiency.

Most proponents of sustainable development include not only the current generation but also future generations.

The World Commission on Environment and Development was not the first to raise awareness of the problems of environment and development; however, its timing was important. Coming at a time when the arms race also had peaked, the Commission first met in October of 1984. The race for natural resources had been going on for decades but was picking up momentum. For over two years Commission members worked to create a report on the key issues. Their report included the following findings:[38]

- The environmental crisis is inseparable from the economic crisis and the energy crisis.

- Accelerating population growth, especially in urban areas.

- Most of the growth of industrial production has occurred since 1950.

- The resources gap is widening between the "have" nations and the "have not" nations.

- The influence of industry in policymaking is heavy; yet the industrial sector has used much of the planet's ecological capital. For decades industries have taken more out of the earth than they have put back.

- The needs of small farms have been largely ignored in developing countries.

- Natural resources in some countries such as Latin America were being used to pay down national debts instead of for development.

- Poverty and unemployment increased.

- Institutions that are interested in finding solutions to specific problems tend to work independently of other institutions trying to solve other problems that are related.

- Economies of countries are linked worldwide. It is not just the economy of a few particular nations that need further development, but the entire world economy needs to be developed in a way that is sustainable rather than unsustainable.

- Some population groups are more vulnerable than other groups. The vulnerable need to be protected.

- Political stability, peace and security also must be established otherwise the other problems cannot be managed.

- Shared leadership is needed to change the policies of nations and international organizations that all nations can agree upon. New policies must emerge from international cooperation and within international legal frameworks.

Economic development needed to be sustained, but the environment also needed to be sustained and cared for, and the poor also needed care. Clearly, these somewhat competing interests needed to be managed together rather than separately. Needed was coordination among government organizations, nongovernment organizations, cultural organizations, scientific researchers and commerce, just to name a few of the key players. Other initiatives related to the work of the World Commission have produced guidelines for businesses, especially multinational enterprises. For example, the UN Global Compact and the CAUX Principles offer guidelines for business in terms of sustainable development.

Following the work of the World Commission, in 1992 the United Nations established the UN Commission on Sustainable Development. In 2009 the UN General Assembly adopted a resolution to convene a Conference on Sustainable Development 2012.

During the intervening years in over a dozen sessions convened by the Commission, the ideas of sustainable development have also become one of the most popular themes across economic sectors and around the world. Goals have been established to guide the efforts of the world community of nations and institutions.

These goals of sustainable development, and the dialogue that has arisen among members of the UN Commission related entities, are essentially attempts to reconcile, or find ways to manage, the sometimes competing goals of economics, social justice for current and future generations, and responsible care for the earth over the long term.

Caring for the poor must include eliminating the twins poverty and hunger. If poverty and hunger are not eliminated or drastically reduced, these evils will diminish the ability of the earth and communities to provide for all. The physical and political safety of food and communities will be threatened. The burden of poverty could become an excessive constraint on economic development. Economic development assumes that most people are contributing to their own needs as well as the needs of others. By caring for the earth in a sustainable way, we increase the carrying capacity of the earth to the benefit of all. Economic development also must encompass rich and poor. To accomplish this, eliminating poverty and hunger requires sharing wisdom.

We conclude that discussions of sustainable development are essentially attempts to reconcile, or find ways to manage, the sometimes competing goals of economics, social justice for current and future generations and responsible care for the earth.

This chapter raises fundamental questions about a firm and its responsibilities to society. This is another way of asking fundamental questions: What is the purpose of business? Is it merely to make a profit or is it something bigger? Readers who wish to explore these deeper questions should read appendix F in conjunction with this chapter.

DOWN TO THE NITTY-GRITTY

Think about scenario at the beginning of this chapter. You are a vice president of a company preparing to make a presentation to the top-level leadership team regarding the best way to approach corporate responsibility. Should you take the Andrew Carnegie approach or the Julius Rosenwald approach? Which approach to corporate responsibility is best? It's time to get down to the nitty-gritty (see table 19.1)!

THROUGH THE LENS OF BIBLICAL THEMES

This part of the chapter will use the biblical story themes as a lens through which to evaluate the topic featured in the chapter. Because the themes are interrelated and interdependent, we should expect to see some overlap in the thinking regarding the issues. Some themes will contribute the same thinking as will other themes. The power of these themes comes from their guidance when a community of people talks about complicated ethical dilemmas faced in business practice.

A close parallel exists between the UN Commission goals and biblical ideas. An important difference also exists: faith relationship with God is characterized by loyalty to absolute, objective moral standards, which lie outside the human community. While the efforts of the UN Commission appear to be efforts toward shalom, nothing in the UN Commission's goals expresses the importance of spirituality and agreement upon fundamental, absolute moral principles.

Table 19.1. Applying the ethical process.

Keeping Your Heart: An Intrapersonal Process	Walking in the Community: An Interpersonal Process

• You are a vice president preparing to make a presentation on corporate responsibility. What does your heart say is the right thing to do regarding corporate responsibility?
• Which biblical themes explored in this book inform your heart on this question?
• Which biblical theme, if any, do you feel yourself resisting? Why do you feel resistance?
• What other influences in your heart seem to be prominent as you think about this situation?
  • Fundamental beliefs
  • Cognitive reasoning
  • Judgments and evaluations
  • Decisions
  • Virtues
  • Will
  • Memory of personal experiences with other people
  • Perceptions of others in the community
  • Personal biases
  • Awareness of interpersonal relationships
  • Commitments to God and to others
  • Intuitions
  • Conscience
  • Human spirit
  • Emotions
	• You are a vice president preparing to make a presentation on corporate responsibility. With whom might you have a conversation about the issues prior to your presentation? Who else might have a helpful perspective?
	• Who should take a leadership role in the conversation about corporate responsibility?
	• Which of the biblical themes in this chapter will most likely come up in the conversation either directly or indirectly? Why? Which one(s) will be the most influential in the conversation?
	• If you have a conversation with someone regarding this situation, which of the fundamental tensions presented earlier in the book might come up?
	• What right-versus-right dilemmas, if any, can be identified? Have a conversation with someone about this now. What is the outcome of the conversation?

Cosmic conflict. As we saw in chapter eighteen (on global business), the conflict between God and Satan is cosmic in scope. If the great conflict between God and Satan occurs in society worldwide as well as in human hearts, what does this say about the battle over sustainable development? Does it not suggest that ultimately the battle over sustainable development is a battle over our conception of God and his character, a battle over our worship to God? Developing this thought a bit further, we might take the perspective of Ignatius and view the earth ecosystems interconnected with earth's social systems as one, if not the chief, field of this cosmic battle. If the physical battlefield of this earth is lost because of human negligence, we contribute little to and probably detract from the divine war effort on the spiritual front. In losing the battle over sustainable development we literally give ground to the armies of the devil.

Creation. Sustainable development is clearly presented in the creation story. The good earth is available for humans to benefit from their labors of managing it. At the same time, humans were also given the responsibility to care for the earth.[39] These two thoughts are shown in table 19.2.

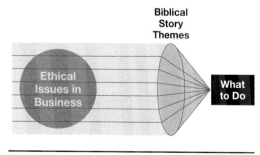

Figure 19.2. Evaluating an ethical process.

Holiness. In terms of sustainable development, the biblical story calls the land holy! It is set apart for a special purpose to serve all of God's creation. When humans abuse the land and take thoughtlessly without provision for its renewal, restoration and rejuvenation, we undermine the holiness of the land for ourselves.

Covenant relationships. Responsibility of enterprises is not a topic that is dealt with explicitly in the Bible. However, the biblical record on several issues may be helpful. Covenant relationships made provision for dealing with poverty through the gleaning laws.[40] Taking advantage of vulnerable community stakeholders (widows, orphans, strangers, legal aliens, disabled) was forbidden. The admonitions not to oppress others are squarely in the context of Israel's slavery in Egypt. Redemption from slavery should cause them to remember not to oppress others. In oppressing their own and others, they would essentially be returning to a culture of bondage from which they had been saved. Heads of the economic units (families) were expected to save 10 percent of their harvest to be contributed to sustenance of the temple and provide for the needs of those who were too poor to pay tithe.[41] As creation is linked with sustainable development, so too is covenant, as is illustrated in table 19.2.

Shalom. When corporate responsibility is narrowed to merely the economic impact on the firm and its close business partners, economic prosperity of the firm becomes isolated from the other dimensions of shalom. In turn, this undermines the idea of true prosperity considered in shalom. Shalom is a community-focused concern, not merely an individual concern. Focusing primarily on financial measures of performance and the degree to which socially responsible actions affect such performance glosses over the broader social context in which business is conducted.

Sabbath. The sabbath is inseparable from sustainable development in Scripture (see table 19.2). Sabbath encompasses all efforts for economic development and all responsibilities for sustaining the earth. Sabbath observance is an expression in action of our responsibilities.

The goals that have come from these international collaborative efforts, though mainly secular, find a parallel with sabbath-shalom

Table 19.2. Sabbath, the center of sustainable development in Scripture.

	Development	Sustainability
	Subdue the earth.	Serve the earth.
Creation	God blessed them; and God said to them, "Be fruitful and multiply, and fill the earth, and subdue it; and rule over the fish of the sea and over the birds of the sky, and over every living thing that moves on the earth." (Gen 1:28)	Then the LORD God took the man and put him into the garden of Eden to cultivate it and keep it. (Gen 2:15) And you shall not defile the land in which you live, in the midst of which I dwell; for I the LORD am dwelling in the midst of the sons of Israel. (Num 35:34)
		Sabbath
Covenant	Six days you shall labor and do all your work. (Ex 20:9) Six years you shall sow your field, and six years you shall prune your vineyard and gather in its crop. (Lev 25:3)	Remember the Sabbath day to keep it holy…in it you shall not do any work. (Ex 20:8,10) During the seventh year the land shall have a sabbath rest, a sabbath to the LORD; you shall not sow your field nor prune your vineyard. (Lev 25:4) Nor shall you glean your vineyard, nor shall you gather the fallen fruit of your vineyard; you shall leave them for the needy and for the stranger. (Lev 19:10)

principles rooted in creation and covenant. Additionally, these goals are examples of the deeper principles at work in sabbath keeping.

The biblical basis of sabbath comes from two other themes: creation and covenant. Some see that sabbath is the biblical basis of the Christian view on sustainable development. The following illustration shows the dual emphases in the sabbath concept directly from Scripture. In the creation account (Genesis) the commission to subdue the earth (development) is coupled with the purpose of serving the earth (sustainability). Also, the giving of the covenant (Exodus–Deuteronomy) includes directions for economic and technological development (work, pruning, harvest) that are constrained by keeping the weekly sabbath and the sabbatical. At the center of this is sabbath as shown in table 19.2.

Justice. Biblical justice is an all-encompassing idea that is to pervade the entire community. Justice is talked about in the biblical story as running like a stream throughout the land to feed and nourish the whole land with life-giving power. This suggests that all our social endeavors will be channels for justice and we will not limit what we define as ethics to only those actions related to lying, cheating and stealing in business transactions. Justice, like a large ocean liner, must have a wide berth at port, wide enough to encompass all.

Righteousness and truth. Corporate responsibility keeps in view the policies and strategic commitments of the entire organization while not forgetting that ethical decision making involves individual persons. While persons affect work teams, and work teams affect departments and divisions, and departments affect the whole organization, the whole organization has an effect on the larger communities in which it participates. This is an interesting setting in which to think of standing firm on principle and being faithful in the organization's relationships to these larger communities. It is in corporate responsibility that righteousness and truth run in close parallel. Here we are concerned about organizational faithfulness to covenant principles when tested by time and circumstance.

Wisdom. Covenant relationships work only when the participants act smart by nourishing long-term relationships with people and with the physical environment. Wisdom involves watching out for the economic interests of the future generation. The organization as a whole will, over time, develop collective wisdom for how to manage the ethical tensions that are faced. Top-level leaders have responsibility to see that this wisdom is disseminated to new workers and to managers.

Loving kindness. Just like persons who are in relationship to each other, organizations are in relationship to markets, industries, the government and the communities where they manage business operations. Loyalty is not founded on verbal promises but on repeated actions that support the relationships. Reciprocity will be encouraged among organizations, some of which will have more bargaining power and others will have less. Organizational leaders will shape organizational policies so that compassion and mercy are tempered with justice.

Redemption. At the organizational level, corporate responsibility is in close alignment with the root ideas of redemption. Living redemptively means that the organization will work to liberate the oppressed and rescue those who are vulnerable to being taken advantage of. Organizations will engage in sustainable development in order to participate in the redemption of society and the physical environment. This does not mean that business no longer needs the salvation provided only by God. Rather, it means that at the organizational level managers will participate with God in the renewal efforts meant to sustain life and resources for the future.

CHAPTER REVIEW QUESTIONS

1. What historical influences led to the idea of corporate responsibility becoming popular?

2. What should be considered when making a business case in support of corporate responsibility?

3. How do proponents of the broad view of corporate responsibility support their point of view?

4. What arguments do proponents of the narrow view of corporate responsibility offer in support of their position?

5. What is sustainable development?

6. What guidance do the biblical story themes offer when considering corporate responsibility?

DISCUSSION QUESTIONS

1. Is it right that a company with more bargaining power as a buyer with respect to its supplier uses its leverage to influence the supplier to engage in corporate responsible actions? Is it right that the company as a supplier with bargaining power with respect to its buyer(s) uses its leverage to influence the buyer(s) to engage in corporate responsible actions?

2. *Instrumental versus intrinsic.* The managers of some companies see corporate responsibility actions as primarily instrumental to benefit shareholder value. Such actions are primarily a means to an economic purpose

either because these are expected by society or required by law. Managers of other companies view corporate responsibility as an end in itself for the good it does for shareholders or for others. Intrinsically valuable responsible actions can also benefit society in general.[42] What is your perspective on this debate?

3. *Doing well, doing good.* In his article on corporate responsibility Peter Drucker said, "Business can discharge its 'social responsibilities' only if it converts them into 'self-interests,' that is, into business opportunities."[43] Do you agree or disagree? What is your rationale?

4. How far does corporate responsibility extend?

ETHICAL VIGNETTES TO DISCUSS

For each of the vignettes, apply the biblical story themes to evaluate the corporate responsibility efforts described.

1. Here are three important facts to consider: First, 80 percent of the world's garment workers are women, but most of them have few opportunities to advance in their knowledge and abilities. Second, thriving communities depend on the education and advancement of women. Third, when they get access to education and technical support, women are agents of real change for their families and their communities. The garment retail giant Gap, Inc., considered these facts and realized there is an opportunity to do something about it. Partnering with two other international organizations, Gap, Inc., created a new program called P.A.C.E., which stands for Personal Advancement and Career Enhancement.[44]

Launched in 2007, the program is designed to improve the education and abilities of female garment workers. Participation is voluntary for factories and workers. The program is adaptable to different cultures (garment workers are in many countries). Participants develop communication skills, problem solving skills, financial literacy and legal literacy. Results have been positive. Even after just one or two years of participating in the program, women in the P.A.C.E program improved their ability to influence their families' decision making, their ability to communicate with others regarding stresses at home and their ability to travel. The program spread to more than sixty factories in seven countries and during its first seven years had an impact on the lives of more than twenty thousand women.

2. Many people have heard about Toms Shoes program of corporate responsibility. You buy one pair of Toms shoes and the company will give one pair to someone in need. The company also provides eye care for each pair of shoes or sunglasses it sells. The shoe give-away program has been around since the founding of the company in 2006. The number of pairs the company has sold (and given away) numbers into the tens of millions. But Toms wanted to expand the concept of social entrepreneurship. So in 2013 the company launched Toms Marketplace to encourage socially conscious shoppers to support other social entrepreneurs who share the vision that business is not just about earning profits.[45] Through their website the company features the efforts and products of entrepreneurs who promote a variety of social causes in different countries.

Evaluating the Morality
of Political-Economic Systems

SCRIPTURE PASSAGE

Submit yourselves for the Lord's sake to every human institution, whether to a king as the one in authority, or to governors as sent by him for the punishment of evil-doers and the praise of those who do right. For such is the will of God that by doing right you may silence the ignorance of foolish men. (1 Pet 2:13-15)

CHAPTER OVERVIEW

In this chapter we will evaluate the morality of economic systems. In particular, we will

- review the characteristics of economic systems
- evaluate the strengths and weaknesses of free-market capitalism
- consider how the morality of contemporary economic systems can be judged
- consider contemporary economic systems through the lens of biblical story themes

MAIN TOPICS

Characteristics of an Economic System
Free-Market Capitalism: Strengths and
    Weaknesses

The Christian Critique and Response
Down to the Nitty-Gritty
Through the Lens of Biblical Themes

KEY TERMS

capitalism, free market, free-market capitalism, laissez-faire, socialism, socialist capitalism

OPENING SCENARIO

According to a report released by the labor union AFL-CIO in 2013, some chief executives of large corporations are paid more than 350 times what the average worker makes.[1] The labor group asserted that it takes just six hours for a highly paid CEO to earn what the average hourly worker earns in a whole year.

The income gap may be widening, which leads some people to worry that a redistribution of income is taking place where the rich are getting richer and the poor are getting poorer. Assuming that this is true, was this caused by the free-market capitalist economy run amuck?

The widening wage gap is just one of several debatable issues that are social currency in the twenty-first century. Controversial independent film producer Michael Moore has catalogued several unsavory effects of the free-market system that, in his opinion, needs radical reformation.[2] For example, in "The Productivity to Paycheck Gap: What the Data Show," Dean Baker cites strong increases in productivity enjoyed by US companies since 1973 while the real income of a typical worker rose very little.[3] Large US corporations earned record profits while at the same time laying off tens of thousands of workers. In 2008 a Rasmussen poll found that a little over half of American adults prefer capitalism over socialism while 20 percent believe that socialism is better.[4]

The gap in income comparing the compensation of top-level leaders with that of frontline employees is one important issue that is talked about in the marketplace. At the larger scale of nations, the gap between wealthy, developed nations and comparatively poor, underdeveloped nations also has captured public attention for years. At this scale the issues become more complicated, as do the solutions to the problems.

Over the years various critics have thought about the good and the bad of the broader economic systems in which they lived and worked. In modern times proponents of the free market evaluate state-controlled economic systems of socialist economies.[5] Supporters of socialism criticize the free-market systems.[6] Within Christianity supporters of the free market criticize socialist systems while others take the opposite view. Although there is not room here to account for all the details of this debate, we will consider the major themes that have emerged.

This chapter will provide a brief review of the differences between the free-market capitalist system and the socialist system that can be found in most introductory economics courses and textbooks. Before we can complete this comparison, we need to consider the characteristics of an economic system.

CHARACTERISTICS OF AN ECONOMIC SYSTEM

We arrive in this chapter at the place where we will look at the broader ethical, social and legal environment of business through the lens of scriptural story themes. Recall from chapter one that ethical and legal thinking can be applied to four levels (see fig. 20.1).

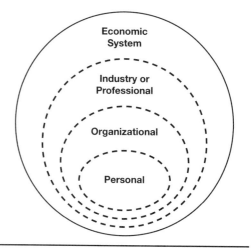

Figure 20.1. Four levels of application of morality, ethics and law.

An economic system is the collection of organizations and individuals that, when they work together, becomes society's answer to key questions about producing goods and services and trading things of value. These organizations include manufacturing companies, service companies, financial institutions, marketing and advertising firms, distribution companies, and many more. Of course we cannot forget that the economic system exists to serve customers! Hundreds of industries and millions of organizations make up the economic system of a typical Western nation. Figure 20.2 presents a highly simplified illustration of an economic system.

Two major economic systems (and variations of each) exist. "The great ideological struggle of the twentieth century has been be-

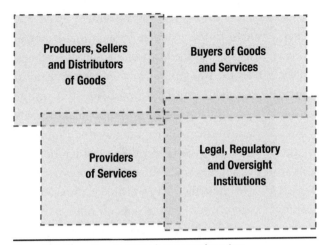

Figure 20.2. The active elements of an economic system.

cision making is decentralized regarding products and prices. Except for a few categories of natural resources, products and services, the market is free from direct control by the government or by a small group of persons. Coordination of production and distribution is accomplished by market forces. Price is the signal of value. Prices for most products and services are set by the market forces of supply and demand as both buyers and sellers place values on the things offered for sale in the market. Freedom to invest money in businesses results in competition.

tween collectivism and liberalism."[7] We sometimes refer to collectivism as socialism. Free-market capitalism is another way to describe liberalism. The term "free market" refers to the relatively limited involvement of civil government in the marketplace. In other words, in the capitalist system the market is more free of civil government intrusion when compared with the socialist system. In reality, most countries have a mix of both capitalism and socialism.

In all economic systems we observe production of goods and services that are traded in marketplaces. Workers are involved in the production of goods and the provision of services. Workers or their families are also consumers. Prices are used to signal to buyers and sellers the monetary value they place on the things that are traded.

As we explore the characteristics of an economic system we begin to see some of the differences between the capitalism and socialism.

Free-market capitalism. Under capitalism private entities (individuals, partners, investors) are the dominant parties that have discretion to accumulate money to invest in property, buildings and equipment needed for production and distribution of goods. De-

> Every person is to be in subjection to the governing authorities. For there is no authority except from God, and those which exist are established by God. Therefore whoever resists authority has opposed the ordinance of God; and they who have opposed will receive condemnation upon themselves. (Rom 13:1-2)

Socialism. Under socialism private entities (individuals, partners, investors) may be allowed to accumulate cash to invest in production and distribution of products, but government organizations also accumulate cash for use in operating businesses. In the more extreme forms of socialism, personal property can be owned, but the ownership of property used in production of goods and services may be more limited than in a free market. State-controlled bureaucracy is needed to manage industries and businesses operated by the government. Decision making is both decentralized and centralized regarding products and prices. Pricing may be set by market forces or government bureaucracy depending on the product. When prices are set by government bureaucrats, this tends to distort the information that price gives to customers.

One can also view the two different economic systems as two structural solutions to the questions related to production and distribution of goods. Each structural option comes with benefits and costs. Neither is perfect in itself. These two opposing types of systems can be seen as two ends of a continuum when we consider the degree to which civil government affects marketplace activities. This is illustrated in figure 20.3.[8]

To better understand the relationship between the two ends of the continuum, we might use the analogy of a traffic system to describe free-market capitalism.[9] The government makes and enforces basic traffic rules and sometimes provides repairs to keep the traffic moving along. The government is present by enforcing the rules of the road. The government also is a major customer of goods and services of business. We can bring socialism into the analogy if the government wants to increase its involvement by directing the flow of traffic in a particular direction or "for the benefit of particular groups."[10]

It is the degree of involvement by governments in the economic system that is one of the issues at the heart of many of the debates over the two types of system. Government involvement can have a positive effect on the economy; too much involvement and the government may unintentionally undermine the economic system from doing well at producing, distributing and trading goods and services.[11]

Without the civil government, the economic system would have a difficult time operating effectively. Even in a relatively free market, the government plays an important role. The government provides a certain minimum level of security and stability among the population by maintaining armed forces ready for defense. The government does not directly provide for worker safety; through regulations it mandates that a minimum level of safety be maintained by companies. In short, the government sets the rules for marketplace behaviors. The domestic justice system offers some, but not perfect, protection for persons and organizations against infringements of property rights. The Constitution, the rule of law and the justice system contribute to general domestic stability. The justice system also provides an impartial third-party means to handle business disputes. The government is the only entity authorized to create currency used in exchanges. The money supply is regulated by the government.

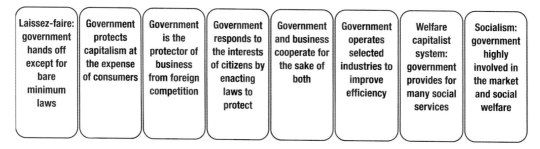

Figure 20.3. Government influence on the free market: a continuum.

Lawmakers and regulators respond to market injustices by making improvements in laws and regulations. In addition, the government is one of the largest customers of goods and services provided by the other two sectors of the economy. It can use its massive buying power to shape marketplace behaviors of both buyers and sellers. It manages large areas of private business. In addition, it uses its vast economic resources to meet social goals.

One way government can increase its involvement in the economic system is to produce and enforce more laws and regulations applicable to business and other organizations. More regulations tend to move a free-market economic system toward a socialist system. Another way is when government increases its involvement in providing public goods for protection or security or in other ways contributes to the overall well-being of society. A public good might be something as simple as a street lighting system that makes it safer for persons to walk at night. Or it might be something more complex (and expensive) such as the military, a healthcare system, an educational system, a road and bridge system, public transportation systems, a general welfare assurance system, and any number of other goods. Public goods are funded by tax revenues. Still another way government can increase its involvement is by subsidizing particular businesses or selected industries. Government can also create monopolies for the purpose of distributing utility resources such as water and electricity.

FREE-MARKET CAPITALISM: STRENGTHS AND WEAKNESSES

Having considered the characteristics of an economic system, including some of the structural tradeoffs (benefits and costs), we consider some of the strengths and criticisms of capitalism.

Free-market capitalism strengths. Vigorous supporters of free-market capitalism have put forward several ideas.[12]

Free-market capitalism promotes morality. Capitalism is based on sound moral principles of honesty and faithfulness to promises. These are principles common to any economic system.[13] The structure of the economic system promotes following these moral principles. Businesses have learned that to survive, customers must trust them. Likewise, suppliers must trust that they will be treated fairly and receive their payments as agreed. Accordingly, reputation is vital to market success with both buyers and sellers. The free-market system is sometimes criticized as promoting selfish self-interest. Sometimes buyers or sellers are tempted to abuse their market power. As much as the market encourages self-interest, it also promotes morality. The value of private property ownership prevents theft and general chaos in society. The presence of competition in the market acts as a moral check and balance to excessive self-serving behaviors. Business encourages the development of highly prized virtues of patience, honesty, self-control, prudence, courage, temperance, hope, faith and love. Furthermore, a free market teaches the value of cooperation, for it is only by cooperating in the marketplace that both buyers and sellers achieve their goals and society receives the benefits of the market.

Free-market capitalism promotes mutuality. This is related to the arguments of morality, because the players of the market are mutually interdependent. It is only the relative freedom of the market players that promotes this.

Free-market capitalism has an inherent moral legitimacy. A free market makes important contributions to the common good of society. It is the risk-taking entrepreneurs who create organizations which offer employment. It is the marketplace where persons and organizations exchange things of value that contribute to flourishing well-being.

Free-market capitalism promotes individualism. Individualism is sometimes criticized; however, the positive side of individualism is that it fosters respect for other persons, which is a fundamental moral principle of the free market. The free market is not nearly as individualistic as some critics try to describe it. The reason is that the family is still the primary economic unit of society. Thus, while individuals make purchase decisions based on self-interests, they cannot discount or forget the interests of others in their community. We, after all, are not merely individuals but rather persons in community.

Free-market capitalism is the most efficient among alternatives. One of the major problems that society as a whole experiences is the distribution of resources necessary for a flourishing life. The free market is an efficient coordinating mechanism. Prices are the signal to buyers and sellers regarding the value of products and services. It is the free market which has been shown to be the most efficient system for production and distribution.

Free-market capitalism protects human freedoms. Capitalism is a necessary (but not sufficient) condition for democracy. In a free market the economic system enjoys a degree of separation from the political processes under a constitutional democracy. Freedom to buy and sell in the market is dependent on political freedoms. History shows that where market freedom is curtailed, political freedoms also are curtailed.

Free-market capitalism improves the position of the disadvantaged, including the poor. Successful free-market capitalists create great

social institutions from which thousands of people benefit for generation after generation. Innovations in one industry spread to other industries and create an interlinked chain of constant improvements in how we serve each other. Commerce is the best system in the world for diminishing abuses of individuals and minorities, but every system is problematic. In spite of the most heroic efforts by policy makers and lawmakers, no economic system is able to remove poverty. Compared with the alternative (socialism), the free market has contributed to alleviation of poverty to a greater degree. The free market provides the best pathways to break free from poverty. Equality of income has never been achieved in any economic system.

Supporters of the free market conclude that overall the system is fair. They point out that the free market promotes individual economic and political freedom. For many, freedom is the basis of justice. Capitalism supports equality of opportunity, not equality of outcomes. Rewards are proportional to the risk, the level of effort and luck. The system rewards innovation and risk taking. Production is the most efficient in a free market. This results in lower prices, higher quality and better accessibility. The system as a whole does not contain any inherently immoral elements. The system benefits society as a whole, as well as the individuals who are active players in the market. It is true that a significant wage gap exists; however, even for the poor who live in this system, their lifestyle and living conditions are improved dramatically over the last two hundred years. The poor have access to many of the same types of products and services once available only to the extremely wealthy.

Free-market capitalism weaknesses. The free-market economic system is not perfect.

Opponents of the free-market system have presented several criticisms.[14]

Laissez-faire (libertarian) capitalism is sometimes the target of criticisms. Opponents of this form of capitalism present several arguments.[15] A market free from government involvement increases the chances that market players will abuse their economic power. A market free from government interference essentially puts businesses beyond the social constraints that might otherwise prevent abuses. Thus, not only is law minimized but also the moral foundation for law that would foster self-restraints is limited. A free market tends to overlook the most disadvantaged members of society such as the poor by denying them dignity. "Not only does capitalism rest on the premise that people are basically acquisitive, individualistic and materialistic, but in practice capitalism strongly reinforces those human tendencies."[16] For all that capitalism does to improve the position of the disadvantaged, it also perpetuates economic inequality. Furthermore, capitalism replaces cultural norms with individual self-interest as the highest good.

Many opponents to the free-market system put forward criticisms pointing out certain weaknesses of capitalism.

Money creates power, and power corrupts. Successful businesses develop a large amount of political and social power. This undermines the very moral principles that are said to be at the foundation of a free-market system.

Capitalism produces moral muteness.[17] Managers and subordinates learn that it is best to keep quiet when you observe fellow workers or your superiors doing things that are unethical. This code of silence perpetuates elements of organizational culture that undermine the moral foundation of the economic system.

This has become a part of the social contract between business and society: "Say you are committed to following generally-accepted moral principles, but don't ask and don't tell what is really going on." Some have argued that it is not only capitalism that produced moral muteness. Silence about the moral issues can be found in every economic system.

The strong emphasis on price oversimplifies some values and ignores others. There are other values of life than the price that is placed on a good or service. But the free market excessively emphasizes price and money to the detriment of other human values. This reduces contribution of businesses to only financial benefits to the few who hold the investment capital. It minimizes the general social benefits that might otherwise be provided by businesses.

The free market does not adequately manage negative externalities. Business causes a host of consequences for society such as pollution that businesses do not pay for. The costs must be covered by society, with no particular organization charged with the responsibility to clean up the messes caused by businesses. Thus, in a free market businesses are allowed to shift some costs to entities outside the enterprise. This increases profits for the businesses but lowers the profit for society.

The free market emphasizes short-term profits. Short-term thinking distorts the value of the present to the detriment of the future. "Jeffrey Skilling, president of Enron, did annual performance reviews based on forced rankings according to income earned for the company and, annually, fired the lowest ranked 20 percent of Enron's employees. Thus, he fostered a culture of 'bring in the numbers any way, any how' and, in time, destroyed the company."[18] Competition can be beneficial to consumers who get better quality and better access and better prices, but competition can also be destructive when it leads competitors to do whatever they can to win.

In addition to these criticisms, Karl Marx presented a few chief complaints about capitalism. These criticisms are still popular among neo-Marxists and some Christians.[19]

Capitalism exploits workers. Socialists start with the premise that the owners of large amounts of cash used in production and distribution of goods have an advantage over everyone else. Workers are merely factors of production which are used to get the highest profit possible in the distribution and sale of products. Workers have little or no bargaining power. If they want to survive, they must work. But workers must work for the persons who control the means of production, that is, the capitalists. Capitalists pay the bare minimum in order to generate profits.

Capitalism alienates workers. It was under capitalism that industrialization developed. Industrialism emphasizes an extreme form of division of labor in order to generate the highest profit. The result is that, over the years, industry workers have increasingly become specialists able to perform just a few highly specialized tasks. Workers' tasks are designed to benefit efficiency of machines. And machines are designed to promote the economic interests of capitalists, not the well-being of workers. Workers are separated from each other whenever efficiency dictates. Craftsmanship has declined as industrial workers have comparably fewer opportunities to develop a wide variety of human skills.

Capitalism protects the vested interests of investors. Profit is the number one goal of each business with all other values becoming subservient to this goal. This prevents many from achieving their economic desires.

Critics of the system point out that certain injustices are tolerated or even fostered by the free market. Some workers are exploited by unscrupulous investors. The system promotes demand for products that are wasteful. Inequities of income are allowed. The wage gap is getting wider.

THE CHRISTIAN CRITIQUE AND RESPONSE

In August 1948, the World Council of Churches (WCC) organized in Amsterdam, the Netherlands. At this first meeting the theme of the conference was "Man's Disorder and God's Design." Members attending the conference contributed to developing a document which, in part, criticized both socialism and laissez-faire free-market economic systems.[20] Four criticisms are noted:

- Capitalism tends to subordinate the meeting of human needs to contributing to the economic advantage of the persons who have power over economic institutions.

- Capitalism tends to produce economic inequalities.

- Capitalism has fostered materialism. The heavy emphasis is on making money so that people can acquire more things.

- Capitalism has caused social catastrophes such as widespread unemployment.

This was not the first time that religious leaders had voiced their concerns over economics.[21] For centuries there has been an uneasy relationship between leaders of the Christian church and economics.

The following responses were offered in answer to the criticisms:[22]

- Capitalism is primarily an attempt to meet human needs. Needs result in demand, and owners of businesses are interested in producing products that satisfy demand. There are evil business leaders in any economic system who look out primarily for their own self-interests.

- Capitalism has done more than any other economic system to meet human needs.

- Capitalism may not have contributed to the reduction of inequalities; however, it has not caused the inequalities. The poor will always be in society.[23] Capitalism has done much to raise the standard of living.

- The doctrine of economic equality is dangerous in that it causes some people to believe that they have equal rights to the property of others.

- Equality is not synonymous with the kingdom of God. Furthermore, equality is

not the primary goal of capitalism. Even so, capitalism has come closer than any other economic system to providing equality.

- Materialism in capitalist economy is not essentially different from the materialism in the socialist economy. Materialism is the fault of government leaders who persuade citizens that luxuries are the right of all persons. Furthermore, the church should not criticize capitalism for excessive amount of materialism when the church teaches that there is nothing evil about things. It is how things are used where the problem lies.

- Unemployment, by itself, does not indicate the morality of the economic system. In Nazi Germany there was low unemployment. In addition, unemployment might occasionally be experienced in other economic systems. One day capitalism may

Table 20.1. Applying the ethical process.

Keeping Your Heart: An Intrapersonal Process	Walking in the Community: An Interpersonal Process
<ul><li>You are a chief executive officer. What does your heart say is the right thing to do regarding your compensation and the wage gap?</li><li>Which biblical themes explored in this book inform your heart on this question?</li><li>Which biblical theme, if any, do you feel yourself resisting? Why do you feel resistance?</li><li>What other influences in your heart seem to be prominent as you think about this situation?<ul><li>Fundamental beliefs</li><li>Cognitive reasoning</li><li>Judgments and evaluations</li><li>Decisions</li><li>Virtues</li><li>Will</li><li>Memory of personal experiences with other people</li><li>Perceptions of others in the community</li><li>Personal biases</li><li>Awareness of interpersonal relationships</li><li>Commitments to God and to others</li><li>Intuitions</li><li>Conscience</li><li>Human spirit</li><li>Emotions</li></ul></li></ul>	<ul><li>You are a chief executive officer. With whom might you have a conversation about the issues of the wage gap in your company? Who else might have a helpful perspective?</li><li>Who should take a leadership role in the conversation about executive compensation and the wage gap?</li><li>Which of the biblical themes in this chapter will most likely come up in the conversation either directly or indirectly? Why? Which one(s) will be the most influential in the conversation?</li><li>If you have a conversation with someone regarding this situation, which of the fundamental tensions presented earlier in the book might come up?</li><li>What right-versus-right dilemmas, if any, can be identified? Have a conversation with someone about this now. What is the outcome of the conversation?</li></ul>

learn how to avoid social catastrophes such as unemployment.

- Criticizing capitalism for its weaknesses should accompany celebration of all the good it has done. To be one-sided with criticism is to be unjust.

This debate established in broad outlines the direction of the conversation among Christians in the second half of the twentieth century and the beginning of the twenty-first century. The debate continues.

DOWN TO THE NITTY-GRITTY

Think about scenario at the beginning of this chapter. You are a chief executive officer of a company. Your annual compensation is about fifty times more than what a front-line, entry-level employee earns. Is this right? It's time to get down to the nitty-gritty (see table 20.1)!

THROUGH THE LENS OF BIBLICAL THEMES

This part of the chapter will use the biblical story themes as a lens through which to evaluate the topic featured in the chapter. Because the themes are interrelated and interdependent, we should expect to see some overlap in the thinking regarding the issues. Some themes will contribute the same thinking as will other themes. The power of these themes comes from their guidance when a community of people talks about complicated ethical dilemmas faced in business practice. Any form of government that stifles either the intrapersonal or interpersonal ethics processes undermines God's plan for flourishing life because it undermines the basic dimensions of human existence.

Scripture supports a differentiation between civil sectors, religious sector and economic sector in the theocracy of ancient Israel. Evidence for this is in the presence of legitimate leadership roles for the government (king), the religious organization (priests, scribes) and the economic sphere (heads of households). Leaders in all three sectors were expected to depend on the principles of the covenant for guidance in their affairs.

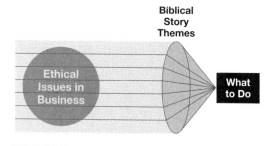

Figure 20.4. Evaluating an ethical process.

In the history of Israel we see what happens under three different political-economic systems. Forced to move to Egypt to get food, Jacob's family became enslaved. The centralization of the Egyptian government efficiently produced grain for use during the famine. The centralized power that was helpful during a crisis later abused its power committing injustices against foreigners.

Escaping the bondage of Egypt, the people agreed to follow the covenant principles under the prophetic leadership of Moses. Moses organized a governing council system of advisors along with a balance of power between the judicial system and religious leaders.

Moses predicted that if the people demand a king, the king must be limited in his powers.[24] The king must be chosen from among the people. He must be limited in military power, limited in the number of international alliances made through marriage and limited economically.

After Moses' death there was no strong

central government. Starting with Joshua, a series of judges, each one less committed to the covenant principles than the previous one, attempted to keep the nation cohesive. Largely they were ineffective. The result was chaos and anarchy, which was just as destructive as the Egyptian bondage.

Finally, as Moses had predicted, the people became exasperated. During the judgeship of Samuel they demanded a limited centralized government under a king. The government established was a limited constitutional monarchy.[25] It was limited in that the directions provided by Moses limited the king's political and economic power. It was constitutional in the sense that the Ten Commandments formed the basis of all law.

Within the reigns of just three kings, Saul, David and Solomon, the nation was once again plunged into the chaos of civil war. Following this a succession of mostly unfaithful kings steadily led the people to the brink of extinction when they were taken into bondage in Babylon.

When Israel went into Babylonian captivity, the prophet Jeremiah called for the people to pray for the prosperity of Babylon: "Seek the welfare of the city where I have sent you into exile, and pray to the LORD on its behalf; for in its welfare you will have welfare" (Jer 29:7).

They were not called on to agitate for structural changes to the economic system they were in.

Through this process we see a few ideas that surface regarding how to interact with the political-economic system. Regardless of what type of government is in power, injustice must be resisted.

When the followers of God are in positions of power in the land, a balance of power must be maintained between the civil government and the religious organization. The constitution of the civil government must be founded on the principles of covenant relationships. All key leaders are encouraged to learn the principles of the covenant and apply them to their sector of society. This includes religious leaders, judicial leaders, civil leaders and economic leaders.

When followers of God find themselves under the authority of a government that does not align with covenant principles, God's people have the responsibilities. Pray for and seek a flourishing life for all persons in the land.[26] Some persons must have the courage to speak out as prophets against injustices perpetrated by leaders in the faith community. Messages given to the faith community will challenge all persons to allow God to write on their hearts the principles of the law of God so that their own lives are transformed.[27] Secular powers should not be blamed for the unfaithfulness of the faith community. When appropriate, work for a better situation that allows for freedom of worship.[28] Some persons must have the courage to speak out against injustices perpetrated by civil power.[29] Messages given to civil powers will show the consequences of continued injustice.

Later, when Judah was under the rule of Rome during the time of Christ, Jesus did not call for revolutionary, structural political-economic changes to the economic system. Instead, he called for persons and communities to develop a clearer and deeper understanding of the law of God.[30]

More than one Christian has put forward biblical criteria that he or she believes should be used to judge the morality of any economic system. We present two such recommendations as examples.

Chewning, Eby and Roels recommend the following criteria for evaluating the morality of any economic system:[31]

- The system should produce adequate supply of products and services to enhance the quality of life.

- The system should provide for the basic needs of marginal and disadvantaged people.

- The system should respond to and allow for individual differences and needs. There should be fair and equitable means of resolving conflicts.

- The system should reward and encourage initiative and hard work.

- The system should provide meaningful work for all people and provide opportunities for them to contribute to the welfare of society.

- The system should use natural and human resources efficiently and carefully.

- The system should respect and care for other countries; it should not exploit them or rob future generations.

- Power and access to power should be spread equitably among sectors of society and special interest groups.

- The benefits of the system and the costs of providing them should be spread equitably throughout the system.

- Human rights should be protected.

- Individuals should be valued and given opportunity to grow and develop.

Volf presents three normative principles on which he believes an economic system should be judged:

- *Guarding individual dignity.* To be based on biblical principles, the economic system must foster individual dignity. "In economic life the individual is thus not to be treated as a thing but as a free and responsible agent."[32]

- *Fostering community.* It is not just individual dignity that must be guarded. We live as persons in community. Fostering community requires us to give the poor preferential treatment because they are the most vulnerable.

- *Care for the natural environment.* The message of the Bible is that the whole earth will participate in redemption. This is a call for protection of nature from the damages that are caused when we engage in work.

To contribute to this discussion, we offer how the biblical story themes can be used to evaluate the morality of an economic system.

Cosmic conflict. Normatively, an economic system will foster a flourishing life rather than destroy. Part of this is to promote freedom of choice within boundaries.

Creation. Economic systems should foster mutual interdependence rather than creating lopsided dependencies on any set of market entities. Furthermore, economic systems should contribute to the restoration of the image of God. The economic system that is aligned with biblical thinking will foster responsibility and promote fundamental principles that are part of the character of God.

Holiness. Although we cannot expect all market entities to be consecrated to God and fully devoted to his service, we should expect that the economic system does not restrict market players from exercising their commitments. Entities in the market system should contribute to the eradication of those elements that are evil or destructive of human flourishing.

Covenant relationships. Biblical thinking is

long term in nature. Short-term gains should be achieved only if long-term needs are taken care of. Such a system will promote loyalty. It will encourage actions that have a positive effect on both individuals and the community. Provisions must be made for reconciliation.

Shalom. Just as with the creation theme, the shalom theme, when followed by the economic system, will contribute to all dimensions of an abundant life, safety, justice and wholeness. The economic system will contribute to health and well-being, as well as to social and political harmony.

Sabbath. Sabbath principles embedded in the economic system will include encouraging meaningful work and at the same time make provision for putting limits on human greed.

Justice. The biblical story considers justice in the context of the whole community. It is not merely an individual matter. For a flourishing life to be enjoyed by the whole community, every institution of society must foster justice in ways that are appropriate for its overall contribution to society. Thus, some persons must take a leadership role to resist injustice.[33]

Righteousness. The economic system will promote doing the right thing. The rule of law, the moral foundation of law, will be honored in the system. Corrections for wrong doing will be honored.

Truth. The economic system should be built on elements that are reliable when tested by time and circumstances. A biblically aligned system will promote faithfulness to promises. It will foster truth telling and truth living.

Wisdom. The economic system must make provisions for market players to protect themselves from being taken advantage of. In short, it will foster the wisdom that honors relationships. The economic system will promote constructive relationships. It will encourage the development of practical skills. It will contribute to practical usefulness.

Loving kindness. The economic system rooted in love will foster loyalty in relationships, loyalty demonstrated in actions. The system will promote mutual reciprocity. Compassion will not be lost in the hustle for profits.

Redemption. Although the economic system cannot solve all ills, prevent all evil or reconcile every difference, it can do its part by collaborating with other sectors of society to transform human life toward a more flourishing existence. Where shalom gets damaged by market players, where flourishing life is harmed, the economic system will accept the encouragement of government and the nonprofit sector to be transformed.

CHAPTER REVIEW QUESTIONS

1. What are the characteristics of an economic system?

2. What are the strengths and weaknesses of a free-market capitalist economic system?

3. What are the arguments and responses of Christians regarding capitalism?

4. What guidance do the biblical story themes offer when considering the political-economic system?

DISCUSSION QUESTIONS

1. Is capitalism a valid context in which to address the problem of poverty, in this nation and the world? Compared with the alternatives, is it the best context?

2. In a global market, should governments simply step aside and allow the dynamics of the markets to oversee companies?

3. On what basis should the economic system be required to contribute to society's

overall well-being beyond the production and distribution of goods and services?

4. To what degree should for-profit businesses be held responsible for all the failings of the market to uphold moral principles?

5. How can an economic system promote moral values such as faithfulness to promises, honesty and integrity while at the same time undermine these values by encouraging greed and selfishness? How can the same economic system be both just and unjust at the same time?

ETHICAL VIGNETTES TO DISCUSS

1. The week before Saturday, December 28, 2013, 1.3 million Americans received the news that their extended federal unemployment benefits were coming to an end. States that would be heavily affected included California, Texas, Florida, New York and Michigan. Proponents of an additional extension of unemployment benefits say that helping the unemployed for another year will be a needed, additional stimulus to the economy. Opponents of the extension say that an additional year will only delay the inevitable, that is, the unemployed will be encouraged to accept jobs that many have turned down hoping to get a better one. They also say that an extension of benefits for such a small proportion of the total work force will have minimal if any additional effect on strengthening the economy. Regardless of the legal action by Congress on the matter, there is an ethical issue at stake. Is it ethically right not to renew an additional extension of federal unemployment benefits for another year?

2. In the fall of 2013, President Barack Obama proposed to Congress that the federal minimum wage be increased from $7.25 to $9.00 and thereafter to be increased using an index tied to inflation. In February 2014, President Obama signed an executive order to raise the minimum wage of federal contract workers to $10.10 per hour. The executive order would take effect in January 1, 2015. The order applied to existing contracts and replacements of expiring contracts. While Congress debates the issues, Mr. Obama encouraged business leaders to do what they can to raise the wages of employees. He argued that doing so would not hurt the economy; it would boost the economy. Was it ethical or unethical for Congress to raise the federal minimum wage?

3. In January 2014, severe cold weather blanketed large sections of the United States. Demand soared for propane, heating oil, electricity and other energy sources used to heat homes and apartment buildings. In rural America, propane is commonly by millions of households to heat their homes, corn driers and livestock buildings. The excess demand caused a propane shortage and increased prices. Regulations require truck drivers to drive no more than a certain number of hours per day. But thousands of customers needed propane as fast as possible. Pat Quinn, governor of Illinois, declared an official propane shortage in the state. This provided the legal basis for relaxing regulations that propane truck drivers must adhere to. Trucks had to be sent farther away to transport propane because the fixed pipelines that distribute the fuel could not keep up with demand. This raised the cost of serving customers and increased the time drivers needed to spend on the road per day. If during a shortage

the propane delivery regulations can be temporarily put on hold, on what basis, if any, might these regulations be considered unethical to begin with?

4. Fisker Automotive, the designer and maker of the Fisker Karma electric automobile, was able to get more than $60 million in capital from investors in 2007 to start its company. But it needed more cash. In 2009 Fisker received a $528.7-million loan from the US Department of Energy. Of that loan, $169.3 million was to be used for engineering integration costs of the Karma sedan and $359 million to fund the development of a lower-cost plug-in hybrid sedan. Fisker had difficulties with the project. The batteries it had purchased from A123 Systems did not work as well as hoped. More than two hundred Karmas had to be recalled. Production delays plagued the firm. In July 2013, many industry experts predicted that Fisker Automotive would file for bankruptcy. Was the government relationship with Fisker Automotive a good thing for the well-being of society?

5. Comparing the structure of government of the Russian Federation with that of the United States, we observe differences in the amount of power that the top political leader of the country is given. Using the biblical themes presented in this book, evaluate the differences in the balance of power in the governments of the two nations. Do the biblical themes support a strong centralized power of the presidency with lesser power given to lawmakers and the courts or a relatively equal power among the presidency, the lawmakers and the courts?

Moral Muteness and
Pressure to Compromise

SCRIPTURE PASSAGE

> If you know these things, you are blessed
> if you do them. (Jn 13:17)

CHAPTER OVERVIEW

In this chapter we will wrestle with the
problem of integrating ethical principles in
the life of a manager who works in the dynamic and competitive ethical, social and
legal environment of business. In particular,
we will

- understand the problem of moral muteness
  among managers

- explore practical ways to push back against
  pressure to compromise ethical values

MAIN TOPICS

Managing Moral Muteness
Dealing with Pressure and Coercion
Is Compromise Inevitable?
Differences of Opinion
Through the Lens of Biblical Themes

KEY TERMS

compromise, dissent, graded absolutism,
moral muteness

MANAGING MORAL MUTENESS

In the introduction of this book we presented
the idea that ethics is a personal process. We
considered that this process is a process of the
heart that involves the whole person, not just
the abstract reasoning ability. Ethics is a response of or expression of faithfulness in our
relationship with God.

Furthermore, we introduced the idea that
ethics is a community process that involves
community dialogue. It is not only pastors,
priests or rabbis who engage in ethical dialogue. It is not just the members of Congress
who debate moral foundation of law.
Members of these groups are important con-
tributors to the community conversation.
Moral issues arise from within a community
setting; they engage members of the community in conversation. Executives, managers and front-line workers talk about these
moral issues which arise from within the
economic sector.

Interestingly, some organizations stifle this
conversation. By relegating business ethics to
purely an intrapersonal, abstract reasoning
process, many contemporary business organizations and nonprofit organizations cut off the
important communal dialogue process that

can enhance moral power that individuals need for making decisions.

Managers and employees often do not talk about business ethical issues at work. This problem is called moral muteness. Moral muteness fosters the idea that morality is a narrowing force in an organization that needs to explore many alternatives for success in the marketplace. Moral muteness is a coping mechanism for the stress that managers experience when facing difficult ethical dilemmas. This has the triple results of neglecting to deal with moral problems, reducing the organizational influence of principles of right and wrong and making it more difficult for managers to recognize moral issues that are present in the decisions that they make.

The causes of moral muteness.[1] Three causes of moral muteness have been observed. First, managers, it has been found, may keep quiet because they anticipate trouble if they speak up. Speaking up about moral issues may result in confrontation which, in turn, disrupts the social harmony at work. A manager may be lenient with a subordinate during the annual performance evaluation out of concerns that if the ethics of the employee's behavior are raised, it will be a threat to harmony. The disharmony could spread outside the organization into society.

Second, some managers believe that talking about moral issues will be a distraction from efficient problem solving. When managers face a decision that results in both harm and good, the organization has a problem to solve: minimize the harm and promote the good. Moral talk, it is perceived, tends to point fingers of blame, which works against the process of finding a solution. If managers are aware that there are wide differences of belief, this may influence muteness because there is

an expectation that the differences will not contribute to problem solving. There may be a fear that morality promotes only simplistic solutions when the moral problems are complicated. Furthermore, some managers believe that talking about moral issues will reduce organizational flexibility because it is believed that morality tends to constrain the alternatives for behavior.

Third, managers avoid moral talk because it is seen as a threat to their influence and effectiveness. Managers have a certain image to maintain. They are paid to be practical. Moral talk, it is believed, requires managers to be too idealistic in a context that requires practicality. The more complicated the moral dilemma, the more likely the conversation will focus on company politics, relationships with competitors or the economic costs and benefits of various alternatives. Many managers do not know how to talk about ethical issues with others.

The moral muteness of managers looks at the problem from the point of view of the person who chooses not to talk about moral issues of business while at work. Another point of view is that of the organization, which sometimes tends to stifle dissent.

Dissent in organizations.[2] In business schools and company training programs you will often hear leaders extolling the virtues of team building, critical thinking, creativity and flexibility. The reality of the marketplace is that many organizations value other things more highly: order, conformity and the hierarchy of authority. Challenging the authority of persons who are above you in the chain of command is often met with resistance. Leaders tend to protect themselves against attempts to undermine their influence. Unless there is an accepted, authorized role to play, such as the loyal opposition or devil's advocate, when everyone else is keeping quiet, the one who speaks up can be quite alone but highly noticeable in the organization. If the one person continues to speak up, he or she is labeled a chronic complainer, and nobody likes a complainer. If the person persists in giving voice to dissent, he or she can be ostracized from the organization.

Organizations that stifle dissent risk muting the very things that need to be heard. If organizational leaders listen to dissent, this can prevent the organization from experiencing catastrophic unsavory consequences. Managers who have legitimate power to make changes in the organization are unwilling to use the power for good while other managers in the same organization are just as willing to use their power for evil. Paradoxically, organizational leaders who are bent on self-protection from dissenters become both the creators and the victims of the shared organizational values that foster muteness.

Dissent is an opportunity to foster organizational well-being. The voice of dissent can be used to enhance organizational influence of a leader rather than see it as a force which undermines the leader's influence. Allowing dissent promotes integrity, which is an important hidden force for organizational success in a marketplace that easily distrusts. Dissent also acknowledges the loyalty of employees who want what is best for the organization. By stifling dissent leaders destroy one of the influences which can make the organization stronger.

Stifling ethical conversations in organizations is one thing. But there is another problem that members of organizations sometimes experience. This is the problem of pressure and even coercion to compromise ethical values.

DEALING WITH PRESSURE AND COERCION

The economic sector has its share of unscrupulous persons, just as do government and nonprofit organizations. Persons in authority will sometimes ask a subordinate to act unethically. If this happens, what should you do? How do you push back effectively against such pressure?

When a Christian manager wants to push back against the pressure to compromise moral values, several alternatives are available. One alternative is to take a position based on religious teachings. In many business environments this will bring only ridicule. Another approach is less direct in terms of religious teachings but in the end may be more effective. The following are some ways to consider.[3]

- *First seek to understand.* Avoid jumping to conclusions before you truly understand what is being asked. Some actions are clearly wrong, and it does not require complicated discussions to get to the truth of the matter. Other actions in the market are part of a more complicated situation. If needed, encourage taking a little more time to explore the alternatives that are both expedient and morally sound.

- *Focus on the business needs.* Deal with ethical issues as a business problem with business goals at stake. Short-term risks are often easier to grasp than long-term risks. Thus, you may need to be explicit in how the long-term risks are tangible. The more concrete the risks, the more urgent they are. Speaking of long term, consider the long-run risks of not speaking up! Identify the company values that are at stake which could be compromised. Place the moral issue in the middle of the organization's overall mission and show how a moral lapse will undermine the purpose of the organization's existence in the short term, in the long term or better yet, both. Show the linkage between the moral issue and the organization's goals. Doing this may require highlighting the goals other than profit that are highly prized by the organization. The clear implication of this is that in order for the organization to achieve some of its goals it sometimes must constrain its efforts toward profit. Most organizations do this all the time in order to keep from breaking the law or making key stakeholder groups angry. Position the issues in terms of the whole company and its needs. Making it personal to your own feelings or beliefs can come across as self-serving and self-righteous, both of which are often offensive to people. To illustrate the consequences of such an action, cite an example from your industry or another industry where a company allowed a moral lapse to go unchecked.

- *Be assertive and positive.* Instead of merely saying no, propose a realistic alternative to consider. When a viable alternative exists, it is more difficult to accept the easy way out. True assertiveness is a way of confirming your individual worth and dignity while simultaneously confirming and maintaining the worth of others.

- *Strengthen an ethical culture.* Every employee is expected to align with ethical standards of the organization; however, it is the manager who must take a leadership role in this. It is part of the manager's job! This is one reason why organizations hire managers. Every manager contributes something to the strength of the corporate culture. You do this by choosing what you pay attention to and this is one of the most important ways that

shared values get embedded in an organization. What you care about is what you talk about, what you ask others to report on, what you measure and what you focus on for making adjustments to efficiency and effectiveness. Reward with recognition people who show moral imagination. When necessary use anecdotes or other narratives from the experience of past leaders and founders that support the moral value at stake. Encourage employees to voice their concerns when ethical values are being challenged.

- *Be wise.* Evaluate how much political capital you have spent defending other issues. The more political capital you have available, the better. The less you have, the more you may need to depend on others for help in defending an ethical issue. Understand how dependent the organization is on you or your work unit. More dependence means the more influence you have on decision making. Learn how influence is built in your organization, and then build your own influence. Awareness of the degree of influence you have will give you courage to speak up in appropriate ways that do not flaunt your power for your own sake but rather use your power for the good of the organization.

- *Set an example.* Be consistent in your behavior. Avoid ethical gray areas. In meetings and conversations mention the ethical dimensions of issues such as mission, values and goals to show that these are matters of fact.

- *Draw strength from others.* Identify others in the organization who are experts and who share the same moral values. The organization is dependent on these experts and because of this they have a degree of influence on decision makers. One key kind of expert in this situation is someone who is adept at developing creative "both-and" alternatives where the company can get its goal accomplished and moral values can be supported.

- *Get familiar with the law.* The law is based on key moral values widely held in society. Paraphrasing a portion of a relevant state or federal statute can redirect a conversation.

- *Show the value of interdependence.* Position the moral issue in terms of the values shared by customers or suppliers. Be ready with evidence that these are their shared values. Position the moral issue in terms of widely held social norms that few would disagree with. If these norms have been highlighted in the regional or national news lately, all the better. You will have a news story or two to illustrate the folly of allowing a moral lapse to go unchecked.

- *Take the high road.* If the question becomes whether or not anyone will ever find out about an immoral action, this may be the time to play the integrity card. The fact that more than one person knows means a higher risk that eventually the truth will be found. Taking the high road of truth telling and integrity will prevent the need for future protection against those who may speak out later. It will also prevent the need for crafting a risky cover-up scheme that will very likely cost the company far more in the long run.

- *Establish the boundaries.* If you are in a job where you think you might be asked to compromise your beliefs, make sure your manager understands what you will and will not be willing to do within the company.

IS COMPROMISE INEVITABLE?

For some ethical dilemmas it sometimes feels like there is no way out. For example, because

> For the grace of God has appeared, bringing salvation to all men, instructing us to deny ungodliness and worldly desires and to live sensibly, righteously and godly in the present age. (Titus 2:11-12)

of changes in the market, such as consumer demand or competitors' actions, the firm may find that it is overextended in its expenses. Managers will be tasked with the responsibility of downsizing. There is no way getting around the fact that downsizing will result in economic chaos for some workers who are let go. It seems that in these types of situations, a compromise between competing duties is unavoidable. To think otherwise seems naive. On the one hand, the manager has the duty to take actions that support the continuation of the organization and its mission. On the other hand, the manager has the duty to be fair to individual workers who will be affected by restructuring.[4]

So when faced with a situation where there is conflict between competing values, what is the faithful person to do?[5] One approach is to avoid the conflict by asking someone else to make the decision. If this is not possible, the person can quit the job. Personally avoiding the conflict does not make the conflict go away. It merely lets someone else deal with it.

Another approach is to use moral imagination to think of another way through so that both conflicting duties can be honored. For some, this will be the preferred approach where it is possible. In reality there may be limitations on the availability of alternatives which offer freedom from the conflicts of duty.

A third approach is to take a graded absolutism approach to the conflict of duty. By doing this, you find a duty that is higher than the two duties that are in conflict and then obey the higher one. This approach assumes that some duties rank higher than others, and because of this, control our obedience options. Some argue that the Scripture itself or our own reasoning can be ambiguous regarding the ranking of duties in certain situations. Because of this, they advocate a fourth approach.

The fourth approach is to do one's best to take the course of action which results in the lesser of two evils. The assumption behind this approach is that the decision is unavoidable and that the conflicts in duty also are ultimately not resolvable, yet life must go on.

Each of these approaches emphasizes the use of reason; however, as we explored in the introduction to this book, the process of deciding what is right and wrong is not limited to abstract reasoning ability and use of logic. The biblical story approach to decision making embraces the whole person in community. This involves dialogue, listening to the perspective of others, listening to the results of abstract reasoning and listening to the reasoning that comes from emotions. These are conversations of the heart in relationship with the hearts of other people.

DIFFERENCES OF OPINION

Even after considering the biblical story themes, will there be differences of opinion among faithful believers regarding what is right and what is wrong for marketplace behaviors? For the clearest, simplest ethical issues, probably not. However, on other more difficult issues, probably yes. I think this is so for the following reasons.

Deceitfulness of the human heart. The Scripture says that the human heart is de-

ceitful.[6] We deceive not only other people but ourselves, too! Our personal biases easily creep into the ethics process whereby we tend to give ourselves a preference over others. Inevitably, this leads us toward moral relativism or egoism even when we attempt to put our ethical process within a faith-based framework. This is not to say that the community conversation is useless. On the contrary! The community conversation can contribute to putting boundaries around our personal biases that check the natural desires for selfishness. If for no other reason than this, community dialogue should be encouraged.

Intermingling egoism, relativism or utilitarianism with biblical story themes. Closely related to the deceitfulness of the human heart is the innate desire to have our own way regardless of the effect on other people. When people are looking, we are willing to move beyond narrow self-interest; however, when we are alone or when we think others are not aware of our actions, the human tendency is to move toward egoism. Perhaps we are not aware that this is antithetical to biblical faith. The same problem can come up when a person attempts to comingle relativism or utilitarianism with biblical story themes.

Proximity to the situation. The closer we are to a given situation, the more we are aware of the tangible, concrete dimensions of ethical actions. This proximity provides us with a perspective that is different from those who have never experienced the situation directly and are at a distance.

Complexity of the situation. The simple issues ("Don't steal money from the cash drawer.") everyone will agree on. The complex issues are the ones where we see disagreements. As the complexity of an ethical issue increases, so does the likelihood that well-meaning persons will have differences of opinion on what is right and what is wrong. This is one reason why a community dialogue is so important. It takes a community to deal with highly complex issues.

Incomplete information about a situation or consequences. One reason that a community dialogue is needed on complex ethical issues in business is that a person has a difficult time gaining access to all the information about the situation. Just as we have incomplete information about the complex issues, so too we have incomplete information about the consequences of our actions on others.

Differences in social roles and social goals. Another reason why community conversations are needed is that the key leaders involved in the dialogue have differences of perspective relative to their social role. This should not be construed to be in support of relativism; however, in reality business leaders see things slightly different from lawmakers and from pastors and theologians. Put three faithful believers in a room: a business professional, a pastor and a politician. See how they differ in how they see a particular ethical situation.

Emphasizing one pole of a paradox to the detriment of the other pole. Emphasizing the short term over the long run will generate differences of opinion, just as does emphasizing individual needs over the community needs. Christians in Western societies tend to emphasize individuality and downplay community. We tend toward applying ethics to the person. This emphasis masks an equally important set of needs experienced in the community.

Emphasizing one biblical theme over others. One beauty of the Scripture themes is that collectively they provide the community with guidance for community conversations about what to do in the marketplace. But when one person emphasizes one theme over the others, this will result in differences of opinion. When taking one theme apart from the others we can lose sight of how the themes are interwoven with each other. For example, it is in the biblical theme of wisdom that we see an important tension. Wisdom includes not only the community perspective but also the individual perspective. It includes not only the perspective of spirituality but also the perspective of material dimensions of life. The presence of this tension in an important biblical theme should give us courage to participate in the community conversations about right and wrong. Imbedded in wisdom we see covenant, shalom, justice, truth, righteousness and loving kindness all wrapped up together. Likewise, in the theme of holiness we see woven the principles of covenant relationships, the hope of shalom, justice, righteousness and truth. Collectively, it is all the biblical story themes that are needed for the most complex ethical dilemmas. Various members of the community can advocate on behalf of each theme as being applicable. The community dialogue that ensues based on the biblical themes will generate, over time, improved and perhaps more sophisticated understandings of the best actions. For some this dialogue will last months, years and even decades.

Emphasizing one dimension of a particular biblical theme over its full understanding. Consider the biblical story theme of wisdom again. One dimension of biblical wisdom is being smart with respect to social exchanges: Do not let others take advantage of you; achieve the best you can. Taken by itself, however, this dimension of wisdom will be allowed to destroy other dimensions and other biblical ideals. Taken by itself this element of wisdom will be allowed to undermine shalom and justice. It is the full understanding of wisdom which is needed to guard against this danger.

Lack of moral leadership. Some persons involved in community dialogue regarding the ethical issues of business need guidance from those who are more experienced and have the courage to get involved. Without moral leadership, community conversations are less efficient. Dialogue can shift to the person who is the most persuasive or the most influential. Political dimensions of community conversations may put unnecessary boundaries on what can be talked about and what are taboos. Without leaders to arise and identify the central issues the conversation will founder. Without courage to point out flaws in reasoning, flaws in information, flaws in assumptions, conversations will be foggy.

Do differences of opinion mean, in the final analysis, that ethics is only relative, even for well-meaning believers? No. In this section we are simply describing the reality of life in community but not prescribing that everyone should do what is right in his or her own eyes. The prescription in this book is that each person participate in the community conversation by earnestly seeking the best understanding of how biblical story themes guide behaviors.

Community dialogue may not remove all doubt regarding right and wrong. In such a case, the well-meaning believer will listen, participate in the dialogue and the make a decision or take an action. Following the action, the humble believer will again participate in the community dialogue and from this become wiser for the next time the ethical issues are complicated. From the experience, the person is better equipped to talk with others who are wrestling with complex issues.

THROUGH THE LENS OF BIBLICAL THEMES

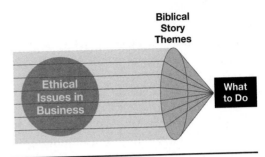

Figure 21.1. Evaluating an ethical process.

We draw an important conclusion after considering the impact of biblical story themes: The standard of behavior prophetically portrayed in the themes is higher than humans are able to achieve on their own.

Consider each of the themes once more. We are in a cosmic conflict that is above our pay grade and abilities to win on our own. We were created in the image of God, an image that was not fully destroyed yet has become powerless to withstand the influence to go contrary to the wonderful plan for life established at creation. The call to a fully consecrated life, separate yet among those we serve, can only partially be accomplished based on human will alone. Such a consecrated life should lead us toward deep commitments in our relationships with God, with each other and with the earth. Yet, we find that humans repeatedly breach this covenant. We are powerless to achieve a full flourishing life of well-being. Indeed, the biblical story themes tell us that flourishing life is a gift of God. One of the interrelated structural influences for recovery from this difficult problem God put in place. Both work and sabbath call us to and contribute to the restoration of the image of God in the human soul. Our contemporary lifestyles pull us away from diligent work and from sabbath rest. We are called to exercise justice, righteousness and truth, yet we continually find ourselves and others being unfair, doing the wrong thing and being unfaithful to promises.

If we are unsuccessful in achieving the ideals prophetically described in the biblical story themes, we often feel that we have conquered the ideal of wisdom especially in the marketplace. Humans have learned creative ways to manage risk and the time value of money. We have learned a lot about customer behaviors, the laws of supply and demand, the power of market structure and industry structure, the importance of core competence and other internal resources to sustain a competitive advantage. But what have we learned about true biblical wisdom? We have not learned as well that biblical wisdom is founded in covenant relationships and that it comes only by steeping the heart in the content of the other biblical themes. Finally, many humans prize love, belonging and loyalty above all other values.

Even after we have become wealthy and seen our balance sheets exceed those of our peers, we learn that all this is nothing without love. Without loving kindness and loyalty, life is shallow and at times miserable. Those around us who demonstrate love remind us how desperate we are to experience it and how weak we are in producing it. Paradoxically, as much as humans value love and loyalty, we continually show our propensity to either not accept it or not give it to others. Of ourselves as a whole the human race is not capable of sustaining the type of loving relationships envisioned in the biblical story. This, too, is part of the story!

We can illustrate this problem with figure 21.2.

The biblical story says that there is only one solution to this difficult problem. There is no way that we will be transformed to live consistently along the ideals of the biblical themes unless we have our hearts transformed by the power of God. In short, to pick up an idea from the introduction to this book, there is no way that we can come to faithfulness without the power of God.

The amazing part of the biblical story is that this occurs when we develop a relationship with Jesus Christ. It is in a relationship with him that we have our minds transformed. It is in a relationship with him that we find deliverance.[7] This is not a one-time event but be-

---

Biblical story themes hold a high standard
+ Human inability to live up to that standard all the time
+ Human propensity to do the opposite of the standard

Recipe for human failure in achieving the ideal of our own will

Figure 21.2. The human dilemma.

Biblical story themes hold a high standard
- Recipe for human failure in achieving the ideal of our own will
+ Relationship with Jesus Christ

Transformation of the human heart, will and behavior for moral success in the market

Figure 21.3. The solution to the human dilemma.

comes a continual process of restoration, character building, will strengthening, wisdom producing and courage tempering. In short, the biblical story theme of redemption provides the power for all the other themes to be successful in our lives.[8] With the relationship with Jesus Christ as part of the equation, we see a different picture possible (see fig. 21.3).

Another conclusion we draw from the study of these biblical story themes is that these are interrelated, interdependent and interwoven with each other. In short, the biblical narrative tells a story of a fully integrated life of the person in relationships with the community. The biblical story themes are not merely a random list of dos and don'ts but rather a description of God's plan for his creatures to live a life of well-being and blessing to each other.

A third and final conclusion we draw is that when applying any one theme or all the themes to a particular situation or ethical dilemma may require dialogue with other community members. The ethics process requires conversations both informal and, at times, formal. The more complex the situation, the more likely that community conversation is required. The more wisdom that a person develops over time from facing ethical dilemmas and from engaging in the community conversation, the better the person is prepared to take actions that are in alignment with biblical story themes; the more prepared persons become to offer meaningful contributions to the community conversations in their own family, in the places they work and in the larger public square of the community.

CHAPTER REVIEW QUESTIONS

1. What does moral muteness mean, and how is it a problem in organizations?

2. What are the causes and consequences of moral muteness in organizations?

3. What is the concept of dissent, and how is it a problem in organizations?

4. What are some of the ways that a person can deal with pressure and coercion to compromise ethical values?

5. Why are there differences of opinion on ethical issues?

6. What is the concept of compromise, and how should the faithful Christian view it?

7. What guidance do the biblical story themes offer for dealing with pressure to compromise ethical values?

DISCUSSION QUESTIONS

1. Why are managers reluctant to express publically the moral dimensions of the decisions they make?

2. How can an employee raise moral issues in an organization without appearing narrowly self-serving, hypocritical or self-righteous?

3. Compare the ideas in this chapter for how to push back against pressure to compromise with the biblical themes we have considered in this book. To what degree do the biblical themes support these practical ideas? What additional imaginative approaches for pushing back come to mind when considering the biblical story thinking?

4. Why does this chapter say that the more complicated the ethical issue, the more likely a community conversation will be required in order to know what is right to do?

5. How can the Christian avoid persecution when remaining faithful to biblical thinking and action in the marketplace?

ETHICAL VIGNETTES TO DISCUSS

For each of the vignettes, apply the biblical story themes to discern what is right and wrong.

1. Peter Drucker, one of the most influential management thinkers of the second half of the twentieth century, wrote in 1973:

   > Management development and manager development are not means to "make man over" by changing his personality. Their aim is to make man effective. Their aim is to enable a man to use his strengths fully, and to make him perform the way he is, rather than the way somebody thinks he ought to be. An employer has no business with a man's personality. Employment is a specific contract calling for specific performance, and for nothing else. Any attempt of an employer to go beyond this is usurpation. It is immoral as well as illegal intrusion of privacy. It is abuse of power. An employee owes no "loyalty," he owes no "love" and no "attitudes"— he owes performance and nothing else.[9]

   Do you agree or disagree with Drucker? What is your rationale?

2. You are involved in the development of a training program where you are collaborating with a group of individuals from multiple departments. You are one of five people who are supposed to do conduct a pilot training event with a small group before rolling it out to the entire organization. The final project date is looming, and all five developers have been unable to complete their parts to the project. The other persons are claiming to the boss to have finished their respective parts even though you know they have not. What should you do?

3. You have noticed that the managers at the company you work for do not closely monitor the employees' use of company property. The company provides unlimited Internet access and electronic devices such as printers, fax machines, telephones, and various office supplies. You notice a co-worker who uses significant amounts of work time to pay bills online, check personal email, place postings on social media and print off her and her daughter's school assignments. She also takes home office supplies for her daughter to use for school. You believe she is taking advantage of the company's property and stealing. She believes the company owes her the right to use those items as an employee. What should you do?

4. The employee handbook of your company states that any employee caught stealing inventory or equipment from the company will be fired. One day you see an employee take two boxes of toner cartridge out of the office work room. Moreover, you observe this employee taking these same two boxes to his car at the end of the day. This employee is one month away from the date that he has said he will retire. What should you do?

PART FIVE

APPENDIXES AND CASE STUDIES

Part V presents additional information that the reader may be interested in. The following appendixes are offered for further study:

- Appendix A: Key Questions from the Biblical Themes. This appendix illustrates the kinds of questions that the biblical story themes pose when deciding what is right and wrong in the marketplace.

- Appendix B: Scriptural Basis for the Biblical Themes. This appendix provides a summary of the biblical references in support of each theme meeting the selection criteria.

- Appendix C: Biblical Themes Summary Tables. This appendix is offered to help students review the major elements of each biblical story theme.

- Appendix D: Ten Principles for Flourishing. This appendix explores the Ten Commandments in terms of the contribution they make to the biblical idea of prosperity.

- Appendix E: Summary of Ethical Models in Comparison. This appendix is a study tool to help students review the major contemporary ethical models.

- Appendix F: The Purpose of Business Through the Lens of Biblical Themes. This appendix addresses the question, What is

the purpose of business? It explores the role of profit.

- Appendix G: Ethical and Social Issue Debate Topics. This appendix provides examples of the many debatable issues in the ethical, social and legal environment of business.

- Appendix H: Prosperity in the Bible: Q & A Bible Study. This appendix leads you on a Bible study on the topic of prosperity.

Seventeen original short cases are presented in Part V. These include the following titles:

1. The 25 Percent Discount Car Rental

2. Praising God for Victory in Court

3. Banker Bashing

4. Volkswagen, the UAW and Community Dialogue

5. Wi-Spy

6. Pushing the Stuck Dune Buggy

7. Frequent Flier Grounded

8. Guarantee but at a Premium

9. Promising the Moon

10. The Boogie Man

11. Who's the Dirtiest Crook?

12. Dirty Tricksters in the Bible

Appendix A

Key Questions from the Biblical Themes

The biblical model of ethics is an intrapersonal process and an interpersonal process. In the intrapersonal process, each person has responsibility to understand and interpret the principles of action designed for a flourishing life. This involves introspection and awareness that the person cannot live in total isolation from others in society. This responsibility involves diligent keeping of the heart (the whole person) in the context of a wider community.[1]

The interpersonal process requires community dialogue even if in just a small group. It involves conversations, testing ideas, exploring different points of view, reflection, sometimes debate, decision making, observing results of our actions and then further reflection and conversation. Through this conversation a communal or shared understanding of right and wrong develops over time. For social issues that are common across many people and people groups, the community takes responsibility through its leaders for establishing organizational policies and, for the wider society, social policies (laws and regulations) which guide behavior across society.

Like the process of nurturing relationships, this is not a mechanical process. At the same time, the biblical story themes give rise to specific questions that should become part of introspection and the group conversation.

Because the biblical story themes are interrelated, interwoven and interdependent, we should expect to see similar questions arising from various themes.

Table A.1. The biblical story themes and key ethical questions.

Biblical Theme	Key Ethical Process Questions
Cosmic Conflict	• Will the action foster freedom within boundaries or will it undermine freedom or boundaries? • Will the action reveal God's character? • Will the action support or undermine long-term relationships? • Will the action support or undermine harmony among members of the community?
Creation	• Will the action I am about to take honor and respect human life? • Will it foster a flourishing life in community for the long run or will it result in harm? • When we take from the earth, how are we fulfilling our responsibility to care for the earth? • Will the actions we are about to take contribute to or undermine the process of God restoring his image in the people who are affected? • Will this action acknowledge God's lordship over all of life? • Will this action support the capabilities of the earth to sustain life into the future? • Will this action be an attempt to exploit the earth as merely a means to an end?

Holiness	• Will this action show my commitment to being faithful to God? • Will the action I am about to take communicate God's holiness? • Will the action honor the sacredness of relationships and resources needed to sustain flourishing life? • Will my action be consistent with what I am called by God to reveal about his character? • Does my action need to be distinctively different from the common actions of the marketplace? • Will my action be an attempt to combine right doing with wrong doing? • Will my action merely be a way for me to show how good I am rather than, in humility, foster good for others? • Will my actions be a form of self-righteousness?
Covenant Relationships	• Will it foster a flourishing life in community for the long run or will it result in harm? • Will the action nourish a long-term relationship or destroy it? • What needs to be done in this relationship in the long run so that the flourishing of abundant life in the community is nourished? • Will this action reveal character of the covenant makers? • Will this action nourish a faithfulness-enhancing interdependent relationship among those involved? • Will this action provide a means by which at least one party can act in redemptive ways when the other party breaches the relationship? • Will the action foster mutual blessings to all involved or all represented here?
Shalom	• Will it foster a flourishing life in community for the long run or will it result in harm and misery? • Will the action attempt to separate one dimension of shalom from the others? • Will the action support or undermine community prosperity? • Will the action support harmony in the community or will it be disruptive to harmony? • Will the action be for the purpose of extending the life of shalom to a broader community by blessing others?
Sabbath	• Will the action feed contentment or discontentment? • Will the action contribute to other members of the community doing their part through productive labor? • Will this action allow for limits to be placed on my drive for acquisition of wealth?
Justice	• Will the action be fair? • Will the action support the rights of others? • Will this action take unfair advantage of someone who is unfamiliar with the situation? • Will the action undermine legitimate processes established by those in authority? • Will the action be an attempt to circumvent legitimate processes of fair distribution of resources?
Righteousness	• Will the larger community consider this action to be right? • Will this action reveal that I am standing firm on principles of right and wrong?
Truth	• Will this action support faithfulness in action when tested by time and circumstance? • Will this action require hiding the truth from others?
Wisdom	• Will this action have an adverse consequence for other people in the relationship? • Will this action result in harm to me, my family and my organization?
Loving Kindness	• Will this promote loyalty in the relationship? • Will the action support doing things for others unselfishly? • Will the action support the relationship even if I do not like the other party?
Redemption	• Will this action provide a means by which at least one party can act in redemptive ways when the other party breaches the relationship? • Will this action serve to remove the influences that undermine relationships?

Appendix B

Scriptural Basis for the Biblical Themes

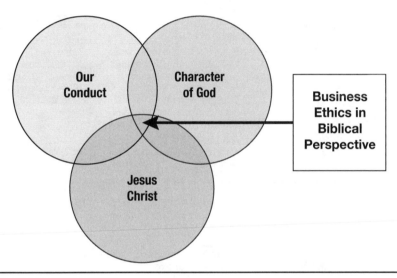

Figure B.1. Evaluating an ethical approach.

Table B.1. Biblical themes and biblical perspectives.

	Jesus Christ and His Work	The Believer's Conduct	The Character of God
Cosmic Conflict	Genesis 3:15; Matthew 10:1; 13:37-39; 28:18; Mark 3:14-15; John 10:10; 12:31-32; 16:8-11; Acts 2:23; 10:38; Hebrews 2:14; 1 John 2:22; 3:8; Revelation 12:7; 17:14	Proverbs 8:13; 28:4; see also Psalm 97:10; Proverbs 9:7-8; 14:16; 15:12; 16:6; 20:26; 22:3; Matthew 10:16; 20:25-26; John 14:30; 1 Corinthians 4:9; 5:13; 2 Corinthians 10:4-5; 11:3; Ephesians 4:27; 5:11; 6:12-17; 1 Thessalonians 5:4-8; 1 Timothy 1:18; 6:12; James 4:7; 1 Peter 5:8-9; 1 John 3:10-14; Revelation 13:17; 14:12	Exodus 14:14; 15:3; 34:6-7; Deuteronomy 1:30; 20:4; Joshua 5:14-15; 10:14, 42; 1 Samuel 17:45-47; 1 Kings 22:19; 2 Chronicles 20:15, 29; Psalm 24:7-10; 46:7; 68:17; 78:65; 136:16; 140:7; Isaiah 13:4; 42:13; Zephaniah 3:17; Zechariah 7:9; 14:3; Matthew 10:1; Luke 2:13; John 10:10; 1 Corinthians 15:24-26; Ephesians 3:8-11; Colossians 1:15-20; 1 Peter 1:18-21; Revelation 16:7; 17:14; 19:11, 14, 19; 20:7-9

	Jesus Christ and His Work	The Believer's Conduct	The Character of God
Creation	John 1:3; Hebrews 1:1-2; Revelation 4:11	Genesis 1:26-28; 2:15; Psalm 8:3-6; 1 Corinthians 3:9; 2 Corinthians 3:18; 5:17; Ephesians 2:10; Colossians 3:10; James 1:18; 1 Timothy 4:4	Genesis 2:7; Psalm 19:1-6; 33:6, 9; 104:24; John 1:3; Acts 17:24-26; Romans 1:18-20; Revelation 21:1
Holiness	Isaiah 53:9; Luke 1:35; Acts 3:14; 4:27; Romans 1:4; 2 Corinthians 5:21; Hebrews 4:15; 7:26; James 1:27; 1 Peter 1:18-19; 2:21-22; 1 John 3:5	Deuteronomy 28:9; Psalm 15:1-5; 34:14; Proverbs 9:10; 2 Corinthians 7:1; Ephesians 1:4; 2 Timothy 2:22; 1 Peter 1:15-16; 2:21-22; 3:11; 2 Peter 3:11	Exodus 15:11; 1 Samuel 2:2; 1 Chronicles 16:10; Psalm 22:3; 77:13; 89:18; Isaiah 5:16; 6:3; 43:15; John 17:11; Revelation 15:4
Covenant Relationships	Deuteronomy 4:13; Malachi 3:1; Matthew 22:36-40; John 17:2; Hebrews 12:24	Deuteronomy 6:6; 7:9; 8:18; Psalm 19:7; Jeremiah 31:33; 2 Corinthians 3:4-6; Galatians 5:14; Hebrews 10:16; Revelation 14:12	Deuteronomy 4:1, 40; 5:33; 7:9; 8:1-3; 30:20; Psalm 111:9; 119:142; Proverbs 3:1; Isaiah 54:10; Jeremiah 32:40; 38:20; Malachi 2:5; Romans 7:10
Shalom	Isaiah 9:6-7; 53:5; Luke 1:79; 2:14; John 14:27; Romans 5:1; Ephesians 2:14; Colossians 1:20	Psalm 29:11; 34:14; Proverbs 16:7; Isaiah 48:18; Romans 14:17; 2 Corinthians 13:11; Galatians 5:22; Philippians 4:7; Colossians 3:15; 1 Thessalonians 5:23; 2 Thessalonians 3:16; 2 Timothy 2:22; 1 Peter 3:11; 2 Peter 3:14	Psalm 34:12-14; 35:27; Isaiah 54:10; Ezekiel 34:25; 37:26; Romans 16:20; 2 Corinthians 13:11; Hebrews 13:20; Revelation 6:4
Sabbath	Mark 2:27-28	Exodus 20:8-11; 31:13-17; Deuteronomy 5:12-15; Mark 2:27-28; 3:4	Genesis 2:3; Exodus 20:8-11; Deuteronomy 5:12-15
Justice	Psalm 89:14; Isaiah 9:6-7; Jeremiah 23:5; Zechariah 9:9; Matthew 12:14-21	Deuteronomy 16:18-20; Psalm 25:9; 82:3-4; 106:3; Proverbs 2:6-9; 8:20-21; 21:3; Ecclesiastes 5:8; Isaiah 10:1-2; Amos 5:24	Genesis 18:25; Deuteronomy 10:18; 16:20; 32:41; Psalm 19:9; 33:5; 89:14; Proverbs 16:11; Isaiah 5:16; Ezekiel 18:21, 27
Righteousness	Psalm 89:14; Jeremiah 23:5; Romans 1:16-17; 1 Corinthians 1:30; 1 John 2:1	Psalm 15:1-2; 106:3; Ezekiel 45:10; Matthew 6:33; Romans 3:21-26; 14:17; 2 Corinthians 5:21; Ephesians 6:12-17; 2 Timothy 2:22; 1 John 3:10-14	Psalm 7:9; 19:9; 33:5; 145:17; Proverbs 10:16; 11:19, 30; 12:28; 16:17; Isaiah 5:16; 9:6-7; Ezekiel 33:16, 19; Romans 3:21-26; 5:18, 21; 2 Peter 3:13
Truth	1 Kings 2:4; John 1:14; 14:6; 2 Corinthians 13:8; Ephesians 4:21; 2 Peter 2:1-3; 1 John 1:6	Psalm 15:1-2; 51:6; Proverbs 3:3; 23:23; John 16:13; 17:17; Galatians 5:22; 1 John 1:6; 5:20; 3 John 1:8	Exodus 34:6; Psalm 19:9; 57:10; 86:15; 89:14; 111:7-8; 117:2; 119:142; Habakkuk 2:4; John 14:6; Revelation 2:10
Wisdom	Proverbs 8:22-30; 1 Corinthians 1:24, 30	Psalm 19:7; 51:6; Proverbs 3:13; 23:23; Jeremiah 9:23-24; Romans 12:16; Colossians 1:28; Revelation 13:18	Psalm 104:24; Proverbs 2:6-9; 3:13-18; 9:6; 13:14; 1 Corinthians 1:24; Ephesians 3:8-11
Loving Kindness	Psalm 33:5; 89:14; John 1:14; 15:13; Romans 8:39; Ephesians 5:2	Micah 6:8; John 13:35; 1 Corinthians 13:13; Galatians 5:14, 22; Colossians 3:14; 2 Timothy 2:22; 1 John 3:10-14	Exodus 34:6; Deuteronomy 7:9; Psalm 63:3; 86:15; 89:14; 117:2; 119:77; Proverbs 21:21; 2 Corinthians 13:11; 1 John 4:8, 10
Redemption	Matthew 1:21; Mark 10:45; Acts 2:23; Romans 3:24; 5:10-11; 8:29; 1 Corinthians 1:30; 2 Corinthians 5:19; Galatians 3:13; Ephesians 1:7; 2:16; 3:8-11; Colossians 1:13-14, 20; Hebrews 9:12; 1 Peter 1:18-21	Isaiah 1:27; Acts 4:12; 1 Corinthians 6:20; 2 Corinthians 5:18-20; Ephesians 6:12-17; 1 Peter 1:18-21	Job 19:25; Psalm 7:10; 18:2; 27:1; 34:18; 79:9; 91:16; 103:4; 111:9; 130:7; 144:2; Isaiah 45:15; 48:17; Jeremiah 50:34; Habakkuk 3:18; Luke 1:47; Romans 6:23; Ephesians 1:13-14; Titus 3:4-5; 1 Peter 1:18-19

Appendix C

Biblical Themes Summary Tables

The following tables can be used for review purposes. They can also be a handy reminder when discussing vignettes and cases.

Every major Bible narrative includes one or more of these themes in the plot of the story. Biblical themes are those recurring concepts that carry or illustrate the central messages of the Bible story. For example, one of the central themes of the Bible is that of salvation or some might say redemption. Some scholars believe that this theme is the universal theme of Scripture and that all other themes are either subdivisions or further explanations of it. Another theme closely related to salvation is that of covenant. Both the theme of redemption and the theme of covenant have ties to economic activity.

One of the elements of aesthetic beauty regarding these biblical story themes is that we should expect to see some repetition of ideas because these themes overlap and are interrelated.

Table C.1. Central messages of the Bible story themes.

	The Believer's Conduct	Character of God	Jesus Christ
Cosmic Conflict	We struggle not against flesh and blood but against principalities and powers.	The conflict is over the character of God: his justice and mercy.	Jesus Christ is the central figure in the battle against the powers of darkness.
Creation	Creation of human beings tells us much about our work in the marketplace.	Creation reveals much about the character of God.	Creation was the action of Jesus Christ that set in motion a great plan of God.
Holiness	Faithful followers are fully consecrated to God, set apart for distinctive service.	God is separate from moral impurity but connected with creation.	The coming of Jesus Christ reveals the holiness of God.
Covenant Relationships	Imitate the covenant relationship modeled by God.	God is the great giver of covenant relations.	Jesus is the fulfillment of the covenantal promises.
Shalom	God's plan for humans included a flourishing life of peace (shalom) in all of its dimensions.	God is the originator of peace.	Jesus obtained and gave peace through his work.
Sabbath	Sabbath is a recurring symbol of loyalty to God and the primary means of maintaining a close relationship with God.	God set apart the sabbath for humankind.	Jesus is the Lord of the sabbath.
Justice	As humans interact in the marketplace, they display justice while they create flourishing peace.	Justice is a central dimension of God's character under attack by Satan.	Jesus Christ revealed the justice of God through his person and work.

	The Believer's Conduct	Character of God	Jesus Christ
Righteousness	Humans foster righteousness and through this flourishing peace.	Righteousness is a central dimension of God's character under attack by Satan.	Jesus Christ revealed the righteousness of God through his person and work.
Truth	Humans foster a life of truth and through this flourishing peace.	Truth is a central dimension of God's character under attack by Satan.	Jesus Christ revealed the truth of God through his person and work.
Wisdom	Humans live a life of wisdom and through this foster flourishing peace.	Wisdom is a central dimension of God's character under attack by Satan.	Jesus Christ revealed the wisdom of God through his person and work.
Loving Kindness	Humans foster loving kindness and through this flourishing peace.	Loving kindness is a central dimension of God's character under attack by Satan.	Jesus Christ revealed the loving kindness of God through his person and work.
Redemption	Humans participate in the redemptive work of God. They also are agents of redemption.	Redemption is one of the universal themes of Scripture that integrate many of the themes present here.	Jesus Christ is the central figure in God's plan of redemption.

Table C.2. How the cosmic conflict theme intersects with other themes.

Theme	God	Versus	Satan
Cosmic Conflict	Fosters freedom within boundaries; supports harmony among members of the community		Offers complete freedom that leads to lawlessness; disrupts harmony among members of the community
Creation	Creates and sustains		Destroys
Holiness	Moral purity; set apart for doing good based on love, righteousness and justice		Moral pollution; undermining love, righteousness and justice
Covenant Relationships	Fosters long-term relationship through broad, mutually beneficial commitments; embraces responsibility in community; freedom within boundaries		Destroys relationships through selfishness; separates from community; avoids responsibility in community; manipulation and coercion
Shalom	Fosters everlasting, flourishing life		Brings destruction, injury, misery and death
Sabbath	Performs meaningful work; rests from grasping for more; fosters contentment; remains faithfully loyal; honor the holiness of God		Destroys the meaningful value of work; unrelentingly grasps for more; incites discontentment; disloyal; dishonor to the holiness of God
Justice	Just actions; impartial judgment		Unjust actions; biased judgment in favor of narrow self-interest
Righteousness	Righteous in actions in community; gives no cause to discredit authority		Unrighteous in actions in community; discredits authority for no cause
Truth	True, faithful, reality-based; reveals, fosters understanding		False, unfaithful, fantasy-based; hides, deceives
Wisdom	Wise		Foolish
Loving Kindness	Loyal commitment; compassionate		Disloyal; cruel
Redemption	Redeems and gains by giving; sets free; resolves the question regarding God's character		Loses by taking; keeps in bondage; questions God's character

Table C.3. Cosmic conflict.

God	Satan
Fosters freedom within boundaries	Slavery; bondage; offers complete freedom that leads to lawlessness
Supports harmony among members of the community	Disrupts harmony among members of the community
Makes provision for reconciliation; acts to take care of sin; permanently removes sin	Leaves others to fend for themselves
Life	Death
Mercy	Cruelty
Reveals character	Hides character
Freedom to choose	Force, coercion
Teaches and models by example	Lives above the principles
Incarnational approach to communication	Aloofness
Impartial evaluation	Partiality
Provides a means of separation to preserve community	Does not separate good from evil
Communicates truthfully and without deceit	Deceitful
Fosters relationships with people of all status	Gives preference for persons of status
Heals	Hurts
Creating, sustaining	Destroying, chaotic
Covenantal relationship	Opposite
Plan for fostering everlasting, flourishing life	Destruction and death
Meaningful work and rest; contentment	Meaningless toil; grasping for more
Justice	Injustice
Righteousness	Unrighteousness
Truth; faithfulness	Falsehood; unfaithfulness
Wisdom	Foolishness
Loving kindness	Opposite
Redemption	Loss
Resolves the issue of God's character	Raises questions regarding God's character

Table C.4. Creation and chaos.

Creation	Chaos
Designed to foster the flourishing life of shalom	Designed to produce misery and wasteland
Order	Chaos
Fertile	Barren
Sustaining	Withering
Dependence; interdependence	Independence
Power of light	Power of darkness
Making a place for loyalty	Making a place for disloyalty
Lordship of Christ over all	Lordship of Christ usurped, challenged
Beautifying, caring, serving environment	Defacing, abusing or destroying environment
Image of God	Image of humans and creation
Interdependent co-workers with God	Independence from God
Happiness = productive; service to others	Happiness = unproductive; served by others
Service	Self-gratification
Responsibility	Irresponsibility
Honor and respect ultimate authority of God	Usurp ultimate authority of God
Maintain healthy relationships with each other	Distort relationships with each other
Restore the image of God	Deface; destroy the image of God
Enjoyment of creation is worship of God	Enjoyment of creation is self-worship

Table C.5. Holiness and defilement.

Holiness	Defilement
Sacred, consecrated fully to God, not for ordinary use	Common, profane, deconsecrated, ordinary use
Wholly other, sanctify for good and righteousness; dwelling among but separate	Join, unify, unite with evil and unrighteousness
Distinctive role	No distinction
In opposition to or intolerant of all that is evil and unfaithful to God	Allowing or encouraging evil and unfaithfulness
Keeping sacred things separate from common things	Combines the holy with the profane, right with wrong
Moral purity	Moral pollution, evil
Being owned by God	Attempting to be free or independent of God
Serving the one true God	Serving other gods
Power and life exercised in moral context	Weakness and death in moral context
Acts of judgment against sin	Encourages sin
Purification from evil	Pollution with evil
Complete break from idolatry and false religion	Acceptance of idolatry and false religion
Cleanness of social justice	Uncleanness of injustice

Table C.6. Covenant and casual relationships.

Covenant Relationship	Casual Relationship
Long-term concerns	Short-term concerns
Deepening permanent commitment	Shallow, casual, temporary commitment
Loyalty	Disloyalty
Fundamental commonly shared principles: Ten Commandments	Rejection of commonly shared principles
Individual and communal	Individual
Created and sustained in the presence of God	Made primarily for self
Vulnerable to being broken	Vulnerable to being broken
Respect for the interests of all considered	Participants look out for their own interests
Gives to nourish the relationship	Takes from and depletes the relationship
Covenant principles are broadly applicable and essentially spiritual in nature, yet comprehend specific duties	Principles are narrowly applicable in principle; duty is whatever works best in a given situation

Table C.7. Shalom and misery.

Shalom	Misery
Loyalty and faith in God and in others	Disloyalty, distrust of God and others
Abundant life	Stealing, killing, destroying
Safety	Danger, calamity
Justice	Injustice
Whole, complete, strong, healthy	Broken, incomplete, weak, sick
Ruled by covenant relationships, right doing and what is good	Ruled by sin and evil
Social and political harmony	Social and political disharmony, conflict, strife
Economic prosperity is integral to other dimensions of shalom	Economic prosperity is independent of other dimensions of well-being

Table C.8. Keeping sabbath and ignoring sabbath.

Keeping Sabbath	Ignoring Sabbath
Encourages meaningful work	Destroys meaningful work
Rests from grasping for more	Unrelentingly grasps for more
Fosters diligent work and contentment	Incites discontentment; devalues work
Loyal, trusting	Disloyal, distrusting
Renounces human autonomy	Embraces human autonomy
Acknowledges God's lordship over all of life; respects God's holiness	Rejects God's lordship over all of life; disrespects God's holiness
Resting in the redemption provided by the Creator	Attempting to provide our own redemption through our works of righteousness
Acknowledges the limits of human power	Ignores the limits of human power
Honors the holiness of God	Dishonors the holiness of God
Spending holy time with God	Avoiding time with God

Table C.9. Justice and injustice.

Justice	Injustice
Basing actions that affect others on covenant relationship principles of God's law	Basing actions that affect others on personal bias
Heroically intervening to correct injustices	Perpetrating or perpetuating or ignoring injustices
Extending justice throughout the entire community beyond the formal justice system	Limiting justice to what is done in the formal justice system
Honoring the rights of others	Jeopardizing or weakening the rights of others

Table C.10. Righteousness and unrighteousness.

Righteousness	Unrighteousness or Wickedness
Firm, straight	Slack, crooked
Strong, enduring, steadfast	Weak, temporary
Doing the right things based on the norms of covenant relationships (God's law); blameless in conduct according to the covenant	Selfish, greedy, destructive, self-sufficient; out of alignment with the covenant
Acting in a way that is faithful to promises made in covenant relationships, including toward those who are most vulnerable	Uncaring toward the vulnerable in the community
Regard for God's character; trusts in God's righteousness	Disregard for God's character; trusts in their own righteousness
Acts that honor, preserve and lend stability to covenant relationships; invests in community; places the interests of others above narrow self-interests	Acts that corrupt, violate, destabilize and ultimately destroy covenant relationships; takes from community
Interventional—making right that which is wrong so that covenant relationships can be renewed	Uncaring about nourishing covenant relationships
A protection against destruction; provides guidance to others in the community	The cause of destruction; leads astray others in the community
Attempts to obey God's law on human power fail; righteousness comes only from God	Attempts to obey God's law on human power fail; righteousness from no other source
Walking on a straight, smooth pathway designed by God	Walking on a crooked, rough pathway designed by humans or Satan

Table C.11. Truth and falsehood.

Truth	Falsehood or Unfaithfulness
Reliability of behavior after being tested	Failure to act in a way that you ought after being tested
Faithfulness to what you ought to be	Unfaithfulness to what you ought to be
Reliable behavior pattern; faithfulness	Unreliable behavior pattern; unfaithfulness
Telling the truth without deception	Deceiving others through our words or actions
Walking in integrity and uprightness	Walking without integrity

Table C.12. Wisdom and foolishness.

Wisdom	Foolishness
Understands how covenant relationships work	Lacks understanding of covenant relationships
Constructive, productive	Destructive, unproductive
Honors God	Dishonors and blames God
Relationship-centered, humble	Self-centered, proud
Morally upright, smart	Morally stupid
Uses discretion, communally prudent	Uses indiscretion, communally reckless
Protects self from being misled; does not mislead others	Blind to being misled; misleads others
Practical skill mastery used for good, useful	Inept, useless, worthless
Listens to counsel from others in the community who are faithful to covenant relationships	Listens to self or those who are adversaries of covenant relationships

Table C.13. Loving kindness and capricious loyalty.

Loving Kindness, Loyalty	Capricious Loyalty
Love based primarily on unchanging loyalty and kindness	Loyalty based primarily on changeable feelings of affection
Respect for the covenant relationship	Shallow commitment to the relationship as long as we feel positively toward the other person
Loyalty that is demonstrated in action	Loyalty in words only
Fostering mutual reciprocity	Promotes selfish gain
Faithfulness in relationships	Unfaithfulness in relationships
Gracious, compassionate	Unkind, coldhearted

Table C.14. Redemption and bondage.

Redemption	Bondage
To act as a kinsman to buy back someone or something of value or to buy back a person, to ransom, liberate or rescue	To put into bondage, to take, to enslave
God's transforming power of good matures	Transforming power of evil matures
Designed to recover lost shalom	Deepens the misery of lost shalom
In Christ because of the grace of God	In self
Cannot be earned by good works; standing achieved by God's power	Attempts unsuccessfully to achieve standing by one's own power
Covenant provides means of redemption	Breaking covenant accentuates the need for redemption
Not limited to spiritual forgiveness of sins; encompasses the whole earth	Encompasses the whole earth
Humans commissioned to participate with God	Humans participate with God's adversary
Reconnecting with God; fosters reconciliation	Separation from God

Appendix D

Ten Principles for Flourishing

SCRIPTURE PASSAGES

So He declared to you His covenant which He commanded you to perform, that is, the Ten Commandments; and He wrote them on two tablets of stone. (Deut 4:13)

How blessed is the man who does not
    walk in the counsel of the wicked,
Nor stand in the path of sinners,
Nor sit in the seat of scoffers!
But his delight is in the law of the LORD,
And in His law he meditates day and night.
He will be like a tree firmly planted by
    streams of water,
Which yields its fruit in its season
And its leaf does not wither;
And in whatever he does, he prospers.
    (Ps 1:1-3)

Those who love Your law have great peace,
And nothing causes them to stumble.
    (Ps 119:165)

So then, the Law is holy, and the commandment is holy and righteous and good. (Rom 7:12)

Love does no wrong to a neighbor; therefore love is the fulfillment of the law. (Rom 13:10)

In this appendix we explore how the Ten Commandments are a summary of the covenant principles designed to foster flourishing life in the community.

The purpose of the Ten Commandments forms the basis of vocation for community members and their leaders regardless of the work they do: Be trustees of covenant relationships so that the promised blessings envisioned in the Decalogue are realized. This duty involves sharing responsibility for oversight, protection and interpretation of the Ten Commandments.[1]

When the promises of a flourishing life are fulfilled, God's creative power is at work. This understanding of the Ten Commandments broadens our understanding of the meaning of prosperity. Unless the other dimensions of flourishing life are included in our thinking about prosperity (spiritual well-being, physical well-being, domestic social harmony, international political harmony), it becomes hollow. Economic well-being achieved at the expense of spiritual well-being, physical health, emotional health, domestic social harmony and international political harmony is ultimately worthless. Yet, without economic thinking as part of well-being an important influence in day-to-day activities of finding, developing, and making available to each other resources needed for living a flourishing life of well-being is made materially impossible.

Similar to a constitution, the Ten Commandments are the basic principles on which other laws are shaped that are designed to foster general well-being in society. Notice the wording of the Preamble to the Constitution of the United States of America. Compare these words with the idea of shalom:

> We the People of the United States, in Order to form a more perfect Union, establish Justice, insure domestic Tranquility, provide for the common defense, promote the general Welfare, and secure the Blessings of Liberty to ourselves and our Posterity, do ordain and establish this Constitution for the United States of America.

The traditional approach is to apply the Ten Commandments at primarily the individual level of behavior. Given the social nature of ethics, a wider, communal perspective must be taken. The commandments are not merely a random, arbitrary list of ethical dos and don'ts for individuals.

They form the prescription for how the community as a whole can experience shalom through individual and collective behaviors.

The community has responsibility to preserve, protect and interpret the covenant. Civil leaders,[2] religious leaders,[3] economic leaders[4] and prophets[5] all play a part in this. Indeed everyone has a role to play to preserve the Ten Commandments for future generations.[6] If just one person has the role of preserving and interpreting the principles of the Ten Commandments, the risk increases that the principles on which flourishing life is based will become corrupted. Thus the whole community has shared responsibility for overseeing, protecting and interpreting the covenant.

A summary of the relationship between the Ten Commandments and flourishing well-being is given in table D.1.[7]

Table D.1. The Ten Commandments and flourishing well-being (shalom).

Context and Purpose
Rom 7:12 Rom 13:10
• Comprehension of the Ten Commandments must be scaled up to include the person, the primary work unit (the family) and the whole community. The Decalogue applies to domestic relationships and international relationships.
• The Decalogue describes a divine-human partnership where humans interpret the moral frameworks established by God in the context of specific situations for specific business organizations and in so doing realize God's promised blessings.
• If the people write the principles of the Law on their hearts allowing these principles to direct their actions to moral right doing, the result is Yahweh's blessing for all who participate in this plan. (Ps 29:11; 34:14)
• The purpose of the Ten Commandments is the experience of shalom (peace): a flourishing life in the community. (Ps 119:165)
• The purpose of the Ten Commandments is also to lead us to a relationship with God. (Rom 3:19-20; 5:20-21; 8:3)

Commandment	Relationship with Flourishing Well-Being
Prologue Ex 20:1-2	The Ten Commandments are given in the context of release from bondage. Whatever comes from this release from bondage in terms of the anticipation of flourishing well-being, is a result of a creative work of God. Redemption from oppression comprehends all dimensions of Shalom: spiritual health, physical health, social harmony, international harmony and economic prosperity.
	• The guidance that the Decalogue gives begins with a statement of God's character.
	• The Decalogue is a description of God's character that he wants to see reproduced in the community in all dimensions of life.
	• Ultimately shalom is a creative work of God.
	• Although the community has a responsibility to observe all the commands, their memory of the redemption narrative is the starting point for the response.
	• Redemption comprehends all dimensions of life: spiritual health, physical health, social harmony, international harmony, economic prosperity.

1. "You shall have no other gods before Me." (Ex 20:3) Deut 5:7; 6:4-5, 14; Ps 73:25; 81:9; Is 43:10; Jer 25:6; Mt 4:10; 1 Cor 8:6; Phil 3:18-19	Whatever we might say about particular commands that when followed promote prosperity, ultimately the contribution to a flourishing life by the commandments depend on the willingness of people to be loyal to the One who gave the covenant principles. Ethics is a confession of faith in a gracious God who is the ultimate source of moral principles. Yet, these principles have rational plausibility when considered in the context of a community. • Faithful believers must review their whole life in community and acknowledge what might be there that might be placed ahead of a relationship with their Creator and Redeemer. • That which we choose to pledge the allegiance of our hearts, minds and actions is the focus of our worship and the ground of ethical standards. • To have another god is to reject God and his plan for full well-being in favor our own ideas for well-being. It means rejecting the Giver of shalom. It mirrors an essential issue in the cosmic conflict.
2. "You shall not make for yourself an idol, or any likeness of what is in heaven above or on the earth beneath or in the water under the earth." (Ex 20:4; see also vv. 5-6) Ex 34:17; Lev 19:4; Deut 5:8; Ps 97:7; 115:4; Is 40:18; 42:8	Idolatry is worship of self since it is the human that creates the idol, but worship of self is a negation of the covenant. This, then, is the essence of idolatry: crossing the line between creature and Creator taking upon ourselves the authority to create a distorted attitude toward God acting as if he is the source of our personal gratification. Whenever humans give reverence to the social order, the structure and forms of culture that we have created, we risk placing these above the principles of right doing outlined in the Decalogue. • When we emphasize one dimension of shalom to the exclusion of the others, we risk creating a false shalom. • Making and worshiping an idol is an attempt to be in a position of power equal to or over the Creator, thus undermining his sovereignty. • The life of the faithful believer becomes the tangible representation of God to others. • Worship of idols decreases personal responsibility and accountability for human actions in the organization and in the community. • Supporting an economic system that produces and uses idols diverts resources. This creates market inefficiencies. • Through our faithfulness to God, we are called to represent the image of God to the world in all dimensions of life, including the marketplace, as imperfect and flawed as such a representation might be. Humans represent God to the world, but in so doing we should not come to believe that such representation is the best that can be offered to the world especially because ultimate knowledge of God's mysterious nature is limited. This command is a call to humility.
3. "You shall not take the name of the LORD your God in vain, for the LORD will not leave him unpunished who takes His name in vain." (Ex 20:7) Lev 19:12; Deut 5:11	True worship to God, claiming loyalty to the Creator and covenant Redeemer, means that the follower of God will follow God into the marketplace by demonstrating the essential characteristic believed to be the essence of God in his relationship with the community (i.e., faithfulness to covenant promises). • Making false promises undermines community trust. This has a downward pressure on communal exchange activities, and as a result, lowers the overall well-being of the community. • False promises attack truth (living faithfully and consistently). • Any statement that deceives is forbidden. • Do not associate with God's name in order to further economic ambitions. • Persons who choose to make promises to others will be circumspect about what they promise. Be circumspect. • Do not parade your religious faith around for others to see, invoking God as the author of strategic plans, operational decisions or business successes, using relationships in religion to build business or making reference to God in order to further personal ambitions.

4. "Remember the sabbath day, to keep it holy. Six days you shall labor and do all your work, but the seventh day is a sabbath of the LORD your God." (Ex 20:8-10; see also v. 11) Gen 2:3; Ex 31:13-14; Lev 19:3; Deut 5:12-15	The sabbath day is a means for humans to continually renounce human autonomy and acknowledge God's lordship in human life. The weekly sabbath day of worship is inseparable from and interdependent with the commission to work. Without working creatively in the material world during the rest of the week, the experience of shalom would be impossible to achieve. One might even say that sabbath would lose some of its meaning if on the other six days no meaningful work was done or if God was not honored in human work. • The Decalogue's plan for shalom included work. • The abundant life of well-being is not a life of leisure. The Decalogue's plan for shalom included humans working. Diligent work supports well-being for the person and the community. Yet, the aim of this work was not accumulation of material personal possessions alone. • Worship to God involves giving up 14.29 percent of productive time each week to community worship. Yet, sabbath is the secret to a fully prosperous life in a community who shares sabbath values. • Worshiping the Creator is the foundation for shalom; it encourages contentment and without contentment, there can be no shalom. • Helping other people who are close to you experience sabbath rest extends shalom from you to them.
5. "Honor your father and your mother, that your days may be prolonged in the land which the LORD your God gives you." (Ex 20:12) Ex 21:15-17; Lev 19:3; Deut 5:16; Prov 1:8-9; 20:20; Mt 15:4; Eph 6:1	The family unit envisioned in the fifth commandment is the primary economic unit considered in the Ten Commandments. But the family, in Scripture, is an extended family which is part of a larger cluster of families in a community. If you want to experience a flourishing life in community, each has a duty to respect and honor the other regardless of the position you are in with respect to power and authority. • The well-being of children and the aged depends on the parents and the children. • Wisdom is mediated through those who are older and more experienced in the ways of God, in the journey of walking with God in daily life and who have responsibility for the well-being of the community as a whole. To refuse instruction provided by the wise is to dishonor God. • Without the double-sided duty of honor this flourishing life of well-being would quickly be undermined and the community would quickly be returned to oppression. This would undermine the redemption narrative. • Persons must earn the right to be honored by how they conduct themselves in community. • Reciprocal honor builds relationships rather than tears them down. • Honor begins in the home. As children learn to honor parents, they learn how to honor others in society. • Honoring each other requires taking actions that result in well-being for each other.
6. "You shall not murder." (Ex 20:13) Gen 9:5-6; Lev 24:21; Deut 5:17; Prov 1:18; Mt 5:21-22; Rom 13:9	Flourishing life depends on a stable, safe civil society where the other blessings of shalom are experienced. This begins with flourishing physical life, without which the other dimensions of well-being are not possible. In general, we keep this command when we foster the fulfillment of promises for well-being in all dimensions. • Physical life is the basis of experiencing shalom. If persons fear for their lives or for their economic stability, if the continuity of life is uncertain because of the presence of murderers who are not stopped, communal activities would be greatly curtailed. True prosperity for all would decline. • Killing a person is a direct attack on covenant relationships, shalom and the image of God. • Killing is a violent expression of the cosmic conflict. • This command requires us to take responsibility for the unintentional harm we cause to others and to take reasonable means to promote safety not only at work but also elsewhere in the community. • We are to be like the tree of life to foster a flourishing life of others in the community, promote the life of all living things, help others to develop to their fullest potential and bring out their best and assist those who cannot care for themselves. • We must take responsibility for what we do to ourselves, including the choices that we make for behaviors that affect our health and well-being. • We should develop ourselves and our workers to the fullest potential possible for service to others. • Fostering life promotes prosperity; taking life destroys prosperity.

7. "You shall not commit adultery." (Ex 20:14) Deut 5:18; Prov 6:32-33; Mt 5:27-28; Eph 5:3; Heb 13:4; Jas 4:4	Anything that would lead toward being unfaithful in a relationship is included in the scope of this commandment. Marriage is not the only relationship that is covenantal in nature, but it illustrates the sacredness of all relationships in a covenant community. Success in the community depends on maintaining solid relationships that are honored by all. • Adultery interferes with the covenant relationship of another while undermining your own covenant relationship. • Adultery signifies that a covenant relationship is broken. • Adultery disrupts creation's plan for community. • Adultery undermines the family solidarity; family is the primary cultural unit of society. • Adultery violates the most important human relationship. • Adultery is theft of covenant relationship.
8. "You shall not steal." (Ex 20:15) Lev 19:11-13; Deut 5:19; 25:13; Rom 13:9; Eph 4:28	Underneath the action of stealing is the meaning that stealing has in the context of the covenant and all that it promised by God in well-being. Because for the believer God is the owner of all things material, theft or fraud is an attack on God. It is also an attack on the dignity of the person and his or her work which was required to achieve shalom. When we steal, we are attacking this great commission and the Creator who gave it when our duty is to work in concert with and imitate the Creator. • Stealing is an attack on sabbath, which is associated with diligent work. • Stealing is an attack on shalom and contentment. It indicates dissatisfaction with life. • Stealing undermines more than just the economic dimension of shalom. • Theft is a refusal to accept what God has given, a refusal to enter into the type of contentment envisioned in shalom. • This command excludes any act of deceit or treachery, any interference by third parties in the family or with property that anyone possesses. • This command includes the use of technology in trade. • This command requires each person in the community to watch out for the interests of others. • The positive dimension of this command represents another invisible hand of the market. The hand of self-interest does contribute to a certain degree of flourishing well-being. But without the invisible hand of other-interest and generosity, flourishing life is only partial.
9. "You shall not bear false witness against your neighbor." (Ex 20:16) Ex 23:6; Lev 19:11; Deut 5:20; Prov 19:5	In this command the primary issue at stake is bringing false testimony against a fellow citizen in the context of the justice system. The cornerstone of civil law and justice in the ancient Hebrew culture was the process of giving testimony whereby the truth is spoken by witnesses to an impartial judge who will not take bribes. Deceit and lying sacrifice true shalom. • Bearing false witness is an attempt to steal the character (reputation) of another. This is an affront to truth (Lev 19:11). • False witnesses steal property, freedom and even life. • False witnesses perpetuate injustice and this, in turn, destroys the fabric of a flourishing society. • False witnesses attempt to hide; they undermine transparency. • Without an impartial justice system, marketplace shalom is destroyed.
10. "You shall not covet your neighbor's house; you shall not covet your neighbor's wife or his male servant or his female servant or his ox or his donkey or anything that belongs to your neighbor." (Ex 20:17) Deut 5:21; Rom 13:9; 1 Tim 6:9-10; Heb 13:5	Part of the responsibilities of acceptance of God's promise of flourishing life was the commitment to work productively six days a week. This is not covetousness. The flip side of this is that faithful followers of God will be content with the rewards of their hard work. • Coveting shows that the heart has not been watched over (see Deut 4:9; Prov 4:23; Jas 1:14-15). • True prosperity is achieved when limits are placed on personal desires so that the needs of the community are taken care of while the needs of the organization are also met. This applies equally to buyers who desire to maximize their utility as it does to sellers who desire to maximize their economic profit. Unfettered desire and greed are destructive. • Coveting reveals that shalom is lacking in the heart of a person. • Coveting mirrors the origin of the cosmic conflict. • Coveting is the fundamental reason why social disorder exists. • Ethics is a confession of faith in a Creator-Redeemer who will supply all our needs. By making a relationship with God the primary focus, we will foster contentment.

Appendix E

Summary of Ethical Models in Comparison

We can compare a summary of the various contemporary ethical models that have been applied to the ethical, social and legal envi-

ronment of business in terms of their greatest weakness or greatest need.

We can see from this summary that some

Table E.1. A comparison of ethical models.

Ethical Model	Greatest Weaknesses and Need
Egoism You have no moral duty to help others unless doing so brings benefits to yourself. There are no moral absolutes that apply to all persons.	Rejects absolute, universal standards of right and wrong. Offers no solution to societal conflicts of interest. Attempts to isolate the person from community. Rejects that moral standards require objective, impartial application to all persons. **Need:** Society as a whole must find a way to reconcile all the differences of opinion regarding what is right and wrong. Egoism offers no guidance for this.
Relativism Standards of right and wrong are socially determined. There are no moral absolutes that apply to all persons in all social groups.	Social group role depends on a valid standard of conduct outside the social role. Relativism offers nothing to define what that standard is. Society's norms may not be based on principles that can be applied universally. **Need:** The interaction between groups or societies requires a bare minimum of standards that apply to more than one social group.
Common Sense Gut instinct Intuition Social consensus Social reasoning Practical judgment Generally accepted moral principles No moral absolutes exist.	It requires the existence of a standard of right and wrong that is commonly accepted. Depends on the popularity of views in society regarding right and wrong. Persons or groups in positions of power can influence common sense. **Need:** A standard of right and wrong that becomes generally accepted in society that helps social groups resolve their differences regarding right and wrong.
Social Contract Set of perceived but unwritten social obligations Common beliefs regarding promises made to each other No moral absolutes exist.	Members of society differ in terms of how they define the elements of the social contract. Does not define what is right and wrong by itself. **Need:** A standard of right and wrong that persons in society can commit to.
Utilitarianism Actions that produce or tend to produce the greatest amount of good for the most people No moral absolutes exist.	It offers no objective standard to define what is good or bad. Right and wrong are defined in terms of culturally determined or individually determined standards of good and bad; utilitarianism may impose unreasonable sacrifices on the few in order to promote the welfare of the many. **Need:** An objective standard of right and wrong that takes into considerations those who are harmed by social actions.

Ethical Model	Greatest Weaknesses and Need
Universalism Use reason alone. Moral standards must be universally applied to all persons without logical contradiction. Respect the autonomy of others.	The categorical imperative places reason above the Bible and independent of God. Does not define what is right and wrong by itself. **Need:** A standard of right and wrong that can be used to determine what should be universally applied without logical contradiction.
Agency Follow directives of those in legitimate authority. No moral absolutes exist.	Does not describe how to manage the tension between what is required of you and duty to others. Moral principles come before and supersede the agency relationship. Does not define what is right and wrong by itself. **Need:** A standard of right and wrong that supersedes or is the basis of the agency relationship.
Justice and Rights Be fair to others. Respect the rights of others. No moral absolute definition of justice and rights exists.	Each person's idea of fairness may be different from an opposing person's idea. Without an objective standard of right and wrong that lies outside personal definitions of fairness, justice can degenerate toward cultural relativism or egoism. **Need:** A standard for justice and rights that can be used to define justice and rights.
Virtues and Character Virtues are rooted in community definition of good. Who you are drives what you do. Be faithful to how the community has shaped you. No moral absolutes exist.	If virtues are ultimately dependent on the community's moral vision, there is no transcendent absolute standard of right and wrong. **Need:** A standard of right and wrong that is used by the community to shape the virtues and character traits of community members considered to be good or excellent.

contemporary ethical models, without an external, absolute objective standard of right and wrong, reduce to either egoism or relativism when pushed to their logical conclusions (see fig. E.1).

When considering these contemporary ethical models we notice something common to them all. Each ethical model lacks something important: a universally applicable set of moral standards that supersedes or is at the foundation of the model.

Universalism stands apart from egoism and cultural relativism in that it permits no logical contradictions when applying a duty universally. However, universalism places the location of standards of right and wrong within each human's reason. Accordingly, like the other models universalism also appears to lack an absolute, objective standard that lies outside the person or social group.

When comparing these contemporary ethical models with the biblical story themes

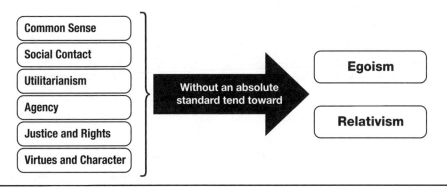

Figure E.1. The relationship among ethical models.

SPECTRUM OF ETHICAL MODELS

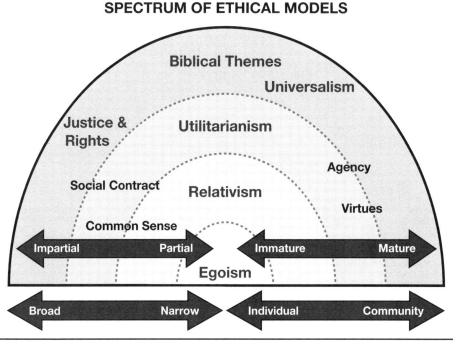

Figure E.2. Diagram of ethical models.

we notice something else. Egoism and cultural relativism stand in direct opposition to the biblical story themes. This finding places the other contemporary ethical models in a weak position with respect to the biblical message for the marketplace.

Saying that you will accept utilitarianism as your ethical model plus the biblical perspective places you in a self-contradictory position. Saying that you will follow agency and the biblical themes puts you into a self-contradictory position. However, if you say that the biblical themes are your foundation and that following biblical thinking you wish to be a faithful marketplace agent, you have identified the objective standards that you will apply to your work as an agent.

Similarly, if you say that the biblical themes are your foundation and you also wish to consider the consequences of your actions on all relevant stakeholders (one of the principles of utilitarianism), you establish

the ground on which to consider the consequences and the net resulting effect of your actions on all relevant stakeholders. You also establish the ground on which to counteract utilitarian weaknesses. Likewise, if you say that common sense or the social contract are your preferred approaches to ethical decision making in the marketplace and you choose biblical teaching as your foundation, you have something substantial with which to evaluate both common sense and the social contract. You have a foundation to determine when what others say is right should be challenged or accepted.

We can make another observation in terms of the spectrum of ethical models considered in part II of this book: In comparison with other models, the biblical themes consider not only individual self-interests but also the interests of society as a whole. Biblical themes are the most impartial, broadest, mature and focused on the larger community.

We come to a basic question that you cannot avoid: Must humans have an objective, absolute standard of right and wrong, a standard that lies outside the person or the social group? Egoists and cultural relativists say no. Essentially all other contemporary ethical models agree. In contrast to this, themes of the biblical story say yes!

Hidden in each of the contemporary ethical models is a kernel of biblical truth that should not be forgotten (see table E.2). In parentheses is noted the biblical story theme that is the primary home for the kernel of truth.

Table E.2. Kernels of biblical themes in ethical models.

Contemporary Ethical Model	Kernels from the Biblical Themes
Egoism	Do not act in a way that is self-destructive. Be responsible and take care of your own legitimate needs as well as the needs of others. Do unto others as you would have them do unto you (covenant). However, be careful that your own narrow self-interests do not keep you from serving others and their interests. Be willing to act altruistically and unselfishly even it if this means that you get no personal benefit from such actions and if it means that it costs you (loving kindness, redemption). Do not isolate your decision from your relationship with others (creation, covenant).
Relativism	Be tolerant of others. Foster freedom to choose. Do not require others to believe the same way you believe. However, represent biblical ideals in a way that offers attractive, plausible and practical alternatives to cultural relativism (cosmic conflict).
Common Sense	Steep your mind in scriptural principles so that your instincts and gut feelings become informed by biblical story themes. Demonstrate to others the attractiveness in the practical wisdom of biblical ideals. However, be careful to not simply accept your gut instinct, social consensus or common wisdom in complicated situations. These may lead you toward a biased, narrow self-interest.
Social Contract	Make the implicit commitment to a standard of right and wrong found in the biblical story themes (covenant, truth). These will more than likely be respected by others. However, be careful not to use the popularity of beliefs regarding right and wrong as your standard. Make your commitment to God supreme in your life. Allow this consecration (holiness) to shape your thinking in social settings.
Utilitarianism	Value the practical utility (wisdom, truth) of your actions because these are designed to help not only yourself but also the larger community that you serve. Foster the well-being of all persons and the community as a whole. However, be careful not to make utility or optimization become the standard of right and wrong. Do not let economic well-being become isolated from the other dimensions of true prosperity (shalom).
Universalism	Apply the biblical standards of right and wrong as equally to yourself as they should be applied to others. Use your God-given reason when interpreting and applying biblical story theme ideals. However, do not make your own reason the standard of right and wrong since it is untrustworthy (cosmic conflict, truth).
Agency	Be faithful in your marketplace agency relationships as long as doing so does not require you to forget the legitimate needs of other stakeholders or forget the biblical ideals which are the foundation (covenant, shalom, truth, righteousness).
Justice and Rights	Foster justice and respect rights of others. Use the biblical story themes to inform you regarding the nature of fairness and rights in different situations. Do not let self-interests shape your definition of fairness and rights. Be assertive in righting wrongs that have been done in the past (justice, sabbath, shalom).
Virtues and Character	Saturate your mind with biblical thinking so that, over time, your character is shaped by biblical ideals. Become a virtuous person by habitually following the biblical story themes (righteousness, truth). Demonstrate your character with your actions (cosmic conflict, truth). When necessary dialogue with others in the faith community regarding how to apply biblical principles in complicated situations. Contribute to the dialogue when others need help in applying biblical story themes to particular situations (shalom).

The Purpose of Business
Through the Lens of Biblical Themes

SCRIPTURE PASSAGE

Depart from evil and do good;
Seek peace and pursue it. (Ps 34:14)

OVERVIEW

In this appendix we wrestle with the issues related to the question, What is the purpose of business? This question has important implications for several topics in business ethics and corporate responsibility. In particular we will

- explore the issues in the current debate regarding the purpose of business

- distinguish between several related ideas

- consider the purpose of business through the lens of biblical story themes

MAJOR TOPICS

Two Contemporary Views
The Business Model: The Context of Profit
Managerial Control Devices
Theory of the Firm
Distinctions
The Point of Profit
The Many Purposes of Business
Through the Lens of Biblical Themes

KEY TERMS

business model, instrumental purpose, level of analysis, profit, ultimate purpose

For at least a generation the claim that profits are the purpose of business has come under increasing scrutiny. Profit might be the result of business operations, but does profit represent the real purpose of a business? Is the purpose to make a profit or something else? Is there only one purpose of business, or can there be more than one? To answer these questions this essay will look at contemporary views on the purpose of business. To set the context in which to understand the concept of profit the essay will review the concept of the business model and the difference between operational and strategic managerial controls. The essay will review the legitimate role of profit. It will suggest that there are multiple purposes of business, some of which are primary and others secondary or instrumental. Finally, the essay will conclude with an exploration of the purpose of business as seen through the lens of biblical story themes.

TWO CONTEMPORARY VIEWS

Although there have been voices to the contrary over the years,[1] to some contemporary thinkers, as stated above, business exists for the purpose of generating profits.[2]

In the first half of the twentieth century Berle and Means were two voices to the contrary. They state that the interests of the community are paramount for the organization.[3] Another purpose of business is that of being an agent for change and material progress in society. Business has the role of organizing activities designed to do things for others on condition that others reciprocate by offering something of value in exchange. Business has a legitimate role in generating innovations that accrue to the benefit of society as a whole. It has a role in maintaining the presence of minimal ethical standards in society.

In the view of Peter Drucker, the famous management expert of the twentieth century, business does not exist for the purpose of employees, managers or even its stockholders. He claimed that only one valid purpose exists for business: to create a customer by offering goods and services that the customer needs and wants.[4] In Drucker's view: "Even the most private of enterprises is an organ of society and serves a social function."[5]

William Kline states simply that "the purpose of business is to produce a good or service for trade."[6] He says that the motivation for business may vary and profit is not necessarily the goal. The business may succeed if it is profitable, but "it does not seem that profit need be" the "primary intention" in order to be a business.[7] "Someone may wish to build a better mousetrap simply because it is a better mousetrap."[8] "The business of business has changed over the ages . . . but the underlying reasons for conducting business are still as constant as the basic requirements for survival."[9]

THE BUSINESS MODEL: THE CONTEXT OF PROFIT

We use models in many places in society. A basketball coach draws Xs and Os on a clipboard to show where the players should move for an inbound pass with three seconds to go before the final buzzer. The drawing is a model of how the coach wants the play to unfold so that the designated shooter can make the final shot.

Models are not perfect. They do not explain everything. They are often limited to specific time frames or specific operating conditions. They often assume, but normally do not explain, the larger purposes of what is being modeled. Models are built on important assumptions. Accordingly, the value of the model as a projection device is dependent entirely on the accuracy of its underlying assumptions. A coach's drawing on a clipboard does not show player motivation, player skill, or everything what the competition will do when the ball is passed inbounds.

In the world of business we use conceptual models to illustrate the underlying influences at work on an organization. The business model of an organization is a story that describes, from the point of view of organizational owners and managers, how the enterprise works within its larger context.[10] This story contains the key assumptions that support the story. The business model encompasses the activities that lead to the provision of value that satisfy the wants of others when there is an expectation of payment from those who receive benefit.

Business, after all, is social activities that involve exchange of payment for value offered by the business. It is only natural for parties in the exchange to be concerned about the amount of value that is received compared with the amount of value incurred as an expense.

However, the value of engaging in marketplace activities is a concern of both buyer and seller. Thus, to the degree that profit raises to the level of concern, we conclude that it is a concern of both parties in the exchange. Further, to allow the buyer but not the seller to be concerned with profit seems inconsistent with the social nature of business. When profit is part of the business model story, it is discussed from the point of view of the organizational managers. In comparison with organizational managers, customers tend to have a narrow perspective that shapes their concerns regarding the transactions of value they engage in.

The business model is explained in part by the financial estimates that describe the ways the organization will buy and sell and as a result of this add cash to investors as it meets its obligations to others in society. These financial estimates include both the revenue stream and expense structure as elements of the story about how the organization operates in its larger environment. Accordingly, the business model can be expressed in terms of any one of several standard financial statements and analyses such as the following: breakeven (cost-volume-profit) analysis, the income statement, the statement of cash flows and the balance sheet. Each of these implies the existence of purposeful work. None describe what that purpose is.

Using breakeven analysis to compare the incoming value with the outgoing value to determine when these are equal suggests that there are purposeful business activities occurring. Businesses do not spend money on just anything. They spend money on things that they hope customers will find of value. The income statement summarizes the gains and losses which reveal the results of business operations for a particular period of time.[11]

The profit and loss statement asks the question, To what degree did our work contribute to our ability to continue pursuing the organization's purpose? It suggests that work activities have a purpose, but by itself it does not define what that purpose is. The statement of cash flows encourages managers to act on the truth of where cash came from and where it goes. Like the income statement the statement of cash flows implies that there is a purpose for the organization but by itself it does not reveal that purpose.

The balance sheet is based on the formula: What we *own* = what we *owe* + *net worth* (assets = liabilities + owner equity). If the organization owed nothing to others, its net worth would be equal to the value of its assets. What we owe (liabilities) is part of what we own (assets) because the organization is responsible to a larger community in which the story of the organization is being played out. Thus, what the firm owns includes its responsibilities to others outside the firm. Assets are the things that give the organization power to meet certain claims on the firm's responsibilities to others. Assets also are those things that are the foundation for the organization's ability to fulfill its promises to society. The balance sheet tells part of the story, but alas, like the other financial statements it does not define the how and why assets are used in serving others.

Collectively, the financial statements tell part of the larger story. Admittedly, these important statements all point to profit as a key measure.[12] However, financial statements of profitability cannot define the purpose of the organization. Instead, they imply that a purpose exists. It is in the rest of the story, after we see the financial and managerial accounting, that we see the purpose of the business.

MANAGERIAL CONTROL DEVICES

Claiming that the purpose of business is profit confuses operational managerial controls with strategic controls. Managerial controls emphasize short-term task-related activities. Examples of operational managerial controls include measures of efficiency such as the profitability-oriented financial measures described by financial statements. In contrast, strategic controls focus on the organization as a whole in the longer term. Strategic controls are focused more on effectiveness (which, in turn, are closer to the purpose of an organization) than efficiency in achieving organizational goals.

Profit is a useful measure of efficiency but less useful as a measure of organizational effectiveness. The reason is that the focus of profit tends to be on the financial results of completing operational tasks during a period of time or at a particular point in time. Profit might be achieved through any number of efficient means in any given organization. Some means might be closely aligned with strategic purpose while other means might not be. By themselves, profit measures do not care which means or which purposes are in view. Thus, measures of profitability, and similarly other managerial control metrics, do not say much about the underlying purposes of an organization.

THEORY OF THE FIRM

Scores of descriptive theories of the firm have been proposed by business scholars. The dominant theories are: agency theory, neoclassical economic theory, the resource-based theory, the behavioral theory, the evolutionary theory, the transaction-cost theory, and the stakeholder theory. Most of the theories of the firm attempt to explain why firms exist, the nature of business organizations, and what contributes to economic performance of firms in highly competitive markets. With few exceptions the theories are predominantly egoistic in perspective, based on the assumption that business exists for building wealth.

DISTINCTIONS

When considering the purpose of business, especially in terms of the role of profit, several distinctions should be drawn. We will consider each one here.

Personal motives versus larger purpose. One difficulty when discussing the questions is the tendency of some to confuse the personal motives of owners and managers with the larger purpose of the organization in society. A person might go into business to make money. Such a person might even say that the purpose of business, as seen from his or her personal motive point of view, is to make a profit. A manager responsible for profit and loss may have as a goal the earning of profit, especially if a cash incentive is associated with that. Achieving a profit on a regular basis is something tangible that can be shown to one's employer or to a prospective employer as a signal that the manager has the abilities needed for the organization to succeed in the future. But motive for a human activity is not necessarily the same thing as the larger, deeper reason for why humans engage in such activity.

How we trade things of value is not instinctive. Business practices have evolved over time and have become social conventions designed by humans to serve humans. Thus, business is a social practice, a set of behaviors and rules for behavior for living life. But to become accepted broadly across many times and places worldwide such social conventions must foster some greater good for the societies that engage in such practices as they develop and learn to survive and thrive.[13] We conclude, therefore, that the deeper purpose of business is related to achieving a greater good for society regardless of the personal motives that may be at play.

Internal versus external perspective. A further distinction that is helpful when talking about the purpose of business is the perspective that one takes whether external or internal when considering a particular situation that an organization is in. An external perspective sees the purpose of an organization from the point of view of those on the outside, such as suppliers and customers who have goals to accomplish. An internal perspective sees purpose from the point of view of those on the inside who are accountable for achieving goals related to producing and distributing goods and services in a manner that is responsible for resources entrusted to them. These perspectives are not necessarily mutually exclusive. For example, an employee of a company can have the external perspective of a consumer at the same time as having the internal perspective of a worker.

Ultimate purpose versus instrumental purposes. Another difficulty is that people sometimes confuse the ultimate purpose of an activity with the instrumental purpose of that activity.[14] These are not always identical. For analogy, you would not spend a Saturday evening playing Rook® for the purpose of racking up points on a piece of scratch paper. Points earned are outcomes of the play and may be instrumental in increasing the perceived social status of a person in a given context, but the ultimate purpose of the game is something different. It may be to have an enjoyable evening of social interaction. Likewise, the outcome or goal of business may be in earning a profit, for

it is in earning a profit that the business is allowed to continue. Thus, the closest we can come to identifying profit with the purpose of business is to see it as an instrumental purpose which allows the organization to continue doing its ultimate purpose which is larger than profit. Admittedly, some organizations are formed and operated for no other purpose than to generate a profit. Even in these cases, what appears to be an ultimate purpose may be only instrumental to achieving some other ultimate purpose. Purpose is generally something larger, that is, to serve others by offering products and services which meet their needs.

Long-term purpose versus short-term obligations. Another important distinction is the long-term purpose of an organization versus its short-term obligations. Purpose drives organizational leaders to make commitments on behalf of the firm as it carries out its service to society. These commitments, by nature, come with short-term financial and legal obligations which cannot be ignored if leaders expect to be faithful to their commitments. Suppliers have to be paid in a timely manner or they will stop supplying. The firm must meet its payroll obligations or it breaks the law and workers will go away. Regulations must be followed or the government will impose unfavorable constraints. Equipment and other property must be acquired now to meet expected future commitments.

The point of this distinction is twofold. First, looking at purpose from external or internal perspectives creates a slightly different emphasis on what the business does. By nature those, especially managers, on the inside of an organization will have a mental orientation different from those on the outside. These mental orientations can be either in concert or in competition. Second, people typically care less about the profitability of another organization if they are on the outside because it is up to the managers of the other organization who are responsible for profit and loss. From the outside it is relatively easy to criticize another firm that, in the process of fulfilling its commitments, generates a profit. In contrast, those with an internal perspective care a lot more about profitability of their own firm because these are the stakeholders who have the responsibility to follow through on commitments to others in a way that uses resources wisely. But pressure on profits can also come from inside the firm when employees or managers desire higher compensation, more organizational influence or a higher social status.

Level of analysis distinction. Another distinction to be made here is that we must consider the broader reason for the *raison d'être* of business as a social institution versus the purpose of a particular business in its particular market or industry. This distinction is applied in much the same way as we might consider the purpose of education, the purpose of civil government or the purpose of an impartial justice-legal system in society. Here the purpose of business, at least in an economic sense, is to facilitate the exchanges that members of society need to complete on a recurring basis in order to obtain the goods and services they need and want for living life.

Employing the other side of this distinction we must consider the purpose of a particular business positioned in a particular market or industry. For example, we might consider the purpose of a company that manufactures metal containers (tin cans) which it sells to food processing businesses for use in preserving food. The purpose of a particular business firm is identical to its mission. It is when the mission of a firm becomes separated from the larger purpose of business in society that moral problems arise.

Peter Drucker counseled long ago that the purpose of business lies outside business in society. The purpose of a particular business is the reason for engaging in business-related endeavors. Such a reason is inseparable from the larger purposes of the society in which the business exists.[15]

THE POINT OF PROFIT

If profit is not the ultimate purpose of business, then what is the point of profit? While profit is important to the ongoing success of a business, it does not adequately express the idea of purpose. The reason is that profit, when emphasized by itself, downplays the shared societal values which are at the root of why we enter into exchange relationships with each other in particular markets. If the purpose of entering into exchanges was to merely gain a profit, the means by which these purposes are achieved would quickly turn to violence and destroy the ability of society to live its shared values. As Charles Handy said, "The purpose of business . . . is to make a profit so that business can do something more and better. That 'something better' becomes the real justification for" why the business exists.[16]

Profit is a signal of how efficiently the business is meeting the needs of others in society. Profit is just one of several outcomes of purposeful activity. An often-used analogy is that of breathing. We do not live for the purpose of taking in oxygen and expelling carbon dioxide. The purpose of life is larger than that, but we cannot live without breathing. Too much oxygen does harm to the human. Likewise, generating too much profit (profit maximization) causes problems for the organization: unwise and perhaps arrogant management decisions, unsafe working conditions or short-changing customers on value.

Some might say, as does Drucker, that profit is good not only for the organization but also for society. Until a business earns an economic profit it uses more resources from society than it returns as value back to society. A business operating at an economic loss destroys the wealth that otherwise could be used to develop and distribute new products and services.[17]

Profit, while beneficial if earned by honest, just means, paradoxically can become destructive if it is earned in excess.[18] Leaders in an organization who are merely interested in making money would become hopelessly focused on short-term gain to the firm's long-term detriment. The pursuit of short-term gains would torpedo investment for the long run. Managers would stop looking for ways to make the organization better. They would have little need to innovate. Thus, even from a practical point of view making profit the purpose of business does not work very well unless you are willing to live a socially or economically destructive existence.

Business is not merely an economic entity. It is a community of people committed to providing products and services that are valued by society, a social institution designed to bring value to the larger society. The primary relationships in this community, those that produce the values prized and therefore purchased by society, are the associations among managers, production workers, technicians, support staff and top-level leaders.

By way of contrast, in the context of the modern corporation the relationships of stockholders, board directors and creditors generally do not produce the value. When the leaders of a corporation focus exclusively on the profit that is earned as a result of the collaborative effort of the people in the firm, the company begins to die even though the financial statements might indicate that it is thriving. Instead, when a corporation contributes to society by offering goods and services, by helping to minimize the transaction costs of customers exchanging with them in the marketplace and by contributing to the greater good of society through how it uses community's resources, it is maximizing its overall contribution to society. But to attempt to separate the economic outcomes of a firm from the social impact of the firm or too narrowly define the social impact of a firm merely in terms of its economic impact is to gloss over or even to tear apart the larger social reason a firm exists.

THE MANY PURPOSES OF BUSINESS

Most organizations have more than one purpose, and sometimes these purposes can be in conflict with each other, thus requiring managers to weigh carefully each purpose with the current situation and make choices that manage the tensions involved. After considering the questions surrounding this theme, we conclude that the following are the categories of purpose that Christian organizational leaders must manage:

- demonstrating the character of God by serving a need in the greater society that contributes to sustaining human interdependencies by offering products and services that are demanded by the market

- serving God by contributing to the well-being of some persons in society that are in proximity to the organization by fostering community wisdom, love, justice, peace, right doing and faithfulness in relationships

- playing a role in a particular industry or market in cooperation (and sometimes in competition) with other organizations

- achieving the instrumental goals that enable the organization to continue serving society into the future (i.e., earning a profit that exceeds the cost of capital)

- returning to society more than the value of the resources consumed in the process of providing products and services

- providing a means of economic sustainability for owners

- providing employment for workers

Some of these purposes cannot be primary. For example, if providing employment is the primary purpose of an organization, its leaders would hire more workers, which would in turn drive up the total labor cost and, correspondingly, the market prices. This, in turn, would drive away customers. Higher market prices would make it more difficult for the workers to purchase the goods they need and want. In a highly competitive market, organizations that employed comparatively fewer workers would be the ones that survive, and the organizations whose purpose was to provide employment would find it difficult to continue its purpose of providing employment. Thus, providing employment is a secondary purpose.

Other purposes must be primary in order for the organization to continue responding to its environment with goods and services that are valued in society. For example, serving a need in the greater society and contributing to the well-being of some persons in society will result in the market responding with demand, which will contribute a positive revenue stream for the ability of the organization to continue its role.

THROUGH THE LENS OF BIBLICAL THEMES

The purpose of business can be seen through the lens of biblical story themes. Seen from the perspective of all the themes as a group, the purpose of business is to provide a space for the qualities described in the themes to take root and flourish in the marketplace experiences of all involved. Business is to provide moral leadership to buyers and sellers, employees, strategic partners, the market and the industry as a whole.

Cosmic conflict. The purpose of business is not just local or even global; business is also cosmic! It is in business as much as in church where persons demonstrate in their actions God's way or Satan's way. Businesses exist not to generate cash flow but rather to reveal God's character. Business can emulate how God managed his economy. Another purpose is to resist Satan and evil in the marketplace. God's program of management in the great cosmic conflict is to foster freedom within boundaries. So, too, it would seem is the purpose of business.

Creation. The purpose of business is to provide a setting where we can be co-workers with God in sustaining and promoting a flourishing life. Everything that we do in business, every resource we use, every person we engage in service, all were created by God and comprise the first elements of the value chain. These resources are holy (consecrated and set apart for special service to the Creator) and should be treated with reverence, as we would treat any holy object. The earth is not something to exploit merely for gain. Rather, it is a gift from God to be used in service to God. The great work of those involved in business involves being a co-worker with God in the restoration of the image of God in humans lost in the Garden of Eden. Accordingly, one purpose of business is to honor the moral authority of God, who established the principles of flourishing life.

Holiness. Business has a role to play: not just in managing the buying and selling processes but also managing these processes in a way that demonstrates God's character. The idea of holiness suggests being separate from the common in the world. Yet, holiness also is the foundation for self-sacrificing love. It is the holiness of God that separates him from us and draws him to us. In the marketplaces of the earth, business followed according to the principles of God's character will be both separate from the world and yet close to the world to reveal God. This requires a distinctive difference in our marketplace behaviors.

Covenant relationships. The purpose of business through the lens of the biblical story is that it serves the many relationships embedded in the community. The purpose is not just profit but rather serving the needs of the relationships so that life is promoted. Business, above all else, is for well-being of persons in community. Business exists for the purpose of revealing the character of those who make commitments to each other. It exists to nourish faithfulness-enhancing, interdependent relationships. It exists to act in redemptive ways and in all things to be a blessing to others.

Shalom. The purpose of business is to provide a structured means in society for people to be a blessing to each other. In this way they extend the experience of shalom to others while experiencing it themselves. Even when one person or one organization cannot create well-being for an entire community by themselves, they can create a taste of shalom for those with whom they connect. While economic prosperity is important (without it, the other dimensions of shalom would practically

be impossible), the larger purpose of business is to work for full prosperity in all its dimensions. Shalom cannot be experienced if injustice exists. Thus, business also exists for the purpose of promoting justice and removing injustices so that the full well-being, including economic wealth, can be realized.

Sabbath. The purpose of business is to foster both work and contentment. Workplaces are the structured institutions where persons can contribute to society and to meeting their own needs. One purpose of business is to promote the work-rest interdependent relationship. Business does not exist for its own narrow self-interest purpose, but rather for the larger purposes of resting from ambition, constraint of unchecked commercialism and liberation from secular pressures.

Justice. The purpose of business is to be a channel of justice in the marketplace so that many can receive blessings. Business exists to reveal God's character of justice. Business is to take the moral leadership in use of technology in ways that foster justice. Business exists to treat market players fairly, to foster the rights of others, to avoid favoritism and to support legitimate processes of exchange and communication.

Righteousness. The biblical purpose of business in society is to lend stability to the larger community by acting in ways that support covenantal relationships. Business should exist to help others remain steadfast in doing the right thing no matter the cost. Business exists to encourage workers to shape their behavior in alignment with biblical principles. Few institutions have such a powerful role. Business exists to be resolute and firm in standing for the basic principles even when faced with changing times. Business exists to help others remain true to duty.

Truth. The purpose of business is to be one of the structures in society that encourages faithfulness, trustworthiness and consistency when values are exchanged. Business has a role to plan by encouraging others toward faithfulness of action. Business should be foremost in working hard to find the truth of every marketplace situation and to take corrective actions based on the truth of a situation.

Wisdom. Business is not only to be the repository of knowledge about how to efficiently exchange things of value in the market or the most practical ways of doing business. In the biblical way of thinking, business is for the purpose of sharing not only practical wisdom but also wisdom about how life in the community can be improved as business leaders work together with other community leaders to solve community problems. Business exists to pursue excellence of insight and understanding. It exists to help persons and the whole community to keep our hearts with diligence.

Loving kindness. The purpose of business seen through the lens of loving kindness is this: Business is about fostering loyalty in relationships within the community. Business offers a space where loyalty can flourish, where giving is encouraged, even toward an enemy, and where market participants show compassion by choosing not to take vengeance.

Redemption. The purpose of business is to bring healing to broken relationships. While business cannot, in a practical sense, heal all broken relationships in the community, it can provide the space were some relationships are healed through persons' participation in the buying and selling processes. As in the creation theme, here business works for the restoration of the image of God in all who participate in the marketplace. Business is not for the purpose of taking but rather for the purpose of giving healing and blessings. It exists to bring healing, blessing and life preservation.

Appendix G

Ethical and Social Issue Debate Topics

Every few months a debate emerges in society regarding what is the right or wrong thing to do about a situation. Every few months a new ethics scandal hits the news media. These events offer opportunities for citizens to become knowledgeable about the facts and the issues. Studying the situations and the issues is an important way to be effective in participating in these larger communal conversations. One might argue that participation in the larger dialogue is one mark of a fully engaged citizen.

The following are examples of ethical, social and legal issues present in the environment of business. Each one emerged into public discussion at one point or another. They represent good opportunities for having thoughtful conversations and debates for the purpose of applying various moral theories, including a biblical perspective carried by the major biblical story themes.

International pricing discrimination. Australian consumers are upset that they must pay almost 70 percent more on average to download from iTunes compared with what customers pay in the United States. Prices for some computer software products are also much higher in Australia compared with the United States. Australian lawmakers are considering making changes to the Australian Copyright Act and the Competition and Con-

sumer Act to stop what they believe to be unjustified price discrimination. Is it wrong for iTunes to charge Australians almost 70 percent more than it charges Americans for downloading the same iTunes product?

Squeezing the small company off the shelf. In August 2013, it was reported that the US Senate is investigating the use of slotting fees that retail food stores charge food manufacturers to gain access to shelf retail shelf space. Grocery store executives say that slotting fees are necessary to offset costs and risks of putting new products on the shelf—products that might not sell as well as expected. Some smaller food manufacturers say that high slotting fees (which can be paid by the larger corporations) are unaffordable and unfair. They also claim that because larger food companies can pay the fees, they are able to squeeze smaller firms out of the market. Is it wrong for food retailers to charge slotting fees that are unaffordable to smaller firms?

Bailing out a failure. Solyndra, LLC, a solar-panel manufacturing firm, received a $535 million loan guarantee in March 2009 under a US Department of Energy program. One year later, in March 2010, auditors raised concerns about the financial viability of Solyndra. On January 1, 2011, the firm owed the US government $527 million. In August 2011, Solyndra operations shut down and most workers were laid off. The next month Solyndra filed for bankruptcy protection. Was the US government relationship with Solyndra a good thing for society?

Support your favorite pirate. Websites that feature pirated movies and television shows are selling advertising space to companies who wish to attract customers to their products. Internet advertising is often purchased using automated technology that asks no questions about the ethics of the companies offering products. Advertisers simply want to get access to Internet users who match a certain profile for their target market segments. Sites that offer pirated videos generate hundreds of millions of dollars annually in advertising revenue from companies buying automated advertising Internet space. Should companies who purchase advertising space on sites that offer pirated videos be held accountable for breaking intellectual property laws?

Bluffing in business. If we define bluffing as an effort to mislead someone through a false show of strength, is it wrong to bluff during business negotiations?

CEO compensation. In 2012 John Hammergren, CEO of McKesson Corporation (MCK), a pharmaceutical distribution company, earned more than $130 million in total annual compensation. According to the Forbes' list of America's highest-paid executives, Hammergren ranked 121 out of 189 in efficiency but very high in compensation. McKesson Corporation ranked 14 on the Fortune 500 list. In contrast, during the same time period Bob Sasser, CEO of Dollar Tree, earned $8.84 million and was ranked third in efficiency while Jeff Bezos, CEO of Amazon.com, ranked first in efficiency and earned $1.68 million dollars. Was John Hammergren paid too much in 2012?

Finders keepers, losers weepers. You just purchased a used motorcycle from someone. Your dream has been to use the motorcycle for road trips. This particular model came complete with accessories such as saddle bags and a beautiful leather tail bag. You put the title to the motorcycle into your pocket and enjoy your first ride home. After you get home, you decide to give your new machine a thorough cleaning and polishing. Sifting through the bits and pieces of trash in the saddle bags you find a small, hard-shell, velvet-covered box. Inside the box is a beautiful diamond ring. The diamond ring alone is probably worth a good portion of the price of the cycle. Should you take the ring back to the previous owner of the motorcycle?

Dumping toxic wastes. Every year hundreds of millions of tons of hazardous toxic wastes are shipped from North America to developing countries for disposal. Is this right?

Sale of violent video games. Hundreds of video games that depict gratuitous violence are produced and sold in the world. Some experts say that repeated exposure to violence in video games has a harmful effect on the psyche of people who indulge in this leisure-time activity. Are the claims of these experts correct? If so, is it right that video game producers create and sell these harmful products?

Big-box retailer price-matching policy. A national chain, big-box retailer advertises that if customers find a current better price for the exact same in-stock product at another retailer, it will match the price and beat it by 10 percent. This retailer then makes arrangements with the appliance manufacturers to carry the exact same appliances sold elsewhere only under different model numbers (i.e., model numbers that no other retailer has available). This form of price matching policy might be legal, but is it moral?

AIDS medication. Should American pharmaceutical industry make AIDS medications available to African countries at or below the cost of production?

Food labeling. Should the US Food and Drug Administration require food labeling that identifies the product as being genetically modified?

Fracking for natural gas. On December 13, 2012, Edward Davey, the Energy Secretary of the United Kingdom, lifted a ban on the drilling for natural gas trapped in shale rock. The lifting of the ban will allow companies to explore for and extract natural gas from across a wide area of Great Britain. Britain has trillions of cubic feet of shale gas covering up to 60 percent of the land. Drilling for natural gas in shale rock is sometimes called fracking. Fracking has become a controversial method of extracting natural resources from the earth. The reason is that the process involves injecting water laced with dangerous chemicals deep into the shale rock beds which forces natural gas out of the earth. Opponents of fracking claim that the process contaminates groundwater supplies, releases methane gas pollution into the atmosphere near the drilling sites and causes earthquakes. Proponents of fracking claim that this method will result in lower energy costs and move the country toward energy independence. Fracking has been a controversial drilling method in the United States also. If the claims of opponents of fracking claim are true, is it ethical for the government of Great Britain to lift the ban on shale rock drilling?

Whistleblowing at Enron. Sherron Watkins, vice president for corporate development at Enron Corporation, became the most spectacular example of whistleblowing in the United States. *Time* selected her as a "Person of the Week" in 2002. Regardless of the ethical and legal problems that came to light as a result of her whistleblowing, did she do the morally right thing by exposing her company to the public?

Senior management—Penn State University scandal. Jerry Sandusky, who had retired from his position as defensive coordinator for the Penn State University football team in 1999, was arrested in early November 2011 under allegations that he had sexually molested several boys. A few days after his arrest, the university board of trustees fired head football coach Joe Paterno and university president Graham Spanier. Was it morally right to fire Paterno and Spanier?

Government and business. The US government claims that WikiLeaks.org posted on the Internet thousands of classified US State Department documents. Julian Assange, director of WikiLeaks.org, has declared that the documents were posted on the Internet because citizens need to know the truth about what is going on inside the government. Until December 1, 2010, Amazon.com had been providing server space to WikiLeaks.org. Assange has been celebrated by some and criticized by others as being a spy. Should the US government establish new laws and regulations limiting what can be uploaded to the Internet?

Sweatshops. Is it immoral for a US company to contract with product suppliers that operate sweatshops?

Morality of advertising. Are all forms of paid advertising fundamentally and inherently exploitive and because of this immoral?

Profit seeking in health care. Is profit seeking by owners of healthcare services organizations moral?

Your favorite iPhone manufacturer. iPhones and iPads are popular products in the United States, products that have boosted the stock price for Apple Computers. Recently

Apple has been criticized for contracting with companies that use labor practices that are illegal in the United States. One of the companies that makes iPhones for Apple and that has come under criticism is Foxconn, located in Shenzhen, China. If the allegations are true, is it ethical for Apple to contract with Foxconn to make iPhones?

Recruiting veterans to for-profit university. Colorado Technical University and University of Phoenix are just two of several for-profit universities that have been at the center of allegations regarding its recruitment practices targeting US military veterans eligible for the G.I. Bill to get a college education. During 2008 and 2009, 36 percent of US government payments for veterans' educational benefits ($640 million) went to for-profit universities. Allegations surfaced around 2010 regarding the claim that some for-profit universities were using ethically questionable practices to recruit veterans, including designing their websites to look like official government websites in an attempt to deceive veterans and using high-pressure tactics with enrollment advisors to enroll students some of whom the advisors expected would drop out or fail. Is it ethical to make the design of a company's Internet web page to appear like it is an official government website discussing veterans' educational benefits?

Fueling growth with bribes. According to a *New York Times* investigative report, a former Walmart executive alleged that the company breached the US Foreign Corrupt Practices Act by paying more than $24 million (US) in bribes to government officials. The money was disbursed in more than 440 payments throughout Mexico to secure building permits for its stores. Allegedly the payments stopped only after construction of Walmart stores was complete in Mexico. Founded by Sam Walton,

Walmart, a company that has publicized its high moral standards, is estimated to be the largest employer in Mexico with more than two hundred thousand employees. The alleged bribes may have been authorized by Walmart general counsel (lawyer). Written evidence that has been uncovered in the scandal by 2006 seemed to support the claim that Walmart's highest-level leaders, including the company lawyers, during the time period knew about the bribes and the internal investigation but attempted to delay and then deflect the investigation away from top-level leaders. They placed in charge of the investigation one of the persons who was a primary target in the allegations. Was it wrong for Walmart leaders to place in charge of the investigation a person who was alleged to be a key person in the bribery actions?

Exporting banned pesticides. Should companies based in the Unites States export to developing nations pesticides which have been banned in the United States?

Energy and the environment—ethanol. Should the US government subsidize the development of a national ethanol production infrastructure to increase supplies of this substitute for gasoline?

Energy and the environment—Kyoto. Should the United States support the Kyoto Protocol?

Immigration policy. Should the United States construct more physical barriers along its borders and implement stricter entrance requirements to tighten control over goods and people entering and exiting the country?

Immigration reform. In April 2010, Governor Jan Brewer of Arizona signed into state law a bill on illegal immigration. The aim of the new law is to identify, prosecute and deport illegal immigrants. Is this law moral?

National health care. Should the United States implement a single-payer national healthcare system?

Compulsory military service. Should the United States activate a program of compulsory military service (such as the draft)?

Job outsourcing. Should the United States continue to give tax breaks for companies that outsource jobs to other countries?

Jobs and unemployment. Should the United States government raise the minimum wage?

Government involvement in business. Should the US government bail out major companies in an industry (such as automobile companies)?

Internet. Is it moral for someone to hack into another organization's website or database to obtain information?

Pollution. Is it moral for pharmaceutical companies to dump waste products into rivers, lakes or streams?

Executive powers. Should the president of the United States be authorized to shut down the US portion of the World Wide Web in the case of a national emergency?

Media biases. Is it moral for a media corporation to operate with a conservative or liberal bias?

Intellectual property. Is it moral for intellectual property law to limit access to copyrighted information such as computer application programming code?

International aid. Is it moral for the government of the United States to provide international aid to other countries when it could use that money to help impoverished communities in the United States?

Retirement fund investments. Is it moral that retirement fund investment fund managers use hedge funds?

Monopolies. Are unregulated monopolies inherently immoral? (Utility companies are regulated monopolies.)

Internet marketing. Is it moral for a current university student using information obtained from the university student and faculty directory to create and use his or her own email mailing list to promote the sale of products or services owned by the student's company?

Employee rights. Is it moral for company leaders to fire an employee who uses the Internet at work to send personal emails or surf the web for personal amusement?

Discrimination. Was the Supreme Court decision on the Bakke v. University of California case moral? (Allan Bakke sued the university because he claimed that affirmative action admissions policies discriminated against him.)

Downloading information. Is it moral to download copyrighted material such as music from someone else's hard drive?

Internet marketing. Is it immoral for a business to promote its products and services through the use of spam email or spam texts?

Internet marketing and information privacy. Is it moral for one organization to sell telephone or email lists to third parties for commercial purposes?

Environmental stewardship and sustainability. Should a federal law be passed requiring fast-food restaurants to switch from polystryrene packaging to paper packaging?

Governance. Should publically traded companies in the United States be required to use a certain percentage of outside directors?

Should CEO compensation be decided by committees who are completely independent of the board of directors or of the corporation who employees the CEO?

Corporate responsibility. Should all publically traded firms be required to engage in a certain amount of corporate social responsibility (as measured by dollar amount of expense) as long as the firms can choose the specific activities?

Environmental care and corporate responsibility. Is BP responsible for the damage that was done by the oil spill in the Gulf of Mexico that occurred during 2010?

Government regulations. Should the US government enact new legislation and regulations limiting deep sea water drilling and pumping of crude oil?

The revised banking information and regulations generally prohibits a management official from serving two nonaffiliated depository institutions, depository institution holding companies or any combination thereof, in situations where the management interlock would likely have an anticompetitive effect. Is this a beneficial regulation?

Prosperity in the Bible: Q & A Bible Study

The following Q & A-style Bible study provides an overview of the biblical idea of prosperity. This forms the anchor for understanding material, financial and economic well-being from the scriptural point of view. After each question, Bible references are provided. The reader is encouraged to have a Bible nearby when going through this study.

From whom does prosperity come?

Regardless of what humans do to foster flourishing well-being in the community, and regardless of what prosperity means, ultimately prosperity is a gift of God (Gen 12:2; 13:2; 39:2-3, 23; Deut 8:11-18; 1 Sam 2:7-8; Job 1:21; Ps 113:7-8; Prov 10:22; Eccles 5:19).

What are some of the ways that the Bible describes prosperity?

The Bible uses many words to refer to prosperity. The dominant word that seems to encompass the broadest meaning of the term is *shalom*, or flourishing well-being in all dimensions. Three relevant descriptions of prosperity come from the writings of Moses (Lev 26:3-9; Deut 7:12-15; 28:1-14). Table H.1 lists some of the Old Testament words used to describe prosperity.

Likewise, in the New Testament several words are used to refer to prosperity (see table H.2).

What are the basic elements of prosperity?

In one of King Solomon's poetic writings that describes the experience of shalom (Ps 72),

we see that shalom comes from God in the forms of righteousness, help to the poor, freedom from oppression, rain for crops that bring abundant harvests, international harmony and political power, economic power and worship to God. Here are some of the key elements:

- faithful covenant relationship with God (Ex 20:3; Deut 6:5; 10:12; Ps 19:7-8)

- safety (Lev 25:18; Job 5:23; Ps 4:8; 12:5; 119:117; Prov 18:10; 1 Sam 20:42; Jer 32:37; 33:16)

- justice (Is 42:4; 59:8; Jer 4:1-2)

- physical health and fertility (Ex 15:26; Deut 30:16; Jer 33:6)

- domestic harmony (Prov 15:16; 16:7)

- economic well-being (Ps 72:16; Is 30:23)

Is prosperity primarily for us to enjoy or for those who come after us?

True prosperity is multigenerational. We should hope, work and pray for shalom for our children and for the well-being of our grandchildren! As we foster well-being for them, we will enjoy a flourishing life, too. This requires us to move beyond narrow self-interests and consider the interests of the broader community in succeeding generations (Gen 45:10; Ex 12:14; 20:5-6, 12; 31:16; Deut 4:40; 6:4-7; 7:9; Ps 10:6; 72:5; 119:90; 128:6; Prov 13:22).

Table H.1. Old Testament words that describe prosperity.

Concepts*	Meanings	English Translations	Select Passages
Shalom	Flourishing well-being, complete, soundness, welfare, peace	Peace, prosperity, welfare	Gen 37:14; 43:27; Exod 18:7; 1 Sam 17:18; Ps 35:27; 37:11; 73:3; Jer 29:7, 11
Barak, berakah	To kneel, bless; a blessing	Blessing	Deut 30:1, 19; Josh 8:34; Ps 72:17; 132:15; Prov 3:33
Tob	Good, welfare, benefit, good things	Good, welfare, prosperity	Deut 23:6; 28:11; 30:15; 1 Kings 10:7; Ps 25:13; 106:5; 128:5; Prov 13:21; Eccl 7:14; Jer 14:11; 39:16
Yatab	To be good, well, glad, pleasing	Do well, go well, prosper, good	Gen 4:7; 12:13; 32:9, 12; 41:37; Ex 1:20; Deut 4:40; 5:16, 29; 28:63; 30:5
Tsalakh	To advance, prosper	Prosper	Deut 28:29; 39:3, 23; Josh 1:8; Ps 118:25; Is 53:10; Jer 2:37; 22:30; Dan 3:30; 8:12, 24
Sakal	Prudence, insight, circumspect	Prosper; skillful, understand; success; be wise; give heed; insight	Gen 3:6; Deut 29:9; Josh 1:7-8; Ps 2:10; 14:2; 101:2; 119:99; Prov 1:3; 17:8; Is 52:13
Parakh	To bud, sprout, shoot	Flourish	Ps 72:7; 92:7, 12-13; Prov 11:28; 14:11
Pissah	Abundance, plenty	Abundance	Ps 72:16†
Dashen	To be fat, to grow fat	Fat, prosper, prosperous, rich	Deut 31:20; Ps 22:29; 92:14; Prov 11:25; 13:4; 28:25; Is 30:23
Shamen	Fat, rich, robust	Fat, rich	Gen 49:20; 1 Chron 4:40; Jer 5:28
Kheleb	Fat	Fat	Gen 45:18; Ex 23:18; Lev 4:31
Shalah	Ease, prosperity	Prosper, ease	Ps 30:6; 122:6-7; Jer 22:21; Lam 1:5; Dan 4:27
Kosharah	Prosperity	Prosperity	Ps 68:6†
Yatar	To remain over	Prosper	Gen 30:36; 44:20; Deut 30:9
Kabod	Abundance, honor, glory	Abundance, wealth, splendor	Gen 31:1; 45:13; Ps 8:6; 49:16-17; 57:5; 84:11; 85:9; Is 61:6
Rab	Much, many, great	Abundance	Gen 13:6; 27:28; 45:28; Ex 1:9; 34:6; Deut 28:47; Ps 72:7
Meod	Muchness, force, abundance	Very good, abundance	Gen 1:31; 7:19; 13:2; 15:1; 41:49
Saba	Plenty, satiety	Abundance, plenty	Gen 41:29-31, 34, 47, 53; Deut 6:11; 8:10; 31:20

*There are other concepts related to prosperity in the Hebrew Bible not included in this table. For example: wealth (*khayil* [Deut 8:18], *ashar* [Prov 23:4]); riches (*nekes, osher* [the most common term], *hon* [Ps 112:3; 119:14; Prov 8:18; 11:4; 24:4], *khosen* [Prov 27:24]); gain (*marbit* [Lev 25:37], *sakhar* [Prov 31:18]); inheritance (*nakhal, nakhalah*) and others.
†This appears to be the only occurrence in the Hebrew Bible.

Is prosperity primarily a community experience or an individual experience?

Just as the covenant (*berit*) is both a communal and individual experience, so too is the biblical idea of prosperity. But the dominant emphasis in Scripture is on community well-being. This means that when we pray for prosperity, we are praying not just for our own narrow self-interests for financial wealth but also for prosperity that the whole community will enjoy. This places our perspective on others, not ourselves. Individual prosperity in the Scripture is interdependent with communal prosperity in all its dimensions.

Table H.2. New Testament words that describe prosperity.

Concepts	Meanings	English Translations	Select Passages
Euodoō	To have a prosperous journey	Prosper	1 Cor 16:2; 3 Jn 1:2
Plousios	Wealthy	Rich	Mt 19:23-24; Mk 10:25; Lk 12:16; 21:1; Eph 2:4; 1 Tim 6:17; Jas 1:10-11; 2:5-6; 5:1; Rev 2:9; 3:17; 13:16
Ploutos	Wealth	Wealth	2 Cor 8:2; Col 2:2
Plouteō, ploutizō	To be rich	Rich	1 Cor 4:8; 2 Cor 6:10; 8:9; 1 Tim 6:9, 18; Rev 3:17-18
Chrēma	A thing that one uses or needs	Wealthy	Mk 10:23; Lk 18:24
Bios	Wealth	Wealth	Lk 15:12, 30
Timiotēs	Preciousness, costliness, worth	Wealth	Rev 18:19
Euporia	Prosperity, plenty	Prosperity	Acts 19:25
Perisseuō	To be over and above, abound	Prosperity, abundance	Mt 13:12; 25:29; Lk 12:15; Rom 5:17; 1 Cor 12:23-24; 2 Cor 1:5; 8:14; Phil 4:12; 4:18
Megas	Great	Abundant	Acts 4:33
Hyperpleonazō	To abound exceedingly	Abundant	1 Tim 1:14

Community Emphasis: Deut 4:40; 8:18; Jer 29:4-7; Ezek 37:26; Zech 1:17; Mal 3:9-12. **Individual Emphasis:** Lev 18:5; Jos 1:7-8; 1 Sam 18:14-15; 1 Chron 4:10; Ps 1:1-3; 92:12.

Does the Bible contrast a flourishing life with anything?

Prosperity in all its fullness is contrasted in the Bible with a life of misery and adversity. Just as there are several ideas that refer to prosperity, so there are several terms that refer to its opposite. The most common among these in the Old Testament is *ra*, or misery, evil and adversity in all dimensions. Tables H.3 and H.4 show the different ways misery is described in the Bible.

Given all this information, can you summarize the idea of prosperity from the Bible?

- Prosperity encompasses the totality of life. Envisioned is a full, flourishing life of well-being in all dimensions.

- Prosperity is multidimensional. Like a diamond, it has many facets: it is multigenera-

tional and primarily communal, but the individual perspective is not forgotten.

Is prosperity something we should pursue and pray for?

Yes. Pursuing prosperity means that we are eager to pursue faithfulness in our covenant relationship with God and with each other. It means that we are interested in others around us enjoying a life of faithfulness. Pursuing prosperity means that we will work for the good of the larger community for a flourishing life in all its dimensions. As a community allows God to work among it for increased faithfulness, prosperity in all dimensions results for the community. As the community prosperity goes, so does the individual prosperity. Yet, individual prosperity contributes to the totality of community prosperity. The two are interrelated and interdependent. Economic prosperity pursued on its own, apart from faithful covenant relationships in all dimensions, will destroy the other dimensions of

Table H.3. Contrasts to prosperity in the Old Testament.

Concept	Meanings	English Translations	Select Passages
Ra, raah	Evil, misery, calamity, distress, injury, wickedness, famine, hunger	Misery, adversity, trouble, wicked	Gen 41:30; Ps 41:1; Prov 21:12; Is 45:7; Jer 29:11; 39:16
Makhsor	Need, a thing needed, poverty	Want	Ps 34:9; Prov 11:24; 28:27
Khaser	To lack, to need, to be lacking, decrease	Want	Ps 23:1; 34:10; Prov 13:25; 28:22
Merah	A curse	Curse	Deut 28:20; Prov 3:33; 28:27
Resh	To take possession, to dispossess	Poverty	Prov 6:11
Ebyon	In want, needy, poor	Poor	Deut 15:4
Qelalah	Curse	Curse	Deut 28:15, 45; 29:27; 30:1; Josh 8:34
Abad	To perish	Perish	Deut 28:63
Shamad	To be exterminated or destroyed	Destroy	Deut 28:63
Natash	Uproot, pluck up	Uproot	Jer 12:14

Table H.4. Contrasts to prosperity in the New Testament.

Concept	Meanings	English Translations	Select Passages
Ptōchos	One who crouches and cowers, beggarly	Poor	Mt 11:5; 26:9, 11; Mk 12:42-43; Lk 4:18; 6:20; 7:22; 18:22; 19:8; 21:3; Jn 12:5-6, 8; Rom 15:26; 2 Cor 6:10; Gal 2:10; Jas 2:2-3; Rev 13:16
Penichros	Needy, poor	Poor	Lk 21:2
Penēs	One who works for his living	Poor	2 Cor 9:9
Talaipōria	Hard work, hardship, distress	Misery	Rom 3:16
Ponēros	Toilsome, bad	Evil	Mt 5:11; 6:13; 12:35; 13:19; 22:10; Lk 6:22, 45; Jn 3:19; 7:7; 17:15; Acts 19:12-13; Eph 5:16; 1 Thess 5:22; 1 Jn 2:13-14; 5:18-19
Kakos, kakia	Bad, evil; wickedness	Evil	Mt 24:48; 27:23; Mk 15:14; Lk 23:22; Acts 23:5; Rom 1:29-30; 3:8; 7:19; 12:17, 21; 16:19; 1 Cor 10:6; 14:20; Phil 3:2; 1 Tim 6:10; Heb 5:14; 1 Pet 3:9-10; Rev 2:2
Phaulos	Worthless, bad	Evil	Jn 3:20; 5:29

Table H.5. Moses' contrast of shalom and misery.

Misery	Shalom
Physical illnesses (Deut 28:22, 27-28)	No diseases (Ex 15:26; Deut 7:15)
Drought, plague, disasters, destruction of crops (Deut 28:23-24, 39, 60-61)	Rain which leads to healthy crops, plenty of food and economic strength (Deut 28:12)
Defeat by enemies (Deut 28:25)	Defeat of enemies (Deut 6:3; 28:7)
Poverty and loss of resources (Deut 28:30-34)	Prosperity (Deut 28:11-12)
Exile (Deut 28:36, 49-53)	World leadership (Deut 4:6-7; 28:1, 13)
International ridicule, war, exile (Deut 28:36-37, 49-53)	International reputation (Deut 4:6-7; 28:1, 10, 13)
Borrowers (Deut 28:44, 48)	Lenders (Deut 28:12)
Social disharmony (Deut 28:54)	Freedom (Deut 6:3)
Decline in population (Deut 28:62)	Growth of population (Deut 28:4)

prosperity (Ps 14:7; 25:22; 34:14; 51:18; 122:6; Prov 4:5-7; 23:23).

What did the prophet Moses teach regarding prosperity?

Moses compared a life of misery with a life of flourishing well-being. Giving the covenant meant giving a prescription for a full life lived in faithfulness to God and with each other. The purpose of the covenant was to foster flourishing life! Table H.5 presents a summary of some of the contrasts that Moses gives.

Faithfulness in following covenantal relationship with God and with each other, when written on the heart and when widely spread throughout the community, results in flourishing well-being in the community. Only when flourishing life is experienced in the community can individuals enjoy true prosperity. Each of the Ten Commandments and all of them collectively, when followed throughout the community, tend toward shalom (Lev 18:5; Deut 1:11; 4:40; 5:29; 6:18; 7:12-15; 8:18; 15:4-11; 28:1-2, 8-11; 29:9-12; 30:5, 9; Ps 119:165). The economic dimension of shalom is the only one with constraints placed on it. It is interesting that the constraint on economic well-being is brought up three times in the Decalogue (sabbath command, eighth commandment, tenth commandment).

What role were humans given to foster flourishing life?

Prosperity is viewed as a gift from God. However, humans have a role to manage the resources they have been given, to devote themselves completely to the service of God in all that they do and in all relationships. For example, among other things we should foster the health of others (Ex 20:13). We should promote social harmony (Ps 15). We are encouraged to work diligently (Prov 12:27), manage our own assets wisely (Prov 27:23-24)

and watch out for the safety of assets that belong to others (Ex 23:4). We are called on to give and lend to the poor (see verses below) and save an inheritance for the grandchildren (Ps 25:13; Prov 13:22; see also Prov 14:21, 31; 19:17; 22:9; Ps 15:1-5; Is 56:1; Mic 6:8).

What should be our attitude toward money?

If we are blessed with financial abundance, we should be grateful to God. We are warned not to be greedy (Prov 11:6). King David and King Solomon encouraged us to keep our priorities straight. There are several things more important than money:

- Truth (faithfulness; Prov 23:23), which is the only thing that Scripture says we should get a monopoly on. Faithfulness increases in value the more you have of it and the longer you keep it!

- Reputation (Prov 22:1)

- Wisdom (Prov 3:14; see also Prov 8:11, 19; 16:16)

- Knowledge (Prov 20:15; see also Prov 8:10)

- Diligence (Prov 12:27)

- The covenant (Ps 119:127; see also Ps 119:14, 72, 162)

- The fear of the Lord (Prov 15:16)

- Righteousness (Ps 37:16)

- Righteousness, godliness, faith, love, perseverance and gentleness (1 Tim 6:11)

How did Jesus talk about economic prosperity?

Jesus cautioned against making economic prosperity separate from faithfulness to God. He emphasized the sustaining power of God (Mt 6:33; 19:24; 26:11; Mk 10:29; 14:7; Lk 4:18; 7:22; Jn 10:10; 14:14). Wealth can be good, but Jesus emphasized how dangerous is the desire for money. Riches are not usually a blessing.

Riches are usually a curse. Riches destroy people. Accordingly and consistent with the teachings of Moses, financial abundance is the only dimension of shalom on which Jesus placed limits.

Did Jesus emphasize economic prosperity over other dimensions of shalom?

No! Far from it. Jesus emphasized, first and foremost, the covenant relationship with God. He also brought out physical and mental health wherever he traveled signifying that the time had come for the fulfillment of God's promises (Mk 1:14-15; Lk 4:18; Jn 6:38).

How did the disciples and apostles understand prosperity?

They seem to emphasize the communal dimension of prosperity (Rom 14:19; Phil 2:4; 3 Jn 1:2). They called for pursuit of shalom, as did David and Solomon (1 Pet 3:11; Heb 12:14). They emphasized the importance of obedience that results in blessings (Jas 1:25).

They identify Jesus Christ as the fulfillment of the promises of shalom (Eph 2:14). Prosperity is centered in Jesus Christ (Mk 6:56; Acts 3:26; 10:38).

Case Studies

CASE 1—THE 25 PERCENT DISCOUNT CAR RENTAL[1]

Frequent flier programs of the major airline companies normally include relationships with other airline companies, hotels and car rental companies. Frequent flier program managers typically send to their frequent flier program members notices and fliers encouraging members to use the services provided by these frequent flier partners.

Using direct mail, the frequent flier program managers at the airline company sent a discount coupon for car rental to frequent flier program members. Knowing that later in the year he would be making a trip and knowing that during this trip he would need to rent a car, one member of the program saved the coupon for later use. He carefully inspected the small print on the back of the coupon noting the expiration date (December 31) of that calendar year. Information on the back of the coupon revealed that the offer was for "up to 25 percent" off the usual rental car prices and that the customer using the coupon would receive double the frequent flier miles for the car rental transaction. Other relevant information included the contract identification number for the offer.

Later in the year when it was time to make specific travel plans, the frequent flier program member went on the Internet and, using one of the travel planning websites, reserved a rental car from the car company that was featured in the offer. He did not see any place to put the contract identification number in the online reservation form, but on the day of travel, he showed up at the rental car agency counter at the airport and presented the coupon to the agent before completing the transaction. She refused to accept the coupon stating that because the coupon contract identification number had not been used to reserve the car, the coupon could not be honored: no discount and no bonus on frequent flier miles would be given. While standing at the counter the customer reviewed the back of the coupon and noted to the customer service agent that nothing was stated anywhere on the coupon requiring the contract identification number to be used at the time of reservation.

She still refused but asked if he would give her the coupon; she would have a discussion with her manager about it later. He offered to let her copy the coupon but stated that he would keep it for use during follow-up conversations because he did not have a copy. She replied that she did not have access to a copy machine to copy the coupon. Needing a car and wanting to complete the transaction so that he would have some chance of obtaining a discount, he signed the rental agreement and took possession of the rental car. The price quoted by the Internet website was stated in the rental agreement.

The next day he called the customer service department of the frequent flier program. They told him to call the rental car company directly stating that even though they had sent the coupon to the customer, they were not part of the relationship between the customer and the rental car company and had simply passed along information to the customer in their marketing materials. He called the rental car company, and they stated something similar to what the agent had said, namely, that he should have used the coupon contract identification number at the time of the reservation. When he asked why the coupon would not be honored at the time he presented at the counter, the agent had no explanation except to say that the coupon was for use at the time of reservation. The agent asked him to send in the coupon by mail and that they would look into the matter further. He refused, stating that he needed to keep the coupon as evidence but that he would send a copy of it to them via email.

Using his camera he took a picture of both sides of the coupon and emailed these images to the rental car company. In an email reply the car rental company stated that the company valued his business and because of this they would give him a 10 percent discount and that this discount would be applied to the account when he returned the car. The email also stated that there would be no bonus frequent flier miles awarded because the coupon was not honored at the time of the reservation. After he returned home, the customer scanned both sides of the coupon and enlarged the small print so that it was easier to read. He sent this via email attachment to the airline frequent flier program agent. In an email from the airline company the agent stated that he would receive bonus miles for bringing the matter to their attention but that the company would not give bonus miles for the car rental. He protested that he had not asked for bonus miles because he brought it to their attention but that the bonus miles should be for the car rental transaction.

DISCUSSION QUESTIONS

1. At this point in the story,[2] who appears to have attempted a dirty trick?

2. Did the customer attempt to do an ethical dirty trick on the car rental company? If so, what was it?

3. Did the car rental company attempt an ethical dirty trick on the customer? If so, what was it?

4. What are the ethical issues at stake?

5. How would the faithful Christian car rental agent handle this?

6. How would the faithful Christian customer handle this?

CASE 2—PRAISING GOD FOR VICTORY IN COURT

As Richard Scrushy emerged from the court room on June 28, 2005, he declared, "God is good!" A jury of his peers had just acquitted him of all thirty-six charges that he had allegedly breached the Sarbanes-Oxley Act and had committed bribery, securities fraud, accounting fraud, conspiracy and mail fraud. He walked out of the court a free man but a person who would be dogged with lawsuits for months to come. He was free but was unemployed. His former employer, HealthSouth, had fired him from his post as chief executive officer in 2003 for allegedly committing accounting fraud.

At the trial, his lawyers persuaded the jury

that Mr. Scrushy is a humble man from Selma, Alabama, who was unfairly targeted by the federal government. Former subordinates testified against him. One of the witnesses against him, William Owens, even produced an audio recording in which Scrushy had allegedly given a confession. The jury thought the statements made on the recording were too ambiguous and left room for doubt. Mr. Owens's testimony was put in jeopardy when it was revealed that he had not filed a tax return for nine years. Prior to Scrushy's trial Owens had plead guilty to fraud and conspiracy in a bargain with the federal government agreeing to testify against his former boss. At the acquittal it appeared that Owens's deal put him in prison while his former boss avoided the long arm of the law.

At the time of the trial Scrushy co-hosted a Christian television show with his wife. During the trial he was seen preaching in local churches in what some observers believed was an attempt to influence the jury through the influence of congregation members.

Six months after the acquittal, Scrushy sued HealthSouth for wrongful termination, demanding his job back along with back pay and reimbursement for legal expenses he had incurred to defend himself in court. He was not an employee, but technically he was still a director on the board of trustees. And he was resisting pressure to resign. A director cannot be removed without the vote of shareholders, and that would not occur for a few months. Finally, after weeks of increasing pressure, Scrushy resigned his position on the board.

In a countersuit HealthSouth demanded that Scrushy pay back over $34 million in bonuses he had been paid from 1996 to 2002, another $12 million in bonuses for reaching financial goals and more than $200 million

from selling stock that had inflated values because of the overstated earnings to the tune of $3.9 billion. HealthSouth also claimed that Scrushy's actions had cost the company hundreds of millions of dollars (see table CS.1).[3]

Table CS.1. HealthSouth estimate of costs.

Estimated Cost of Fraud (in Millions)	
Restatement books	225
SEC settlement	100
Restructuring credit agreements	89
Litigation	68
Transition management	56
Documenting internal controls	31
Audit	10
Total	579

The countersuit also claimed that Scrushy's employment agreement had never been fully executed by the board because it had been signed only by Scrushy and one of the members of the board's compensation committee and the chief financial officer at the time, William Owens. Signatures of these two persons do not carry the same legal authority as official board action.

Almost exactly one year to the day after Scrushy's joyful praise to God for his victory over the evil government forces in court, he was in court again. On June 29, 2006, the outcome was not as joyful: no proclamation of God's favor this time. Scrushy was convicted in US District Court of bribery, conspiracy and four counts of mail fraud. He had bribed then Governor Don Siegelman to gain political favors. At the same trial Siegelman was convicted of charges of corruption. The court required Scrushy to repay $47.8 million dollars. Siegelman and Scrushy vowed to appeal the conviction.

Yet another year would go by before the legal wrangling would come to a conclusion: in June, 2007 Scrushy was sentenced to pay a fine of $150,000 and serve nearly seven years in prison for bribery. The district court judge denied Scrushy's request to remain free pending appeal. In a civil settlement for charges brought by the Securities and Exchange Commission (SEC), Scrushy agreed to pay $81 million for the $2.6 billion accounting fraud charges. As part of the settlement Scrushy would be banned for five years from working with securities. Scrushy did not admit guilt.

Two years later Scrushy still denied that he had any knowledge of the $2.6 billion fraud actions. Furthermore, he denied that subordinates had informed him of the fraudulent actions. In spite of his denials, Scrushy lost again in court when shareholders for HealthSouth brought a class-action suit against him. Perhaps some of them were saying privately, "God is good!" The court required Scrushy to pay a $2.88 billion civil judgment on behalf of HealthSouth.

One year later the story was not yet complete. The US Supreme Court reversed the judgment by the US district court and ordered an appellate court to review the case.

In January 2012, Scrushy was expected to be released from prison to a halfway house. He had not paid the $2.88 billion and was expected to be dogged by HealthSouth to pay.

Fast forward almost a year later. Scrushy was out of prison and living in Houston, Texas. He filed a document in federal court in Birmingham, Alabama, stating that he was talking with investors about starting a company to take advantage of the new healthcare law signed by President Barack Obama. Scrushy's attorney filed a motion in US District Court in Birmingham to have the SEC ban lifted so that Scrushy would work with investors. Concurrent with this, Scrushy was actively trying to get his name cleared for the alleged wrongdoing. At the time Scrushy filed the paperwork, creditors began looking to see what kind of

business venture Scrushy might get involved with. As of 2013 he had not paid back the massive civil judgment.

Conduct some follow-up research and reflection:

- Where is Richard Scrushy today? Is he working with investors? How much has he paid of the $2.88 billion judgment from the civil suit?

- Should Scrushy be allowed to be involved in business investments and investors?

- Would you work for Richard Scrushy?

- What biblical story themes are relevant in this case? How do the biblical themes guide your thinking regarding Scrushy's actions?

CASE 3—BANKER BASHING

From 2008 through 2013 many nations had economies that were a mess. The mortgage banking crisis of 2008 had spiraled out of control affecting the United States, several countries in Western Europe, and other places as well. Whole nations teetered on the brink of bankruptcy. While scores of nations, notably the Group of Eight (G8), debated whether or not and how to bail out countries such as Greece and Spain, millions of people lost their jobs.

At the height of the crisis, popular criticism of financial institutions, banks in particular, grew to a crescendo. The media and lawmakers alike called for investigations. The Occupy! movement swept the world, affecting more than a hundred of the world's largest cities in 2011. Occupy! protested the outrage the movement's members felt at the widening wage gap between wealthy chief executives and front-line workers struggling to make ends meet.

The unemployment problem in the United States started to abate, and with better times, criticisms of banks also waned. But in Western

Europe, like a bulldog protecting a bone someone is trying to take away, populist critics were not letting go of the fight. Most bank executives kept quiet in the face of continuing public criticisms. But by the end of 2014 Sergio Ermotti, the new chief executive officer of UBS AG, a Swiss bank, was fed up with the continuing criticisms. "Life is hard enough," he complained. "It's not going to be very helpful to be constantly bashing banks."[4] His frustrations reached a peak just as the distrust of banks by many people was it its lowest in decades.

Mr. Ermotti is rare among bank executives in publicly voicing such frustrations, at a time when banks are widely held in low regard. One of the reasons for the bank bashing was the low performance of UBS. As was the case in the United States, Swiss taxpayers had contributed to a bailout package. Then employees at UBS were caught in trading scandals. UBS was accused of manipulating benchmark interest rates. The widening wage gap added to the underlying discontent. Then top managers received generous compensation packages after the company lost $2.7 billion dollars. To add insult to injury for Mr. Ermotti, the Swiss, British and United States governments have been probing into the allegations of currency exchange manipulation by UBS.

One of Ermotti's complaints is that politicians, bank customers and shareholders who criticize UBS are attempting to hold UBS to a standard higher than they would hold their own organizations. He questioned the basis that critics seem to have for attacking UBS when their own organizations are under suspicion for unethical practices.

Mr. Ermotti seems to want society to move beyond calls for change and demands for accountability and apology. He reasons that there is only a limited amount of good that can come

from industry leaders repeating apologies and commitments to do better. At some point you have to let the industry leaders get to work making the kinds of changes that will prevent injustices. Continuing public criticisms can turn into distractions. Ermotti disputed the claim that it is the banking industry that is the cause of the economy that was out of control. Furthermore, he claimed that most of the problems that his bank experienced were caused by small groups of employees who are not representative of the larger corporate culture of UBS. Even so, Ermotti focused much of his efforts on the changes to corporate culture.

DISCUSSION QUESTIONS

1. Is the continuing public criticism of UBS (and other banks) justified?

2. If people believe that injustices have been perpetrated by managers of a company like UBS, can you blame persons from continuing to speak with strident voices against the alleged injustices?

3. What does a company like UBS that has been the target of bank bashing need to do in order to regain public trust?

4. To what degree might a code of ethical conduct be sufficient in regaining public trust in UBS?

CASE 4—VOLKSWAGEN, THE UAW AND COMMUNITY DIALOGUE

For a brief time the eyes of the nation were focused on Chattanooga, Tennessee, where workers at the Volkswagen assembly plant were given a chance to decide whether they wanted to become unionized. In the months leading up to the vote, advocates on behalf of the unionization of the Chattanooga Volkswagen plant argued that the union would accomplish several objectives of benefit to the workers:

- Organized labor can use its leverage to get better pay, benefits and working conditions for workers.

- Workers will be given more influence in decisions that affect not only their work but also the organization as a whole.

Opponents of unionization voiced their concerns, too:

- Some claim that it was organized labor which demanded ever higher pay and benefits and other restrictions which caused the downfall of US automakers in Detroit, Michigan.

- Workers are already getting more money than workers in unionized assembly plants.

- Adding a union would only put money in the pockets of the union organization, not in the pockets of the workers.

- The union cannot be trusted. Evidence provided included claims that union organizers told lies and tried to use tangible inducements to get workers to support the vote.

The debate going on inside the plant made it onto the local evening news on more than one occasion. The position of both supporters and opponents were given television air time on local news.

Volkswagen officials said that they favor a German works council approach which includes workers in decision making. Under US law, unionization is necessary in order to form a works council. In the months leading up to the vote it appeared to most people that Volkswagen officials supported the presence of organized labor in the assembly plant. But these officials are from Germany, where people have different opinions about organized labor than do executives of American companies. The UAW pres-

ident had voiced his desire that US labor unions join forces with labor unions from other countries in order to become more influential.

The week before the vote, UAW officials claimed that they would garner an easy majority vote. But, as their optimism soared, US Senator Bob Corker spoke publically about his disfavor of the assembly plant becoming unionized. Tennessee Governor Bill Haslam also chimed in, stating that the UAW was more concerned about German shareholders than American workers.

Apparently Senator Corker was not the only one who thought that way. In the end, when workers were asked if they wanted a union in the Chattanooga plant, the vote was 626 in favor and 712 opposed to the union; 89 percent of the eligible workers cast votes. The outcome of the vote was one more snubbing of the union by Southern auto assembly workers from more than one state. For years the UAW's influence has declined as its number of members also declined. After the vote the UAW was required to cease its attempt to promote a union for at least one year.

US labor law does not prohibit public officials from commenting on the pros and cons of unionizing a plant. Senators, governors and other elected officials have opinions and have a legal right of free speech. But did Senator Corker's comments go beyond free speech? People supportive of the UAW position said that Volkswagen leaders agreed not to interfere with workers' freedom to choose. But the senator made public remarks which implied that if the workers voted no, the plant would be strengthened and grow because a new vehicle, a mid-sized SUV, would be added to the production lines. If the vote was yes, in support of the union, there would be trouble. Some thought that Corker's remarks contained a thinly veiled threat which some workers might have found intimidating. If the senator had stated that the union would be bad for the state of Tennessee, it would not be considered interference. However, if the senator's statements created an atmosphere of coercion, that might have tainted the vote.

After the vote, UAW lawyers filed a complaint with the National Labor Relations Board (NLRB) accusing Corker of interfering. If the NLRB finds that statements tainted the election, it could order a new vote. Key determinants in the NRLB ruling include whether or not the statements made by the senator are factually correct, whether the opposition had an opportunity to respond with counter arguments and the nature of the effect of the statements.

DISCUSSION QUESTIONS

1. Is it ethical for public officials to speak out either in favor of or in opposition to the efforts of organized labor to form a union at an assembly plant?

2. What was the outcome of the UAW complaint with the NLRB? Conduct some follow-up research on the situation in the Chattanooga Volkswagen assembly plan. Has the UAW been successful in rekindling interest for the union to represent workers at Volkswagen?

3. How should the community dialogue on the ethics of the relationship between employers and employees be managed?

4. What kinds of restrictions should be placed on community dialogue regarding the ethics of labor unions and the interests of workers?

CASE 5—WI-SPY

Not many people have seen the compact hatchback cars roaming the streets of the land capturing photos of the streets. But millions of people have seen the images captured and made available on the Google maps website. The result of the massive Google effort provides a monster database of images from which Google users can benefit.

With Google maps Street View you can virtually drive up to the house where your parents lived when they were children. You can look around the neighborhood and get a feel for the terrain using the panorama viewpoint of the camera system that sat atop the vehicle that drove by that spot a few years ago. If you want to visit a certain business in a far-away town and want to know what it looks like so that when you get there you will recognize it, click on Google maps and find the link for the Street View and you are instantly transported to the spot. You will see vehicles passing. You can look over your shoulder and see what is behind you. You can zoom in on a particular building for a closer look.

If you do not like the street you are on, virtually turn the corner at the next block and take another street to see what it looks like. If you get bored some evening, take a journey from some random small town in America and virtually drive somewhere else. It is like taking that road trip you have always wanted to take but do not want to spend the time and money (for gas, motels, and restaurants) for. Some areas that are not large enough for a car to drive on have been mapped using Google tricycles, snowmobiles and boats.

Street Views are not limited to roads in the United States. The Google mapping program that began in 2007 expanded to include views of streets in scores of countries. To accomplish this Google vehicles have roamed millions of miles through thousands of cities and towns. Google Street View vehicles are outfitted with nine digital cameras which create images which can be stitched together for continuous viewing pleasure. Since 2008 the system has been using high-resolution cameras to improve how images look. What many people may not realize is that in some locations, some Google vehicles were packing more than just a digital imaging package. Some Google vehicles were looking for WiFi hot spots to include in the Google map system.

Concerns of privacy surfaced soon after Google started the program. Some people complained that Google was capturing images of people doing things that they might not want posted on the Internet. The concerns increased in 2010 when it was revealed that Google had collected and stored data gathered from unprotected (unencrypted) WiFi connections present in buildings that the Google car drove past. Apparently the Street View system in some locations was helping itself to email addresses, medical information, names, passwords and complete emails and snooping on private conversations between people as they actively used WiFi systems.

Google officials claimed that the software code accidently caught a ride on the Google vehicle and was created by a rogue software engineer known only as Engineer Doe. Furthermore, they claim that the Google Street View program leaders did not want to use the data gathered from WiFi systems that the vehicle encountered. They also claimed that the massive amount of data gathered was something that occurred by error.

Officials in more than one country complained. Complaints were filed with the Federal Communications Commission (FCC) of the United States government. The FCC investigated, but Engineer Doe refused to answer questions citing the Fifth Amendment of the Constitution. While the FCC could have slapped a much stiffer fine on Google, it chose a token: $27,000. This may not be the end of the story because a class-action law suit started in California against Google for invasion of privacy. There could be other lawsuits that arise also.

Google claims that as soon as the company became aware of the problem, it grounded the Street View cars and segregated the captured WiFi signal data from the digital photo image data.

DISCUSSION QUESTIONS

1. What is unethical about using software to snoop on unprotected WiFi hot spots?

2. Conduct some follow-up research regarding the privacy concerns with the Google Street View system. What is the latest on the class-action lawsuit? What additional issues have surfaced in the story?

3. What do the biblical story themes indicate for how we should view the actions of the Wi-Spy system that snooped on WiFi hot spots?

4. If Google leaders followed the biblical story themes, how might they have handled the situation any differently?

CASE 6—PUSHING THE STUCK DUNE BUGGY

You have probably seen the television advertisements showing how much fun in the sun people can have when they are riding in an open-air dune buggy. Wind through their hair, sunglasses aimed at the next jump, the gleeful riders have the time of their life. But have you ever thought what these fun-loving people would do if they ever got their dune buggy stuck on the side of a steep sand hill?

If you are driving your dune buggy up a steep sand dune hill and get stuck, what are you to do? In one of its television advertisement Nissan suggested that if one of your friends is driving a Nissan Frontier mid-size pickup, the problem of a stuck dune buggy is solved. Just do what is shown in the Nissan television commercial: let a Nissan Frontier push your dune buggy up and over the top, and you have it made.[5] In the commercial the crowds watching such a seemingly impossible feat cheered wildly and made comments like "What's this guy doing?" "Man, no way!" "Are you kidding?" "Did you see that?"

Whoa! Not so fast. Is a Nissan pickup pushing a dune buggy up an extremely steep sand dune hard to believe? If you answered no, maybe you have not seen a pickup drive up a really steep sand dune. If you answered yes, it may be because it was not true. The viewers of the commercial did not realize (until it came out in the news later) that both the dune buggy and the Nissan Frontier were being dragged up the hill with hidden cables.[6] When you watch the video, you cannot see cables. All you see is this amazing truck apparently pushing the stranded dune buggy over the top.

After an investigation by the Federal Trade Commission (FTC), a Nissan spokesperson stated that the Frontier cannot do what was shown in the commercial. Nissan claimed that the commercial was intended to depict fantasy rather than reality; however, the commercial comes across as if an amateur video camera operator is capturing the video with a group of friends, some of whom are commenting on the exploits of the Frontier during and after the action. In spite of the special effects that were used, this, some say, gave the video a realistic feel to it. In the video the steepness of the sand dune was modified to make it appear steeper

than it was in reality. "Nissan," the representative stated, "takes its commitment to fair and truthful advertising seriously."

When you watch the television advertisement, you will notice the words "Fictionalization. Do not attempt" show on the screen before the Nissan Frontier comes into view.

As a result of the investigation Nissan and its brand management advertising agency TBWA agreed to not use potentially misleading product demonstrations in the future. Neither company was required to pay a fine. In addition, Nissan is allowed to use special effects in future product commercials.

DISCUSSION QUESTIONS

1. What, if anything, is wrong with using special effects in product videos?

2. Should the Nissan commercial have stated that the vehicles shown in the video were being pulled up the hill with hidden cables?

3. Does the disclaimer "Fictionalization" release Nissan and its advertising agency from responsibility?

CASE 7—FREQUENT FLIER GROUNDED

Airline frequent flier programs have been around since the early 1970s. In the late 1970s the tracking systems and reward programs became more sophisticated. In 1981 American Airlines introduced its innovation in customer loyalty management: make their loyal frequent flier members even more loyal by offering them attractive fares. Frequent flier programs were so effective that eventually almost all airlines instituted some type of program just to remain competitive.

The economics of frequent flier programs goes deeper than the hope for customer loyalty.

For example, the effectiveness of a frequent flier program depends on the size of network that the airline is a part of: The bigger the network, the more attractive the frequent flier program becomes. In addition, airlines that dominate a particular airport can charge a hub premium price on tickets. Airport dominance is also related to frequent flier program effectiveness. Travelers are more likely to enroll in a frequent flier program of the airline that is dominant at the airport they prefer. In other words, customers are willing to pay more for tickets just to be in a frequent flier program of an airline that dominates their preferred airport. In spite of this some customers are still very price sensitive when it comes to purchasing airline tickets. Tourists are more price sensitive than business travelers when it comes to purchasing airline tickets. This seems to be true when business travelers spend frequent flier miles to make trips.[7]

For all the work they do in maintaining customer loyalty, frequent flier miles are not worth very much (one or two cents per mile), but they do add up. Over the years tens of trillions of frequent flier miles have been racked up worldwide.

Even if the miles are not worth much cash, airline companies have learned that if you try to take away or devalue the miles, frequent fliers get upset. For example, fliers complained when airlines raised the minimum number of miles required to get a free trip. As in other areas of business, disputes arise occasionally between the customer and the airline over frequent flier program administration. Frequent flier lawsuits are not a frequent occurrence, but they do happen. One of the issues that can come up is the relationship between state contract law and the federal Airline Deregulation Act of 1978, which preempts state law. Whether the federal law nullifies the duties under state laws is something that the Supreme Court has to decide. Which brings up the frequent flier in this story who was grounded by his frequent flier program.[8]

Rabbi Binyomin Ginsberg, an educational consultant and a member of the Northwest Airlines frequent flier program, was kicked out of his program. Ginsberg took them to court.

Haven't heard of Northwest Airlines? That may be because Northwest was acquired by Delta Airlines. When Delta Airlines bought Northwest, not only did they get an air carrier; they also got the lawsuit from Rabbi Ginsberg. At the acquisition, Ginsberg's frequent flier miles were transferred to Delta Airline's frequent flier program. Over the months since his lawsuit, the case made its way to the US Supreme Court.

Ginsberg's attorney asserted to the Supreme Court that contract law in the state of Minnesota contains a duty to deal in good faith and deal fairly. Because the frequent flier arrangement is a contract between the carrier and the flier, the attorney reasoned that there is a duty by the airline to treat the member fairly and that arbitrarily removing the member from the program while canceling all earned miles is unfair. Second, Northwest Airlines used the frequent flier program to induce Mr. Ginsberg to spend a lot of money over many years to purchase tickets from their company instead of from a competitor. Third, although Ginsberg acknowledges that he frequently complained to the Northwest Airline customer service department, the airline gave him no warning that he should change airlines. He was also a loyal customer for many years, as shown by the number of frequent flier miles he had accumulated signifying the hundreds of thousands of dollars the airline had earned from the fares he had paid. Instead, the airline merely canceled his frequent flier account, erased hundreds of thousands of miles that he had accumulated during his business travel and stopped him from earning miles in the future.

The attorney representing the airline stated to the Supreme Court that Rabbi Ginsberg is guilty of several things. First, he intentionally booked tickets on full flights for the purpose of getting bumped off for compensation. Second, Ginsberg was not only a frequent flier; he was also a frequent complainer. In short, the airline asserted that he was abusing his membership in the program. The attorney also argued that the Northwest Airline frequent flier rules gave the airline discretion when determining whether or not a program member was abusing the program. Furthermore, the attorney argued that because the federal law preempts the state law, it is acceptable for the airline company to be unfair to the frequent flier member.

DISCUSSION QUESTIONS

1. Conduct some research on the Internet regarding the Supreme Court case involving Rabbi Ginsberg. What was the final decision by the US Supreme Court? What explanation did the court provide that helps us understand their legal reasoning?

2. If a person shows a pattern of booking tickets on full flights and then gets bumped off those flights in order to get compensation, is this by itself a valid reason to remove the person from the airline's frequent flier program? Doesn't the fact that airlines overbook flights and then ask for volunteers suggest that passengers are free to take the offers that are made? On what basis should a passenger who frequently takes these offers be punished by the airline?

3. If a frequent flier member complains a lot to the customer service department of the airline, is this a valid reason to remove the member from the frequent flier program if the complaints are legitimate concerns?

4. Is it right that the airline took away all the frequent flier miles that Rabbi Ginsberg had accrued over the years? Shouldn't the airline be responsible to compensate Mr. Ginsberg in some way for taking the miles away?

5. What part should fairness play in the determination of what is ethically right and wrong in this case?

6. Is it fair that the airline companies raise the minimum number of miles needed to cash in on a free trip?

CASE 8—GUARANTEE BUT AT A PREMIUM

You are the purchasing manager for small metal fabrication company that provides punching, welding, laser cutting, riveting, bending, assembly and finishing for a variety of metal containers and other products.[9]

Mike Jones, vice president for marketing at Advanced Structural Steel, Ltd., one of your main suppliers, is on the telephone talking to you about the impact on the market from a United Steelworkers of America strike.[10] "We are in the same boat with every other steel distributor. We usually get shipments of steel in every week. But with the strike, we expect that Friday will be our last shipment for at least two weeks. We are scrambling to do deals with Japan, Brazil, or anywhere we can get steel so that we can keep you guys working, but these deals take time to put into place."

You had heard on the news of the strike. Mike's statement about the market impact of the strike made sense, and you are starting to feel uneasy. "What does this mean, Mike?" you ask.

"We have contracts with large fabrication companies that we supply and these large-order customers are coming first because they have paid a premium price for their steel. We have had to make deals with some of our competitors to buy some of their inventory. It might mean that you will have to wait a while. It all depends on how long the strike lasts."

"Yes, but what does this mean for us? We have orders we are obligated to fill."

"I hate to break the news to you, but essentially this means that you will probably have to wait until the strike is over before we can guarantee shipment. We have to protect ourselves and not promise more than we can deliver."

"What is the premium rate that the larger companies have paid to get assurance of deliveries? We will match whatever the big boys are paying!" you say.

Mike puts you on hold and then returns to the line. "Premium prices are for the smaller gauges 3 through 12." He reports the price to you.

"You're killing me, Mike! That is a huge premium," you say. "But we simply have no choice at least for the next forty-five days. I'll see if we can pass some of the cost along to our customers, but they are not going to be happy about this. Let's do it, but let's put in the deal that if the strike ends during the next forty-five days, the premium is refunded."

"This makes me feel terrible!" Mike says. "I hate to take a premium from you, but I understand that situation you are in." Reluctantly Mike agrees. "The premium will mean that you get shipments, but it won't guarantee that the shipments will come exactly on time every week. I mean, like I said, we are scrambling to get alternative suppliers lined up, but their supplies may be disrupted, too."

A few days later your order for steel comes through with the premium price noted on the invoice. Thankful that you do not have to stop operations, you pay the premium.

DISCUSSION QUESTIONS

1. What is the essence of what Mike Jones is doing with his phone call?

2. Is there anything wrong with what Jones has done? Is it illegal?

3. Doesn't a shortage of steel mean that the value will go up and that companies that really need the inventory will be willing to pay the extra cost?

4. What is the right thing for Advanced Structural Steel to do?

CASE 9—PROMISING THE MOON[11]

Darrin knew that Charlene was probably looking elsewhere for employment. He had heard this through the company grapevine. He assumed that in this case the grapevine was carrying accurate information. Darrin did not want to lose Charlene, but he could not give her a raise. So Darrin decided to give Charlene a more clear vision of what could come in the future if she stayed with the firm.

"Charlene, I wanted to talk with you today about your situation," Darrin started in after she entered his office.

"Thank you!" Charlene said.

"You are an important person on our team, Charlene," Darrin continued.

"Yes, I know that."

"I wish we could pay now you what you are truly worth. Unfortunately in these kinds of cases there is often a lag time between the valuable contributions that employees make and growth in market demand for the company's products and services. And it is during this lag time that I am concerned about in your case." Darrin hoped that this introduction would ease Charlene's mind about whether he was truly concerned about her.

"Darrin, I appreciate your concern; however, if the firm truly believed that my contribution would make the kind of difference you allude to in terms of market demand, doesn't it make sense that the company would want to compensate me now if for no other reason than to keep me here so that the growth can be realized? After all, it is the contribution I am making now which is going to payoff in stronger demand, isn't it?"

"I don't want to argue with you about timing. But I agree with you that we should look to your future with this company. This is why I wanted to talk with you. In your case I see a very bright future if you stay with us. I think that within a reasonable amount of time you will have more flexibility in terms of your responsibilities. I think that major opportunities will come your way to broaden your usefulness here. I'm very sure that the company will be able to show you in tangible ways how much it values your work. I mean, I'm thinking big numbers for you. This is something that I have already started to talk about with my boss. She knows you and has watched your work." Darrin stopped and waited for Charlene's reaction.

"Let's talk specifics in terms of what the company can do for me in the future. What do you mean when you say 'big numbers?'" Charlene asked.

"Without a firm go-ahead from my boss, I can't make specific promises to you, Charlene. If you were in my position, would you want to say something that would obligate the company to something that it is not prepared to honor?"

"If you cannot talk specifics, how do I know that my situation will change?" she asked.

DISCUSSION QUESTIONS

1. How would you describe what Charlene's boss is doing?

2. Do you think that Darrin intends to give Charlene a raise? What is your rationale?

3. Is Darrin's action a dirty trick or just good management to try to keep a valued employee?

4. What, if anything, is wrong with how Darrin handled the situation? If you were Charlene, how would you handle this?

CASE 10—THE BOOGIE MAN[12]

Your firm, an outsource partner under contract with a large corporation, provided a specialized set of tasks that helped them manage the supply chain more efficiently. The mantra around your company has been, "Never Forget: Our Customers Can Always Do What We Do!" In one staff meeting you heard the top boss remark that if your firm did not do its job, your customers would find a way to do the work themselves. "Just remember that every day we do our job well, we teach them how to do the same work without us," he said.

Some employees' employment status was recently changed from hourly employee to exempt professional employee, meaning that exempt employees are not paid overtime pay. Lately managers have been asking these professional employees to put in longer hours to get the work done. Obviously, no one is talking about raises, and this stands to reason given that your firm is an outsource partner and must perform the tasks for less money than it would cost the corporation that contracts for your services. Plus, your firm must interact with the employees of the corporation as if your team were insiders but be more polite with them than they are with you.

Lately, your boss has been making statements about the need to "make changes" if the team cannot get its work done with less. He sent around an article about rising unemployment. The previous month he sent around an article on the state of the economy. During staff meeting he hinted of the possibility of layoffs, but when staff members asked about the specifics, he denied that a specific layoff had been planned.

Then one day you notice on his desk a copy of *The Black Book of Outsourcing*, an annual survey report that evaluates the satisfaction that corporations have with their outsource partner contractors.[13] You notice a piece of paper sticking out of the report marking one page. On the top of the book mark is written "Staff meeting agenda."

You have heard other employees talk about looking for work elsewhere. One said openly in the lunch room the other day, "I'm not going to wait around for this company to axe me. I'm out of here the first chance I get." You are getting concerned.

DISCUSSION QUESTIONS

1. How would you describe what the boss is doing?

2. Is there anything wrong with this?

3. Do you think that he intends to lay off employees?

4. How would you respond in this situation?

CASE 11—WHO'S THE DIRTIEST CROOK?[14]

Some would say that Robert Maxwell, the legendary CEO of Mirror Group Newspapers, takes the prize of dirtiest crook.

But John Major, at the time prime minister of the United Kingdom, trumpeted Maxwell as a "great character." Maxwell had led his company to the pinnacle of newspaper publishing success as he acquired hundreds of companies great and small into the Mirror Group's investment portfolio. In March 1991 he was hailed as the savior of the *New York Daily News* when he rescued it for $60 million and agreed to accept its massive liabilities.

Then, in early November 1991, while on an Atlantic Ocean voyage in his luxury yacht, this sixty-eight-year-old former Member of Parliament (1964–1970), former captain in the British Army and one of the richest people in the world mysteriously fell into the bowels of the sea near the Canary Islands.

Then the rest of the story began to unfold. Banks called in their loans to the Mirror Group. The corporation was massively in debt. Then the real scandal hit the news: Maxwell had manipulated the stock price of his firm by diverting more than £1.5 billion (British pounds sterling) from the corporate operating funds and employee pension funds to purchase stock in his own company. Some thirty thousand employees were affected by the £440 million that Maxwell took from their pension funds.

Maxwell was not a person you wanted to criticize. He was known for filing lawsuits against people who criticized him. He bugged the offices of his sons Kevin and Ian to spy on them during merger and acquisition talks.

Mirror Group leaders filed for bankruptcy protection in 1992. In June 1992 the chairman of the board and the chief financial officer resigned. Top-level leaders were caught in the investigations. The British Serious Fraud Office brought charges against Kevin Maxwell and Ian Maxwell and two other Mirror Group employees. Subsequently they were acquitted of charges that they conspired to transfer pension fund assets. As the scandal unfolded the Mirror

Group was not the only firm to get dragged through the mud. The highly regarded accounting firm of Coopers & Lybrand Deloitte received its share of criticism. Lehman Brothers received a fine of £80,000 by the British Securities and Futures Authority for "keeping inadequate records and for maintaining lax procedures" in its dealings with Maxwell.

The Mirror Group repaid some of the pension fund money; the British government, and indirectly its taxpayers, contributed funds. Mirror Group pensioners lost about half of their money.

How could a person of Maxwell's character be allowed to run a corporation using dirty tricks? Twenty years prior to his demise the British Department of Trade had found him "unfit" to head a public company because he had a chronic problem of comingling personal funds with corporate funds to the detriment of shareholders. In 1971 public accountants did not see their role as giving a message to their clients that the client's firm is being managed badly. Coopers & Lybrand could have tipped off regulators to their concerns. Apparently they did not. In 1971 there was no law prohibiting someone with Maxwell's problem from being a director. Such a British law was not passed until 1986. Yet, it was common knowledge in the industry that a dominant personality who demands centralized decision-making authority is considered to be a high-risk leader. A year prior to Maxwell's death an article appeared in a London newspaper asserting that money from a large pension fund was being invested in a corporation in which Maxwell had a financial interest. Few paid attention.

In the wake of the Maxwell scandal the British government enacted new rules that governed the management of employee pension funds.

DISCUSSION QUESTIONS

1. What does it mean to be a dirty crook?

2. What is wrong with comingling funds?

3. Is it wrong to appropriate money from one company fund to help strengthen the company as a whole?

4. On what basis should we consider it a dirty trick?

CASE 12—DIRTY TRICKSTERS IN THE BIBLE

Dirty tricks are not something that developed in modern times. People have been tricking each other for centuries. Here are a few examples of tricksters that we find in the Bible.[15]

- One of the famous stories is that of Samson and Delilah.[16] Samson the strong man was hiding in the wilderness after killing Philistines and burning their fields. Three thousand of his own people of Judah came to him and complained that the Philistines had arrayed for battle for the purpose of capturing Samson. Samson asked them not to kill him but instead to take him to the Philistines. They first made an oath not to kill him. Then they bound Samson in new ropes and carried him to the enemy. On arrival Samson burst the bonds, took the jawbone of an ass and killed a thousand of the enemy. Sometime later, after Samson fell in love with Delilah, she asked him what it would take to bind him. He told her that seven new ropes would be too strong for him. Delilah tied him up with the seven new ropes, but when the Philistines who had been hiding in the next room grabbed him, Samson broke free. Time after time Delilah pressed Samson for the way that would bind him. Time after time she tricked him and he tricked her until finally Samson relented and told her the real reason for his strength. One last time Delilah tricked him, only this time Samson's strength was gone and he was held prisoner until the day he died.

- Trickery occurred in a love story that started as a business relationship between Jacob and his uncle Laban. By the time Jacob met Laban, Jacob already had developed a reputation for being a deceiver: he tricked his father, Isaac, into giving him the inheritance which should have been given to the older brother, Esau.[17] Jacob fled the wrath of Esau and was in need of work and a wife. He traveled to Laban's region hoping to get both.[18] Jacob knew how to raise sheep, and he made a deal with Laban that if he worked reliably for Laban for seven years in return he wanted Laban's daughter Rachel to be his wife. Laban agreed. Jacob fulfilled his part of the contract, and at the end of seven years the wedding was planned. Jacob was very surprised after his first night with his new bride to find out that Laban had not given Rachel to Jacob but had substituted the older daughter, Leah, instead. Laban said something to the effect that "Oh, I'm sorry. Didn't you know that it is the firstborn daughter who always gets married first?" You may be familiar with the rest of the story. Jacob loved Rachel so much that he worked another seven years so that he could have Rachel as his wife. Laban had used special knowledge to trick Jacob, but in the end Jacob used his specialized knowledge of how to raise sheep to trick Laban. As a result Jacob became very wealthy.

- Joseph, the prime minister of Egypt, who used trickery when his own people came to him asking to purchase food.[19] It was Joseph's Hebrew brothers whom his father had sent to purchase the food to prevent starvation, the same brothers who had sold him into slavery many years before. Joseph used the situation to see his younger brother Benjamin before he sold his brothers food. First, Joseph required his brothers to bring him Benjamin knowing that this would cause them and his father great anxiety. Then he planted an expensive article in one of their grain sacks and accused them of stealing it from him. This also caused them great anxiety. In the end, however, he was reconciled to his brothers and paved the way for his family to get more than grain: a permanent place to live during the famine.

DISCUSSION QUESTIONS

1. Which of these three Bible stories involves trickery at its worst?

2. Because these (and other similar) stories are in the Bible, does this mean that dirty tricks are acceptable to God?

3. Are there some dirty tricks that are illegal?

4. Are there other dirty tricks that are not illegal but also not moral?

5. What, if anything, is wrong with using a little trickery in business relationships? What makes it wrong?

CASE 13—DIRTY TRICKS WITH ANCIENT BUSINESS TECHNOLOGY

"Can you sell me one-fourth *qab* of cinnamon? My family is having a special celebration next month. Make sure there are no bugs in the cinnamon," Miriam said as she stood with hands behind her back. Miriam was the daughter of Abiram, one of the wealthy men in the village, one of the families that Jacob ben David desired most as customers. Abiram and his family were looked up to by other villagers.

"Yes, and can I interest you in looking at the newest purple silk I have brought with me?" Jacob was an itinerant spice and fabric trader. He had seen Miriam before on one of his trips through the village and had watched how other girls had gathered around her to talk about what she was wearing.

"If you give me a good price on the cinnamon today, I might bring Mother to see the silk tomorrow," said Miriam.

Jacob ben David put his hand into the light brown leather bag that hung from the corner of his folding table on which he displayed samples of his products. The bag contained Jacob's small ceramic measuring cups of different sizes. On the side of each cup had been engraved in bold letters a label promising the amount it contained. Jacob always turned this side of the cup so that his customer could read the label. Hanging on the other corner was a black leather bag containing stones used for weighing. Jacob kept all his weights and measures out of sight in leather bags while he waited for customers. He could not take the chance that a village hoodlum would steal something this important for trading.

"Let's see, one-fourth *qab* of cinnamon. Ah, here it is. Would you like to purchase the cup, too, or have you brought your own jar?" Jacob said as he retrieved the ceramic cup from his bag.

"I have my own," said Miriam.

Jacob nodded. He wiped out the inside of the cup with a clean cloth and dipped it into the large sack of ground cinnamon. He gently tapped the cup with his finger to settle the contents, and then he scraped the top of the cup so that the cinnamon filled it just to the brim. Jacob named the price, and Miriam responded by holding out to Jacob a small ceramic cup that looked very similar in size to Jacob's measuring cup.

"Just pour it in here," she said.

"Are you sure you want to carry cinnamon home in this?" Jacob asked. "It might spill out."

"I will be careful. Mother told me to make sure I got everything I paid for," said Miriam.

Jacob shrugged and poured the cinnamon from his cup into hers. Strangely, her cup was not full. This sparked a frenzied discussion that turned into heated debate over measures and prices. During the debate Miriam quoted the words of the prophet Moses and King Solomon:

> You shall do no wrong in judgment, in measurement of weight, or capacity. You shall have just balances, just weights, a just ephah, and a just hin; I am the LORD your God, who brought you out from the land of Egypt. (Lev 19:35-36)

> A just balance and scales belong to the
> LORD;
> All the weights of the bag are His concern.
> (Prov 16:11)

"My cup is the standard measure based on the *qab*," insisted Jacob. "I've been selling *qabs* of spices in this village for three years now and no one has ever questioned it. Where did you get your one-fourth *qab* measure cup?"

"We purchased our cup the last time we were in Capernaum. We learned that we cannot always trust the traders that come to our village," Miriam argued.

"What do Capernaum potters know about standard measures?" Jacob asked.

"How do I know that I can trust *you*?" Miriam asked.

Back and forth the debate went with Jacob defending and Miriam attacking his measures and prices until Jacob finally said, "Do you want cinnamon or not? If you want to buy cinnamon that fills your measure, it will cost you a little more. If you don't want cinnamon, someone else will buy it."

DISCUSSION QUESTIONS

1. Which person in this story had the correct measuring cup? What needs to be done to establish the truth of the matter? Read Deuteronomy 25:13-16 and Proverbs 11:1.

> You shall not have in your bag differing weights, a large and a small. You shall not have in your house differing measures, a large and a small. You shall have a full and just weight; you shall have a full and just measure, that your days may be prolonged in the land which the LORD your God gives you. For everyone who does these things, everyone who acts unjustly is an abomination to the LORD your God. (Deut 25:13-16)

> A false balance is an abomination to the LORD,
> But a just weight is His delight.
> (Prov 11:1)

2. Why would having two different measures (large and small) be a problem?

3. Why does Solomon state that weights and measures belong to God and are something he is concerned about?

4. Why does the Bible consider unjust measures an abomination?

5. From the point of view of business success, what is the biggest issue at stake in this story?

CASE 14—CANCELING AN ORDER FOR MACHINED PARTS[20]

As vice president of operations your job is to coordinate the delivery of inventory, production and the shipment of finished goods. Whenever you have the opportunity to minimize the amount of finished goods sitting in your warehouse unsold, you take it.

Most months of the year your production quota matches pretty closely (within ± 3 percent) to the sales projections made by the vice president of sales and her team. This month, however, sales dropped into the abyss, falling by 20 percent from expected, and you do not know why. After having a discussion with the warehouse manager and the vice president of sales, you decide to call your supplier of machined parts.

"Hello, Marc. I'll need to cancel this month's order. Something happened to sales and we are not sure what it is, but I can't afford to have half-a-million dollars' worth of unsold inventory sitting on the shelves around here."

Your supplier has a quick response. "It's fifteen days into the month already! We have already processed most of your order. There is the cost of fabricating the jigs needed for cutting and drilling. That cost I can't make go away. The specialty items that we normally subcontract are already in process at other shops so that we can meet your deadlines. They may have most of it done already, for all I know. We can stop production today, I might be able to get subcontractors to stop production tomorrow, but we've got to charge you for the work we've already completed."

"Nuts," you reply. Reluctantly you agree to pay for the goods.

DISCUSSION QUESTIONS

1. Who has attempted to play a dirty trick on whom in this scenario: you or your supplier?

2. What, if anything, is wrong with your supplier's response?

3. What might be done to prevent this situation from being a dirty trick on your part?

4. What could be done to prevent your supplier from playing a dirty trick on you?

5. If you were the vice president of operations, what creative solutions might be available so that your supplier gets his payment but you do not incur a liability this month?

6. How would you define a business trick as being dirty?

CASE 15—ALL FOR THE NPO MISSION OR RAW OPPORTUNISM?

A religious nonprofit organization (NPO) based in the United States hired three independent consultants to serve on a temporary contract basis alongside three of its full-time employees. Together they were to work on a project in the Russian Federation. The three independent consultants worked as freelance specialists and were not part of the same organization. The American nonprofit organization had contracted with a religious nonprofit organization based in Western Europe to provide services to a third religious nonprofit organization based in Russia. It was the European NPO that was paying the costs, including travel and consultant fees.

The project was organized into three phases that spanned four years, but the consulting agreement was established at the beginning of the project. Phase one involved a ten-day trip to Russia. The consultants were paid for their travel and an agreed-on consulting fee. Phase two required the review of documents that had been translated into English from Russian. The agreement was that payment for document reviews would come at the end of the project when phase three was complete. Phase three involved another ten-day trip to Russia for face-to-face meetings with employees of the Russian religious NPO where the consultants gave the results of their document re-

views and evaluated the validity of the feedback from the Russians.

About five days into the third phase, while the American consultants and full-time employees of the American organization were on site in Russia and had already completed some of the face-to-face meetings, the leader of the American contingent called a breakfast meeting for the American team. At breakfast he suggested that the contract consultants forego part of their consulting fee designated for some, but not all, of the face-to-face meetings. The reason he gave for this was to do the European nonprofit organization a "good turn" because they were paying for services provided to the Russians. The amount of money at stake was approximately 10 percent of the total, not including travel expenses.

After the leader made this statement, the people around the table were silent. Apparently no one wanted to blurt out, "But we signed an agreement, and we have already provided some of the service! And now you say you don't want to pay us?"

Later that day, the American leader brought up the subject again. "You know, I really did not bring this issue up very well this morning. I should have presented more information about the financial health of the European organization. I should have brought it up indirectly at first in order to discern your reactions. Clearly, I made a mistake in how I brought the subject up." All but one of the consultants remained silent. The one who spoke said, "Well, if you really think this is needed, we will do what you think is right."[21] The other consultants gave him a cool stare in response.

Later that night one of the consultants was restless and had a hard time sleeping for thinking about the interest in the American leader in not paying part of the agreed-on fee.

His mind turned to all the reasons why it was not a good idea to withdraw some of the payment. He did not like that the American leader wanted to avoid some of the responsibilities under the agreement. He did not like that this conversation occurred while the team was in Russia after some of the services had already been provided. He did not like being put in a difficult internal political position that made the contract consultants look bad if they insisted on getting paid according to the terms of the contract. Then he thought about the spiritual mission of the Russian organization and all the good that the Americans and Europeans were attempting to do.

After the consultants had returned home, one of them had a conversation with an older, more experienced consultant. The other consultant said, "This is the way they do business over 'there.' I wouldn't be surprised if it was the leader of the European NPO who had thought of this and the American was merely a spokesperson."

DISCUSSION QUESTIONS

1. What do you think about actions of the American team leader?

2. Was it wrong for the American team leader to suggest that part of the agreed-on fee not be paid?

3. What, if anything, is wrong with using opportunistic behavior after an agreement has been made if it is done for a good cause?

4. Would the same action be considered wrong if done in a for-profit setting? If so, why?

5. If you had been one of the contract consultants on that team and attended the breakfast meeting when the American leader had made his proposal, what would you have said?

6. Would you have stated your reaction openly in that group setting or later in private to only the American leader?

CASE 16—MARTIN LUTHER ON DIRTY BUSINESS TRICKS[22]

In his essay on money Martin Luther lists several common business practices of his day which sixteenth-century German merchants allegedly used to increase their wealth at the expense of others. Evaluate each of the dirty tricks. Is each truly a dirty trick or merely a solid business activity that should not be criticized? On what basis, if any, should any of these dirty tricks be avoided by a Christian? Which of these dirty tricks is the worst? What makes it so bad? What current laws are in place to prevent these tricks?

- *Selling on credit*. "There are some who have no conscientious scruples against selling their goods on time and credit for a higher price than if they were sold for cash. Indeed, there are some who will sell nothing for cash but everything on time, so they can make large profits on it."[23]

- *Shortages of supply*. "Again, there are some who sell their goods at a higher price than they command in the common market, or than is customary in the trade; they raise the price of their wares for no other reason than because they know that there is no more of that commodity in the country, or that the supply will shortly be exhausted, and people must have it."[24]

- *Creating a monopoly*. "Again, there are some who buy up the entire supply of certain goods or wares in a country or a city in order to have these goods entirely under their own control; they can then fix and raise the price and sell them as dear as they like or can. . . . Even the imperial and secular laws forbid this; they call it *monopolia*, . . . transactions for selfish profiteering, which are not to be tolerated in country or city."[25]

- **Selling on promise of future delivery**. "Another fine bit of sharp practice is for one man to sell to another, on promise of future delivery, wares that the seller does not have. It works this way: A merchant from a distance comes to me and asks me if I have such and such goods for sale. Although I do not have them I say Yes anyway and sell them to him for ten or eleven gulden, when they could otherwise be bought for nine or less, promising delivery in two or three days. Meanwhile, I go out and buy the goods where I knew in advance that I could buy them cheaper than I am selling them to him. I deliver them, and he pays me for them. Thus I deal with his [the other man's] own money and property without any risk, trouble, or labor, and I get rich."[26]

- **Living off the street**. "Another practice called 'living off the street' is this: When a merchant has a purseful of money and no longer cares to venture on land and sea with his goods, but to have a safe business, he settles down in a large commercial city. When he hears that some merchant is being pressed by his creditors and lacks the money he must have to satisfy them, but still has good wares, he gets someone to act for him in buying the wares, and offers eight gulden for what is otherwise with ten. If this offer is turned down, he gets someone else to make an offer of six or seven gulden. This poor man begins to be afraid that his wares are depreciating, and is glad to accept the eight gulden so as to get hard cash and not to suffer too great a loss and disgrace."[27]

- **Collusion**. "Here is another piece of selfish profiteering: Three or four merchants have in their control one or two kinds of goods which others do not have, or do not have for sale. When these men see that the goods are valuable and are advancing in price all the time because of war or some disaster, they join forces and let it be known to others that the goods are much in demand, and that not many have them for sale. If they find any who have these goods for sale, they set up a dummy to buy up all such goods. When they have cornered the supply, they draw up an agreement to this effect: Since there are no more of these goods to be had, we will hold them at such and such a price, and whoever sells cheaper shall forfeit so and so much."[28]

- **Re-buying inventory**. "Again, I must report this little trick: I sell a man pepper or the like on six months' credit, knowing that he has to sell it again immediately to get ready money. Then I go to him myself, or send someone else, and buy the pepper back from him for cash, but on such terms that what he bought from me on six month's credit for twelve gulden I buy back for eight, while the market price is ten. Thus I buy it from him at two gulden less than the current market, while he bought it from me at two gulden above the market. So I make a profit going and coming, simply because he has to have the money to maintain his credit standing; otherwise, he might have to suffer the disgrace of having no one extend him credit in the future."[29]

- **Working capital loans**. "Another little trick is customary in the trading companies. A citizen deposits with a merchant perhaps two thousand gulden for six years. The merchant is to trade with this and, win or lose, pay the citizen a fixed *zinse* [interest, tax] of two hundred gulden a year. What the merchant makes over and above this is his own, but if he makes no profit he must still pay the *zinse*. In this way the citizen is doing the merchant a great service, for the latter anticipates a profit of at least three hundred gulden from the two thousand. On the other hand, the merchant is doing the citizen a great service, for his money would otherwise lie idle and bring him no return. That this common practice is wrong and is in fact usury, I have shown sufficiently in the treatise on usury."[30]

- *Inflating the weight or bulk of goods*. "Again, they have learned to store their goods in places or under conditions where they will increase in bulk. They put pepper, ginger, and saffron in damp cellars or vaults where they will take on more weight. Woolen good, silks, furs of marten or sable, they sell in dimly-lit vaults or shops, keeping them from the air. This custom is so general that almost every sort of commodity has its special kind of air. There are no goods but what some way is known of taking advantage of the buyer, whether it be in the measure or the count of the dimensions or the weight. They know how to give them an artificial color; or the best-looking items are put at top and bottom and the worst in the middle. There is no end to such cheating; no merchant dare trust another out his sight or reach."[31]

DISCUSSION QUESTIONS

1. The ideas that Martin Luther put forward come from the early sixteenth century—approximately five hundred years ago. What really is new in terms of lying, stealing and cheating in our contemporary world of business?

2. Why might someone object to selling on credit at a higher price than selling for

cash? What, if anything, is wrong with selling on credit?

3. In the "shortages of supply" scenario, Luther implies that the decision to change prices is at the capricious whim of the seller. Is this completely true? What influence does the buyer have on the change in price when there are shortages?

4. How easy or how difficult is it for someone in business to create a monopoly by purchasing large amounts of a particular good?

5. Consider each of the other dirty tricks described by Martin Luther. What, if anything, is wrong with each one? Do you agree or disagree with Luther?

CASE 17—THE ITALIAN HORTICULTURE JOB

Bill and Mary are a retired couple. Three or four times a week they walk for one hour with a small group of friends at the local shopping mall. The friends are members of the local horticulture club. While walking through the mall one morning Mary noticed some unusual Italian flowering plants that the managers of the mall had put out in many places around for the shoppers to enjoy.

She stopped and admired these. Later that day she and Bill visited the local garden supply stores to search for this plant. None of the stores had any of the plants.

Mary figured that she could grow her own plant from cuttings from someone else's plant. She returned to the mall with scissors and plastic bags. Without getting permission from the mall management, she took one cutting from three of the many plants. Mary knew that these few cuttings would not harm the plants in any way. She also knew that growing new plants is a way to enhance the environment. Was it ethical for Mary to take these cuttings without permission?

Think about the other alternatives that Mary has. Mary could

- purchase the plants through mail order.

- purchase seeds and plant them.

- talk with the managers at the mall and ask permission get three cuttings.

- ask permission to take three cuttings, nurture the three plants, keep two of them and then bring the third plant back to the mall.

- talk with the nine other members of her horticulture club about the opportunity. Ask permission from the managers at the mall to obtain twenty cuttings. Each club member would nurture two of the cuttings into healthy plants. Nine of the plants would be given to families in one of the poor neighborhoods who want to beautify their property. One of the plants would be brought back to the mall. The horticulture club members would each keep one plant.

Use your imagination. What other alternatives might Mary have?

What if Mary and five of her closest horticulture friends broaden their viewpoint? What if they went to the mall and asked permission to get ten cuttings? In exchange, the group promised to bring back two healthy plants that the mall could use. Assuming that permission is granted, what if the six people carefully nurtured the cuttings into healthy plants? Two of the ten plants are brought back to the mall as promised. From the remaining eight plants, more cuttings are made and this process continues for three years so that instead of just eight plants, the small group of horticulturists has 216 healthy plants. Some of these they give away. Others they use to continue gleaning more cut-

tings and propagating more and more plants.

Now, what if Mary broadened her view point even more? What if Mary makes it a campaign to beautify the downtown shopping area with these hundreds of flowering plants which she donates to businesses in exchange for their commitment to continue nurturing them?

The beautification program can continue to grow. What if the Chamber of Commerce picks up the idea and makes the commitment, with Mary's encouragement, to beautify every street in town with these same flowering plants? Every organization encourages employees, volunteers and customers to plant one or more of the plants at the front of homes, apartment buildings, city parks, businesses, schools, churches, community centers and other places around town. Mary and two friends from the horticulture club start a small business selling these plants. Other plants are given away to people in need. Mary and her friends host educational sessions on how to nurture and care for cuttings so that they mature into beautiful flowering plants. Now think what this type of leadership will do!

Mary and her husband will start a specialty plant growing and nurturing business to supply the plants at wholesale prices to local garden centers and other local businesses that want to sell the plants to tourists. Oh, yes, tourists! By the time this community commitment reaches about eight or ten years of expansion, the town will have a reputation for the place to see these plants during their peak of blooming. Every year the town hosts a Bloom Festival to celebrate the beauty of the flowers. The Bloom Festival gets listed in travel guides. It is featured on television news magazine shows. The town becomes one of the most heavily photographed towns from the air during the height of bloom season. Many vendors in town sell the beautiful plants.

The business that Mary and Bill start is joined by many other businesses that start to serve the growing tourist trade: restaurants, hotels, craft shops, along with businesses that support the flower growing trade in and around town. New jobs are created. Unemployment drops. Exciting new shopping areas are developed. Property values gradually start to increase. The local high school and college begin horticulture training programs for students. The poorer neighborhoods are cleaned up. One farmer devotes an entire hillside, visible from the highway leading into town, to the growth of these flowering plants. Another landowner takes the risk of turning dozens of acres into fruit orchards. Fruit harvests spawn new trading adventures by serving new markets and attracting tourists during a different season.

Not everything is pure bliss. As the flowering plant trade shows itself to be profitable, new companies begin supplying products. The market price of the plants comes down, attracting even more tourists and sparking innovations in growing and nurturing technology in order to lower costs. Some entrepreneurs misjudge the market, start businesses and then fail. They had incorrect assumptions. These are replaced by entrepreneurs who study more carefully the market and refine their assumptions about the business model that must be in place in order to succeed. For a while an oversupply of flowering plants depresses the profits of the organizations who supply the market. This encourages innovation.

Mary and Bill's business expands to mail order. They sell not only plants but also plant cutting and nurturing equipment and supplies. Over the years Mary and Bill become expert in how to safely propagate new plants. They publish a book on how to grow these special plants. In the book is the story of how it all got started. As their business expands, they decide to expand the product line and go public. Mary and Bill are wealthy beyond their imagination. But their wealth did not come easily. They had to work hard for other people! But they now live in a community where jobs are plentiful, real estate prices are solid and steadily increasing, crime declines and the economy in town is becoming diversified around the knowledge of how to care for and propagate these beautiful plants.

Tourists begin asking how the Bloom Festival got started. The story people tell includes the bit about Mary's decision not to take cuttings without permission but instead to ask permission and with the permission began with a few friends a whole interest in town beautification, education and entrepreneurship. The moral foundation becomes part of the reputation and self-identify of community as a whole.

Consider the dramatic long-term differences between two scenarios.

- Mary takes three cuttings from mall plants without permission. She is nervous and even a bit ashamed about planting these on the front of her property. She plants them in her back yard. She lives in fear that someone might ask her where she got such beautiful plants. To cover for her egoism she might even tell a lie. Mary keeps this little escapade to herself while she tries to enjoy the beauty of the plants.

- Mary takes a moral and entrepreneurial leadership role. She respects the property of others and finds several ways to broaden her self-interests to include the interests of others. With a few friends, she secures permission to make a few cuttings, but then the small group leverage this into community benefit over the long run. Her goal of having a few beautiful plants on her property is widened to embrace the entire community. Her possibility thinking moves beyond narrow self-interests. In the end, she and her husband become wealthy, but what is more important, they help many families improve their economic position, and the community as a whole develops a reputation which drives economic development for the long run.

From this hypothetical situation several tentative observations might be drawn.

1. While self-interest does result in a certain degree of flourishing life, egoism does not result in shalom.

2. Shalom is community-oriented. While one family can enhance its enjoyment in life by taking a few plants from the mall, nourishing them and growing them into healthy flowering plants, this falls far short of the shalom envisioned in Scripture.

3. Fostering shalom requires commitment to helping not only yourself but also other people and other organizations.

4. Fostering shalom requires leadership. Someone with a wider scope of awareness needs to step forward and take actions that are designed to help many. Someone needs to organize the stakeholders, to negotiate for reducing barriers and to communicate the vision of what can happen when concerted efforts by many are harnessed.

5. Fostering shalom requires entrepreneurial risk taking. By nature shalom is communal, but improving health, well-being, knowledge, skill (wisdom), economic prosperity and social harmony requires risk taking by a few on behalf of the many.

DISCUSSION QUESTIONS

1. Will this example of the journey toward shalom apply to all other types of businesses?

2. Will everyone who participates in Mary's plan want to take a leadership position?

3. What connection do you see between the story and the following Scripture passages?

> But you shall remember the LORD your God, for it is He who is giving you power to make wealth, that He may confirm His covenant which He swore to your fathers, as it is this day. (Deut 8:18)

> Depart from evil and do good;
> Seek peace [shalom] and pursue it.
>   (Ps 34:14)

> Those who love Your law have great peace [shalom]. (Ps 119:165)

> Her [wisdom] ways are pleasant ways
> And all her paths are peace [shalom].
>   (Prov 3:17)

> The steadfast of mind You will keep
>   in perfect peace,
> Because he trusts in You. (Is 26:3)

> And the work of righteousness will be peace,
> And the service of righteousness, quietness and confidence forever. (Is 32:17)

> So then we pursue the things which make for peace and the building up of one another. (Rom 14:19)

> Now flee from youthful lusts and pursue righteousness, faith, love and peace, with those who call on the Lord from a pure heart. (2 Tim 2:22)

> He must turn away from evil and do good;
> He must seek peace and pursue it.
>   (1 Pet 3:11)

Notes

PREFACE

[1]M. E. Cafferky, *Management: A Faith-Based Perspective* (Upper Saddle River, NJ: Pearson Education, 2012).

[2]Rom 10:17.

GENERAL INTRODUCTION

[1]This is one of the more beautiful, poetic passages of Scripture in which the ethical ways of God are contrasted with the ways of humans. It includes a wonderful promise of what life can be like when the person and a whole community are open to the possibility of being faithful in a relationship with God.

[2]A PIN is a personal identification number used for security purposes to protect the identity of a person using a bank card to make purchases. This scenario comes from the information provided on the Federal Bureau of Investigation website: www.fbi.gov/news/stories/2011/july/atm_071411/atm_071411. When caught the perpetrators were convicted in court, fined and sentenced to spend years in federal prison.

[3]L. T. Hosmer, *The Ethics of Management*, 6th ed. (New York: McGraw-Hill Irwin, 2008); R. T. DeGeorge, *Business Ethics*, 7th ed. (Upper Saddle River, NJ: Prentice Hall, 2010). Similar descriptions of the process can be found in the writings of other scholars.

[4]Jas 2:14-26; see also Deut 32:20, 51; Hab 2:4; Rom 5:1; 10:10; Eph 2:8; 2 Pet 1:5-9.

[5]This book is based on both Testaments of the Bible. "The ethics of the Old Testament are an absolute necessity for formulating New Testament ethics or any kind of Christian ethics, for only in the Old Testament can the proper foundations be laid for all biblical, theological, or Christian ethical theory or action." W. C. Kaiser Jr., *Toward Old Testament Ethics* (Grand Rapids: Zondervan, 1983), p. 33.

[6]In the Scripture, the belly is also a place where emotions are sensed; however, emotions can also be experienced in the heart (Prov 12:25; 14:10; 15:13, 15; 17:22; 23:7; Neh 2:2; Is 35:4; Jn 14:1).

[7]Deut 32:46; Ps 37:31; 40:8; 119:11; Is 51:7; Jer 31:33; Heb 8:10.

[8]The biblical story describes four primary types of leaders who were wisdom leaders for persons in the community. These leaders have a responsibility to safeguard and interpret the principles of God's Word: the leader(s) of government such as the king (Deut 17:14-20), leaders of the religious organization foremost of whom were the priests (Lev 10:10-11), the prophets (Deut 18:15; 2 Chron 20:20) and the leaders of the economic organizations, that is, heads of households (Deut 6:6-7).

[9]See also Prov 19:20.

[10]Lk 6:47-49; 11:28; Jas 1:21-22, 25.

[11]Some Christian ethics writers approach the ethics process implicitly as primarily a personal matter. See as examples S. B. Rae, *Moral Choices: An Introduction to Ethics* (Grand Rapids: Zondervan, 1995); H. H. Barnette, *Introducing Christian Ethics* (Nashville: Broadman, 1961); M. E. Cafferky, "The Moral-Religious Framework for Shalom," *Journal of Religion and Business Ethics* 3, no. 1 (2014): Article 7 [1-36].

[12]Gen 17:1; Ex 16:4; 18:20; Deut 5:33; 6:7; 10:12; Ps 32:8; 86:11; 101:2; 119:1, 35; 138:7; Prov 6:20-23; Mk 7:5; Jn 8:12; 12:35; Rom 6:4; 1 Cor 7:17; 2 Cor 5:7; Eph 2:10.

[13]The community dimension of biblical ethics has been observed by more than one scholar. See J. Rogerson, "Discourse Ethics and Biblical Ethics," in *The Bible in Ethics*, ed. J. Rogerson, M. Davies and M. Daniel Carroll R. (Sheffield, UK: Sheffield Academic Press, 1995), pp. 17-26; B. C. Birch, "Divine Character and the Formation of the Moral Community in the Book of Exodus," in *The Bible in Ethics*, ed. J. Rogerson, M. Davies and M. Daniel Carroll R. (Sheffield, UK: Sheffield Academic Press, 1995), pp. 119-35; B. C. Birch and L. L. Rasmussen, *Bible and Ethics in the Christian Life* (Minneapolis: Augsburg, 1976); B. C. Birch, *Let Justice Roll Down: The Old Testament, Ethics and Christian Life* (Louisville, KY: Westminster/John Knox, 1991).

[14]Gen 13.

[15]See the story in Ex 5:1-23 in which a community conversation was silenced by the Egyptian overlords but then taken up by Moses and Aaron with God.

[16]Ex 15:23-24; 16:2-9; 17:2-3; Num 11:1; 20:2; 21:5.

[17]Judg 17:6; 21:25. Birch believes that the phrase "doing what was right in his own eyes" refers to the discontinuance of communal dialogue regarding right and wrong.

[18]Prov 12:20.

[19]Ps 72:12; 82:3; Prov 29:4; Is 1:17; Dan 4:27.

[20]Is 9:6.

[21]2 Chron 22:3.

[22]Is 3:3.

[23]Lev 19:11.

[24]Ex 18:16-26; Lev 19:15; Deut 1:15-17.

[25]Ps 1:1-2; Is 8:20.

[26]Mk 7:7-9.

[27]See Deut 4:9-10; 6:7; 11:19; Ps 37:30; 40:9-10; 78:4-6; Prov 6:22.

[28]Amos 5:15.

[29]Ps 99:4.

[30]Deut 6:6-7; 11:19; Ps 34:11; 78:5.

[31]Gen 5:22-24; 17:1; 48:15; Lev 26:12-13; Deut 5:33; 8:6; 11:22.

[32]Jn 14:26.

[33]Eph 6:17.

[34]Col 3:16.

[35]I appreciate my colleague Dr. Rob Montague for calling my attention to this distinction.

[36]Ps 19:7-8; 2 Cor 3:17-18.

[37]2 Cor 3:18.

[38]The connection between the character of God and moral content has been drawn by scholars. For example, see B. C. Birch, "Divine Character and the Formation of the Moral Community in the Book of Exodus," in *The Bible in Ethics*, ed. J. Rogerson, M. Davies and M. Daniel Carroll R. (Sheffield, UK: Sheffield Academic Press, 1995), pp. 119-35.

[39]Ex 6:7; 7:5; 10:2; 31:13; Deut 4:35, 39; 7:9; Ps 9:10; 25:4; Judg 2:10; Jn 17:3.

[40]Rom 8:11; Col 3:16; Rev 3:20.

[41]By using two types of persons in terms of religious experience, I do not intend to convey the idea that religious experience is confined to just these two categories. Indeed, a variety of religious experiences exists.

[42]Deut 29:29; Ps 25:14; 92:5; Is 55:8-9; Rom 11:33-34.

[43]Eph 4:1.

[44]Heb 12:2.

[45]From a theological point of view, the circles representing the character of God and Jesus Christ and his word should overlap more than is portrayed in the illustration. However, in Scripture the work and divine identity of Jesus is presented as an important topic. Thus, in this text we use the visual illustration of three circles throughout to remind the reader of the three types of Bible passages that can be observed. These three circles correspond with the columns presented in appendix B.

1 WHY ETHICS IN BUSINESS IS IMPORTANT

[1]Similar thoughts are expressed in Deut 6:18; 12:18, 28; Ps 19:9-11; 25:12-13; Mk 10:28-31; Lk 18:29-30; Jn 6:51; 10:10; 1 Tim 4:8; 6:6.

[2]S. Leung, "Despite Best Efforts, Doughnut Makers Must Fry, Fry Again; Low-fat Version of the Treat Proves Hard to Roll Out; Mr. Ligon Lands in Hole," *Wall Street Journal*, January 5, 2004, A.1-A.; C. Lewis, "The Case of the (Not So) Skinny Treats," *FDA Consumer* 35, no. 4 (2001): 38-39.

[3]Many factors influence profitability in the short run: prices, costs, demand, competitors, debt.

[4]D. Quinn and T. Jones, "An Agent Morality View of Business Policy," *Academy of Management Review* 20, no. 1 (1995): 22-42.

[5]Even though there does not appear to be any direct measurable financial impact of honesty, the customer, the supplier or the employee must believe that you are honest; otherwise they may not choose to have a business relationship with you.

[6]That unethical people get wealthy was recognized in ancient Hebrew times. See Ps 37:7, 16, 35; 49:5-6; 52:7; 62:10; 73:3, 12; 92:7; Jer 12:1-2; Mt 5:44-45.

[7]We will explore this more in chapter 2.

[8]Today we would call this a direct marketing company. Story told to the author by a descendant of the salesman.

[9]Monotheist (mono-theist = one God) religions believe in the existence of one God.

[10]J. Dalla Costa, *The Ethical Imperative: Why Moral Leadership Is Good Business* (Reading, MA: Addison-Wesley, 1998); "Do Good Ethics Ensure Good Profits?," *Business & Society Review* 70, no. 3 (1989): 4-10; D. Collins, *Essentials of Business Ethics: Creating an Organization of High Integrity and Superior Performance* (Hoboken, NJ: John Wiley & Sons, 2009), p. 8; B. Weinstein, "Ask the Ethics Guy: Why Should We Be Ethical?," *The Monitor*, Knight-Ridder/Tribune News Service, November 3, 2008; C. C. Verschoor, "Ethical Behavior Brings Tangible Benefits to Organizations," *Strategic Finance* 82, no. 11 (2001): 20-21; L. S. Paine, "Managing for Organizational Integrity," *Harvard Business Review* 72, no. 2 (1994): 106-17; L. S. Paine, "Does Ethics Pay?," *Business Ethics Quarterly* 10, no. 1 (2000): 319-30; P. Jessup, "Business Ethics Does Pay," *New Zealand Management* 58, no. 1 (2011): 38-39; O. C. Ferrell, J. Fraedrich and L. Ferrell, *Business Ethics: Ethical Decision Making and Cases*, 8th ed. (Boston: Houghton Mifflin, 2008), pp. 17-24; G. Becker, "The Competitive Edge of Moral Leadership," *International Management Review* 3, no. 1 (2007): 50-71; G. Dutton, "Do Strong Ethics Hurt U.S. Global Competitiveness?," *World Trade* 21, no. 3 (2008): 36, 38, 40-41; A. Sen, "Does Business Ethics Make Economic Sense?," *Business Ethics Quarterly* 3, no. 1 (1993): 45-54; M. W. Sheffert, "The High Cost of Low Ethics," *Financial Executive* 17, no. 6 (2001): 56-58; D. Koehn, "Integrity as a Business Asset," *Journal of Business Ethics* 58 (2005): 125-36; R. B. Cialdini, P. K. Petrova and N. J. Goldstein, "The Hidden Costs of Organizational Dishonesty," *MIT Sloan Management Review* 45, no. 3 (2004): 67-73; A. Bhide and H. H. Stevenson, "Why Be Honest If Honesty Doesn't Pay?," *Harvard Business Review* 68, no. 5 (1990): 121-29; M. Velasquez, "Why Ethics Matters: A Defense of Ethics in Business Organizations," *Business Ethics Quarterly* 6, no. 2 (1996): 201-22; R. Duska, "Business Ethics: Oxymoron or Good Business?," *Business Ethics Quarterly* 10, no. 1 (2000): 111-29.

[11]W. D. Thompson, "Restoring Integrity to Business," *Vital Speeches of the Day* 69, no. 1 (2002): 12.

[12]This point is part of a larger discussion called the "divine command" theory of ethics.

[13]M. D. Long and S. Rao, "The Wealth Effects of Unethical Business Behavior," *Journal of Economics and Finance* 19, no. 2 (1995): 65-73; P. E. Varca and M. James-Valutis, "The Relationship of Ability and Satisfaction to Job Performance," *Applied Psychology: An International Review* 42, no. 3 (1993): 265-75; Josephson Institute, *Josephson Institute Reports:* The Hidden Costs of Unethical Behavior (Los Angeles: The Josephson Institute, 2004); S. Webley and E. More, "Does Business Ethics Pay?" (London: Institute of Business Ethics, 2003).

[14]R. A. Brealey and S. C. Myers, *Principles of Corporate Finance*, 6th ed. (New York: Irwin McGraw-Hill, 2000), pp. 27-28.

[15]Long and Rao, "Wealth Effects of Unethical Business Behavior," pp. 65-73; J. W. Weiss, *Business Ethics: A Stakeholder and Issues Management Approach*, 3rd ed. (Mason, OH: Thomson South-Western, 2003).

[16]Here the thoughts of Peter Drucker are extended. P. F. Drucker, "The Information Executives Truly Need," *Harvard Business Review* 73, no. 1 (1995): 54-62.

[17]F. Snare, *The Nature of Moral Thinking* (New York: Routledge, 1992), p. 3.

[18]T. M. Jones, "Ethical Decision Making by Individuals in Organizations: An Issue-Contingent Model," *Academy of Management Review* 16, no. 2 (1991): 366-95. See also T. Barnett, "Dimensions of Moral Intensity and Ethical Decision Making: An Empirical Study," *Journal of Applied Social Psychology* 31 (2001): 1038-57; D. S. Carlson, K. M. Kacmar and L. L. Wadworth, "The Impact of Moral Intensity Dimensions on Ethical Decision Making: Assessing the Relevance of Orientation," *Journal of Managerial Issues* 14, no. 1 (2002): 15-30; J. M. Kukerich, M. J. Waller, E. George and G. P. Huber, "Moral Intensity and Managerial Problem Solving," *Journal of Business Ethics* 24 (2000): 29-38; R. Haines, M. D. Street and D. Haines, "The Influence of Perceived Importance of an Ethical Issue on Moral Judgment, Moral Obligation and Moral Intent," *Journal of Business Ethics* 81 (2007): 387-99.

[19]These and many other examples of white-collar crime are presented on the website of the Federal Bureau of Investigation: www.fbi.gov/news/stories/story-index/white-collar-crime.

[20]These and other dilemmas that have some ambiguous elements are presented at the end of every chapter and in an appendix.

[21]Adapted from M. E. Cafferky, *Management: A Faith-Based Perspective* (Upper Saddle River, NJ: Pearson Education, 2012), pp. 149-52; M. H. Bazerman and D. A. Moore, *Judgment in Managerial Decision Making*, 8th ed. (Hoboken, NJ: John Wiley & Sons, 2013), pp. 132-59; G. Yukl, *Leadership in Organizations*, 5th ed. (New York: Pearson, 2013), p. 345; C. Moore, "Moral Disengagement in Processes in Organizations," *Journal of Business Ethics* 80 (2008): 129-39; A. Bandura, "Selective Moral Disengagement in the Exercise of Moral Agency," *Journal of Moral Education* 31, no. 2 (2002): 101-19.

[22]T. L. Beauchamp and N. E. Bowie, eds., *Ethical Theory and Business*, 7th ed. (Upper Saddle River, NJ: Pearson Prentice Hall, 2004), pp. 1-2.

[23]L. T. Hosmer, "Strategic Planning as If Ethics Mattered," *Strategic Management Journal* 15 (1994): 17-34.

[24]We will consider some of these in later chapters.

[25]Mt 22:37-38; see also Deut 6:5; Lev 19:18.

[26]Ex 20:1-17; Deut 5:1-22; Rom 13:9.

[27]For examples see Ex 22–23; Mt 5–7; Rom 12:17-21.

[28]Beauchamp and Bowie, *Ethical Theory and Business*, pp. 1-2; Hosmer, "Strategic Planning as If Ethics Mattered," pp. 17-34.

[29]Many people in business avoid the use of the word *moral* preferring instead to use the word *ethics*. The terms "moral" and "morality" sometimes carry connotations of personal judgment or religious belief which many prefer not to include in the business environment.

[30]O. W. Holmes, "The Path of the Law," *Harvard Law Review* 10 (1897): 459. The essay was reprinted in 1997.

[31]W. Blackstone, *Commentaries on the Laws of England*, vols. 1-4 (Boston: T. B. Wait & Sons, 1818), p. 34.

[32]J. Nesteruk, "The Moral Dynamics of Law in Business," *American Business Law Journal* 34, no. 2 (1996): 134.

[33]H. C. Black, *Black's Law Dictionary*, 5th ed. (St. Paul, MN: West Publishing, 1979), p. 975.

[34]J. M. Grcic, "Democratic Capitalism: Developing a Conscience for the Corporation," *Journal of Business Ethics* 4, no. 2 (1985): 147-48.

[35]Holmes, "Path of the Law," p. 459.

[36]Paine, "Managing for Organizational Integrity," pp. 106-17.

[37]K. G. Denhardt, *The Ethics of Public Service: Resolving Moral Dilemmas in Public Organizations* (Westport, CT: Greenwood, 1988).

[38]This reference to moral standards coming from within a person is not meant that each person is the original source of a moral standard, but rather that each person has accepted a moral standard and holds it in his or her mind with which to judge the rightness or wrongness of actions.

[39]These four levels have also been identified in E. M. Epstein, "Business Ethics, Corporate Good Citizenship and Corporate Social Policy Process: A View from the United States," *Journal of Business Ethics* 8 (1989): 583-95; Cafferky, *Management*, pp. 495-96.

[40]R. C. Chewning, J. W. Eby and S. J. Roels, *Business Through the Eyes of Faith* (San Francisco: HarperSan-Francisco, 1990), pp. 26-28.

2 FUNDAMENTAL TENSIONS IN THE ENVIRONMENT OF BUSINESS

[1]"Carving Up the Industry," *The Economist* 347, no. 8075 (1998): 62-63; "Contractors Call for Code to End Rivals' Dirty Tricks," *Caterer & Hotelkeeper* 192, no. 4271 (2003): 10.

[2]One reason for this may be that traditionally business education has focused primarily on the practical knowledge, activities and skills of business. Another reason may be that the fundamental core of the business environment is highly abstract. Because of this, it can be difficult to grasp the first time you think about it.

[3]A paradox is a social situation that contains mutually exclusive, contradictory elements existing together and for which no resolution is possible. Hundreds of paradoxes have been identified in social groups such as business organizations. For examples see K. S. Cameron and R. E. Quinn, "Organizational Paradox and Transformation," in *Paradox and Transformation: Toward a Theory of Change in Organization and Management*, ed. R. E. Quinn and K. S. Cameron (Cambridge, MA: Ballinger, 1988), pp. 1-18; M. W. Lewis and G. E. Dehler, "Learning Through Paradox: A Pedagogical Strategy for Exploring Contradictions and Complexity," *Journal of Management Education* 24, no. 6 (2000): 708-25.

[4]In addition to the tensions described in this chapter, there are other tensions as well. For example: "Business ethics is cursed (or blessed depending on one's perspective) with certain seemingly constant and irresolvable difficulties. Prime among these are the following: (1) inconsistent results when multiple ethical theories are applied in judgment of a particular business practice; (2) conflicts among multiple societal moral norms which all appear applicable to a single business decision; and (3) fact gathering and methodological constraints which encumber efforts to apply traditional ethical theories to complex business practices" (p. 23). T. W. Dunfee, "Business Ethics and Extant Social Contracts," *Business Ethics Quarterly* 1, no. 1 (1991): 23-51.

[5]J. J. Rousseau, *The Social Contract and Discourses* (1763; New York: E. P. Dutton, 1913).

[6]H. Fayol, *General and Industrial Management* (1916; London: Sir Isaac Pitman and Sons, 1949), p. 26.

[7]P. Selznick, *Leadership in Administration: A Sociological Interpretation* (Berkeley: University of California Press, 1957), p. 9.

[8]C. Perrow, *Complex Organizations: A Critical Essay*, 3rd ed. (New York: McGraw-Hill, 1986), p. 66. Examples of other scholars that have identified this paradox include E. Durkheim, *The Division of Labor in Society* (New York: The Free Press, 1984), pp. 174, 295; T. Parsons and E. A. Shils, *Toward a General Theory of Action: Theoretical Foundations for the Social Science* (New York: Harper & Row, 1962).

[9]R. G. Olson, *The Morality of Self-Interest* (New York: Harcourt, Brace and World, 1965), p. 1; M. E. Cafferky, "Leading in the Face of Conflicting Expectations: Caring for the Needs of Individuals and of the Organization," *Journal of Applied Christian Leadership* 5, no. 2 (2011): 38-57; M. E. Cafferky, "Exploring the Fundamental Paradox of Being an Organizational Leader," *Journal of Biblical Integration in Business* 13 (2011): 140-57.

[10]These elements are adapted from J. M. Grcic, "Democratic Capitalism: Developing a Conscience for the Corporation," *Journal of Business Ethics* 4, no. 2 (1985): 145-46; Parsons and Shils, *Toward a General Theory of Action*; Olson, *Morality of Self-Interest*, p. 28; H. C. Triandis, *Individualism and Collectivism* (Boulder, CO: Westview Press, 1995), pp. 38-39; J. K. Fletcher and K. Käufer, "Shared Leadership: Paradox and Possibility," in *Shared Leadership: Reframing the Hows and Whys of Leadership*, ed. C. L. Pearce and J. A. Conger (Thousand Oaks, CA: Sage Publications, 2003), pp. 21-47; K. R. Andrews, *The Concept of Corporate Strategy* (Homewood, IL: Dow Jones-Irwin, 1971), pp. 231-32; P. F. Drucker, *The Practice of Management* (New York: Harper & Brothers, 1954), pp. 265-66; B. M. Bass, "From Transactional to Transformational Leadership: Learning to Share the Vision," *Organizational Dynamics* 18, no. 3 (1990): 19-31; C. W. Langfred, "The Paradox of Self-Management: Individual and Group Autonomy in Work Groups," *Journal of Organizational Behavior* 21, no. 5 (2000): 563-85; R. Wilson, *Economics, Ethics and Religion: Jewish, Christian and Muslim Economic Thought* (New York: New York University Press, 1997), p. 64; C. I. Barnard, *The Functions of the Executive* (Cambridge, MA: Harvard University Press, 1938), pp. 88, 293; R. Perloff, "Self-Interest and Personal Responsibility Redux," *American Psychologist* 42, no. 1 (1987): 3-11; A. Ryan, *Utilitarianism and Other Essays: J. S. Mill and Jeremy Bentham* (New York: Penguin Books, 1987), p. 66.

[11]The tension between short term and long run has been identified by many. Consider D. Dodd and K. Favaro, "Managing the Right Tension," *Harvard Business Review* 84, no. 12 (2006): 62-74; D. Dodd and K. Favaro, "Managing the Short Term/Long Term Tension: How Small Changes to Traditional Strategic Planning Processes Can Make a Big Difference," *Financial Executive* 22, no. 10 (2006): 22-25; R. T. De-George, *Business Ethics*, 6th ed. (Upper Saddle River, NJ: Pearson Prentice Hall, 2006); A. Rappaport, "The Economics of Short-Term Performance Obsession," *Financial Analysts Journal* 61, no. 3 (2005): 65-79; R. F. Vancil, "Strategy Formulation in Complex Organizations," *Sloan Management Review* 17, no. 2 (1976): 1-18; Andrews, *Concept of Corporate Strategy*, pp. 230-31; H. A. Simon, *Administrative Behavior*, 4th ed. (New York: The Free Press, 1997); M. H. Bazerman, *Judgment in Managerial Decision Making*, 6th ed. (New York: John Wiley & Sons, 2006), p. 62; R. A. Webber, *Time and Management* (New York: Van Nostrand Reinhold, 1972), p. 126.

[12]R. W. Emerson, "Society and Solitude," in *Selected Writings of Emerson* (New York: The Modern Library, 1981), p. 816.

[13]G. Hamel and C. K. Prahalad, *Competing for the Future* (Boston: Harvard Business School Press, 1994).

[14]Perhaps coupled with unfavorable changes in metabolism or decreases in physical exercise.

[15]Dodd and Favaro, "Managing the Short Term/Long Term Tension," pp. 22-25; Dodd and Favaro, "Managing the Right Tension," pp. 62-74.

[16]J. Ugelow, "Short-Term/Long-Term Solutions in Waste Management: Economics and the Transition Process," *Waste Management & Research* 12, no. 3 (1994): 243-56.

[17]M. H. Bazerman and D. A. Moore, *Judgment in Managerial Decision Making*, 8th ed. (Hoboken, NJ: John Wiley & Sons, 2013), p. 108.

[18]Ibid., pp. 109-10.

[19]DeGeorge, *Business Ethics*, p. 59; Bazerman, *Judgment in Managerial Decision Making*, p. 62.

[20]Webber, *Time and Management*, p. 126.

[21]Selznick, *Leadership in Administration*, p. 151.

[22]Bazerman, *Judgment in Managerial Decision Making*, p. 62.

[23]Grcic, "Democratic Capitalism," pp. 145-50.

[24]Simon, *Administrative Behavior*, p. 107.

[25]S. Young, *Moral Capitalism: Reconciling Private Interest with the Public Good* (San Francisco: Berrett-Koehler, 2003), pp. 7-8.

[26]See a survey of this issue in M. E. Cafferky, *Management: A Faith-Based Perspective* (Upper Saddle River, NJ: Pearson Education, 2012), p. 210.

[27]Selznick, *Leadership in Administration*, p. vi.

[28]Ex 20:15.

[29]R. C. Solomon, "Business and the Humanities: An Aristotelian Approach to Business Ethics," in *Business as a Humanity*, ed. T. J. Donaldson and R. E. Freeman (New York: Oxford University Press, 1994), pp. 45, 58; P. H. Warehane, "Moral Character and Moral Reasoning," in *Business as a Humanity*, ed. T. J. Donaldson and R. E. Freeman (New York: Oxford University Press, 1994), pp. 98, 100; J. Nesteruk, "The Moral Dynamics of Law in Business," *American Business Law Journal* 34, no. 2 (1996): 133-40; J. J. Piderit, *The Ethical Foundations of Economics* (Washington, DC: Georgetown University Press, 1993), p. 34; R. M. Kidder, "Ethical Decision-Making and Moral Courage," in *The Accountable Corporation*, vol. 2, ed. M. J. Epstein and K. O. Hanson (Westport, CT: Praeger, 2006), p. 83; Y. Lurie and R. Albin, "Moral Dilemmas in Business Ethics: From Decision Procedures to Edifying Perspectives," *Journal of Business Ethics* 71 (2007): 195-207; Parsons and Shils, *Toward a General Theory of Action*.

[30]For discussions of casuistry see K. E. Kirk, *Conscience and Its Problem: An Introduction to Casuistry* (1927; Louisville, KY: Westminster John Knox, 1999); S. Hauerwas, *The Peaceable Kingdom: A Primer on Christian Ethics* (Notre Dame, IN: University of Notre Dame Press, 1983); A. R. Jonsen and S. Toulmin, *The Abuse of Casuistry: A History of Moral Reasoning* (Los Angeles: University of California Press, 1988); M. Calkins, "Casuistry and the Business Case Method," *Business Ethics Quarterly* 11, no. 2 (2001): 237-59; D. C. Jones, *Biblical Christian Ethics* (Grand Rapids: Baker Books, 1994), pp. 138-40.

[31]Piderit, *Ethical Foundations of Economics*, p. 9. As we will see, this is nothing more than egoism.

[32]R. M. Kidder, *How Good People Make Tough Choices: Resolving the Dilemmas of Ethical Living* (New York: Fireside Publications, 1995); J. L. Badaracco, *Defining Moments: When Managers Must Choose Between Right and Right* (Cambridge, MA: Harvard Business School Press, 1997).

[33]One might even argue from this that managing the complex right-versus-right dilemmas is one of the biggest reasons that we need leaders in society.

[34]P. Block, *Community: The Structure of Belonging* (San Francisco: Berrett-Koehler, 2008), p. 93.

[35]See appendix A for additional questions that can be asked in a group setting.

[36]Cafferky, "Leading in the Face of Conflicting Expectations," pp. 38-55.

[37]Num 32:1-32.

[38]2 Thess 3:6-15.

[39]Ex 20:5; 34:7; Num 14:18; Deut 5:9.

[40]Prov 27:23-27.

[41]Lk 14:28-30.

[42]Tit 3:14.

[43]Mk 12:31.

[44]Deut 29:23; 2 Kings 2:19; Prov 26:7; Ezek 15:3-5; Lk 13:6-9; Heb 6:8.

[45]Eccles 3:2; Mt 3:10; Lk 3:9.

[46]Ex 20–23.

[47]Mt 5–7; 9:13; 12:7; 20:23; Lk 11:42. For a contemporary discussion of casuistry see J. F. Keenan, "The Return of Casuistry," *Theological Studies* 57, no. 1 (1996): 123-39.

[48]Kidder, *How Good People Make Tough Choices*.

[49]www.parkrangers.org.

3 BIBLICAL THEMES FOR BUSINESS ETHICS—PART 1

[1]Theme in a narrative has been defined as "a generalized, abstract paraphrase of the inferred central or dominant idea of a story." C. E. Bain, J. Beaty and J. P. Hunter, *The Norton Introduction to Literature* (New York: W. W. Norton, 1995), p. 244. It is the dominant ideas of the Bible that are considered in this text.

[2]Scholars have wrestled with the relationship between theology and business ethics. For examples see T. F. McMahon, "The Contributions of Religious Traditions to Business Ethics," *Journal of Business Ethics* 4 (1985): 341-49; R. T. DeGeorge, "Theological Ethics and Business Ethics," *Journal of Business Ethics* 5, no. 6 (1986): 421-32; O. F. Williams, "Can Business Ethics Be Theological? What Athens Can Learn from Jerusalem," *Journal of Business Ethics* 5, no. 6 (1986): 473-84; O. F. Williams and J. W. Houck, *Full Value: Cases in Christian Business Ethics* (San Francisco: Harper & Row, 1978); D. A. Wren, "Medieval or Modern? A Scholastic's View of Business Ethics," *Journal of Business Ethics* 28 (2000): 109-19; L. L. McSwain, "Christian Ethics and the Business Ethos," *Review & Expositor* 81, no. 2 (1984): 197-207; F. R. McCurley and J. H. P. Reumann, "Ethical Guidance Provided by the Bible—Confusion, Chimera or Prophetic Realism?," in *Corporation Ethics: The Quest for Moral Authority*, ed. G. W. Forell and W. H. Lazareth (Philadelphia: Fortress, 1980), pp. 35-51; M. Novak, *Toward a Theology of the Corporation*, rev. ed. (Washington, DC: American Enterprise Institute, 1981); I. R. Harper and S. Gregg, eds., *Christian Theology and Market Economics* (Northampton, MA: Edward Elgar, 2008); G. Magill, "Theology in Business Ethics: Appealing to the Religious Imagination," *Journal of Business Ethics* 11, no. 2 (1992): 129-35; M. Calkins, "Recovering Religion's Prophetic Voice for Business Ethics," *Journal of Business Ethics* 23 (2000): 339-52; G. J. Rossouw, "Business Ethics: Where Have All the Christians Gone?," *Journal of Business Ethics* 13, no. 7 (1994): 557-70; M. E. Cafferky, "The Moral-Religious Framework for Shalom," *Journal of Religion and Business Ethics* 3, no. 1 (2014): Article 7 [1-36].

[3]Biblical themes and their connection with Bible stories are studied and emphasized in the field of biblical theology. For descriptions of the field see B. S. Rosner, "Biblical Theology," in *New Dictionary of Biblical Theology*, ed. T. D. Alexander and B. S. Rosner (Downers Grove, IL: InterVarsity Press, 2000), pp. 3-11; J. K. Mead, *Biblical Theology: Issues, Methods and Themes* (Louisville, KY: Westminster John Knox, 2007), pp. 169-239; R. B. Gaffin Jr., "Systematic Theology and Biblical Theology," *Westminster Theological Journal* 38, no. 3 (1976): 281-99. Biblical themes specifically related to business ethics have been identified by A. Hill, *Just Business* (Downers Grove, IL: InterVarsity Press, 2008); D. A. Hay, *Economics Today: A Christian Critique* (Grand Rapids: Eerdmans, 1989); D. P. McCann, "Business Corporations and the Principle of Subsidiarity," in *Rethinking the Purpose of Business: Interdisciplinary Essays from the Catholic Social Tradition*, ed. Cortright and Naughton (Notre Dame, IN: University of Notre Dame Press, 2002), pp. 169-89; M. E. Cafferky, *Management: A Faith-based Perspective* (Upper Saddle River, NJ: Pearson Education, Inc., 2012).

[4]The following works were consulted when selecting and summarizing the themes used in this book: G. K. Beale, *A New Testament Biblical Theology: The Unfolding of the Old Testament in the New* (Grand Rapids: Baker Academic, 2011); J. M. Hamilton, *God's Glory in Salvation Through Judgment: A Biblical Theology* (Wheaton, IL: Crossway, 2010); T. D. Alexander, *From Eden to the New Jerusalem: An Introduction to Biblical Theology* (Grand Rapids: Kregel Academic & Professional, 2008); W. C. Kaiser Jr., *The Promise-Plan of God: A Biblical Theology of the Old and New Testaments* (Grand Rapids: Zondervan, 2008); S. J. Hafemann and P. R. House, *Central Themes in Biblical Theology: Mapping Unity in Diversity* (Grand Rapids: Baker Academic, 2007); Mead, *Biblical Theology*; C. G. Bartholomew, *Out of Egypt: Biblical Theology and Biblical Interpretation* (Grand Rapids: Zondervan, 2004); J. Goldingay, *Old Testament Theology*, 3 vols.; vol. 1: *Israel's Gospel*, vol. 2: *Israel's Faith* (Downers Grove, IL: IVP Academic, 2003, 2006); W. Dyrness, *Themes in Old Testament Theology* (Downers Grove, IL: InterVarsity Press, 1977); W. Brueggemann, *Theology of the Old Testament: Testimony, Dispute, Advocacy* (Minneapolis: Fortress, 1997);

C. H. H. Scobie, *The Ways of Our God: An Approach to Biblical Theology* (Grand Rapids: Eerdmans, 2003); Alexander and Rosner, *New Dictionary of Biblical Theology*; J. Barr, *The Concept of Biblical Theology: An Old Testament Perspective* (Minneapolis: Fortress, 1999); W. A. Elwell, ed., *Evangelical Dictionary of Biblical Theology* (Grand Rapids: Baker Books, 1996); B. S. Childs, *Biblical Theology of the Old and New Testaments: Theological Reflection on the Christian Bible* (Minneapolis: Fortress, 1993); I. H. Marshall, *New Testament Theology: Many Witnesses, One Gospel* (Downers Grove, IL: InterVarsity Press, 2004); T. R. Schreiner, *New Testament Theology: Magnifying God in Christ* (Grand Rapids: Baker Academic, 2008); U. Schnelle, *Theology of the New Testament* (Grand Rapids: Baker Academic, 2009).

[5]Samson's incredible story is told in Judg 13–16.

[6]Mk 1:35; Lk 6:12; 9:18; Jn 6:15; Heb 5:7.

[7]A study resource for reviewing the content of the various themes introduced in chapters 3 and 4 is located in appendix C.

[8]Here are a few examples of the many books and articles about evil bosses: J. Dixit and P. Doskoch, "Bosses from Hell," *Psychology Today* 29, no. 5 (1996): 24; B. Dumaine, "America's Toughest Bosses," *Fortune* 128, no. 9 (1993): 38-52; R. I. Sutton, *Good Boss, Bad Boss: How to Be the Best and Learn from the Worst* (New York: Business Plus, 2010); J. Kirby, "Evil at Work: Bad Bosses," *Maclean's* 121, no. 40 (2008): 70; M. Haight, *Who's Afraid of the Big, Bad Boss? How to Survive Thirteen Types of Dysfunctional, Disrespectful, Dishonest Little Dictators* (West Conshohocken, PA: Infinity Publishing, 2008); H. A. Hornstein, *Brutal Bosses and Their Prey* (New York: Penguin Riverhead Trade, 1997); B. L. Katcher and A. Snyder, *Thirty Reasons Employees Hate Their Managers: What Your People May Be Thinking and What You Can Do* (New York: AMACOM, 2007).

[9]More than one biblical scholar has identified this theme of Scripture. The following are examples: F. Thielman, *Theology of the New Testament: A Canonical and Synthetic Approach* (Grand Rapids: Zondervan, 2005), pp. 681-90; T. Longman III, D. G. Reid and W. A. VanGemeren, *God Is a Warrior: Studies in Old Testament Biblical Theology* (Grand Rapids: Zondervan, 1995); Alexander, *From Eden to New Jerusalem*; Scobie, *The Ways of Our God*; D. A. deSilva, *New Testament Themes* (St. Louis, MO: Chalice Press, 2001); N. R. Gulley, *Systematic Theology* (Berrien Springs, MI: Andrews University Press, 2003); G. A. Boyd, *God at War: The Bible and Spiritual Conflict* (Downers Grove, IL: InterVarsity Press, 1997); G. A. Boyd, *Satan and the Problem of Evil: Constructing a Trinitarian Warfare Theodicy* (Downers Grove, IL: InterVarsity Press, 2001); C. A. Evans, "Inaugurating the Kingdom of God and Defeating the Kingdom of Satan," *Bulletin for Biblical Research* 15, no. 1 (2005): 49-75; P. D. Miller Jr., "God the Warrior," *Interpretation* 19, no. 1 (1965): 39-46; L. S. Chafer, "Angelology," *Bibliotheca Sacra* 99, no. 396 (1942): 391-417; L. S. Chafer, "Angelology," *Bibliotheca Sacra* 99, no. 395 (1942): 262-96; L. S. Chafer, "Angelology," *Bibliotheca Sacra* 99, no. 394 (1942): 135-56; L. S. Chafer, "Angelology," *Bibliotheca Sacra* 99, no. 393 (1942): 6-25; L. S. Chafer, "Angelology," *Bibliotheca Sacra* 99, no. 392 (1941): 389-420; B. J. Macdonald-Milne, "The Eucharist as Witness to the Kingdom of God and Experience of God's Reign," *International Review of Mission* 69, no. 274 (1980): 143-50; H. K. LaRondelle, "The Biblical Concept of Armageddon," *Journal of the Evangelical Theological Society* 28, no. 1 (1985): 21-31; T. Longman III, "The Divine Warrior: The New Testament Use of an Old Testament Motif," *Westminster Theological Review* 44, no. 2 (1982): 290-307; T. N. D. Mettinger, "Fighting the Powers of Chaos and Hell: Towards the Biblical Portrait of God," *Studia Theologica* 39, no. 1 (1985): 21-38; B. A Stevens, "Jesus as the Divine Warrior," *Expository Times* 94, no. 11 (1983): 326-29; S. R. Garrett, "Christ and the Present Evil Age," *Interpretation* 57, no. 4 (2003): 370-83. Also brief reference is made to this theme in the spiritual warfare of ideas in series preface of K. L. Wong and S. B. Rae, *Business for the Common Good: A Christian Vision for the Marketplace* (Downers Grove, IL: IVP Academic, 2011), p. 14.

[10]Gen 3.

[11]1 Sam 17.

[12]Mt 4; 10:1; Lk 10:18; Jn 12:31; 16:11; 1 Jn 3:8.

[13]Acts 19.

[14]Mt 13:37-39; 20:25-26; 28:18; Jn 12:30-32.

[15]Mt 10:1; 12:28.

[16]Acts 10:38; 26:18; Rom 8:38; Col 1:13-20; 2:15; Eph 1:20-22; 2:13-18; Heb 2:14; 10:12-13; 2 Tim 1:10; 1 Pet 3:18-22; Rev 3:21.

[17]Rom 13:12; 2 Cor 6:7; 10:3-5; Eph 2:2; 3:8-11; 4:27; 6:12-17; 1 Thess 5:4-8; 1 Pet 5:8-9; Jas 4:7.

[18]Job 1–2; Lk 22:3; a.k.a. Dragon (Rev 12:9; 20:2), Serpent (Rev 12:9), the devil (slanderer, false accuser; Mt 4:1-11; Lk 4:1-13). See also Gen 3; Lk 12:18; Acts 10:38; 13:10; 2 Cor 4:4; 11:3, 14; Heb 2:14; 1 Pet 5:8; 1 Jn 3:8; 5:3; Rev 12:9-11.

[19]Is 14:13; Ezek 28:2-9; 2 Thess 2:3-4; Rev 13:6-7.

[20]Gen 1-3; Ex 34:6-7; Deut 7:9; Ps 7:10; 35:27; 57:10; 79:9; 86:15; 89:14; 104:24; 119:142; Is 54:10; Jer 32:40; Ezek 37:26; Acts 17:24-26; Rom 1:18-20; 3:21-26; 16:20; Eph 1:13-14; 3:8-11; Col 1:15-20; Tit 3:4-5; 1 Jn 4:8-10; Rev 16:7; 19:11.

[21]D. J. Elazar, "Covenant and Community," *Judaism* 49, no. 4 (2000): 387-98.

[22]Eph 5:1.

[23]Eph 6:12-17.

[24]Jas 4:7.

[25]The markets of the world are also the places where a lot of good is done. It is in the ethical, social and legal environment of business where we find loyalty, trust, healing and helping. We find good people counteracting the forces of marketplace evil, heroes who are willing to put their careers on the line for good. From front-line employees and low-level supervisors to top-level executives there are thousands of people in business who are honest, caring, serving for the good of others.

[26]A. Hall, " 'I'm Outta Here!' Why Two Million Americans Quit Every Month (and Five Steps to Turn the Epidemic Around)," March 11, 2013, www.forbes.com/sites/alanhall/2013/03/11/im-outta-here-why -2-million-americans-quit-every-month-and-5-steps-to-turn-the-epidemic-around (accessed May 17, 2013). Hall's recommended treatment for the epidemic of job quitters parallels some of the elements of the conflict between God and Satan: (1) take care of your employees (foster a flourishing life); (2) empower your people; (3) eliminate negative politics; (4) be trustworthy; (5) recognize your people.

[27]Gen 1–2; Ps 104:5; Prov 3:19-20.

[28]Gen 1:26-29; Ps 8:3-6; Acts 17:24-28.

[29]C. J. H. Wright, "Ethics," in *New International Dictionary of Old Testament Theology and Exegesis*, ed. W. A. VanGemeren, 5 vols. (Grand Rapids: Zondervan, 1997), 4:585-94.

[30]For the connection between the imagery of the sanctuary and the Garden of Eden see L. B. Schachter, "The Garden of Eden as God's First Sanctuary," *Jewish Bible Quarterly* 41, no. 2 (2013): 73-77; G. K. Beale, "Eden, the Temple and the Church's Mission in the New Creation," *Journal of the Evangelical Theological Society* 48, no. 1 (2005): 5-31; Alexander, *From Eden to the New Jerusalem*.

[31]P. Copan, *Is God a Moral Monster? Making Sense of the Old Testament God* (Grand Rapids: Baker Books, 2011), p. 59.

[32]Ps 33:6-9; Jn 1:1-3; Heb 1:1-10; Rev 3:14; 4:11.

[33]1 Tim 4:4.

[34]Gen 1:26-28; 2:15. See also "Oxford Declaration on Christian Faith and Economics," *Transformation* 7, no. 2 (1990): 1-9.

[35]See also Rom 12:4-5; 1 Cor 10:17; 12:12-27; Eph 5:30; Col 2:19.

[36]A more complete comparison chart is available in appendix C.

[37]Wright, "Ethics," pp. 585-94.

[38]R. Mason, "Restoration," in *New International Dictionary of Old Testament Theology and Exegesis*, ed. W. A. VanGemeren, 5 vols. (Grand Rapids: Zondervan, 1997), 4:1137-40.

[39]Ps 40:9; 51:12; Jer 31:33; 32:39-40; Ezek 11:19; 2 Cor 3:18; 5:17; Col 3:10.

[40]Is 65:17-19; Rev 21:1-5.

[41]Ps 19:7.

[42]In Deut 6:6-7 this is introduced when Moses tells the people that the heads of household, the leaders of the primary economic unit of the day, should teach their children the principles of the Ten Commandments. This role of preservation and protection of the Ten Commandments was a role also shared by the civil leaders (Deut 17:14-20), religious leaders (Deut 33:9-10), independent prophets (Deut 18) and the community as a whole (Deut 13).

[43]M. L. Stackhouse, "The Location of the Holy," *Journal of Religious Ethics* 4, no. 1 (1976): 63-104; A. Hill, *Just Business: Christian Ethics for the Marketplace* (Downers Grove, IL: IVP Academic, 2008), pp. 23-36; L. K. Mullen, "Holy Living—The Adequate Ethic," *Wesleyan Theological Journal* 14, no. 2 (1979): 82-95; D. R. Griffin, "The Holy, Necessary Goodness and Morality," *Journal of Religious Ethics* 8, no. 2 (1980): 330-49; J. A. Naudé, "*qds*," in *New International Dictionary of Old Testament Theology and Exegesis*, ed. W. A. VanGemeren, 5 vols. (Grand Rapids: Zondervan, 1997), 3:877-87; W. Brueggemann, *Reverberations of Faith: A Theological Handbook of Old Testament Themes* (Louisville, KY: Westminster John Knox, 2002), p. 98.

[44]Hill, *Just Business*, p. 23.

[45]T. E. McCominsky, "qadash," in *Theological Wordbook of the Old Testament*, ed. R. L. Harris, 2 vols. (Chicago: Moody Press, 1980), 2:786-89.

[46]Lev 18:3; 20:26; Num 23:9.

[47]W. J. Dumbrell, *The Faith of Israel: A Theological Survey of the Old Testament* (Grand Rapids: Baker Book House, 2002); D. G. Peterson, "Holiness," in *New Dictionary of Biblical Theology*, ed. T. D. Alexander and B. S. Rosner (Downers Grove, IL: InterVarsity Press, 2000); E. A. Martens, *God's Design: A Focus on Old Testament Theology* (Grand Rapids: Baker Book House, 1981); W. A. Dyrness, *Themes in Old Testament Theology* (Downers Grove, IL: InterVarsity Press, 1977), p. 51; Naudé, "*qds*," p. 879; S. B. Rae, *Moral Choices: An Introduction to Ethics* (Grand Rapids: Zondervan, 1995), pp. 22-23.

[48]Ex 31:17.

[49]Ps 22:3-5; 33:21; Ezek 20:41; 28:25; 39:27; Hab 1:12.

[50]Ex 29:42-46; Hos 11:9. See the comments on this in Peterson, "Holiness," p. 545.

[51]Is 53:9; Mk 1:24; Lk 1:35; 4:34; Acts 4:27; Phil 2:1-11; 2 Cor 5:21; Heb 4:15; 7:26; 9:14; Rev 3:7.

[52]Lev 20:26; Deut 7:6; 14:2; 26:19. W. C. Kaiser Jr., *Toward an Old Testament Theology* (Grand Rapids: Zondervan, 1978), pp. 110-19; B. K. Waltke, *An Old Testament Theology: An Exegetical, Canonical and Thematic Approach* (Grand Rapids: Zondervan, 2007); W. A. Dyrness, *Themes in Old Testament Theology* (Downers Grove, IL: InterVarsity Press, 1977); Dumbrell, *Faith of Israel*.

[53]Ex 19:5-6; Lev 11:44-45; 19:2; 20:7, 26; see also Num 16:3; Deut 7:6; 14:2; 26:19; 28:9; 1 Pet 2:5-11; Rev 5:10.

[54]Dyrness, *Themes in Old Testament Theology*, p. 139.

[55]Martens, *God's Design*, p. 96; Naudé, "*qds*," p. 883; Dumbrell, *Faith of Israel*, p. 47. See also Lev 11:44; 19:2; 20:7; Rom 12:2; Col 3:12; 1 Thess 4:7; Jas 1:27; 1 Pet 1:15-16; 1 Jn 2:15-17.

[56]Lev 19:13; Deut 24:14. The book of Leviticus is sometimes referred to as the Holiness Code.

[57]Lev 19:9-10; Deut 24:19.

[58]Lev 19:14, 32; Deut 27:18.

[59]Lev 19:15; Deut 16:18-20.

[60]Lev 19:16; Deut 22:8.

[61]Lev 19:23; Deut 20:19-20.

[62]Lev 19:33-34; Deut 24:17.

[63]Lev 27:28.

[64]Lev 19:35-36; Deut 25:13ff.

[65]Josh 24:19-21; Ezra 6:21; Ps 1:1; 2 Cor 7:1; Rev 18:4. Waltke, *Old Testament Theology*, p. 407; Dyrness, *Themes in Old Testament Theology*, pp. 52-53; Naudé, "*qds*," p. 884; Peterson, "Holiness," pp. 545-46.

[66]Deut 7:6; 1 Cor 6:17.

[67]Jn 17:15.

[68]Deut 26:19. As we will see, the biblical idea of prosperity is much broader than economic wealth.

[69]Hill, *Just Business*, pp. 23-36.

[70]Mt 20:28; Rom 3:20-27; Gal 1:4; Eph 5:2; 1 Tim 2:6; Tit 2:14; 1 Pet 2:24; 1 Jn 2:2.

[71]Is 61:1; Rom 6:18; Gal 5:1, 13.

[72]Wright, "Ethics," pp. 585-94; O. P. Robertson, *The Christ of the Covenants* (Grand Rapids: Baker Book House, 1980); W. J. Dumbrell, *Covenant and Creation: A Theology of the Old Testament Covenants* (Grand Rapids: Baker Book House, 1984); L. L. Nash, *Good Intentions Aside: A Manager's Guide to Resolving Ethical Problems* (Boston: Harvard Business School Press, 1991); S. W. Herman, *Durable Goods: A Covenantal Ethic for Management and Employees* (Notre Dame, IN: University of Notre Dame Press, 1997); M. L. Pava, *Leading with Meaning: Using Covenantal Leadership to Build a Better Organization* (New York: Palgrave Macmillan, 2003); H. K. LaRondelle, *Our Creator Redeemer: An Introduction to Biblical Covenant Theology* (Berrien Springs, MI: Andrews University Press, 2005); D. P. McCann, "On Moral Business: A Theological Perspective," *Review of Business* 19, no. 1 (1997): 12; J. Lee, *The Two Pillars of the Market: A Paradigm for Dialogue Between Theology and Economics* (New York: Peter Lang, 2011); K. Shin, *The Covenantal Interpretation of the Business Corporation* (Lanham, MD: University Press of America, 2001); D. Sturm, "Corporations, Constitutions and Covenants on Forms of Human Relation and the Problem of Legitimacy," *Journal of the American Academy of Religion* 41, no. 3 (1973): 331-53; C. Caldwell, "Leading With Meaning: Using Covenantal Leadership to Build a Better Organization," *Business Ethics Quarterly* 15, no. 3 (2005): 499-505; L. J. Moisan, *Leadership Is a Covenant: Leading People and Living Life More Effectively* (Bloomington, IN: Author House, 2007); Hill, *Just Business*, pp. 179-80; S. B. Young, "Fiduciary Duties as a Helpful Guide to Ethical Decision-Making in Business," *Journal of Business Ethics* 74 (2007): 1-15.

[73]Deut 6:18.

[74]The biblical idea of "blessing" combines the idea of covenant and shalom. When you bless someone, you are attempting to bring the promises of shalom into a reality for that person while you reaffirm the deep, mutually beneficial relationship with him or her. An important blessing that conveys the idea of shalom is in Num 6:24-26. Common greetings found in the Bible were in the form of blessing. Thus, when you greeted someone in the community, you pronounced a blessing on that person. In what might otherwise seem like a simple "hello" and "good-bye" you stated your hope that the other person will experience an abundant life in all of his or her relationships. See Gen 26:29; 44:17; Ex 4:18; Num 25:12; Judg 18:6; 19:20; 1 Sam 1:17; 2 Sam 15:9. Seventeen letters to the early church in the New Testament began with such a greeting. For examples see Rom 1:7; 1 Cor 1:3; 2 Cor 1:2; Gal 1:3; Eph 1:2; Rev 1:4. See also M. E. Cafferky, "The Religious-Ethical Framework for Shalom," *Journal of Religion and Business Ethics* 3, no. 1 (2014): Article 7 [1-36].

[75]This is relevant for business where organizations typically have differing degrees of bargaining power.

[76]This is one reason why marriage is a good example of how biblical covenants work.

[77]Ex 20:1-17; Deut 5:1-22. Scripture summaries of the Ten Commandments can be found in the Old Testament in Ps 15; Is 33:14-15; 56:1; Mic 6:8. The New Testament also contains summaries of the Decalogue: Mt 5–7; 22:37-40; Mk 10:19; Lk 18:20; Rom 13:8-10. More than one scholar has stated that the Ten Commandments recorded by Moses are the foundation not only of Jewish ethics but also Christian ethics.

Some have gone farther by stating that the Decalogue is the basis of ethics in many societies. On this see W. Barclay, *The Ten Commandments for Today* (Grand Rapids: Eerdmans, 1973); M. F. Rooker, *The Ten Commandments: Ethics for the Twenty-First Century* (Nashville: B&H Academic, 2010).

[78]Cafferky, "Ethical-Religious Framework for Shalom."

[79]Here an important distinction is being made between justification and sanctification, even though both are a work of God. Obedience to God is best associated with sanctification (transforming our living for God) rather than justification (making us right with God). On this see Rooker, *Ten Commandments*.

[80]Deut 4:40; 5:16; 6:6-9; Josh 1:8; Ps 19:7; Jer 38:20; 42:6. See how Jesus relates this idea to his own work (Jn 10:10). The Ten Commandments are traditionally referred to as the Halakah, which means "to walk." See as examples Deut 6:6-7; 8:6; 10:12; 11:19. This imagery is used in Eph 5:1-2. Walking is the biblical imagery for all social interactions and endeavors, including marketplace activities.

[81]D. Melé, "Religious Foundations of Business Ethics," in *The Accountable Corporation*, ed. M. J. Epstein and K. O. Hanson, 4 vols. (Westport, CT: Praeger, 2006), 2:11-43.

[82]Many Christians believe that Jesus Christ gave the Ten Commandments to Moses and that when he came to earth, he demonstrated the principles of the commandments in his life and work. See R. K. Hughes, *Disciplines of Grace* (Wheaton, IL: Crossway, 1993), p. 20; E. P. Clowney, *How Jesus Transforms the Ten Commandments* (Phillipsburg, NJ: P & R, 2007), p. 40. See also Mt 5:17; Lk 16:17; Rom 3:31; Gal 3:17-24.

[83]The Bible says that faithful followers of God are servants or ambassadors of God's covenant relationship with us. See Mk 16:15-16; 2 Cor 3:6; 5:18-20; 6:1.

[84]See also Lk 6:30-31. Various forms of the Golden Rule can be found in many world religions and in philosophy. This has led some to say that the Golden Rule is the most important principle of ethics. Most contemporary versions of the Golden Rule have stripped it of its biblical covenant roots. Accordingly, the biblical version is distinctly different because it incorporates all of the precepts of the Ten Commandments and, by extension, the life and work of Jesus Christ as its basis.

[85]Mt 22:34-40; Mk 12:28-34; Lk 10:25-28.

[86]Jesus also mentioned the prophets when he gave the two great commands and the Golden Rule because the work of the prophet was to call wayward people back to a close relationship with God in which the law of God is written on their hearts (Ezek 11:19; Jer 31:33; 32:40). The prophets lived and worked in particular circumstances where people's behaviors were destroying covenant relationships. The prophets also drew attention to the promises of God related to covenantal living in community first envisioned by Moses (Deut 28).

[87]For a more complete exploration of the principles of the Ten Commandments, see appendix D.

4 BIBLICAL THEMES FOR BUSINESS ETHICS—PART 2

[1]For similar biblical exhortations see also Mt 5:9; Rom 12:18; Gal 5:22; Heb 12:14; 1 Pet 3:11.

[2]The Preamble establishes the goal or purpose of the Constitution.

[3]W. Eichrodt, "Covenant and Law," *Interpretation* 20, no. 3 (1966): 302-21; T. M. Gregory, "Peace," in *The Zondervan Encyclopedia of the Bible*, ed. M. C. Tenney, 5 vols. (Grand Rapids: Zondervan, 2009), 4:747-50; H. Gross, "Peace," in *Encyclopedia of Biblical Theology*, ed. J. B. Bauer (New York: Crossroad, 1981), pp. 648-51; J. P. Healey, "Peace," in *The Anchor Bible Dictionary*, ed. D. N. Freedman, 6 vols. (New York: Doubleday, 1992), 5:206-7; P. J. Nel, "8966 *slm*," in *Encyclopedia of Biblical Theology*, ed. W. A. VanGemeren (Grand Rapids: Zondervan, 1997), 4:130-35; P. Potter, "Peace: The Fruit of Justice," *Theology Today* 36, no. 4 (1980): 498-503; G. E. Schaefer, "Peace," in *Evangelical Dictionary of the Biblical Theology*, ed. W. A. Elwell (Grand Rapids: Baker Books, 1996), pp. 597-98; F. J. Stendebach, "Shalom," in *Theological Dictionary of the Old Testament*, ed. G. J. Botterweck, H. Ringgren and H.-J. Fabry, 15 vols. (Grand Rapids: Eerdmans, 2006), 15:13-49; W. M. Swartley, *Covenant of Peace: The Missing Peace in New Testament Theology and*

Ethics (Grand Rapids: Eerdmans, 2006); E. Waltner, "Shalom and Wholeness," *Brethren Life and Thought* 29 (1984): 145-51; D. L. Smith-Christopher, "Shalom," in *The New Interpreters Dictionary of the Bible*, ed. K. Doob Sakenfeld, 5 vols. (Nashville: Abingdon, 2009), 5:211-12; J. Van Duzer, *Why Business Matters to God (And What Still Needs to Be Fixed)* (Downers Grove, IL: IVP Academic, 2010), p. 55; K. L. Wong and S. B. Rae, *Business for the Common Good: A Christian Vision for the Marketplace* (Downers Grove, IL: IVP Academic, 2011), p. 71; M. E. Cafferky, "The Ethical-Religious Framework for Shalom," *Journal of Religion and Business Ethics* 3 (2014): Article 7 [1-36].

[4]Num 25:12; Josh 9:15; 1 Kings 5:12; Is 54:10; Ezek 34:25; 37:26.

[5]See these passages in which life is related to themes descriptive of God: Deut 30:15, 19; 32:39; Ps 36:9; Prov 9:10; 12:28; 13:14; Rom 8:6; 1 Jn 4:9.

[6]Ps 29:11; 34:14; 119:133; 122:6; Is 26:3; 32:17; Rom 6:12-14; 14:17; 2 Cor 13:11; Gal 5:22; Phil 4:7; Col 3:15; 1 Thess 5:23; 2 Tim 2:22; 1 Pet 3:11; 2 Pet 3:14.

[7]Is 9:6-7; see also Ezek 37:26.

[8]Is 53:5; Lk 1:79; 2:14; Rom 5:1; Eph 2:14-15; Col 1:20; 3:15; 2 Thess 3:16; Heb 13:20.

[9]Although Jesus does not specifically use the word *peace* it seems that complete well-being of shalom is what he has in mind. In this passage he seems to be equating his own life and work with the fulfillment of the community's hopes and dreams for shalom.

[10]See also Is 32:17.

[11]For a short study of the other Bible concepts related to shalom, see appendix H.

[12]Ps 122:6; Jer 29:4-14; Zech 8:19. The connection between business and the biblical ideal of shalom has been drawn by more than one scholar. For examples, see R. C. Chewning, J. W. Eby and S. J. Roels, *Business Through the Eyes of Faith* (San Francisco: HarperSanFrancisco, 1990), pp. 194-95; R. P. Stevens, *Doing God's Business: Meaning and Motivation for the Marketplace* (Grand Rapids: Eerdmans, 2006), pp. 19-27; M. E. Cafferky, *Management: A Faith-Based Perspective* (Upper Saddle River, NJ: Pearson Education, 2012), p. 12; T. P. Steen, S. VanderVeen and J. Voskuil, "Finance: On Earth as It Is in Heaven?," *Managerial Finance* 32, no. 10 (2006): 802-11.

[13]The theme of sabbath is intertwined with creation, covenant, shalom and other themes. Like shalom, sabbath is closely identified with covenant and is even called a perpetual sign of the covenant relationship between God and his people (see Ex 31:16; Is 56:6). Some believe that the sabbath command is the most important. On this see M. F. Rooker, *The Ten Commandments: Ethics for the Twenty-First Century* (Nashville: B&H Academic, 2010), pp. 75-102.

[14]Many scholars have contributed to the dialogue regarding sabbath. The following represent various viewpoints: W. Brueggemann, *Sabbath as Resistance: Saying No to the Culture of Now* (Louisville, KY: Westminster John Knox, 2014); Rooker, *Ten Commandments*, pp. 75-102; N.-E. A. Andreasen, *Rest and Redemption: A Study of the Biblical Sabbath* (Berrien Springs, MI: Andrews University Press, 1978); W. J. Dumbrell, *Covenant and Creation: A Theology of the Old Testament Covenants* (Grand Rapids: Baker Book House, 1984); W. Eichrodt, "The Law and the Gospel: The Meaning of the Ten Commandments in Israel and for Us," *Interpretation* 11, no. 1 (1957): 23-40; J. Goldingay, *Old Testament Theology*, vol. 2: *Israel's Faith* (Downers Grove, IL: InterVarsity Press, 2006); S. J. Hafemann, "What Does It Mean to Know God? The Covenant God of the Sabbath," in *The God of Promise and the Life of Faith: Understanding the Heart of the Bible* (Wheaton, IL: Crossway, 2001), pp. 41-60; H. K. LaRondelle, *Our Creator Redeemer: An Introduction to Biblical Covenant Theology* (Berrien Springs, MI: Andrews University Press, 2005); P. D. Miller, *The Ten Commandments* (Louisville, KY: Westminster John Knox, 2009).

[15]Brueggemann says, "No wonder our most familiar Sabbath blessing ends: 'The Lord lift up his countenance upon you and give you peace (*shalom*),' . . . for the benediction is the affirmation of Sabbath, the conclusion of creation, when harmony has been brought to all the warring elements of our existence."

W. Brueggemann, *Peace* (St. Louis, MO: Chalice Press, 2001), p. 16. On the comprehensiveness of sabbath benefits for the whole creation see Rooker, *Ten Commandments*, pp. 75-102.

[16]Is 56:6; 66:23; Ezek 44:24; 45:17; 46:1-12.

[17]B. Gert, *Common Morality: Deciding What to Do* (New York: Oxford University Press, 2004), p. 4.

[18]The creation narrative does not call the seventh day of creation week "sabbath"; however, later references to sabbath connect it with creation suggesting the possibility that the Bible writers may have believed that sabbath had its origin at creation. The most direct connection between sabbath and creation is given in Ex 20:8-11.

[19]Rooker, *Ten Commandments*, pp. 75-102.

[20]The story of the manna illustrates this core principle of loyalty and faith. So closely was sabbath tied to covenant that if you broke the sabbath you were breaking the covenant. On this see the comments of Rooker, *Ten Commandments*, pp. 75-102.

[21]Lev 25:1-6.

[22]Amos 8:1-6.

[23]C. D. Marshall, *The Little Book of Biblical Justice: A Fresh Approach to the Bible's Teachings on Justice* (Intercourse, PA: Good Books. 2005), p. 13.

[24]Many writers have contributed to our understanding of the Bible term "justice." The following are representative: J. P. Burnside, *God, Justice and Society* (New York: Oxford University Press, 2011); J. M. Coomber, *Bible and Justice: Ancient Texts, Modern Challenges* (Oakville, CT: Equinox Publishing, 2011); W. J. Houston, *Justice: The Biblical Challenge* (Oakville, CT: Equinox Publishing, 2010); W. J. Houston, *Contending for Justice: Ideologies and Theologies of Social Justice in the Old Testament* (London: T & T Clark, 2008); Marshall, *Little Book of Biblical Justice*; C. J. H. Wright, *Old Testament Ethics for the People of God* (Downers Grove, IL: InterVarsity Press, 2004); R. B. Hays, *The Moral Vision of the New Testament: Community, Cross, New Creation* (San Francisco: HarperSanFrancisco, 1996); B. C. Birch, *Let Justice Roll Down: The Old Testament, Ethics and the Christian Life* (Louisville, KY: Westminster John Knox, 1991).

[25]Potter, "Peace," pp. 498-503.

[26]H. V. Bennett, "Justice, OT," in *The New Interpreters Dictionary of the Bible*, ed. K. Doob Sakenfeld, 5 vols. (Nashville: Abingdon, 2008), 3:476-77. See Deut 18:3-5.

[27]Prov 22:2; Gal 3:28; Col 3:11; Jas 2:1-4.

[28]Marshall, *Little Book of Biblical Justice*, p. 6.

[29]See also Prov 2:8; 31:8; Is 59:8.

[30]Deut 10:18; Ps 10:18; 17:2; 37:6; 82:3-4; Prov 31:8-9; Eccles 5:8-9; Is 10:1-2; 51:4; Amos 5:24. The comparison with flowing water is also used to describe shalom in Is 66:12.

[31]Ex 23:6; Deut 24:7; Prov 17:23.

[32]Deut 16:20; 25:13-16; Ps 106:3.

[33]Discussions of the relationship of the theme of righteousness to other themes can be found in the works of many biblical scholars, including those cited above. The following are additional examples: Potter, "Peace"; W. Brueggemann, *Reverberations of Faith: A Theological Handbook of the Old Testament* (Louisville, KY: Westminster John Knox, 2002), pp. 177-80; M. L. Soards, "Righteousness in the New Testament," in *The New Interpreter's Dictionary of the Bible*, ed. K. Doob Sakenfeld, 5 vols. (Nashville: Abingdon, 2009), 4:813-18; N. Declaisse-Walford, "Righteousness in the Old Testament," in *The New Interpreter's Dictionary of the Bible*, ed. K. Doob Sakenfeld, 5 vols. (Nashville: Abingdon, 2009), 4:818-23.

[34]Ps 15:2; Prov 2:10-20.

[35]Ex 9:27; Deut 32:3-4; Ps 15; 24; 31:1; 36:10; 37; 40:10; 71:2; 88:10; 89:14; 112; 145:17; Is 46:13; 51:5-8; Jer 9:24; Mt 5:20; 6:1; Lk 1:6; 23:47; Jn 16:8-10; 1 Cor 1:30; 1 Pet 3:10-12.

[36]Job 17:9; Ps 48:10; Prov 20:28; Is 59:16.

[37]Deut 9:4; 2 Kings 18:6; 23:1-3; Phil 3:9.

[38]Rom 1:16-17.

[39]Gen 18:23; Ex 9:27; Deut 25:1; Ps 1; 10:3-11; 37; 45:7; Prov 3:33; 4:14-18; 10:2-11; 11:5-10; Neh 9:33; Mal 3:18.

[40]Gen 4:1-8.

[41]2 Kings 9.

[42]Prov 12:26.

[43]Gen 42:16; Ex 18:21; Josh 24:14; 1 Sam 12:24; 1 Kings 22:16; Prov 3:3.

[44]E. Berkovitz, "Emeth, the Concept of Truth," in *Man and God: Studies in Biblical Theology* (Detroit: Wayne State University Press, 1969), pp. 253-91; W. C. Kaiser Jr., *Toward Old Testament Ethics* (Grand Rapids: Zondervan, 1983), pp. 222-25; L. J. Kuyper, "Grace and Truth: An Old Testament Description of God and Its Use in the Johannine Gospel," *Interpretation* 18, no. 1 (1964): 3-19.

[45]Prov 20:6. When the prophet Zechariah predicted the fulfillment of all the hopes and dreams for God's work of bringing shalom, he described the experience as truth. See Zech 8:3-19.

[46]Living a consistent life begins by not deceiving yourself. See, for example, Prov 25:14; 26:16; 28:11; 30:12; Lk 14:11; Rom 12:16; Gal 6:3; Rev 3:17.

[47]Prov 28:20; 29:14.

[48]Ps 5:6; 12:2; 119:29, 113, 128, 163; Rom 12:9; Eph 4:25; Rev 22:15.

[49]2 Kings 12:15.

[50]W. Dyrness, "Wisdom," in *Themes in Old Testament Theology* (Downers Grove, IL: InterVarsity Press, 1977), pp. 189, 195; G. von Rad, *Old Testament Theology*, vol. 1: *The Theology of Israel's Historical Traditions* (New York: Harper & Row, 1962), p. 418; H. P. Müller, "Chakham," in *Theological Dictionary of the Old Testament*, ed. G. J. Botterweck and H. Ringgren, 15 vols. (Grand Rapids: Eerdmans, 1980), 4:370-85.

[51]Ps 104:24; Prov 3:19.

[52]Prov 3:13.

[53]Eph 3:8-11.

[54]J. A. Grant, "Wisdom and Covenant: Revisiting Zimmerli," *European Journal of Theology* 12, no. 2 (2003): 103-13; D. A. Hubbard, "The Wisdom Movement and Israel's Covenant Faith," *Tyndale Bulletin* 17 (1966): 3-33. See also F. E. Eakin Jr., "Wisdom, Creation and Covenant," *Perspectives in Religious Studies* 4, no. 3 (1977): 218-32; L. Hoebeke, "The Decalogue and Practical Wisdom: Rereading a Seminal Text," *The Journal of Management Development* 29, no. 7/8 (2010): 736-46.

[55]Prov 1:3-7; 2:6-9; Jer 9:23-24; Goldingay, *Old Testament Theology*, vol. 2: *Israel's Faith*, p. 583.

[56]B. K. Waltke, "The Gift of Wisdom," in *An Old Testament Theology: An Exegetical, Canonical and Thematic Approach* (Grand Rapids: Zondervan, 2007), p. 913. See also M. V. Fox, "Aspects of the Religion of the Book of Proverbs," *Hebrew Union College Annual* 39 (1968): 55-69; C. J. Collins, "Proverbs and the Levitical System," *Presbyterion* 35, no. 1 (2009): 9-34.

[57]H. Ringgren, "Byn," in *Theological Dictionary of the Old Testament*, ed. G. J. Botterweck and H. Ringgren, 15 vols. (Grand Rapids: Eerdmans, 1977), 2:99-107. See the survey of research on wisdom in R. J. Sternberg, G. B. Forsythe, J. Hedlund, J. A. Horvath, R. K. Wagner, W. M. Williams, S. A. Snook and E. L. Grigorenko, *Practical Intelligence in Everyday Life* (New York: Cambridge University Press, 2000), pp. 59-64.

[58]Ex 28:3; 31:6.

[59]Eccles 4:13; Jer 50:35.

[60]1 Kings 5:7.

[61]Is 10:13.

[62]1 Kings 3:28; 4:29-34; Prov 20:26; Is 11:1-6.

[63]2 Sam 14:20; Job 39:17.

[64]1 Kings 10:2-4; Waltke, *An Old Testament Theology*.

[65]H. W. Holloman, "Prudence," in *Kregel Dictionary of the Bible and Theology* (Grand Rapids: Kregel Academic & Professional, 2005), p. 433.

[66]V. H. Kooy, "Discretion and Prudence," in *The Interpreter's Dictionary of the Bible*, ed. G. A. Buttrick, 4 vols. (Nashville: Abingdon, 1962), 1:847.

[67]Ps 14:1; 74:18, 22; Prov 10:8, 14, 23; 14:1; 15:20; 19:23; 30:32; Jer 4:22; 5:4.

[68]See the following examples of fools who lack sense: Prov 1:7, 22; 6:32; 7:7; 10:23; 11:12; 12:11; 15:5, 21; 17:16, 18; 18:2; 24:30; Eccles 2:14; 10:3, 15.

[69]M. L. Pava, "The Many Paths to Covenantal Leadership: Traditional Resources for Contemporary Business," *Journal of Business Ethics* 29, nos. 1, 2 (2001): 85-93.

[70]God's love is presented in a variety of ways in the Bible. In the Old Testament the affection side of God's love is described as God's compassion (Deut 13:7; 30:3; 32:36; Ps 25:6; 40:11; 51:1) or his willingness to show favor (Gen 43:29; Ex 33:19; Num 6:25; 2 Sam 12:22; Ps 4:1). In the New Testament God's love is called *agape*, or unconditional, selfless giving (Jn 5:42; 14:21, 23; 15:10, 13; Rom 8:39; 1 Tim 1:14; 1 Jn 2:5; 3:1; 4:8). God's love also is referred to by New Testament writers who mention God's grace (Jn 1:14-17; Acts 4:33; 14:3; 15:11; Rom 3:24; 4:16; 6:14; 16:20; 1 Cor 15:10) and God's mercy (Jn 6:36; Lk 18:13; Heb 8:12; Jas 5:11).

[71]Kuyper, "Grace and Truth," pp. 3-19; G. R. Clark, "The Word *Hesed* in the Hebrew Bible," JSOT Supplement Series 157 (Sheffield: Sheffield Academic Press, 1993); R. Routledge, "*Hesed* as Obligation: A Re-examination," *Tyndale Bulletin* 46, no. 1 (1995): 179-96; L. E. Toombs, "Love and Justice in Deuteronomy," *Interpretation* 19, no. 4 (1965): 399-411; J. C. McCann Jr., "The Hermeneutics of Grace: Discerning the Bible's Single Plot," *Interpretation* 57, no. 1 (2003): 5-15.

[72]Ps 33:5; 119:64.

[73]Prov 3:3; 19:22; Hos 12:6; Mic 6:8; Zech 7:9.

[74]D. J. Elazar, "Covenant and Community," *Judaism* 49, no. 4 (2000): 387-98.

[75]Ex 6:6; Lev 25:48-49; 2 Sam 4:9; Ruth 3:13; Job 6:23; Ps 25:22; 31:5; 69:18; 72:14; 111:9; 119:154; 130:3; Lam 3:58; Lk 1:68; Rom 3:24; Gal 4:5; Tit 2:14.

[76]Rom 8:19-22.

[77]This metaphor was suggested, but no graphic illustration was provided, by Elazar, "Covenant and Community," pp. 387-98.

PART II CONTEMPORARY APPROACHES

[1]H. B. Arthur, "Making Business Ethics Useful: Summary," *Strategic Management Journal* 5, no. 4 (1984): 319-33.

[2]Such an approach can be called an eclectic approach.

[3]E. Goldberg, *The New Executive Brain: Frontal Lobes in a Complex World* (Oxford: Oxford University Press, 2009), pp. 173-82; M. Oscar-Berman and K. Marinković, "Alcohol: Effects on Neurobehvioral Functions and the Brain," *Neuropsychology Review* 17 (2007): 239-57.

[4]L. Kohlberg, *The Psychology of Moral Development: The Nature and Validity of Moral Stages*, 2 vols. (New York: Harper & Row, 1984).

5 EGOISM

[1]See also Prov 22:16; 27:12; 28:27.

[2]These are hypothetical street names based on the scenario presented in O. C. Ferrell and J. Fraedrich, *Ethical Decision Making and Cases* (Boston: Houghton Mifflin, 1991), p. 41.

[3]www.fhwa.dot.gov/bridge/deficient.cfm (accessed May 31, 2013).

[4]www.dnr.mo.gov/geology/geosrv/geores/historymoeqs.htm (accessed May 31, 2013).

[5]hsv.com/genlintr/newmadrd/ (accessed May 31, 2013).

⁶Fictitious name.

⁷This is a hypothetical case for illustration purposes only.

⁸Other possible definitions exist. The ones explored here are commonly discussed and seem to be at the heart of the debate over self-interest.

⁹J. C. Worthy, "Religion and Its Role in the World of Business," *Religious Education* 53, no. 4 (1958): 331-39; R. R. Richards, *God and Business: Christianity's Case for Capitalism* (Maitland, FL: Xulon, 2002), pp. 263-66; D. E. Frey, "The Good Samaritan as Bad Economist: Self-Interest in Economics and Theology," *Cross Currents* 46, no. 3 (1996): 293-302.

¹⁰Because all persons have interests, it is redundant to say "self-interest"—all interests belong to the self. Even so, this is the term that has become popular. See R. W. Faulhaber, "The Rise and Fall of 'Self-Interest,' " *Review of Social Economy* 63, no. 3 (2005): 405-22.

¹¹Altruism is any act that seeks to advance the good of others for their sake and not for the sake of advancing the narrow self-interest of the actor. Thus, altruism is often defined as the opposite of egoism (using the narrow view of the term). Altruism as a normative theory of behavior states that humans sometimes should act in the interest of others and not in their selfish self-interest. B. Russell, "Egoism," in *Cambridge Dictionary of Philosophy*, ed. R. Audi, 2nd ed. (Cambridge: Cambridge University Press, 1999), p. 255.

¹²The tension between what we want to do and what we should do is an important source of internal conflict. For a discussion on this through the lens of emotion and cognition, see M. H. Bazerman and D. A. Moore, *Judgment in Managerial Decision Making*, 8th ed. (Hoboken, NJ: John Wiley & Sons, 2013), pp. 103-18.

¹³Corresponding to the two views presented here, for clarity some people prefer to use different terms. Some use the term "self-interest" referring to the broad view and the term "selfishness" when speaking of the narrow view. See P. T. Heyne, "Moral Misunderstanding and the Justification of Markets," *The Region* 12, no. 4 (1998): 31-32; I. Maitland, "The Human Face of Self-Interest," *Journal of Business Ethics* 38 (2002): 3-17; B. Griffiths, *The Creation of Wealth: A Christian's Case for Capitalism* (Downers Grove, IL: InterVarsity Press, 1984), pp. 64-70; H. S. James Jr. and F. Rassekh, "Smith, Friedman and Self-Interest in Ethical Society," *Business Ethics Quarterly* 10, no. 3 (2000): 659-74.

¹⁴J. Rachels, *The Elements of Moral Philosophy* (New York: McGraw-Hill, 2002), p. 77; T. Tännsjö, *Understanding Ethics: An Introduction to Moral Theory* (Edinburgh: Edinburgh University Press, 2002), pp. 17-41; Russell, "Egoism," p. 255; H. J. Gensler, *Ethics: A Contemporary Introduction* (New York: Routledge, 2004), pp. 143-45; F. Snare, *The Nature of Moral Thinking* (New York: Routledge, 1992), p. 44.

¹⁵Tännsjö, *Understanding Ethics*, pp. 17-41.

¹⁶S. M. Honer, T. C. Hunt and D. L. Okholm, *Invitation to Philosophy: Issues and Options*, 8th ed. (Belmont, CA: Wadsworth, 1999), p. 160.

¹⁷Ferrell and Fraedrich, *Ethical Decision Making and Cases*, p. 42.

¹⁸Some may be careless criticizers of the term "self-interest" by equating it with "self-absorption and disregard for the rights and interests of others, money-making, avarice and greed, materialism, hedonism and the profit motive." See Maitland, "Human Face of Self-Interest," pp. 3-4.

¹⁹W. H. Shaw and V. Barry, *Moral Issues in Business*, 10th ed. (Belmont, CA: Thomson Wadsworth, 2007), p. 53.

²⁰Ibid., p. 54.

²¹Maitland, "Human Face of Self-Interest."

²²Rachels, *Elements of Moral Philosophy*, p. 79.

²³Ibid.

²⁴Shaw and Barry, *Moral Issues in Business*, p. 55. See also Gensler, *Ethics*, pp. 143-45.

²⁵Rachels, *Elements of Moral Philosophy*, pp. 87-88; Gensler, *Ethics*, pp. 143-45; A. Rand, *The Virtue of Self-*

ishness: A New Concept of Egoism (New York: Penguin Putnam, 1964), p. 33.

[26]Rachels, *Elements of Moral Philosophy*, pp. 85-86.

[27]Ibid., p. 89.

[28]Faulhaber, "Rise and Fall of 'Self-Interest,' " pp. 405-22.

[29]Positive illusions are described in Bazerman and Moore, *Judgment in Managerial Decision Making*, pp. 14-30.

[30]R. T. DeGeorge, *Business Ethics*, 6th ed. (Upper Saddle River, NJ: Pearson Prentice Hall, 2006), p. 606.

[31]Non-Christians also recognize this. See P. F. Hodapp, *Ethics in the Business World* (Malabar, FL: Krieger Publishing Company, 1994), pp. 7-10.

[32]Deut 12:8; Prov 21:2.

[33]1 Kings 11; 2 Kings 21; Mt 2; Jn 11:47-53.

[34]Gen 40:12-15; 45–46; 2 Kings 5; Dan 1; Mt 9:20-22; Mk 2:1-5, 25-28.

[35]D. P. Hollinger, *Choosing the Good: Christian Ethics in a Complex World* (Grand Rapids: Baker Academic, 2002), p. 31.

[36]Gen 3:1-6.

[37]Mt 4:3-9.

[38]Is 56:11.

[39]Gen 2:18.

[40]Gen 1:26-28; 2:15.

[41]Ex 18:18; Num 11:14; Deut 1:9-12; Prov 27:16; Eccles 4:9-12; 1 Cor 3:6.

[42]D. Hicks, "Self-Interest, Deprivation and Agency: Expanding the Capabilities Approach," *Journal of the Society of Christian Ethics* 25, no. 1 (2005): 147-67; D. Straton, "Love, and the Self, in the Teachings of Jesus," *Journal of Religious Thought* 21, no. 2 (1964/1965): 95-107.

[43]Other Scripture passages implicitly appeal to self-interests: see Mt 6:33; 1 Cor 5:10.

[44]D. J. Elazar, "Covenant and Community," *Judaism* 49, no. 4 (2000): 387-98.

[45]J. Boersema, *Political-Economic Activity to the Honor of God: The Foundation* (Winnipeg, MB: Premier Publishing, 1999), pp. 162-65.

[46]See also 1 Cor 10:24; Gal 6:2-5.

[47]1 Thess 2:9.

[48]Ex 20:5; 34:14; 2 Kings 19:34; Is 43:25; 48:9-11.

[49]Deut 32:4; Ps 33:5; 89:14; 145:16-17; Mt 18:14.

[50]See also Mt 5:7.

[51]A. Hill, *Just Business: Christian Ethics for the Marketplace* (Downers Grove, IL: IVP Academic, 2008), pp. 61-62.

[52]Developed after considering D. Fozard Weaver, *Self-Love and Christian Ethics* (New York: Cambridge University Press, 2002); Hicks, "Self-Interest, Deprivation and Agency." The topics of self-love and self-interest also have been taken up by other authors. For a deeper consideration of the issues see Straton, "Love, and the Self, in the Teachings of Jesus"; J. Lippitt, "True Self-Love and True Self-Sacrifice," *International Journal of the Philosophy of Religion* 66 (2009): 125-38; J. E. Leightner, "Utility Versus Self-Sacrificing Love," *Christian Scholar's Review* 32, no. 3 (2003): 317-28; J. E. Leightner, "Response: 'Not My Will . . .' Further Thoughts on Utility Versus Self-Sacrificing Love," *Christian Scholar's Review* 34, no. 1 (2004): 17-20; J. T. Rose, "Reflection: Utility Versus Self-Sacrificing Love," *Christian Scholar's Review* 34, no. 1 (2004): 11-15.

[53]Gen 1:26-28; Ps 8.

[54]See also Rom 15:1-3; Phil 2:3-4; Jas 2:8.

[55]Deut 4:40. See also appendix H.

[56]Prov 22:2; Gal 3:28; Col 3:11; Jas 2:1-4.

[57]See also Rom 15:1-2; 1 Cor 12:25; Gal 5:13.

[58]Rom 12:2.

[59]Ps 51:10; Rom 13:14; 1 Cor 10:33; 2 Cor 5:17; Eph 2:2; 4:22; Col 3:10; 1 Pet 1:14; 4:2.

[60]Adapted from some of the stories told in L. Dodson, *The Moral Underground: How Ordinary Americans Subvert an Unfair Economy* (New York: The New Press, 2009).

[61]This vignette is based on S. V. Bruton, "Teaching the Golden Rule," *Journal of Business Ethics* 49 (2004): 179-87.

6 RELATIVISM

[1]K. O'Keefe, "Cambodian Garment Factories Come Under Scrutiny," *Wall Street Journal*, September 23, 2013.

[2]R. Benedict, *Patterns of Culture* (Boston: Houghton Mifflin, 2005); H. J. Gensler, *Ethics: A Contemporary Introduction* (New York: Routledge, 1998), p. 11.

[3]J. W. Cook, *Morality and Cultural Differences* (Oxford: Oxford University Press, 1999), p. 26.

[4]J. P. Moreland, "Moral Relativism," in *Readings in Christian Ethics*, vol. 1: *Theory and Method*, ed. D. K. Clark and R. V. Rakestraw (Grand Rapids: Baker Books, 1994), p. 24.

[5]Cook, *Morality and Cultural Differences*, p. 34; L. T. Hosmer, *The Ethics of Management*, 6th ed. (New York: McGraw-Hill Irwin, 2008), pp. 100-103; R. M. Kidder, *How Good People Make Tough Choices: Resolving the Dilemmas of Ethical Living* (New York: Fireside Books, 1996), pp. 92-99; T. L. Beauchamp and N. E. Bowie, eds., *Ethical Theory and Business*, 7th ed. (Upper Saddle River, NJ: Pearson Prentice Hall, 2004), pp. 8-10.

[6]For a discussion and critique of these levels see R. E. Freeman and D. R. Gilbert, *Corporate Strategy and the Search for Ethics* (Englewood Cliffs, NJ: Prentice-Hall, 1988), pp. 22-41.

[7]This is not necessarily the same as narrow self-interest egoism because the person may be taking into considerations the needs of others when deciding what is right and wrong. This type of relativism says that it is up to each person to decide what to do. A similar concept to this is that of "agent relativism." On this see N. L. Sturgeon, "Relativism," in *The Routledge Companion to Ethics*, ed. J. Skorupski (New York: Routledge, 2010), pp. 356-65.

[8]The perspective taken here is akin to that of "appraiser relativism," where persons other than the one taking an action are judging the rightness or wrongness of an action that someone else has taken. On this see Sturgeon, "Relativism," pp. 356-65.

[9]Social role relativism requires the belief that those in the profession have, in fact, found what is right and adhere to this standard. It also requires the belief that the moral priorities that persons in the particular role have established are valid.

[10]This belief has sparked a debate regarding the manager's obligation to other stakeholders. We will address this in a later chapter.

[11]An organization or an industry is one example of a social group. Employees of a particular work team may look to the team for indicators of what is right and wrong.

[12]D. Collins, *Essentials of Business Ethics: Creating an Organization of High Integrity and Superior Performance* (Hoboken, NJ: John Wiley & Sons, 2009), pp. 84-85.

[13]Notice how important it is to select a particular social setting as the one where standards of right and wrong are established. Even the relativist recognizes the need for a standard of right and wrong. For the relativist it is merely a matter of identifying the appropriate social group.

[14]B. B. Schlegelmilch and D. C. Robertson, "The Influence of Country and Industry on Ethical Perceptions of Senior Executives in the U.S. and Europe," *Journal of International Business Studies* 26, no. 4 (1995): 859-81; T. Donaldson, "Just Business Abroad," *Responsive Community* 1, no. 4 (1991): 48-55.

[15]L. T. Hosmer, *The Ethics of Management*, 6th ed. (New York: McGraw-Hill Irwin, 2008), pp. 100-101. This view emerged from the teaching about evolution and the origin of the species.

[16]R. E. Freeman and D. R. Gilbert, *Corporate Strategy and the Search for Ethics* (Englewood Cliffs, NJ: Prentice-Hall, 1988), pp. 22-41.

[17]Ibid.

[18]Ibid.

[19]Ibid.

[20]Ibid.

[21]R. T. DeGeorge, *Business Ethics*, 7th ed. (Upper Saddle River, NJ: Prentice Hall, 2010).

[22]Gen 1:26-28; Ps 8.

[23]Lev 25:23.

[24]Ex 12:48-49; 23:12; Lev 24:22; Num 9:14; 15:14-16, 26-30; Deut 16:14; 29:9-13.

[25]Deut 31:12.

[26]Lev 20:2; 22:25.

[27]Deut 26:12.

[28]Jer 5:19; Ezek 11:9.

[29]Deut 15:3; 23:20.

[30]Lev 24:16.

[31]Deut 12:8; Judg 17:6; 21:25; Prov 12:15.

[32]The story in 1 Chron 13 is interesting in terms of doing what was right in the eyes of all the people.

[33]Is 1:7.

[34]Ex 22:21; 23:9; Lev 19:33-34; Deut 1:16; 27:19; Ps 146:9; Is 14:1; Zech 7:10; Gal 6:10; 1 Tim 5:10; 6:17-18; Heb 13:2; 3 Jn 1:5.

[35]Deut 24:17; Josh 20:9.

[36]Ex 34:16; Deut 7:2-3; Ps 106:35; Prov 11:15; Ezra 9:12; Amos 3:3; 1 Cor 15:33; 2 Cor 6:14.

[37]Prov 27:2; elders should have a good reputation with others—1 Thess 4:12; Col 4:5; 1 Tim 3:7.

[38]Prov 12:15.

[39]Prov 14:12.

[40]Mt 7:1-2; 1 Kings 3:9; Prov 2:1-9; Rom 2:1; 14:13; Jas 4:11.

[41]Deut 10:18-19; 23:7.

[42]Lev 19:10; Deut 24:19-21.

[43]Ex 34:14-16.

[44]Deut 4:5-6, 14; 5:32; 6:14-19.

[45]Judg 2:12; Jer 13:10; 25:6; 1 Chron 5:25.

[46]Deut 7:3.

[47]Josh 11:17.

[48]Based on the description of a dirty trick in G. Kennedy, *Essential Negotiation* (New York: Bloomberg Press, 2004), pp. 69-71.

[49]S. Z. Al-Mahmood and S. Banjo, "Deadly Collapse—Bangladesh Garment Factory Crumbles, Killing at Least 159," *Wall Street Journal*, April 25, 2013, A1; "Death Toll in Bangladesh Garment Factory Collapse Crosses 700," RTTNews, May 7, 2013; M. McDonald, "Survivors Rescued from Collapsed Bangladesh Garment Factory," *Manufacturer's Monthly,* April 2013; S. Z. Al-Mahmood, "Bangladesh to Raise Pay for Garment Workers," *Wall Street Journal Online*, May 13, 2013; S. Z. Al-Mahmood, K. Chu and S. Banjo, "Bangladesh Shuts Three Factories of Top Exporter; Government Closes Facilities of Largest Garment Manufacturer in Industry Cleanup; Death Toll in Collapse Passes 1,000," *Wall Street Journal Online,* May 9, 2013.

7 COMMON SENSE

[1]Common sense has been considered by more than one writer. See as examples M. J. Adler, *The Time of Our Lives: The Ethics of Common Sense* (New York: Holt, Rinehart and Winston, 1970); R. M. Veatch, "Is There a Common Morality?," *Kennedy Institute of Ethics Journal* 13, no. 3 (2003): 189-92; R. W. McGee, *Business Ethics and Common Sense* (Westport, CT: Quorum Books, 1992); E. P. Kinsey, "Where Has All the Common Sense Gone?," *Mid-American Journal of Business* 19, no. 2 (2004): 7-11; L. Klein, "Applied Social Science: Is It Just Common Sense?," *Human Relations* 59, no. 8 (2006): 1155-72; C. R. Morgan and P. Thiagarajan, "The Relationship Between Ethics, Common Sense and Rationality," *Management Decision* 47, no. 3 (2009): 481-90; T. Reid, *Practical Ethics*, ed. K. Haakonssen (Princeton, NJ: Princeton University Press, 1990); T. Reid, *Essays on the Intellectual Powers of Man* (1785; Cambridge: Cambridge University Press, 1969); S. A. Rosenfeld, *Common Sense: A Political History* (Cambridge, MA: Harvard University Press, 2011); C. Geertz, "Common Sense as a Cultural System," *Antioch Review* 33, no. 1 (1975): 5-26.

[2]S. Zhao, "The Nature and Value of Common Sense to Decision Making," *Management Decision* 47, no. 3 (2009): 441-53.

[3]L. L. Nash, *Good Intentions Aside: A Manager's Guide to Resolving Ethical Problems* (Boston: Harvard Business School Press, 1990), p. 28.

[4]Ibid., pp. 28-29.

[5]Prov 14:12; 1 Cor 3:18; Gal 6:3; 1 Jn 1:6-8; Jas 1:26.

[6]M. H. Bazerman, *Judgment in Managerial Decision Making*, 6th ed. (Hoboken, NJ: John Wiley & Sons, 2006), p. 131. See also E. Bonabeau, "Don't Trust Your Gut," *Harvard Business Review* 81, no. 5 (2003): 116-22, 131.

[7]J. Haidt, *The Righteous Mind: Why Good People Are Divided by Politics and Religion* (New York: Pantheon Books, 2012); J. D. Greene, R. B. Sommerville, L. E. Nystrom, J. M. Darley and J. D. Cohen, "An fMRI Study of Emotional Engagement in Moral Judgment," *Science* 293 (2001): 2105-8; G. Ugazio, C. Lamm and T. Singer, "The Role of Emotions and Moral Judgments Depends on the Type of Emotion and Moral Scenario," *Emotion* 12, no. 3 (2012): 579-90.

[8]Most who hold this view believe that ethics is the result of the process of evolution.

[9]H. J. Gensler, *Ethics: A Contemporary Introduction* (New York: Routledge, 2004), pp. 47-57.

[10]E. Dane and M. G. Pratt, "Exploring Intuition and Its Role in Managerial Decision Making," *Academy of Management Review* 32, no. 1 (2007): 33-54; C. C. Miller and R. D. Ireland, "Intuition in Strategic Decision Making: Friend or Foe in the Fast-Paced Twenty-First Century?," *Academy of Management Executive* 19, no. 1 (2005): 19-30; L. A. Burke and M. K. Miller, "Taking the Mystery out of Intuitive Decision Making," *Academy of Management Executive* 13, no. 4 (1999): 91-99; E. Sadler-Smith and E. Shefy, "The Intuitive Executive: Understanding and Applying 'Gut Feel' in Decision Making," *Academy of Management Executive* 18, no. 4 (2004): 76-91; D. G. Myers, "The Powers and Perils of Intuition," *Psychology Today* 35, no. 6 (2002): 42-52; Bazerman, *Judgment in Managerial Decision Making*; S. Sachdeva, P. Singh and D. Medin, "Culture and the Quest for Universal Principles in Moral Reasoning," *International Journal of Psychology* 46, no. 3 (2011): 161-76.

[11]B. Faber, "Intuitive Ethics: Understanding and Critiquing the Role of Intuition in Ethical Decisions," *Technical Communication Quarterly* 8, no. 2 (1999): 193.

[12]L. T. Hosmer, *The Ethics of Management*, 6th ed. (New York: McGraw-Hill Irwin, 2008), pp. ix, 5.

[13]J. Z. Nitecki, "In Search of Common Sense in Common Sense Management," *Journal of Business Ethics* 6, no. 8 (1987): 639-47.

[14]Ibid., p. 643.

[15]K. Albrecht, *Practical Intelligence: The Art and Science of Common Sense* (San Francisco: Jossey-Bass, 2009); R. J. Sternberg, G. B. Forsyth, J. Hedlund, J. A. Horvath, B. K. Wagner, W. M. Williams, S. A. Snook

and E. Grigorenko, *Practical Intelligence in Everyday Life* (New York: Cambridge University Press, 2000); F. O'Connell, *The Competitive Advantage of Common Sense: Using the Power You Already Have* (Upper Saddle River, NJ: Prentice Hall, 2003).

[16]Zhao, "Nature and Value of Common Sense to Decision Making."

[17]D. Robin, "Toward an Applied Meaning for Ethics in Business," *Journal of Business Ethics* 89 (2009): 139-50.

[18]C. McMahon, "Morality and the Invisible Hand," *Philosophy & Public Affairs* 10, no. 3 (1981): 247-77.

[19]B. Gert, *Common Morality: Deciding What to Do* (New York: Oxford University Press, 2004), p. 4.

[20]B. Gert, "Common Morality and Computing," *Ethics and Information Technology* 1, no. 1 (1999): 58.

[21]J. Rachels, *The Elements of Moral Philosophy*, 4th ed. (New York: McGraw Hill, 2002), p. 77.

[22]Ibid.

[23]Gert, *Common Morality*, p. 5.

[24]T. L. Beauchamp, "A Defense of the Common Morality," *Kennedy Institute of Ethics Journal* 13, no. 3 (2003): 260-61.

[25]Including the United Nations Global Compact (1999), the CAUX Round Table Principles for Business (1994) and the Interfaith Declaration report (1993) produced by a group of religious organizations.

[26]M. S. Schwartz, "Universal Moral Values for Corporate Codes of Ethics," *Journal of Business Ethics* 59 (2005): 27-44. See also T. Donaldson and T. W. Dunfee, *Ties That Bind: A Social Contracts Approach to Business Ethics* (Boston: Harvard Business School Press, 1999); J. C. O'Brien, "The Urgent Need for a Consensus on Moral Values," *International Journal of Social Economics* 19, nos. 3-5 (1992): 171-86; J. Dalla Costa, *The Ethical Imperative: Why Moral Leadership Is Good Business* (Toronto: HarperCollins, 1998); CAUX Round Table, *CAUX Round Table Principles for Business* (The Hague, 1994); T. L. Beauchamp and N. E. Bowie, eds., *Ethical Theory and Business*, 7th ed. (Upper Saddle River, NJ: Pearson/Prentice Hall, 2004). See also Sachdeva, Singh and Medin, "Culture and the Quest for Universal Principles in Moral Reasoning."

[27]Schwartz, "Universal Moral Values for Corporate Codes of Ethics," p. 39.

[28]D. Quinn and T. Jones, "An Agent Morality View of Business Policy," *Academy of Management Review* 20, no. 1 (1995): 22-42.

[29]Hosmer, *Ethics of Management*, p. 33.

[30]R. M. Hare, "One Philosopher's Approach to Business Ethics," in *Business Ethics: Perspectives on the Practice of Theory*, ed. C. Cowton and R. Crisp (New York: Oxford University Press, 1998), p. 49. See also J. A. Barach and J. B. Elstrott, "The Transactional Ethic: The Ethical Foundations of Free Enterprise Reconsidered," *Journal of Business Ethics* 7, no. 7 (1988): 545-51; P. Ulrich and J. Feams, *Integrative Economic Ethics: Foundations of a Civilized Market Economy* (Cambridge: Cambridge University Press, 2010); Donaldson and Dunfee, *Ties That Bind*; O'Brien, "The Urgent Need for a Consensus on Moral Values."

[31]Donaldson and Dunfee, *Ties That Bind*, pp. 27, 44.

[32]Zhao, "Nature and Value of Common Sense to Decision Making"; Morgan and Thiagarajan, "Relationship Between Ethics, Common Sense and Rationality," p. 487; B. Hoose, "Intuition and Moral Theology," *Theological Studies* 67, no. 3 (2006): 602-24.

[33]E. A. Locke, "Business Ethics: A Way Out of the Morass," *Academy of Management Learning & Education* 5, no. 3 (2006): 326.

[34]B. Hooker, "Sidgwick and Common-Sense Morality," *Utilitas* 12, no. 3 (2000): 347-60.

[35]Gensler, *Ethics*, p. 56.

[36]Deut 4:6; Ps 19:7; 111:10; 119:34, 98; Prov 3:3; 7:3; 9:10; Eccles 10:2; Jer 31:33; Jas 1:25.

[37]W. L. Hathaway, "Common Sense Professional Ethics: A Christian Appraisal," *Journal of Psychology and Theology* 29, no. 3 (2001): 224-33.

[38]Prov 12:15.

[39]Prov 12:26.

[40]Ps 1:1-6; Prov 14:7; 22:3; 26:12.

[41]See also Prov 3:7; 14:12, 16.

[42]Prov 6:32; 7:7; 11:12; 12:11; 15:21; 17:16, 18; 24:30; Eccles 10:3.

[43]Based on the vignette presented at www.smallbusinessnotes.com/managing-your-business/business -ethics.html.

8 SOCIAL CONTRACT

[1]A true story based on the author's experience.

[2]T. Donaldson and T. W. Dunfee, *Ties That Bind: A Social Contracts Approach to Business Ethics* (Boston: Harvard Business School Press, 1999).

[3]The social contract is sometimes referred to as the "contractarian business ethics." See B. Wempe, "On the Use of the Social Contract Model in Business Ethics," *Business Ethics: A European Review* 13, no. 4 (2004): 332-41.

[4]Donaldson and Dunfee, *Ties That Bind*, p. 39.

[5]J. A. Thompson and D. W. Hart, "Psychological Contracts: A Nano-level Perspective on Social Contract Theory," *Journal of Business Ethics* 68 (2006): 230. Also see G. P. Latham, *Work Motivation: History, Theory, Research and Practice*, 2nd ed. (Los Angeles: Sage Publications, 2012), pp. 270-75; D. M. Rousseau, "Developing Psychological Contract Theory," in *Great Minds in Management: The Process of Theory Development*, ed. H. Smith and M. Hitt (Oxford: Oxford University Press, 2005), pp. 190-214.

[6]Rousseau, *Psychological Contracts in Organizations*, p. 9.

[7]Plato, *Republic*, ed. R. Kraut (New York: Rowman & Littlefield, 1997).

[8]T. Hobbes, *Leviathan*, ed. R. Tuck (1651; Cambridge: Cambridge University Press, 1996).

[9]J. Locke, *Two Treatises of Government*, ed. I. Shapiro (New Haven, CT: Yale University Press, 2003).

[10]J. J. Rousseau, *The Social Contract and Discourses* (1763; New York: E. P. Dutton, 1913); Harvard Law Review, "Jean Jacques Rousseau and the Doctrine of the Social Contract," *Harvard Law Review* 31, no. 1 (1917): 27-39.

[11]Rousseau, *Social Contract and Discourses*, p. 5.

[12]J. Rawls, *Political Liberalism* (Cambridge, MA: Harvard University Press, 1995); J. Rawls, *A Theory of Justice* (Cambridge, MA: Harvard University Press, 1971); J. Habermas, *Between Facts and Norms: Contributions to a Discourse Theory of Law and Democracy*, trans. William Rehg (Cambridge, MA: MIT Press, 1996).

[13]Wempe, "On the Use of the Social Contract Model in Business Ethics."

[14]J. Hasnas, "The Normative Theories of Business Ethics: A Guide for the Perplexed," *Business Ethics Quarterly* 8, no. 1 (1998): 19-42; T. W. Dunfee, "Business Ethics and Extant Social Contracts," *Business Ethics Quarterly* 1, no. 1 (1991): 23-51; T. Donaldson and T. W. Dunfee, "Toward a Unified Conception of Business Ethics: Integrative Social Contracts Theory," *Academy of Management Review* 19, no. 2 (1994): 252-84; Donaldson and Dunfee, *Ties That Bind*; T. Donaldson, *Corporations and Morality* (Englewood Cliffs, NJ: Prentice-Hall, 1982); E. Palmer, "Multinational Corporations and the Social Contract," *Journal of Business Ethics* 31 (2001): 245-58; R. E. Karnes, "A Change in Business Ethics: The Impact of Employer-Employee Relations," *Journal of Business Ethics* 88 (2009): 189-97; M. Keeley, *A Social-Contract Theory of Organizations* (Notre Dame, IN: University of Notre Dame Press, 1988).

[15]Dunfee, "Business Ethics and Extant Social Contracts," p. 24.

[16]E. J. Conry, "A Critique of Social Contracts for Business," *Business Ethics Quarterly* 5, no. 2 (1995): 187-212; Hasnas, "Normative Theories of Business Ethics."

[17]Hasnas, "Normative Theories of Business Ethics."

[18]C. M. Horvath, "The Social Equation: Freedom and Its Limits," *Business Ethics Quarterly* 5, no. 2 (1995): 334.

[19]Thompson and Hart, "Psychological Contracts," p. 229.

[20]T. W. Dunfee and T. Donaldson, "Contractarian Business Ethics: Current Status and Next Steps," *Business Ethics Quarterly* 5, no. 2 (1995): 176.

[21]Hasnas, "Normative Theories of Business Ethics," p. 33.

[22]P. F. Hodapp, "Can There Be a Social Contract with Business?," *Journal of Business Ethics* 9 (1990): 127-31.

[23]Hasnas, "Normative Theories of Business Ethics."

[24]Hodapp, "Can There Be a Social Contract with Business?"

[25]K. J. Clark, "Why Be Moral? Social Contract Theory Versus Kantian-Christian Morality," *Journal of Markets and Morality* 6, no. 1 (2003): 81-98.

[26]Ps 119:45; Jas 1:25.

[27]Clark, "Why Be Moral?," p. 95.

[28]www.theblackbookofoutsourcing.com.

9 UTILITARIANISM

[1]Based on the description in G. Kennedy, *Essential Negotiation* (New York: Bloomberg Press, 2004), pp. 69-71.

[2]C. Bird, *An Introduction to Political Philosophy* (New York: Cambridge University Press, 2006).

[3]E. A. Opitz, *Religion and Capitalism: Allies, Not Enemies* (New Rochelle, NY: Arlington House, 1970), pp. 128-24.

[4]In this there may be some parallels between *eudaimonia* and the Hebrew idea of *shalom*.

[5]N. L. Geisler, *Christian Ethics* (Grand Rapids: Baker, 1989), p. 31.

[6]A. Ryan, *Utilitarianism and Other Essays: J. S. Mill and Jeremy Bentham* (New York: Penguin Books, 1987), pp. 293-94.

[7]Ibid., pp. 288-89.

[8]Ibid., pp. 337-38.

[9]C. R. McConnell and S. L. Brue, *Microeconomics: Principles, Problems and Policies*, 15th ed. (New York: McGraw-Hill Irwin, 2002), p. 22.

[10]In economics this is also known as the Pareto Optimality.

[11]R. T. DeGeorge, *Business Ethics*, 7th ed. (Upper Saddle River, NJ: Prentice Hall, 2010), p. 44.

[12]These and other assumptions are reviewed in Bird, *Introduction to Political Philosophy*, pp. 47-66.

[13]Bird, *An Introduction to Political Philosophy*, p. 48.

[14]T. Tännsjö, *Understanding Ethics: An Introduction to Moral Theory* (Edinburgh: Edinburgh University Press, 2002), p. 34.

[15]Ibid., p. 26; DeGeorge, *Business Ethics*, p. 56.

[16]DeGeorge, *Business Ethics*, p. 59.

[17]A. Sen, *The Idea of Justice* (Cambridge, MA: Belknap Press, 2009), p. 218.

[18]L. T. Hosmer, *The Ethics of Management*, 6th ed. (New York: McGraw-Hill Irwin, 2008), pp. 106-7; R. M. Kidder, *How Good People Make Tough Choices: Resolving the Dilemmas of Ethical Living* (New York: Fireside Books, 1996), pp. 156-57; DeGeorge, *Business Ethics*, pp. 50-53.

[19]Geisler, *Christian Ethics*, p. 75. See also Prov 14:12.

[20]Geisler, *Christian Ethics*, p. 75.

[21]R. M. Green, *Religion and Moral Reason* (New York: Oxford University Press, 1988), p. 7.

[22]J. Rawls, *A Theory of Justice* (Cambridge, MA: Harvard University Press, 1971).

[23]Bird, "Utilitarianism," p. 48.

[24]Ibid., p. 61.

[25]E. A. Cochran, "Utilitarianism," in *Dictionary of Scripture and Ethics*, ed. J. B. Green (Grand Rapids: Baker Academic, 2011), p. 801.

[26]Mt 25:31-46.

[27]Mt 9:10-13; Mk 2:13-17; Lk 5:27-32; 19:1-10; Jn 4:7-39.

[28]Mt 19:13-15.

[29]Mt 18:10-14; Lk 15:3-7.

[30]M. E. Cafferky, "Toward a Biblical Theology of Efficiency," *Journal of Biblical Integration in Business* 16, no. 1 (2013): 41-60.

[31]Deut 8:18; 1 Sam 2:7; 1 Chron 29:12; Prov 22:2.

[32]Ps 128:1-2; 1 Thess 2:9; 4:11-12; 2 Thess 3:11-12; Tit 3:14; Rom 12:11; Eph 4:28; Heb 6:10-12.

[33]Prov 6:6-11; 10:4-5, 16, 26; 12:9, 24, 27; 13:4, 11; 14:23; 15:19; 18:9; 19:15, 24; 20:4, 13; 21:5, 25; 22:29; 23:4; 24:30-34; 26:14-16; 27:23; 28:19; 31:13-17, 26-27; Eccles 5:15; 9:10; 10:18; 11:4-6; Mt 20:6-7; Rom 12:11; 2 Thess 3:10-12; 1 Tim 5:8-13.

[34]2 Tim 4:11; Phil 1:11; Heb 6:7.

[35]Lev 25:3-4.

[36]Gen 30–31; Prov 27:23-24.

[37]Gen 26:12; Mt 13:8, 23; Mk 4:8, 20.

[38]Deut 29:23; 2 Kings 2:19; Prov 26:7; Ezek 15:3-5; Lk 14:35; Heb 6:8.

[39]Prov 1:17; 24:27; Eccles 10:9-10.

[40]Mt 3:10; 7:18-19; Lk 3:9; 13:7; 14:35; Jn 15:1-2; Heb 6:8; Jude 12.

[41]Eccles 3:2.

[42]Eph 5:16; Col 4:5.

[43]Ex 20:15; Lev 19:11; Deut 5:19; 1 Kings 21; Mt 19:18; Mk 10:19; Lk 18:20; Rom 13:9; Eph 4:28.

[44]J. Cottingham, "Partiality and Impartiality," in *The Routledge Companion to Ethics*, ed. J. Skorupski (New York: Routledge, 2010), pp. 617-27.

[45]J. E. Leightner, "Utility Versus Self-Sacrificing Love," *Christian Scholar's Review* 32, no. 3 (2003): 320.

[46]Leightner, "Utility Versus Self-Sacrificing Love," p. 323. See also J. E. Leightner, "Response: 'Not My Will . . .' Further Thoughts on Utility Versus Self-Sacrificing Love," *Christian Scholar's Review* 34, no. 1 (2004): 17-20.

[47]J. T. Rose, "Reflection: Utility Versus Self-Sacrificing Love," *Christian Scholar's Review* 34, no. 1 (2004): 11.

[48]Ibid., p. 14.

[49]This vignette is based on a conversation the author had with people in a company where this event happened.

10 UNIVERSALISM

[1]J. E. Hare, "Immanuel Kant (1724–1804)," in *Key Thinkers in Christianity*, ed. A. Hastings, A. Mason and H. Pyper (New York: Oxford University Press, 2003), pp. 92-97. See also S. Palmquist, "'The Kingdom of God Is at Hand!' (Did *Kant* Really Say *That*?)," *History of Philosophy Quarterly* 11, no. 4 (1994): 421-37; L. Dupré, *The Enlightenment and the Intellectual Foundations of Modern Culture* (New Haven, CT: Yale University Press, 2004), p. 187.

[2]R. P. Wolff, *The Autonomy of Reason: A Commentary on Kant's Groundwork of the Metaphysics of Morals* (Gloucester, MA: Peter Smith, 1972), p. 55.

[3]Ibid., p. 117.

[4]T. E. Hill Jr. and A. Zweig, *Immanuel Kant: Groundwork for the Metaphysics of Morals* (New York: Oxford University Press, 2002), p. 20.

[5]F. Snare, *The Nature of Moral Thinking* (New York: Routledge, 1992), p. 39.

[6]Wolff, *The Autonomy of Reason*, p. 159.

[7]Hill and Zweig, *Immanuel Kant*, p. 237. See also C. M. Korsgaard, "Kant's Formula of Universal Law," *Pacific Philosophical Quarterly* 66, no. ½ (1985): 24-47.

[8]Hill and Zweig, *Immanuel Kant*, p. 222.

[9]Scholars have different opinions regarding which type of contradiction Kant had in mind.

[10]Dupré, *Enlightenment and the Intellectual Foundations of Modern Culture*, p. 134.

[11]To live in a logical contradiction like this is to attempt to live in a world of absolute moral standards and at the same time live in a world of relativism. We imagine that Immanuel Kant would say that this is to attempt the logically impossible because both absolutism and relativism are mutually exclusive.

[12]Some might argue that in such an instance the person who steals is aware of the rule and agrees with the rule but is willing, on a particular occasion, to take the risk of getting caught and the resulting penalty in order to achieve another short-term goal. In such an instance, no contradiction occurs. Rather, it is merely a matter of engaging in a calculated risk-reward. Such an argument, we say in response, unintentionally removes the moral issue from the situation.

[13]Hill and Zweig, *Immanuel Kant*, p. 230.

[14]Mt 7:12.

[15]Hill and Zweig, *Immanuel Kant*, p. 231.

[16]Wolff, *The Autonomy of Reason*, p. 175; H. J. Gensler, *Ethics: A Contemporary Introduction* (New York: Routledge, 2004), p. 104.

[17]Wolff, *The Autonomy of Reason*, p. 176.

[18]Ibid., p. 182.

[19]W. C. Reuschling, *Reviving Evangelical Ethics: The Promises and Pitfalls of Classic Models of Morality* (Grand Rapids: Brazos, 2008), p. 40.

[20]L. T. Hosmer, *The Ethics of Management*, 6th ed. (New York: McGraw-Hill Irwin, 2008), pp. 108-9; R. M. Kidder, *How Good People Make Tough Choices: Resolving the Dilemmas of Ethical Living* (New York: Fireside Books, 1996), pp. 157-58; E. A. Opitz, *Religion and Capitalism: Allies, Not Enemies* (New Rochelle, NY: Arlington House, 1970).

[21]Reuschling, *Reviving Evangelical Ethics*, p. 67. Some Christians would object to this criticism as an over-simplification of Kant's philosophy. For example, some might argue that Kant simply recognizes a fundamental scriptural principle that moral duties are universal. They would also argue that humans must use their power of reason to interpret the Bible and discern right from wrong.

[22]Dupré, *Enlightenment and the Intellectual Foundations of Modern Culture*, pp. 137-38.

[23]Wolff, *The Autonomy of Reason*, p. 85.

[24]Dupré, *Enlightenment and the Intellectual Foundations of Modern Culture*, p. 138.

[25]One response to this supposed weakness may be if we asked the thief whether or not he or she would want another thief to steal his or her property. In other words, apply the second and third test of the categorical imperative.

[26]Lev 19:18, 34; Mt 5:43-44; 7:12; 19:19; 22:39; Mk 12:31-33; Lk 10:27; Rom 13:8-10; Gal 5:13-14; 1 Thess 4:9; Jas 2:8.

11 AGENCY

[1]L. Kwoh, "Memo to Staff: Take More Risks; CEOs Urge Employees to Embrace Failure and Keep Trying," *Wall Street Journal*, March 20, 2013, B.8.

[2]W. Grajetzki, *Court Officials of the Egyptian Middle Kingdom* (London: Duckworth, 2009).

[3]J. J. Finklestein, "An Old Babylonian Herding Contract and Genesis 31:38f," *Journal of the American Oriental Society* 88 (1968): 30-36; M. A. Morrison, "The Jacob and Laban Narrative in Light of Near Eastern Sources," *Biblical Archeologist* 46, no. 3 (1983): 155-64; J. N. Postgate, "Some Old Babylonian Shepherds and Their Flocks," *Journal of Semitic Studies* 20 (1975): 1-20; A. Mein, "Profitable and Unprofitable Shepherds: Economic and Theological Perspectives on Ezekiel 34," *Journal for the Study of the Old Testament* 31, no. 4 (2007): 493-504.

[4]S. B. Young, "Fiduciary Duties as a Helpful Guide to Ethical Decision Making in Business," *Journal of Business Ethics* 74 (2007): 1-15.

[5]N. A. Shankman, "Reframing the Debate Between Agency and Stakeholder Theories of the Firm," *Journal of Business Ethics* 19, no. 4 (1999): 319-34; Young, "Fiduciary Duties."

[6]H. R. Cheeseman, *The Legal Environment of Business and Online Commerce: Business Ethics, E-Commerce, Regulatory and International Issues*, 5th ed. (Upper Saddle River, NJ: Pearson Prentice Hall, 2007), pp. 388-413.

[7]R. S. Pindyck and D. L. Rubinfeld, *Microeconomics*, 5th ed. (Upper Saddle River, NJ: Prentice Hall, 2001), p. 609.

[8]M. C. Jensen, *Foundations of Organizational Strategy* (Cambridge, MA: Harvard University Press, 1998), p. 45.

[9]Shankman, "Reframing the Debate."

[10]J. R. Boatright, "Fiduciary Duties and the Shareholder-Management Relation: Or, What's So Special About Shareholders?," *Business Ethics Quarterly* 4, no. 4 (1994): 393-407; Young, "Fiduciary Duties."

[11]There are exceptions such as when the corporation sells shares in an initial public offering (IPO) or some other stock sale event.

[12]Boatright, "Fiduciary Duties and the Shareholder-Management Relation," p. 399.

[13]D. Quinn and T. Jones, "An Agent Morality View of Business Policy," *Academy of Management Review* 20, no. 1 (1995): 22-42.

[14]K. E. Goodpaster, "Business Ethics and Stakeholder Analysis," *Business Ethics Quarterly* 1, no. 1 (1991): 53-73.

[15]Quinn and Jones, "An Agent Morality View of Business Policy."

[16]Boatright, "Fiduciary Duties and the Shareholder-Management Relation."

[17]Ibid., p. 404.

[18]R. E. Freeman, *Strategic Management: A Stakeholder Approach* (Boston: Pittman Ballinger, 1984); R. E. Freeman, "A Stakeholder Theory of the Modern Corporation," in *Ethical Theory and Business*, ed. T. L. Beauchamp and N. E. Bowie (Upper Saddle River, NJ: Pearson Prentice Hall, 2004), pp. 55-64.

[19]Goodpaster, "Business Ethics and Stakeholder Analysis."

[20]J. Heath, "The Uses and Abuses of Agency Theory," *Business Ethics Quarterly* 19, no. 4 (2009): 497-528.

[21]Jensen, *Foundations of Organizational Strategy*, p. 54; S. A. Ross, "The Economic Theory of Agency: The Principal's Problem," *American Economic Review* 63, no. 2 (1973): 134-39; M. C. Jensen and W. H. Meckling, "Theory of the Firm: Managerial Behavior, Agency Costs and Ownership Structure," *Journal of Financial Economics* 3, no. 4 (1976): 305-60.

[22]D. Besanko, D. Dranove, M. Shanley and S. Schaefer, *Economics of Strategy*, 5th ed. (Hoboken, NJ: John Wiley & Sons, 2010), pp. 185-91.

[23]J. H. Davis, F. D. Schoorman and L. Donaldson, "Toward a Stewardship Theory of Management," *Academy of Management Review* 22, no. 1 (1997): 20-47.

[24]K. M. Eisenhardt, "Agency Theory: Assessment and Review," *The Academy of Management Review* 14, no. 12 (1989): 57-74.

[25]Young, "Fiduciary Duties."

[26]Heath, "Uses and Abuses of Agency Theory."

[27]Shankman, "Reframing the Debate"; Quinn and Jones, "An Agent Morality View of Business Policy."

[28]Quinn and Jones, "An Agent Morality View of Business Policy"; Goodpaster, "Business Ethics and Stakeholder Analysis."

[29]Quinn and Jones, "An Agent Morality View of Business Policy."

[30]Heath, "Uses and Abuses of Agency Theory."

[31]Ps 50:10; Gen 1:26-28.

[32]Prov 27:23-27.

[33]Ex 23:4; Deut 22:1.

[34]Lk 12:42-48; 1 Cor 4:2.

[35]Ezek 34:8; Jn 10:12-13.

[36]A. D. Hill, "The Loyal Christian Agent," in *Christianity and Business: A Collection of Essays on Pedagogy and Practice*, ed. Edward J. Trunfio (n.p.: Christian Business Faculty Association, 1991), pp. 109-24.

[37]1 Pet 2:18-19; Col 3:22; Eph 6:5-9.

[38]2 Sam 12:1-15; Daniel; Acts 5:20.

[39]Heath, "Uses and Abuses of Agency Theory," p. 498.

[40]1 Sam 3:20.

[41]Mt 10:16.

12 JUSTICE AND RIGHTS

[1]D. Kahneman, J. L. Knetsch and R. H. Thaler, "Fairness as a Constraint on Profit Seeking: Entitlements and the Market," *American Economic Review* 76, no. 4 (1986): 728-41.

[2]Survey research results indicate the following: For item 1, 82 percent consider raising the price of snow shovels unfair. For item 2, 62 percent of respondents consider decreasing wages unfair. For item 3, 22 percent of respondents view a 5 percent salary increase as unfair. For item 4, 75 percent of people tend to view raising rent acceptable.

[3]J. Rawls, "Justice as Fairness," *The Philosophical Review* 67, no. 2 (1958): 164-94; J. Rawls, "Justice as Fairness: Political Not Metaphysical," *Philosophy and Public Affairs* 14, no. 3 (1985): 223-51; J. Rawls, *A Theory of Justice* (Cambridge, MA: Harvard University Press, 1971); J. R. Boatright, *Ethics and the Conduct of Business*, 4th ed. (Upper Saddle River, NJ: Prentice Hall, 2003), p. 73; W. H. Shaw and V. Barry, *Moral Issues in Business*, 10th ed. (Belmont, CA: Thomson Wadsworth, 2007), p. 105.

[4]A. Sen, *The Idea of Justice* (Cambridge, MA: Belknap Press, 2009), pp. 155-56.

[5]M. H. Bazerman and D. A. Moore, *Judgment in Managerial Decision Making*, 8th ed. (Hoboken, NJ: John Wiley & Sons, 2013), p. 142.

[6]Kahneman, Knetsch and Thaler, "Fairness as a Constraint on Profit Seeking"; Bazerman and Moore, *Judgment in Managerial Decision Making*, pp. 132-59.

[7]Kahneman, Knetsch and Thaler, "Fairness as a Constraint on Profit Seeking," p. 731.

[8]Ibid., p. 732.

[9]Bazerman and Moore, *Judgment in Managerial Decision Making*, pp. 93-94.

[10]Boatright, *Ethics and the Conduct of Business*, p. 74.

[11]The word *commutative* is derived from the Latin word which means to exchange or substitute one thing for another.

[12]D. M. Rousseau, *Psychological Contracts in Organizations: Understanding Written and Unwritten Agreements* (Thousand Oaks, CA: Sage Publications, 1995), p. 128.

[13]R. T. DeGeorge, *Business Ethics*, 6th ed. (Upper Saddle River, NJ: Prentice Hall, 2006), pp. 97-98.

[14]Rawls, *Theory of Justice*; M. Clayton, "Justice and Distribution," in *The Routledge Companion to Ethics*, ed. J. Skorupski (New York: Routledge, 2010), pp. 692-703.

[15]*Contractarian* is in reference to the concept of social contract.

[16]Rawls, *Theory of Justice*.

[17]R. Nozick, *Anarchy, State and Utopia* (New York: Basic Books, 1974).

[18]Shaw and Barry, *Moral Issues in Business*, p. 110.

[19]T. L. Beauchamp and N. E. Bowie, eds., *Ethical Theory and Business*, 7th ed. (Upper Saddle River, NJ: Pearson Prentice Hall, 2004), p. 29. The distinction between positive rights and negative rights will be explained in the next section.

[20]Discussions of rights can be found in the works of several authors. One helpful summary of the issues on which this section is based is in T. Campbell, "Rights," in *The Routledge Companion to Ethics*, ed. J. Skorupski (New York: Routledge, 2010), pp. 669-79.

[21]Beauchamp and Bowie, *Ethical Theory and Business*, p. 29.

[22]Ibid., p. 30.

[23]The Christian ideas of justice have been reviewed by J. Dengerink, "The Idea of Justice in Christian Perspective," *Westminster Theological Journal* 39, no. 1 (1976): 1-59.

[24]Jer 9:24; Zeph 3:5.

[25]See also Gen 18:25; Prov 2:6-9.

[26]C. Marshall, *The Little Book of Biblical Justice: A Fresh Approach to the Bible's Teachings on Justice* (Intercourse, PA: Good Books, 2005), p. 7.

[27]Prov 22:2; Gal 3:28; Col 3:11; Jas 2:1-4.

[28]Marshall, *Little Book of Biblical Justice*, p. 23. The Hebrew word for justice is *mishpat*.

[29]Gen 1:26-28.

[30]S. Greidanus, "Human Rights in Biblical Perspective," *Calvin Theological Journal* 19, no. 1 (1984): 5-31.

[31]Marshall, *Little Book of Biblical Justice*, pp. 25-26.

[32]1 Kings 10:9; Ps 89:14; 97:2.

[33]P. Enns, "Mispat," in *New International Dictionary of Old Testament Theology and Exegesis*, ed. W. A. VanGemeren, 5 vols. (Grand Rapids: Zondervan, 1997), vol. 2, pp. 1142-44. In Ex 21:1 the Hebrew word is translated into English as ordinances (New American Standard Bible) or judgments (King James Version).

[34]P. H. Sedgwick, *The Market Economy and Christian Ethics* (Cambridge: Cambridge University Press, 1999), p. 225.

[35]B. Johnson, "Mispat," in *Theological Dictionary of the Old Testament*, ed. G. J. Botterweck, H. Ringgren and H.-J. Fabry, 15 vols. (Grand Rapids: Eerdmans, 1998), 9:94; Enns, "Mispat," p. 1143.

[36]Marshall, *Little Book of Biblical Justice*, pp. 14-15.

[37]Ps 106:3.

[38]Ex 23:6; Deut 24:7; Prov 14:31; 17:23.

[39]Ex 20:15; Mal 3:5; Lk 10:7; 1 Tim 5:18.

[40]Marshall, *Little Book of Biblical Justice*, p. 13. See Is 32:16-18; 60:17-19; D. G. Groody, "Globalizing Justice: The Contribution of Christian Spirituality," *International Review of Mission* 98, no. 389 (2009): 259-71.

[41]P. Potter, "Peace: The Fruit of Justice," *Theology Today* 36, no. 4 (1980): 498-503.

[42]Deut 16:20.

[43]Marshall, *Little Book of Biblical Justice*, pp. 11-12. See Ps 72:1-2; Is 32:1; Amos 5:24.

[44]Johnson, "Mispat," p. 89; H. V. Bennett, "Justice, OT," in *The New Interpreters Dictionary of the Bible*, ed. K. Doob Sakenfeld, 5 vols. (Nashville: Abingdon, 2008), 3:476-77.

[45]Bennett, "Justice, OT," p. 476.

[46]Ex 23:8; Deut 1:17; 10:17; 16:19; 27:25; 1 Sam 8:3; Jer 26:11; Ezek 22:12; Amos 5:7, 12, 15; 6:12; Zech 7:9; Mic 3:1, 9.

[47]Enns, "Mispat," p. 1144. For examples, see Is 1:17, 21; 5:7; 10:2; 59:8-9; Hab 1:4.

[48]E. Berkovitz, "*Emeth*, the Concept of Truth," in *Man and God: Studies in Biblical Theology* (Detroit: Wayne State University Press, 1969), pp. 253-91.

[49]See also Deut 25:13-16.

[50]Prov 1:3-7; 2:6-9; J. Goldingay, *Old Testament Theology*, vol. 2: *Israel's Faith* (Downers Grove, IL: Inter-Varsity Press, 2006), p. 583.

[51]Is 16:5; Jer 9:24; Hos 2:19.

[52]R. N. Kanungo, "Alienation and Empowerment: Some Ethical Imperatives in Business," *Journal of Business Ethics* 11, no. 5/6 (1992): 413-22; M. Sashkin, "Participative Management Is an Ethical Imperative," *Organizational Dynamics* 12, no. 4 (1984): 5-22.

[53]Kanungo, "Alienation and Empowerment," p. 414.

13 VIRTUES AND CHARACTER

[1]Mt 12:35.

[2]This is scenario is based on the description of a hypothetical situation presented in D. Koehn, "A Role for Virtue Ethics in the Analysis of Business Practice," *Business Ethics Quarterly* 5, no. 3 (1995): 533-39.

[3]Ibid., p. 535.

[4]S. Valentine and L. Godkin, "Professional Ethical Standards, Corporate Social Responsibility and the Perceived Role of Ethics and Social Responsibility," *Journal of Business Ethics* 82, no. 3 (2009): 657-66.

[5]This is not the first time someone has identified virtue ethics with both duty and consequences. See M. C. Nussbaum, "Virtue Ethics: A Misleading Category?," *Journal of Ethics* 3, no. 3 (1999): 163-201.

[6]D. P. Hollinger, *Choosing the Good: Christian Ethics in a Complex World* (Grand Rapids: Baker Academic, 2002), p. 46.

[7]S. Hauerwas, "Virtue," in *Readings in Christian Ethics*, vol. 1: *Theory and Method*, ed. D. K. Clark and R. V. Rakestraw (Grand Rapids: Baker Books, 1994), pp. 251-56.

[8]E. M. Hartman, "Socratic Questions and Aristotelian Answers: A Virtue-Based Approach to Business Ethics," *Journal of Business Ethics* 78 (2008): 315.

[9]Ibid., p. 317.

[10]Hauerwas, "Virtue," p. 254.

[11]R. C. Solomon, "Victims of Circumstances? A Defense of Virtue Ethics," *Business Ethics Quarterly* 13, no. 1 (2003): 45.

[12]Hartman, "Socratic Questions and Aristotelian Answers," p. 322.

[13]Typical discussions about virtue ethics start by analyzing the writings of Aristotle. Such discussions either ignore or grossly gloss over the contribution of ancient Hebrew writings. We will address this later in this chapter.

[14]M. Slote, "Virtue Ethics," in *The Routledge Companion to Ethics*, ed. J. Skorupski (New York: Routledge, 2010), pp. 478-89.

[15]Ibid.

[16]Aristotle, *Nicomachean Ethics* (Indianapolis: Bobbs-Merrill, 1962).

[17]W. C. Reuschling, *Reviving Evangelical Ethics: The Promises and Pitfalls of Classic Models of Morality* (Grand Rapids: Brazos, 2008), p. 52.

[18]Ibid., pp. 55-56. See also G. F. Cavanagh and M. R. Bandsuch, "Virtue as a Benchmark for Spirituality in Business," *Journal of Business Ethics* 38 (2002): 109-17.

[19]Slote, "Virtue Ethics," p. 478; Hollinger, *Choosing the Good*, p. 45.

[20]Hollinger, *Choosing the Good*, p. 47.

[21]D. D'Souza, *The Virtue of Prosperity: Finding Values in an Age of Techno-Affluence* (New York: Simon & Schuster, 2000), p. 169.

[22]Hauerwas, "Virtue," pp. 251-56.

[23]The debate over the distinction between character and virtue is surveyed in Solomon, "Victims of Circumstances?"

[24]Hollinger, *Choosing the Good*, p. 46. Here he is quoting T. R. Anderson, *Walking the Way: Christian Ethics as a Guide* (Toronto: United Church Publishing House, 1993), p. 111.

[25]R. Bondi, "The Elements of Character," *Journal of Religious Ethics* 12, no. 2 (1984): 201-18; E. C. Gardner, "Character, Virtue and Responsibility in Theological Ethics," *Encounter* 44, no. 4 (1983): 315-39.

[26]R. T. DeGeorge, *Business Ethics*, 7th ed. (New York: Prentice Hall, 2010), p. 84.

[27]Slote, "Virtue Ethics," pp. 478-89.

[28]Hollinger, *Choosing the Good*, p. 57.

[29]Koehn, "A Role for Virtue Ethics in the Analysis of Business Practice."

[30]Solomon, "Victims of Circumstances?"

[31]Koehn, "A Role for Virtue Ethics in the Analysis of Business Practice."

[32]Ibid.

[33]Ibid.

[34]Slote, "Virtue Ethics," pp. 478-89.

[35]Hartman, "Socratic Questions and Aristotelian Answers."

[36]Hollinger, *Choosing the Good*, p. 46.

[37]Prov 4:23; Ezek 11:19-21; Jer 17:9; Mt 22:37; Mk 7:21-23; Lk 6:43-45; Rom 12:2; Gal 5:22-23; Phil 4:8; 2 Cor 3:18.

[38]Reuschling, *Reviving Evangelical Ethics*, p. 117.

[39]Ibid., pp. 115-41.

PART III CONTEMPORARY ISSUES

[1]Or those who receive services from nonprofit organizations and government agencies.

[2]Lev 19:11.

[3]M. M. Jennings, *Business Ethics: Case Studies and Selected Readings*, 4th ed. (Mason, OH: Thomson South-Western, 2003), pp. 6-8. Here Jennings cites an article by J. O. Cherrington and D. J. Cherrington, "Ethics: A Major Business Problem," *Exchange*, Fall 1989, pp. 30-33.

14 ETHICAL ISSUES IN CONSUMER BEHAVIOR

[1]S. J. Vitell and J. Muncy, "Consumer Ethics: An Empirical Investigation of Factors Influencing Ethical Judgments of the Final Consumer," *Journal of Business Ethics* 11 (1992): 585-97.

[2]H. R. Dodge, E. A. Edwards and S. Fullerton, "Consumer Transgressions in the Marketplace: Consumers' Perspectives," *Psychology & Marketing* 13, no. 8 (1996): 821-35; L. Neale and S. Fullerton, "The International Search for Ethics Norms: Which Consumer Behaviors Do Consumers Consider (Un)acceptable?," *Journal of Services Marketing* 24, no. 6 (2010): 476-86.

[3]M. J. Polansky, P. Q. Brito, J. Pinto and N. Higgs-Kleyn, "Consumer Ethics in the European Union: A Comparison of Northern and Southern Views," *Journal of Business Ethics* 31, no. 2 (2001): 117-30; A. d'Astous and A. Legendre, "Understanding Consumers' Ethical Justifications: A Scale for Appraising Consumers' Reasons for Not Behaving Ethically," *Journal of Business Ethics* 87 (2009): 255-68.

[4]For discussions of these trends from an existential perspective, including the variety of Christian social ethics points of view, see P. H. Sedgwick, *The Market Economy and Christian Ethics* (Cambridge: Cambridge University Press, 1999), pp. 82-150; T. Smith, "The Existential Consumption Paradox: An Exploration and Meaning in Marketing," *The Marketing Review* 7, no. 4 (2007): 325-41; H. Rempel, *A High Price for Abundant Living: The Story of Capitalism* (Scottdale, PA: Herald Press, 2003), pp. 69-83; K. R. Himes,

"Consumerism and Christian Ethics," *Theological Studies* 68, no. 1 (2007): 132-53; C. M. Wallace, "Readings at the Intersection of Culture and Faith: Consumerism and Christian Community," *Anglican Theological Review* 85, no. 3 (2003): 581-88; P. M. Cooey, "Christian Perspectives on Overcoming Greed in a Consumeristic Society: Buying Fear as Collusion with Greed Versus an Economy of Grace," *Buddhist-Christian Studies* 24 (2004): 39-46; M. G. Nixon, "Satisfaction for Whom? Freedom for What? Theology and the Economic Theory of the Consumer," *Journal of Business Ethics* 70 (2007): 39-60; W. T. Cavanaugh, "When Enough Is Enough," *Sojourners* 34, no. 5 (2005): 8-10, 12, 14.

⁵Early articles by scholars who began studying the economic dimension of consumerism are represented by the following: W. J. Regan and L. Germann, "The Productified Way of Life," *California Management Review* 8, no. 1 (1965): 73-82; G. S. Day and D. A. Aaker, "A Guide to Consumerism," *Journal of Marketing* 34, no. 3 (1970): 12-19; P. Kotler, "What Consumerism Means for Marketers," *Harvard Business Review* 50, no. 3 (1972): 48-57; B. A. Morin, "Some Negativisms About Consumerism," *Journal of Small Business Management* 10, no. 3 (1972): 6-10; L. L. Berry, "Consumerism, Marketing and the Small Businessman," *Journal of Small Business Management* 10, no. 3 (1972): 14-19; S. A. Greyser and S. L. Diamond, "Business Is Adapting to Consumerism," *Harvard Business Review* 52, no. 5 (1974): 38-58; N. Kangun, K. K. Cox, J. Higginbotham and J. Burton, "Consumerism and Marketing Management," *Journal of Marketing* 39, no. 2 (1975): 3-10.

⁶This paradox is also observed by Smith, "Existential Consumption Paradox."

⁷Here the idea of communication went beyond the use of communication technology (cell phones). It was the possession of the technology that became the symbolic communication of self-identity.

⁸The growth of consumerism has led to the use of the term "retail therapy," which refers to a form of self-medication through shopping experiences.

⁹P. Odou and P. de Pechpeyrou, "Consumer Cynicism: From Resistance to Anti-Consumption in a Disenchanted World?," *European Journal of Marketing* 45, no. 11/12 (2011): 1799-1808.

¹⁰This is not to deny the problem with consumer scams. Indeed, marketplace scam artists are still active and successful because of inexperienced or uneducated consumers in each new generation.

¹¹Vitell and Muncy, "Consumer Ethics."

¹²S. J. Vitell and J. Muncy, "The Muncy-Vitell Consumer Ethics Scale: A Modification and Application," *Journal of Business Ethics* 62 (2005): 267-75.

¹³These and other questionable activities are not condoned here. They are reported to encourage the reader to reflect on how consistently he or she desires to live life in the marketplace. Some of these items come from self-reports of university students. See also reports from W. C. Lesch and J. Brinkmann, "Consumer Insurance Fraud/Abuse as Co-Creation and Co-Responsibility: A New Paradigm," *Journal of Business Ethics* 103 (2011): 17-32; D. McCorkle, J. Reardon, D. Dalenberg, A. Pryor and J. Wicks, "Purchase or Pirate: A Model of Consumer Intellectual Property Theft," *Journal of Marketing Theory and Practice* 20, no. 1 (2012): 73-86; T. King and C. Dennis, "Deshopping Behavior Using the Qualitative Analysis of Theory of Planned Behavior and Accompanied (De)shopping," *Qualitative Market Research: An International Journal* 9, no. 3 (2006): 282-96; Dodge, Edwards and Fullerton, "Consumer Transgressions in the Marketplace."

¹⁴Other influencing factors that have been studied in terms of unethical consumer behaviors include age, gender, education level and personality type.

¹⁵D. R. Forsyth, "A Taxonomy of Ethical Ideologies," *Journal of Personality and Social Psychology* 39, no. 1 (1980): 175-84; D. R. Forsyth, "Individual Differences in Information Integration During Moral Judgment," *Journal of Personality and Social Psychology* 49, no. 1 (1985): 264-72. This taxonomy can be applied in other contexts of business ethics in addition to consumer ethics.

¹⁶S. Steenhaut and P. Van Kenhove, "An Empirical Investigation of the Relationships Among a Consumer's Personal Values, Ethical Ideology and Ethical Beliefs," *Journal of Business Ethics* 64 (2006): 137-55.

[17]A. Chatzidakis, S. Hibbert, D. Mittusis and A. Smith, "Virtue in Consumption?," *Journal of Marketing Management* 20 (2004): 527-44; D. Strutton, S. J. Vitell and L. E. Pelton, "How Consumers May Justify Inappropriate Behavior in Market Settings: An Application on the Techniques of Neutralization," *Journal of Business Research,* 30 (1994): 253-60; M. J. Carrington, B. A. Neville and G. J. Whitwell, "Why Ethical Consumers Don't Walk Their Talk: Towards a Framework for Understanding the Gap Between the Ethical Purchase Intentions and Actual Buying Behavior of Ethically Minded Consumers," *Journal of Business Ethics* 97 (2010): 139-58; M. Autio, E. Heiskanen and V. Heinonen, "Narratives of 'Green' Consumers—The Antihero, the Environmental Hero and the Anarchist," *Journal of Consumer Behavior* 8 (2009): 40-53; d'Astous and Legendre, "Understanding Consumers' Ethical Justifications"; K. Fukukawa and C. Ennew, "What We Believe Is Not Always What We Do: An Empirical Investigation into Ethically Questionable Behavior of Consumption," *Journal of Business Ethics* 91 (2010): 49-60; A. Chatzidakis, S. Hibbert and A. Smith, " 'Ethically Concerned, Yet Unethically Behaved': Towards an Updated Understanding of Consumer's (Un)ethical Decision Making," *Advances in Consumer Research* 33 (2006): 693-98; T. De Bock and P. Van Kenhove, "Double Standards: The Role of Techniquest of Neutralization," *Journal of Business Ethics* 99, no. 2 (2011): 283-296.

[18]This is sometimes referred to as moral disengagement and moral justification. For examples see G. P. Latham, *Work Motivation: History, Theory, Research and Practice* (Los Angeles: Sage Publications, 2012), pp. 240-42; P. R. Murphy and M. T. Dacin, "Psychological Pathways to Fraud: Understanding and Preventing Fraud in Organizations," *Journal of Business Ethics* 101, no. 4 (2011): 601-18; C. Moore, "Moral Disengagement in Processes of Organizational Corruption," *Journal of Business Ethics* 80, no. 1 (2008): 129-39; A. Bandura, "Selective Moral Disengagement in the Exercise of Moral Agency," *Journal of Moral Education* 31, no. 2 (2002): 101-19.

[19]J. M. Ntayi, W. Byabashaija, S. Eyaa, M. Ngoma and A. Muliira, "Social Cohesion, Groupthink and Ethical Behavior of Public Procurement Officers," *Journal of Public Procurement* 10, no. 1 (2010): 68-92; Yi-Hui Ho, "A Review of Research on Ethical Decision-Making of Purchasing Professionals," *Information Management and Business Review* 4, no. 2 (2012): 72-78; R. Landeros and R. E. Plank, "How Ethical Are Purchasing Management Professionals?," *Journal of Business Ethics* 15 (1996): 789-803; D. C. Robertson and T. Rymon, "Purchasing Agents' Deceptive Behavior: A Randomized Response Technique Study," *Business Ethics Quarterly* 11, no. 3 (2001): 455-79; A. Saini, "Purchasing Ethics and Inter-Organizational Buyer–Supplier Relational Determinants: A Conceptual Framework," *Journal of Business Ethics* 95 (2010): 439-55; J. A. Badenhorst, "Unethical Behavior in Procurement: A Perspective on Causes and Solutions," *Journal of Business Ethics* 13, no. 9 (1994): 739-45; K. M. Atwater, "Whistleblowers Enforce Procurement Ethics," *Summit* 10, no. 4 (2007): 4-8, 13-14.

[20]US Environmental Protection Agency, *Energy Trends in Selected Manufacturing Sectors: Opportunities and Challenges for Environmentally Preferable Energy Outcomes* (March 2007), p. 2-1.

[21]A. Fry, "Facts and Trends: Water," *World Business Council for Sustainable Development* (August 2005), www.unwater.org/downloads/Water_facts_and_trends.pdf.

[22]Source: www.yearbook.enerdata.net/ (accessed August 2014).

[23]Source: www.eia.gov/forecasts/ieo/.

[24]Source: www.eia.gov/cfapps/ipdbproject/iedindex3.cfm?tid=44&pid=45&aid=2&cid=regions&syid=2005&eyid=2009&unit=QBTU.

[25]Ibid.

[26]S. J. Vitell, "The Role of Religiosity in Business and Consumer Ethics: A Review of the Literature," *Journal of Business Ethics* 90 (2010): 155-67; S. J. Vitell, J. J. Singh and J. G. P. Paolillo, "Consumers' Ethical Beliefs: The Roles of Money, Religiosity and Attitude Toward Business," *Journal of Business Ethics* 73, no. 4 (2007): 369-79; C. A. Lopes, "Consumer Morality in Times of Economic Hardship:

Evidence from the European Social Survey," *International Journal of Consumer Studies* 34 (2010): 112-20; S. J. Vitell and J. G. P. Paolillo, "Consumer Ethics: The Role of Religiosity," *Journal of Business Ethics* 46 (2003): 151-62; H. Schneider, J. Krieger and A. Bayraktar, "The Impact of Intrinsic Religiosity on Consumers' Ethical Beliefs: Does It Depend on the Type of Religion? A Comparison of Christian and Moslem Consumers in Germany and Turkey," *Journal of Business Ethics* 102 (2011): 319-32; A. M. Patwardhan, M. E. Keith and S. J. Vitell, "Religiosity, Attitude Toward Business and Ethical Beliefs: Hispanic Consumers in the United States," *Journal of Business Ethics* 110 (2012): 61-70; S. J. Vitell, J. G. P. Paolillo and J. J. Singh, "The Role of Money and Religiosity in Determining Consumers' Ethical Beliefs," *Journal of Business Ethics* 64 (2006): 117-24; B. Cornwell, C. C. Cui, V. Mitchell, B. Schlegelmilch, A. Dzulkiflee and J. Chan, "A Cross-Cultural Study of the Role of Religion in Consumers' Ethical Positions," *International Marketing Review* 22, no. 5 (2005): 531-46; R. N. Gerlich, J. J. Lewer and D. Lucas, "Illegal Media File Sharing: The Impact of Cultural and Demographic Factors," *Journal of Internet Commerce* 9 (2010): 104-26.

[27]Acts 13:10.

[28]Gen 3:6-13.

[29]Deut 2:6; 5:21; 14:26.

[30]1 Thess 4:6; see also Mk 10:19.

[31]Prov 25:16; Lk 15:14.

[32]M. E. Cafferky, "Toward a Biblical Theology of Efficiency," *Journal of Biblical Integration in Business* 16, no. 2 (2013): 41-60.

[33]Amos 8:5.

[34]W. C. Kaiser Jr., *Toward Old Testament Ethics* (Grand Rapids: Zondervan, 1983), p. 213.

[35]Landeros and Plank, "How Ethical Are Purchasing Management Professionals?," p. 793.

15 ETHICAL ISSUES IN MANAGEMENT

[1]The name of the company is fictitious; all the events are real. They occurred over a three-year period in an organization for which the author worked. These events have been compressed into a shorter time period for this written description and have been applied to a different industry.

[2]E. Fehr and S. Gächter, "Fairness and Retaliation: The Economies of Reciprocity," *The Journal of Economic Perspectives* 14, no. 3 (2000): 159-81.

[3]For discussions of employment at will see R. T. DeGeorge, *Business Ethics*, 7th ed. (New York: Prentice Hall, 2010), pp. 349-51; H. R. Cheeseman, *The Legal Environment of Business and Online Commerce: Business Ethics, E-Commerce, Regulatory and International Issues* (Upper Saddle River, NJ: Pearson Prentice Hall, 2010), pp. 415-16.

[4]And the employer may not have this information at the time of hiring a new worker.

[5]In some cases it is known or can reasonably be assumed that the job is temporary because of the seasonality of the business. For example, some retail stores hire extra employees the last quarter of the year to staff their stores for the year-end holiday shopping season. At the end of the season, they lay off some or all of these workers. In some agricultural businesses, the number of employees needed varies by the planting and harvesting seasons. For a biblical example of this, see Mt 20.

[6]If the worker is fired for such an action and if the employee wants to contest the employer's action, the harmed employee will most likely need to sue the employer in court.

[7]There are ethical issues surrounding price discrimination. Some believe that price discrimination that is based on anything other than differences in economic value is wrong.

[8]Some organizations, such as religious nonprofit organizations that have religious beliefs regarding the use of alcohol, may have the legal right to forbid employees from using alcohol.

[9]The literature on bullying at work has increased since 1990. See as examples L. M. Andersson and C. Pearson, "Tit for Tat? The Spiraling Effect of Incivility in the Workplace," *Academy of Management Review* 24 (1999): 454-71; P. Lutgen-Sandvik, S. J. Tracy and J. K. Alberts, "Burned by Bullying in the American Workplace: Prevalence, Perception, Degree and Impact," *Journal of Management Studies* 44, no. 6 (2007): 837-62; D. Van Fleet and E. Van Fleet, "Towards a Behavioral Description of Managerial Bullying," *Employee Responsibilities & Rights Journal* 24, no. 3 (2012): 197-215; J. D. Bible, "The Jerk at Work: Workplace Bullying and the Law's Inability to Combat It," *Employee Relations Law Journal* 38, no. 1 (2012): 32-51; A. K. Samnani, "The Early Stages of Workplace Bullying and How It Becomes Prolonged: The Role of Culture in Predicting Target Responses," *Journal of Business Ethics* 113, no. 1 (2013): 119-32; S. Branch, S. Ramsay and M. Barker, "Workplace Bullying, Mobbing and General Harassment: A Review," *International Journal of Management Reviews* 15, no. 3 (2013): 280-99.

[10]D. Salin, "Ways of Explaining Workplace Bullying: A Review of Enabling, Motivating and Precipitating Structures and Processes in the Work Environment," *Human Relations* 56 (2003): 1214 (emphasis in original).

[11]Lutgen-Sandvik, Tracy and Alberts, "Burned by Bullying in the American Workplace," p. 841.

[12]Ibid., p. 851.

[13]1 Cor 14:33; 2 Cor 13:11; 2 Thess 3:16.

[14]Gen 3:14-15.

[15]1 Pet 4:11.

[16]Num 12:13; 2 Sam 9:7; 1 Kings 21:29; 2 Chron 12:6-7; Is 2:12; Ezek 28:3; Mt 18:4; 20:25-28; Mk 10:42-45; Lk 3:15; 10:34-35; Jn 3:28; Eph 4:32; Col 3:12-17; 1 Pet 4:1.

[17]Prov 3:27; Mt 7:1-4; Rom 12:9-21; 1 Cor 13:4-7.

[18]Mt 7:12.

[19]Ps 133:1; Rom 12:18; 13:13-14; 14:17-19; Eph 4:1-3; Phil 2:3-4, 13-16; 1 Thess 5:13; Heb 12:9-14; 1 Pet 3:11.

[20]Mt 15:12-14; 16:6-12; 17:24-27; 21:12-13; 22:15-21; Mk 2:16-19; 3:1-6; Lk 5:30-32; 11:38-47.

[21]Jn 8:4-9; see also Prov 15:1; 25:15.

[22]Eccles 2:24; 3:22; 5:18.

[23]As told in N. R. Pearcey, *Total Truth: Liberating Christianity from Its Cultural Captivity*, study guide edition (Wheaton, IL: Crossway, 2005), pp. 371-72.

[24]This vignette is based on the research regarding cheating on management reports reported in G. P. Latham, *Work Motivation: History, Theory, Research and Practice* (Los Angeles: Sage Publications, 2012), pp. 208-9.

16 ETHICAL ISSUES IN ACCOUNTING AND FINANCE

[1]This story and many others are posted on the Federal Bureau of Investigation website: www.fbi.gov/news /stories/2014/february/historic-insider-trading-scheme/historic-insider-trading-scheme. Many other news stories about Mathew Martoma can be found on the Internet.

[2]The testing phase of drug research is called a drug trial.

[3]F. C. Militello Jr., and M. D. Schwalberg, *Integrity-Based Financial Leadership and Ethical Behavior* (Morristown, NJ: Financial Executives Research Foundation, 2003), p. 14.

[4]S. P. Green, *Lying, Cheating and Stealing: A Moral Theory of White-Collar Crime* (New York: Oxford University Press, 2006), pp. 148-60.

[5]J. T. Wells, "So That's Why It's Called a Pyramid Scheme," *Journal of Accountancy* 190, no. 4 (2000): 91-95; J. T. Wells, "Follow Fraud to the Likely Perp," *Journal of Accountancy* 191, no. 3 (2001): 91-94.

[6]*Report to the Nations on Occupational Fraud and Abuse: 2012 Global Fraud Study* (Austin, TX: Association of Certified Fraud Examiners, 2012), p. 45.

[7]Green, *Lying, Cheating and Stealing*, pp. 34-47.

[8]Ibid., p. 55.

[9]Ibid., pp. 76-77.

[10]Some argue that insider trading should be allowed so that the market will have more complete information leading to a more efficient market.

[11]R. T. DeGeorge, *Business Ethics*, 7th ed. (Upper Saddle River, NJ: Prentice Hall, 2010), pp. 241-47.

[12]H. A. Ryan, W. Bottiglieri and S. L. Kroleski, "Fraud Versus Ethics: The Case of the Backdating of Stock Options," *Journal of Business & Economics Research* 6, no. 4 (2008): 13-23.

[13]Ibid., p. 14 (emphasis in the original).

[14]*Report to the Nations on Occupational Fraud and Abuse.*

[15]Ibid., p. 57.

[16]For a description of the many different types of white-collar crime see the Federal Bureau of Investigation website, www.fbi.gov/about-us/investigate/white_collar/whitecollarcrime, and the website of the Cornell University law school, www.law.cornell.edu/wex/white-collar_crime. For reading on how the concept of white-collar crime has developed over the years see E. H. Sutherland, "White-Collar Criminality," *American Sociological Review* 5 (1940): 1-12; V. Aubert, "White-Collar Crime and Social Structure," *American Journal of Sociology* 58 (1952): 263-71; G. Geis, "Toward a Delineation of White-Collar Offenses," *Sociological Inquiry* 32 (1962): 160-71; G. Robin, "White-Collar Crime and Employee Theft," *Crime and Delinquency* 20, no. 3 (1974): 251-62; D. O. Friedrichs, "White-Collar Crime and the Definitional Quagmire: A Provisional Solution," *Journal of Human Justice* 3, no. 3 (1992): 5-21; D. O. Friedrichs, "Occupational Crime, Occupational Deviance and Workplace Crime," *Criminal Justice* 2, no. 3 (2002): 243-56; E. Podgor and J. Israel, *White-Collar Crime in a Nutshell* (Eagan, MN: West Group, 2004); K. F. Brickey, *Corporate and White-Collar Crime* (New York: Aspen Publishers, 2006).

[17]From the Federal Bureau of Investigation website: www.fbi.gov/stats-services/publications/financial-crimes-report-2010-2011.

[18]Trading stocks based on material, nonpublic information.

[19]Giving or receiving money in return for doing something illegal or unethical.

[20]Making a material misstatement, misrepresentation or omission relating to a real estate transaction which is relied on by one or more parties to the transaction. Other types of real estate fraud can include illegal flipping of property (property is purchased, falsely appraised at a higher value and then quickly sold), nondisclosed second mortgage, loan modification schemes and equity skimming.

[21]This can come in any of several forms, such as diverting insurance premiums, raiding the premium revenue and disaster fraud.

[22]Ponzi schemes are investment frauds where investors are paid cash returns on their investment using the funds collected from new investors. Ponzi schemes fall apart when the Ponzi scheme leader(s) do not invest the money but keep it themselves.

[23]In affinity fraud, investors trust people who are respected members of a social group comprised of persons similar to themselves. These investors trust members of their social group, which leaves the investors open to fraud.

[24]In a pyramid scheme, money collected from new participants is paid to people who joined the scheme earlier. People who get others to join earn commissions.

[25]Criminals say that they represent a special investment program that only the largest banks get access to. They represent that the return on investment is high and the risk is low.

[26]Victims are told that they must pay a fee up front in order to participate in an investment deal. The fees are described as covering taxes and processing of the account.

[27]Small, nonexistent companies sometimes get investors to pay money in return for a promissory note. These companies have not registered with the Securities and Exchange Commission (SEC) and offer promises of high returns and low risk. The money given in exchange for a promissory note is not repaid.

[28]Unscrupulous foreign exchange investment firms may take investment cash from unwary investors not in hopes of earning a return but for the purpose of churning the account by trading in order to collect a trading fee. Others may produce false investment account statements that indicate how much has been earned when no earnings have been achieved and the criminal has diverted the investor's funds into personal use. False claims and high-pressure tactics may be used to secure the sale.

[29]See the note for foreign currency exchange fraud. These practices are similar to those employed by unscrupulous gold and silver traders.

[30]*United States Attorney's Annual Statistical Reports*, Table 3: White Collar Crime. Fiscal Years 2007–2012 (Washington, DC: US Department of Justice).

[31]U.S. Department of Justice Executive Office for United States Attorneys, "United States Attorneys' Annual Statistical Report: Fiscal Year 2010," p. 26, http://www.justice.gov/sites/default/files/usao/legacy/2011/09/01/10statrpt.pdf.

[32]Source: Various sections of the US Code as noted in table 16.2.

[33]M. Graham, "White-Collar Crime and the United States Economy," honors thesis, University of New Hampshire (unpublished paper, University of New Hampshire's Scholars' Repository, 2012).

[34]Prov 13:11; see also Prov 10:2; 28:22; Jer 17:11.

[35]For a presentation on why white-collar crime sentences should be harsher than they typically are, see J. S. Dutcher, "Comment from the Boardroom to the Cellblock: The Justifications for Harsher Punishment of White-Collar and Corporate Crime," *Arizona State Law Journal* 37 (2005): 1295-1319.

[36]For additional case studies see V. Christian and A. Gumbus, "Shades of Gray: Applying Professional Codes of Ethics to Workplace Dilemmas," *Organization Management Journal* 6 (2009): 178-99.

[37]Based on a similar case described in C. M. Bradley, "Mail Fraud After McNally and Carpenter: The Essence of Fraud," *Journal of Criminal Law and Criminology* 79, no. 3 (1988): 573-622.

[38]Prov 28:16; Is 33:15.

[39]C. Fleck, "Living in Limbo," *AARP Bulletin* 52, no. 7 (2011): 18, 20-21.

17 ETHICAL ISSUES IN MARKETING

[1]Stories about this historic price-fixing scheme can be found in several publications. The following are examples: R. Narisetti, "Justice Department Is Investigating Tire Makers for Possible Price-Fixing," *Wall Street Journal*, Eastern edition, August, 24, 1995, A3; M. Moore, "Bridgestone Pleads Guilty to Price Fixing," *Rubber & Plastics News* 43, no. 15 (2014): 1.

[2]R. P. Bagozzi, "Marketing as Exchange," *Journal of Marketing* 39, no. 4 (1975): 32-39.

[3]S. L. Vargo and R. F. Lusch, "Evolving to a New Dominant Logic for Marketing," *Journal of Marketing* 68 (2004): 1-17.

[4]This can be applied to intangible services as well as to tangible products.

[5]Reported by the Institute for Advertising Ethics: www.aaf.org/images/public/aaf_content/images/ad%20ethics/IAE_Principles_Practices.pdf.

[6]M. E. Cafferky, *Let Your Customers Do the Talking* (Chicago: Upstart Publishing, 1996).

[7]For more information on the ethics of word-of-mouth marketing, see www.womma.org/ethics/womma-code-of-ethics. Also see the Federal Trade Commission (FTC) regulations regarding the use of endorsements and testimonials in the Code of Federal Regulations: 16 C.F.R. §§ 255.0–255.5, www.ecfr.gov/cgi-bin/text-idx?tpl=/ecfrbrowse/Title16/16cfr255_main_02.tpl.

[8]www.womma.org/ethics/womma-code-of-ethics.

[9]For several examples of marketing situations, see Federal Trade Commission Code of Federal Regulation (C.F.R.) 16 C.F.R. §§ 255.0–255.5, www.ftc.gov/sites/default/files/attachments/press-releases/ftc-publishes-final-guides-governing-endorsements-testimonials/091005revisedendorsementguides.pdf.

[10]www.aaf.org/images/public/aaf_content/images/ad%20ethics/IAE_Principles_Practices.pdf.

[11]www.fcc.gov/encyclopedia/do-not-call-list.

[12]Some of these examples are based on T. A. Shimp, *Advertising, Promotion and Supplemental Aspects of Integrated Marketing Communications*, 6th ed. (Boston: Thomson South-Western, 2003).

[13]J. Hookway, "'Flappy Bird' Creator Pulled Game Because It Was 'Too Addictive': Amid Speculation of a Publicity Stunt, Developer Says Fuss Was Overwhelming," *Wall Street Journal* (online), February 11, 2014, www.wsj.com/articles/SB10001424052702303874504579376323271110900.

[14]www.dellproduct.com/Program.aspx?PI=GNbVEXZPZu8=.

[15]Consumers can obtain information on recalled products from a clearing house website sponsored by the US government: www.recalls.gov.

[16]J. Muncy, "Ethical Issues in Multilevel Marketing: Is It a Legitimate Business or Just Another Pyramid Scheme?," *Marketing Education Review* 14, no. 3 (2004): 47-53.

18 ETHICAL ISSUES IN GLOBAL BUSINESS

[1]N. Vardi, "Many of the Bribery Allegations Against Walmart May Not Be Illegal," *Forbes* April 24, 2012, p. 32; www.forbes.com/sites/nathanvardi/2012/04/24/many-of-the-bribery-allegations-against-wal-mart-may-not-be-illegal; K. Ellis, "Walmart Scrutiny Mounts," *Women's Wear Daily* 205, no. 8 (2013): 1.

[2]www.unodc.org/unodc/en/treaties/CAC/signatories.html.

[3]M. Blowfield and A. Murray, *Corporate Responsibility: A Critical Introduction* (New York: Oxford University Press, 2008), p. 71.

[4]P. H. Werhane, "Globalization and its Challenges for Business and Business Ethics in the Twenty-First Century," *Business and Society Review* 117 (2012): 383-405.

[5]J. R. Boatright, *Ethics and the Conduct of Business*, 4th ed. (Upper Saddle River, NJ: Prentice Hall, 2003), p. 413.

[6]J. R. DesJardins and J. J. McCall, *Contemporary Issues in Business Ethics*, 5th ed. (Belmont, CA: Wadsworth/Thomson Learning, 2005), pp. 471-72.

[7]R. T. DeGeorge, "International Business Ethics," *Business Ethics Quarterly* 4, no. 1 (1994): 1-9.

[8]T. Donaldson, *The Ethics of International Business* (New York: Oxford University Press, 1989), p. 14.

[9]Other ethical issues that arise in the context of global business include child labor, sweatshops, extortion, stealing intellectual property, industrial espionage, industrial sabotage, fair trade pricing, employee safety, kickbacks, insider trading, fraud, counterfeiting and money laundering.

[10]Some think of corruption as merely another form of theft or extortion without the use of physical force.

[11]L. A. Breuer and R. H. Khuzami, *A Resource Guide to the U.S. Foreign Corrupt Practices Act* (Washington, DC: US Department of Justice and the Securities and Exchange Commission, 2012), pp. 2-3; United Nations Office on Drugs and Crime, *United Nations Convention Against Corruption* (New York: United Nations, 2004). See also S. P. Green, *Lying, Cheating, and Stealing: A Moral Theory of White-Collar Crime* (New York: Oxford University Press, 2006), pp. 193-211.

[12]www.transparency.org.

[13]www.justice.gov/criminal/fraud/fcpa.

[14]Ibid.

[15]www.justice.gov/criminal/fraud/fcpa/guide.pdf.

[16]R. Audi, *Business Ethics and Ethical Business* (New York: Oxford University Press, 2009), pp. 109-28; J. A. Fadiman, "A Traveler's Guide to Gifts and Bribes," *Harvard Business Review* 64, no. 4 (1986): 122-36.

[17]H. S. James Jr., "When Is a Bribe a Bribe? Teaching a Workable Definition of Bribery," *Teaching Business Ethics* 6, no. 2 (2002): 199-217; S. Turow, "What's Wrong with Bribery," *Journal of Business Ethics* 4, no. 4 (1985): 249-51; Fadiman, " Traveler's Guide to Gifts and Bribes"; S. R. Salbu, "Transnational Bribery: The Big Questions," *Northwestern Journal of International Law & Business* 21, no. 2 (2001): 435-70; Green,

Lying, Cheating, and Stealing, pp. 193-211; P. Steidlmeier, "Gift Giving, Bribery and Corruption: Ethical Management of Business Relationships in China," *Journal of Business Ethics* 20, no. 2 (1999): 121-132.

[18]Green, *Lying, Cheating, and Stealing*, pp. 193-211; Audi, *Business Ethics and Ethical Business*, p. 113.

[19]J. Reed and E. Portanger, "Bribery, Corruption Are Rampant in Eastern Europe," *Wall Street Journal* 234, no. 92 (1999): A21; M. Esterl and D. Crawford, "Siemens to Pay Huge Fine in Bribery Inquiry," *Wall Street Journal* 252, no. 141 (2008): B1, B5; R. Gold and B. Casselman, "Corporate News: Halliburton to Pay $559 Million to Settle Bribery Investigation," *Wall Street Journal* 253, no. 21 (2009): B3; R. Gold and D. Crawford, "U.S., Other Nations Step Up Bribery Battle," *Wall Street Journal* 252, no. 62 (2008): B1-B6.

[20]Breuer and Khuzami, *Resource Guide to the U.S. Foreign Corrupt Practices Act*, p. 3.

[21]Donaldson, *Ethics of International Business*, pp. 146-47.

[22]www.icj-cij.org/homepage/index.php?lang=en.

[23]J. Cameron and K. R. Gray, "Principles of International Law in the WTO Dispute Settlement Body," *International and Comparative Law Quarterly* 50 (2001): 248-98.

[24]www.oecd.org/unitedstates.

[25]Its predecessor organization, The Organization for European Economic Cooperation (OEEC), was established in 1948 to manage the operations of the United States Marshall Plan for the reconstruction of Europe, which had been devastated in World War II.

[26]*Criminal Law Convention on Corruption* (Strasbourg: Council of Europe, 1999), conventions.coe.int/Treaty/Commun/QueVoulezVous.asp?NT=173&CL=ENG.

[27]The treaty went into effect in 2002.

[28]United Nations Office on Drugs and Crime, *United Nations Convention Against Corruption*.

[29]For a more complete list of international organizations that cooperate in combating corruption see the website of the International Association of Anti-Corruption Authorities, www.iaaca.org/AntiCorruptionAuthorities/ByInternationalOrganizations/.

[30]www.cauxroundtable.org/. Other examples include the Sullivan Principles for Africa (1999), www.thesullivanfoundation.org/gsp/endorsers/charter/default.asp; the OECD *Guidelines for Multinational Enterprises* (Paris: OECD Publishing, 2011), http://dx.doi.org/10.1787/9789264115415-en.

[31]INSEAD is an international graduate school of business located in France.

[32]www.cauxroundtable.org/index.cfm?&menuid=142.

[33]www.unglobalcompact.org/AboutTheGC/TheTenPrinciples/index.html. See also O. Williams, "The United Nations Global Compact: What Did It Promise?," *Journal of Business Ethics* 122, no. 2 (2014): 241-51.

[34]Mt 28:18; 1 Cor 4:9; Col 1:15-20; Rev 12:7.

[35]Mt 4:1-11; Mk 1:9-13; Lk 4:1-13; Heb 2:18; 4:15.

[36]Mt 6:13; 26:41; Mk 14:38.

[37]An interesting example of attempting to win favor is found in Gen 32–33, where Jacob gives gifts to his estranged brother Esau. See also the importance of receiving social favor from others in Prov 11:27; 14:35; 16:15; 19:6; 22:1; 29:26.

[38]Ps 119:158; Prov 3:4; 22:1.

[39]Deut 8:17-18; Prov 10:22; Mt 5:44-45; 6:33; Lk 6:32-38; Jn 3:16; 15:12-13; Rom 5:7-8; 8; 12:1-6; 1 Cor 12; Jas 1:17.

[40]Prov 19:6.

[41]L. E. Toombs, "Love and Justice in Deuteronomy," *Interpretation* 19, no. 4 (1965): 399-411.

[42]Rev 21:1.

[43]Rom 8:19-23.

[44]Ex 23:8; Deut 10:17; 16:19; 27:25; 1 Sam 8:3; 12:3; 2 Chron 19:7; Job 6:22; Ps 15:5; 17:8, 23; 21:14; 26:10; Prov 15:27; 29:4; Eccles 7:7; Is 1:23; 5:23; 33:15; Ezek 16:33; 22:12; Amos 5:12; Mic 3:11; 7:3.

[45]Ex 23:8; Deut 10:17; 16:18-20; 27:25; Ps 15:5; Prov 17:8, 23; Eccles 7:7.

[46]Phil 2:1-11.

[47]This complex vignette was inspired by Salbu, "Transnational Bribery."

[48]This is a fictional account based on the account of a true story told to the author by an executive of an oil and gas company that did business with another African country, not Togo. The company name is fictional.

19 CORPORATE RESPONSIBILITY

[1]Based on P. F. Drucker, "The New Meaning of Corporate Social Responsibility," *California Management Review* 26, no. 2 (1984): 53-63.

[2]Fair trade practices focus on improving the wages and working conditions of workers in developing markets.

[3]M. E. Porter and M. R. Kramer, "Strategy and Society: The Link Between Competitive Advantage and Corporate Social Responsibility," *Harvard Business Review* 84, no. 12 (2006): 78-92.

[4]These examples were posed by Milton Friedman, "The Social Responsibility of Business Is to Increase Its Profits," *New York Times Sunday Magazine*, September 13, 1970.

[5]M. Luther, "Trade and Usury," in *Luther's Works*, vol. 45: *The Christian in Society II*, ed. W. I. Brandt (Philadelphia: Fortress, 1962), pp. 233-310.

[6]B. Griffiths, *The Creation of Wealth: A Christian's Case for Capitalism* (Downers Grove, IL: InterVarsity Press, 1984), p. 9.

[7]A. B. Carroll, "A History of Corporate Social Responsibility: Concepts and Practices," in *The Oxford Handbook of Corporate Social Responsibility*, ed. A. Crane, A. McWilliams, D. Matten, J. Moon and D. S. Siegel (Oxford: Oxford University Press, 2008), pp. 19-46; R. Marens, "Recovering the Past: Reviving the Legacy of the Early Scholars of Corporate Social Responsibility," *Journal of Management History* 14, no. 1 (2008): 55-72; H. R. Bowen, *Social Responsibilities of the Businessman* (New York: Harper and Row, 1953); E. Dale, "Management Must Be Made Accountable," *Harvard Business Review* 38, no. 2 (1960): 49-59; M. Heald, "Management's Responsibility to Society: The Growth of an Idea," *Business History Review* 31 (1957): 375-84; K. Davis, "Can Business Afford to Ignore Social Responsibilities?," *California Management Review* 2 (1960): 70-76.

[8]Negative externalities are results of business activities which cause a cost to be incurred by others.

[9]R. Carson, *Silent Spring* (New York: Houghton Mifflin, 1962).

[10]www.earthday.org/earth-day-history-movement.

[11]S. Waddock, "Building a New Institutional Infrastructure for Corporate Responsibility," *Academy of Management Perspectives* 22, no. 3 (2008): 87-108.

[12]Sometimes referred to as corporate social responsibility. Here the word *social* is dropped because responsibility issues are broader than just social impacts of business. As we explore in this chapter, responsibility also encompasses concerns regarding the physical environment.

[13]A. T. Lawrence and J. Weber, *Business and Society: Stakeholders, Ethics, Public Policy* (New York: McGraw-Hill Irwin, 2008), pp. 45-46.

[14]Porter and Kramer, "Strategy and Society," p. 82.

[15]M. Blowfield and A. Murray, *Corporate Responsibility: A Critical Introduction* (New York: Oxford University Press, 2008), p. 135.

[16]Ibid., p. 138.

[17]Ibid., pp. 130-57.

[18]Ibid., p. 136.

[19]Ibid., pp. 130-57.

[20]Drucker, "New Meaning of Corporate Social Responsibility."

[21]Ibid.

[22]Porter and Kramer, "Strategy and Society"; P. F. Drucker, *The Practice of Management* (New York: Harper & Brothers, 1954), pp. 386-87. Also adapted from L. T. Hosmer, *The Ethics of Management*, 6th ed. (New York: McGraw-Hill Irwin, 2008), pp. 125-31.

[23]Hosmer, *Ethics of Management*.

[24]J. W. Weiss, *Business Ethics: A Stakeholder and Issues Management Approach*, 3rd ed. (Mason, OH: South-Western, 2003).

[25]K. Davis and R. Blomstrom, *Business and Its Environment* (New York: McGraw-Hill, 1966); P. F. Drucker, *Management: Tasks, Responsibilities, Practices* (New York: HarperBusiness, 1974), pp. 326-51; D. Windsor, "Corporate Social Responsibility: Cases For and Against," in *The Accountable Corporation: Corporate Social Responsibility*, ed. M. J. Epstein and K. O. Hanson, 4 vols. (Westport, CT: Praeger, 2006), 3:31-50; Lawrence and Weber, *Business and Society*, p. 51; Porter and Kramer, "Strategy and Society."

[26]Lk 12:48.

[27]Windsor, "Corporate Social Responsibility"; Porter and Kramer, "Strategy and Society."

[28]Lawrence and Weber, *Business and Society*, p. 51.

[29]Ibid., p.52; see also Windsor, "Corporate Social Responsibility"; Porter and Kramer, "Strategy and Society"; Weiss, *Business Ethics*.

[30]Lawrence and Weber, *Business and Society*, p. 52.

[31]Drucker, *Practice of Management*, p. 386; M. Friedman, *Capitalism and Freedom* (1962; Chicago: University of Chicago Press, 2002), pp. 133-36; Friedman, "Social Responsibility of Business"; Windsor, "Corporate Social Responsibility"; Lawrence and Weber, *Business and Society*, p. 53; Blowfield and Murray, *Corporate Responsibility*, pp. 338-61.

[32]Lawrence and Weber, *Business and Society*, p. 54.

[33]A. L. Svenson, "Whose Social Responsibility?," *SAM Advanced Management Journal* 35, no. 3 (1970): 14-19.

[34]Windsor, "Corporate Social Responsibility."

[35]Blowfield and Murray, *Corporate Responsibility*, pp. 338-61.

[36]Ibid., p. 235.

[37]F. Hermans and L. Knippenberg, "A Principle-Based Approach for the Evaluation of Sustainable Development," *Journal of Environmental Assessment Policy and Management* 8, no. 3 (2006): 299-319.

[38]G. H. Brundtland, *Report of the World Commission on Environment and Development: Our Common Future* (Oslo, March 1987).

[39]Gen 1:26-28; 2:15.

[40]See H. E. von Waldow, "Social Responsibility and Social Structure in Early Israel," *The Catholic Biblical Quarterly* 32 (1970): 182-204.

[41]Deut 14:22-28; 16:14; 26:12; Jer 22:3.

[42]R. L. Martin, "The Virtue Matrix: Calculating the Return on Corporate Responsibility," *Harvard Business Review* 80, no 3 (2002): 68-75.

[43]Drucker, "New Meaning of Corporate Social Responsibility," p. 59.

[44]www.gapinc.com/content/csr/html/community/advancing-women.html.

[45]www.toms.com/Marketplace.

20 EVALUATING THE MORALITY OF POLITICAL-ECONOMIC SYSTEMS

[1]www.aflcio.org/Corporate-Watch/CEO-Pay-and-You/CEO-to-Worker-Pay-Gap-in-the-United-States.

[2]www.michaelmoore.com/books-films/facts/capitalism-love-story.

[3]D. Baker, "The Productivity to Paycheck Gap: What the Data Show" (Washington, DC: Center for Economic and Policy Research, 2007).

[4]www.rasmussenreports.com/public_content/politics/general_politics/april_2009/just_53_say_capitalism_better_than_socialism.

[5]F. A. Hayek, *The Road to Serfdom* (1944; Chicago: University of Chicago Press, 1994); M. Friedman, *Capitalism and Freedom* (Chicago: University of Chicago Press, 1962).

[6]K. Marx, *Capital: A Critique of Political Economy* (1867; New York: Penguin Books, 1990).

[7]R. Skidelsky, *The Road from Serfdom* (New York: Penguin Books, 1995), p. 17. For a standard comparison between the two competing systems, see P. R. Gregory and R. C. Stuart, *Comparative Economic Systems*, 5th ed. (Boston Houghton Mifflin, 1995).

[8]Based on R. T. DeGeorge, *Business Ethics*, 7th ed. (Upper Saddle River, NJ: Prentice Hall, 2010).

[9]Sidelsky, *Road from Serfdom*, p. 20.

[10]Ibid.

[11]Ibid., p. 26.

[12]This is not intended to be a comprehensive review of all the arguments, but these are representative. See R. H. Nash, "Does Capitalism Pass the Moral Test?," in *Readings in Christian Ethics*, vol. 2: *Issues and Applications*, ed. D. K. Clark and R. V. Rakestraw (Grand Rapids: Baker, 1994), pp. 345-54; R. H. Nash, "Is Capitalism Immoral?," in *Social Justice and the Christian Church* (Milford, MI: Mott Media, 1983), pp. 111-38; S. Young, *Moral Capitalism: Reconciling Private Interest with the Public Good* (San Francisco: Berrett-Koehler, 2003); M. J. Miller, "Business as a Moral Enterprise," in *Christian Theology and Market Economics*, ed. I. R. Harper and S. Gregg (Northampton, MA: Edward Elgar, 2008), pp. 113-18; A. Carden, "The Market's Benevolent Tendencies," in *Business and Religion: A Clash of Civilizations?*, ed. N. Capaldi (Salem, MA: M&M Scrivener Press, 2005), pp. 55-64; M. Novak, *Business as a Calling: Work and the Examined Life* (New York: The Free Press, 1996); M. Novak, "Profits with Honor," *Policy Review* 77 (1996): 50-56; Friedman, *Capitalism and Freedom*; A. Sen, *Development as Freedom* (New York: Random House, 1999); W. H. Shaw and V. Barry, *Moral Issues in Business*, 10th ed. (Belmont, CA: Thomson Wadsworth, 2007); Hayek, *Road to Serfdom*.

[13]See the discussion about common sense (chap. 7).

[14]Shaw and Barry, *Moral Issues in Business*; E. N. Wolf, *Top Heavy: The Increasing Inequality of Wealth in America and What Can Be Done About It* (New York: The New Press, 2002); Young, *Moral Capitalism*; Nash, "Is Capitalism Immoral?"; G. F. Cavanagh, *American Business Values: A Global Perspective*, 5th ed. (Upper Saddle River, NJ: Pearson Prentice Hall, 2006); Edgar H. Schein, "Learning When and How to Lie: A Neglected Aspect of Organizational and Occupational Socialization," *Human Relations* 57, no. 3 (2004): 260-73.

[15]Young, *Moral Capitalism*.

[16]Shaw and Barry, *Moral Issues in Business*, p. 160.

[17]R. Jackall, *Moral Mazes: The World of Corporate Managers* (New York: Oxford University Press, 1988); F. B. Bird and J. A. Waters, "The Moral Muteness of Managers," *California Management Review* 32, no. 1 (1989): 73-88.

[18]Young, *Moral Capitalism*, p. 144.

[19]Marx, *Capital*; A. Gorz, *Division of Labor: The Labor-Process and Class-Struggle in Modern Capitalism* (Atlantic Highlands, NJ: Humanities Press, 1976); H. Braverman, *Labor and Monopoly Capital: The Degradation of Work in the Twentieth Century* (New York: Monthly Review Press, 1998); D. Katz, "Satisfactions and Deprivations in Industrial Life," in *Industrial Conflict*, ed. A. Kornhauser, R. Dubin and A. M. Ross (New York: McGraw-Hill, 1954), pp. 86-106; C. B. Saunders, H. M. O'Neill and O. W. Jensen, "Alienation in Corporate America: Fact or Fable?," *Journal of Business Ethics* 5, no. 4 (1986): 285-89.

[20]J. C. Bennett, "Capitalism and Communism at Amsterdam," *The Christian Century* 65, no. 50 (1948): 1362-64; N. S. Ream, "In Defense of Capitalism," *The Christian Century* 66, no. 1 (1949): 14-15. These and related

criticisms have been put forward by Christians for decades. For a few examples, see S. C. Mott, *Biblical Ethics and Social Change*, 2nd ed. (New York: Oxford University Press) 2011; P. H. Sedgwick, *The Market Economy and Christian Ethics* (Cambridge: Cambridge University Press, 1999); D. S. Long, *Divine Economy: Theology and the Market* (New York: Routledge, 2000); C. Beed and C. Beed, *Alternatives to Economics: Christian Socio-economic Perspectives* (Lanham, MD: University Press of America, 2006); V. V. Claar and R. J. Klay, *Economics in Christian Perspective: Theory, Policy and Life Choices* (Downers Grove, IL: InterVarsity Press, 2007); A. Barreera, *Market Complicity and Christian Ethics* (Cambridge: Cambridge University Press, 2011); D. K. Ma, "Destructive Creation: The Covenantal Crisis of Capitalist Society," *Theology Today* 63 (2006): 150-64; M. Volf, *Work in the Spirit: Toward a Theology of Work* (Eugene, OR: Wipf & Stock, 1991); C. Johnson, "A Christian Critique of Economics," *Buddhist-Christian Studies* 22 (2002): 17-29.

[21]D. K. Finn, *Christian Economic Ethics* (Minneapolis: Fortress, 2013).

[22]Ream, "In Defense of Capitalism," pp. 14-15. In later decades other Christians joined to defend capitalism. See for a few examples R. Benne, *The Ethic of Democratic Capitalism* (Philadelphia: Augsburg Fortress, 1981); M. Novak, *The Spirit of Democratic Capitalism* (New York: Simon & Schuster, 1982); Nash, "Is Capitalism Immoral?"; B. Griffiths, *The Creation of Wealth: A Christian's Case for Capitalism* (Downers Grove, IL: InterVarsity Press, 1984); E. A. Opitz, *Religion and Capitalism: Allies, Not Enemies* (New Rochelle, NJ: Arlington House, 1992); R. R. Richards, *God and Business: Christianity's Case for Capitalism* (Maitland, FL: Xulon, 2002); P. Heyne, *Are Economists Basically Immoral? And Other Essays on Economics, Ethics and Religion* (Indianapolis: Liberty Fund, 2008); P. Wehner, Arthur C. Brooks and Philip Jenkins, *Wealth and Justice: The Morality of Democratic Capitalism* (Washington, DC: AEI Press, 2010).

[23]Mt 26:11; Mk 14:7; Jn 12:8; see also Deut 15:11.

[24]Deut 17:14-20.

[25]J. A. Hutchison, "Biblical Foundations of Democracy," *Journal of Bible and Religion* 15, no. 1 (1947): 34-37; Y. Hozony, *The Philosophy of Hebrew Scripture* (Cambridge: Cambridge University Press, 2012), pp. 149-51.

[26]Jer 29:7.

[27]Jer 31:31-33.

[28]Ex 3–12; Nehemiah.

[29]The experiences of the prophets illustrate this.

[30]Mt 5–7.

[31]R. C. Chewning, J. W. Eby and S. J. Roels, *Business Through the Eyes of Faith* (San Francisco: HarperSanFrancisco, 1990), pp. 9-10.

[32]Volf, *Work in the Spirit*, pp. 15-16.

[33]1 Tim 2:1-2.

21 MORAL MUTENESS AND PRESSURE TO COMPROMISE

[1]F. B. Bird and J. A. Waters, "The Moral Muteness of Managers," *California Management Review* 32, no. 1 (1989): 73-88; N. Shahinpoor and B. F. Matt, "The Power of One: Dissent and Organizational Life," *Journal of Business Ethics* 74, no. 1 (2007): 37-48; J. D. Stanley, "Dissent in Organizations," *The Academy of Management Review* 6, no. 1 (1981): 13-19.

[2]Shahinpoor and Matt, "Power of One."

[3]Adapted from M. C. Gentile, "Keeping Your Colleagues Honest," *Harvard Business Review* 88, no. 3 (2010): 114-17.

[4]This is another example of the individual-community tension (see chap. 2).

[5]This was proposed by K. Wong and J. Van Duzer, *Navigating Muddy Waters: Preparing Students to Handle Moral Compromise in the Context of Managerial Roles*, paper presented at the Christian Business Faculty Association annual conference (Cedarville, OH: Cedarville University, 2006). A similar discussion can

be found in N. L. Geisler, *Christian Ethics* (Grand Rapids: Baker, 1989), pp. 79-132.

[6]Job 15:14; Prov 28:26; Jer 17:9.

[7]Rom 7:19–8:14.

[8]Some Christian faith traditions call this the process of sanctification.

[9]P. F. Drucker, *Management: Tasks, Responsibilities, Practices* (New York: HarperBusiness, 1973), pp. 424-25.

APPENDIX A: KEY QUESTIONS FROM THE BIBLICAL THEMES

[1]Deut 4:9; Prov 3:1; 4:4.

APPENDIX D: TEN PRINCIPLES FOR FLOURISHING

[1]This appendix is based on M. E. Cafferky, "The Ethical-Religious Framework for Shalom," *Journal of Religion and Business Ethics* 3, no. 1 (2011): Article 7 [1-36].

[2]Deut 17:14-20.

[3]Deut 33:9-10.

[4]Deut 6:6-7. The primary economic unit in Hebrew society was the family. Heads of households had the responsibility to teach the next generation the principles of the Ten Commandments.

[5]Deut 18:15-18.

[6]Deut 13.

[7]In this table the Reformed Protestant structure of the Ten Commandments is used. The perspective of Roman Catholic and Anglican churches can be used without materially changing the thesis of this appendix.

APPENDIX F: THE PURPOSE OF BUSINESS THROUGH THE LENS OF BIBLICAL THEMES

[1]As early as 1878 Edwin T. Freedley considered the "object" of business to "supply the wants of others in exchange for the means of satisfying our own wants or desires." Freedley also states that the fundamental idea underlying all kinds of business is "mutual help, or, as it has been expressed, *ministry*, not gain. In the earliest periods of society, when men were gathered together in tribes, each pursued a particular art or industry, not entirely for his own profit but for the good of the community in which he dwelt" (emphasis in original). E. T. Freedley, *Common Sense in Business or, Practical Answers to Practical Questions on the True Principles and Laws of Success* (Philadelphia: S. A George & Co., 1878), pp. 34-35. Freedley goes on to quote a respected business scholar "Dr. Johnson," that "there are few ways in which a man can be more innocently employed than in getting money."

[2]In the modern era the purpose of business is described in terms of profit by T. Veblen, *The Theory of Business Enterprise* (New York: Charles Scribner's Sons, 1904), p. 87: "Gain, they feel, is normal, being the purpose of all their endeavors; whereas a loss or a shrinkage in the values invested is felt to be an untoward accident which does not belong in the normal course of business, and which requires particular explanation." See also in Veblen (p. 93) where he states that profit is the business man's "object." See also M. C. Jensen, "Agency Costs of Free Cash Flow, Corporate Finance and Takeovers," *American Economic Review* 76, no. 2 (1986): 323-29; M. C. Jensen, "Value Maximization, Stakeholder Theory and the Corporate Objective Function," *Journal of Applied Corporate Finance* 22, no. 1 (2010): 32-42.

[3]A. A. Berle and G. C. Means, *The Modern Corporation and Private Property* (New York: Macmillan, 1933), p. 356.

[4]J. W. McGuire, "The Finalité of Business," *California Management Review* 8, no. 4 (1966): 89-94; B. Daviss, "Profits from Principle: Five Forces Redefining Business," *The Futurist* 33, no. 3 (1999): 30; P. F. Drucker, *Management: Tasks, Responsibilities, Practices* (New York: HarperBusiness, 1974), pp. 42-61; W. J. Byron, "Twin Towers: A Philosophy and Theology of Business," *Journal of Business Ethics* 7, no. 7 (1988): 526; D.

Ahlstrom, "Innovation and Growth," *Academy of Management Perspectives* 24, no. 3 (2010): 11-24; O. Harari, "You're Not in Business to Make a Profit," *Management Review* 81, no. 7 (1992): 53-55; W. Kline, "Business as an Ethical Standard," *The Journal of Private Enterprise* 24, no. 2 (2009): 35-48; E. Sternberg, *Just Business: Business Ethics in Action* (London: Warner Books, 1995).

[5]P. F. Drucker, *The Practice of Management* (New York: Harper & Brothers, 1954), p. 381.

[6]W. Kline, "Business Ethics from the Internal Point of View," *Journal of Business Ethics* 64, no. 1 (2006): 62.

[7]Ibid., p. 65.

[8]Ibid.

[9]M. Kooskra, "Perceptions of Business Purpose and Responsibilities in the Context of Radical Political and Economic Development: The Case of Estonia," *Business Ethics: A European Review* 15, no. 2 (2006): 184.

[10]J. Magretta, "Why Business Models Matter," *Harvard Business Review* 85, no. 5 (2002): 86-92; L. Schweizer, "Concept and Evolution of Business Models," *Journal of General Management* 31, no. 2 (2005): 37-56; T. Harford, *The Undercover Economist* (New York: Random House, 2005), pp. 11-17.

[11]C. H. Gibson, *Financial Statement Analysis: Using Financial Accounting Information* (Cincinnati: South-Western College Publishing, 1995), p. 46.

[12]Here the term "profit" is used from the perspective of financial accounting rather than economics.

[13]Byron, "Twin Towers," pp. 525-30; R. F. Duska, "The Why's of Business Revisited," *Journal of Business Ethics* 16, no. 12/13 (1997): 1401-9.

[14]R. C. Solomon, *Ethics and Excellence* (Oxford: Oxford University Press, 1992); R. E. Ewin, "The Virtues Appropriate to Business," *Business Ethics Quarterly* 5, no. 4 (1995): 833-42; M. J. King and B. Rigby, "How Business Confuses Outcomes with Purpose," *ABA Banking Journal* 97, no. 4 (2005): 10.

[15]Drucker, *Management*, p. 61. See also Ahlstrom, "Innovation and Growth"; Ewin, "Virtues Appropriate to Business"; Duska, "The Why's of Business Revisited"; J. Kay, "A Stakeholding Society—What Does It Mean for Business?," *Scottish Journal of Political Economy* 44, no. 4 (1997): 425-37; C. Handy, "What's a Business For?," *Harvard Business Review* 80, no. 12 (2002): 49-56; Kline, "Business Ethics from the Internal Point of View."

[16]Handy, "What's a Business For?," p. 51.

[17]He states, "What we generally call profits, the money left to service equity, is usually not profit at all. Until a business returns a profit that is greater than its cost of capital, it operates at a loss. Never mind that it pays taxes as if it had a genuine profit. The enterprise still returns less to the economy than it devours in resources. It does not cover its full costs unless the reported profit exceeds the cost of capital. Until then, it does not create wealth; it destroys it." P. F. Drucker, "The Information Executives Truly Need," *Harvard Business Review* 73, no. 1 (1995): 59. Not all Christians will agree with Drucker.

[18]Drucker, *Practice of Management*, p. 62.

CASE STUDIES

[1]Based on a story that the car rental customer told to the author.

[2]After a series of emails between the customer and the rental car company and between the customer and the airline, the frequent flier program managers eventually gave bonus frequent flier miles for the use of the coupon in addition to the bonus miles for bringing the matter to their attention. The whole process took two months to get resolved.

[3]Joseph Mantone, "HealthSouth Responds," *Modern Healthcare* 36, no. 1 (2006): 4.

[4]D. Enrich and F. Guerrera, "UBS Chief's Plea: Stop 'Lecturing,'" *Wall Street Journal,* January 28, 2014, C.1.

[5]You may be able to find on YouTube the Nissan Frontier advertisement: www.youtube.com/watch?v=mhhwQmNQzNE. You may also find interesting news stories on YouTube about the situation: www.youtube.com/watch?v=XD_ymapyjPU.

[6]Stories about this advertisement were published in the *Wall Street Journal* and *Automotive News.*

[7]M. Bar, K. Chernomaz and D. Escobari, "Pricing and Travelers' Decision to Use Frequent Flier Miles: Evidence from the U.S. Airline Industry," in *Airline Industry: Strategies, Operations and Safety*, ed. C. R. Walsh (Hauppauge, NY: Nova Science Publishers, 2011), pp. 1-19.

[8]Stories about Rabbi Ginsberg's lawsuit can be found in the *Wall Street Journal.*

[9]Based on the description of a dirty trick in G. Kennedy, *Essential Negotiation* (New York: Bloomberg Press, 2004), pp. 69-71.

[10]This is a fictitious company and a fictitious event.

[11]Based on a description at www.bnet.com/blog/salesmachine/the-7-dirty-tricks-that-bosses-play-and-how -to-cope/15211?pg=5.

[12]Based on a description at www.bnet.com/blog/salesmachine/the-7-dirty-tricks-that-bosses-play-and-how -to-cope/15211?pg=6.

[13]www.theblackbookofoutsourcing.com.

[14]"Pension Changes Urged After Maxwell Scandal," *New York Times*, March 10, 1992, p. 22; E. Ipsen, "How to Account for Maxwell Scandal," *New York Times*, December 10, 1991; "Lehman Division Is Fined in Maxwell Case," *New York Times*, March 5, 1996, p. 8; S. Prokesch, "British Investment Agency Criticized in Maxwell Case," *New York Times*, July 10, 1992, D3; "Two Top Officials of Mirror Group Quit," *New York Times*, June 18, 1992, p. 8; T. McCarroll, "Maxwell's Plummet," *Time* 138, no. 24 (1991): 54; T. Nash, "Coming Clean on Dirty Tricks," *Director* 45, no. 13 (1992): 38; W. A. Henry III, "Captain Bob's Amazing Eleventh-Hour Rescue," *Time*, March 25, 1991, p. 52.

[15]Other examples of tricksters include Lot's daughters (Gen 19), Tamar (Gen 38), Rahab (Josh 2). See N. Steinberg, "Israelite Tricksters: Their Analogues and Cross-Cultural Study," *Semeia*, no. 42 (1988): 1-13; M. Jackson, "Lot's Daughters and Tamar as Tricksters and the Patriarchal Narratives as Feminist Theology," *Journal for the Study of the Old Testament* 98 (2002): 29-46; R. D. Patterson, "The Old Testament Use of an Archetype: The Trickster," *Journal of the Evangelical Theological Society* 42, no. 3 (1999): 385-94; S. Niditch, *Underdogs and Tricksters: A Prelude for Biblical Folklore* (New York: Harper & Row, 1997); S. Niditch, "Samson as Culture Hero, Trickster and Bandit: The Empowerment of the Weak," *Catholic Biblical Quarterly* 52 (1999): 608-24.

[16]Judg 14–16.

[17]Gen 27:36.

[18]Gen 29–31.

[19]Gen 42–43.

[20]Based on the description of a dirty trick in G. Kennedy, *Essential Negotiation* (New York: Bloomberg Press, 2004), pp. 69-71.

[21]On the following day the American leader had another discussion with the team. This time he stated that he was withdrawing his suggestion that the contract consultants forego some of their fees. He apologized for how he had brought up the topic. The contract consultants thanked him. Nothing further was said about the matter during team meetings; however, individually the contract consultants had follow-up conversations among themselves about the team leader's proposal. They each gave their opinions to each other regarding what was right or wrong about the proposal.

[22]M. Luther, "Trade and Usury," in *Luther's Works*, vol. 45: *The Christian in Society II*, ed. W. I. Brandt (Philadelphia: Fortress, 1962), pp. 233-310.

[23]Ibid., p. 261.

[24]Ibid., p. 262.

[25]Ibid.

[26]Ibid., p. 265.

[27]Ibid.
[28]Ibid., p. 266.
[29]Ibid., p. 267.
[30]Ibid.
[31]Ibid., p. 269.

Subject Index

About the Author

Michael E. Cafferky is The Ruth McKee Chair for Entrepreneurship and Business Ethics and professor of business and management at Southern Adventist University, where he has served since 2003. Prior to this he served for twenty years in the healthcare industry in middle and senior management. He also has experience working in the construction and manufacturing industries. In addition to serving in entry-level positions of janitor, factory worker and construction worker, he has served as a marketing director, medical clinic administrator, hospital chief operating officer, chief financial officer and hospital interim chief executive officer.

Dr. Cafferky has consulted for companies in a variety of industries, including health care, services and manufacturing. He has helped entrepreneurs create successful business plans and improve their operational efficiency and their organizations.

Dr. Cafferky earned the Doctor of Business Administration (DBA) from Anderson University, Falls School of Business, Anderson, Indiana, and a Master of Divinity degree from Andrews University Theological Seminary. He is the author of eight books, including the college textbook *Management: A Faith-Based Perspective* (Pearson, 2012), a peer-reviewed, full-length principles of man-

agement textbook written from a Christian worldview; *Scriptural Foundations for Business* (Andrews University Press, 2013); *Managing Word of Mouth for Leadership Success: Connecting Healthcare Strategy and Reputation* (Health Administration Press, 2004); and *Breakeven Analysis* (Business Expert Press, 2010), coauthored with colleague Jon Wentworth, and now in its second edition. His articles have been published in the *Journal of Biblical Integration in Business*, *Christian Business Academy Review*, *Journal of Religion and Business Ethics*, *Faith in Business Quarterly* and the *Journal of Applied Christian Leadership*.

Dr. Cafferky teaches management and leadership courses, including Principles of Management, Organizational Behavior, Leadership in Organizations, Ethical, Social and Legal Environment of Business, Integrating Faith and Business, Organization Theory, and Strategic Decision Making.

In 2011 the faculty at Southern Adventist University presented Dr. Cafferky with the university President's Award for Excellence in Scholarship. In 2013 he received the Sharon G. Johnson Award from the Christian Business Faculty Association, a national recognition for his efforts in integrating faith and business scholarship. For three years Dr. Cafferky served as a volunteer examiner for the Malcolm Baldrige National Quality Award program. He has lectured on faith and business in several countries, including the United States, Canada, Mexico, Australia, the Russian Federation, South Africa, France, Rwanda and Ghana.

Dr. Cafferky and his wife, Marlene, have two grown sons, Bryan and Nolan. Some of his leisure interests include international and domestic travel, film, "making stuff from scratch" and low-power amateur radio (AA6WQ/4) communicating with Morse Code (CW).

Other publications by the author:

Patients Build Your Practice, McGraw-Hill
Managed Care and You, McGraw-Hill
Let Your Customers Do the Talking, Upstart Publishing
Managing Word of Mouth for Leadership Success, Health Administration Press
Breakeven Analysis: The Definitive Guide to Cost-Volume-Profit Analysis, Business Expert Press
Management: A Faith-Based Perspective, Pearson Education
Scriptural Foundations for Business, Andrews University Press

Finding the Textbook You Need

The IVP Academic Textbook Selector
is an online tool for instantly finding the IVP books
suitable for over 250 courses across 24 disciplines.

ivpacademic.com